CRIMINAL EVIDENCE

CRIMINAL EVIDENCE

Sixth Edition

Judy Hails, J.D., LL.M.

California State University, Long Beach

WADSWORTH
CENGAGE Learning

Australia • Brazil • Japan • Korea • Mexico • Singapore • Spain • United Kingdom • United States

WADSWORTH
CENGAGE Learning

Criminal Evidence,
Sixth Edition
Judy Hails

Executive Editor: Marcus Boggs

Acquisitions Editor:
Carolyn Henderson-Meier

Assistant Editor: Beth Rodio

Editorial Assistant: Jill Nowlin

Marketing Manager:
Terra Schultz

Marketing Communications
Manager: Tami Strang

Project Manager, Editorial
Production: Samen Iqbal

Creative Director: Rob Hugel

Art Director: Maria Epes

Print Buyer: Paula Vang

Permissions Editor:
Roberta Broyer

Production Service:
Aaron Downey, Matrix
Productions Inc.

Copy Editor: Dan Hays

Cover Designer: Yvo Riezebos
Designs

Cover Image: Corbis Images/
William Whitehurst

Compositor: International
Typesetting and Composition

For product information and technology assistance, contact us at **Cengage Learning Academic Resource Center, 1-800-423-0563**

For permission to use material from this text or product, submit all requests online at **www.cengage.com/permissions**
Further permissions questions can be e-mailed to
permissionrequest@cengage.com

Library of Congress Control Number: 2007940633

Student Edition:

ISBN-13: 978-0-495-09581-1

ISBN-10: 0-495-09581-8

Wadsworth Cengage Learning
10 Davis Drive
Belmont, CA 94002-3098
USA

Cengage Learning products are represented in Canada by Nelson Education, Ltd.

For your course and learning solutions, visit
academic.cengage.com

Purchase any of our products at your local college store or at our preferred online store, **www.ichapters.com**

Printed in the United States of America
1 2 3 4 5 6 7 12 11 10 09 08

To my daughters
Miriam Soto and Kahina Kaci
I'm so proud of both of you

CONTENTS

Chapter 3

Types of Evidence   57

Chapter 4

Direct and Circumstantial Evidence   75

Chapter 5

Witnesses   101

Chapter 6

Crime Scene Evidence and Experiments   135

Chapter 7

Documentary Evidence, Models, Maps, and Diagrams   167

Chapter **8**

Hearsay and Its Exceptions   193

Chapter **9**

Privileged Communications   241

Chapter **10**

Developing Law of Search and Seizure   267

Chapter **11**

Field Interviews, Arrests, and Jail Searches   309

Chapter 12

Plain View, Consent, Vehicle, and Administrative Searches   337

Chapter 13

USA PATRIOT Act, Foreign Intelligence, and Other Types of Electronic Surveillance Covered by Federal Law   363

Chapter 14

Self-Incrimination   385

Chapter 15

Identification Procedures   417

Chapter 16

Preparing the Case for Court   437

TABLE OF CASES

PREFACE

This book has been written for use in introductory-level criminal evidence courses. It is introductory in the sense that it is intended for students who have no legal background. It is *not* introductory in the sense of being superficial.

Criminal Evidence is a comprehensive evidence text. All evidentiary topics that commonly occur in criminal proceedings are included. Hearsay and privileges are thoroughly covered. Six chapters are devoted to constitutional issues that are essential to the collection of admissible evidence.

Mastery of the material presented in *Criminal Evidence* will enable a law enforcement officer to analyze the evidence collected with an eye toward building a solid case. Interaction with the prosecutor will be improved because the officer will understand what is required to admit crucial evidence in court. On the witness stand, the officer will be better prepared to testify because he or she has a better understanding of the strategies used to establish credibility and impeach witnesses.

All legal texts, except those designed for use in only one state, must deal with the diversity that exists in the laws of the 50 states. The Federal Rules of Evidence provide a starting point because they are in use in the federal courts as well as in the courts of several states. *Criminal Evidence* makes frequent reference to the Federal Rules of Evidence for this reason. The approach used in the text is to state the most common rules and definitions. Where wide variation exists among the states, students are specifically urged to consult their local laws.

Most definitions have been converted to itemized lists that are easy for the student to understand. Whenever possible, legal jargon has been avoided. Key terms are **boldfaced** throughout the chapters, as well as listed at the beginning of each chapter, in order to draw the reader's attention to the importance of these terms. All concepts have been amply illustrated with examples arising in criminal cases; examples of situations in which the rules do not apply are also given. Chapters are carefully subdivided into suitable teaching units.

Organization

Chapters 1 and 2 provide a basic introduction to the American legal system. State criminal trials are placed in the larger context of the state and federal judicial systems. Variations among states and the ever-changing nature of law are explained. Chapter 2 provides a detailed explanation of the trial process and related court activities. New trends, such as allowing judges to conduct *voir dire* during jury selection, expanding the use of hearsay at preliminary hearings, and giving the judge authority to decide if new scientific tests should be admitted at trial, are covered.

Chapter 3 defines basic concepts of evidence: relevance, direct evidence, circumstantial evidence, testimonial evidence, real evidence, stipulations, judicial notice, and presumptions.

Chapter 4 explores direct and circumstantial evidence in more depth. A wide variety of situations in which circumstantial evidence can play a key role in criminal trials is discussed. A discussion of the use of the Battered Child Syndrome, Rape Trauma Syndrome, and Battered Woman Syndrome as circumstantial evidence is included.

Witnesses are covered in Chapter 5. Topics related to the handling of trial witnesses include competence, impeachment, rehabilitation, and corroboration. The Opinion Rule is covered in depth with the role of the expert witness illustrated by examples related to sanity, ballistics, and blood matching.

Chapters 6 and 7 focus on real evidence. Preservation of evidence at the crime scene and maintaining the chain of custody are emphasized. Basic rules on the use of scientific evidence are given with background information on the scientific basis for fingerprints, blood tests, and ballistic testing. The section on DNA matching has been expanded to include a wider array of tests. Specialties in areas such as forensic accounting, age progression photography, and forensic anthropology that may play a role in a criminal trial are reviewed. Documentary evidence is covered in detail. Authentication requirements are enumerated. The capabilities of forensics documents examiners are discussed. The need to account for the original document is included in this section along with rules that authorize the use of substitutes when the original is unavailable.

Chapter 8 is devoted to the Hearsay Rule. Recent Supreme Court cases restricting the use of testimonial hearsay are covered. More than a dozen exceptions to the Hearsay Rule are discussed in detail. The use of itemized lists in place of more traditional definitions is one of the strong points of this chapter. Numerous examples that illustrate each exception make the Hearsay Rule easier to understand.

Privileges are covered in Chapter 9. Again, definitions are turned into itemized lists in order to assist in the learning process. Eight different privileges are covered in detail. Examples are included for each.

Chapters 10 through 15 are devoted to constitutional issues. The framework of the Fourth Amendment and the Exclusionary Rule are covered in Chapter 10. The numerous exceptions to the Exclusionary Rule are explained. This chapter also contains a detailed discussion of the procedures that must be followed in order to obtain a warrant.

Chapter 11 focuses on detentions. Field interviews, arrests, booking, and custodial situations are discussed. In each of these situations, the grounds for detaining a subject are established, as is the extent of the search that accompanies the detention.

A thorough discussion of other warrantless searches is contained in Chapters 12. This chapter cites more than 45 major Supreme Court cases. Topics covered in Chapter 12 include the Plain View Doctrine, the Open Fields Doctrine, abandoned property, consent searches, vehicle searches (incident to arrest, probable cause, inventory, and reasonable suspicion), the appropriate use of roadblocks, and administrative searches.

Chapter 13 has major revisions. It now focuses on both physical and electronic eavesdropping. It contains detailed discussion of the USA PATRIOT Act and electronic surveillance (wiretaps, "bugs," pen registers, and e-mail), as well as physical searches and National Security Letter subpoenas used in domestic criminal investigations and foreign intelligence purposes.

Self-incrimination is covered in Chapter 14. *Miranda,* of course, is the key to this discussion. A wide variety of situations that complicate the application of *Miranda* are discussed. The right to counsel during post-arraignment interrogation is also covered.

Chapter 15 is devoted to identification procedures. Constitutional aspects of lineups, showups, and photographic lineups are discussed. This short but comprehensive chapter serves as a guide for avoiding the pitfall of improperly handling witnesses during the identification process.

The role of the officer once the case goes to court is covered in Chapter 16. A convenient record-keeping system is suggested to help collect all needed information. Tips are given on courtroom demeanor and dress, along with suggestions for dealing with jurors and the media.

A comprehensive glossary and index are at the end of the book. Both are designed to make it easy for a student to look up information and/or for people to quickly refresh their memories.

What's New in the Sixth Edition

Each chapter starts with a recent, high publicity case selected with care so that it is appropriate for discussion while studying the chapter. Following the case study, many chapters have a table of myths and corresponding facts about the topic under discussion. The entries in these tables are intended to pique interest and do not attempt to be comprehensive. A writing assignment is found at the end of each chapter. Students are told to go online and find a case on a specific topic covered in each chapter. Writing across the curriculum is emphasized in each chapter as well as Internet research skills.

Additional examples have been added throughout the book. In many instances, they are in chart form so that it is easier for the student to catalog the rules that apply. Some chapters also have mini scenarios that illustrate situations that at first glance appear to be governed by the rule under discussion but, upon more thorough analysis, do not. The reasons for the final conclusion are clearly stated.

Chapter 6, Crime Scene Evidence and Experiments, now contains information on a wider variety of DNA tests and points out the reason for utilizing each test. Several new areas of expertise, such as forensic accounting, age progression photography, and forensic footwear analysis, are discussed to help students understand the role of the expert witness.

Every effort has been made in Chapters 10–15 to cover the most recent U.S. Supreme Court cases that apply during criminal investigations. It is important to recognize that the vast majority of Supreme Court decisions in the past 20 years have made subtle refinements in existing rules; the barrage of new rules typical of the Warren and Berger Courts has disappeared. In its place are cases the Court carefully selects in order to fine-tune the brash opinions of the past. These refinements are included in the discussions of the rules police officers must follow. The text was updated and now includes Supreme Court cases that were decided before January 1, 2008, as well as revisions of other material.

The portion of Chapter 11 that discusses an officer's right to use force has been expanded. In addition to stating the rule that deadly force may only be used when a life is in imminent danger, the discussion of what is reasonable force has been expanded as well as the role that reasonable appearances play in the legal analysis of the decision to use physical force in reaction to a tense situation.

Chapter 13, USA PATRIOT Act, Foreign Intelligence, and Other Types of Electronic Surveillance Covered by Federal Law, now focuses on the post-September 11, 2001, fight against terrorism. Most of the new laws provide additional tools for federal agencies, particularly the FBI; they are discussed in *Criminal Evidence* because of their broad general interest. The Federal Wiretap Act, which is used in criminal investigations involving U.S. citizens and residents, is also discussed.

A glossary containing more than 200 terms (including all key terms) is conveniently located at the back of the book. It has been revised in order to make it easier for students to use. Terms were selected on the basis of what a student would be likely to look up. Exceptions to the Hearsay Rule and exceptions to the Exclusionary Rule are identified in a manner that will help students recognize which rule is discussed. Some terms have been cross-referenced so that they could be found by both their legal designation and their common moniker.

The Table of Cases has been updated to enable the reader to quickly locate the discussion and full citation for each of the more than 190 U.S. Supreme Court cases covered in the book.

A number of changes were made based on suggestions by many teachers who use *Criminal Evidence*. Chapter layout has been changed to make it easier to find the definitions. Many more examples are included; in a number of chapters, mini scenarios were added to illustrate situations in which specific rules would and would not apply.

Supplements

An extensive test bank is available for *Criminal Evidence*. It has been revised and now includes true–false, multiple-choice, and essay questions. Annotated chapter outlines, useful frameworks for classroom presentations, are also available. PowerPoint presentations will be available for all chapters.

Acknowledgments

Many reviewers generously provided feedback in preparation for the sixth edition of this text. I would like to thank each one. I also thank the editors and production staff at Wadsworth for their assistance and support in bringing this book to you. Particularly, Carolyn Henderson-Meier, Beth Rodio, Jill Nowlin, and Samen Iqbal. Dan Hays did an outstanding job as copy editor, as did Aaron Downey from Matrix Productions Inc.

I thank James Young, Esq., Deputy City Prosecutor, Long Beach, CA, and adjunct professor in the Department of Criminal Justice at California State University, Long Beach. Without his assistance in editing and updating Chapters 12–16, I would not have been able to complete this project.

About the Author

Judy Hails has taught in the criminal justice field for more than 35 years. She is currently a professor in the Department of Criminal Justice at California State University, Long Beach, where she received the Distinguished Faculty Teaching Award in 1998. She was a visiting assistant professor at Illinois State University (1981–1983) and an adjunct professor at John Jay College in New York City (1978–1980). From 2000 to 2002, she was also an adjunct instructor at Los Angeles Harbor College and Long Beach City College. During the Fall 2007 semester, she taught at the China Criminal Police College in Shenyang, China.

Dr. Hails is a former sergeant with the Los Angeles County Sheriff's Department. Her education includes: B.S. in mathematics from Loma Linda University; M.S. in criminology from CSU Long Beach; J.D. from Southwestern University School of Law; and an LL.M. in criminal justice from New York University School of Law.

She has published four well-received textbooks: *Criminal Evidence, Criminal Procedure, Criminal Procedure: A Case Approach,* and *Criminal Law.* She has also published numerous articles in professional journals on criminal procedure, prisoners' rights, and domestic violence.

Dr. Hails is a past president of the California Association of Administration of Justice Educators and also the Western and Pacific Association of Criminal Justice Educators. She served a 3-year term as Trustee for Region V of the Academy of Criminal Justice Sciences. She is a life member of the Academy of Criminal Justice Sciences and the Western Society of Criminology. She is an inactive member of the California State Bar.

CHAPTER 1

Introduction

Feature Case: Michael Jackson

Once known as the King of Pop, one of his most unforgettable roles was that of Defendant Jackson in a 14-week trial in a small California county where he lived in the secluded ranch he called Neverland. Jackson had been charged with multiple counts of sexual acts with a boy who was underage at the time, and the prosecutor presented witnesses who testified about events that fall under nearly every category we discuss in this book: eye witnesses who presented direct evidence, claiming they watched as Jackson had sex with the boy; circumstantial evidence, such as witnesses who observed Jackson and the victim's behavior and concluded that a sexual relationship existed; witnesses called to establish Jackson's *modus operandi* based on the fact that Jackson had molested them even though there could be no prosecution of those cases because the statute of limitations had expired; expert witnesses from both the behavioral sciences and the physical sciences who analyzed the evidence and tried to persuade the jury to believe their conclusions; and physical evidence introduced by the person who found it, analyzed by the person who performed the tests on it, and explained by the person who claimed to be an expert witness. Jackson's attorney carefully cross-examined all the prosecution witnesses, impeaching many of them, and put his own witnesses on the stand.

In the end, the prosecution was for naught; the jurors acquitted Jackson. We discuss the role of the jury and how it can come to conclusions that are out of sync with public opinion.

Learning Objectives

After studying this chapter, you will be able to

- Define the term *evidence*.
- Explain who has the burden of proof in a criminal case.
- Describe the role of the judge and jury in a criminal case.
- Specify the historical changes that have occurred in the way evidence is presented at trial.
- Identify three sources of the law governing evidence.
- Discuss the relationship between federal and state rules of evidence.
- Clarify how case law can change statutory rules of evidence.
- Describe what materials are used for legal research.
- Look up a case if provided with the correct legal citation.

Key Terms

- Beyond a reasonable doubt
- Burden of persuasion
- Burden of proof
- Case law
- Evidence
- Federal Rules of Evidence
- Harmless Error Rule
- Judicial discretion
- Probative force
- *Stare decisis*
- Trier of the facts
- Trier of the law

What Is Evidence?

We all use **evidence** every day. For example, we might look out the window to see what the weather is like and use this evidence to decide what to wear. Commercial companies collect sales statistics and use that evidence to guide their marketing strategy. Teachers give tests to see how much their students are learning and use this evidence to assign grades. Scientists conduct experiments and use the evidence to find cures for diseases.

There are many definitions of evidence. Two found in *Black's Law Dictionary* (pocket), third edition (2006), are given to help you understand the concept:

Evidence Defined

Something (including testimony, documents, and tangible objects) that tends to prove or disprove the existence of an alleged fact.

The collective mass of things, especially testimony and exhibits, presented before the court in a given dispute.

Police investigators also try to gather as much evidence as possible. If they are convinced a case has been established, they take all the information to the prosecutor. The prosecutor evaluates the evidence in order to decide if the case should be filed. Ultimately, the jury (or the judge if both sides decide to forego the jury) will hear all the evidence and decide if the defendant is guilty.

Along with other aspects of evidence, this book is interested in the process of introducing evidence at trial. You will find it helpful to understand the legal definition of evidence. *Black's Law Dictionary* (pocket), third edition (2006), gives comprehensive definitions and the pocket edition is a convenient size for students.

Evidence, in the legal sense, includes only what is introduced at trial. Lawyers and judges use the phrase "introduced into evidence." Only the things that have been formally introduced at trial are evidence. Some commonly used terms, such as "inadmissible evidence," are misleading. If the object is not admissible, it cannot be evidence. One side may attempt to admit something into evidence, but if it is not admitted it does not become evidence in the case.

A wide range of things can be used as evidence. If you go to court and watch a trial, the most obvious evidence is the testimony of the witnesses. What a person says from the witness stand while under oath is evidence. All evidence must be introduced via the testimony of a witness. For example, a physical object, such as a gun, may be introduced into evidence only after a witness has testified about it, thus providing a foundation for its admission. Such testimony might include, among other facts, the circumstances under which the gun was found. The variety of things that can be used as evidence is only limited by the facts of the case. A gun might be evidence in a murder case where the victim was shot, but a gun would be not be evidence in a murder case where poison was used by an unarmed assailant.

A survey of recent murder cases reveals a vast assortment of things that could be used as evidence, such as guns, knives, scissors, lead pipes, baseball bats, blunt objects, bombs, cars, poisons, lye, acids, water, ice picks, and even pillows and knitting needles.

Many types of documents can also be evidence. Anything written or printed, pictures (whether still, movies, or videos), sound recordings, and electronic files are also considered documents when introduced into evidence. A forged check is a document; the demand note given to a bank teller during the robbery is another example. Counterfeit money would also be considered documents, as well as graffiti on a wall or inscriptions on tombstones. An e-mail message is also a document. Court records can also be important documents if the prosecutor needs to prove that the defendant had a prior conviction.

Some evidence is developed just for the trial. A wide variety of tests are done in forensics laboratories to prepare cases for trial. The defendant may be fingerprinted solely for the purpose of comparing his or her prints with those found at the scene. The case may be reenacted to determine if the scenario given by a witness could possibly be true. Scale models may even be constructed for submission as evidence.

Several chapters in this book are devoted to explaining what evidence is legally admissible in court. The mere fact that something *could* be admitted is not enough. The proper groundwork must be laid before the judge will allow the evidence to be introduced. These requirements are also covered.

Since the U.S. Supreme Court decided *Mapp v. Ohio* in 1961, the police have also had to be concerned with how the evidence was obtained. Information and physical objects obtained in violation of the defendant's constitutional rights are generally not admissible as evidence in a case. Later chapters deal with these problems.

Burden of Proof

It is widely said that the prosecution has the **"burden of proof"** in criminal cases. This means that the prosecution is required to produce credible evidence to prove every element of each crime charged. The proof must be **"beyond a reasonable doubt."** This places a heavy burden on the prosecution. Our society, however, has decided that it is better to let the guilty go free than to convict innocent people.

Black's Law Dictionary (standard edition) (2004) gives a brief definition of proof beyond a reasonable doubt.

Beyond a Reasonable Doubt Defined

Proof that precludes every reasonable hypothesis except that which the law requires for the case. In criminal cases, the accused's guilt must be established "beyond a reasonable doubt," which means that facts proven must, by virtue of their probative [tending to prove] force, establish guilt.

There have been many attempts to explain the reasonable doubt standard. Pattern Criminal Jury Instruction 1.03 used by the U.S. Court of Appeals for the Sixth Circuit gives a useful explanation:

> The defendant starts the trial with a clean slate, with no evidence at all against him, and the law presumes that he is innocent. The presumption of innocence stays with him unless the government presents evidence here in court that overcomes the presumption, and convinces you beyond a reasonable doubt that he is guilty.

This means that the defendant has no obligation to present any evidence at all, or to prove to you in any way that he is innocent. It is up to the government to prove that he is guilty, and this burden stays on the government from start to finish. You must find the defendant not guilty unless the government convinces you beyond a reasonable doubt that he is guilty.

The government must prove every element of the crime charged beyond a reasonable doubt. Proof beyond a reasonable doubt does not mean proof beyond all possible doubt. Possible doubt or doubts based purely on speculation are not reasonable doubts. A reasonable doubt is a doubt based on reason and common sense. It may arise from the evidence, the lack of evidence, or the nature of the evidence.

Proof beyond a reasonable doubt means proof which is so convincing that you would not hesitate to rely and act on it in making the most important decisions in your own lives. If you are convinced that the government has proved the defendant guilty beyond a reasonable doubt, say so by returning a guilty verdict. If you are not convinced, say so by returning a not guilty verdict.

Thus, the prosecutor is required to fully satisfy the jury that the defendant committed each crime charged. Prosecutors must look at the definition of each crime and make sure that proof has been presented on each element of every offense. Many states have pattern jury instructions for each offense that the judge will read to the jury at the end of the trial. Prosecutors frequently use these instructions to help itemize what they will be required to establish.

The defense does not have to prove that the defendant did not commit the crime. Even so, the defense attorney frequently calls witnesses. The defendant may also take the witness stand even though the Fifth Amendment gives him or her the right to refuse to do so. These acts are usually the result of a "game plan" developed by the defendant and his or her attorney. Although it is true the defense does not have to do anything, as a practical matter the defendant is more likely to be convicted if no defense evidence is presented. It is usually safer to call defense witnesses and try to convince the jury that the prosecution's evidence does not establish the case beyond a reasonable doubt. For example, the defense could try to show any or all of the following: that the prosecution's witnesses are lying, the case rests on mistaken identity, the defendant has an alibi, or the defendant is "not guilty by reason of insanity."

Another way to explain this adversarial relationship between defense and prosecution is that the prosecution has the burden of producing evidence that establishes the crime(s) beyond a reasonable doubt. The defense, on the other hand, will have the **burden of persuasion**. This means that the defense can try to persuade the jury that the prosecution has not established the defendant's guilt.

There are some special situations in which the defendant does have the burden of proof. These are the so-called "affirmative defenses." Self defense, duress, intoxication, entrapment, and insanity are good examples. The defense must introduce evidence on these issues. Some states even require the defendant to prove them, usually by a preponderance of the evidence. The U.S. Supreme Court has upheld this allocation of the burden of proof as long as the defendant is not required to disprove an element of the crime. Due to the variations between the states, you should consult local laws to determine who bears what burden on each affirmative defense.

In cases in which the defense is attacking the constitutionality of the methods used to obtain evidence, the burden may be altered by the fact that the police obtained a warrant. Searches without a warrant are usually presumed to be unconstitutional; that is, the prosecution has the burden of proof. Search warrants are frequently treated differently. The defense has the burden of proving that the search incident to a warrant was illegal.

Role of Judge and Jury

In a jury trial the roles of judge and jury are distinct: The judge is the **"trier of the law"** and the jury is the **"trier of the facts."** If the case is heard without a jury, the judge plays both roles.

The "trier of the law" determines what laws apply to the case. This is clearly shown in the selection of jury instructions. After consultation with the attorneys for both sides, the judge selects instructions that inform the jury what the law is. Errors in selecting jury instructions may be grounds for reversal of a conviction.

Not as obvious, but equally important, is the role of the judge in deciding what evidence is admissible at trial. This is easier in some areas than others. For example, if a statement is privileged, the judge must exclude it unless there is an applicable exception to the privilege. If a confession was obtained by coercion, the judge must exclude it. Even in these examples, the judge must analyze the facts and conclude that the privilege applied to the conversation or that the tactics used to obtain the confession were coercive. This is done, of course, after each side has had a chance to argue what ruling should be made. The judge may have the benefit of reviewing written briefs, submitted by both sides, giving legal points and authorities relevant to the decision. Judges are also allowed to do legal research or have their law clerks check the legal basis for the decision.

Perhaps the most difficult decisions are those where the judge must rule on specific questions the attorneys want to ask the witnesses. Although some questions are obviously permitted and others are not, there is a gray area in between. The judge must try to apply the law to these situations and make a ruling. This is referred to as **"judicial discretion."** The judge has the legal right to decide if the questions should be allowed and must rule on numerous objections by the lawyers during each trial. Higher courts will uphold the trial judge's rulings unless there is an obvious abuse of discretion.

A good example of this use of discretion is the right to ask questions to test the witness's memory. The Sixth Amendment gives criminal defendants the right to cross-examine their accusers. Obviously, this includes the right to try to show the jury that the witness has a bad memory. On the other hand, it is unrealistic to expect a witness to recall every minute detail of an event that may have happened 6 months or a year ago. Additionally, excessive questioning wastes time and may confuse the jury. At some point, the judge will rule that no more questions on this issue will be allowed.

Questions that attempt to introduce evidence that has only slight value to the case are also involved here. The side wishing to introduce the evidence will probably argue that the evidence is very important. The opposing side will tell the judge that the information is useless. The judge must use discretion and decide if there is a valid reason for introducing the evidence.

Other rules of evidence call for similar determinations by the judge. For example, evidence that is too prejudicial or photographs that are too graphic are inadmissible. The individual judge is left to decide where the line is to be drawn between what is acceptable and what is too prejudicial—what is merely a realistic depiction and what is too graphic or gruesome.

The jury is the "trier of the facts." This means that the jury reviews the evidence presented, decides which evidence to believe, and applies the legal instructions the judge gave to the facts. If two witnesses have given conflicting testimony, the jury must decide whom to believe. The jury decides how much weight to give to the testimony of each witness and which witnesses are telling the truth.

This function of determining the truthfulness of the witnesses is particularly important. Our legal system gives jurors almost total responsibility for determining the credibility of witnesses. Very few cases successfully argue credibility of a witness as grounds for reversal.

History and Development of Rules of Evidence

The rules of evidence were designed to control both the judge and the jury. They were also intended to make the trial more businesslike and efficient. The evolutionary process that resulted in our present rules of evidence is a reflection of both English and American history.

In the Middle Ages, glaring abuses of the trial process, such as the Star Chamber and the Inquisition, developed. Strangely enough, the Star Chamber was originally developed to cure abuses by the royalty. At their height, both the Star Chamber and the Inquisition became obsessed with forcing the suspect to confess. The noble ideal that a person could not be convicted solely on the allegations of others dissolved into a nightmare of torture chambers designed to force the suspect to confess.

The earliest forms of juries differed greatly from our current jury. At one time, jurors were selected based on their knowledge of the case. Unlike our present system in which jurors are not supposed to have an opinion about the case prior to the trial, early jurors were only selected if they had personal knowledge of the facts. Busybodies made excellent jurors. Juries were also given the right to conduct their own investigations into the cases.

During the sixteenth century, the rule developed that anyone having a personal interest in the case was disqualified from testifying. This was based on a belief that someone with an interest in the case would more likely be biased and untruthful. In addition to disqualifying people with a financial interest in the outcome of the lawsuit, this rule prevented the parties to the case from testifying. The spouses of parties were also disqualified as witnesses. Connecticut was the first state in the United States to abolish this rule, but that did not happen until the 1840s. Some states retained the rule until after the Civil War.

Old transcripts indicate that trials were much less formal between 1776 and 1830 than they are today. Hearsay was freely admitted, witnesses were allowed to give long narrative answers, and opposing attorneys broke in to cross-examine whenever they wished. Many of our present rules of evidence were developed to correct problems posed by these unruly trials.

As with many reforms, the rules that emerged were found to be too rigid. Exceptions to the rules were developed to make the new rules work better. The numerous exceptions to the Hearsay Rule are good examples of this process. From time to time, legal reformers have attempted to replace old rules with more modern ones. Some prestigious national organizations, such as the American Law Institute and the National Conference of Commissioners on Uniform State Laws, have solicited input from the leading scholars in the field and attempted to draft model laws.

Unfortunately, our federal system of government makes systemwide reform nearly impossible. Except where the U.S. Constitution is controlling, each state is free to enact its own rules of evidence and other laws. Somewhere in the legislative process the model codes are frequently altered or amended. Therefore, in evidence, as in many areas of the law, each state's law is unique.

Sources of Evidence Law

Evidence law reflects both historical evolution and the strengths and weaknesses of our federal system of government. Both statutory law and case law have definite impacts; federal law and state law interact.

United States Constitution

As you learned in high school, the U.S. Constitution is the supreme law of the land. But there is very little in the Constitution that has a direct bearing on evidence. Several provisions of the Bill of Rights, however, do restrict the actions of government in criminal prosecutions. Although early Supreme Court decisions found no connection between these protections and the admission of evidence, the mid-twentieth century saw a reversal of those rulings.

Generally speaking, nothing obtained in violation of the defendant's constitutional rights may be used at trial. Later chapters of this book deal with how specific provisions of the Bill of Rights are currently being applied in criminal trials.

The U.S. Constitution is not static. Each year, the U.S. Supreme Court rules on a variety of cases. Every one of these decisions, in some small way, interprets the Constitution, Bill of Rights, or federal laws. This process has allowed the Constitution to be a living document. The Fourth Amendment is a prime example of this process. As recently as 1948, it was believed that the amendment did not apply to the states. The rulings of the Supreme Court have so drastically altered this view that many have nearly forgotten that the Fourth Amendment has not always been applied to acts of state government.

Where there are no provisions of the Constitution or Bill of Rights involved, our federal system allows each state to enact its own rules of evidence. The common heritage of English law in most of the states has resulted in a great deal of similarity. Even so, there are many differences.

United States Supreme Court

Evidence is only one of the many topics addressed each year in the opinions of the U.S. Supreme Court. Two important functions of the Supreme Court should be noted: (1) The Court is the final arbiter of the meaning of the U.S. Constitution, and (2) the Court acts as supervisor of the federal court system. Rulings of the Court that interpret the Constitution are binding on all federal and state courts. On the other hand, if the Court is acting in its supervisory capacity, the decision does not control the state courts.

When ruling on the meaning of the Constitution, the Supreme Court has the authority to overrule any court in the nation. It also has the power to overrule its own prior decisions. Gradual changes can be seen in the Court's decisions as justices retire and are replaced.

The Court is very selective about which cases it hears. It obviously does not have the time to review every case filed in the United States. The vast majority of appeals to the U.S. Supreme Court and requests for review are denied. This means the Court does not hold a hearing on the cases. It does not mean that the Court agreed with the rulings of the lower courts. Refusal to hear a case sets no legal precedent. Due to the enormous number of requests received by the Court, only a small percentage can be heard each year.

Federal Courts

The federal courts hear cases involving violations of federal statutes. A panel of three judges at a U.S. Court of Appeals can rule on the constitutionality of state and federal laws. If the U.S. Supreme Court has not made a definitive statement on a particular issue, the federal Court of Appeals decision is binding on all states within its boundaries. This may cause confusion because the 13 Courts of Appeals can make conflicting rulings. Ultimately, the problem will be resolved by a U.S. Supreme Court case on point. Such a case takes precedence over the lower court decision.

Federal Rules of Evidence

The **Federal Rules of Evidence** are laws governing the admission of evidence in federal courts. They are enacted by Congress in the same manner as any other federal regulations. A comprehensive set of rules of evidence for federal courts were adopted by the U.S. Supreme Court in 1972. They were forwarded to Congress, where they were duly enacted. The Federal Rules of Evidence became effective January 2, 1975. Some of the rules have been amended since then.

Enactment of the Federal Rules of Evidence was significant for several reasons. The rules represented a comprehensive set of rules designed to work together as a whole. The authors believed they incorporated the best of the old law and corrected the problems that had developed. The new rules replaced both the existing statutory and case law.

The process of developing the new Federal Rules of Evidence received a great deal of publicity within the legal profession. The drafting committee had input from nationally renowned judges, attorneys, and legislators. The final draft was viewed by many as the best evidence code ever drafted.

The new Federal Rules of Evidence immediately affected all federal courts—but the long-term impact was even greater. Many states imitated the federal rules. Some simply declared that the federal rules would be the binding law of evidence in their state. Nearly half of the states now take that approach. Additionally, many other states modeled portions of their evidence laws after the federal rules.

As with any other piece of legislation, the federal rules have been subject to court interpretation. Title 28 of the *United States Code (Annotated)* lists the decisions of all federal courts that relate to the rules. The U.S. Constitution is controlling. When interpreting this type of legislation, the courts also consider the drafting committee's comments that accompanied the legislation. If there was no comment, or the comment does not cover the question that is raised by the appeal, common law will also be considered. Due to the fact that the rules were enacted as a comprehensive package, the courts usually try to make their rulings reflect the overall purpose of the code if none of the above sources is controlling.

State Rules of Evidence

Each state has the right to enact its own evidence code. As mentioned previously, many states now follow the Federal Rules of Evidence. Some, such as Arizona and California, have placed all their rules of evidence in one code. Determining the evidence law in states that follow either of these approaches is fairly easy.

Unfortunately, there are quite a number of states whose legislatures have not enacted comprehensive evidence codes. In these states, the law of evidence is spread over several codes and usually involves case law as well. For example, the law of privilege may be in the Code of Civil Procedure, but the "dying declaration" exception to the Hearsay Rule may be in the Penal Code. There may not be any specific legislation on many kinds of evidence. If a rule is needed, case law is the only place to look. This obviously complicates the task of discovering what law to apply to specific situations.

State Case Law

Each state is free, within Constitutional limits, to enact and interpret its own laws. The laws of other states are not binding, but they may influence the judge. Where there is no binding case law on a point, or where one side is seeking to modify the existing law, an attorney may try to convince the judge that case law from another state is persuasive. If the judge studies the case law presented and finds the reasoning sound, he or she may apply that same logic when making a decision in the current case. Although the case law of a sister state has no legal effect, it may informally affect the final outcome of the case.

Impact of Case Law

Our legal system is based on the concept that the legislature enacts laws but the courts have the right to interpret them. The courts also have the right to rule that a statute is invalid because it violates the state or federal constitution. The U.S. Supreme Court interprets the federal constitution. Those rulings apply to the entire country. State courts can also rule that a state law violates the U.S. Constitution. These rulings will stand until the U.S. Supreme Court has ruled in a contrary manner on a similar law.

Prior cases are considered binding. This is called *stare decisis.* These earlier decisions are what we are referring to when we talk about **"case law."** The rule of a case will continue to be in effect until it is reversed, vacated, or overruled. A higher court can change the rule by making a new ruling on the same issue. This is done by reversing the original decision or making the new rule in a later case that presents the same issue. If there is no higher court, or the higher court has not ruled on the issue, the original court can change the case law in the same manner.

One problem that arises in using case law is that there is no automatic feedback from the courts to the legislature. Even though the U.S. Supreme Court or the highest court in the state has ruled that a code section is void, there is no way to change the code except for the legislature to pass a new law. This causes a delay in revising the codes. Sometimes the legislature does not follow through with the process and the codes retain invalid laws for years. This makes the study of case law very important.

The highest court of the state (called the Supreme Court in most states and not to be confused with the U.S. Supreme Court) has authority over all of the state's courts as long as its rulings do not violate the U.S. Constitution and Bill of Rights. Figure 1-1 illustrates the organization of the typical state judicial system. Below the high court are several appellate

Figure 1-1
Typical State Judicial System

courts of equal authority. Each makes decisions that control the actions of all courts below it on the organizational chart. If a higher court has not ruled on an issue, the intermediate appellate courts may make their own rulings. These may differ from the decisions other courts of equal authority have made on the same issue. When these differences occur, the lower courts must follow the decisions of the courts immediately above them.

The following examples refer to the organization chart in Figure 1-1. Suppose the state has divided the Court of Appeals into two districts. The Court of Appeals for the First District held that the physician–patient privilege does not apply in criminal trials. The Court of Appeals for the Second District held that the physician–patient privilege applies in criminal matters except when the doctor was consulted to help the patient commit a crime. If Defendant Doe commits a crime in a county whose trial courts must follow the precedents from the First District, the physician–patient privilege cannot be claimed. If Doe's offense was perpetrated in a county located in the Second District, the privilege can be used unless the doctor helped Doe commit a crime. These discrepancies will continue until the state's Supreme Court makes a ruling on the use of the physician–patient privilege in criminal cases or one of the District Courts changes its ruling.

Each court has the power to reverse its earlier rulings as long as it continues to follow the rulings of the higher courts, including the U.S. Supreme Court. Again using the example of the physician–patient privilege, the Second District Court of Appeals could decide that the privilege does not apply in criminal cases. This would result in both the First District and the Second District having the same rule.

Review of Evidentiary Matters on Appeal

In most situations, evidentiary matters are considered on appeal only if the issue was raised in the trial court. Attorneys are expected to make objections before the evidence is introduced. This is done to make the trial more efficient—the trial judge has the chance to make a ruling and prevent inadmissible things from being introduced into evidence. Hopefully, the judge has made the correct rulings and a retrial can be avoided. It is part of our adversary system that you only have the right to exclude evidence if your attorney makes the proper objection at the right time.

Some questions regarding what evidence is admissible are decided during the trial, whereas others are customarily ruled on before the trial begins. Objections to specific questions asked a witness are usually made immediately after the question is asked. If one side claims that a witness should not be allowed to testify at all, arguments are usually heard before the witness takes the stand. On the other hand, questions related to the legality of a search, or attacks on the interrogation methods that produced a confession, are usually settled before the trial date.

When the judge's ruling on the admissibility of evidence is challenged on appeal, the attorneys are required to submit briefs giving their legal arguments. Specific statutes and case law must be cited as authority for the court to make a ruling. The easiest example would be when one side can cite a case that is an exact match for the facts and issues of the present case. This is referred to as being "on all fours." Otherwise, each side will try to persuade the judge regarding the appropriate way to interpret the law. Analogies will be drawn from prior decisions to the current case. An attorney may also base arguments on public policy, common law, or the intent of the legislature when it enacted the law. This last rationale is more commonly seen when the court is ruling on a new law.

If the appellate court finds that the trial judge made an error, one question remains: Does the error justify reversal? Unless there is a substantial likelihood that the error was serious enough to affect the outcome of the case, the **"Harmless Error Rule"** will be applied.

The Harmless Error Rule Defined

The Harmless Error Rule states that an error will not cause a case to be reversed on appeal unless the appellate court believes the error was likely to affect the outcome of the case.

In other words, would the jury have been likely to arrive at a different verdict if the judge had made the correct ruling? In many cases, the conclusion is that the error had no impact on the verdict.

The Appellate Process

The side that loses in the trial court frequently appeals to a higher court. When a defendant is acquitted, double jeopardy prevents the prosecution from re-filing the charges; therefore, the prosecution rarely appeals. On the other hand, a conviction can be reversed on appeal, so defendants frequently appeal. Under the American view of double jeopardy, a successful appeal by the defendant does not prevent the prosecution from refiling the charges. Therefore, some defendants who win appeals go free, whereas others are convicted again and serve sentences for their crimes.

The basic rule is that a person who has been convicted is entitled to one appeal. If you follow the news, you know that sometimes there are many appeals in the same case. The entitlement to one appeal means that a person who cannot afford an appeal has the right to have the government pay for a lawyer and necessary documents for one appeal. Traffic tickets and other infractions do not qualify for appeals at government expense. Neither do appeals taken after the first one is complete; for example, the state government does not have to pay for appeals to the state's highest court or appeals to the U.S. Supreme Court.

The appellate process starts when a Notice of Appeal is filed at the end of the trial. This is done in the trial court. All necessary documents are prepared and transferred to the appellate court. A clerk's transcript and a reporter's transcript, or their equivalents, are prepared. Most of the paperwork in the case will be copied and put in the clerk's transcript. The reporter's transcript includes a verbatim account of what was done during pretrial hearings as well as the trial and sentencing hearings. The verbal sparring between the attorneys and judge will be in the reporter's transcript as well as a record of what the witnesses said in court under oath.

A different set of titles is used on appeal. Suppose the defendant in the trial court files an appeal because she believes the trial judge made an incorrect ruling on an evidentiary matter; specifically, the judge ruled that a witness could answer a question that the prosecution asked. The defendant will become the appellant (person who appeals). The prosecution will become the respondent (person that responds to the appellant). If the case goes to a higher level, the titles *appellant* and *respondent* will be used, but they will be assigned based on who filed the second appeal. After the direct appeals are over, the defendant may file actions such as **habeas corpus**, which challenges the legality of confining the person, or a variety of civil suits. The titles will be different in these cases, too.

Both sides prepare a brief of the case. This brief must reference legal issues at trial that are found in either the clerk's transcript or the reporter's transcript. Some states allow pretrial issues, such as the legality of the arrest, to be included; others have separate hearings and appeals for pretrial issues. The appellant (defendant at trial) files the first brief and states the issues that the appellant wants the court to consider. This may involve constitutional issues, such as violation of Fourth Amendment when the arrest was made or a Sixth Amendment violation when the judge did not allow a witness to answer a question that the defense asked. The judge's rulings on whether or not a witness can testify, and the content of the jury instructions, are among the most frequent issues appealed. Each issue appealed must be referenced to a specific page of one of the transcripts. When the appellant's opening brief is complete, copies are given to the trial court judge, the appellate court judges, and the respondent. State rules determine how long the appellant has to complete the brief, but it is rarely more than 60 days.

The respondent answers (cites legal references, references to pages of the transcripts, and its own legal reasoning) the appellant's issues. This will probably take at least 1 month and sometimes much longer. After the appellant's opening brief and the respondent's opening brief are complete, the appellate court will consider the case. Sometimes the case is considered solely on the briefs, whereas other times there will be a hearing. No witnesses are called at the hearing before the Court of Appeals. All discussions are restricted to the evidence presented before the trial court and the legal reasoning presented to the appellate court.

Often, the appellant will successfully point out an error that occurred in the trial court but still lose the appeal. This is because of the Harmless Error Rule. When the Supreme Court established this rule, it reasoned that a case should be reversed only if the appellate court was convinced that the errors contributed to the outcome of the case in a significant way.

There is no right to a second level of appeal. Assuming the side that loses the first appeal wants to take the case to a higher court, a formal brief is usually prepared stating the issues to be heard and presented to the higher court. The case is heard only if the judges of the higher court vote to hear the case. State law specifies how many votes are required. It is more difficult for the trial defendant at this level because the U.S. Supreme Court ruled that states do not have to provide an attorney to handle legal actions after the first appeal.

How Legal Research Is Conducted

A variety of books are available in the law library to help you discover what the law is on any given issue. A great number of legal materials are available on the Internet. These resources take several forms. Some, such as *American Jurisprudence* (Am. Jur.), are similar to encyclopedias. They are carefully indexed for ease in finding the issue. They give a summary of the law with numerous footnotes. Treatises, such as *McCormick on Evidence*, more closely resemble lengthy textbooks. They frequently are on only one subject, but they carefully explain it in minute detail.

Legal digests are organized by topic. They usually give short quotes from individual cases rather than a textbook-style explanation of the law. The annotated codes also use quotations from many cases. These quotes are usually listed immediately after the code section that they interpret. The researcher looks for the quotes that appear to be on point and then reads the cases. Cases are then checked to verify that they are still good precedent (currently prevailing law). Special books and databases are published for this latter purpose.

Most cases can be found in two or more books. This is because the content of the opinions cannot be copyrighted. Judicial opinions are printed by the publishing company authorized by the state or federal government. They are published by other companies as well. The digests and other legal references frequently give all the places a case can be found. These are called parallel citations. Reading any one of these is sufficient because the full text of the case is given in each one.

For example, the opinions of the U.S. Supreme Court can be found in three series of books: *United States Reports* (U.S.), *United States Supreme Court Reports, Lawyers Edition* (L.Ed.), and *Supreme Court Reporter* (S.Ct.). If we wanted to look up the *Miranda* decision, we would first look up the citation: *Miranda v. Arizona*, 384 U.S. 436, 16 L.Ed. 2d 694, 86 S.Ct. 1602 (1966). We would then determine which books containing Supreme Court decisions are in our library. Law libraries frequently have all three, but other libraries may have only one. If the *United States Reports* are available, we look up the citation 384 U.S. 436: We find volume 384 and the *Miranda* case will start on page 436. We would find the same case in volume 86 of the *Supreme Court Reporter* on page 1602. The procedure for finding a case in *United States Supreme Court Reports, Lawyers Edition,* is slightly different. The Lawyers Edition started with volume 1 and numbered consecutively, then a new series was started that also began with volume 1 and was numbered consecutively. The second set of volumes is called the "Second Series." "Second Series" is printed on the spine of the book and "2d" appears in the citation. Thus, if we look up 16 L.Ed. 2d 694 to find *Miranda,* we first find the second series of books for the *United States Supreme Court, Lawyers Edition,* then open volume 16 and look on page 694.

Cases from state courts and the lower federal courts are located in much the same way. Due to variations in publishing companies, not all cases from a state may be available from the same source. Some states have one set of publications for opinions from the highest court and another for lower appellate court cases. Some states do not publish all of the appellate court decisions. Unpublished decisions do not set precedents. Trial court opinions are not considered precedent and therefore are not usually published. Students should become familiar with how to find both the decisions of the U.S. Supreme Court and the published decisions of the courts in their state.

Computerized research materials are readily available. Penal codes and other statutes may be purchased on CD-ROM. Major publishers sell their digests, case reports, and other materials on CD-ROM. Subscriptions are available that provide frequent updates. Online services make codes, case law, and other materials for every state as well as the federal courts available. These Internet databases are updated almost daily.

One of the advantages of computerized material is the speed with which an experienced researcher can locate material. Key word searches can be used to identify every case in the file that discusses a topic or every case that discusses a particular code section or case. General terms, such as *due process* or *Fourth Amendment,* are not useful because there are thousands of cases that use these words. To use the database efficiently, the person conducting the search must know the specific words or phrases used by the courts when discussing the topic. For example, a search of U.S. Supreme Court cases using "vehicle search based on probable cause" would produce every case that used exactly that phrase but miss cases in which the court used the phrase "car search based on probable cause." Browsers can combine words and phrases, such as "arrest" and "exigent circumstances," for more efficient searches. These search engines usually make it possible to download relevant materials from the Internet to a disk or directly into a word processor file for use in briefs and other materials. This saves a great deal of time.

Summary

In a trial, *evidence* refers to all items that are admitted to prove any issue in the case. This includes testimony of sworn witnesses, documents, physical objects, and other items that are relevant to the case.

The prosecution bears the burden of proof in criminal cases. The jury must be convinced beyond a reasonable doubt that the defendant committed the crime(s). The defense usually has the burden of persuasion when affirmative defenses are used.

The judge is the trier of law at trial. Selection of jury instructions is part of the duties of the trier of the law. The judge also rules on the admissibility of all items either side wants to use to prove its case. Judicial discretion is used to determine admissibility if there is no clear-cut law that applies.

The trier of the facts is the jury, or if there is no jury, the judge. The trier of facts determines credibility of witnesses, the weight to be given to testimony of each witness, how the facts match the definition of the crime, and if the prosecution has established the case beyond a reasonable doubt.

Rules of evidence have changed over time. Whereas jurors were once selected on the basis of their personal knowledge of the case, we now try to have jurors who have no knowledge of the facts prior to trial. The procedures used in trial have generally become more formal. Exceptions to the rules of evidence have developed when specific rules have been shown to be too rigid.

The U.S. Supreme Court interprets the U.S. Constitution. These decisions are binding on all courts in the country. It also makes decisions that involve the Federal Rules of Evidence. These opinions are binding only on the federal courts.

Each state has the right to enact its own laws as long as those laws do not violate the U.S. Constitution. State courts interpret state laws and the state constitutions. Each state court is bound by the decisions of higher courts within the organization of its own state court system. Opinions of other states may be considered in order to decide if the appellate courts agree with their reasoning, but they do not have any direct effect on decisions in any state except the one where they were issued.

Evidentiary issues usually must be raised at the trial court in order to preserve them for appeal. When an appellate court decides that there was an error at trial, the case is normally reversed only if the error is believed to have had an impact on the verdict.

Resources for legal research are available in book form, on CDs, and on the Internet. Codes and case law are available as well as digests and other tools.

Review Questions

1. Define the general term *evidence.*
2. Explain the term *burden of proof.*
3. Define what is meant by *beyond a reasonable doubt.*
4. Who has the burden of proof on affirmative defenses?
5. In a criminal trial, who is the trier of the law, who is the trier of fact, and what are their respective roles?
6. List three sources of law that govern evidence.
7. What is the role of the U.S. Supreme Court in determining the rules of evidence for federal courts and for state courts?
8. Define *stare decisis* and explain how it applies.
9. Describe the role of state courts in interpreting the laws of evidence.
10. Explain how the courts determine if a decision should be reversed based on a question of admissibility of evidence.
11. Define the term *judicial discretion.*
12. Explain the Harmless Error Rule.
13. Explain the basis for a court's interpretation of a new statute.
14. What effect does the law of State "A" have on a court's decision of a case tried in State "B"?
15. Explain how to find the opinion of the U.S. Supreme Court in *Terry v. Ohio,* 392 U.S. 1, 20 L.Ed. 2d 889, 88 S.Ct. 1868 (1968).

Writing Assignment

Log on to the Internet and go to www.findlaw.com. Click on "For the Legal Profession" at the top of the page. Scroll down and click on "Newsletter Signup." In the first column, put a check mark beside U.S. Supreme Court. In the third column, put a check mark on Legal News Headlines, Writ, and other items of your choice. After you have done this, go to the next web page and sign up and give your e-mail address. This will result in e-mails being sent to you every time a new issue is released. As items arrive in your e-mail, keep track of all of them that might relate to this course. If you do not have e-mail, you should go to the www.findlaw.com website at least once a week and look under the items you checked.

Today's assignments: On the "Newsletter Signup" page of www.findlaw.com (second page), click on Writ (bottom of third column). Find a headline that interests you and scroll down to the article. Read one of the commentaries on the current issues of Writ. Write a 250-word (one-page) summary about the article that you read.

CHAPTER **2**

The Court Process

Feature Case: Phil Spector

Music producer for the Beatles, Sony and Cher, and Ike and Tina Turner. Elected to the Rock and Roll Hall of Fame. Phil Spector was arrested and charged with first-degree murder in February 2003. After a night on the town, Spector took actress Lana Clarkson to his mansion. Two hours later, the Brazilian-born chauffeur who was waiting in a limousine in front of the house heard a shot. Seconds later, Spector emerged from the house holding a gun. According to the chauffeur, he said, "I think I killed somebody." Clarkson was found in the foyer of the house with a gunshot through her mouth. She was in a seated position on the floor with her purse over her shoulder. The defense claimed that she shot herself. The chauffeur's testimony was questioned by the defense based on the fact that he spoke English with a heavy accent. It was inferred that he did not understand what Spector said moments after the gunshot. The chauffeur was adamant that he heard Spector correctly.

The prosecution presented three witnesses who had dated Spector. Each woman said that Spector, after drinking, threatened her with a gun when she said she was leaving his house.

Forensic testimony focused on blood spatters, fibers, gunshot residue, DNA, and the path the bullet took when it killed Clarkson. Even here, there was controversy. Renowned forensic expert Dr. Henry Lee, who was testifying for the defense in this case, withheld evidence from the prosecution. This enabled the prosecution to cast doubt on his credibility.

After twelve days of deliberation, the jury was unable to reach a verdict. They hung 10 to 2 in favor of conviction. The prosecution announced plans to try the case again.

Learning Objectives

After studying this chapter, you will be able to

- List what evidence is considered by the prosecutor when filing criminal charges.
- Identify what evidence is needed at the preliminary hearing.
- Identify the types of evidence considered by grand juries.
- Explain what information the prosecutor must give the defense during discovery.
- Describe what evidence the defense can use at suppression hearings.
- Explain how juries are selected.
- List the order of events at a criminal trial.
- Describe what law and evidence juries are allowed to consider when they decide a case.
- Explain what evidence can be considered at a sentencing hearing.
- Identify what evidence can be used for an appeal of a criminal conviction.

Key Terms

- Affidavit
- Arraignment
- Challenge for cause
- Charge bargaining
- Clerk's transcript
- Contemporaneous Objection Rule
- Direct appeal
- Direct examination
- Discovery
- Double jeopardy

- *Habeas corpus*
- Harmless Error Rule
- Hold the defendant to answer
- Impeachment
- Indictment
- Information
- Laying the foundation
- Leading question
- Peremptory challenges
- Plea bargaining

- Polling the jury
- Preliminary hearing
- *Prima facie* case
- Probable cause
- Rebuttal
- Rejoinder
- Reporter's transcript
- Sequestered
- Suppression hearing
- *Voir dire*

Introduction

The evidence that is required at various stages of any court proceeding varies according to the type of proceeding and the crime charged. In order to adequately prepare for each court appearance, it is necessary to understand what evidence will be needed at each stage of the proceeding. It must be remembered that preparation of the case begins with the officer's initial observations in the case, not when the prosecutor is doing the final preparation to take the case to court. For example, if an officer stops a car based on reasonable suspicion, the officer should make notes on all of the facts that were used to establish reasonable suspicion. If an arrest is made, the officer needs to record all facts used to establish probable cause for that arrest.

This chapter briefly discusses the different court proceedings in a criminal case, along with what evidence will be used. Issues relating to illegal search and seizure and obtaining confessions are covered in Chapters 10 through 14.

The Criminal Complaint

Criminal cases come to court from three main sources: the police, private persons ("citizen's arrests"), and grand jury **indictments**. Some states allow police officers to bring misdemeanor cases directly to court. Others have the prosecutor's office handle the filing of the first court documents for police and private persons. If an arrest warrant has been issued, it may serve in lieu of filing additional documents to charge the suspect with a crime. The grand jury procedure is somewhat different and will be outlined in a later section of this chapter.

There are several variations of the procedure for cases brought to the prosecutor by the police. If the police made the arrest based on an arrest warrant, the application for the warrant will be the first official document filed with the court. Some states require the officer to obtain an arrest warrant after the arrest if none was issued earlier. If there is no arrest warrant, the complaint will be the first document filed.

The prosecutor decides which cases should be filed and what crimes will be charged. In order to do this, he or she will need a report that clearly states the facts of the case and what information is available to the police. Although the Fourth Amendment establishes **probable cause** as the standard for arrest, there is no precise standard for the prosecutor to use when filing the charges.

The following are some of the things the prosecutor will consider:

1. How strong is the case against the suspect?
2. Did police conduct their investigation thoroughly?
3. Based on the facts in the police report, what crime was committed?
4. Were the suspect's constitutional rights violated?
5. Are the witnesses credible?

The prosecutor does not want to file criminal charges against an innocent person. Since most prosecutor's offices are overworked, cases that do not appear to be "winnable" frequently are not filed.

The way a prosecutor handles the case at this stage varies. In the most serious cases, the prosecutor may interview witnesses prior to filing the charges. On the other hand, for misdemeanors the prosecutor may proceed after only reading the police report. Many states allow the prosecutor to consider information that is not given under oath or otherwise admissible in court.

In some cities and counties, one officer takes all of the minor cases to the prosecutor at once, rather than having each arresting officer go to the prosecutor's office. Other areas of the country require the arresting officer to personally swear out the complaint.

The complaint must state the facts for each charge. This includes at least a description of what crime was committed, where it occurred, and when. The description of the crime must cover every element in the definition of that crime; this is frequently done by using the wording from the penal code. At a minimum, the place where the crime occurred must show that the event occurred within the court's jurisdiction. The date is needed to satisfy the statute of limitations. Figure 2-1 shows an example of how charges are listed in a complaint.

Some states have attempted to reduce paperwork by allowing specially formatted police reports to substitute for complaints. The traffic ticket is probably the most common example. Some states also use the citation in lieu of an arrest for misdemeanors and do not require the drafting of a formal complaint in these cases.

If the police seek an arrest warrant prior to taking the person into custody, the formal procedures for obtaining a warrant must be followed. These include making out an **affidavit** that includes all the facts of the case. The affidavit is made under oath. Normally, the prosecutor reviews the warrant application. The final decision on issuing the warrant must be made by a judge or magistrate. If the judge accepts the affidavit as sufficient, the warrant will be issued. Arrest warrants frequently use the same

---

Charges

COUNT I: John Smith is hereby charged with the violation of Section 459 of the Penal Code, burglary, in that on or about May 1, 2007, he entered a residence located at 123 Main Street, Los Angeles, CA with the intent to steal.

COUNT II: John Smith is hereby charged with the violation of Section 242 of the Penal Code, battery, in that on or about May 1, 2007, he willfully, and without consent, hit Jane Jones. Said event occurred at 123 Main Street, Los Angeles, CA.

COUNT III: John Smith is hereby charged with the violation of Section 488 of the Penal Code, petty theft, in that on or about May 1, 2007, he took merchandise valued at $124.99 without consent and without paying for it from Lucky Market located at 125 Main Street, Los Angeles, CA.

Figure 2-1
Sample Complaint

type of wording as complaints. Many states allow the arrest warrant to take the place of the complaint after the arrest has been made.

When a private person wants to file charges, he or she is usually required to go to the prosecutor's office and give all the information needed under oath. Some states require the prosecutor to file the charges requested by a private person; other jurisdictions give the prosecutor the right to decide if the cases should proceed. When the prosecutor files the case, the complaint is usually in the same format as the one used for cases handled by the police. The prosecutor handles the case from this point on in the same way as if the police had requested the complaint.

After the prosecutor decides what charges to file, the complaint will be typed and taken to the court clerk. The clerk's office will handle the paperwork, including scheduling the case for future court dates. Delivering the complaint to the clerk is called "filing the complaint." Once the complaint has been filed, the suspect is legally known as the defendant.

Arraignment

The **arraignment** is the defendant's first court appearance on the charge. Nationwide, a variety of names are used, such as the "first appearance" and "preliminary hearing." To avoid confusion, it will be referred to as an arraignment in this text. It is a brief court proceeding with the following purposes:

1. Inform the defendant what charges have been filed.
2. Make sure the defendant has an attorney.
3. Set bail.
4. Enter a plea.
5. Set the next court appearance.

If the defendant does not have an attorney, the judge will try to determine if the defendant qualifies for a free, court-appointed lawyer or if the defendant wishes to represent him- or herself. This is a high priority because in many states the defendant cannot enter a plea without counsel or a formal waiver of the right to counsel.

At the arraignment, the defense may seek to dismiss the case because the complaint does not contain all the required information. This is a challenge to the wording of the complaint. Witnesses are usually not called; neither is the evidence in the case evaluated at the arraignment.

The defendant will be asked to enter a plea. Guilty and Not Guilty are the most common. If a defendant pleads *Nolo Contendere* (no contest), the criminal courts will treat the case the same as if a guilty plea was entered, but civil courts may treat it differently. Other pleas, such as Not Guilty by Reason of Insanity, are frequently entered at a later time because the attorney needs more time to determine if they are appropriate.

The arraignment can also serve as a probable cause hearing. To qualify as a probable cause hearing, the arraignment must be held within 48 hours of arrest, and the judge must review sworn statements to determine if there is probable cause. A probable cause hearing is not required if a judge previously issued an arrest warrant for the defendant or if the defendant will not be held in custody pending trial.

Preliminary Hearing

In most states, felony cases that have not been heard by a grand jury must have a **preliminary hearing** (also called a *preliminary examination*), unless the defense waives it. Statutes rarely require preliminary hearings in cases involving only misdemeanors. As with arraignments, names of the hearing may vary from state to state.

The preliminary hearing is a "mini-trial" without a jury. The defendant is present with his or her attorney; the prosecutor represents the State. In many states, the preliminary hearing is held in a lower court than the one in which felony trials are conducted.

The primary purpose of the preliminary hearing is to have a judge hear the case and decide if there is enough evidence to

1. Prove that a crime was committed by the defendant, and
2. Require the defendant to face trial on the charge.

In some states, this is done at the arraignment instead of holding a separate hearing at a later time. In cases in which an arrest warrant was not obtained, this is the first time a judge reviews the facts of the case.

Some states permit hearsay that would not otherwise be admissible at trial to be used at the preliminary hearing. For example, California allows police officers to testify to hearsay at the preliminary hearing even though the statement is not covered by an exception to the Hearsay Rule. This makes it possible to reduce the number of times the victim must appear in court.

In many cases, the preliminary hearing will also be the first time the witnesses are required to take an oath that what they are saying is true. The defense has the right to ask these witnesses questions for the purpose of showing that they have not been truthful or they are mistaken. By listening to all of the witnesses, the defense can also decide how strong a case the prosecutor has. This information may become very helpful during plea bargaining.

The defense also has the right to call witnesses. The defendant may testify in his or her own defense. It is very common for the defense to decide that it is not to its advantage to call any witnesses at this stage of the proceedings.

At the end of the preliminary hearing the judge decides if there is enough evidence to **"hold the defendant to answer,"** which means allowing the prosecution to go to trial on the charges. The prosecution's evidence must establish that it is more likely than not that the defendant committed the crime charged. This is called a ***prima facie*** (on its face) **case**. The judge relies on what each witness said and whether or not he or she believes the witness was telling the truth. If there was more than one charge filed, the judge must make a decision on each felony charge. Assuming sufficient evidence was presented, at the end of the hearing the judge announces that the defendant is bound over for trial.

If the judge holds the defendant to answer, the prosecutor will prepare the appropriate form, usually called an **"information."** The information is similar in form and wording to the complaint. If the judge does not hold the defendant to answer on all of the original felonies, the information will only contain the felonies authorized by the judge. The prosecutor may also drop charges from the case at this time. The information will be filed in the clerk's office of the court where the trial will take place. A second arraignment (at a higher court in some states) will be held on the information.

Grand Jury

The purpose of the grand jury in criminal cases is to take testimony, review evidence, and decide if the suspect should be charged with a crime. Grand juries have other duties as well, primarily verifying efficient and honest county government. The grand jury is composed of citizens, not prosecutors.

Grand jurors are typically chosen by lot at a drawing held once each year. They come from lists of names submitted by judges, people who have volunteered for grand jury service, or the list from which trial jurors are selected. Each state is free to establish its own rules on how grand jurors are selected, provided there is no racial or gender discrimination involved. States also set the size of the grand jury and decide how many grand juries can be empanelled at the same time.

For historical reasons, the grand jury operates separately from either the police or the prosecutor. The grand jury has the right to investigate criminal activity on its own, but in many states it rarely does this. The prosecutor can also present cases to a grand jury. This can be done either before or after the suspect is arrested.

No matter which route the case takes, the grand jury can call witnesses and ask questions regarding the crime. The proceedings are held in secret; the suspect does not have to be informed that he or she is being investigated. The suspect does not have the right to be at the grand jury proceedings unless called to testify, and while testifying he or she does not have the right to have an attorney present in the grand jury room. He or she does not have the right to call witnesses, be present when others testify, or have an attorney cross-examine witnesses called by the prosecutor. Some states even refuse to give defendants a copy of the transcript of the grand jury proceedings after they have been indicted. State laws prohibiting witnesses from discussing their testimony after they appear before the grand jury violate the First Amendment. The U.S. Supreme Court held that prosecutors are not required to present evidence to the grand jury that tends to show that the suspect is not guilty of the crime; some states have either statutes or case law that mandates that grand jurors receive this information.

The minimum number of grand jurors who must vote for prosecution in a case is set by state law; unanimity is not required. Some states allow all charges to go to trial if the grand jury is convinced that any one of the alleged felonies was committed by the suspect. If the grand jury decides the suspect should be brought to trial, a document usually called a "True Bill of Indictment" will be filed with the court clerk. At this point, the defendant will be considered indicted. If the suspect is not in custody, a warrant will be issued and bail will be set (if the offense is bailable) by the court. An arraignment will be held on the indictment, usually in the court where the trial will be held.

Suppression Hearing

The purpose of a **suppression hearing** is to allow a judge to decide if evidence can be used at trial. Most states require the defense to make suppression motions prior to trial if they know of any legal grounds to object to evidence due to illegal search and seizure or an illegally obtained confession. Some states also allow other evidentiary issues to be decided at the suppression hearing. By knowing what evidence can be used before the trial starts, both sides can more efficiently plan their trial strategy. If enough of the evidence in the case is suppressed, the defense can successfully ask for the case to be dismissed.

Unless local court rules state a time for the suppression hearing, the defense may schedule it anytime before trial. In practice, suppression hearings are normally held after the preliminary hearing in felony cases. There are two main reasons for this: If the case is dismissed at the preliminary hearing no suppression hearing will be necessary, and testimony given at the preliminary hearing may alert the defense to the need for a suppression hearing.

The normal rules of evidence apply at suppression hearings. This gives both sides the right to call witnesses and cross-examine. If the issue is the admissibility of the defendant's confession or the defendant is charged with possession of the item in question (for example, possession of marijuana), the defendant's testimony at the suppression hearing cannot be introduced at trial. If this rule was not used, a person could not claim the Fourth or Fifth Amendment without admitting guilt. Many states allow the defense to submit the suppression motion solely on the transcript of the preliminary hearing if the defense believes the sworn testimony at that proceeding established that the evidence was obtained illegally. The prosecution, of course, would have the right to call witnesses to refute the defense's claim.

The judge will either make a decision on the motion at the time of the hearing or take the matter "under submission" and issue a ruling at a later date. Some states permit either party to appeal the ruling before trial. Due to the fact that this is done before the trial begins, the defense cannot claim **double jeopardy** if the decision is reversed on appeal.

Examples of Issues Heard at Suppression Hearings

- Motion to suppress drugs found in the defendant's pocket. Defense alleges that the police did not have probable cause to stop the defendant; therefore, the drugs were found during an illegal search.
- Motion to suppress drugs found during search incident to an arrest. Defense alleges that there was no probable cause to arrest; therefore, the search was illegal.
- Motion to suppress guns found during the execution of a search warrant. Defense alleges that the warrant should not have been issued because the facts in the affidavits do not state probable cause for the search.
- Motion to suppress stolen jewelry found during the execution of a search warrant. Defense alleges that the officers improperly executed a warrant authorizing them to look for assault rifles; therefore, the jewelry found in a drawer was not legally seized.
- Motion to suppress two kilograms of marijuana found during the execution of a warrant that authorized the search of the house. Defense claims that the police failed to comply with "knock-and-announce" before entering the house; therefore, the search that produced the marijuana was illegal.
- Motion to suppress the defendant's confession. Defense alleges that officers questioned the suspect after the arrest and *Miranda* warnings were not given until after the first incriminating statement was made.
- Motion to suppress the defendant's confession. Defense alleges that the officers continued to interrogate the defendant after she requested an attorney; therefore, the statements she made are inadmissible.

Discovery

The idea behind **discovery** is that each side should have ample warning of what the other side will present at trial. This should make the trial more efficient and promote the process of truth finding. It also reduces the number of times it is necessary to stop the trial so that either side can try to challenge surprise witnesses. The growing practice of pretrial discovery has eliminated most of the dramatic surprises at trial.

Discovery (the right to know what evidence the other side has) varies greatly from state to state. There are two areas where the U.S. Supreme Court has required discovery:

1. The name of an informant must be disclosed when the true identity of this person is necessary for the defendant's case.
2. The prosecution must disclose any evidence it has that tends to indicate the defendant is not guilty. This material is often referred to as "*Brady* material" because the case of *Brady v. Maryland* established the rule.[1]

Until recently, discovery in criminal cases was largely one-sided. The prosecution had to disclose information to the defense, but the defense was allowed to withhold information from the prosecution. The reason for this was the interpretation of the Fifth Amendment protection against self-incrimination. Neither side is required to disclose privileged information, such as legal opinions on what strategies it plans to use at trial. Reciprocal discovery is a growing trend. Both sides must disclose names of witnesses, physical evidence, copies of laboratory tests performed on evidence, and statements potential witnesses made to investigators. Statements by the defendant to his or her attorney are still considered exempt from discovery.

Examples of Items Covered by Discovery Rules in Many States
- List of all witnesses (except the defendant) that each side intends to call.
- Recorded statements made by people on the witness list except statements the defendant made to the defense attorney.
- Itemized list of the physical evidence either side has in the case.
- Results of lab tests performed on the evidence by either side that will be introduced in court.
- Reports made by expert witnesses that are scheduled to testify in the case for either side.
- Statements made by all co-defendants.

Requiring a defendant to notify the prosecution that an alibi defense is planned does not violate the privilege against self-incrimination. Disclosure

of where the defendant claims to have been at the time the crime was committed and the names of alibi witnesses has been upheld. Statutes that
require both sides to make pretrial disclosure of intended witnesses have
also been upheld.

Discovery can be conducted at either a formal or an informal level.
Informal discovery is conducted by the attorneys without making requests
in court. Where the courts or the legislature have established clear-cut
rules on what must be given to the other side, it is common for the attorneys to exchange information that they know the court would order them
to provide to the other side.

Formal discovery motions are made in court for a variety of reasons,
such as the following:

1. There is no established rule on releasing the information requested.
2. One side is claiming that the information should not be released.
3. The attorneys do not have a good working relationship.
4. A discovery issues needs to be preserved.

A formal discovery motion must state exactly what is wanted (for
example, "all statements made by Mrs. Jones to the police").

When the defense requests information from the prosecutor, the prosecutor is responsible for disclosing what is in his or her file and what the
police have in their files. Because it is the prosecutor's duty to know what
is in the police files, it is important that the police keep the prosecutor fully
informed about the case.

Failure to comply with discovery rules can result in the items being
declared inadmissible in court or the judge not allowing a witness to take
the stand. The prosecutor's refusal to give information that the court
ordered released can be grounds for dismissing the case. This applies even
to cases in which the prosecutor intentionally refuses to name an informant
for fear the informant will be killed. A case can also be dismissed because
the prosecutor erroneously said information did not exist when, in fact, the
police had it in their files but did not tell the prosecutor about it.

Plea Bargaining

Plea bargaining is the process whereby the prosecution and defense work
out an agreement for the defendant to plead guilty to one or more charges
without a trial. In return, the prosecutor usually agrees to drop some of the
original charges or sentencing demands. When the agreement is reached
before the charges are filed, the process is called **"charge bargaining"**;
after the charges are filed, the process is called **"plea bargaining."** It is now

recognized as a legitimate part of the legal system in many jurisdictions. In some states, as many as 97 percent of defendants use plea bargaining to avoid trials.

Either the prosecutor or the defense attorney may initiate the plea bargaining process. Many factors will be considered. One that is very important is the strength or weakness of the evidence in the case. Both sides will consider the police reports and testimony given at the preliminary hearing. Information from further investigations may be reviewed. The results of any laboratory tests will be scrutinized. Both sides will try to guess which witnesses the jury will believe. Nonevidentiary issues will also be considered; for example, what is the difference in the sentence if the defendant is convicted compared to if he or she agrees to the plea bargain? Are there mitigating circumstances that justify giving the defendant a less severe sentence? Is the court calendar so full that the case will be dismissed for lack of a speedy trial? Has the defendant worked as an informant or in some way helped the police and thereby "earned" special treatment?

The final result is an agreement that the defendant plead guilty to one or more crimes and the prosecutor dismiss the rest of the original charges. For example, if there were five counts of burglary, the defendant may plead guilty to two counts of burglary and the remaining three will be dismissed. If the original charge was for driving under the influence, the defendant may plead guilty to a lesser charge of reckless driving.

The U.S. Supreme Court has set the following requirements for plea bargaining:

1. The defendant must have an attorney during plea bargaining if he or she would have the right to one at trial on the same charges.
2. There must be no threats or promises in the plea bargaining process.

Prior to accepting a plea bargain, the judge will ask questions to show that the defendant's rights have been protected. It is also generally recognized that the defendant has the right to withdraw a plea if the judge does not honor the agreement made by the prosecutor. Many states restrict plea bargaining, whereas others allow the prosecutor to enter into plea bargains on the charges but not on the sentence the defendant will receive.

The Trial

The trial is the highest-profile action in the criminal case. In reality, trials are relatively rare because of plea bargaining and pretrial dismissals. Trials in most states follow the same format: selection of the jury, opening statements, prosecution witnesses, defense witnesses, rebuttal witnesses "called by either side," closing statements, instructions on the law from the judge to the jury, jury deliberation, and verdict. Unique situations may arise that require departures from this format.

Jury Selection

The Sixth Amendment guarantees the right to a speedy trial by a jury of one's peers in criminal cases. Although the U.S. Supreme Court has said this only applies to defendants facing more than 6 months in jail, many states provide jury trials in all criminal cases. Some states even allow jury trials for infractions. The defendant has the right to demand a jury. Although less commonly used, the prosecution also has this right. The case may be heard by a judge only if both the prosecution and the defense agree to waive the right to a jury.

Historically, the criminal jury was composed of 12 people. The U.S. Supreme Court has ruled that the Sixth Amendment sets a minimum size of 6 for juries in criminal cases. Each state legislature has the right to set the jury size as long as there are at least 6 jurors. Many states still require 12 jurors.

The idea of a jury of our "peers" has been interpreted to mean that the jury must be from a cross section of the adult population. Discrimination on the basis of race or gender is not allowed in the jury selection process.

The initial phase of jury selection is conducted by the jury commissioner or someone at the courthouse who handles assembling jurors. A master list of everyone eligible for jury duty must be compiled. Traditionally, voter registration records were used for this purpose. More recently, the master jury lists have been enlarged in order to cover a greater portion of the population. Some states now combine voter registration and driver's license information.

Names of people to be called for jury duty are randomly selected from the master list. Each state has its own list of reasons a person may use to be legally excused from jury duty. Financial hardship, caused by loss of wages during jury duty, is commonly accepted in many jurisdictions. Those not exempt from jury duty will be told to report to the courthouse on a given date. The length of jury service varies. Some courts require jurors to attend daily for 1 or more months. Others require jurors to come in 1 day a week for 1 month, whereas some only ask for 1 day. Once selected to sit on a jury, they must serve until the trial is over, except when excused for cause by the judge.

Prospective jurors spend a great deal of time waiting to be called to a courtroom. There is usually a jury assembly room where they can read, watch television, etc. When a judge is ready to start jury selection, the Jury Commissioner's office is asked for a group of prospective jurors. Thirty people are frequently sent to the courtroom; the judge may ask for more if this does not turn out to be enough. Names may be drawn randomly each time a jury panel is requested or some other method, such as assigning jurors to groups before they arrive at the courthouse, may be used.

Once in the courtroom, names are randomly drawn to fill the jury box. Prospective jurors take an oath to answer questions truthfully. **Voir dire** (the process of questioning to determine if a person is qualified) is conducted to determine if these people can consider the evidence in the case with open minds. Although *voir dire* was traditionally done by the attorneys, many states now allow the judge to ask the questions in order to save time. When jury questionnaires are used, a set of written questions is completed by each prospective juror and the answers are reviewed by the attorneys before *voir dire* begins.

Examples of Questions Jurors Are Asked during *Voir Dire*

1. Do you know the defendant in the case?
2. Do you know the victim in the case?
3. Do you know any of the people who will be called to testify?
4. Have you heard anything in the news about this case?
5. Do you believe that the police always arrest the right person?
6. Do you understand that the defense does not have to prove that the defendant is innocent?
7. Do you understand that the defendant does not have to testify? And that if he does not testify, you cannot hold it against him?
8. Have you been on a jury before today? If so, which side did you vote for?

The attorneys will ask the judge to dismiss anyone whose answers during *voir dire* indicate that he or she will not decide the case solely on the facts introduced at trial and the law as stated in the jury instructions. This request is called a **"challenge for cause"** and may be used as often as believed necessary. Reasons for being excused at this stage include racial bias against the defendant, belief that police only arrest the guilty, and exposure to pretrial publicity to the extent that the prospective juror has already formed a conclusion regarding the defendant's guilt or innocence. In order to successfully challenge for cause, the attorney must convince the judge that the prospective juror will not base his or her decision on what occurs inside the courtroom. Generalities, such as friendship with a police officer or even being a police officer, are not enough.

If a juror is excused, a new name will be drawn. The new juror will be asked similar questions, and the attorneys will have a chance to challenge him or her. This process is repeated until there are enough people in the jury box to form a jury.

Next come the **"peremptory challenges."** These are used to allow each side to replace jurors whom they subjectively feel cannot be fair. No reason need be stated for using a peremptory challenge, but a juror may not be excluded solely on the basis of race or gender. The prosecution and defense alternate in using their peremptory challenges. If a juror is excused, a new juror will be called, questioned, and possibly challenged. The jury selection is completed when either the maximum allowed peremptory challenges have been used or both sides agree to accept the people then seated in the jury box.

State law establishes how many peremptory challenges there are in any given case. A typical state might allow each side 6 for misdemeanors, 12 for felonies, and 20 in death penalty cases. When there is more than one defendant, the procedure becomes more complicated. Generally, however, the number of challenges is increased in proportion to the number of defendants.

Alternate jurors are normally selected last. They become members of the jury only if one or more jurors become unable to complete the trial due to illness or other reasons. Alternates also may be challenged for cause. A separate number of peremptory challenges to be used on alternates may be set by state law.

Once the jury and alternates are selected, they take an oath to decide the case on the evidence admitted at trial and under the rules of law given them by the judge. "Jeopardy" attaches to the defendant(s) at this point. The trial officially starts when the jury is given the oath.

In most states, jurors are given paper and urged to take notes as the case is presented. They will be told that they are not to discuss the case with people who are not on the jury; discussions of the case among jurors should not start until deliberations at the end of the trial. Recent excesses by tabloid journalists in high-publicity cases have led some states to enact laws prohibiting jurors from accepting money for telling about the case even after the verdict is returned. The judge may order the jury **"seques-tered"** if it is believed this is the best way to protect jurors from outside influences that might affect their vote.

When a jury is sequestered, the bailiff keeps the jury together and pre-vents all contact with nonjurors. In high-publicity cases, in which jurors may be prejudiced by media coverage, sequestering the jury may include housing them in a local hotel at night and requiring them to eat all of their meals together under the watchful eye of the bailiff. Due to the expense to the government and inconvenience to the jurors, sequestering of the jury is rarely done while testimony is being taken. It is common during delibera-tions, however, to require the jury and bailiff to eat meals together without outsiders present, but jurors are allowed to go home each night.

The Courtroom Setting

The center of attention in the courtroom is a dais on which the judge's desk and witness chair are located, usually enclosed by wood paneling. Facing the judge in the middle of the courtroom are two tables, one for the prosecution and the other for the defense. The prosecutor usually sits on the side of the room closest to the jury. There is usually a lectern for the attorneys to use when addressing the judge or questioning witnesses. The court clerk's desk is usually at the side of the judge's platform. If there is a court reporter, a small desk is usually located between the judge's platform and the tables for the attorneys. The bailiff's desk is frequently to one side of the room. The jury box is along one side of the room, perpendicular to the judge and attorneys. Facing the judge in the back of the room are seats for spectators and the press. Figure 2-2 illustrates the layout of a courtroom.

Technology is gradually coming to courtrooms, although the expense is still prohibitive for many jurisdictions. Where the only visual aids available in the past were chalkboards and easels with pads of newsprint, some courtrooms are now equipped with computer systems and large projection screens that make it possible for the jury to instantly see each item

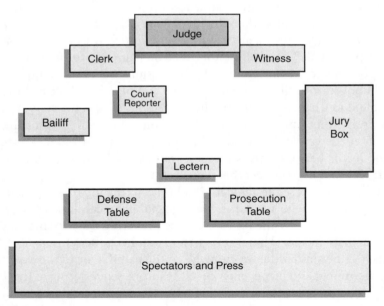

Figure 2-2
The Courtroom Setting

the attorneys and witnesses are discussing. The attorneys may be required to have all photographs and diagrams transferred to laser disk so that they can be shown in this manner. Videotapes may also be shown.

Another useful innovation is real-time stenographic reporting. In the past, the court reporter used the stenotype machine to keep a verbatim record of the proceedings, but only a person with special training could read the tape produced by the machine. Eventually, the notes were transcribed and included in the court record. Computerized stenotype machines use software that automatically generates a transcript. Some courtrooms are equipped with monitors so the judge and attorneys can review the exact wording of questions if an objection is made or the witness asks to have the question repeated. The monitor can replace a sign language interpreter if a witness who has a hearing impairment is testifying. Some systems also allow the attorneys to mark the transcript with reference notes; such markings are confidential and not visible to other parties viewing the transcript on other monitors. Printouts of the transcripts are available at the end of the court session so the attorneys can prepare for the next day. This system also facilitates the process if the jury makes a request to have the testimony of a witness read to them during deliberations.

Opening Statements

An opening statement is a speech an attorney makes to the jury. It is *not* evidence in the case. Only evidence given at trial by witnesses under oath may be considered by the jury when they decide the case.

The purpose of the opening statement is to introduce the jury to the case. Two things are usually discussed in the opening statement—the facts of the case and the role of the jury in deciding guilt or innocence. Opening statements are particularly important in long cases because the jurors need help fitting the pieces of the puzzle together, especially if the facts will not be presented in chronological order.

Opening statements are optional. If the case is tried without a jury, it is common for both sides to skip the opening statement. When there is a jury, the prosecutor will normally give an opening statement. This will usually be the first thing that happens after the jury is sworn in and the charges are read.

Meanwhile, the defense has three options: (1) give an opening statement immediately after the prosecutor, (2) give an opening statement after the prosecution has called all of its witnesses, or (3) not give an opening statement at all. The defense attorney will make a tactical decision on the best way to proceed in each case.

The advantage of waiting to give an opening statement until after the prosecution has called its witnesses is that the presentation can be tailor-made for the evidence that has already been introduced against the defendant. It also allows the defendant to avoid revealing what the main defenses will be until after the prosecution has called all of its witnesses. The disadvantage of waiting is that the jurors will only hear the prosecution's side of the case prior to listening to the witnesses. This may result in the jurors placing too much weight on their testimony.

Prosecution's Case in Chief

The prosecution presents its case first. During the prosecution's case in chief, the prosecutor must establish every element of each crime charged beyond a reasonable doubt. Each witness will be called to the witness stand, given the oath, and asked questions. Questioning by the attorney who called the witness is called **direct examination.** During direct examination the attorney asks questions and the witness answers them. Questions are limited to things that are relevant to the case. A question that suggests the desired answer is called a **leading question** and is not usually allowed during direct examination; if such a question is asked, the opposing side may object. For example, on direct examination the prosecutor could ask, "What color shirt was he wearing?" It would be considered a leading question to ask, "Was he wearing a blue shirt?"

Questions are usually short and to the point so the witness can easily understand them. Argumentative questions, such as "Isn't it true that you drove the getaway car while he went inside the liquor store to commit the robbery?" are not allowed. Normally, the witness will be asked specific questions and will not be allowed to tell what happened in story form. A question that asks the witness "Tell me what happened" is called a narrative question and is rarely permitted.

Example of Direct Examination

Prosecutor: Where were you at 7:00 p.m. on August 27, 2007?

Witness: I was at John's house watching the Angels game.

Prosecutor: Who was there with you?

Witness: John, my brother Bill, and some guy who is a friend of John but I don't know his name.

Prosecutor: Was there an argument?

Witness: Yes. John and Bill were yelling at each other about whether the umpire should have called a pitch a strike.

Prosecutor: Did you observe anything other than their shouting at each other?

Witness: Yes. John hit Bill.

While the prosecutor is conducting direct examination of a witness, the defense may make objections to the questions asked. The proper time to object is immediately after the question is asked and before the witness has a chance to answer. This is called the **Contemporaneous Objection Rule**.

The purpose of the rule is to allow the judge to decide if the question is proper before the jury hears the witness's answer. The attorney who made the objection will be required to state the legal rule that makes the question improper (for example, hearsay or a leading question). The attorney who asked the question will have a chance to explain why the question should be permitted before the judge makes a final decision. If the judge agrees that the objection is valid, the ruling will be "objection sustained" and the witness will be instructed not to answer the question. If the objection is considered improper, the ruling will be "objection overruled" and the witness will be told to answer the question.

Example of Contemporaneous Objection Rule

Prosecutor: Tell us what John said.

Defense: Objection, your Honor. Hearsay.

Prosecutor: Your Honor, John is the defendant in this case. His statements are admissible under the admissions exception to the Hearsay Rule.

Judge: Objection overruled.

All evidence is introduced by calling witnesses to the stand. If any physical evidence, such as the murder weapon, is to be introduced into evidence, a witness must be called who can tell where the object was found and what happened to it since it was found. This is called **laying the foundation.** Once it has been shown that the object is relevant and it has been authenticated (shown that it has not been altered or tampered with), it will be given an identification number or letter. Frequently, objects introduced by one side are given numbers and the other side's evidence is given letters. For example, the prosecution may introduce the murder weapon and it will be marked "People's Exhibit 1," whereas the defense introduces fingerprints found at the scene and they are marked "Defense's Exhibit A."

Example of Laying the Foundation to Admit Physical Evidence

Prosecutor: Did John hit Bill with his bare hand?

Witness: No, he picked up a heavy ashtray and hit him with it.

Prosecutor: Can you describe the ashtray?

Witness: Yes, it was about four inches square and maybe two inches deep. I think it was made of glass. It had an Angels logo on it.

Prosecutor:	Is this the ashtray?
Witness:	Yes.
Prosecutor:	How can you tell?
Witness:	I gave it to John for his birthday because he was an Angels fan. I had it engraved "John, I hope your Angels win the series." If you look on the back of the ashtray, that is what it says.

The Sixth Amendment right to confront witnesses has been inter-preted to mean that the defendant has the right to be present when prosecution witnesses testify. Reforms intended to ease the trauma child abuse victims suffer while testifying have had to comply with the Sixth Amendment. Screens or other physical barriers and closed circuit televi-sion can be used so that witnesses do not have to look at the defendant only if there is a clear showing that the physical confrontation would cause severe emotional trauma. The need for these protective measures must be determined on a case-by-case basis. The defendant and jurors watch the victim testify via television monitors. Although closed circuit television can be used when necessary to protect the abuse victim, the child who is testifying must be available for normal cross-examination.

After the prosecutor finishes questioning a witness, the defense attor-ney will have the opportunity to do so. This is called cross-examination. The purposes of cross-examination are to

1. Follow up on statements made during direct examination.
2. Ask relevant questions that were not asked during direct examination.
3. Show that the witness should not be believed.

The Sixth Amendment confrontation clause gives the defendant the constitutional right to cross-examine all prosecution witnesses. Figure 2-3 shows how attorneys narrow the focus of a witness's testimony during ques-tioning. Cross-examination is considered essential in the search for the truth. Most states follow the rule that cross-examination is limited to the scope of the direct examination (plus impeachment; see Figure 2-3 and Chapter 5). This means that the cross-examination may only cover topics asked during direct examination. For example, if a prosecution witness testified about what happened during a robbery, the defense attorney could ask questions about details of the robbery that the prosecutor did not cover. However, the defense could not ask about some other crime, such as a burglary commit-ted by the defendant on a different day. The jury has the job of deciding who is telling the truth. Therefore, a witness may be cross-examined to show why

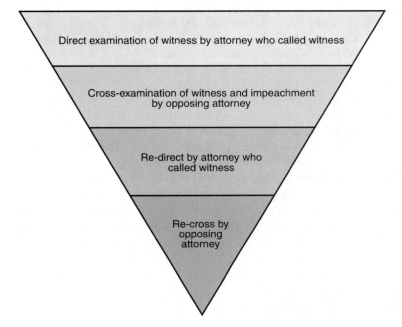

Figure 2-3
Narrowing Focus of Testimony

he or she should not be believed. This is called **impeachment.** Any witness who takes the stand can be impeached. The following are some of the ways to impeach:

1. Showing that the witness is lying by submitting prior statements the witness made that are inconsistent with what he or she just said.
2. Calling witnesses to show that the person testifying has a reputation for dishonesty.
3. Proving that the witness is biased and might be distorting the facts.
4. Proving that the witness has a prior felony conviction.

If a witness is impeached, the attorney who called him or her may in turn attempt to show why the jury should believe the witness. This is called "rehabilitation." Impeachment and rehabilitation are covered in more detail in Chapter 5.

Example of Impeachment and Rehabilitation

Defense: You testified that you heard John say, "If the Giants win I will kill you." Where were you when this statement was made?
Witness: On the other side of the room, maybe 10 feet away.
Defense: Do you have a hearing impairment?
Witness: Yes, I have a moderate loss in my left ear.
Prosecutor (after cross-examination is finished): Are you sure you heard what John said correctly?
Witness: Oh, yeah, he was shouting. You would have to be deaf not to hear him.

After cross-examination the attorney who called the witness will have the opportunity to ask the witness more questions. This is referred to as re-direct examination. There are strict limits on what can be done during re-direct. It can be used to rehabilitate a witness who has been impeached or to ask questions aimed at clarifying what the witness said during cross-examination. Attorneys are not allowed to treat this as an opportunity to ask questions they forgot to ask earlier. After re-direct, the opposing attorney has a similar right to question the witness. This is referred to as re-cross-examination. The attorney conducting re-cross is allowed to ask questions to clarify information obtained during re-direct. Both re-direct and re-cross are optional and may be skipped if the attorney deems that further questioning is not necessary.

The trial will proceed with the prosecutor calling witnesses and conducting direct examination and the defense cross-examining them until the prosecutor is satisfied that each element (*corpus delicti*) of the crime(s) charged has been established beyond a reasonable doubt. The prosecutor is not required to call all possible witnesses, but the jury may decide that the case has not been proven if a person who apparently has important information is not called. When the prosecutor decides that no more witnesses will be called, he or she will inform the judge that the prosecution "rests its case."

Example of Prosecution Resting Its Case

Prosecutor: No more questions for this witness.
Judge: The witness may step down. Prosecutor, call your next witness.
Prosecutor: The prosecution rests.

Defense's Case in Chief

Since the burden of proof in a criminal case rests with the prosecution, the defense is not required to prove anything. At the end of the prosecution's case in chief, the defense may immediately make a motion to acquit the defendant. This motion would be based on the prosecution's failure to establish every element of the crime. The judge will normally grant such a request only if the prosecution has failed to introduce testimony regarding one or more elements of the crime.

The defense does not have to call any witnesses. The defense may use cross-examination of prosecution witnesses to show that the defendant should not be convicted. The defendant and his or her attorney will decide whether it is necessary to call defense witnesses. It must be kept in mind that any witnesses the defense calls can be cross-examined and possibly impeached by the prosecution. This includes the defendant if he or she decides to testify. The defense may rely on the fact that the prosecution did not prove its case beyond a reasonable doubt.

If the defense does call witnesses (which is usually the case), the defense attorney will conduct the direct examination of each witness followed by cross-examination by the prosecutor. One unique choice for the defense is calling character witnesses. The defense has the right to introduce evidence that the defendant has a good reputation for honesty, integrity, and other relevant traits. The defense hopes the jury will conclude that since the defendant is a "good person," he or she could not have committed the crime. If the defense does call character witnesses, the prosecution will be allowed to cross-examine them regarding both the defendant's character and the credibility of the character witness. The prosecution will also be allowed to call its own character witnesses during **rebuttal** to show that the defendant, in fact, has a poor reputation.

Example of Use of Character Witness

Defense Attorney:	Mr. Jones, are you familiar with the reputation of John, the defendant in this case?
Witness:	Yes.
Defense Attorney:	On what do you base your conclusions about his reputation?
Witness:	I have lived next door to him for the last 5 years. Most of the neighbors are friendly and I have talked to them about John.
Defense Attorney:	Based on these contacts with the neighbors, what is John's reputation?
Witness:	Everyone thinks he is a good guy. He is very involved with his children. He is very gentle with them. He never gets angry. He is very helpful when someone is having trouble fixing something. If he gives you his word, he keeps it.

Once the defense has called all of its witnesses and they have been cross-examined, the defense rests.

Rebuttal and Rejoinder

Sometimes defense witnesses raise new issues, such as alibi or character. Rebuttal gives the prosecution a chance to call witnesses on these new issues. It is not used to fill gaps in the case accidentally left by the prosecution during the case in chief. The judge has the power to decide if the prosecution may call rebuttal witnesses. If rebuttal witnesses are called, the defense may cross-examine them.

Rejoinder is the calling of witnesses by the defense to attack the evidence introduced by the prosecution during rebuttal. If the judge allows rejoinder, the prosecution will be allowed to cross-examine.

Closing Arguments and Summation

Closing arguments (also called summations) resemble opening statements in many ways. The main difference is that the attorneys may discuss only the evidence actually introduced during trial. The closing argument is each attorney's last chance to persuade the jurors to find for his or her side.

In most states, the prosecution goes first. It will review the evidence and emphasize everything that points to the defendant's guilt. The defense follows, trying to show that the prosecution has not proven guilt beyond a reasonable doubt. The defense will stress its witnesses' versions of the facts and point out weaknesses in the prosecution's case. Many states allow the prosecution to reply after the defense has given its closing statement, provided the defense called witnesses during its case in chief. The reason for this is that the prosecution has such a heavy burden of proof.

Jury Instructions

Near the end of the case the judge will meet with the attorneys and select applicable jury instructions. Jury instructions are statements of law that will be read to the jury to tell them what rules to use when deciding the case. Important terms will be defined, such as "beyond a reasonable doubt," "malice," and "competency of a witness." Each crime will be defined. The jury will be told it has the right to decide which witnesses to believe and how important each witness's testimony was. The process of discussing the facts and voting on the verdicts will be explained.

Each attorney will prepare a list of jury instructions that he or she wants given. The individual instructions may be taken from a published book of jury instructions or written by the attorney. The instructions are usually based on the wording of prior court decisions or statutes. At their conference the judge will review prosecution and defense requests. Instructions requested by both sides will be included and given to the jury.

If one side objects to the other's request, the judge will hear arguments from both sides and make a ruling. If no one has requested key instructions, the judge has the responsibility to add these instructions to the list.

Example of a Jury Instruction for Unarmed Bank Robbery

Based on U.S. Court of Appeals for First Circuit
Model Criminal Jury Instructions for 18 U.S.C. § 2113(a)

The defendant is accused of robbing the [bank, savings and loan association, or credit union]. It is against federal law to rob a federally insured [bank, savings and loan association, or credit union]. For you to find the defendant guilty of this crime, you must be convinced that the Government has proven each of these things beyond a reasonable doubt:

<u>First</u>, that the defendant intentionally took money belonging to the [bank, savings and loan association, or credit union], from a [bank, savings and loan association, or credit union] employee or from the [bank, savings and loan association, or credit union] while a [bank, savings and loan association, or credit union] employee was present;

<u>Second</u>, that the defendant used intimidation or force and violence when he did so; and

<u>Third</u>, that at that time, the deposits of the [bank, savings and loan association, or credit union] were insured by the [_____]. [The parties have so stipulated.]

Intimidation is actions or words used for the purpose of making someone else fear bodily harm if he or she resists. The actual courage or timidity of the victim is irrelevant. The actions or words must be such as to intimidate an ordinary, reasonable person.

After closing arguments, the judge will give the instructions to the jury. In some states this is done by reading the prepared statements. These states frequently give the jury a copy of the instructions to take to the jury room during deliberations. Other states allow the judge to instruct the jury about the case in a more informal manner.

Jury Deliberations

The judge will instruct the jurors regarding the selection of a foreman before they start deliberating the case. They will be told to discuss all the evidence before voting on any of the charges. Each charge must be voted on separately.

Jury deliberations normally take place in the jury room, which is usually located near the courtroom where the trial was held. The exhibits that were introduced into evidence are usually sent to the jury room. No one except the jurors is allowed in the jury room during deliberations. Alternate jurors are not present during deliberations unless they have taken the place of jurors who have been excused due to illness or other emergency. If a juror is excused after deliberations have begun, an alternate will be appointed, and the jury will be instructed to start deliberations over. Traditionally, total secrecy surrounded jury deliberations to the point that jurors could not even be called at a later time to testify about jury misconduct. Some states have changed this rule and now allow jurors to testify if the defendant moves to have a conviction reversed due to jury misconduct.

The jurors should discuss the case and consider each other's viewpoints. If there is disagreement about what a witness said, the jury can ask to have the verbatim record of key points of the testimony read to them. The judge will normally meet with the attorneys and discuss what should be said in response to these types of questions. Reading of testimony or giving additional instructions for the jury will be formally done in the courtroom with the prosecutor, defendant, and defense attorney present. Jurors will then return to the jury room.

The deliberation process allows the jurors to discuss the case and vote on each charge. If the vote is not decisive, they may continue the discussion and voting process. No time limits are set; deliberations may run from a few minutes to several days. Usually, the jury will finally agree on the outcome of the case; in other words, reach a verdict. Historically, criminal cases required a unanimous verdict. The U.S. Supreme Court has held that the Sixth Amendment only requires a unanimous verdict when the state uses six-member juries. When larger juries are used, unanimity is not necessary. The Supreme Court has approved verdicts of 9-3, 10-2, and 11-1. Each state's legislature must determine which standard will be used. Most states still require unanimous verdicts.

If the jurors cannot reach a verdict (that is, are "deadlocked"), the jury foreman will notify the judge of the problem. At this point, neither side is told what the last vote was. The jurors return to the courtroom and the judge will ask questions to determine if there is any chance that the jurors can discuss the case further and reach a verdict. If any of the jurors indicates he or she might change his or her mind, the jury will be sent back for more deliberations. If the judge believes there is no chance of reaching a verdict, the jury will be dismissed and the trial will be over. This is referred to as having a "hung jury."

Example of Jury Instruction Used When Jury Cannot Reach a Verdict

Based on U.S. Court of Appeals for Ninth Circuit Model Criminal Jury Instructions

Members of the jury, you have advised that you have been unable to agree upon a verdict in this case. I have decided to suggest a few thoughts to you.

As jurors, you have a duty to discuss the case with one another and to deliberate in an effort to reach a unanimous verdict if each of you can do so without violating your individual judgment and conscience. Each of you must decide the case for yourself, but only after you consider the evidence impartially with your fellow jurors. During your deliberations, you should not hesitate to reexamine your own views and change your opinion if you become persuaded that it is wrong. However, you should not change an honest belief as to the weight or effect of the evidence solely because of the opinions of your fellow jurors or for the mere purpose of returning a verdict.

All of you are equally honest and conscientious jurors who have heard the same evidence. All of you share an equal desire to arrive at a verdict. Each of you should ask yourself whether you should question the correctness of your present position.

I remind you that in your deliberations you are to consider the instructions I have given you as a whole. You should not single out any part of any instruction, including this one, and ignore others. They are all equally important.

You may now retire and continue your deliberations.

The defense usually requests that the charges be dismissed. If the case is dismissed the prosecutor cannot re-file the case. The judge rarely dismisses the charges unless the jury verdict was overwhelmingly in favor of the defendant (10-2, for example). If the charges are not dismissed, the prosecutor will have the right to re-file a case that was dismissed if he or she believes it is worth the additional time and effort.

Verdict

When the jury reaches a final decision, the foreman notifies the judge that a verdict has been reached. The defendant and all the attorneys will be told to return to the courtroom. Each charge and the corresponding verdict will be read. Figure 2-4 is an example of a verdict form that might be used in a trial. The attorneys have the right to ask each juror to state that he or she agrees with each verdict. This is called **"polling the jury."** The purpose

We the jury find the defendant, John Jones, Case No. CR-1234,

☐   Guilty

☐   Not Guilty

Of the crime of murder in the first degree, Penal Code Section 187.

Signed: _____   _____

         Jury Foreman   Date

Figure 2-4
Example of a Verdict Form

of polling the jury is to make sure that there has been no mistake. It also gives each juror one last chance to change his or her mind. After these procedures have been completed, the court clerk will officially enter the verdict on each count (charge) into the court records.

Sentencing

If the verdict is guilty on any of the charges, the next step is sentencing. In many states, sentencing does not occur on the day the verdict is read. The main reason for this is the request by the court for a pre-sentence investigation report. Except when the statute gives the judge no choices regarding the sentence, this additional information will help the judge decide on the appropriate punishment. The exact content of these reports varies, but they usually include information on the defendant's past life and prior convictions (called a "social history"), as well as any aggravating or mitigating circumstances in the present case. Depending on the seriousness of the crime and local court rules, procedures range from having a probation officer prepare the report while the defendant is free on bail to having a diagnostic study done while the defendant is confined in the reception center of the state prison. The defense is usually allowed to submit a similar report prepared by its own experts.

The purpose of the sentencing hearing is to determining what sentence should be imposed. The judge frequently has the option to sentence the defendant to probation, fine, and jail or prison. The length of the prison sentence is decided by the judge. The Supreme Court, in a series of cases starting with *Apprendi v. New Jersey* (2000)[2], increased the role of the jury in determining the defendant's sentence. If the judge wants to impose a longer sentence than the norm that the legislature set for the crime, the only facts that judge can use are those the jurors unanimously agreed had been established at trial.

Both sides usually have the right to call witnesses at the sentencing hearing. The person making the pre-sentence investigation report may be called and cross-examined. Victims may be given the right to make a statement to the judge. After reviewing all of the information, the judge will make a final decision at the sentencing hearing. Death penalty cases are somewhat unique because it is usually the jury, instead of the judge, that decides the sentence. Most states do not have juries sentence the defendant in non-capital cases.

Example of Judge Sentencing the Defendant

Judge: Mr. Jones, you have been convicted of the crime of robbery. I find that you committed this crime intentionally and there were no mitigating circumstances. I therefore sentence you to serve 5 years in the state prison. You are to pay a fine of $5,000 and make restitution to the victim in the amount of $3,251, the amount you took during the robbery. I hereby remand you to the custody of the State Department of Corrections.

At the close of the sentencing hearing, the defense attorney frequently informs the judge that an appeal will be filed. The judge will then decide if the defendant should be allowed out on bail while the appeal is in progress. The attorneys will be permitted to introduce evidence that the defendant is (or is not) likely to leave the state to avoid serving the sentence or that he or she may commit additional crimes if bail is granted. Figure 2-5 summarizes the stages of a trial.

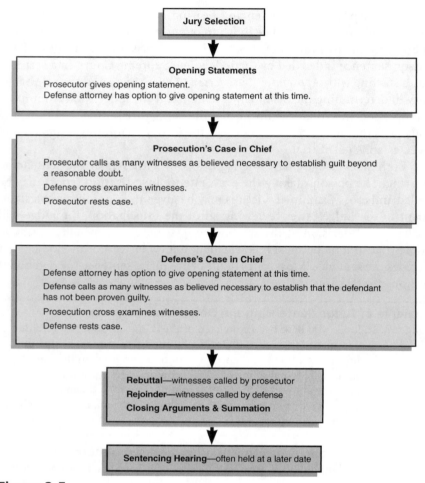

Jury Selection

Opening Statements
Prosecutor gives opening statement.
Defense attorney has option to give opening statement at this time.

Prosecution's Case in Chief
Prosecutor calls as many witnesses as believed necessary to establish guilt beyond a reasonable doubt.
Defense cross examines witnesses.
Prosecutor rests case.

Defense's Case in Chief
Defense attorney has option to give opening statement at this time.
Defense calls as many witnesses as believed necessary to establish that the defendant has not been proven guilty.
Prosecution cross examines witnesses.
Defense rests case.

Rebuttal—witnesses called by prosecutor
Rejoinder—witnesses called by defense
Closing Arguments & Summation

Sentencing Hearing—often held at a later date

Figure 2-5
The Trial

Appeal

There are several ways to change a guilty verdict. After the jury returns a guilty verdict, the defense attorney may ask the trial judge to set aside the verdict and grant a new trial or enter an acquittal. The most common appeal is made to a higher court based on what happened at the trial. This is called a **"direct appeal."** *Habeas corpus* can also be used to seek reversal and is explained later in this section.

The following are the most common reasons for setting aside a conviction: (1) The jury convicted the defendant even though the judge believes no reasonable person could believe that he or she was guilty, or (2) the judge realizes there were legal errors committed during trial that are sure to result in a reversal on appeal. Double jeopardy prevents the prosecution from having the verdict set aside if the jury acquitted the defendant.

The direct appeal can be based only on what is included in the record of prior court hearings, including the preliminary hearing, any suppression hearings, and the trial. The record is frequently divided into two documents—the **reporter's transcript** and the **clerk's transcript.** The reporter's transcript is a typed, verbatim record based on the notes the court reporter made at the proceeding (frequently with the help of a stenotype machine). It will include what the attorneys and judge said as well as what the witnesses said under oath. In courts in which court reporters are not used, the attorneys are usually required to meet and agree on a statement of what happened during the trial. This is frequently called a "settle statement of facts."

The clerk's transcript includes copies of all documents filed with the court clerk during the case. This would include the complaint, information, indictment, any motions made to suppress evidence, requests for jury instructions, and the entries of the clerk during court days. The daily entries list the names of the judge, defendant, and attorneys present, the purpose of the hearing, and the names of witnesses called (but not a summary of their testimony). During jury selection, the clerk's record lists the names of every person called to the jury box, as well as the names of the jurors selected. If a juror is excused and replaced by an alternate, this event is also indicated.

Direct appeals must be filed within a short time after conviction. The time for appeal is set out in the state statutes or court rules. Notice of appeal is usually required within 30 days or less after the sentencing hearing. The statutes or court rules also give the length of time the attorneys have to prepare briefs—30 days is common. The court can extend the length of time if the attorney makes a timely request and states a valid reason.

When the defense files a notice of appeal, the court will have the reporter's transcript and clerk's transcript prepared. Due to the expense of typing the reporter's transcript, it is usually not made prior to this time. If the defendant cannot afford the transcripts, the government is required to pay for them. The defense reviews all of the transcripts and then prepares a brief that will be filed with the appellate court. The brief usually begins with a summary of the facts of the case, listing the page numbers where this information can be found in the transcripts. Legal arguments for reversing the conviction follow. Each reason for reversal is usually discussed separately and includes statutes, court cases, and other legal references in support of the argument.

The American legal system places great reliance on the jury's ability to determine which witnesses are telling the truth. Therefore, cases are rarely reversed if the defense bases its appeal primarily on the credibility of witnesses. Occasionally, a conviction is reversed because the court of appeals believes the case was so weak the jury should not have convicted. If a case is reversed on grounds of insufficient evidence, the legal consequences are the same as if the jury had acquitted the defendant. The prosecutor cannot re-file the case. Most appeals are based on legal problems with the case.

Examples of Issues That Can Be Raised on Appeal
- Confession obtained in violation of *Miranda* rules.
- Search violated the Fourth Amendment.
- Improper jury instruction given by judge.
- Judge improperly sustained objections and refused to allow a witness to testify on important questions.

Examples of Issues That Cannot Be Raised on Appeal
- Weight to be placed on testimony of individual witnesses.
- Credibility of each witness.
- Possible testimony of witnesses who were not called during trial.

Appellate courts often rule an error harmless even when the defense correctly points to errors that occurred at trial. The **"Harmless Error Rule"** allows the conviction to stand unless the court believes that the error had a substantial influence on the outcome of the case. If the conviction is reversed on one of these legal grounds, the prosecution has the right to re-file the case.

The defense can also appeal on the grounds that the judge improperly sentenced the defendant. If this is the only grounds for reversal, the case will be sent back to the trial court for a new sentencing hearing, but the conviction will still stand.

The defendant has the right to one appeal immediately after being convicted. The appellate court cannot refuse to review the case. If the defendant cannot afford to hire an attorney to handle the appeal, the court must appoint one for this purpose. After the first appeal, the court has the right to reject further appeals. Both the highest state court and the U.S. Supreme Court have formal procedures that allow the defendant to request review of the case, but only a small percentage of the cases are given full hearings. In many states, the highest court handles the first appeal if the defendant was given a death sentence.

Habeas corpus is a separate civil lawsuit used to challenge illegal confinement. Being in jail, prison, or on probation or parole due to an improper conviction is considered to be illegal confinement. The defense files a Petition for a Writ of *Habeas Corpus*. The petition briefly states why the person filing the petition believes the defendant should be released. The prosecution must file a reply giving reasons the conviction is valid. If the judge reviewing the petition believes there are valid legal grounds to consider the case, a hearing will be held. At this hearing, unlike on direct appeal, both sides can call witnesses who will be subject to both direct and cross-examination. Another dissimilarity between *habeas corpus* and the direct appeal is that *habeas corpus* can be filed at any time as long as the defendant is still in custody; direct appeals are restricted to the time period immediately following the trial.

Examples of Issues That Should Be Raised by *Habeas Corpus*
- Person was illegally arrested and is being held in county jail.
- Person was placed in a mental hospital against his or her will and claims to be legally sane.
- Person is in jail and has served the entire sentence but has not been released.
- Defendant was denied his or her right to an attorney at trial because the defense attorney was incompetent.

Examples of Issues That Should Not Be Raised by *Habeas Corpus*
- The judge did not give proper jury instructions during the trial.
- The evidence presented at trial was not sufficient to convict the defendant.
- The defendant was illegally arrested and therefore should receive monetary payment from the arresting officer and police department.

Habeas corpus is usually the best way to request reversal on the grounds that the defense attorney at trial was incompetent. The hearing is usually needed to determine how much research and preparation the attorney did prior to trial. *Habeas corpus* has also been successfully used when the U.S. Supreme Court made retroactive rules that affected cases that were beyond the time limits for direct appeals. One such case was *Gideon v. Wainwright*, which declared that a criminal defendant who cannot afford to hire an attorney has a constitutional right to have the state provide a free lawyer for his or her trial.

Summary

The prosecutor may consider all facts and evidence available when deciding what charges to file. At the preliminary hearing, witnesses must be called to testify regarding every element of each crime charged. In many states using a grand jury, testimony regarding all elements of all crimes must be presented.

Suppression hearings are based on testimony made under oath. This is taken from transcripts of previous hearings, such as the preliminary hearing, or witnesses are called at the suppression hearing.

Attorneys exchange information during discovery. If a formal discovery motion is filed, it will contain legal references showing the right to receive what has been requested. Witnesses are not usually called at this hearing.

The trial process begins with jury selection. Jurors are under oath to truthfully answer questions regarding their ability to serve. Jurors who have already made up their minds about the defendant's guilt are excused. Attorneys also have the right to remove a limited number of jurors for other reasons.

The attorneys may preview the evidence in the case during opening statements, but opening statements are not evidence in the case. The attorneys have a duty to discuss only evidence that they believe will be presented during the trial.

The prosecution must convince the jury beyond a reasonable doubt that the defendant committed the crimes charged. This is done by calling witnesses and introducing physical evidence. When the prosecutor calls a witness, he or she conducts the direct examination of that witness. The defense attorney will cross-examine the witness in order to show the direct examination left out information and to attack the truthfulness of the witness.

After the prosecution has finished calling its witnesses, the defense may call witnesses. When the defense calls witnesses, the defense attorney conducts direct examination and the prosecutor will cross-examine. Since the prosecution has the burden of proof, the defense is not required to call any witnesses.

Closing statements are not evidence in the case. During closing statements the attorneys summarize the evidence, point out the weaknesses in the other side's evidence, and urge the jury to vote for their side.

The jury will be given instructions that the judge and attorneys have selected. The jury will go into deliberations and decide the outcome of the case based on the legal rules provided in the jury instructions. If the jury is unable to reach a verdict (hung jury), the prosecutor may retry the case unless the judge dismisses the charges.

Witnesses may be called at the sentencing hearing. Their testimony is usually focused on facts the judge can use to decide what is an appropriate sentence. This frequently includes facts about prior crimes, physical trauma suffered by victims, and other information that would not be allowed at trial.

Neither the direct appeal nor the motion to set aside a verdict involve calling new witnesses. They are based on what happened at trial. Witnesses may be called at a *habeas corpus* hearing to show why the conviction is illegal.

Review Questions

1. What facts may the prosecutor consider when deciding what charges to file?
2. What is the standard of proof at the preliminary hearing?
3. What types of evidence may the prosecution and the defense introduce at the preliminary hearing?
4. Explain the role the grand jury serves in criminal cases.
5. What facts may the grand jurors consider when deciding what charges to include in the indictment?
6. What information must the prosecution and the defense exchange during discovery?
7. Discuss what evidence the defense may introduce at a suppression hearing.
8. Describe how juries are selected.
9. What is the purpose of the opening statement and the closing argument?
10. How does cross-examination differ from rebuttal evidence?
11. What is a jury instructed to do during deliberations?
12. Describe what happens if the jury cannot reach a verdict.
13. What evidence may be considered by the judge at the sentencing hearing?
14. What evidence may the judges consider when deciding a case on direct appeal?
15. What evidence may the judge consider when ruling on a Petition for Writ of *Habeas Corpus*?

Writing Assignment

On the Internet, go to www.cnn.com/crime. Find a case that interests you. Write a 250-word (one-page) summary of the case.

Notes

1. *Brady v. Maryland* 373 U.S. 83, 10 L.Ed. 2d 215, 83 S.Ct. 1194 (1962).
2. *Apprendi v. New Jersey* 530 U.S. 466, 147, L.Ed. 2d 435, 120 S.Ct. 2348 (2000).

CHAPTER 3

Types of Evidence

Feature Case: Martha Stewart

Domestic diva. Star of her own TV show that tells millions of housewives and others charming tricks to make their homes showcases. Martha Stewart's friend Samuel Waksai submitted an application to the Food and Drug Administration (FDA) for a new colon cancer drug. Stock in his company rose to $75. When Waksai learned that his application for the drug would be denied, he and his family attempted to sell $7.5 million worth of stock in the company before the denial was made public. Martha's stock broker heard of the sale and called her office, leaving a message that was logged in, suggesting that stock in the company would be trading for less. By the time Martha sold, the stock had dropped to $58. The next day, the FDA publicly disclosed the application was denied. Within 3 days the stock was selling for $43. The sale profited Martha approximately $51,000.

The FBI, Securities and Exchange Commission, and federal prosecutor launched an investigation. Waksai, the owner of the company that produced the cancer drug, was prosecuted, convicted, and sent to prison for insider trading. Martha's stock broker alleged that she had previously told him to sell the stock if it went below $60. If this was the reason for the sale, there was no crime.

An interview with the FBI was set up. Phone calls were made between Martha and the stock broker before the interview. Martha changed an entry in the phone log. When Martha was interviewed by the FBI, she denied any conversation about the failed company or selling its stock. Martha made several public statements reiterating that she would be exonerated. Authorities extensively studied her phone records and documents related to her stock holdings but were unable to find sufficient evidence to prosecute her for insider trading.

Martha was charged with lying during an FBI interview and ultimately convicted. She served 4 months in federal prison.

Learning Objectives

After studying this chapter, you will be able to

- Define relevant and material evidence and explain when each is admissible in court.
- Define circumstantial evidence and explain how it differs from direct evidence.
- Explain the difference between testimonial and real evidence.
- Define stipulation and judicial notice and explain how each applies in court.
- Describe presumptions and how they are used in court.

Key Terms

- At issue
- Circumstantial evidence
- Conclusive presumption
- Corroborative evidence
- Cumulative evidence
- Direct evidence

- Documentary evidence
- Inference
- Judicial notice
- Limited admissibility
- Material evidence
- Presumption

- Probative value
- Real evidence
- Rebuttable presumption
- Relevant evidence
- Stipulation
- Testimonial evidence

Relevant Evidence

In the study of the rules of evidence, there are several basic terms that must be understood before discussing specific issues. This chapter discusses the more important of these key terms.

One of the basic concepts of evidence is that only **relevant evidence** is admissible in court. There are situations, however, in which even relevant evidence will not be admitted. One is when the evidence was obtained in violation of the defendant's constitutional rights. This rule is discussed later in detail (see Chapter 10). Two other common reasons for excluding evidence are violations of the Hearsay Rule (see Chapter 8) or the fact that the information is privileged (see Chapter 9).

To put it as simply as possible, something is relevant if it tends to prove (or disprove) a disputed point or issue in the case. One of the keys to what is relevant is the question of what is **"at issue"** in the case. "At issue" refers to all disputed facts that are required to establish the elements of the crime(s) charged and the defendant's guilt beyond a reasonable doubt; facts necessary to establish the defense are also "at issue." When the defendant enters a plea of "Not Guilty," all the facts needed to establish the crimes charged are, in effect, disputed. Evidence can be admitted to establish these facts. If the prosecution believes it is necessary, more than one witness may be called to testify about the same fact or event. On the other hand, if the defendant admits something, such as the prior conviction, the facts regarding the crime that resulted in that conviction are no longer in issue. No evidence can be admitted to prove facts that are not at issue.

Consider the Martha Stewart case at the beginning of the chapter. It is important to note that she was charged with lying to the FBI, not with insider stock trading. What was "at issue"? The issue in her trial was whether or not she told the truth when interviewed by the FBI. It is easy to become sidetracked with the precise time that phone calls were made, when Martha received word that the cancer drug was not being approved, etc. If Martha had been charged with insider trading, those facts would have been important because the exact time she learned of the company's problems would have been "at issue." But she was charged with intentionally lying to the FBI. The facts that were "at issue" were the ones that showed that she knew she was not telling the FBI the truth.

Relevant Evidence Defined

Relevant evidence is any evidence that tends to prove or disprove any disputed fact in the case. It merely needs to show that it is more probable that the fact exists than it appeared before the evidence was introduced. No single piece of evidence has to make a fact appear more probable than not.

Another key to admissibility is **probative value.** This means that the evidence must make it appear that a fact probably occurred. Sometimes there is one piece of evidence that conclusively proves the case. This is rare, however. More commonly, there are a variety of pieces of evidence that, when considered together, convince the jury that the defendant is guilty beyond a reasonable doubt. It is difficult to decide what weight any one piece of evidence will have in convincing the jury that the defendant is guilty or innocent. Any evidence that might have some impact on the jury has probative value. If an attorney makes an objection based on lack of relevance, the judge must decide if the evidence is likely to have any effect on the jury. If not, the evidence will not be admitted. This determination is made on a question-by-question basis during both direct and cross-examination.

Examples of Relevant Evidence in a Murder Trial
- Defendant's fingerprints were on the murder weapon.
- Defendant bought the murder weapon the day before the victim died.
- The victim's blood was found on the defendant's hands.
- Defendant was the last person seen with the victim before her death.

- Defendant was the beneficiary of a large life insurance policy on the life of the murder victim.
- Defendant had previously threatened to kill the victim.
- Defendant disappeared the day after the victim died.

Relevant evidence must also be **"material."** There currently appear to be two different definitions of material:

1. Evidence is material if it is logically connected with some fact that is at issue.
2. Material evidence is evidence that is important to the case—it cannot be too remotely connected to the facts at issue.

In practice, relevant evidence is material only if it meets both of these tests:

1. It must be relevant to some fact that is at issue in the case, and
2. It must have more than just a remote connection to the fact.

There are several other limits to the admissibility of relevant evidence. These restrictions apply to evidence that does not have very great probative value. A balancing test is used to determine if the value of the evidence outweighs the problems it may cause at trial. As the Federal Rules of Evidence state, there are other reasons to exclude evidence.

Federal Rule 403. Exclusion of Relevant Evidence

Although relevant, evidence may be excluded if its probative value is substantially outweighed by the danger of unfair prejudice, confusion of the issues, or misleading the jury, or by consideration of undue delay, waste of time, or needless presentation of cumulative evidence.

Relevant evidence is not admissible if it would be unduly prejudicial due to its emotional impact on the jury. The court is cautious about admitting evidence if it would be likely to arouse either hostility or sympathy toward either side. The defendant's prior convictions are in this category. In most cases, the prior conviction has only slight relevance, but the chance that the jury will believe that the defendant was more likely to have committed the current crime merely because of the prior conviction is great. Therefore, evidence of prior conviction is usually not admissible by the prosecution during its case in chief. If the defendant takes the witness stand, his or her prior record may be used to impeach. Prior convictions are also admissible at the sentencing hearing.

On the other hand, pictures of the murder victim may arouse the hostility of the jury toward the defendant, but they are usually admissible because of their greater relevance to the case. Even in these types of cases, prosecutors face restrictions on the number of photographs or their size (for example, limited to 8 × 10 inches); in the past, some judges allowed black-and-white pictures but not color photographs because they thought that the gruesome color pictures would inflame the jury.

Other reasons for rejecting relevant evidence are that it might distract the jury from the main issues of the case or that it would take too much court time to prove a fact that had only minimal relevance. An example of this is the court's reluctance to allow testimony regarding laboratory tests that do not have a record of very high accuracy. In one case, a child had contracted a rare form of venereal disease when she was sexually molested. The court refused to admit the laboratory tests showing that the defendant had the same disease because the test could only show that there was a 20% probability that a person had transmitted the disease to the victim. Another example is the limitation placed on calling a witness to impeach someone who has already testified. If the testimony is being questioned because of inconsistencies on minor details, the judge will not allow the opposing side to call another witness because this is unduly time-consuming and distracts the jury from the main issues of the case.

Cumulative evidence may also be excluded. Cumulative evidence merely restates what has already been admitted into evidence. For example, if there were 10 eyewitnesses to the crime and they all gave basically the same account of what happened, their testimony would be cumulative. How many eyewitnesses will be allowed to testify is up to the judge. Probably, after 2 or 3 have said the same thing, the judge would sustain an objection that the testimony is merely cumulative and should not be allowed. On the other hand, if their testimony corroborates what has already been introduced, it is usually admissible.

Examples of Cumulative Evidence
- John testified that he was at 3rd and Main at 10:00 p.m. on November 3 and saw a man flee the scene in a Ford.
- Henry testified that he was at 3rd and Main at 10:00 p.m. on November 3 and saw a man flee the scene in a red Ford sedan.
- Jack testified that he was at 3rd and Main at 10:00 p.m. on November 3 and saw a man run from the store, get in a red car, and leave in a hurry.

The distinction is that cumulative evidence basically repeats the same thing that has already been introduced, whereas **corroborative evidence** supports the prior testimony by providing additional evidence to confirm what the previous witness has said, without merely duplicating it. Real evidence may be used to corroborate testimonial evidence. For example, a ballistics test that shows a gun has been fired corroborates the testimony of a witness who said she saw the defendant fire the gun.

Examples of Corroborative Evidence
- Adam testified that he was at 1st and Cedar at midnight on November 3 and he saw a red car speed past. As it went by, someone threw an apparently empty bank bag out the window.
- Sam testified that he walked through the intersection of 1st and Cedar at 11:55 p.m. on November 2 on his way to buy cigarettes at the liquor store and there was nothing unusual on the ground. On his way home 10 minutes later, he found an empty bank bag in the street.
- Tom testified that he was working at the liquor store on the corner of 2nd and Cedar and he remembers Sam buying cigarettes at a couple of minutes before midnight.

When there is a question about the admissibility of relevant evidence, the judge will be called upon to exercise discretion. Both sides will be allowed to argue why their requests should be granted. The judge will then make a ruling that may be appealed at the end of the trial. Such rulings are upheld as long as they are logical and do not violate common sense.

Evidence may be relevant if introduced for one purpose but irrelevant for some other purpose. This is called **"limited admissibility."** For example, a prior statement of the defendant may be admitted to show inconsistencies between what he or she testified to in court and what was said to the police. The purpose of introducing this earlier statement is to show that the defendant is lying, and it is relevant for this purpose. The same statement, however, may be irrelevant if used to show that the earlier statement is true and the in-court statement is false.

Examples of Relevant Evidence
- Witness to bank robbery wrote down the license number of the "getaway" car. Records show that defendant owned the car with that license.

  This evidence is relevant because it makes it more probable that the defendant committed the robbery. It is, however, far from conclusive. The defense can introduce evidence to show that the witness did not copy the license number correctly or that the defendant's car was stolen the day before the robbery.

- Five minutes after a theft, the defendant was stopped near the scene. Defendant had a unique ring in his pocket that had been taken in the theft.

  This evidence is relevant because it makes it appear more probable that the defendant committed the theft. It is not conclusive. The defense can show that there is some other explanation for the defendant having the ring.

- In a trial for rape, the defendant has admitted that he had sexual intercourse with the victim. His defense is based on his claim that the victim consented to the sexual act. The prosecutor wants to admit evidence that the defendant matches the physical description given the police by the victim immediately after the crime.

Ordinarily this evidence would be relevant, but under the facts of this case it is not. Due to the defense of consent, the defendant has admitted that he is the person who had intercourse with the victim. His identity is not in issue. Therefore, evidence that shows that he is the person the victim described is not relevant.

- In a prosecution for the theft of a TV from an apartment, the owner of the TV did not know the serial number for the TV. The defendant was discovered trying to sell a similar TV a month later.

This is relevant but very weak unless there is some distinctive marking on the TV that can identify it from thousands of similar TV sets manufactured at the same plant.

Direct and Circumstantial Evidence

One method of classifying evidence divides all evidence into two types: direct and circumstantial. A conviction can be based on either direct or **circumstantial evidence** or a combination of both. The defense attorney's favorite argument, "It is only circumstantial evidence," may be reassuring to the defendant, but it is legally possible to convict a person solely on the basis of circumstantial evidence.

   Direct evidence of a fact in issue is always relevant. In a criminal case, direct evidence usually involves eyewitness testimony regarding the commission of the crime. For example, it would be considered direct evidence if a witness testified that he saw the defendant shoot the murder victim. If the jury believes the witness is telling the truth, it has no choice but to conclude that the defendant shot the victim. On the other hand, it is only circumstantial evidence if the witness testified that he heard a gunshot and ran to the scene of the crime just in time to see the defendant run from the location with a smoking gun in her hand. This is not direct evidence because it is necessary to draw a conclusion from the facts given, namely that the person with the smoking gun is the same person who shot the victim. Even though the jury believes the witness, it can still conclude that someone else shot the victim and the defendant merely picked up the gun after the shooting and ran with it.

Direct Evidence Defined

Direct evidence is based on personal knowledge or observation of the person testifying. No inference or presumption is needed. If the testimony is believed by the jury, the fact it relates to is conclusively established.

Circumstantial Evidence Defined

Circumstantial evidence indirectly proves a fact. It requires the trier of fact to use at least one inference or presumption in order to conclude that the fact exists.

Circumstantial evidence may be so strong that it is nearly conclusive or so weak that it is immaterial. Admissibility of weak circumstantial evidence is at the discretion of the judge.

An **inference** is a logical conclusion that a person can make based on a fact or group of facts. The jury decides when to draw inferences. A **presumption** is a conclusion that the law requires the jury to make. In the example of the woman with the smoking gun, it is a logical conclusion that she shot the victim if there was no one else at the shooting scene between the time the gunshot was heard and when she was observed running away with the smoking gun. The jury will make the final determination on whether to draw this conclusion. The defense may be able to offer a logical explanation for her conduct that convinces the jury that someone else actually shot the victim. If a presumption had been involved, the jury would have been told what conclusion the law required them to draw. (Presumptions are discussed in more detail later in this chapter.)

There are many common situations in which circumstantial evidence is frequently used in criminal cases. Some states have actually enacted these into law; others merely allow the jurors to use their common sense and draw the logical conclusions.

Examples of Direct and Circumstantial Evidence

- **Fact**: The defendant was seen running from the scene immediately after the crime occurred.
  Inference: The defendant committed the crime.
- **Fact**: A man working at the scene of the robbery hid behind large boxes and watched as the robber shot the clerk who would not hand over the cash.
  Inference: None. This is direct evidence. The witness saw the entire event; if the jury believes him, there is no need for an inference.
- **Fact**: The defendant was the only person who knew the combination to the safe.
  Inference: The defendant opened the safe.
- **Fact**: The victim had a reputation for being an obnoxious bully.
  Inference: The victim started the fight and the defendant was acting in self-defense.
- **Fact**: Eyewitness saw the defendant put poison in the food and watched while the victim ate it.
  Inference: None. This is direct evidence that the defendant poisoned the victim. If the jury believes the witness, there is no need for an inference.

Direct and circumstantial evidence are discussed in more detail in Chapter 4.

Testimonial and Real Evidence

Another method of classifying evidence is by the way it is presented in court. There are a variety of terms that are used for this purpose. This book divides evidence into two types: testimonial and real. Note that this is a separate classification system. An item, such as the defendant's gun that was found near the murder scene, can be correctly classified as both circumstantial evidence and real evidence.

The key concept in **testimonial evidence** is that a person is testifying under oath or affirmation.

Testimonial Evidence Defined

Testimonial evidence is evidence given by a competent witness while testifying under oath or affirmation in a court proceeding. Affidavits and depositions are frequently included in testimonial evidence.

> *Note*: An affirmation is a solemn formal declaration used in place of an oath for those persons whose religious beliefs forbid oath-taking.

All evidence must be introduced through the testimony of a person on the witness stand. The verbal content of what the witness says is testimonial evidence. This includes both direct and cross-examination. If the witness tells about seeing the defendant shoot the victim, this is testimonial evidence. However, if the gun is admitted into evidence, the gun is real evidence.

A witness must be under oath or affirmation. This is the normal procedure at trial. A written statement made out of court under oath or affirmation is called an affidavit. A deposition is a pretrial procedure mainly used in civil cases. An attorney for each side and a stenographic reporter are usually present when a deposition is taken. The witness is placed under oath and asked questions. Cross-examination may be permitted; attorneys are allowed to make objections. In many states, the transcript of this session may be read into evidence if the witness later becomes unavailable to testify. Testimonial evidence is discussed in more detail in Chapter 5.

There is some confusion regarding the correct term for objects that are admitted into evidence. **Real evidence,** physical evidence, demonstrative evidence, and tangible evidence are all commonly used terms. Various authors define one term so that it includes the others. Students should be aware that the previous terms are frequently used interchangeably. **Documentary evidence** is a subgroup of real evidence (see Chapter 7).

Real Evidence Defined

Real evidence is anything (except testimonial evidence) that can be perceived with the five senses that tends to prove a fact that is at issue.

Many states only consider objects that are admitted into evidence as exhibits to be real evidence. Some authors use a broader approach and apply the term *real evidence* to items such as drawings on blackboards or butcher paper that were made while a witness was testifying but not formally introduced into evidence. Real evidence is discussed in more detail in Chapters 6 and 7.

Examples of Real Evidence
- Physical items: guns, knives, blood-soaked clothing, key to the safe deposit box
- Documents: checks, contracts, letters, ransom notes, newspapers, maps, deeds, wills, fingerprint cards, computer files
- Exhibits made for trial: models, scale drawings, charts, demonstrations
- Pictures: still photographs, enlargements, motion pictures, videos, digital images, photocopies, X-ray films, jpegs, etc.

Substitutes for Evidence

There are some situations in which the jury is specifically told what facts to believe rather than having the opposing sides introduce evidence on the issue. These can be divided into three categories: stipulations, judicial notice, and presumptions.

Stipulations

An agreement between the opposing attorneys to admit that one or more facts exist is called a **stipulation**. If the agreement is made before trial, the stipulation will usually be introduced in court in the form of a written document. When stipulations are reached during trial, they are usually stated orally for the record. The judge will tell the jurors that they must conclude that the stipulated fact exists and give it the same weight as if it had been proven during the trial. This statement may be made both at the time the stipulation is entered and again in the jury instructions.

Attorneys may agree to make a stipulation for a variety of reasons. Probably the most common is that one side knows the other side can easily prove the facts involved. For example, all the prosecution has to do to prove that the defendant has a prior conviction is to give the judge a certified copy of the conviction. For this reason, the defense frequently agrees to stipulate to the prior.

Another reason for stipulating may be that the facts would prejudice the jury against the defendant. For example, the prosecutor is charging that the defendant has a prior felony conviction. Since the prior is for a gruesome crime almost identical to the present one, the defendant does not want the jury to hear the details. By agreeing to stipulate to the prior, the defendant can keep the prosecution from telling the jury the details of the prior crime.

Stipulations are also made on minor points of the case. Both sides agree that proving these small details is too time-consuming; therefore, they stipulate to them.

Since stipulations involve a voluntary agreement between the attorneys, there are also cases in which there obviously should have been a stipulation but there was none. This can be caused by antagonism between the attorneys, failure to communicate, or lack of preparation. Occasionally, it is a trial tactic.

Examples of Stipulations

- The charges include the fact that the defendant has a prior conviction. The defense may be willing to stipulate that the prior conviction exists and prevent the prosecution from introducing details of that crime.
- The event happened at 10:00 p.m. Both sides may be willing to stipulate that the crime occurred at night. *Note:* This fact could also come in under judicial notice.
- In a drunk driving case, it may be stipulated that the emergency room staff used proper techniques in taking the blood sample from the defendant.

Judicial Notice

Judicial notice is a procedure in which the judge, on his or her own authority, tells the jury to conclude that a fact exists. The jury is required to follow this instruction in civil cases, but it is only advisory in criminal cases. An attorney may request that the judge take judicial notice of some point or the judge may decide to do it without a request.

The idea behind judicial notice is that it is a waste of time to require proof of commonly known facts. Some states break this down and make it mandatory that judicial notice be taken, if requested, of the state's own laws, the federal constitution, and well-known scientific facts. They let individual judges decide whether to take judicial notice of lesser known facts and out-of-state law.

As used in judicial notice, "commonly known facts" refers to facts that are well-known in the community, including the scientific community. The judge's personal knowledge of the fact is not important. If the judge has a doubt about how well-known the fact is, it is the duty of the attorney who requested judicial notice to convince the judge that the fact qualifies.

Judicial notice is not requested if the parties enter into a stipulation. On the other hand, if the attorneys know that the judge will automatically grant judicial notice, they may not bother to draft a stipulation. One side may request judicial notice because the other side refused to stipulate. In these cases, the opposing counsel may argue that judicial notice is not properly taken. It seems to be a contradiction that there could be dispute on what are "commonly known facts." The issues would most likely arise when the attorney requesting judicial notice is attempting to abuse the procedure or the attorney objecting to it is unfamiliar with local law on judicial notice. In the case of scientific facts, it is also common to see debates on the propriety of judicial notice when the scientific fact involved has been recently established or is still controversial.

The Federal Rules of Evidence provide a useful outline on the use of judicial notice. Rule 201 states the following:

(a) **Scope of rule**. This rule governs only judicial notice of adjudicative facts.
(b) **Kinds of facts**. A judicially noticed fact must be one not subject to reasonable dispute in that it is either (1) generally known within the territorial jurisdiction of the trial court or (2) capable of accurate and ready determination by resort to sources whose accuracy cannot reasonably be questioned.
(c) **When discretionary**. A court may take judicial notice, whether requested or not.
(d) **When mandatory**. A court shall take judicial notice if requested by a party and supplied with the necessary information.
(e) **Opportunity to be heard**. A party is entitled upon timely request to an opportunity to be heard as to the propriety of taking judicial notice and the tenor of the matter noticed. In the absence of prior notification, the request may be made after judicial notice has been taken.
(f) **Time of taking notice**. Judicial notice may be taken at any stage of the proceeding.
(g) **Instructing jury**. In a civil action or proceeding, the court shall instruct the jury to accept as conclusive any fact judicially noticed. In a criminal case, the court shall instruct the jury that it may, but is not required to, accept as conclusive any fact judicially noticed.

Examples of Items Subject to Judicial Notice
• Law: U.S. Constitution, state constitution, United States Code, state codes. Out-of-state laws and foreign laws usually have to be shown to the judge before judicial notice is taken.

- Court records and court rules.
- Scientific facts: temperature at which water freezes, time of sunset and sunrise, probabilities of occurrences of various blood types, accuracy of properly maintained radar equipment used to determine the speed a car was traveling, high and low tides.
- Local facts: which cities are in the court district, which streets run north–south, location of landmarks, fact that a given area is uninhabited.

Presumptions

When a presumption is involved, the judge instructs the jury to draw specific conclusions from the facts. Unlike stipulations and judicial notice, in order to use a presumption the attorney must convince the jury that at least some of the facts exist. When discussing presumptions, two terms are commonly used. The basic fact is that fact which must be established in order to use a presumption. The presumed fact is the fact that the judge will tell the jurors they must assume happened if the basic fact is established. Keep in mind that if the basic fact is not established, the presumption cannot be used.

Presumption Defined

A presumption is a conclusion that the law requires the jury to draw from facts that have been established at trial. The judge instructs the jurors when they are to use a presumption.

There are two constitutional limitations on presumptions in criminal cases: (1) A presumption must be based on a logical assumption rather than mere policy, and (2) when used by the prosecution, the basic fact must be established beyond a reasonable doubt. A presumption that a person intends the ordinary consequences of his or her voluntary acts is unconstitutional because the jury could believe it shifts the burden of persuasion to the defendant.

The following rather complicated presumptions have also been found to be unconstitutional: Intent to commit theft by fraud is presumed when there is a failure to return rental cars within 20 days of the owner's demand, and a person is presumed to have embezzled a rental car if the car was not returned within 5 days of the expiration of the rental agreement.

Some states list specific presumptions in their codes and specify the effect of each presumption. Others rely on the common law or the local state's case law. The Federal Rules of Evidence do not contain any presumptions for use in criminal cases.

Presumptions are generally divided into two types: conclusive and rebuttable. **Rebuttable presumptions** can be further divided into strong

Figure 3-1
Conclusive, Strong Rebuttable, and Weak Rebuttable Presumptions

and weak. Which category a presumption falls into is governed by the social policy behind it. Not all states will find the same policy reason for a presumption, so it may not be considered to be in the same category in all states.

In its simplest form, a presumption requires the jury to conclude that the presumed fact is true if the jury believes the basic fact has been established. In all presumptions, the opposing side can try to convince the jury that the basic fact did not occur. This can be done by attacking the credibility of the witnesses who testified about the basic fact or presenting witnesses who are in a position to know that the fact never occurred. Figure 3-1 illustrates each of the presumptions.

The role of the presumed fact changes according to the social policy involved. In cases in which social policy is strongest (that is, **conclusive presumptions**) no one is allowed to refute the existence of the presumed fact, but attacks on the basic fact may be used to avoid the conclusion that the presumption directs the jury to draw. There are very few conclusive presumptions.

When a rebuttable presumption is involved, the opposing side can attempt to disprove either the basic fact or the presumed fact. With a strong rebuttable presumption, many states give the opposing side the task of either disproving the basic fact or disproving the presumed fact. Merely casting doubt on the existence of the presumed fact is not enough.

The lowest level of social policy is involved in weak rebuttable presumptions. These are usually created to expedite the trial rather than to enforce the interests of society. In these cases, the presumption completely disappears if the opposing side has introduced evidence to disprove the presumed fact; the jury will not even be told that the presumption exists.

It is helpful to work through several presumptions in order to understand how they operate. First, consider the conclusive presumption that a child born to a married couple who are living together was fathered by the husband unless the husband is impotent or sterile. There is a strong social policy favoring the legitimacy of children that resulted in the creation of this presumption. Sometimes it resulted in a man being ruled the father of a child when blood tests established a high probability that he was not the father. With advances in DNA testing making it scientifically possible to disprove paternity, and a lowering of the social stigma of illegitimacy, there has been pressure on state legislatures to do away with this presumption.

Now let's examine a strong rebuttable presumption. A presumption that many states place in this category is that a person who has disappeared and has not been heard from in 5 years is presumed to be dead. The basic fact is that a person has disappeared and not been heard from in 5 years. The presumed fact is that the person is dead. The purpose of this presumption is to allow property rights to be settled among the heirs of the person who disappeared and to allow the remaining spouse to remarry. It is not used as a basis for homicide prosecutions.

The party that wishes to use this presumption must establish that the person has disappeared and not been heard from in 5 years. If this is done, and the other side introduces no evidence on the issue, the jury must conclude that the person in question is dead.

The opposing side can attack the presumption in two ways: show that the person has been heard from during the past 5 years (disprove the basic fact) or show that the person is not dead (disprove the presumed fact). Testimony from people who claim to have seen the person recently can be used to attack the basic fact. Evidence that there was a motive for the disappearance, such as escaping prosecution for a serious felony, can be used to attack the presumed fact.

The jurors are usually instructed that if they believe the person has disappeared and has not been heard from, they must conclude that he or she is dead unless they believe the other side's explanation for the disappearance.

The next illustration involves a weak rebuttable presumption: A letter that is properly mailed (correctly addressed, stamped, and put in the U.S. mail) is presumed to reach its destination. This is a presumption established solely to facilitate normal business transactions because it would be very difficult for the person who mails a letter to prove that it reached its destination.

Everyone knows that the mail service is not perfect, but it is easier to start with the general assumption that a letter will get to its destination. If the opposing side tries to show that the letter was not correctly mailed—for example, it was mailed to the wrong address (attacks the basic fact)—the jury will be instructed that if they believe the letter was correctly mailed they must conclude that it got to its destination. During deliberations, the jury will have to decide if the letter was mailed correctly. On the other hand, if the opposing side introduces testimony that the letter never reached the addressee, the presumption ceases to exist, and the jury will not even be told about the presumption.

Summary

Only relevant evidence can be admitted in court. This means that the evidence must tend to prove something that is required in the case. Not only must it be relevant but also the value of the evidence must be sufficient to make the evidence material.

Evidence can be divided into direct or circumstantial. Direct evidence proves the point without the need to draw any conclusions. Circumstantial evidence requires the jury to draw a conclusion that some relevant fact occurred.

Another system of classification divides evidence into two categories: testimonial and real. Testimonial evidence covers what witnesses say under oath or affirmation. Real evidence includes all types of tangible objects.

There are three main substitutes for evidence. The opposing attorneys may agree that a fact exists without proving it to the jury. This is called a stipulation. A judge may take official notice of commonly known facts. Judicial notice is the name for this procedure. Presumptions require the jury to draw specific conclusions if certain basic facts have been established. In all of these situations, the jury is told to assume that a fact has been proven when in fact it has not been. This is done to expedite the trial and, in some cases, to protect strong social policies.

Review Questions

1. Define *relevant* and *material evidence* and explain how they differ.
2. List two situations in which relevant evidence would not be admissible in court.
3. Define *direct* and *circumstantial evidence* and give two examples of each.
4. Define *testimonial* and *real evidence* and give two examples of each.
5. Compare and contrast stipulation and judicial notice, and give two examples of facts that could be judicially noticed.
6. Define *inference* and give an example of its application.
7. Differentiate between a rebuttable presumption and a conclusive presumption.
8. Give an example of a conclusive presumption and a rebuttable presumption.

Writing Assignment

Go to www.cnn.com/crime and click on a case that is currently being tried. Read all you can about that case at the website. Write a 250-word (one-page) paper identifying each piece of evidence as direct, circumstantial, testimonial, real, document, stipulation, judicial notice, and presumption.

Note:

1. Many items will fit in more that one of the previous categories.
2. You may not be able to find something for every one of the previous categories.

CHAPTER 4

Direct and Circumstantial Evidence

Feature Case: Kobe Bryant

Star player for the Los Angeles Lakers. Charged with rape of a Colorado hotel concierge in July 2003. Faced 4 years to life in prison if convicted. Throughout the proceedings, Kobe Bryant maintained that it had been consensual sex.

When the victim was taken to the hospital the day following the sexual encounter for an examination (commonly called a "rape kit"), she had bruises on her neck and in the vaginal area. Her undergarments were sent to the laboratory for testing and it was discovered that there was evidence that she had had multiple sex partners. The defense argued that the evidence indicated the victim had three sex partners, one possibly in the interval between leaving Bryant and arriving at the hospital for the rape exam, and any one of the three could have inflicted the injuries. The defense appealed to the Colorado Supreme Court and won the right to question the victim about her past sexual history despite the Colorado "Rape Shield Law" that made a rape victim's past inadmissible.

As the trial approached, the victim became reluctant to testify or participate in the trial in any way. After jury selection was under way, a settlement was reached and the charges were dropped on September 1, 2004. Bryant issued the following statement: "Although I truly believe this encounter between us was consensual, I recognize now that she did not and does not view this incident the same way I did. After months of reviewing discovery, listening to her attorney, and even her testimony in person, I now understand how she feels that she did not consent to this encounter."

Learning Objectives

After studying this chapter, you will be able to

- Define both *direct* and *circumstantial evidence*.
- Explain how the jury determines the weight to be given to the testimony of each witness.
- Describe circumstantial evidence that can be used to show *modus operandi* and to establish motive.
- Identify situations in which the defendant's knowledge or skills can be used as circumstantial evidence of guilt.
- Describe the types of situations in which the defendant's acts prior to the crime may be used in evidence.
- Identify situations in which the defendant's acts after the crime was committed can be used as circumstantial evidence of guilt.
- Explain when character evidence is admissible at trial and describe how character is established at trial.

Key Terms

- Character
- Circumstantial evidence
- Credibility of the witness
- Direct evidence
- Matter of law
- *Modus operandi*
- Reputation
- Weight of each piece of evidence

Myths about Direct and Circumstantial Evidence	Facts about Direct and Circumstantial Evidence
A conviction cannot be based on circumstantial evidence.	There is no rule that mandates which types of evidence are used to convict.
Direct evidence is given more weight than circumstantial evidence.	The jury decides how much weight will be placed on each piece of evidence. The credibility of the witness has a lot to do with the weight the jury assigns to the evidence.
Direct evidence means a physical object—the murder weapon, the ransom note, etc.	Direct evidence is based on firsthand knowledge—personal knowledge or observation of the person testifying.
Circumstantial evidence means hearsay and rumors surrounding the case.	Circumstantial evidence means testimony that indirectly proves a fact—the jury must use an inference to connect circumstantial evidence to the commission of the crime.

Basic Definitions

In Chapter 3, we briefly discussed direct and circumstantial evidence. The following were the key definitions:

Direct Evidence Defined

Direct evidence is based on personal knowledge or observation of the person testifying. No inference or presumption is needed. If the testimony is believed by the jury, the fact it relates to is conclusively established.

Circumstantial Evidence Defined

Circumstantial evidence indirectly proves a fact. It requires the trier of the facts to use an inference or presumption in order to conclude that the fact exists.

Direct evidence will be admissible if it was legally obtained and is not privileged. **Circumstantial evidence** is admitted at the discretion of the judge. The judge considers whether the evidence is relevant and balances other factors such as the amount of time it will take to introduce the evidence, confusion that may result from the evidence, and the possibility that the evidence may be unduly prejudicial. Direct and/or circumstantial evidence can be used to establish guilt. The law does not favor direct evidence over circumstantial. The jury decides whether the fact has been established.

Weight of Evidence

In American courts, questions of law are decided by the judge. Questions of fact are decided by the jury, unless the trial is being heard by a judge without a jury. Stipulations and items judicially noticed are determined as a **"matter of law"** by the judge; the jury decides all disputed facts.

The jury, as trier of the facts, is given the duty to decide the effect and **weight of each piece of evidence.** This requires the jury to decide which evidence to believe if there is a conflict in the facts. If there is more than one possible interpretation of the facts, the jury has to decide which one is correct. The jury also decides what inferences to draw from circumstantial evidence and which witnesses should be believed.

When direct evidence is introduced, the jury's main function is to decide the **credibility of the witness.** This usually revolves around two factors: the demeanor of the witness and the likelihood that what the witness said could have happened. Demeanor includes all types of body language. The jury also considers whether the witness was evasive or antagonistic. Common sense may be applied to the facts in order to decide if it was possible for the events in question to occur in the manner the witness described. Facts disclosed during impeachment, such as personal bias or prior felony convictions of the witness, may also be considered. Jury instructions usually explain all of this. Impeachment is covered in detail in Chapter 5.

Examples of Ways to Test Credibility of a Witness
- The witness refused to look at the prosecutor or the jury.
- The witness gave evasive answers and refused to be pinned down on details.
- The witness cooperated with one side but was very hostile toward the attorney for the opposing side.
- The witness previously told the police a totally different story than he gave while testifying.
- The witness has previously been convicted for perjury.
- The witness has previously been convicted for any crime involving truthfulness.

Circumstantial evidence is more difficult to evaluate. The jury must decide the credibility of the witness, what inference should be drawn from the evidence, and the weight to be given to each piece of evidence. There is frequently more than one inference that can be drawn from the facts, and sometimes the possible conclusions are quite contradictory. Also, individual jurors will have different ideas on the correct weight for various pieces of evidence. All of these conclusions are obviously affected by the credibility of the witnesses. These issues must be resolved during jury deliberations. The jurors are told to listen to each other's opinions and try to reach a consensus. Lengthy discussions and many ballots may be required. If an impasse occurs, the judge may intervene with additional instructions on the need to consider all points of view in order to reach a verdict, but the jurors are the only ones who can decide what conclusions to reach.

Circumstantial Evidence of Ability to Commit the Crime

Some crimes are committed in a manner that indicates that the suspect had special skills or abilities that the average person would not have had. The more unique the skill, the stronger the inference that the defendant is the one who committed the crime if he or she has that skill. Obviously, the case must be based on more than this one inference. The prosecutor hopes that the jury will conclude that the defendant is guilty if the defendant has the rare skill or ability that was required to commit the crime. The defense can also use the reverse of this approach. If the crime was committed by a person with a special skill or ability, the fact that the defendant does *not* have the requisite skill or ability can be used to infer that the defendant did not commit the crime.

Skills and Technical Knowledge

Most street crimes require few special skills or technical knowledge, but there are circumstances in which even these crimes are committed in such a way that the suspect must have had some specialized training or experience. On the other hand, most white-collar crimes require uncommon skills or technical knowledge.

For example, "safe cracking" is a skill that the average person does not have. In a case in which an unauthorized person opened a locked safe, the fact that the defendant has been known to "crack" safes in the past is relevant. This circumstantial evidence is not conclusive, of course, but combined with other admissible evidence it may convince the jury that the defendant committed the crime. The opposite approach can also be used by the defense. If the defense attorney can convince the jury that the defendant has no idea how to open a safe, the jury would likely conclude that the defendant did not commit the crime (at least not alone).

Computer crimes are another example. Many elaborate embezzlement schemes are accomplished by altering a company's computer software. High-tech extortion plots may involve the unauthorized use of computer access codes or the placing of "logic bombs" and "viruses" in a software program. The Internet may be used to obtain credit card numbers. These crimes require advanced programming techniques that the average person does not possess. In these types of cases, the fact that the defendant had the ability to do sophisticated programming is very relevant circumstantial evidence. Other examples of skills that can be used as circumstantial evidence include etching and printing (counterfeiting cases), locksmithing (burglary without signs of forced entry), bookkeeping (embezzlement), and advanced training in electronics (entry by avoiding a highly sophisticated alarm system).

Examples of Skills and Technical Knowledge Needed to Commit the Crime

- The burglar bypassed an elaborate alarm system in order to enter the building.
- The door was opened with a "lock pick."
- Someone programmed the company computer to pay invoices submitted by a fictitious business.
- The artists made and sold paintings that looked exactly like famous masterpieces.
- Identity theft.

Means to Accomplish the Crime

The fact that the defendant had the means to accomplish the crime can also be used as circumstantial evidence if the average person would not have access to the necessary equipment or location. A simple example of this is if the defendant owned a gun that was the same caliber as the bullet taken from the body of the murder victim. If the bullet is damaged so that no further testing can be done, and there are many similar guns, the inference would be weak. On the other hand, if a ballistics test matches the bullet to the defendant's gun, the inference would be strong.

Examples of Means to Accomplish a Crime
- A person who worked at a company making explosives would have access to the chemicals necessary to manufacture bombs.
- A person caught with a lock pick in his or her possession may have committed a burglary without leaving signs of forcible entry.
- A person who had a large quantity of small, clear plastic envelopes might be selling illegal drugs.
- A person has the combination to the safe that was opened without any sign of prying or other physical damage.
- A person owns a rare gun that is the same make and model as the one used to commit the crime.
- A person was recently fired by the business that was burglarized and still has a key to the back door.

In a similar manner, the fact that the defendant had a stolen pass key for the area where the theft occurred can be used as circumstantial evidence that the suspect was in the area; unauthorized possession of the password for a computer that has been tampered with is circumstantial evidence that the defendant illegally used the computer; and possession of someone else's credit card numbers or telephone calling card numbers is circumstantial evidence that the defendant made the unauthorized charges.

Physical Capacity

Physical capacity can also be used to infer guilt in some cases. An obvious example is the defendant's height, if the physical facts show that only a very tall person could have committed the crime. The ability to run very fast, or the fact that the defendant is disabled and could not possibly have run that fast, can also be used if the situation makes speed relevant. The ability to lift heavy weights would be relevant if the suspect carried away heavy objects, or impotence may be relevant in sex crime cases.

Examples of Physical Capacity to Commit the Crime
- The burglar carried 50-pound bags out of the building.
- The burglar entered the building through a window that would only open a few inches.
- The suspect outran the victim.
- The victim was severely injured by karate kicks to his head.
- The kidnapper picked up the victim and carried her a substantial distance.

Mental Capacity

Mental capacity may also be relevant. This is probably obvious if the defendant is pleading "not guilty by reason of insanity" or "diminished capacity." Juvenile cases may turn on the maturity and mental capacity of the child. Specific intent crimes and crimes requiring premeditation also make mental capacity more important.

On the other hand, since adults are presumed to know things that are common knowledge, the defense may need to establish that the defendant has minimal mental capacity and, therefore, did not know something that was obvious to everyone else. The facts of a crime may also make mental capacity relevant. It can be inferred that sophisticated crimes could only have been committed by very intelligent people. Childish pranks may be circumstantial evidence that the suspect was an adult with below average mental capacity or that juveniles were the culprits.

Examples of Mental Capacity to Commit the Crime
- The defendant developed a very sophisticated plot to kill the victim.
- The defendant used a very complicated chemical formula to manufacture illegal drugs.
- The defendant memorized 20 ten-digit account numbers.
- The ransom demand note was written in perfect Shakespearean English.
- The adult suspect acted like a 7-year-old.

Circumstantial Evidence of Intent

Circumstantial evidence is frequently needed to establish intent. This is doubly true in specific intent crimes. The two most common approaches to establishing intent are modus operandi and motive. Definitions used for these items vary from state to state.

Modus Operandi

Modus operandi literally means the method of operation. Many criminals become creatures of habit and rather methodically commit the same crimes repeatedly in the same way. When this happens, the prosecutor can introduce evidence of the defendant's prior crimes that were substantially similar to the current one and let the jury conclude that the defendant also committed the crime he or she is now charged with. The fact that the defendant has been previously charged with violation of the same penal code section is not enough. There must be a great similarity in the method of committing the crime. If there are many common features, the jury will be more likely to infer that the defendant also committed the crime for which he or she is now on trial. The prosecutor may also be allowed to introduce evidence of very similar crimes committed by the defendant, even if the defendant was never charged with those offenses.

The judge has the discretion to admit or reject this type of circumstantial evidence. The normal rule is that prior crimes are not admissible. The jury should not infer that the defendant is guilty merely because he or she has been guilty of other crimes. The prosecutor must convince the judge that the method of committing the crime was sufficiently unusual to amount to the defendant putting his or her "signature" on it.

An example would be the person who enters liquor stores late at night, asks for a specific brand of cigarettes, and, while the clerk is getting the cigarettes, pulls a gun and demands all the money in the cash register. The combination of time of day, type of store, and diversionary technique make this person's crimes distinctive. The prosecutor will be allowed to introduce evidence so the jury can see that the defendant has committed very similar crimes in the past. Based on this, the jurors will be allowed to conclude, if they see fit, that the defendant also committed the current liquor store robbery.

In a case involving a woman who was charged with bank robbery, the judge ruled that her prior conviction for bank robbery was admissible because there were very few women who rob banks. Normally, the prosecutor will have to show several common features of the past and present crimes in order to convince the judge that the prior offenses can be introduced.

Examples of *Modus Operandi*—Same Method Used on Several Occasions

• A rape suspect frequented "singles bars" and offered to take the victim to dinner. On their "dinner date" he suddenly told the victim he would cook dinner for them. Once they had entered his apartment, he became very aggressive and raped the victim if she did not consent.

- The suspect knocked on the front door. If anyone answered, he asked for Fred. When told that no one by that name lived there, he asked to use the phone. Once inside, he stole expensive items.
- A man walked in parks where children frequently played. He would approach a child, show the child a picture of a puppy, and tell the child he had lost his puppy. The child was asked to help find the puppy. If the child went to an isolated spot with the man, he would molest the child.
- The suspect avoided burglar alarms by entering through the roof. He used a grappling hook to scale the wall and then chopped a hole in the roof.

Motive

Motive does not have to be proven by the prosecution unless it is included in the definition of the crime. Even though it is not an element of the crime, it may be a key to convincing the jury that the defendant is guilty. This is particularly true when there is no direct evidence in the case. Depending on the facts of the case, possible motives could include hate, prejudice, revenge, retaliation, greed, lust, profit, economic need, love, and mercy.

Greed is a motive in many crimes. In a murder case, it usually means the criminal will profit financially from the death of the victim. This could include being hired to commit murder, inheriting money or something else of value from the victim, being the beneficiary of the victim's life insurance policy, eliminating business competitors, and preventing the victim or witness from reporting a crime. Any of these could be used as circumstantial evidence of intent to kill.

Hatred and prejudice also motivate many criminals. Hatred may be obvious if there has been a long-running feud between the victim and the suspect. Racial prejudice may appear as the motive in other cases. Less obvious examples include gang violence and terrorism. Love and mercy may even be motives. "Lovers' triangles" (and other geometric patterns) can erupt into violence and even murder. Euthanasia, or mercy killing, may be based on the belief that a loved one should not be allowed to suffer.

Motive may also be important if the defendant is claiming that a murder was committed in self-defense or in the heat of passion. Evidence that there was a motive for the killing, such as revenge, jealousy, or hate, may help convince the jury that an opportunistic defendant's claim to mitigating circumstances is not valid.

Examples of Motive to Commit the Crime
- Husband was involved in an affair and wanted a divorce. The divorce was never complete because the couple could not agree on a property settlement. Wife was found dead.

- A business owner was deeply in debt. He falsified inventory records to show that many expensive items were stored in the warehouse. He took out a fire insurance policy. Two weeks later the warehouse burned to the ground.
- A woman had a double indemnity life insurance policy that paid twice as much if death was by natural causes but did not pay anything if death was by suicide. Her husband, who was the beneficiary of the insurance policy, hid evidence that indicated the woman took her own life.
- A husband and wife were in the midst of a fierce custody battle. The wife coached one of the children to tell a police officer that the father had sexually abused him.
- A defendant had been charged with capital murder. Only one witness could positively identify the defendant as the killer. Someone killed the witness.

Threats

The fact that the defendant has threatened to commit the crime is circumstantial evidence that he or she committed the crime. Although a person may make threats without planning to carry them out, the fact that the threat was made has some probative value. Specific threats will carry more weight than vague ones. How recently the threat was made, the credibility of the person reporting it, and other circumstances surrounding it will also be relevant. On the other hand, if it can be shown that someone else threatened to commit the crime, the defense can try to convince the jury that the other person committed the crime and the defendant is innocent.

Threats may also be relevant in self-defense cases. The standard used to determine if self-defense justified the use of force is whether a reasonable person would have used the same amount of force in the same circumstances. Jurors may consider the fact that the victim had previously threatened to harm the defendant. The question becomes what force would a reasonable person who had received the same threat believe was necessary to protect him- or herself when confronted by the person who made the threats.

Examples of Relevant Threats to Commit the Crime
- Two days before the victim's death, the victim and suspect got into a fight. The suspect shouted, "I'll kill you for that!"
- A battered woman told her batterer that she was going to leave him. He made a menacing gesture and said, "If you ever leave me you will never see your kids again!" The next day the children disappeared.
- A bully continually threatened another high school student. He taunted, "I'm going to kill you!" One day the bully approached the student with his hand in his jacket pocket simulating a gun. Believing the bully was about to shoot him, the student grabbed a rock and hit the bully in the head.

- Someone repeatedly phoned and in a loud whisper said, "You won't live to see the morning sun." At approximately 2:00 a.m., someone tried to open the back door. The person who received the calls became very frightened and fired a rifle through the door.
- An employee was caught stealing. He told the security staff that if he got fired they would pay for it. A week later, someone slashed the tires on all the cars in the area where the security staff parked.

Circumstantial Evidence of Guilt

What the suspect does following the crime may also be circumstantial evidence of guilt. Flight to avoid prosecution, attempts to hide evidence, possession of stolen property, sudden wealth, and attempts to silence witnesses are commonly put in this category.

Although the average juror probably considers the fact that the defendant has invoked the Fifth Amendment to be evidence of guilt, the U.S. Supreme Court has made it clear that the jury must not draw this conclusion.[1] Invoking *Miranda* rights also comes under the same protection.[2] The Court's reasoning was that constitutional rights would be meaningless if the jury could conclude that a person is guilty if he or she used them.

Flight to Avoid Punishment

This category includes almost anything a suspect does to avoid conviction and serving a sentence. Probably the first to come to mind is fleeing from the scene of the crime. Later attempts to flee to avoid arrest are also included. Hiding raises a similar inference. After arrest, the more common ways to avoid punishment include jumping bail and attempts to escape from jail.

Examples of Flight to Avoid Punishment
- The suspect ran from the scene immediately after the crime.
- The suspect fled the country after being released on bail.
- The police tried to arrest the suspect on an outstanding warrant. The suspect attacked the officer and escaped.

Concealing Evidence

Hiding or concealing evidence raises an inference of guilt, as does destroying evidence. Falsifying evidence or tampering with it can also be used to infer guilt.

Many fact patterns raise this type of inference. Some, such as arson to conceal theft or staging an auto accident to hide the fact that the victim had been murdered, involve detailed planning and can only be disproved by testimony from expert witnesses. Others, such as throwing a ski mask in a trash can while running from the scene of a robbery, can be more easily established.

The defendant may try to hide evidence from the jury by asking witnesses to lie at trial. This information can be used as circumstantial evidence of guilt. The fact that the defendant tried to get a witness to alter testimony is admissible whether or not the witness agreed. It does not matter if the witness was willing to cooperate with the defendant, or if bribery, extortion, or some other means was used to get the witness to comply. The fact that the prosecutor does not plan to file charges for the perjury (lying under oath) or subornation of perjury (recruiting someone to lie under oath) is irrelevant.

Tampering with real (physical) evidence also raises an inference of guilt. This includes altering the evidence in the case or manufacturing evidence for use at trial.

Examples of Concealing Evidence
- The suspect killed the victim and set the house on fire to hide the murder.
- The suspect carved a hole in the wall, hid the evidence, and then paneled the wall to hide the hole.
- The suspect gave evidence to a friend and told him to hide it.

Possession of Stolen Property

In a theft case, the fact that the defendant was in possession of something taken during the theft is circumstantial evidence that the defendant was the thief. The inference is much stronger if the defendant had the property immediately after the theft. Receiving stolen property (called theft by possession in some states), rather than theft, may be a more appropriate charge when there is a substantial time lag between the theft and the discovery that the defendant had the property.

Examples of Possession of Stolen Property
- The suspect was stopped approximately 1 mile from the scene of the robbery. When he searched the suspect, the officer found cash in his pocket that was exactly equal to the amount stolen.
- The suspect had shiny new rims on his car that matched the description of ones stolen approximately 1 week ago. He stated that he had received the

rims as a birthday gift from his girlfriend but could not give the name of his girlfriend.
- The suspect was wearing an antique ring that matched the description of one stolen in a recent home-invasion robbery.

Sudden Wealth

The fact that the suspect suddenly had a lot of money soon after a property crime occurred can be used as circumstantial evidence. This is also true if the defendant profited from a violent crime such as murder. The prosecutor will ask the jury to infer that the money came from committing the crime. The jury may be told how much the defendant earns (or that he or she was unemployed), the defendant's normal spending habits, or that he or she recently tried to obtain charity or loans because he or she had no money. The defense will attempt to convince the jury that there was a legal source for this sudden wealth. Evidence that the defendant inherited a large sum of money from a recently deceased relative, won the lottery, or even won the money by gambling may be introduced into evidence.

Examples of Sudden Wealth
- The suspect, who was unemployed, went to his favorite bar and paid cash for several rounds of drinks for everyone present.
- The suspect, who worked at a low-paying job, deposited $10,000 in cash into his checking account.
- The suspect, who previously took the bus to work, suddenly started driving an expensive automobile.

Threatening Witnesses

If the defendant threatens or abuses the victim or witnesses in order to prevent prosecution and conviction, it can be inferred that the defendant is guilty. Killing the victim, either during the original crime or later, in order to prevent the victim from testifying is the most extreme case. The same inference also applies if threats were used in an attempt to prevent the victim or witness from reporting the crime, to pressure the victim to drop the charges, or to prevent the victim or witness from testifying in court. It does not matter if the defendant makes the threats or if he or she has someone else do it. The jury will decide how much weight the threats should be given based on what the defendant did.

These types of activities frequently amount to separate crimes. Their use as circumstantial evidence is separate from any prosecution for intimidating witnesses.

Examples of Threatening Witnesses
- Prior to leaving the scene of the crime, the robber told the victim, "You call the police and I'll come back and kill you!"
- Someone believed to be the defendant telephoned a person who had been subpoenaed to testify at trial and said in a menacing voice, "You'd better not show up in court if you love your kids."
- John, the defendant, had friends talk to the potential witness on several occasions. These friends appeared to be armed and they said, "We want what is best for John."

Character

"Character witnesses" are used to try to convince the jury that a person did something consistent with his or her character. Most states use reputation as evidence of character. For example, if a person has the reputation for telling the truth, the jury may infer that the person is currently telling the truth. This is circumstantial evidence, and the jury will have to decide how much weight to give the character evidence.

In most states, character witnesses are only allowed to testify about a person's reputation. **Reputation** is what other people believe about a person's character. **Character** describes what a person's moral traits really are. In some cases, there may be a major difference between what the person is and what others believe he or she is.

The most common rule is that the character witness may only testify about what he or she knows of a person's reputation in the "community." Community usually means neighborhood, but it can also refer to a group of people who work together. To testify about reputation in the community, the character witness must tell what he or she has heard other people say. The personal opinion of this witness is not admissible under the traditional rule.

Some states have expanded the traditional rule and allow character witnesses to give their personal opinion of a person's character. This gives the jury more information to use when drawing a conclusion.

The use of character witnesses is restricted to three basic situations:

1. The defendant may try to use his or her good character to convince the jury that he or she did not commit a crime.
2. Specific character traits of the defendant may be used to infer that the defendant did (or did not) commit the crime.
3. Specific character traits of the victim may be used when relevant to the crime.

The Defendant's Character in General

The prosecution is not allowed to attack the defendant's character unless the defendant has placed character at issue. If the defense called character witnesses, the prosecution may call character witnesses during rebuttal. The prosecution's character witnesses will testify that the defendant's reputation is not what the defense witnesses said it was. For example, the defendant may call his priest to testify that the defendant has a reputation for being an honest, law-abiding citizen. The prosecutor may call the defendant's former business partner, who testifies that the defendant has a reputation for being a lying thief.

Cross-examination can be used effectively on character witnesses. Since the witness is supposed to be telling the jury what the defendant's reputation is in the community, showing that the character witness does not know what very many people think of the defendant reduces the impact of the testimony. The testimony of a character witness is also weakened if it is shown that the witness knows the defendant has done things that are inconsistent with his or her reputation. It is also easy to impeach many defense character witnesses for bias. Since the defendant's friends and family frequently testify about his or her good reputation, they probably view things in the light most favorable to the defendant. The character witnesses may also be shown to be liars. The defense, of course, will use the same tactics to impeach the prosecution's character witnesses.

Examples of Evidence on Defendant's Character in General
- The defendant calls her pastor to testify that she is an outstanding member of the congregation and does many acts of charity.
- The prosecutor calls character witness after the pastor testifies. The prosecution witness states that the defendant is known to be a hypocrite who goes to church regularly but otherwise leads the life of a hardened criminal.
- The defendant calls a character witness who testifies that the prosecution's character witness has the reputation for being a liar.

Specific Character Traits of the Defendant

In some trials, one of the defendant's specific character traits may be relevant. Since this evidence is relevant to a specific issue, it can be raised by either side. The prosecution does not have to wait for the defense to call character witnesses first.

The use of specific character traits is most common in trials for violent crimes. If the trial is based on the defendant's killing his wife after finding out that she was having an affair, the defense may try to use his reputation for going into jealous rages in an attempt to reduce the murder charge to voluntary manslaughter. The defendant's reputation as a bully may be useful for the prosecution if the defendant is claiming that he or she acted in self-defense. On the other hand, the defense may try to establish a reputation for being timid to show that the defendant would never have started the fight.

The defendant's reputation for being cautious or reckless may also be relevant in some cases. If the defendant is charged with manslaughter based on gross negligence, his or her reputation for being reckless may be very damaging to a defense based on the contention that the defendant was acting with due care when the death occurred. The defense could use the reverse of this if it could show that the defendant had a reputation for being careful.

Examples of Evidence of Specific Character Traits of the Defendant
- The defendant is charged with murder and claims self-defense. The defense calls character witnesses who testify that the defendant is known to be a gentle person who never becomes violent.
- The prosecution then calls a character witness who testifies that the defendant has the reputation for threatening anyone who disagrees with him.
- The defense calls character witnesses who testify that on several occasions they heard that someone violently attacked the defendant but the defendant did not return the assault.

Character Traits of the Victim

Sometimes the character of the crime victim may be relevant. This is most common in cases in which the defense is based on self-defense. If it can be shown that the victim was a violent person, it is much easier to convince the jury that the defendant acted in self-defense. The inference would be even stronger if the victim's reputation included being a bully. The prosecution can use the reverse of this approach; for example, showing the jury that the victim had a reputation for being a nonviolent person may defeat the self-defense claim.

At one time, the reputation of a rape victim was considered to be at issue. The oldest cases allowed the jury to conclude that the woman who was single and not a virgin would consent to sex with almost anyone. More recently, the reputation of the rape victim for being promiscuous has been used to infer that she consented. This type of questioning is now usually reserved for rape cases in which the defendant admits having sex with the victim but claims that she consented. Some states now refuse to allow questions about the sex life of the victim unless there was a prior relationship between the defendant and the victim.

Examples of Relevant Character Traits of the Victim
- The defendant is charged with murder and claims self-defense. The defense introduced a character witness who testified that the victim had the reputation of being very violent and getting angry very quickly.
- The defendant is charged with rape. The defense calls character witnesses who state that the victim has a reputation for making false accusations against men she dates.
- The defendant is a battered woman charged with killing her batterer. The defense introduced character evidence that the victim was violent and had beaten several of his former girlfriends.

Other Acts Evidence

"Other acts evidence" includes a variety of situations in which prior actions of the defendant are relevant to the current case. In these situations, the prior acts can be used to infer that he or she committed the crime alleged in the current trial. Normally, the defendant's history is not admissible. The use of this type of evidence is permitted in response to specific issues raised by the defense. Since introduction of this type of evidence is contrary to the normal rules, the judge must first decide whether the evidence is relevant and then whether the value of the evidence is outweighed by the potential prejudice against the defendant.

Federal Rules of Evidence, Rule 404(b) combines a number of rules that are discussed in this book under separate headings.

Federal Rules of Evidence, Rule 404(b): Other Crimes, Wrongs, or Other Acts

Evidence of other crimes, wrongs, or acts is not admissible to prove the character of a person in order to show action in conformity therewith. It may, however, be admissible for other purposes, such as proof of motive, opportunity, intent, preparation, plan, knowledge, identity, or absence of mistake or accident, provided that upon request by the accused, the prosecution in a criminal case shall provide reasonable notice in advance of trial, or during trial if the court excuses pretrial notice on good cause shown, of the general nature of any such evidence it intends to introduce at trial.

Identity

Prior similar crimes can be used to infer that the witness correctly identified the defendant. The defendant does not have to have been arrested or charged with the prior crime as long as the prosecutor can call a credible witness who can convince the jury that the defendant committed the crimes.

Circumstantial evidence is most commonly used in this way when an eyewitness claims that he or she saw the defendant commit the crime, but the defendant claims that it is a case of mistaken identity. This method of establishing identity is very similar to the use of prior crimes to show *modus operandi.* Unless there is a great deal of similarity between the current offense and the prior acts, the judge will not allow the prosecutor to admit the prior crimes because they would be unduly prejudicial to the defendant.

Example of Other Acts Evidence Used to Prove Identity

- A 72-year-old man is on trial for bank robbery. He claims the witness wrongly identified him as the robber. The prosecution is allowed to show that robberies by senior citizens are very rare and the defendant has been arrested for two bank robberies in the past 3 years.
- The defendant is charged in an elaborate fraud scene. The prosecution was only able to tie him to the crime by the use of fingerprints found on the documents involved. The defendant claims there is an innocent explanation for how the fingerprints were placed on the documents. The prosecution introduces evidence that the suspect has been involved in the same type of fraud scheme in three states.

Habit or Custom

The fact that the defendant had a habit or custom of doing something can be used to infer that he or she did it when the crime was committed. The victim's habits and customs can also be used to show that he or she was not voluntarily involved in criminal conduct. Habits and customs are easily confused with character traits. Habits and customs are more specific than character traits. A person's character may include being a liar; lying about one's age can be a habit.

In most states, evidence is admissible if the person's habit or custom is so strong that it becomes a semiautomatic response to a particular type of situation. This creates stronger circumstantial evidence than a character trait would. Since the potential for prejudicial impact is less, the judge is usually more likely to admit it if it is relevant to the case. The habit or custom does not have to relate to doing criminal acts. It merely needs to be relevant to the way in which the crime was committed. This type of evidence can also be used to infer that the defendant did not commit the crime because it was his or her habit or custom to act in a different way than the way the person committing the crime acted.

Habitual neatness could be relevant, for example, if the suspect went to great lengths to clean up after the crime was committed. A person's obsession for punctuality could be used to infer that he or she would be at a scheduled appointment unless forced to go somewhere else. In a homicide case in which the body has not been recovered, habit or custom could be used to show that a missing person did not voluntarily leave town without telling anyone.

Examples of Other Acts Evidence to Prove Habit or Custom

- The victim was a very tidy housekeeper. When the police were called to the scene, the house was a mess and the victim was gone. The prosecution asked the jurors to infer that the victim was forced to leave the scene against her will.
- The victim was an elderly man who was very frugal. The prosecution asked the jury to infer that the large check written on the victim's account for an extravagant gift was not written by the victim.
- The victim was an old lady who was inseparable from her dog. After her house burned down, her dog was found dead inside with a bullet hole in his head. Police were never able to locate the old lady or her remains. The prosecution asked the jury to infer that the lady was kidnapped.

Lack of Accident

In some cases, the defendant admits doing the criminal act but claims it was done accidentally. In these situations, the defendant's prior acts can be used to show that the current crime was not an accident.

A good example would be a theft case in which the defendant knew that the victim carried something very valuable in his or her briefcase and attempted to switch briefcases with the victim. The defense might try to prove that picking up the victim's briefcase was an honest mistake. This defense could be very convincing until the prosecutor calls a witness who testifies that the defendant pulled a similar switch a few months ago.

Another example would be the burglar who was caught in a secluded area of Al's Market soon after closing time. His or her claim of not knowing that the store had closed could be countered by testimony of an employee of Bob's Grocery who caught the defendant soon after the defendant had committed a similar burglary by hiding in Bob's Grocery at closing time.

Examples of Other Acts Evidence Used to Show Lack of Accident

- The defendant was charged with carrying a concealed weapon and claimed he did not know the law covered the type of weapon he had. The prosecution showed that the defendant had previously been convicted for carrying the same model of a handgun.

- The defendant was at a party and left with an expensive coat that was not hers. She claimed it was an innocent mistake. The prosecution introduced evidence to show that similar incidents had occurred at two other parties the defendant attended that year.

Prior False Claims

If a person has previously filed false claims, it can be inferred that the current claim is also false. In fraud cases, it may be very helpful to show that the defendant has previously filed false claims in order to recover on insurance policies. Some states also allow the prosecutor to show that the defendant has repeatedly filed claims and ask the jury to conclude that this is evidence that the current claims are false. This, of course, is weaker evidence than the situation in which it can be shown that at least one of the prior claims was actually fraudulent.

A different use of this type of evidence is to discredit the complaining witness. If the witness can be shown to have previously made a false report of a crime, or falsely accused a person of committing a crime, it can be inferred that the present allegations are also untrue. This type of evidence usually comes out during cross-examination if the attorney has done his or her homework. Asking this type of question would only support the credibility of the witness if it turned out that no prior reports had been made.

Examples of Other Acts Evidence—Prior False Claims
- The defendant was charged with staging a traffic accident in order to defraud an insurance company. He claimed it was an accident. The prosecution introduced evidence that the defendant had been involved in three similar accidents and filed excessive claims in each case.
- The defendant was on trial for rape. The defense introduced evidence that the alleged victim had previously filed police reports for rape and then withdrew them when confronted with conflicting evidence.

Offers to Plead Guilty

If the jury knew that the defendant had tried to plea bargain, it would be likely to conclude that the defendant was guilty. Although this is a very logical conclusion, there are strong policy reasons for denying the jury access to this information. Making offers to plead guilty admissible would interfere with nearly all attempts to plea bargain. The need to expedite court proceedings through the use of plea bargaining is considered much more important than allowing the jury to know this evidence. For this reason, most states do not allow the introduction of any testimony about attempts to plea bargain or the fact that the defendant entered a guilty plea but for some reason was allowed to withdraw it. A similar public policy usually covers attempts to settle civil cases. The Supreme Court held that statements made during plea negotiations are admissible, however, if there is an agreement between the defendant and prosecutor that stipulates that the statements can be used in court if the defendant fails to follow through with the actions he or she promised to take. This type of procedure is used when the prosecution offers a plea bargain in exchange for the defendant giving information about other suspects involved in the crime or acting as an undercover operative.

Circumstantial Evidence Involving the Victim

The victim's injuries can provide circumstantial evidence that a crime occurred. This usually requires testimony of an expert witness to explain that the injuries are inconsistent with the defense's theory of the case. For example, in a rape case in which consent of the victim is claimed, a medical expert may testify that the genital bruises sustained by the victim rarely occur during consensual intercourse.

Parents frequently claim that an abused child was injured accidentally. An expert can testify that the X-rays show broken bones that were at different stages of healing. This is consistent with the battered child syndrome and indicates that there were multiple violent attacks on the child.[3] From this it can be inferred that the latest injuries were the result of battering and were not accidental. This type of evidence is admissible even though the defendant has not been previously charged with child abuse. The Supreme Court held that it is not necessary to establish beyond a reasonable doubt that the defendant has previously beaten the child.[4]

In addition to the physical evidence of the battered child syndrome, psychological evidence may also be introduced. This focuses on the child's behavior toward the abuser and others. Experts in psychology may testify to help the jurors understand the types of behavior that frequently result. For example, the abused child frequently is very loving and protective toward the abusive parent. Jurors might conclude that this is a sign that the parent is a loving parent while the behavior may be an attempt to prevent future abuse.

Behavior of the victim can be used to infer that the crime occurred. Not all victims conform to popular stereotypes of how a victim should behave, however. Many courts allow expert witnesses to testify about the Rape Trauma Syndrome and the Battered Woman Syndrome. The expert witness cannot positively state that the crime occurred, but he or she can explain common symptoms so that the jury can make inferences from the victim's conduct.

The Rape Trauma Syndrome is used by the prosecution to overcome jurors' stereotypes of how victims react after being raped. Symptoms include withdrawal from the external world, sleep disorders, exaggerated startle responses, guilt, memory impairment, difficulty concentrating, and avoidance of stimuli that make the victim recall the rape.[5]

The Battered Woman Syndrome has become an issue in the defense of women who kill (or attempt to kill) their abusive partners. This final act of aggression may come while the man is sleeping and clearly does not qualify as self-defense. In courts allowing this defense, expert testimony focuses on studies that show that battered women may accept abuse for years, downplay episodes of violence, defend the abuser by claiming he was justified in beating her, rarely report abuse to family or the police, and pass up chances to flee until some event causes them to strike back and kill. The mental state of the typical abused woman is used to explain why the defendant feared for her life when she used deadly force.[6]

Examples of Circumstantial Evidence Involving the Victim

- In a trial for child abuse, X-rays are introduced that show numerous fractures. The expert witness concludes that the child was beaten on numerous occasions based on the state of healing shown for each broken bone.
- In a trial for sexually molesting a 3-year-old girl, witnesses may testify that the girl's behavior was very sexually oriented. An expert witness may testify that the behavior was not normal for a child that age, and that such behavior usually indicates the child has been involved in sexual activities.
- In a trial of a wife charged with the murder of a husband, the defense claims that the wife acted in self-defense. The defense may introduce evidence that the husband had physically abused the wife on many occasions. An expert witness may testify that a battered woman frequently becomes hypervigilant and interprets small signs of aggression as indicators that a serious beating is about to happen.

Rape Shield Laws

Prior to the 1970s, it was a common defense tactic in rape trials to dredge up a rape victim's prior sexual history. The inference that the jury was encouraged to draw was that if a woman had ever been sexually active, it was more likely that she consented to sex with the defendant. This approach was taken in stranger rape cases as well as when a person alleged that a prior intimate had committed rape.

Legislatures were called on to enact laws to stop this practice. Those laws are referred to as Rape Shield Laws. Some are found in the Evidence Code, and others are found in the Penal Code. Just as there are similarities in them, minor differences are also present. For the purposes of this book, the one in the Federal Rules of Evidence will be discussed.

Federal Rules of Evidence, Rule 412: Sex Offense Cases; Relevance of Alleged Victim's Past Sexual Behavior or Alleged Sexual Predisposition

(a) **Evidence generally inadmissible**. The following evidence is not admissible in a civil or criminal proceeding involving alleged sexual misconduct except as provided in subdivisions (b) and (c):

    (1) Evidence offered to prove that any alleged victim engaged in other sexual behavior.

    (2) Evidence offered to prove any alleged victim's sexual predisposition.

(b) **Exceptions**.

    (1) In a criminal case, the following evidence is admissible, if otherwise admissible under these rules:

        (A) Evidence of specific instances of sexual behavior by the alleged victim offered to prove that a person other than the accused was the source of semen, injury, or other physical evidence;

        (B) Evidence of specific instances of sexual behavior by the alleged victim with respect to the person accused of the sexual misconduct offered by the accused to prove consent or by the prosecution; and

        (C) Evidence the exclusion of which would violate the constitutional rights of the defendant.

    (2) [This exception applies to civil cases and is not reproduced in this text.]

(c) [This section sets out the procedures for determining if this evidence should be admitted and is not reproduced in this text.]

Exceptions (A) and (B) are meant to balance the constitutional right to present a defense against the privacy rights of the victim. This is another way of determining if the evidence is relevant. In the Kobe Bryant case, the Colorado Supreme Court made a ruling similar to exception (A) of the federal code because it was necessary, based on the physical evidence, to account for other possible sources of the victim's injuries. Sub (B) applies to cases in which the victim and the defendant had previously been intimates. It is assumed that these cases are the ones in which it is most likely that there would be a false rape allegation; therefore, the evidence of their relationship is admissible. The final subdivision, (C), leaves the judge the option to make appropriate rulings in unusual cases that do not fit under the other subsections.

Summary

Circumstantial evidence may be used to establish any element of a crime. It is usually weaker than direct evidence because the jury must infer that a fact exists in addition to assessing the credibility of the witness. The jury must also decide the weight to be given to each fact introduced into evidence.

Circumstantial evidence can be used to show that the defendant had the ability to commit the crime. This is done when the crime is committed in such a manner that the suspect must have had some ability that the average person would not possess. Examples include special skills, technical knowledge, tools to accomplish the crime, access to the location where the crime occurred, or unusual physical or mental capacity.

Prior crimes, which are very similar to the current one, can be used to infer that the defendant also committed the present crime. The *modus operandi* needs to be quite distinctive to be used in this manner.

Motive can also be used as circumstantial evidence of guilt. A wide variety of motives can be involved in crimes. Greed, hatred, and jealousy are among the most common.

Prior threats can be used to show that the defendant probably committed the crime. Only fairly recent threats would carry much weight.

Attempts to avoid apprehension after the crime may be used to show guilt. These include flight from the crime scene, attempts to avoid arrest or trial, and intimidating witnesses.

Possession of the fruits of the crime infers guilt. Sudden wealth can also be used to indicate that a person profited from the crime.

Character witnesses may be called by the defense to establish that the defendant has a good reputation. The inference is that a person with a good character would not commit the crime. Once the defense has placed character at issue, the prosecution may also call character witnesses. In some crimes, specific character traits may be at issue; if so, either side may introduce character evidence on the relevant trait. The character of the victim is frequently relevant if self-defense is raised. Attacking the character of rape victims is now more restricted than in the past.

Some defenses may make additional circumstantial evidence relevant. Alleging mistaken identity will make evidence that the defendant committed very similar crimes in the past admissible. Habits and customs may be admissible if they are so firmly established that they are nearly automatic responses. Prior acts may be relevant to show that the current crime was not done by accident or mistake. The fact that a person has previously filed false claims, either to collect on an insurance policy or as crime reports, can be used to infer that the current claim is also false.

There is a strong policy reason, based on judicial efficiency, to exclude evidence that the defendant attempted to plea bargain the charges or that the defendant withdrew a plea bargain. It is not admissible because allowing this evidence into court would result in many more cases going to trial.

Review Questions

1. Define and compare *direct evidence* and *circumstantial evidence*.
2. Explain how the jury decides what weight to give each fact in evidence.
3. List three technical skills and three means of accomplishing the crime that can be used as circumstantial evidence. Describe a crime in which each would be relevant.
4. When can physical and mental capacity be used as circumstantial evidence? Give three examples of each.
5. Define *modus operandi*. Explain how it may be used as circumstantial evidence.
6. When is motive relevant? Give three examples of how motive can be used to infer guilt.
7. Explain how (1) threats, (2) flight from the scene, and (3) attempts to destroy evidence can be used as circumstantial evidence. Give two situations in which each may be relevant.
8. Explain what evidence a "character witness" may present to the jury and when the defendant's general character is admissible.
9. Explain what evidence a "character witness" may present to the jury and when the defendant's general character is admissible evidence.
10. When is the prosecution allowed to call "character witnesses," and when are the defendant's specific character traits admissible?
11. Under what circumstances is the victim's character admissible? Explain.
12. What circumstantial evidence is admissible if the defendant is claiming mistaken identity? Explain.
13. Distinguish "habit" and "character." Explain when "habit" is admissible.
14. What evidence can be used to discredit the defendant's claim that the crime was accidentally committed without criminal intent? Explain.
15. When, if ever, is the fact admissible that (1) the defendant previously attempted to make false claims under an insurance policy or (2) the defendant offered to plead guilty to the crime? Explain.

Writing Assignment

Go to www.findlaw.com for Legal Professionals. Click on Legal News. Scroll down to US Law. Read a story about a case. Write a 250-word (one-page) report identifying the various types of circumstantial evidence mentioned.

Notes

1. *Griffin v. California* 380 U.S. 609, 14 L.Ed. 2d 106, 85 S.Ct. 1229 (1962).
2. *Wainwright v. Greenfield* 474 U.S. 284, 88 L.Ed. 2d 623, 106 S.Ct. 634 (1985).
3. Sylvia I. Mignon, Calvin J. Larson, and William M. Holmes, *Family Abuse: Consequences, Theories, and Responses* (Boston: Allyn & Bacon, 2002); Harvey Wallace, *Family Violence: Legal, Medical and Social Perspectives,* 3rd ed. (Boston: Allyn & Bacon, 2002), Chapter 2.
4. *Estelle v. McGuire,* 502 U.S. 62 (1991).
5. Tammi D. Kolski, Michael Avriette, and Arthur E. Jongsma, Jr., *The Crisis Counseling and Traumatic Events Treatment Planner* (New York: Wiley, 2001); Sylvia I. Mignon, Calvin J. Larson, and William M. Holmes, *Family Abuse: Consequences, Theories, and Responses* (Boston: Allyn & Bacon, 2002), Chapter 3; Harvey Wallace, *Family Violence: Legal, Medical and Social Perspectives,* 3rd ed. (Boston: Allyn & Bacon, 2002), Chapter 13.
6. Lenore E. Walker, *The Battered Woman Syndrome,* 2nd ed. (New York: Springer, 2000); Mark Costanzo and Stuart Oskamp, eds., *Violence and the Law* (Thousand Oaks, CA: Sage, 1994); Harvey Wallace, *Family Violence: Legal, Medical and Social Perspectives,* 3rd ed. (Boston: Allyn & Bacon, 2002), Chapter 8.

CHAPTER 5

Witnesses

Feature Case: Andrea Yates

Andrea Yates had five children and a miscarriage during her 8-year marriage to Rusty Yates. In June 1999, Andrea attempted suicide by taking an overdose of pills. She was briefly hospitalized, diagnosed as having a major depressive disorder, and given antidepressants. Once she returned home, she quit taking her medications, began self-mutilating, and refused to feed her children because she believed they were eating too much. She also began having hallucinations but did not seek psychiatric help. In July 1999, Andrea put a knife to her neck and begged Rusty to let her die. She was again hospitalized, this time remaining in a catatonic state for 10 days. Prior to her release, her doctor warned that another baby might bring on more episodes of psychotic behavior.

In March 2000, at her husband's urging, Andrea became pregnant again and stopped taking her antipsychotic medication. Mary was born in November 2000. On March 12, 2001, Andrea's father died and her mental state immediately began to deteriorate. She stopped talking, refused liquids, mutilated herself, and would not feed Mary. She also frantically read the Bible. By the end of March, Andrea was back in a psychiatric hospital, but after brief treatment her doctor decided she was not psychotic and released her. Andrea returned to the hospital in May. This time she spent 10 days in the hospital. At her last follow-up visit, she was told to think positive thoughts and see a psychologist. Two days later, after Rusty left for work, Andrea filled the bathtub with water and systematically drowned the three youngest boys and then Mary, the baby. The oldest boy saw Mary floating in the tub and ran away. Andrea caught him, dragged him to the bathroom, overcame his desperate resistance, and held him down until he was dead. The three youngest boys were found in a neat row on Andrea's bed with Mary in their arms; the oldest was left floating in the tub. Andrea called Rusty and asked him to come home. She then called 911 and, in a nearly incoherent conversation, asked for a police officer. She later confessed, stating that she was not a good mother, that the children were "not developing correctly," and she needed to be punished.

Andrea Yates was charged with capital murder. The trial lasted 3 weeks and included the testimony of doctors who had treated Andrea as well as expert witnesses. A psychiatrist testified that shortly before the killings, an episode of the *Law & Order* TV show had aired featuring a woman who drowned her children and was acquitted of murder by reason of insanity. Andrea was convicted but the jurors recommended life in prison rather than the death penalty.

An appeal was based on 19 trial errors. One of the most serious was the fact that the episode of *Law & Order* referred to at trial did not exist. The conviction was reversed. The case was tried again in 2006. Andrea was found Not Guilty by Reason of Insanity.

Learning Objectives

After studying this chapter, you will be able to

- Define competency of a witness and give examples of incompetent witnesses.
- Explain the process of impeaching and rehabilitating a witness. List five ways a witness can be impeached.
- Explain the legal methods of refreshing the memory of a witness. Describe the process of introducing reports if the witness has no memory of the events described in the reports.
- State the Opinion Rule and explain its application.
- Explain the prerequisites for allowing an expert witness to testify.
- List three types of evidence that require the testimony of an expert witness.
- Explain what a lay witness is allowed to testify about.

Key Terms

- Competent witness
- Corroboration
- Expert witness
- Hypothetical questions
- Impeachment
- Lay witness
- Opinion Rule
- Past Recollection Recorded Exception
- Present Memory Refreshed Rule
- Rehabilitation
- *Voir dire*

Myths about Witnesses at Trial	Facts about Witnesses at Trial
Only people older than the age of 7 years can testify at a criminal trial.	There is no specific age limit. The person who testifies at a trial must be able to understand the duty to tell the truth and be able to communicate with the jury.
Any witness at a trial can testify about his or her personal opinions on what happened.	Expert witnesses are allowed to give their opinions. Lay witnesses can only testify about the facts they observed with their five senses.
Impeachment means the witness is not allowed to testify.	Impeachment means that during cross-examination the attorney established one or more reasons the jury should not believe what the witness testified about. During deliberations, the jurors will decide whether or not to believe each witness.
Hypothetical questions are not allowed at a criminal trial.	Expert witnesses may be asked hypothetical questions—to state their expert opinion about the facts that have been introduced in the trial. Lay witnesses are not allowed to answer hypothetical questions.
Expert witnesses must have a Ph.D. and teach at prestigious universities.	Expert witnesses must have education and training in the field they are testifying about. There is no requirement that experts always have a Ph.D. There is no requirement that they teach at a college or university.

Competency of Witness

All evidence is introduced at trial by the testimony of a witness. Therefore, the role of the witness in the criminal justice system is very important. This chapter addresses the following five key issues related to the trial witness:

1. Who is competent to testify
2. How the credibility of a witness is attacked
3. What can be done if the witness's memory is faulty
4. What a lay person is allowed to testify about
5. How and when expert witnesses are used

Every witness who testifies in court must be competent. In addition to being competent, the witness must possess relevant information. The standard for competency to testify refers to the person's ability to communicate with the jury. It is not equivalent to the test used to determine if the defendant is mentally competent to stand trial.

Competent Witness Defined
A **competent witness** is a person who
1. Understands the duty to tell the truth
2. Can narrate the events in question

Competence is the first issue addressed. If a person is not competent, he or she will not be allowed to testify. If the witness is competent, the adversary system unfolds. The attorney who called the witness asks questions. Opposing counsel should object if the question calls for an answer the witness is not qualified to answer. The judge rules on the objections. The jurors who watch this interplay must decide whether they believe the witness and how much weight to give the testimony.

Duty to Tell the Truth

The most common oath administered to witnesses today includes the traditional promise to "tell the truth, the whole truth, so help me God." Although each witness must understand the duty to tell the truth, neither the Bible nor swearing is currently mandatory. For the person who is an agnostic or atheist, swearing on the Bible may be a meaningless gesture. Also, some people have religious beliefs against taking an oath on the Bible. As discussed in Chapter 3, an "affirmation" is administered instead of an oath in such instances.

The purpose of the oath or affirmation is to make it clear to a witness that he or she is testifying under penalty of perjury. The witness swears to tell the truth, but the jurors decide whether to believe the witness. No immediate action is taken if the witness is suspected of lying while on the stand. If the witness knowingly lies about a material matter, perjury charges may be filed at a later time. The threat of being punished in this manner is commonly assumed to be sufficient to keep witnesses from lying. The truth is, however, that some witnesses lie but prosecutors rarely file perjury charges. In most situations, administering an oath or affirmation is all that is done to qualify a witness. There is a common exception in cases involving children as witnesses. Young children do not understand the meaning of the term "under penalty of perjury." So the attorney who calls a child as a witness usually has the task of showing the court that the witness knows that he or she is required to tell the truth. Simple questions are asked in language that a child can understand. A typical line of questioning focuses on the fact that the child has been taught that it is wrong to tell a lie. Once it is established that the child knows that lying is wrong and he or she will be punished for lying, the testimony is usually allowed.

A related problem is posed by the person who cannot distinguish fact from fantasy. Again, children pose the most frequent problem. Young children frequently have very active imaginations. They may have invisible friends who are quite real to them. Unfortunately, when a child is a crime victim, this same creativity that is a healthy part of childhood may result in a serious injustice. It is the task of the prosecutor to convince the judge, and later the jury, that the child is able to differentiate between fact and fantasy and to testify about events that actually took place.

Senility and certain types of mental illness can result in the inability to tell fact from fiction. The questions asked in court to determine if a witness knows what the truth is are not based on medical or psychiatric diagnosis. Factual questions are used in order to show that the potential witness is out of touch with reality. This is done before the person testifies in the presence of the jury.

Some courts have ruled that a person who has been hypnotized cannot testify about things discussed while under hypnosis. Proponents of hypnosis claim that a person can recall things under hypnosis that he or she cannot remember in the conscious state. Opponents claim that during hypnosis information can be embedded in a person's memory. When this occurs in hypnosis, the person believes that he or she is recalling what was previously observed but cannot distinguish between what actually happened and what was added to memory during hypnosis. Courts that exclude testimony enhanced by hypnosis usually exclude only testimony about topics that were covered in a hypnotic session. Statements made to the police before hypnosis are usually admissible. Controversy about the use of hypnosis will probably continue until there is conclusive scientific evidence on the effects of hypnosis on memory.

Ability to Narrate

To be a witness, a person must be able to communicate with the judge and jury and must be able to tell about the events in question. This is referred to as the ability to narrate.

Several problems may be raised. Probably the most obvious is the ability to coherently answer questions. To do this, the witness must have the ability to understand the questions. Severely mentally retarded persons, very young children, and people with certain other types of physical and mental illness may not be able to do this.

Other more practical problems may be raised. For example, the witness may not be able to speak English. This is usually solved by using an interpreter or translator. The witness will need an interpreter or translator to understand the questions, and the judge, jury, and defendant may need a translation of the answers. A similar problem arises if a witness speaks through sign language. Again, interpreters are the solution.

Procedure to Establish Competency

If there is a question of the witness's competency, a hearing will be held before the person takes the stand. The jury leaves the courtroom during this session. Questions will be asked of the witness to determine if he or she is competent to testify. This is called *voir dire.* The side wishing to call the witness will bear the burden of convincing the judge that the person is competent. Opposing counsel will be allowed to cross-examine.

This screening process is limited to the two key questions of competency—knowing that there is a duty to tell the truth and being able to narrate. The fact that one side suspects that the witness will commit perjury is not grounds to prevent that person from taking the stand. Neither is the fact that a prospective witness has a severe personality disorder, as long as it does not affect the ability to narrate. Some states do not allow a witness to testify if he or she has previously been convicted of perjury.

Testimony taken during *voir dire* is not used to prove any of the issues in the case. If the person is found competent, he or she will then be put on the witness stand in the presence of the jury. Direct and cross-examination will proceed as with any other witness.

Impeachment

One of the key functions of cross-examination is convincing the jury that they should not believe the other side's witnesses; this is called **impeachment.** In some situations, witnesses may be called solely for the purpose of impeaching someone who has already testified.

A witness is impeached by asking questions. If the answers indicate that the witness lacks credibility, those answers will be emphasized by the opposing attorney during closing arguments. The witness is not asked to leave the witness stand, nor is he or she prevented from testifying at future trials.

The opposing attorney must make a tactical decision on impeachment. Although each witness may be attacked with any or all of the six impeachment methods, questioning usually focuses on one or two that are believed to be the most effective. Both the vulnerability of the witness and the impact on the jury must be considered. Trying to intimidate a witness who has the jury's sympathy may backfire. Every witness, including the defendant (if he or she takes the stand), is subject to impeachment. This frequently discourages defendants in criminal cases from taking the stand if they have prior records. The prosecution is rarely allowed to show the defendant's past if he or she does not take the stand, but if the defendant does take the stand, both prior convictions and crimes that never went to trial may be admissible.

Impeachment Defined

Impeachment is the process of attacking the credibility of a witness. Six main methods of impeachment are allowed:

1. Bias or prejudice
2. Prior felony convictions
3. Immoral acts and uncharged crimes
4. Prior inconsistent statements
5. Inability to observe
6. Reputation

Bias or Prejudice

If a person is biased or prejudiced, either for or against one side of the case, it can be inferred that he or she cannot testify objectively. This includes bias or prejudice toward a defendant, a witness, one of the attorneys, or the police. Bias and prejudice, as used in impeachment, have very broad definitions.

A person can be biased due to friendship. Even though the witness has sworn to tell the truth, if he or she is called to testify against a close friend there may be a conscious or unconscious distortion of the facts. This friendship is a proper subject for cross-examination. The jury will have to decide if the witness was truthful or allowed the friendship to affect his or her testimony.

Example of Impeachment Based on Bias or Prejudice—Friendship

Prosecutor:	Mr. Green, you just testified that John, the defendant, was at your house on the evening of November 15.
Mr. Green:	Yes.
Prosecutor:	How well do you know John?
Mr. Green:	We have been friends for about 5 years.
Prosecutor:	Is John your best friend?
Mr. Green:	Yes.
Prosecutor:	Would you try to help John if he were in trouble?
Mr. Green:	Well, yes, I would do whatever I could.

Hatred and lesser degrees of animosity toward a party to the case may also cause a witness to distort the facts. During cross-examination, questions may be asked to explore bad feelings between the witness and others concerned with the case. Once again, the jury has the task of deciding how these personal feelings may have affected the testimony.

Example of Impeachment Based on Bias or Prejudice—Hatred

Defense: Mr. Brown, you testified that John hit you on November 15. Did you know John prior to November 15?

Mr. Brown: Yes.

Defense: Describe your prior encounters with John.

Mr. Brown: John dated my sister Mary for about a year.

Defense: During that year did you and John become friends?

Mr. Brown: No.

Defense: Why didn't you become friends?

Mr. Brown: He done my sister wrong. He cheated on her and he hit her several times.

Defense: Describe your feelings toward John.

Mr. Brown: I hate him. I hope he gets what's coming to him.

Family ties are generally assumed to form strong bonds that would cause a witness to testify more favorably toward a relative. Obviously, some family feuds result in just the opposite bias. Cross-examination is once again the key to discovering the extent of the distortion.

Example of Impeachment Based on Bias or Prejudice—Family Ties

Prosecution: Mrs. White, you just testified that you observed a fight on November 15. Did you know any of the people involved?

Mrs. White: I know John but not the other guys.

Prosecution: How well do you know John?

Mrs. White: He is my son.

Prosecution: Do you have a good relationship with your son John?

Mrs. White: Yes. He is a very good boy.

Prosecution: Do you believe it is a mother's duty to provide love and support for her children?

Mrs. White: Yes, I do. There isn't anything I wouldn't do to help my children.

Racial prejudice can also cause a witness to distort the truth. Questions regarding racial bias would only be allowed if the facts of the case indicate they are relevant (e.g., the victim and/or defendant are from different racial groups than the witness or there is evidence that the witness is prejudiced about his or her own racial group). Prejudice toward the police officer or one of the attorneys might also be involved. However, the fact that the witness is a bigot is not admissible if there are no aspects of the case that are likely to cause him or her to distort the facts.

Example of Impeachment Based on Bias or Prejudice—Racial Prejudice

Defense: Mr. Allen, you just testified that John, the defendant who is sitting over there, was the man that started the fight.

Mr. Allen: Yes. That is exactly what he did.

Defense: And you are sure it was John?

Mr. Allen: Absolutely.

Defense: Mr. Allen, are you prejudiced against African Americans?

Mr. Allen: No.

Defense: Have you ever said, "They all look alike to me"?

Mr. Allen: Yeah, I've said that.

Other forms of bias or prejudice may arise in individual cases. Sexual biases may be relevant. For example, the witness may testify in a very critical manner at a rape trial because of a belief that women should not go to bars alone. Sexual preference may also become grounds for impeachment. A witness with very strong feelings on this topic (either anti- or pro-homosexuality) can be cross-examined on these attitudes if they are relevant.

Any relationship with the defendant, or anyone else in the case, that could result in a financial impact on the witness can also be used to impeach. This is based on the idea that a person would possibly alter testimony if he or she would be harmed (or helped) financially. For example, an employee may not be able to be totally objective on the witness stand if he or she fears being fired because of what was said. Whether consciously or unconsciously, a witness might also alter the facts if he or she could be promoted, earn a commission from a sale, or make a profit in the stock market if the side calling him or her wins the case.

Example of Impeachment Based on Bias or Prejudice—Financial Gain

Defense: Mr. Smith, are you the owner of the building involved in this case?

Mr. Smith: Yes.

Defense: Did you operate a business at that location?

Mr. Smith: Yes. A video game store.

Defense: Was your business profitable?

Mr. Smith: Don't I wish. We have been losing money for over a year.

Defense: Did you have fire insurance on the building and its contents?

Mr. Smith: Yes. I always pay my insurance premiums.

Defense: Has your insurance paid you for fire damages caused by the crime we are discussing today?

Mr. Smith: Yes.
Defense: How much were you paid?
Mr. Smith: $51,000.

The list of possible biases is quite long (age, occupation, regional, religious, educational, etc.). Only the facts of the case determine what could be relevant in any one case. If there is a question of relevance, the attorneys will debate the issue with the judge outside the hearing of the witness and jury.

Motive to distort the truth or fabricate evidence can also be inferred from the fact that the witness is being paid to testify. The jury is more likely to conclude the payment influenced the testimony when a large amount of money is at stake. Expert witnesses can be impeached by showing the fees they receive for testifying. This also applies to the person who provides evidence in hopes of receiving a reward the city posted for information leading to a conviction. The witness who has accepted money from a journalist for information about the case fits into this category. Paid police informants are also suspect. Entering into a plea bargain in exchange for testifying against a co-conspirator also implies a motive.

Example of Impeachment Based on Bias or Prejudice—Motive

Defense: Mr. Johnson, you just testified that you observed the fight involving John, the defendant in this case. What were you doing when the fight started?
Mr. Johnson: I was talking to John.
Defense: So you knew John prior to the events in question?
Mr. Johnson: Yes, we were friends.
Defense: Have you ever been arrested?
Mr. Johnson: Yes.
Defense: When and for what charges?
Mr. Johnson: I was arrested at the same time John was. They said they were going to charge me with battery.
Defense: Did they take you to court on the battery?
Mr. Johnson: No. They told me that they wouldn't file the charges if I testified against John at his trial.

Prior Felony Convictions

We have a long history of distrusting convicts. At one time, anyone convicted of a felony was considered untrustworthy and not allowed to testify in court. Although most states now allow everyone to testify, impeachment is permitted on prior felony convictions even if the prior crime is totally unrelated to the current case.

Prior convictions may be introduced at trial for two very different purposes. They may come in as "other acts" evidence, mentioned in Chapter 4. When used in this manner, they imply that the defendant is guilty because the defendant has done very similar acts in the past. A separate use of felony convictions is to impeach a witness. Anyone who takes the stand is subject to impeachment. On cross-examination, opposing counsel can ask about prior felony convictions and thus undermine the credibility of the witness. The threat of impeachment is one of the main reasons why defendants with criminal records frequently do not testify at their own trials.

The Federal Rules of Evidence allow prior felony convictions to be used to impeach but give the judge discretion to not allow them. Misdemeanor convictions that involve dishonesty or false statements are also admissible for impeachment. If it has been 10 years since the person was released from prison, the conviction is not admissible unless the judge determines that there is a special reason that warrants telling the jury about the conviction.

Federal Rules of Evidence, Rule 609: Impeachment by Evidence of Conviction of Crime

(a) **General rule.** For the purpose of attacking the credibility of a witness,

    (1) evidence that a witness other than an accused has been convicted of a crime shall be admitted, subject to Rule 403 [Exclusion of Relevant Evidence on Grounds of Prejudice, Confusion, or Waste of Time], if the crime was punishable by death or imprisonment in excess of one year under the law under which the witness was convicted, and evidence that an accused has been convicted of such a crime shall be admitted if the court determines that the probative value of admitting this evidence outweighs its prejudicial effect to the accused; and

    (2) evidence that any witness has been convicted of a crime shall be admitted if it involves dishonesty or false statement, regardless of the punishment.

Most states allow impeachment on prior felony convictions. If the conviction was for a crime committed in another state, it must be similar to a felony as defined by the law of the state where the trial is held. Some states allow impeachment on crimes of moral turpitude. Moral turpitude usually includes all felonies, plus misdemeanors involving dishonesty. A few states include all criminal convictions as grounds for impeachment. Probably the newest, and least used, rule is that impeachment based on prior convictions is limited to crimes relevant to honesty on the witness stand. Truthfulness of the witness is always relevant, but violence would not be considered relevant to honesty.

Example of Impeachment Based on Prior Felony Conviction

Prosecutor:	Mr. Adams, you just testified that John was provoked into hitting the victim.
Mr. Adams:	Yes. That's what I said.
Prosecutor:	Mr. Adams, have you ever been convicted?
Mr. Adams:	Uhh, yes, I was. But only once.
Prosecutor:	And was this conviction for a felony?
Mr. Adams:	Yes.

Even when all prior felony convictions are admissible to impeach, judicial discretion can be used to exclude this evidence. Most commonly, this is done if the conviction is very old and the witness has had no other convictions. Some states have enacted laws that limit this type of impeachment to crimes that occurred in the past 10 years (some use 5 years or some other number). Even where there is no specific law, judicial discretion can be used to prevent attacks on a witness with a long record of exemplary conduct.

If a witness denies a prior conviction, another witness may be called to show the jury that the conviction exists. This witness would usually testify about the court records on the conviction. A certified copy of those records might even be admitted into evidence.

Uncharged Crimes and Immoral Acts

Even crimes that did not result in convictions can be used to impeach. Immoral acts that do not violate any penal laws can also be used. The judge has more discretion since the use of this evidence is very time-consuming and may confuse the jury. Also, the witness has not had the right to a trial on the prior acts.

Generally, the same types of restrictions apply here as with prior convictions. The acts must be relevant to the truthfulness of the witness. Minor crimes are usually inadmissible. If a person has lived a law-abiding life for many years, old crimes are normally inadmissible.

Crimes that were charged but resulted in neither a conviction nor an acquittal may be used. In some situations, cases dropped due to procedural errors may be admissible. Good faith errors on searches and seizures would be in this category. Some states even allow impeachment based on convictions where the witness received a pardon.

Example of Impeachment Based on Uncharged Crimes and Immoral Acts

Prosecutor:	Ms. Young, you testified that you are an in-home aide for elderly patients. How many people have you cared for?
Ms. Young:	About 20, I guess.

Prosecutor: And in caring for those 20 people, have you ever taken any of their possessions home?
Ms. Young: Well, yes, I do that once in a while.
Prosecutor: Did the patients give you permission to do that?
Ms. Young: Not specifically.
Prosecutor: So, you stole from your clients?
Ms. Young: Hey, that's not the same as stealing. I never got arrested or anything.

Prior Inconsistent Statements

A witness can be impeached if he or she has previously made any statement that is inconsistent with the testimony at trial. The statement does not have to totally contradict the testimony; it merely needs to show that there is a reason to suspect the accuracy of the testimony.

The appropriate procedure is to ask the witness if he or she made a specific statement. The date, place, and name of the person to whom the statement was made are also given so that the witness has a fair chance to remember the event. If the witness denies making the statement, the judge may allow another witness to be called to testify about the statement in question. It is misconduct for an attorney to ask a witness about a prior statement unless the statement is believed to have been made.

Example of Impeachment Based on Prior Inconsistent Statements
Prosecutor: Mrs. White, you just testified that John was at your house on the evening of November 15.
Mrs. White: Yes, he sure was.
Prosecutor: Please think back to November 16. On that morning didn't you tell your friend Mabel that you visited your sister the night before?
Mrs. White: I sure don't remember saying that.

The U.S. Supreme Court has ruled that statements obtained in violation of *Miranda* may be used to impeach. The only restriction is that no coercion was used to obtain the statement. Most states follow this rule.

Inability to Observe

The credibility of a witness is weak if he or she was not able to clearly observe the events in question. Impeachment is used to raise this question. Inability to observe usually has one of the following causes: (1) physical handicaps of the witness, (2) obstruction at the scene, or (3) the witness was too far away to see or hear the event in question. Sometimes more than one of these problems arise at the same time; for example, the witness might have a physical handicap (bad eyesight) and also be too far away to see clearly.

Since a witness can testify about anything observed with the five senses, a defect in any of these senses that is relevant to the case may be grounds for impeachment. For example, the eyesight of a person who identified the defendant at the scene could be challenged, though a hearing problem cannot be used to attack testimony about what the witness saw. The jury usually is not very impressed with minor impairments.

Suppose the witness claims to have observed a drug sale while standing across the street. A witness with 20/20 vision is more likely to have seen the transaction clearly than a person whose vision is 20/400. Poor vision may be irrelevant if the person wore proper corrective lenses.

Example of Impeachment Based on Inability to Observe—Physical Problem of Witness

Defense:	Mr. Allen, you testified that you saw John start the fight. Where were you sitting at the time you made this observation?
Mr. Allen:	I was on my front porch.
Defense:	How far is it from your front porch to the spot where the fight started?
Mr. Allen:	Maybe 50 feet.
Defense:	Mr. Allen, have you had your eyes checked lately?
Mr. Allen:	About 6 months ago.
Defense:	What did your doctor tell you about your eyesight?
Mr. Allen:	He said I needed new glasses really, really bad.
Defense:	And did you get new glasses?
Mr. Allen:	No. They cost too much.

The second problem is not with the witness but, rather, the layout of the crime scene. Something may be blocking the view, muffling sounds, etc. Weather and lighting conditions are important. Simple examples would be that there was a tree in the way, a bus drove by at the crucial moment, or it was a dark and stormy night. It might turn out that there was no window on the side of the building where the observation allegedly was made. Both of these avenues of impeachment require the police and attorneys to do their homework.

Example of Impeachment Based on Inability to Observe—Obstruction of View

Prosecutor:	Ms. Morris, you testified that you saw John being attacked before he hit anyone. Where were you at the time you made that observation?
Ms. Morris:	I was sitting in a chair in my front yard.
Prosecutor:	Why were you in your front yard?
Ms. Morris:	We were having a party and there were too many people to fit in the house. Anyway, it was hot in the house.
Prosecutor:	And you were sitting down.

Ms. Morris:	Yes. I was lucky. Most of the people had to stand up.
Prosecutor:	Were there any people between you and where John was?
Ms. Morris:	Yeah. A whole bunch of people.
Prosecutor:	And they were standing up while you were sitting down?
Ms. Morris:	Yeah.
Prosecutor:	With all those people in the way, how could you tell what was happening to John?
Ms. Morris:	I got little glimpses when someone moved.

Reputation

Impeachment based on reputation is usually restricted to the trait of honesty (also called truth and veracity). The credibility of a witness is easily diminished if it is shown that other people believe the witness is a liar.

As discussed in the previous chapter, reputation is usually shown by the testimony of people who claim to know what the community thinks about someone. For impeachment, the question rests on the general reputation of the witness for honesty.

Example of Impeachment Based on Reputation

Prosecutor:	Mr. Evans, do you know Mr. Brown who is a witness in this case?
Mr. Evans:	I don't know him personally.
Prosecutor:	Are you familiar with his reputation?
Mr. Evans:	Yes. I've heard a lot of people talk about him.
Prosecutor:	Have you heard people talk about Mr. Brown's honesty?
Mr. Evans:	Yes. I've heard a whole lot of people say that he is a liar. No one trusts him.

Rehabilitation

Rehabilitation is the restoration of the credibility of a witness. Once a witness has been impeached, the side that originally called the witness will try to convince the jury that their witness testified truthfully and should be believed. Redirect examination is usually used to attempt to rehabilitate witnesses. Sometimes the judge will allow new witnesses to be called to support the credibility of an impeached witness. Figure 5-1 shows the relationship of testimony to the impeachment and rehabilitation of witnesses.

Where impeachment focused on prior criminal conduct, rehabilitation frequently tries to publicize good deeds. If possible, the years of exemplary conduct since the last serious offense will be emphasized. Sometimes an attorney decides that the best defense is a strong offense. The witness's

Figure 5-1
Impeachment and Rehabilitation of Witnesses

unsavory past may be acknowledged during direct examination so the impeachment will lack dramatic effect. Another tactic is to try to show that the witness can be objective despite a criminal record. The nature and extent of the criminal acts will probably be the most significant facts used to determine what rehabilitation will be attempted.

Example of Rehabilitation Based on Good Behavior

Defense:	Mr. Williams, you just testified that you have a prior felony conviction. When did that conviction occur?
Mr. Williams:	In 1988.
Defense:	Was that your only conviction?
Mr. Williams:	Yes.
Defense:	And in the 20-plus years since that conviction, have you ever been arrested?
Mr. Williams:	No.
Defense:	In that 20-plus year period, have you committed any crimes for which you were not arrested?
Mr. Williams:	No.

Three common approaches are used to rehabilitate a witness who was impeached by prior inconsistent statements. One is to try to convince the jury that there was a reason for lying earlier, but the witness is telling the truth now. These reasons might include fear of the police, intimidation by a co-defendant, or misunderstanding the questions. A second method of rehabilitation is to show that the statement used to impeach was taken out of context. The attorney may attempt to show there really was no inconsistency with testimony that tells about the whole conversation. The third method is to introduce statements that were made before the inconsistent statement. If these statements are consistent with the trial testimony, the witness may be rehabilitated.

Example of Rehabilitation Based on Witnesses Currently Telling the Truth

Prosecution: Ms. Benson, you just admitted to the defense attorney that you told the police, on the night we are discussing in this case, that John was not involved in the fight. Was your statement to the police true?

Ms. Benson: No.

Prosecution: Why did you tell the police something that was not true?

Ms. Benson: I was afraid.

Prosecution: Why were you afraid?

Ms. Benson: John's friend was standing there. About 10 feet from me. And he kept staring at me and making a fist.

Prosecution: So why did you lie to the police?

Ms. Benson: I was afraid that I would get beat up if I told the police that John was involved.

A wide array of approaches can be used when the impeachment was based on inability to observe. Sometimes the witness explodes when attacked on cross-examination. For example, the elderly neighbor who is asked about wearing a hearing aid replies, "Even a deaf person could have heard them, the way they were shouting." Asking further questions in this type of situation is not necessary. More commonly, rehabilitation will take the form of asking the witness questions in order to show that the physical handicaps emphasized on cross-examination are not such severe impediments to the ability to observe as they might seem.

Example of Rehabilitation Based on Lack of Impairment by Handicap

Prosecution: Mr. Allen, you just testified that you did not get new glasses when your doctor recommended them. Are you nearsighted or farsighted?

Mr. Allen: I am farsighted.

Prosecution: Does that mean you can see things that are far away?

Mr. Allen: Yes. I can drive and see things just fine but I can't read a book without glasses. It's just stuff that is near to me, like within 5 feet, that I can't read.

Sometimes expert witnesses are called if the ability of one witness to observe is crucial to the case. These experts might discuss how lighting or distance would affect the ability to observe. Models may be constructed to demonstrate that a person at a given location could, or could not, have observed events in question.

Example of Rehabilitation by Use of Expert Witness

Prosecution: Dr. Davis, is Mr. Allen one of your patients?
Dr. Davis: Yes.
Prosecution: When did you last give Mr. Allen an eye examination?
Dr. Davis: About 6 months ago.
Prosecution: Was Mr. Allen nearsighted or farsighted?
Dr. Davis: He is farsighted.
Prosecution: Please explain what farsighted means.
Dr. Davis: In layman's terms, it means that a person is unable to focus properly on items that are close to the person. There is no impairment of vision for things that are far away.
Prosecution: Based on your examination of Mr. Allen, could he clearly see an event that occurred 20 feet from where he was standing?
Dr. Davis: Yes.

If reputation was used to impeach, there are usually two possible methods of rehabilitation. The credibility of the impeaching witness can be attacked. This is done during cross-examination. The other approach is to call reputation witnesses and try to convince the jury that these witnesses, who testify about a very good reputation, are the most credible.

Example of Rehabilitation Based on Reputation

Defense: Mr. Franks, do you know Ms. Benson who testified in this case?
Mr. Franks: Yes.
Defense: And do you know what other people say about Ms. Benson?
Mr. Franks: Yes. We work at the same store so I know a lot of people who know Ms. Benson.
Defense: Based on what the people you work with say, what is Ms. Benson's reputation?
Mr. Franks: They think she is honest. Everybody trusts her.

Table 5-1 summarizes the methods used to impeach and rehabilitate witnesses.

Corroboration

The credibility of a witness is stronger if there is additional evidence to support the witness's testimony. This supporting evidence is called **corroboration.** Either the testimony of another witness or physical evidence may be used.

T A B L E **5-1 Summary of Impeachment and Rehabilitation of Witnesses**

	Impeach	Rehabilitate
Bias, Prejudice, Motive	Show that witness may be less than objective.	Show that despite apparent reason to distort the truth, the witness is being objective.
Prior Felony Convictions	Introduce evidence that witness has prior conviction.	Show that defendant led moral life after conviction.
Immoral Acts and Uncharged Crimes	Ask questions about immoral act and uncharged crimes that indicate the witness may not be testifying to truth.	Testimony to show that despite past immoral acts and uncharged crimes, the witness is currently telling the truth.
Prior Inconsistent Statement	Introduce statement that is inconsistent with testimony at trial.	Introduce prior statements that are consistent with testimony at trial.
Inability to Perceive	Show bad eyesight, hearing, etc. and/or Show layout, distance, etc. made it impossible to hear, see, etc.	Show that witness wore glasses, hearing aid, etc. Show that there were no obstructions, etc.
Reputation	"Character witness" testifies about reputation for lack . of honesty	"Character witness" testifies about reputation for honesty.

There are a few situations in which corroboration is mandatory. One involves the testimony of an accomplice. When one party to the crime testifies against the other, there is always the suspicion that this was done to reduce his or her own culpability. Due to this motive to falsify, a person cannot be convicted based solely on the testimony of an accomplice; there must be corroboration.

Many states also follow the common law rule that there must be some corroboration in cases of false pretenses. A few still follow the old rule that required corroboration in rape cases, although this has been highly criticized; nearly all other crimes can be established solely on the testimony of the victim.

Where corroboration is mandatory, the law usually does not require that all of the testimony be supported by other evidence. Most states merely require that there be some additional evidence to show that the testimony is true.

Even when corroboration is not required, both sides frequently try to introduce as much evidence as possible to corroborate the testimony of their witnesses. Although the judge normally instructs the jury that neither

party is required to introduce all possible evidence in the case, strong corroboration is likely to convince the jury that the witness should be believed.
The jurors still retain the power, however, to reject the evidence because
they do not believe either the original witness or the witness called for
corroboration.

Example of Corroboration

Bob testified that he was at the corner of Third and Main at 7:30 p.m. on
November 15 and saw John hit Sam. Bob said John was wearing black leather
gloves at the time.

The following items were introduced to corroborate Bob's testimony:
- A parking ticket that was dated November 15 at 7:29 p.m. It indicated that a car
  owned by Bob was parked at an expired meter in front of the store located at 301 N.
  Main Street. A city map shows that 301 N. Main Street is the first building north of
  the intersection of Third and Main.
- A sales receipt that shows that John bought a pair of black leather gloves.
- Laboratory tests that show that DNA tests done on tissue samples removed from a
  pair of black leather gloves match a DNA sample taken from Sam.
- Testimony by Tom that he was also at Third and Main at 7:30 p.m. on November 15
  and he saw Bob there.

Corroboration must be distinguished from cumulative evidence.
Evidence is corroborative if it confirms previous testimony by the use of
another source. For example, Mr. Jones testified that he saw the defendant
choke the murder victim. This would be corroborated by the autopsy
report that indicated that there were bruises around the victim's neck.
Physical evidence, such as the rope that the witness saw the defendant
place around the victim's neck, could also be used to corroborate the testimony. Cumulative evidence merely repeats what was said. If another witness was called who testified that he or she also saw the defendant choke
the victim, this evidence would be cumulative. The judge usually allows
several eyewitnesses to testify even though it is cumulative but will eventually refuse to let additional witnesses take the stand on this issue.

Memory Failures

It is not uncommon, especially when there is a long period between the
crime and the trial, for a person to forget details of the case. This includes
victims, witnesses to the crime, and the police officers. When this happens,
it will be necessary to attempt to refresh the person's memory. This can be

done either before taking the witness stand or by asking appropriate questions during direct or cross-examination.

The basic rule is that anything can be used to refresh memory. Witnesses must, however, be able to testify from memory and not merely repeat what was used to refresh their memory. Cross-examination is used to attempt to point out that the testimony is not accurate. It can also be used to show that the witness was coached to the point that the current testimony was memorized or that the attorney told the witness what to say and what not to say.

Although unusual things may be used to refresh the witness's memory, the most common thing used is the report written about the event. Notes that were taken in a field notebook can also be used. For this reason, it is important that police officers take accurate notes and that they are not destroyed until all possibility of a trial (or retrial) has passed.

So far, we have described what is called the **Present Memory Refreshed Rule.** The witness now remembers the events in question and can testify. Sometimes the attempt to refresh memory fails. When this happens, it may still be possible to introduce reports written near the time of the event in question. This is done through the **Past Recollection Recorded Exception** to the Hearsay Rule. The following are the basic requirements for the admission of these reports:

1. The statement would be admissible if the declarant testified at the current trial.
2. The witness currently has insufficient present recollection to testify fully and accurately.
3. The report was made at a time when the facts were fresh in the memory of the witness.
4. The report was made by the witness, someone under his or her direction, or by another person for the purpose of recording the witness's statement.
5. The witness can testify that the report was a true statement of the facts.
6. The report is authenticated as accurate.

The key to using Past Recollection Recorded is that an accurate report was made at a time when the events were fresh in the witness's memory. The legislature does not set a maximum length of time; the jury makes the decision after listening to direct and cross-examination. This topic is discussed in more detail in Chapter 8. Table 5-2 shows the differences between present memory refreshed and past recollection recorded.

T A B L E **5-2 A Witness's Present Memory Refreshed and Past Recollection Recorded**

Present Memory Refreshed	Past Recollection Recorded
Event	Event
Memory dims	Memory dims
Read report, etc. to refresh memory	Read report, etc. to refresh memory
Memory revived	Memory still inadequate
Testify in court from memory	Introduce document written near time of original event

Unavailable Witnesses

Sometimes a witness is not available to testify at trial. This can happen for a variety of reasons (e.g., death, relocation, or the witness has gone into hiding). Under the Hearsay Rule exception for former testimony, statements made under oath at a prior court hearing in the same case may be introduced at trial if the witness is not available to testify at the subsequent trial or hearing. This is discussed in more detail in Chapter 8.

Many states have established other procedures to preserve testimony if it is believed that a material witness will be unavailable at trial. Some allow sworn testimony to be recorded on videotape for later use at trial. Others take sworn statements in a manner similar to depositions that are taken during discovery in civil cases. State laws vary on whether the opposing side is allowed to be present and cross-examine the witness when the statements are obtained.

A material witness can be arrested and detained in the county jail until trial. This is an extreme measure and usually requires a court hearing. A judge usually can require the material witness to post bond in lieu of being jailed if it appears this will be sufficient to guarantee appearance at trial. Some states permit the prosecution to have material witnesses jailed if it appears flight is a serious risk but do not provide similar measures to prevent defense witnesses from leaving the jurisdiction.

Types of Witnesses

The general meaning of "witness" is someone who observed something. When we talk about a witness at a trial, we mean the person who has been sworn and takes the witness stand. There are two main types of witnesses: **lay witnesses** and **expert witnesses.**

In most trials there are far more lay witnesses than experts. Lay witnesses saw the crime occur, talked to the suspect before or after the crime, or otherwise observed what happened and/or gave information to the police. The fact that a person routinely testifies in court as an expert does not affect his or her ability to testify as a lay witness if he or she saw the crime occur. For example, if a forensic pathologist observed a robbery while driving to work, he or she would be allowed to testify about the robbery as a lay witness. If he or she did the autopsy on the robbery–murder victim, he or she may also be called as an expert.

Lay Witness Defined

A lay witness is a person who observed an event that is relevant to the case on trial. Lay witnesses are allowed to testify about any relevant event that was observed with one or more of the five senses (sight, hearing, smell, touch, or taste). Lay witnesses are not allowed to give opinions.

Expert witnesses are called to help the jury understand the evidence. They are in court to explain things to the jury. Experts are not allowed if the facts can be understood by the jurors without their help. There are a wide variety of specialties in which experts can be useful at trial. Some require extensive education, whereas others are based on specialized training and experience.

Testimony by Experts: Federal Rules of Evidence, Rule 702

If scientific, technical, or other specialized knowledge will assist the trier of fact [jury] to understand the evidence or to determine a fact in issue, a witness qualified as an expert by knowledge, skill, experience, training, or education, may testify thereto in the form of an opinion or otherwise, if
  (1) the testimony is based upon sufficient facts or data,
  (2) the testimony is the product of reliable principles and methods, and
  (3) the witness has applied the principles and methods reliably to the facts of the case.

Federal Rule 702 sets out two prerequisites that must be satisfied before an expert witness is allowed to take the witness stand. First, the jury needs help in interpreting scientific, technical, or other specialized facts. Second, the person who will testify is qualified to testify about these facts. These are referred to as the foundation for calling an expert witness. The side that wants to call the expert has the responsibility to lay the foundation for that witness to testify. If the opposing side challenges the need for the expert, a hearing will be held without the jury present to determine if an expert will be allowed to testify. This same type of hearing can be used to challenge the test on the grounds that it is too new to be trustworthy, or that it has not been recognized by an appropriate group of scientists.

After the jury has returned to the courtroom, the opposing side will try to show that the person who is testifying is either not competent in the field or has made mistakes in conducting tests for the trial. The accuracy of the equipment used, as well as human error in conducting the tests, can be attacked on cross-examination.

Opinion Rule

The jury, or the judge if the jury has been waived, is the trier of the facts. For this reason, the general rule is that only facts may be introduced into evidence. Opinions of the witnesses are not admissible because it is the function of the trier of the facts to analyze the evidence. This is called the **Opinion Rule.** The trial process revolves around asking specific questions in order to obtain concrete answers. The Opinion Rule fits into this by seeking to eliminate testimony not directly relating to the facts. Conclusions are left to the jury. In practice, however, the rule really is that lay witnesses are generally not permitted to draw conclusions, but expert witnesses may give their professional opinions.

Lay Witnesses

Even the Opinion Rule has exceptions. Whereas the older view was that lay witnesses were only allowed to express opinions when they were absolutely necessary, the more common practice today is to allow opinions for the sake of convenience. Some courts go so far as to follow Wigmore's view that lay opinions should only be rejected if they have no value to the jury.[1] Much is left to the discretion of the trial judge.

Opinion Testimony of Lay Witness Defined: Federal Rules of Evidence, Rule 701

If the witness is not testifying as an expert, the witness's testimony in the form of opinions or inferences is limited to opinions or inferences which are:
  (a) Rationally based on the perception of the witness, and
  (b) Helpful to a clear understanding of the witness's testimony or the determination of the facts in issue, and
  (c) Not based on scientific, technical, or other specialized knowledge within the scope of Rule 702.

Some statements of opinion are so common that we do not realize they are opinions. For example, an eyewitness attends a lineup and identifies the defendant. This is really a statement of the witness that it is his or her opinion that the defendant is the person that he or she saw committing the crime. Another example would be the statement, "He was drunk." This is an opinion. The facts may have been that the person smelled of alcohol, had watery eyes, slurred speech, unsteady gait, poor muscular coordination, and did not talk rationally. Nearly all courts would allow both of these opinions into evidence.

A wide variety of lay opinions may actually be admissible, including the following:

- Identification of someone's handwriting.
- Statements about the emotional state of someone (he or she was sad, angry, happy, etc.).
- Statements about the physical condition of someone (e.g., he or she was weak, strong, sick, or drunk).
- Voice identification.
- General statements about mental condition (e.g., he or she was coherent, smart, seemed to have low intelligence, etc.).
- Identity of a person based on in-person lineup or looking at a photograph.
- General statements about speed of vehicles (e.g., he or she was going too fast).

If one or more of these opinions is given, additional questions are usually asked so the jury will know the basis for forming the opinion. Cross-examination can also be used to show that there was an inadequate basis for the opinion or that a different conclusion could have been drawn. Table 5-3 presents examples of opinion testimony allowed and not allowed by a lay witness.

Expert Witnesses

Expert witnesses are allowed to give opinions based on their professional judgment. Even though experts have broader rights than lay witnesses, there are still some areas in which they are not allowed to testify. Table 5-4 compares examples of testimony by a lay witness with testimony by an expert witness.

T A B L E **5-3 Opinion Testimony by Lay Witness**

Allowed	Not Allowed
The man had bloodshot eyes and staggered when he tried to walk.	The man was drunk.
The man was disoriented and incoherent.	The man was crazy.
The man carefully aimed before shooting the gun.	The man maliciously killed the victim.
The car was driving faster than the other cars and left skid marks when it tried to stop.	The car was going 85 miles per hour.

T A B L E   **5-4 Comparison of Testimony by a Lay Witness and an Expert Witness**

Lay Witness	Expert Witness
The man smelled of alcohol and failed the field sobriety test.	The man's blood alcohol was 0.12%.
The man hid from everyone and said he was protecting himself from invisible rays.	The man suffered from paranoid schizophrenia.
The car was going faster than the other cars and was unable to stop before hitting the tree.	Based on the skid marks, the car was going 74 miles per hour.
There was a man at the scene of the crime who looks just like the defendant.	DNA tests on blood found at the scene and a sample taken from the defendant indicate that the blood came from the same person.

Experts' testimony cannot invade issues that the judge or jury is required to decide. This means that they usually may not state conclusions on legal issues. For example, a psychiatrist may state a diagnosis (paranoid schizophrenia), but in most states he or she cannot testify that a person is criminally insane.

Experts are only allowed to testify if they are needed. If the facts can be understood by lay jurors, no expert witness will be allowed. Things that are common knowledge do not require an expert to interpret them. Before a judge will allow an expert to testify, he or she must be convinced that there is a sufficiently established body of knowledge on the subject. Even then, the courts may be reluctant to allow testimony. Psychiatrists have developed many diagnoses, including the 47XYY (abnormal male chromosome) syndrome, which the courts have been very reluctant to accept.

For years, most state and the federal courts followed *Frye v. United States* (D.C. Cir. 1923), which held that a scientific technique was admissible in court *only if* it was "generally accepted" as reliable in the relevant scientific community.[2] This test focuses on opinions of large groups of scientists; in many cases, it looks at the official position of professional organizations, such as the American Academy of Forensic Medicine. The Supreme Court in *Daubert v. Merrell Dow Pharmaceuticals, Inc.* (1993) adopted a new standard for use with the Federal Rules of Evidence: The judge must make a preliminary assessment that the reasoning or methodology underlying the testimony is scientifically valid *and* that the reasoning or methodology properly can be applied to the facts in issue.[3] This allows new tests to be used at trial that have not become established in the scientific community. The trial judge makes the key ruling on whether the test provides relevant information. In practice, a hearing is held without the jury present and attorneys for both sides call expert witnesses who testify about the new test. After listening to the experts for both sides and reading briefs that the attorneys wrote, the judge makes a ruling on whether or not the new test will be admissible. The *Daubert* decision is binding on the federal courts. State courts are free to decide whether to adopt the *Daubert* rule; many states still use the *Frye* standard.

Sometimes the courts refuse to accept a new technique as sufficiently accurate. The polygraph is a good example. Although many people believe a well-trained polygraph operator can accurately test for deception, the courts have been very reluctant to accept polygraph results in criminal cases. Opponents argue strongly that there are too many errors to justify giving the jury information that may sound like it is conclusive evidence that a person lied. Many states refuse to admit the results of polygraph examinations.

Still other types of expert testimony are excluded because the courts refuse to believe there is any "scientific" basis for the opinion. Psychics and astrologers would be in this class.

Foundation for Expert Witness

In order to use an expert witness at trial, a foundation must be laid that establishes three main things:

1. The jury needs the help of an expert.
2. There is a recognized area of expertise that applies.
3. The person called to testify has the appropriate background to qualify as an expert.

The court will first address the *Frye* and *Daubert* issues. In most cases, the tests that are used are well established and do not require a separate hearing. The next step focuses on the qualifications of the person who is being called to testify. The exact qualifications vary with the type of expertise. In a few situations, the legislature sets qualifications, such as being a licensed psychologist with 5 years of clinical experience. Most often, there is no rule that requires advanced college degrees, and in some areas, such as accident reconstruction and ballistic examinations, a combination of training and experience is required. In other areas, such as the probabilities involved in a pyramid scheme or the chance of two people having the same DNA, purely theoretical study may be sufficient. The jury is given the task of deciding which expert witness to believe. To do this, the jury will decide which expert is best qualified, did the appropriate test accurately, and interpreted the results correctly.

Even if a person is an expert, he or she cannot give opinions on many things. The testimony must be restricted to factual descriptions of observations, much as a lay witness does, and opinions within the area of his or her expertise. Opinions that are outside the area of expertise are not allowed.

Experts do not have a special right to use privileged communications, such as statements made to a doctor or lawyer. They can base their opinions on these statements only if the privilege has been waived or there is an exception to the privilege that applies in the case. See Chapter 9 for a detailed discussion of privileged communications.

Voir Dire of Experts

The expert will be subjected to *voir dire* to establish his or her qualifications before testifying unless the opposing side is willing to accept the witness without a challenge. *Voir dire* is done without the jury present. The side calling the expert will ask relevant questions to show that the witness has the necessary education and experience. Opposing counsel can cross-examine and attempt to show that the expert does not qualify.

Examination of Expert Witnesses

Immediately after the expert witness takes the stand, questions will usually be asked regarding his or her professional background, education, and training. Since this has already been covered in *voir dire*, the only function of these questions is to impress the jury. It is common to have experts called by both sides in a case. Therefore, the jury needs to know about the expert's qualifications to help them decide how much weight should be given to the testimony.

On direct examination, the expert may be asked about his or her inspection and testing of the evidence in the case. Opinions based on this evidence may be given. Additionally, experts may be asked **hypothetical questions.** Hypothetical questions ask the witness to draw conclusions based on the facts given in the question. Prior to asking a hypothetical question, all of the facts used in the question must have been admitted into evidence via testimony of witnesses (either lay witnesses or expert witnesses).

It is not necessary that the witness has personally examined any of the evidence in a hypothetical question. For example, a civil engineer might be asked, "Would it be safe to drive a car with good tires on a dry surface at 55 miles per hour if there was a 10% downhill grade with a 90-degree turn that was banked 5 degrees?" The engineer would be allowed to give a professional opinion even though he or she had never seen the curve that was actually involved in the case.

Examples of Hypothetical Questions

- "Based on your microscopic examination of the slides containing lung tissue specimens that were prepared during the autopsy, is it your professional opinion that the victim was dead prior to being placed in water?"
- "Based on the fact that the room in question was illuminated with a 60-watt bulb and there were no windows, would you conclude that a person with normal eyesight could accurately determine if the currency was counterfeit?"
- "Based on the testimony regarding the defendant's prior mental illness, the defendant's repeated claims that he was from Mars, and the fact that the defendant repeatedly said, 'You are the devil!' prior to shooting the victim, would you conclude that the defendant understood the nature and quality of his acts?"

In addition to the normal methods of cross-examination, experts may be questioned regarding the sources of information used to form their conclusions. The expert may be asked who he or she considers the leading authors and texts in the field. This also includes asking if he or she has read specific books or articles. If he or she admits reading a given work, questioning may continue on why the expert agrees or disagrees with the opinions stated in it.

Some experts always testify for the defense, whereas others always testify for the prosecution. This can be used to impeach for bias. The amount of the expert's fee is also subject to cross-examination. If the fee appears too large, the jury may discredit the testimony.

Examples of Expert Testimony

Insanity

A lay witness can describe symptoms that he or she observed, but an expert witness is required in order to introduce diagnosis of mental disorders. The expert can explain the effect of the condition on the personality and how it probably affected the defendant's actions. Opinions can also be given on the defendant's ability to form criminal intent, premeditation, or to comprehend what was going on. Although the expert psychiatrist or psychologist usually examines the defendant, hypothetical questions are also utilized. In most states, the expert may not testify that a person is criminally insane because this is a legal, not medical, opinion.

Consider the Andrea Yates case. As long as the psychiatrists told the jury their professional opinions regarding Andrea's psychotic state, the testimony was admissible. This rule applies even though the opinions of two experts are in direct conflict with each other. The jurors have the responsibility to listen to all of the testimony and then decide which witnesses to believe. The expert testimony that caused Andrea's conviction to be reversed was statements about something that had not occurred—that is, testimony that there had been a recent TV show that featured a plot similar to what Andrea had done. Later, it was determined that although a producer may have considered such a script, it was never on TV, therefore allowing the jury to consider the expert's conclusion that Andrea was not insane because she had the mental capacity to copy the plot was a serious error that required reversal.

Examples of Expert Witness Testimony on Issue of Defendant's Sanity

- "Based on my diagnostic interview of the defendant which lasted 6 hours, I diagnosed the defendant as having a bipolar disorder. Due to this condition I believe the defendant knew what he was doing but could not premeditate the murder."
- "After reviewing the reports submitting by the two court-appointed psychiatrists, it is my professional opinion that the defendant suffers from severe depression with suicidal tendencies. It is my opinion that the defendant planned to commit suicide and was unaware that any other person was in the area."

Ballistics

Firearms tests can often reveal if a recovered slug could have been fired from a specific gun, depending on the condition of the slug. The pattern of lands and grooves in the barrel of the gun imprints a pattern on the bullet as it leaves the gun. Since manufacturers use the same configuration in all their guns, the pattern can be used to state what type of gun was used. Microscopic comparison of the recovered slug and one that was test-fired is required to make a positive match. Firing pin marks on the shell casing can often be matched with a suspect gun.

Examples of Expert Witness Testimony about a Ballistics Test

- "After comparing Exhibit A, the bullet recovered from the victim, with Exhibit B, the bullet that was test-fired from the gun found in the possession of the defendant, it is my opinion that the two bullets were fired from the same gun."
- "I have studied the two bullets, Exhibits C and D, under a comparison microscope and it is my professional opinion that the two bullets were not fired from the same weapon."

Blood and Tissue Matching

Blood testing is important because the blood contains substances that can be used to match blood samples to saliva, tears, perspiration, semen, vaginal fluids, mucus, gastric contents, etc. In the past, blood testing was limited to typing by the ABO system. If the suspect did not have the appropriate blood type, he or she could be eliminated, but if there was a match it still was not possible to indicate that the suspect committed the crime. If the suspect had type A blood, test results were not very useful because type A is present in 40% of the U.S. public.

Today, we have much more sophisticated tests. For example, scientific analysis of the DNA (deoxyribonucleic acid) molecule found in all cells reveals the body's genetic code and can identify blood, hair, semen, or skin left at the crime scene as accurately as fingerprints. Each state will decide on the admissibility of each new technique as it becomes recognized in its respective scientific community.

Examples of Expert Witness Testimony on DNA Testing

- "As I have explained, DNA testing was done on semen recovered from the victim when the rape kit was done at the emergency room. Similar tests were performed on a blood sample taken from the defendant at the time of booking. Based on these tests, there is a 1 in 20 million chance that the two samples came from two different individuals."
- "DNA tests were performed on blood samples taken from the rape victim, the defendant, and the child born to the rape victim. Based on these tests I can conclusively state that the defendant is not the father of this child."

Summary

All trial witnesses must be competent. This means that they must understand the duty to tell the truth and be able to answer questions about the events in issue. If there is doubt about the competency of a witness, a *voir dire* examination will be conducted.

The truthfulness of each witness is in issue. The opposing side may ask questions for the purpose of convincing the jurors that they should not believe the witness. This is referred to as impeachment. A witness can be impeached because he or she is biased or prejudiced toward a person involved in the case. The prior crimes committed by the witness, whether or not there has been a conviction, can be used to infer that current testimony is not true. Prior statements that are inconsistent with what the witness said during direct examination may be used to show that the current testimony is not true. A witness can be impeached because he or she could not have accurately observed the events in question. The reputation of the witness for untruthfulness can also be used to impeach.

If a witness is impeached, the side that called the witness will have a chance to attempt to convince the jury that the testimony should be believed anyway. This is called rehabilitation and is usually done on redirect examination.

When a witness cannot remember the events in question, attempts may be made to refresh his or her memory. If this is successful, the witness will testify just like any other witness. Memory problems, of course, will probably be emphasized on cross-examination. If the memory cannot be refreshed, an accurate report made by the witness near the time of the event may be used instead of testimony.

Testimony can be corroborated by another witness or physical objects related to the case. Very few cases require corroboration, but attorneys frequently introduce this additional evidence to help support their case.

A lay witness is allowed to testify about anything observed with the five senses. Opinions are allowed only if they are expressions in such common usage that the jury will understand. Even then, a good attorney will ask the witness to explain what facts led to the conclusion.

Expert witnesses are allowed to express professional opinions. Before an expert can testify, it must be established that the jury needs assistance with the facts. It also must be shown that there is a recognized body of knowledge that applies.

Each expert must show that he or she has the necessary education and experience to qualify as an expert. On the witness stand, the expert can testify about the facts and give opinions. Hypothetical questions may be used so the expert can give an opinion even if he or she has not personally examined the evidence.

Review Questions

1. Define *competency of a witness*, and explain the procedure for establishing the competency of a witness.
2. Give two examples of incompetent witnesses. Explain why each one is incompetent.
3. Define *impeachment*. Explain how impeachment is done, and give six ways a witness can be impeached.
4. Define *rehabilitation of a witness*, and give two examples of how a witness can be rehabilitated.
5. Explain how the memory of a witness can legally be refreshed, and list the requirements for introducing a document under the Past Recollection Recorded Rule.
6. State the Opinion Rule, and explain how it affects testimony.
7. Explain what a lay witness may testify about, and give three examples of opinions a lay witness can give.
8. When is an expert witness used in a criminal case? What arguments must be made to the judge before a specific type of expert witness may be called to the stand?
9. What is the purpose of *voir dire* of an expert witness? Why are the qualifications of an expert witness given to the jury?
10. Explain what hypothetical questions are, and tell how they are used.
11. Give three examples of how an expert witness can be impeached.
12. Give three examples of the use of expert witnesses in criminal trials.

Writing Assignment

Find an expert witness, or a consulting agency that provides expert witnesses, for criminal trials in your state. Write a 250-word (one-page) report on the types of evidence this expert witness can testify about in court.

To find the information for this report:

If you know a person who testifies as an expert witness, you may interview that person and base your report on what you learned from the interview.

If not, go to the "For Legal Professionals" page at www.findlaw.com. Find the section on expert witnesses. Select a specialty frequently used in criminal trials. Find a consulting agency that provides experts in your state and read the material that it has posted on the web. Base your report on what you read.

Notes

1. Wigmore is a famous legal scholar on the subject of evidence.
2. *Frye v. United States*, 293 F. 1013 (D.C. Cir. 1923).
3. *Daubert v. Merrell Dow Pharmaceuticals, Inc.*, 509 U.S. 579, 125 L.Ed. 2d 469, 113 S.Ct. 2786 (1993).

CHAPTER 6

Crime Scene Evidence and Experiments

Feature Case: Scott Peterson

Scott Peterson was convicted for the murder of Laci Peterson, his wife, and Connor, his unborn son. Laci, who was 8 months pregnant, was last seen on December 24, 2002, in Modesto, California. Midmorning, a neighbor found the Peterson family dog running loose in the neighborhood wearing a collar and muddy leash. Laci's car was in the driveway and her purse, cell phone, and keys were in their usual spot in the bedroom. At the time, Scott had taken his boat on a fishing trip in San Francisco Bay. The police were called at 6 p.m. The police, neighbors, and friends searched the area on foot, in all-terrain vehicles and police vehicles, and by helicopter. The search widened to cover several counties. No trace of Laci was found. Police suspected foul play because it was totally out of character for Laci to go off alone without contacting anyone. During the investigation, police discovered that Scott had had numerous infidelities. He met Amber Frey, his current mistress, 2 weeks before Laci disappeared, and he told Amber that he was a widower. When Amber discovered that Scott's wife was missing, she allowed the police to record her phone calls with Scott. She testified for the prosecution at trial and some of the recorded calls were played for the jury.

On April 13, 2003, the decomposed body of a late-term male fetus with umbilical cord attached washed up on the shore of San Francisco Bay approximately 3 miles from where Scott claimed to have gone fishing. One day later, the body of a recently pregnant woman washed up approximately 1 mile from where the baby was found. Due to the decomposition of the body, it was impossible to determine the woman's cause of death. DNA tests showed that the bodies were those of Laci and Connor Peterson.

Scott was arrested 5 days later in La Jolla, California (near the California–Mexico border). At the time, he had $10,000 in cash, four cell phones, camping equipment, a gun, a map showing how to get to his mistress's workplace, Viagra, and his brother's driver's license. His hair and goatee had been dyed. The police believed Scott was planning on fleeing to Mexico. Biological samples were taken from Scott. Based on a theory that Scott had suffocated or strangled Laci in their home and disposed of the body while on his supposed fishing trip, the police searched the couple's house, Scott's truck, a tool box in the back of his truck, his warehouse, and his boat. The only piece of forensic evidence recovered was a single hair found in his boat.

The trial began in January 2004. The prosecution presented circumstantial evidence that Laci had been killed by Scott. Witnesses testified about Scott's behavior (almost immediately selling Laci's car, changing his appearance, adding hardcore pornographic channels to his cable service, and attempting to sell the house), which indicated that Scott knew Laci was not coming home. A hydrologist with the U.S. Geological Survey who was an expert on tides was called as an expert witness. He testified that the tidal systems in San Francisco were sufficiently chaotic to account for Laci and Connor's bodies washing up at the locations where they were found. The affair with Amber Frey was not presented as a motive to kill Laci. Instead, it was presented as evidence of Scott's character.

The defense based its case on lack of direct evidence. It also suggested that Connor's body indicated that he was full-term. The defense theorized that Laci had been kidnapped, held until she gave birth, and then both Laci and Connor had been dumped into the bay. Prosecution medical experts were able to prove that Connor was not full-term and he had died at the same time that Laci died. The medical expert called by the defense tried to show that Connor died 1 week later than the prosecution claimed. On cross-examination, the witness became confused and also admitted that there were no medical records that supported his theory.

The jury convicted Scott of first-degree murder. Scott is now in San Quentin prison on death row. He has never admitted guilt.

Learning Objectives

After studying this chapter, you will be able to

- Properly mark and package real evidence found during the investigation of a criminal case.
- Maintain the chain of custody for real evidence found at a crime scene.
- Explain the importance of scientific evidence in a criminal case.
- Describe how the prosecutor lays the foundation for the admission of crime scene evidence, experiments, and models.

- List commonly accepted laboratory tests used in criminal cases, and explain their respective evidentiary value.
- Explain what conditions must be met before experiments can be introduced into evidence.
- Describe common types of experiments used in criminal trials.
- Explain the most common conditions that must be met before a model or diagram can be introduced into evidence.

Key Terms

- Ballistics expert
- Blood alcohol
- Blood typing
- Chain of custody
- DNA testing
- Experiment
- Laying the foundation
- Latent prints
- Real evidence

Myths about Crime Scene Evidence and Experiments	Facts about Crime Scene Evidence and Experiments
All cases are solved by DNA tests.	DNA tests can only be done on biological evidence (blood, semen, etc.). Although newer DNA tests make it possible to do tests on smaller sized evidence samples, there are still many cases in which no DNA is found.
Crime scene investigators solve most of the cases.	Some cases are solved by scientific tests, but in many cases no tests are performed. There are two main reasons for this: There is no physical evidence to test in many cases, and there are not enough forensic labs to handle all of the samples from convicted felons in order to make a comprehensive database for "cold" DNA testing.
The police can bring anyone who is a suspect to the emergency room to take DNA samples.	The police must have probable cause to arrest in order to take a person to the station or emergency room. Samples could be taken in the field if there is reasonable suspicion the person has committed a crime, but this is limited to fingerprints and mug shots.
New scientific tests are admissible in federal court only if they are accepted by a majority of the professional groups in that branch of science.	In federal court the judge determines if a newly developed test is sufficiently reliable to be admitted in evidence in a criminal trial.
Once a new scientific test is accepted in federal court, it is automatically admissible in all state courts.	Each state determines the admissibility of scientific tests in its courts.

Introduction

In Chapter 3, we defined **real evidence** to include anything that can be perceived with the five senses except trial testimony. This includes physical items, documents, exhibits, and pictures. Since this is such a broad category, it will be divided into two chapters. Evidence recovered at the crime scene and by criminal investigations, scientific evidence, experiments, models, and diagrams are discussed in this chapter. Chapter 7 discusses documents, pictures, models, and exhibits.

All types of real evidence have two things in common: They must be marked and formally introduced into evidence, and the attorney who wishes to introduce them must lay a foundation to establish the admissibility of the items in question.

The formal process of marking evidence has four steps. First, the item must be shown to opposing counsel before testimony about it is introduced. This gives the attorney a chance to see what is to be discussed and form appropriate questions. Second, the side that intends to introduce the item has the court clerk assign it a number (or letter) for identification purposes. Third, the foundation is laid to establish that the item is admissible. Lastly, a formal request is made to admit it into evidence. If the judge rules that the item is admissible, it is given an exhibit number (or letter) and becomes evidence in the case. The following example illustrates the process involved for the prosecution to introduce the murder weapon (e.g., a gun) into evidence.

Example of Introduction of Evidence

Prosecutor shows gun to defense attorney and allows him or her to examine it if desired.

Prosecutor: Your Honor, the prosecution requests that the clerk mark this .38-caliber Smith & Wesson revolver for identification as People's No. 1. (Gun is given to clerk, who attaches tag to gun with "People's No. 1" written on it.)

Prosecutor calls witness(es) and lays foundation to show that the gun is the one found at crime scene and that ballistic tests show that the slug test-fired from this gun matches the slug removed from the victim's body.

Defense cross-examines and raises objections to admission of the gun into evidence.

Prosecutor: Your Honor, the prosecution requests that the gun which was marked for identification as People's No. 1 be admitted into evidence as Exhibit No. 1.

Defense: [May make objection.]

Judge: [Rules on objection; allows evidence if no objection or objection overruled] Let the gun be received into evidence as Exhibit No. 1. (Clerk attaches tag that reads "Exhibit No. 1.")

Exhibits that have been admitted into evidence may be examined by the jury and can usually be taken to the jury room during deliberations.

The two requests to mark the gun, first for identification and later as an exhibit, appear to be a waste of time. The reason for marking it twice is that not all items displayed during trial will be admitted into evidence. To keep the trial record straight, all of those items are marked for identification purposes. The prosecutor or defense attorney may use something to illustrate a point or help a witness describe an event but not ask to have it introduced as evidence in the case. Opposing counsel may successfully argue that the item is inadmissible. Sometimes the testimony of several witnesses is needed to lay the foundation. Assigning the identification number the first time any testimony is given about the item makes it easier to determine which piece of evidence is being discussed. By the time all of the witnesses have testified and the foundation for admitting the item into evidence is complete, one or more other items may have been introduced into evidence. Most judges like to have the exhibits numbered in chronological order; to do this, exhibit numbers are not assigned until the judge rules the item is admissible. To avoid confusion, one side usually uses letters and the other numbers. For example, the prosecution might begin with "1," whereas the defense starts with "A." If a large number of exhibits is anticipated, each side will be assigned a block of numbers, such as 100 to 299 for the prosecution and 300 to 599 for the defense.

Crime Scene Evidence

All items that are admitted as exhibits must be authenticated. Authentication means to show that an item is genuine. To authenticate evidence found at the crime scene, or during other parts of the investigation of the case, it is necessary to show that the item is the same one described by the witness. The item needs to be in the same condition that it was in at the time it was found by the police unless it was necessary to conduct laboratory tests on it. If tests have altered its appearance, this must be explained to the jury. Careful handling of evidence and accurate report writing are crucial. Most police department procedure manuals give detailed instructions on how to handle many different types of crime scene evidence.

For example, at the crime scene it is very important to protect evidence so that it is not destroyed or damaged. Restricting public access to the area is important to prevent people from stepping on evidence, handling it, or removing it from the scene. Officers must also be careful not to accidentally damage potential evidence. No one should be allowed to try to clean up the area before the investigation is completed because evidence could be destroyed.

The police usually try to save everything that might have evidentiary value. The prosecutor will make the final decision on what is needed at trial. Things that are not properly preserved will not be admissible. *It is much better to have many items in the evidence locker that are not used than to discover that something that is needed was not kept.*

The series of questions that the attorney asks witnesses in order to establish that a piece of real evidence is admissible is called **"laying the foundation."** The first step in laying the foundation for the admission of crime scene evidence is to have someone identify the object and testify about where the item was found. For example, "Yes, this is the gun that I took from the defendant's pocket at the time of the arrest." If the item has a serial number or some other unique form of identification, this process is easier. Merely describing it, even in rather specific terms (Smith & Wesson .38-caliber revolver), is usually not good enough if there were more than one of these items made. After the piece of evidence has been identified, one or more witnesses will be needed to testify about what has been done with it since it was taken into the custody of the police.

The most common solution to this problem of identifying an object is to make a mark, usually the officer's initials, on the item at the time it was originally collected. It is very important, however, that identifying marks are only made in locations where they do not interfere with the use of the item as evidence. Marks should not be placed where they will be in the way when laboratory tests are done. Extreme caution must also be used to preserve fingerprints, traces of blood, etc. that may be on an object.

The officer needs to be familiar with what laboratory tests may be done in order to be able to handle crime scene evidence properly. For example, blood-stained clothing needs to be air-dried before packaging because mold and mildew that grow in airtight containers where damp clothing is stored can interfere with tests for blood types. On the other hand, charred remains from a suspected arson fire need to be stored in airtight containers immediately to avoid evaporation of gasoline or other volatile fluids used to start the fire. Knowing the types of tests that can be performed will also help the officer decide what evidence should be collected.

Before collecting and packaging evidence for storage, the officer should make a detailed record of the crime scene with clear indications of where each item was found. This can be done by sketching the location, taking photographs of the area, or making detailed notes. Ideally, all three will be done. Figure 6-1 is an example of a police sketch of a crime scene.

Figure 6-1
Typical Police Sketch of Homicide Crime Scene

Sketches should be to scale, with all relevant facts, such as locations of doors, windows, and furniture, included. Distances between key objects should be noted in the drawing. The points of the compass are usually included to help orient the viewer. Photographs also need to show these facts. Additionally, photographs need to have something in them that clearly indicates the size of the items shown. A ruler is frequently placed near the object that is the focus of the picture for this purpose.

The process of packaging evidence for storage is very important. The evidence needs to be preserved for trial so that it will not be damaged, evaporate, or be contaminated by other things. Each piece of evidence must be packaged individually. It is useful to have a variety of clean envelopes and containers on hand for this purpose. Appropriate packing materials, such as sterile cotton, should also be kept on hand. Extra precautions may need to be taken to avoid damaging the evidence if it will be mailed to the crime laboratory.

| Blood sample | Beverage can, may have fingerprints | Gun, believed to be the weapon used to commit the crime |

At a crime scene, police restrict public access to the area, record the details of the scene, and gather evidence.

Figure 6-2
Collecting Evidence at a Crime Scene

The evidence should be marked or tagged and the container should have the necessary identification information on it because the evidence may be removed from the envelope for examination and laboratory tests. Each container should be labeled so that it is not necessary to open it to find out what is inside. This reduces the chance of losing or damaging the evidence. There should also be space (either on the envelope or on a form attached to the package containing the evidence) so that each person who handles it can indicate the time, date, and reason for having it. This detailed procedure is used to establish the **"chain of custody"** (also called chain of possession or continuity of possession). It will be necessary to account for everyone who has had possession of the evidence in order to show the judge and jury that the evidence has not been tampered with. Figure 6-2 illustrates the appropriate steps for collecting evidence at a crime scene.

Scientific Evidence

The modern forensics laboratory can perform a wide variety of scientific tests. Forensic evidence can be used to establish the elements of the crime, conclusively associate the defendant with the crime, and/or help reconstruct the crime.

Evidence found at the crime scene can be sent to a forensics laboratory for testing. If evidence samples, such as blood or urine, are needed so that tests can be performed, the suspect's Fourth Amendment rights must be honored. If the suspect is not already in custody, the police must have probable cause in order to bring the person to an emergency room or other facility to take the samples. This is frequently done in "drunk driving" cases. A person can be detained in the field based on reasonable suspicion, but the person cannot be transported to another location.

If there is no probable cause to arrest, it may be necessary to obtain a search warrant in order to obtain the samples needed for a specific test. The judge will weigh the need for the tests against the potential danger to the suspect when obtaining the evidence. Blood and urine samples are low risk and routinely granted as long as there is probable cause to connect the suspect to the crime. More invasive tests, such as surgery to retrieve a bullet from the suspect's torso for ballistic tests, may be denied if the surgery poses a danger of serious injury.

Types of Cases Commonly Using Scientific Evidence

Research by Peterson[1] showed that police are far more likely to clear a case if scientific evidence is gathered and analyzed. Prosecutors are less likely to plea bargain in these cases, and judges tend to give more severe sentences. Results of a survey suggested that jurors gave scientific evidence serious consideration but that it usually was not the key element in deciding the case.

Peterson also reported on a nationwide survey of crime labs. Approximately two thirds of their caseloads involved drugs, narcotics, and drunk driving cases. Only approximately one fourth of their work was related to crimes against persons or property.

Forensic evidence was used in nearly all murder and drug possession cases. Use in rape prosecutions varied considerably between the jurisdictions (from 30% to 70%). Burglary, robbery, and attempted murder or aggravated battery cases were less likely to have tests from a crime laboratory introduced.

Laying the Foundation

The foundation for the introduction of scientific evidence involves successfully answering three questions: (1) Is this a valid scientific test? (2) Was accurate equipment used for the test? and (3) Was the test performed in an appropriate manner by a qualified person?

The first question, which requires the side offering the test results to establish the scientific validity of the test, is in many ways similar to the requirement that expert witnesses may only be called if there is a valid field of scientific knowledge. This is no problem when a test has become widely accepted. In fact, in those situations it is rare for either side to even ask questions about the scientific basis for the test. Fingerprint comparisons are a good example of a well-established test. Newer tests must be carefully explained to the judge. This is done on *voir dire*. Expert witnesses will be called to provide the necessary background on the test and explain the scientific principles behind it. The federal courts and many state courts allow the judge to determine if the test is sufficiently reliable to be admitted. The judge considers the following factors: whether a theory or technique presents scientific knowledge that will assist the jury, whether it has been subjected to peer review and published in professional journals, the known or potential rate of errors, and how widespread the acceptance of the test is. See discussion of the *Frye* and *Daubert* cases in Chapter 5.

The opposing side can cross-examine and call its own experts. After the witnesses have given their testimony, the judge will decide if the test is sufficiently accepted in the appropriate scientific community. Due to the highly technical nature of these scientific explanations, they are seldom repeated for the jury. Table 6-1 reviews what must be done in court when an expert witness testifies.

Any test can be attacked on the basis of faulty equipment. States frequently require certain types of equipment, such as the machines designed to measure breath alcohol, to be checked regularly and to be certified as accurate. Failure to have the machines tested can cast doubt on the test results. If the results appear to be wrong, the opposing side will attempt to show defects in the test equipment even if routine testing and maintenance have been done. This tactic may be used merely because the test results are damaging to its case. Doing this is the equivalent of impeaching the laboratory equipment. Although the trend in discovery is to share evidence and require each side to reveal the results of laboratory tests before trial, there is no duty to preserve evidence in order to allow the other side to perform tests on it.

Human error can also cause inaccurate test results. The side introducing the test will call the technician who performed it. Questions will be asked to show that the technician has had the appropriate training and that the test was done correctly. The questions will try to point out the skill of the operator and how carefully the required procedures were followed. Cross-examination will be used to try to show that deviations from the required testing procedures could cause the results to be inaccurate. Redirect can be used to try to establish that minor mistakes made during

T A B L E   **6-1 Summary of Procedures Used When Expert Witness Testifies in Court**

	Side Calling the Expert Witness	Opposing Side
Establish that jury needs the assistance of an expert in order to understand the evidence.	*Voir dire* hearing Present arguments to judge explaining why the jury will not be able to understand the evidence.	*Voir dire* hearing Present arguments to judge explaining why the jury will be able to understand the evidence.
Establish that there is a "science" that can be introduced at trial that will help the jury understand the facts of the case. *Note:* This step will be skipped if a well-established test will be introduced.	*Voir dire* hearing Establish scientific validity of test used, based on either *Frye* or *Daubert* (depending on which test is used in the court district).	*Voir dire* hearing Establish that the test does not have scientific validity based on either *Frye* or *Daubert* (depending on which test is used in the court district).
Establish that an expert witness should be allowed to testify.	*Voir dire* hearing Put the expert on the witness stand and ask questions about education, training, and experience in the area that he or she will testify about if allowed to testify in front of the jury.	*Voir dire* hearing Cross-examine the expert and show that he or she does not have the education, training, and experience in the area needed to testify in front of the jury.
Expert testifies during trial.	At trial, ask questions to show 1. Qualifications of expert. 2. Correct facts were used. 3. Equipment used for the tests was appropriate and accurate. 4. Appropriate tests were done. 5. Tests were done properly. 6. Interpretation of test results was correct.	At trial, ask questions on cross-examination to show 1. Expert is not qualified. 2. Wrong facts were used or facts that were used were insufficient. 3. Equipment that was used was not appropriate and/or the equipment did not produce accurate results. 4. Wrong tests were done. 5. Tests were not done properly. 6. Test results were not correctly interpreted.

the test were not likely to affect the results. Sometimes expert witnesses will be called to testify about the effect of procedural errors on the test results. Table 6-2 summarizes what must be done in court to introduce test results.

TABLE **6-2 Introducing Results of Scientific Tests during Trial**

	Side That Wants to Introduce the Evidence	Side That Wants to Prevent Introduction of the Evidence
New lab test	Jurisdiction using *Frye* Introduce facts during *voir dire* to show that the test is recognized as valid in the scientific community. Jurisdiction using *Daubert* Introduce facts during *voir dire* so judge can determine that the test has scientific validity.	Jurisdiction using *Frye* Introduce facts during *voir dire* to show that test is not recognized as valid in scientific community. Jurisdiction using *Daubert* Introduce facts during *voir dire* so judge will not conclude that the test has scientific validity.
Lab test in common usage	Ask judge to have lab test report marked as evidence and then introduce testimony about it.	Object and state facts indicating that the test is not recognized as valid.
Competency of person who did the test	Introduce testimony and documents to show that the person was properly trained to conduct the test.	Introduce testimony and documents to show that the person was not properly trained to conduct the test.
Accuracy of equipment used to conduct test	Introduce testimony and documents to show that the equipment used to conduct the test is working properly and has been checked recently for accuracy.	Introduce testimony and documents to show that the equipment is not working properly and/or has not been checked recently for accuracy.
Test performed properly	Introduce testimony by person who did test to show how the test was conducted.	Introduce testimony by person who did test or an expert to show that the test was not conducted properly.

Commonly Accepted Scientific Tests

Many scientific tests are so well established that they are admitted at trial without a challenge to their validity. This does not mean that the opposing side will not challenge the equipment used or the way the test was performed. This section discusses the basis for accepting a few of the most common scientific tests.

Fingerprints[2]

Use of fingerprints for identification purposes in the United States dates back to 1901 when the New York City Civil Service Commission first used fingerprints for certifying all civil service applicants. Law enforcement began using fingerprints soon thereafter. Centralized fingerprint files, which evolved into the National Crime Information Center files maintained by the FBI today, were started in 1924.

Fingerprint identification is based on three key principles: (1) A fingerprint is an individual characteristic, (2) fingerprints remain unchanged during an individual's lifetime, and (3) fingerprints have general ridge patterns that permit them to be systematically classified.

Identification of a fingerprint is based on a study of the ridge pattern characteristics. Both the number and the relative location of the characteristics are considered. In the approximately 90 years that fingerprints have been collected, no two have been found that were identical.

The typical fingerprint may have as many as 150 ridge characteristics. There has been considerable debate about how many ridge comparisons must match before it can be concluded that the fingerprints are from the same person. Some experts have said anywhere from 8 to 16. In 1973, the International Association for Identification concluded that there is no number that can answer this question in all cases. The final determination is based on the experience, skill, and knowledge of the fingerprint expert.

The ridge characteristics of the finger are formed where the epidermis and dermis meet. Perspiration, salts, and skin oil on the fingertips combine to leave a pattern on surfaces that the skin touches. An injury must produce a scar that goes 1 or 2 millimeters beneath the skin's surface to affect the fingerprint. Even then, there are usually enough matching points left to allow an expert to make a comparison. Also, a scar can be used for identification purposes.

There are three classes of fingerprints: loops (60% to 65% of the population), whorls (30% to 35% of the population), and arches (5% of the population). Each of these classes can be subdivided into distinct groups. Figure 6-3 shows the six common fingerprint patterns. Classification systems, used to help locate fingerprints on file, were based on the presence of one type of pattern on each of the 10 fingers. Such classification systems are now largely replaced by automated filing and searching.

In the past, individual prints had to be compared to prints on file by skilled fingerprint examiners. Now, advanced computer technology is making it easier to match single prints. Flying spot scanners can be used to input fingerprints. All ridge characteristics are given numeric identifiers that can be compared with those already in the database.

A separate question that must be answered when fingerprints are used in court relates to how the prints were preserved. The easier part of the answer relates to how the comparison set of prints was obtained. This

| Plain Arch | Tented Arch | Double Loop |

| Loop | Pocket Loop | Plain Whorl |

Figure 6-3
Six Common Fingerprint Patterns

focuses on the act of making the fingerprint card that was used. Many attorneys do not question this, but some demand testimony about the procedure used to roll the comparison prints.

Fingerprints that are recovered at the crime scene or from other evidence are commonly called **"latent"** (not developed) **prints.** A detailed explanation of how the latent prints were recovered is usually required. For many years, prints on hard, nonabsorbent surfaces (e.g., mirrors, glass, and painted surfaces) were obtained by applying fingerprint powder to the surface with a camel-hair brush. The powder stuck to the skin oil in the fingerprint, thus making it visible. The fingerprint, as seen by the pattern in the powder, was photographed. It was also preserved by "lifting" it from the surface with a special adhesive tape (which may be clear or opaque) made for this purpose. If the object with the print on it is small enough, the actual object bearing the print may be kept for evidence.

Prints on porous surfaces (paper, cardboard, etc.) were obtained by the use of iodine fuming, ninhydrin, and silver nitrate. Laser light has been discovered to produce fluorescent fingerprints that can be photographed. Ninhydrin development, laser techniques, and cyanoacrylic ester fuming are now routinely used to obtain fingerprints on both porous and nonporous surfaces.

Caution must be taken, of course, when collecting and processing latent prints to avoid contaminating them with the fingerprints of investigators or others at the crime scene. The victim's attempts to clean the crime scene may also destroy valuable prints. Additionally, investigators must be aware of other types of laboratory tests that may be needed in the case because fingerprint powder or other substances used to develop latent prints may interfere with another test that must be performed.

Blood Alcohol[3]

The most common use of **blood alcohol** testing is in drunk driving cases. It is also used in cases in which intoxication is an element of the crime and in other cases in which the defendant's sobriety has a bearing on criminal intent.

Alcohol is absorbed into the body from the stomach and small intestine. Although it does not require digestion, absorption will be delayed if there is any food in the stomach. Alcohol is rapidly absorbed into the body's blood and circulatory system and distributed to all parts of the body. The molecular structure and weight of alcohol is such that it is able to cross cell membranes by a simple diffusion process. It can quickly achieve equilibrium in the body. The result is that alcohol rapidly becomes associated with all parts of the body in concentrations proportionate to body water content. It is therefore possible to estimate the total alcohol content of the body using a small sample of the blood.

The most common test for alcohol is done on breath samples; blood alcohol tests are also common. Capillary and arterial blood give the best prediction of brain alcohol concentration. Blood samples should be taken by qualified medical personnel (e.g., doctor, nurse, and laboratory technician) and witnessed by a law enforcement officer. Special procedures are required, such as cleansing the skin with alcohol-free disinfectant, before taking the blood sample.

Kits are available with all the necessary supplies including chemicals to preserve the specimen until it reaches the laboratory. The chain of custody for the blood sample must be recorded. Having an officer witness the taking of the blood sample will eliminate the need to have the person who drew the sample testify in court.

Blood alcohol test results state the percentage of alcohol in the blood. Many states use the 0.08% level as conclusive evidence of driving under the influence; a lower standard may apply to juveniles. The number of drinks that it takes to achieve any specific level of alcohol in the blood varies with the weight of the person. Approximately one drink per hour can be removed from the body by the normal metabolic process.

Blood Typing[4]

There are many questions that a forensic serologist can help to answer: Is it blood? If so, is it human blood? If it is human blood, what group does it belong to? Can additional information be obtained by testing that will help identify the source of the blood? DNA testing is the most accurate way to determine if blood matches, but this type of testing is expensive and takes several days or weeks. Blood typing is inexpensive and can be done quickly; therefore, it is still in use.

Tests performed on a stain to determine if it is blood generally are based on the presence of blood cells or compounds characteristic of blood. These include erythrocytes and leukocytes, blood serum proteins, and hemoglobin and its derivatives.

Once it has been determined that the sample is blood, the next step is to determine if it is human blood. If it is not, laboratory tests can also determine what species of animal the blood is from. Most of these tests are based on the response of the immune system to foreign substances in the blood.

Blood typing is done on human blood. The ABO system is the most common. Four major blood groups are used: A (41% of U.S. population), B (10%), AB (4%), and O (45%). The smallest subgroup in this system is present in 0.5% of the population.

Another blood group system is based on the Rh factor of the blood. This is totally separate from the ABO system. There are eight Rh determinants in common use. Their frequency in the U.S. population ranges from 33.2% for one of the Rh+ subgroups to very rare occurrences in three of the Rh- subgroups. Forensic laboratories in the United States do not rely heavily on the Rh system.

A third blood group system is also in use. The MN system has nine categories. The frequency of these blood types in the U.S. Caucasian population ranges from 24% (MNS group) to 1% (NS group). This system is separate from both the ABO and the Rh systems.

Each of these three blood typing systems has the same problem in court. If the defendant has a different blood type from the one found at the crime scene, it can be shown that it was not his or her blood. The tests cannot conclusively show that the blood came from one specific individual. Unless the suspect has a very rare blood type, the test only points to a large segment of the population. Scientists are constantly seeking better blood grouping systems so that blood can be identified on a more individualized basis.

DNA Testing[5]

Identical DNA molecules are found in each cell of a person's body. With the exception of identical twins, each individual's DNA is unique. Whereas some DNA tests require a blood stain the size of a quarter or a semen stain the size of a dime to determine if the evidence found at the crime scene matches a sample extracted from a criminal suspect, other DNA tests can be done on minute samples. Due to the uniformity of DNA throughout the body, a semen sample found at the crime scene can be matched to a blood sample taken at a clinical laboratory.

The laboratory tests to match DNA samples are very complex and the details are not discussed in this text. Once the tests have been completed, the matching is done both by visual inspection and by computer matching. The complete results of the test are sometimes called a "DNA profile." Comparison calculations are given in two forms: a statement that there is (or is not) a match and a probability calculation for such a match. For example, there is a 1 in 7 million chance that the match would have occurred at random.

DNA testing, first used in criminal prosecutions in 1985, is now admissible in all states. It is most commonly used in sexual assault cases in which semen samples are available and violent crime scenes where blood samples can be retrieved; however, DNA can be used on any type of biological evidence left by the perpetrator. Tests are now available to compare DNA from plants. DNA also has been used to establish that a person did not commit a crime. The Innocence Project has utilized DNA tests between 1989 and 2007 to obtained the reversal of more than 200 convictions and the release of inmates serving prison sentences for crimes they did not commit.

Although the scientific principle involved is unchallenged, there are a variety of errors that can occur. First, the sample recovered from the crime scene may be contaminated by bacteria, virus, or other nonhuman DNA. It may also be contaminated by detergents, salt, and cleaning fluids. Second, the laboratory equipment, gel, enzymes, and DNA probe used in the test may be contaminated. These errors may result in DNA prints that are fuzzy or blurred. Although the major part of the matching technique is computerized, a technician makes the final determination that the total pattern matches; this means the technician's subjective impression is part of the matching process. Some authors estimate that the error rate caused by all of these factors is between 1% and 4%. Finally, and subject to the most controversy, the probability calculation has been attacked because the current database is too small and based on a nonrandom sample. Each testing laboratory maintains its own database; most are developed from samples obtained from blood banks and hospitals. DNA patterns vary for different racial groups and subgroups. The result is that the databases currently being used may not adequately reflect the variety of racial groups in the U.S. population.

Five types of DNA testing are discussed here to give you an idea of what resources are available (from www.ornl.gov/sci/techresources/Human_ Genome/elsi/forensics.shtml, accessed June 5, 2007). Keep in mind that time, money, and availability of DNA laboratories restrict the number of samples that can be tested.

Restriction Fragment Length Polymorphism (RFLP)

This was one of the original DNA analyses used in forensic investigation. It is not used as much now because it requires a larger DNA sample (as large as a quarter) to conduct the test. Samples degraded by environmental factors, such as dirt or mold, do not work as well for RFLP.

Polymerase Chain Reaction (PCR) Analysis

This test reproduces the cells in the sample until there are enough to conduct a DNA test. It can be done on a sample as small as a few cells. This test is not harmed by environmental factors, but great care must be exercised to avoid contamination by other biological materials when collecting and preserving the sample.

Short Tandem Repeat (STR)

STR technology is used to evaluate specific regions (loci) within nuclear DNA. Variability in STR regions can be used to distinguish one DNA profile from another. The FBI uses a standard set of 13 specific STR regions for CODIS, the database that can be operated at the local, state, and national level for convicted offenders, unsolved crime scene evidence, and missing persons. The odds of two individuals having the same 13-loci DNA profile are approximately 1 in 1 billion.

Mitochondrial DNA Analysis (mtDNA)

This test can be used on samples that cannot be submitted for RFLP, PCR, or STR analysis because it does not rely on nuclear DNA. mtDNA analysis uses DNA extracted from another cellular organelle called mitochondrion and can be used to test hair, bones, and teeth. All mothers have the same mitochondrial DNA as their daughters; therefore, mtDNA analysis can be done on cells of unidentified human remains and any female relative of a missing person.

Y-Chromosome Analysis

The Y chromosome is passed directly from father to son, so the analysis of the genetic markers on the Y chromosome is useful for tracing relationships among males or for analyzing biological evidence involving multiple male contributors.

Identification of Controlled Substances[6]

In cases involving possession, distribution, or manufacture of controlled substances, laboratory analysis plays a major role. Testing for controlled substances is essentially qualitative and quantitative organic chemical analysis. As the number of drug cases has increased the demand on the forensic laboratory, new techniques have been developed to do the job faster and more accurately.

A variety of tests may be employed to identify a substance. These usually start with screening tests, but they may also include separation tests, confirmatory tests, and quantitative analysis.

Samples are frequently tested rather than the whole quantity of suspected drugs. This is almost always the case when there was a large seizure. Laboratories follow different approaches to this problem. Some test a given percentage of the evidence. Others do screening tests on a large number of samples, but if the screening tests indicate that only one substance is present, further testing is only done on a small sample.

Representative sampling techniques are important. This is always true when only a sample is tested, but it is even more important when illegally manufactured drugs are in question because of the lack of knowledge about their source. The evidence seized may not be homogeneous. Therefore, it is important to make sure that the sample comes from different locations within the seized containers. A visual inspection of both the sample and the entire quantity seized is useful to ensure that the mathematical formula used produces a truly representative sample. These techniques need to be applied to solid substances, such as bricks of marijuana, as well as large barrels of pills.

When marked tablets are sent for analysis, the marks, along with the color and shape of the tablets, may provide presumptive evidence of their content. Laboratories vary with regard to the amount of testing that is done on these samples. One screening test may be sufficient if there is a known tablet available for comparison that has the same appearance. The appearance of numerous counterfeit or "look-alike" drugs increases the need to carefully test all samples. Due to the fact that capsules are easily tampered with, the presumption arising from their physical appearance is not as strong as the one for tablets.

If the quantity of drugs submitted for examination is very small (e.g., residue in a pipe), it may be necessary to perform tests in a different order than usual. Those tests that can be done on small quantities of the questioned material and have a high degree of accuracy are done first. Screening tests that destroy the test substance, or tests that have a low probability of conclusively identifying the sample, may not be used at all.

Three main types of screening tests are used: spot tests, microscopic tests, and ultraviolet spectrophotometry. Based on the results of these tests, the chemist will select one or more appropriate tests to identify the substance. Additional tests may be done to confirm the identity of the substance tested.

Infrared spectrophotometry is the most popular because it is the least expensive and easiest to use. Scientists also give gas chromatography–mass spectrometry high ratings because it requires only micrograms of material to do the test. Test instruments are frequently connected to computers that store extensive libraries of data on known compounds for comparison.

Due to the wide variety of tests that are now in use, individual crime labs may not be using the same tests. The fact that one specific test that has a high degree of accuracy was not used may be emphasized by the defense. It does not necessarily indicate that the lab work was shoddy.

Identification of Firearms[7]

Firearms can be identified from their fired bullets and cartridges. The firearms examiner is commonly called a **ballistics expert,** even though technically ballistics refers to the motion of projectiles rather than matching the expelled object to the weapon.

Pistols (revolvers, "semiautomatics," and "automatics"), rifles, assault rifles (i.e., automatic rifles such as the M-16), machine guns, and submachine guns are rifled firearms. Their barrels have spiraling lands and grooves that leave patterns of parallel scratches, called striations or striae, on the projectile. Shotguns, on the other hand, have smooth-bore barrels and do not leave striations.

The history of modern firearms examination in the United States began with Dr. Albert Llewellyn Hall in 1900. His technique of pushing, rather than firing, bullets through the weapon's barrel was in use until after World War I. A 1902 appellate case affirmed the use of firearms identification evidence in court, but the practice did not become commonly accepted until the 1930s. The admission of testimony regarding marks on fired cartridges began in 1906 and gained acceptance much faster than other methods of firearms identification.

Microscopic examinations of recovered bullets can be useful even if no weapon has been recovered. They can show the caliber of the gun and many facts about the barrel of the weapon involved. If more than one bullet was recovered, it may also be possible to determine whether more than one gun was used.

Prior to testing a weapon for identification purposes, it should be checked for latent prints and trace evidence, such as blood, bits of skin or fat that may have been deposited on it if the gun was fired at close range. Recovered bullets should also be checked for these substances. Fibers from the pocket in which it was carried may also be present.

Preliminary examination of the weapon should cover make or manufacturer, type of weapon, caliber, serial number, model, number of shots, and barrel length. Prior to test firing, the functioning of the weapon's action and the operation of any safeties should be checked. One purpose of this is to determine if it is safe to test-fire the weapon; another is to refute any defense claim that the gun went off accidentally. Determination of the trigger's pull is also important for this purpose.

If the examiner determines that the bullet recovered from the crime scene has the same characteristics as the suspect's weapon, and the gun passed the safety check, the gun will be test-fired into a bullet trap. Cotton waste or cotton waste soaked in oil is frequently used in a bullet trap; water traps are also used. The ammunition used to test-fire the gun should match that used in the crime as closely as possible. A comparison microscope and special bullet holders allow the examiner to simultaneously view a bullet recovered at the crime scene and one test-fired into the bullet trap.

The examination typically begins with careful checking for land impressions near the base of the bullets. It should then systematically proceed to check the land impressions on one bullet with those on the comparison sample until the entire surface of both bullets has been covered. The bullets are rotated synchronously to determine if there are matching striation patterns. Other distinctive markings, such as skid and shaving marks caused inside the barrel, may also be noted.

Rust in the barrel causes problems because rust particles can cause striations. Each firing may disturb the rust and result in different striations. Alterations in the barrel, including shortening, flattening, or bending, also cause variations in the striation pattern. Studies have shown that some guns, particularly .22 caliber rifles, may not produce identical striations, even when there has been no damage to the gun. Particularly in automatics and very inexpensive handguns (e.g., "Saturday night specials"), the firing of large numbers of bullets may cause wear that makes comparisons difficult.

Due to the fact that striations are caused by imperfections in the metal used to manufacture a gun, the marks left on a bullet are unique. Unfortunately, there is no exact standard for the number of striations that must match before it can be concluded that the bullets were fired from the same gun. If there is a match between the recovered bullet and the test-fired one, it can conclusively be stated that they came from the same gun.

The factors mentioned in the preceding paragraph indicate that two bullets can be fired by the same gun and not have exactly the same markings. The fact they do not match is not conclusive evidence that the bullets were fired from different guns. One study showed that only approximately 20% of the striations on bullets fired from the same weapon matched. This means that many comparisons will result in inconclusive evidence.

If a shotgun cartridge or shells from an automatic were recovered, the examination should also begin with a check for latent prints and trace evidence. The initial examination with a low-powered microscope should note the size, shape, and type of cartridge. Size and position of the firing pin impression and location of extractor and ejector marks are also important. These can be used to determine the make and model of weapons that could have fired the cartridge. This is complicated by adapters that can be used to fire certain types of cartridges from guns designed for different ammunition. Alterations that may have been made to the weapon also interfere with accurate comparisons.

If these preliminary examinations indicate the cartridge could have been fired from the weapon in question, microscopic comparisons will be made of the recovered cartridge and one that was test-fired. The test-fired cartridge should be as similar as possible to the one in question. Special holders are used so that the cartridges can be mounted on a comparison microscope. Firing pin impressions, firing pin drag marks, and breechblock marks are usually compared first.

A match of these markings indicates that the same weapon was involved. Extractor and ejector marks, chambering marks, and magazine marks are compared next. These can indicate that the cartridges were run through the action of the same gun. A variety of problems may arise: (1) Reloaded cartridges may bear markings from more than one gun, (2) low-powered cartridges may not produce enough force to be marked, and (3) the extractor may not grip the cartridge with enough force to mark it.

Other Forensic Specialties and Tests

A variety of forensic tests are listed here. This is not a complete list of every type of forensic evidence used in court.

Forensic Anthropology[8]

Investigators frequently turn to forensic anthropologists for help in identifying human skeletal remains and decomposing bodies. The trained anthropologist works with pathologists and odontologists to estimate age, sex, ancestry, stature, and unique bony features of the deceased. Specialists in facial reconstruction may make three-dimensional sculptures of the face based on a portion of a skull.

Age Progression Photography and Models[9]

Pictures of children may accurately portray what they looked like at the time they were last seen, but after a few years the pictures are nearly useless. Age progression software is used to make a picture of what the child will look like as a teenager. This helps when searching for missing children who have been gone for a long time.

Geographic Profiling[10]

This technique operates on the assumption that serial murderers (or rapists) balance their desire to kill (or rape) far from home and avoid recognition with their desire to remain in familiar territory. Mapping of the locations of serial crimes is facilitated by software developed for this purpose. It is estimated that use of the software helps police narrow their target zone by 95%.

Forensic Footwear Analysis[11]

Making plaster casts of footprints dates back nearly 100 years. Current advancement in this technique focuses on details in the wear pattern of the shoe to estimate the height, weight, and physical impairments of the suspect.

Digital Image Processing[12]

Many new techniques and software are available to help investigators improve the quality of pictures. What were once discarded as blurry pictures can now be enhanced so that an identification can be made.

Forensic Accounting[13]

This specialty is used in fraud and embezzlement cases to establish that financial records have been falsified or altered. Although some accountants are able to do this type of work, a Certified Fraud Examiner or a Fraud Certified Public Accountant has extensive training and experience in this type of work and makes a good witness in court.

Computing/Digital Forensics[14]

When an investigation involves the possibility that evidence has been stored on a computer, it is important to call someone who is specifically trained in this area. Police officers should not boot up the computer and try to find the information on their own because the computer may be set to automatically erase files if a stranger logs on. Unskilled detectives can also delete important files or alter them. The dates the files were used may be important; this data would be changed by merely opening the file.

The specialist in this field has extensive training in recovering data as well as many other ways to search the computer. A Certified Forensics Computer Examiner, or someone with similar credentials, is highly trained in this area. A person who specializes in computing/digital forensics can determine if files have been deleted from a computer or other digital device. Hidden files can also be found. This includes searching for pictures, documents, and e-mail messages.

Other Forensic Specialties

Almost any specialty has a forensic component—for example, forensic economics, forensic engineering, forensic linguistics, forensic photography, forensic psychiatry, and forensic psychology. If an investigator believes assistance is required, a search should be made for a person with appropriate expertise. When the case is prepared for court, it may be necessary to search for an expert who works in the field and is familiar with testifying in court.

Tests That Are Not Commonly Accepted

Scientific tests must be accepted in their field before the courts are willing to allow their use at trial. The amount of evidence needed to show that a test is valid is left to the judge in most state courts and the federal courts. For this reason, newly developed tests are usually not admissible. Since the determination is made on a state-by-state basis, there is usually no nationwide agreement on the use of a test during its developmental stages. There have also been some instances in which courts initially accepted a test but, based on research published at a later time, decided the test was no longer admissible. Spectrographic voice recognition ("voiceprints") and hypnotically refreshed memory fall into this category.

Some tests have been in use for many years but are still rejected by many courts. This section discusses two of them: polygraph examinations and hypnosis.

Polygraph[15]

The principal features of the polygraph are its ability to record changes in respiration, blood pressure, and pulse. Attachments can be added to record galvanic skin reflex (perspiration in hands), muscular movements, and pressures. Use of only one of these features is considered to be inadequate.

The skill of the polygraph examiner is of utmost importance. An internship is required in which the trainee can make frequent observations of an expert conducting polygraph examinations, as well as perform the procedure personally. Ideally, the polygraph examiner should have a minimum of 6 months of training.

The test should be conducted in a quiet, private location. Outside noise should be eliminated where possible. Police investigators should not be allowed to be present during the exam.

A pretest interview is done to explain the procedure to the subject. It is also used to gather information for test questions. Questions asked during the polygraph examination fall into three categories: control questions, relevant questions, and irrelevant questions. Control questions are designed to illicit a dishonest response to something that is not relevant to the case. This shows what the body's response is to lying. Relevant questions relate to the matter under investigation. Irrelevant questions have no bearing on the case but give the examiner the chance to see the subject's response to questioning. During the pretest interview, the subject is usually told what the irrelevant questions will be.

An assessment of truthfulness is made by comparing the responses to control questions with those to relevant questions. Deception is indicated if there is a greater response to the relevant questions than to the control questions. A good examiner should be able to discount the effects of nervousness. This is done in two ways: (1) The pretest interview is designed to relax the subject, and (2) nervousness should be indicated by uniformly irregular polygraph tracings—nerves have a similar effect on control, relevant, and irrelevant questions.

It is estimated that truthfulness/dishonesty are *clearly* indicated in approximately 25% of the cases. In 5% to 10% of the cases, even a highly trained examiner will not be able to make a conclusive analysis. The remaining 65% to 70% of the cases yield subtle indications of truthfulness/dishonesty that trained examiners cannot fully explain to nonexperts.

There are sizable numbers of experts on each side of the argument about polygraph examinations. In 2002, the National Research Council of the National Academy of Sciences published a report finding that polygraph testing has a weak scientific basis and that insufficient attempts have been made to verify the results. The council concluded that polygraph tests should not be used for national security purposes.

The high frequency of inconclusive results makes the courts distrust the polygraph. Judges also fear that jurors will attach too much weight to the results of a polygraph examination. Although states vary in their approaches to the admissibility of polygraph tests, most refuse to admit them. Some allow them in criminal cases if there was a pretest stipulation by both sides that the results may be used in court. When this type of stipulation is made, the polygraph examiner usually must be agreed upon in advance by both sides. If the suspect is in custody at the time of the examination, *Miranda* waivers must be obtained in addition to any other stipulations that are made.

Hypnosis[16]

Hypnosis is commonly described as a trancelike state in which the subject is unconsciously responsive to the suggestions and commands of the hypnotist. It is this state of suggestibility that concerns the courts.

Numerous articles were written in the 1970s and 1980s about the effectiveness of hypnosis in criminal investigations. Some authors claim that new information can be obtained under hypnosis in 60% to 90% of cases. At least 5,000 police officers have been trained to conduct hypnosis. Hypnosis has been used in criminal cases as far back as 1898, but most courts are still hesitant to admit the testimony.

The U.S. Supreme Court, in *Rock v. Arkansas* (1987)[17], reversed a manslaughter conviction in which the state had a rule that hypnotically refreshed testimony is always inadmissible because it is unreliable. The only statements that were admissible were those Rock made to her doctor prior to hypnotic treatment. In this case, the defense appealed on the grounds that the defendant had not been allowed to testify because she had been hypnotized at her attorney's suggestion. The Supreme Court balked at an absolute rule that prevented a defendant from exercising Due Process and Sixth Amendment rights without consideration of the facts of the case.

Several state court decisions allowed testimony from hypnotically refreshed memory, but the majority view is that this type of testimony is inadmissible. For example, a pair of cases decided by the New York Court of Appeal (*People v. Hults* [1990] and *People v. Schreiner* [1991])[18] reaffirm the state's rule that posthypnotic statements (including testimony in court) cannot be used by the prosecution to establish the defendant's guilt or by the defense for impeachment. The states that still allow posthypnotic testimony impose safeguards, such as videotaping of the hypnotic session and detailed records of the information that was given to the hypnotist before the session(s) began. A psychiatrist or psychologist trained and experienced in hypnosis is usually mandated.

Psychiatrists sometimes make a different use of hypnosis when trying to evaluate competency to stand trial and "not guilty by reason of insanity" cases. Due to the fact that this technique is recognized in the field of psychiatry, it is admissible on the mental issues if the proper foundation has been laid. The foundation must include the following: (1) a showing that hypnosis is reliable for this purpose, and (2) a showing that the witness is qualified as an expert on the psychiatric use of hypnosis. This testimony is not used to establish guilt or innocence, but has limited admissibility on the issue of the mental state of the defendant.

Experiments

The ideal **experiment** screens out all extraneous variables so that the experimenter can measure the impact of one factor. Although there are numerous situations that lend themselves to experiments in criminal trials, few experiments are introduced in court. This is largely due to attorneys' lack of knowledge in this area. Some experiments are quite simple, such as going to the crime scene under lighting conditions that are similar to those that existed at the time of the crime to determine if the stop sign is visible, or having someone walk from one location to another to determine if is possible to cover the distance in the time stated by the defendant. Others are very complex and require expensive equipment such as electron microscopes and X-ray analyzers.

Some basic concepts apply to experiments. One is that the conditions must be similar to those that existed when the event in question occurred. Although this similarity is meant to control outside variables, courts are frequently very flexible when it comes to admitting experiments that were not conducted under totally similar conditions. Second, the experiments must be based on sound scientific principles. This is the same basic criteria that applies to all uses of expert witnesses and scientific evidence. Both the testing procedure and the equipment used must conform to standards generally accepted in the scientific community. Third, the judge may refuse to admit experimental evidence if it will be confusing to the jury or take up an undue amount of time at trial. The weight to be given to an experiment is left to the jury.

The Federal Rules of Evidence and some states do not distinguish between experiments and other types of evidence. The normal rules of relevance are used to judge admissibility.

The normal procedure for introducing experiments is the following: (1) have either the person conducting the experiment or someone who witnessed it take the stand, (2) lay the foundation, and (3) ask questions so that the witness can present the results of the experiment. The foundation should include that (1) the witness is familiar with the facts of the case,

(2) the witness knows how to use the equipment used in the experiment, (3) the witness compares the actual event with the results of the experiment, and (4) the witness believes the experiment fairly simulates the events in question.

In a number of cases, a bowl of ice cream has been found at the crime scene. The assumption is that the person who was eating the ice cream was interrupted and left without finishing it. Determining the time between this interruption and the arrival of someone who discovered the bowl of ice cream will help establish the time of the crime. Absent a witness who knows the length of time involved, an experiment may be done to determine the length of time the ice cream sat on the table. Obviously, the room temperature should be the same as it was when the incident occurred. A number of other factors must also be controlled: temperature of the ice cream when it was placed in the bowl, amount of ice cream, size of bowl, etc. It is also important to use the same brand and flavor of ice cream if possible. This is important because the ingredients used to make ice cream are not always the same, and in commercially prepared ice cream, stabilizers are added to slow the melting process. If there are facts that indicate how long the ice cream had been out of the freezer before the crime occurred, the results of the experiment will give a better estimate of when the crime occurred. Otherwise, the results will provide an interval during which the crime occurred.

Establishing how long it takes ice cream to melt sounds like a simple task, but it is important to treat it as a carefully controlled experiment if the results are to be used in court. It is also important because the opposing side will be allowed to point out procedural errors in an effort to convince the jury that they should disregard the results of the experiment.

Experiments may be conducted to determine if it is possible to have committed a crime in a particular manner. For example, the prosecution may believe that the defendant packed the body of the murder victim in ice to prevent *rigor mortis* from setting in until after the defendant was able to establish an alibi.[19] A pathologist would be consulted to determine all the necessary conditions that would need to be set up for the experiment. An object similar in size, weight, and retention of body heat to the victim's body would be used with the body temperature of a living person. It would then be packed in ice and placed in a room in which the temperature was kept the same as the conditions where the body was believed to have been placed by the defendant.

At trial, the effect of temperature changes on *rigor mortis* would be established by an expert witness. A comparison would be made between what would be expected under the temperature present at the time of the crime and what happened when the body was packed in ice under those same weather conditions.

Test crashing of automobiles also is included within the category of experiments. Cars are set to collide under the same road conditions as were alleged in the case (e.g., weather, road surface, incline, angle, banking of the curve, and speed of the vehicle). Based on the results of the test crash, it may be demonstrated that one version of the facts is impossible. Due to the expense of this type of experiment, it is rarely done. Models may be used instead. Computer simulations are becoming more popular.

Summary

All real evidence must be marked before it can be introduced into evidence. The attorney must also lay a foundation to show that it is admissible. Evidence recovered at a crime scene must be carefully handled so that it is not damaged. Detailed records must be kept to show where it was found and what has been done with it since it was taken into police custody.

The foundation for scientific evidence includes a showing that the test used is valid, the person doing it is well trained, and the equipment used is accurate. The exact procedures used during the test are also subject to challenge.

There are many scientific tests that are currently recognized by the courts. Among the most common are fingerprint comparisons, blood alcohol and DNA tests, and tests to identify drugs.

Latent print identification is based on the fact that each person has unique fingerprints. The prints recovered at the crime scene are compared with a set of fingerprints on file. If a match is found, it conclusively establishes that the person left the prints at the scene. There may, of course, be innocent explanations of how the prints got there.

When alcohol enters the human body, it is rapidly distributed throughout the entire system in the same proportion. Blood tests can be used to establish the level of intoxication because the sample taken reflects the alcohol content of all parts of the body.

Laboratory tests can be done to determine if a stain was made by human blood. If it was, the blood type may also be determined. Although traditional tests have been able to identify a person's blood type, this has not been very useful in many cases because a large proportion of the population has the same blood type. The fact that the blood types did not match can establish that the blood was from a different person. DNA testing provides a method that can conclusively identify one person as the source of blood, semen, or other body fluids.

Many tests have been developed to identify drugs. Caution should be taken to test an adequate sample of the seized drugs. This is especially true when illegally manufactured drugs are involved because clandestine drug labs do not have the same quality controls that the legitimate drug industry uses.

In many cases, bullets and cartridges can be tested to determine if they were fired from a particular gun. Microscopic examinations are done to compare unique patterns that are left when the bullet exits the barrel or the cartridge is processed through the firing chamber. An exact match indicates that the gun that was test-fired is the same one used in the crime. Unfortunately, the fact that an exact match was not observed cannot exclude a gun.

The polygraph has not been accepted by most courts. The conflicting views of experts on the reliability of the polygraph have caused the courts to doubt its reliability. The situation is similar for hypnosis. Although once claimed to enhance memory, it is now largely discredited.

Experiments must be conducted under similar conditions to those that existed when the event in question occurred.

Review Questions

1. Explain what should be done to protect evidence at a crime scene, and list three things that should be done to document the scene before evidence is removed.
2. Describe how various items of crime scene evidence should be identified and packaged for storage.
3. Define *chain of custody,* and explain how it is maintained for trial.
4. What scientific tests are most commonly introduced in criminal trials?
5. What foundation must be laid for the admission of a piece of evidence found at the crime scene and for the admission of the results of a scientific test?
6. Explain the scientific basis for fingerprint identification.
7. Explain the reason why blood tests can accurately show alcohol levels in the body.
8. Describe how blood typing can be used in a criminal case.
9. Explain what can be determined by conducting scientific tests on bullets and cartridges.
10. Explain how DNA testing can be used to identify the defendant as the person who committed the crime.
11. Explain why the courts rarely admit polygraph test results and seldom permit witnesses to testify after having been hypnotized.
12. Define *experiment* and give two examples of experiments that could be used in criminal trials.

Writing Assignment

Enter "DNA testing" in Google or another search engine. Find a DNA lab in your area that publishes its price list.

Write a 250-word (one-page) report on the types of DNA testing that the lab does and what it charges for each type of test.

Notes

1. Joseph L. Peterson, "Use of Forensic Evidence by the Police and Courts," *Research in Brief* (Washington, DC: National Institute of Justice, October 1987).
2. Richard Saferstein, "Fingerprints," *Criminalistics: An Introduction to Forensic Science*, 9th ed. (Englewood Cliffs, NJ: Prentice-Hall, (2006), Chapter 14; H. C. Lee and R. E. Gaensslen (Eds.), *Advances in Fingerprint Technology*, 2nd ed. (Boca Raton, FL: CRC Press, 2001); "Fingerprint," downloaded June 9, 2007 from http://en.wikipedia.org/wiki/Fingerprint.
3. Richard Saferstein, "Blood Alcohol," *Forensic Science Handbook*, vol. I, 2nd ed. (Englewood Cliffs, NJ: Prentice-Hall, 2002), Chapter 12.
4. Richard Saferstein, "Blood Typing," *Criminalistics: An Introduction to Forensic Science*, 9th ed. (Englewood Cliffs, NJ: Prentice-Hall, 2006), Chapter 12; G. Nordenson, *Gale Encyclopedia of Medicine: Blood Typing and Crossmatching* [Digital] (Farmington Hills, MI: Thomas Gale, 2004).
5. S. M. Gerber and R. Saferstein (Eds.), "DNA," *More Chemistry and Crime: From Marsh Arsenic Test to DNA Profile* (Washington, DC: American Chemical Society, 2003); R. Saferstein, *Forensic Science Handbook*, vol. I, 2nd ed. (Englewood Cliffs, NJ: Prentice-Hall, 2001), Chapter 3; Human Genome Project. DNA Forensics. Downloaded June 5, 2007, from http://www.ornl. gov/sci/techresources/Human_Genome/elsi/forensics.shtml; U.S. Department of Justice, "Using DNA to Solve Crimes," DNA Policy Book. Downloaded June 5, 2007, from http://www.usdoj. gov/ag/dnapolicybook_solve_crimes.htm; U.S. Department of Justice, "Using DNA to Protect the Innocent," DNA Policy Book. Downloaded June 5, 2007, from http://www.usdoj.gov/ag/ dnapolicybook_protect_innocent.htm; U.S. Department of Justice, "Using DNA to Identify Missing Persons," DNA Policy Book. Downloaded June 5, 2007, from http://www.usdoj.gov/ag/ dnapolicybook_miss_persons.htm; K. Ramsland, "All about DNA Revolution." Downloaded June 6, 2007, from http://www.crimelibrary.com/criminal_mind/forensics/dna/1.html; *The New York Times*, "DNA Reversals Hit 200" (May 26, 2007).
6. Richard Saferstein, "Identifying Controlled Substances," *Forensic Science Handbook*, vol. II, 2nd ed. (Englewood Cliffs, NJ: Prentice-Hall, 2004), Chapter 3.
7. F. J. Jury, J. Weller, and J. S. Hatcher, "Identifying Firearms," *Firearms Investigation Identification and Evidence* (Philadelphia: Ray Riling Arms Books, 2006); R. Quertermous and S. Quertermous, *Modern Guns: Identification & Values*, 14th ed. (Paducah, KY: Collector Books, 2002); National Institute of Justice, *The Future of Forensic DNA Testing* (Washington, DC: U.S. Department of Justice, 2000); G. W. Steadman, *Survey of DNA Crime Laboratories* (Washington, DC: U.S. Bureau of Justice Statistics, 1998).
8. M. Nafte, "Forensic Anthropologists," *Flesh and Bone: An Introduction to Forensic Anthropology*, 2nd ed. (Durham, NC: Carolina Academic Press, 2007); S. N. Byers, *Introduction to Forensic Anthropology: A Textbook*, 2nd ed. (Boston: Allyn & Bacon, 2004); B. Greenbert and J. C. Kunich, *Entomology and the Law: Flies as Forensic Indicators* (Cambridge, UK: Cambridge University Press, 2002); K. Ramsland, "The Body Farm: Tennessee Anthropology Research Facility," *Time of Death*. Downloaded June 6, 2007, from http://www.crimelibrary.com/ criminal_mind/forensics/time/2.html; R. Locke, "The Body Farm," *Discovering Archaeology* (March/April 2000).
9. R. H. Walton (ed.), "Age Progression," *Cold Case Homicides: Practical Investigative Techniques* (Boca Raton, FL: CRC Press, 2006); S. Irsay, "Missing Faces: Age-Progression and Facial Recognition Techniques," *Hidden Traces*. Downloaded on June 6, 2007, from http://www.courttv. com/news/hiddentraces/boyinthebox/recon_side1.html.
10. F. Wang (ed.), "Geographic Profile," *Geographic Information Systems and Crime Analysis* (Hershey, PA: IGI Global, 2005); D. K. Rossmo, *Geographic Profiling* (Boca Raton, FL: CRC Press, 1999); C. Lewis, "In the Search for a Killer, a High-Tech Tool," *Trail of a Suburban Sniper*. Downloaded June 6, 2007, from http://www.courttv.com/news/sniper/100802_ctv.html; "Profiling and Geography." Downloaded June 8, 2007, from http://www.crimelibrary.com/criminal_mind/

profiling/geographic/2.html; "The Global Positioning System," Forensic Files. Downloaded June 5, 2007, from http://www.courttv.com/onair/shows/forensicfiles/techniques/gps.html.

11. W. J. Bodziak, "Forensic Footwear Analysis," *Footwear Impression Evidence* (Boca Raton, FL: CRC Press, 1995); "Casting of Shoeprints." Downloaded June 5, 2007, from http://www.courttv.com/onair/shows/forensicfiles/techniques/casting.html; "Characteristics of Shoeprints." Downloaded June 9, 2007, from http://www.courttv.com/onair/shows/forensicfiles/techniques/print.html; "Forensic Footwear Analysis." Downloaded June 9, 2007, from http://en.wikipedia.org/wiki/Forensic_footwear_evidence.

12. P. Jones, "Digital Imaging," *Practical Forensic Digital Imaging: Applications and Techniques (Practical Aspects of Criminal & Forensic Investigation)* (Boca Raton, FL: CRC Press, 2008); E. Casey, *Digital Evidence and Computer Crime* (San Diego: Academic Press, 2000); H. L. Blitzer and J. Jacobia, *Forensic Digital Imaging and Photography (with CD-ROM)* (San Diego: Academic Press, 2001; "Digital Image Processing." Downloaded June 9, 2007, from http://www.courttv.com/onair/shows/forensicfiles/techniques/digital_image.html; "A Short Introduction to Digital Processing." Downloaded June 9, 2007, from http://web.uct.ac.za/depts/physics/laser/hanbury/intro_ip.html.

13. T. Singleton, A. J. Singleton, G. J. Bologna, and R. J. Linquist, "Forensic Accounting," *Fraud Auditing and Forensic Accounting*, 3rd ed. (New York: Wiley, 2006); T. W. Golden, S. L. Skalak, and M. M. Clayton, *A Guide to Forensic Accounting Investigation* (New York: Wiley, 2005); "Forensic Accounting." Downloaded June 9, 2007, from http://en.wikipedia.org/wiki/Forensic_accounting. "Forensic Accounting: Litigation Support." Downloaded on June 9, 2007, from http://www.forensicaccounting.com.

14. K. J. Jones, R. Bejtlich, and C. W. Rose, "Computing/Digital Evidence," *Real Digital Forensics: Computer Security and Incident Response* (Boston: Addison-Wesley, 2005); B. Carrier, *File System Forensic Analysis* (Boston: Addison-Wesley, 2005); "Gathering Electronic Evidence." Downloaded June 9, 2007, from http://www.nz-lawsoc.org.nz/lawtalk/564wolfe.htm; "Computer Forensics." Downloaded June 9, 2007, from http://en.wikipedia.org/wiki/Computer_forensics; "Information Forensics." Downloaded June 9, 2007, from http://en.wikipedia.org/wiki/Information_forensics; P. Gutmann, "Secure Deletion of Data from Magnetic and Solid-State Memory," *Journal of Digital Evidence* 2(2) (2003); B. Carrier and E. H. Spafford, "Getting Physical with the Digital Investigation Process," *Journal of Digital Evidence* 2(2) (2003); Xiaoyun Wang and Hongbo Yu, "How to Break MD5 and Other Hash Functions," paper presented at EUROCRYPT 2005 (2005); "Computer Forensic Services." Downloaded June 9, 2007, from http://www.protiviti.com/portal/site/pro-us/menuitem.a4be00474b124842bdd22d10f5ffbfa0; "Providing Expert Computer Forensics Analysis, Electronic Discovery and Computer Expert Testimony." Downloaded June 9, 2007, from http://www.evestigate.com; "Digital Discovery in the Criminal Context." Downloaded June 9, 2007, from http://cyber.law.harvard.edu/digitaldiscovery/digdisc_library_3.html.

15. P. A. Granhag and L. A. Stromwall (eds.), "Polygraph," *The Detection of Deception in Forensic Contexts* (Cambridge, UK: Cambridge University Press, 2005); Committee to Review the Scientific Evidence on the Polygraph, *The Polygraph and Lie Detection* (Washington, DC: National Research Council, 2002); M. H. Moore, C. V. Petrie, and A. A. Braga (Eds.), *The Polygraph and Lie Detection* (Washington, DC: National Academy Press, 2003; K. Alder, *The Lie Detectors: The History of an American Obsession* (New York: Free Press, 2007).

16. "Forensic Hypnosis: What Is It?" *Subconsciously Speaking* 19(5): 11 (Royal Oak, MI: Infinity Institute International, September 1, 2004); M. L. Eisen, J. A. Quas, and G. S. Goodman (Eds.), *Memory and Suggestibility in the Forensic Interview*, LEA's Personality and Clinical Psychology Series (Mahwah, NJ: Erlbaum, 2001); A. W. Newman and J. W. Thompson Jr., "The Rise and Fall of Forensic Hypnosis in Criminal Investigation," *Journal of the American Academy of Psychiatry and the Law* 29(1): 74–85 (2001); H. V. Hall and J. Poirier, *Detecting Malingering and Deception: Forensic Distortion Analysis*, 2nd ed. (Boca Raton, FL: CRC Press, 2000).

17. *Rock v. Arkansas* 479 U.S.1079, 94 L.Ed. 2d 136,107 S.Ct, 1276 (1987).

18. *People v. Hults* 76 N.Y. 2d 190, 556 N.E. 2d 1077, 557 N.Y.S. 2d 270 (1990); *People v. Schreiner* 77 N.Y. 2d 733, 573 N.E. 2d 552, 570 N.Y.S. 2d 464 (1991).

19. D. Lucy, "Experiments," *Introduction to Statistics for Forensic Scientists* (New York: Wiley, 2006); A. Field and G. J. Hole, *How to Design and Report Experiments* (Thousand Oaks, CA: Sage, 2003).

CHAPTER 7

Documentary Evidence, Models, Maps, and Diagrams

Feature Case: Enron

Once one of the most respected natural gas, electricity, and communications companies in the country, its name became synonymous with scandal. It also tainted President Bush and other political candidates whom it had supported with large donations. Enron's stock, which had been considered "blue chip," fell from a high of more than $90.00 to 30 cents.

For years there were persistent rumors of bribery and political pressure by Enron in order to secure contracts in Central America, South America, Africa, India, and the Philippines. There were a series of scandals throughout the 1990s involving Enron's irregular accounting procedures that bordered on fraud. Enron created offshore "off-the-books" companies that it used to avoid taxes and make its main business appear very profitable. Company losses were transferred to these companies while profits were shown on the Enron balance sheets. Each quarter management had to find additional ways to hide losses and make it appear that the company was more profitable than before. As these "paper profits" grew, bookkeeping became more "creative," and company stock hit new highs. Arthur Anderson, one of the country's largest and most respected accounting firms, certified balance sheets without mention of these shenanigans.

Executives, who knew of the fraudulent bookkeeping and were afraid that Enron's stock would crash, began using insider information to trade millions of dollars worth of Enron stock at huge profits. Kenneth Lay, Enron CEO, sold $90 million worth of stock he owned. At the same time, investors were told that their stock would continue to climb, possibly to $140 per share. As stock prices started to fall, investors were told the shares would rebound. Lay remained calm in public and thereby convinced investors that all was well. Investors trusted him and bought more stock even though their shares had already lost approximately 75% of their value.

Enron filed for bankruptcy on December 2, 2001. It was the largest bankruptcy ever filed in the United States. More than 4,000 employees lost their jobs, their pensions, 401k's, and college funds that they had established for their children. On January 9, 2002, the U.S. Department of Justice announced it would pursue a criminal investigation of Enron. Voluminous amounts of accounting records and computer files had to be retrieved, studied, summarized, and indexed.

Lay and numerous high-ranking executives of Enron were indicted in federal court for various forms of fraudulent bookkeeping, stock fraud, and insider trading. Many accepted plea bargains. Lay's case went to trial. The jury convicted him on all six counts. He died of a heart attack before his sentencing hearing.

Learning Objectives

After studying this chapter, you will be able to

- Describe how documents are authenticated in court.
- Identify what a forensics documents examiner can determine from a document.
- Define the Best Evidence Rule.
- Recognize the foundation necessary for admitting photographs into evidence.

Key Terms

- Ancient documents
- Authentication
- Documentary evidence
- Forensics document examiner
- Parol evidence
- Posed picture (photograph)
- Primary evidence
- Secondary evidence
- Self-authenticating

Myths about Documentary Evidence, Models, Maps, and Diagrams	Facts about Documentary Evidence, Models, Maps, and Diagrams
The category of documentary evidence only covers documents that the parties intended to have legal consequences.	All types of documents are covered by this category regardless of the intent of the parties making the document.
Only notarized documents are admissible in court.	It is easier to authenticate a notarized document, but the fact that the document is not notarized will not prevent it from being admitted at trial.
The term "document" only covers things written on paper.	The term "document" covers things written on paper as well as photographs, microfiches, audio recordings, videos, and things on CDs and DVDs.
Photographs, models, maps, and diagrams are admissible at trial only if the person who made them testifies.	Photographs, models, maps, and diagrams can be admitted at trial as long as someone testifies who is able to state that the item to be introduced is an accurate presentation of the real thing.

Definitions Used to Describe Documents

In the Federal Rules of Evidence, the definition of "writing" is considerably different than what is used in everyday conversation. Make sure you keep it in mind while you study this chapter.

Definitions of Writings and Photographs

Federal Rules of Evidence, Rule 1001(1) and (2)

For purposes of this article, the following definitions are applicable:
1. **Writings and recordings**. "Writings" and "recordings" consist of letters, words, or numbers, or their equivalent, set down by handwriting, typewriting, printing, photostating, photographing, magnetic impulse, mechanical or electronic recording, or other forms of data compilation.
2. **Photographs**. "Photographs" include still photographs, X-ray films, videotapes, and motion pictures.

Authentication

In addition to being relevant, all types of documents must be authenticated to be admissible as evidence. When we are discussing **documentary evidence,** the term **authentication** means that the party who wants the document to be admitted at trial must establish that the document is what it claims to be.

Authentication must not be confused with the document being accurate. For example, suppose I take a piece of paper, write "4 + 2 = 9," and sign it. It is obvious that my addition is not correct (not accurate). However, if that piece of paper is introduced in court, you could authenticate it. The fact that I did not add the numbers correctly will help you authenticate it.

The reason for the authentication requirement is to prevent a person from fraudulently claiming a document was created. Authentication also protects in situations in which a person claims that a proposed contract is binding when in fact the negotiations on the contract broke down and no contract was ever finalized.

Federal Rules of Evidence Rule 901 provides a long list of ways to authenticate documents. Note that it explicitly states that the list is intended "by way of illustration only" and is "not by way of limitation." This means that the list contains examples of ways to authenticate a document, but the list was not intended to be complete. An attorney in a criminal case can devise additional ways to show that a document is authentic. Even though the new method the attorney proposes is not included in Rule 901, the judge has the power to rule that the new method of authentication can be used in trial if there is a valid basis for the new rule.

Requirement of Authentication for Identification

Federal Rules of Evidence, Rule 901

(a) General provision

The requirement of authentication or identification as a condition precedent to admissibility is satisfied by evidence sufficient to support a finding that the matter in question is what its proponent claims.

(b) Illustrations

By way of illustration only, and not by way of limitation, the following are examples of authentication or identification conforming with the requirements of this rule:

(1) **Testimony of witness with knowledge**. Testimony that a matter is what it is claimed to be.

(2) **Nonexpert opinion on handwriting**. Nonexpert opinion as to the genuineness of handwriting, based on familiarity not acquired for purposes of the litigation.

(3) **Comparison by trier or expert witness**. Comparison by the trier of fact or by expert witnesses with specimens which have been authenticated.

(4) **Distinctive characteristics and the like**. Appearance, contents, substance, internal patterns, or other distinctive characteristics, taken in conjunction with circumstances.

(5) **Voice identification**. Identification of a voice, whether heard firsthand or through mechanical or electronic transmission or recording, by opinion based on hearing the voice at any time under circumstances connecting it with the alleged speaker.

(6) **Telephone conversations**. Telephone conversations, by evidence that a call was made to the number assigned at the time by the telephone company to a particular person or business, if

    (A) in the case of a person, circumstances, including self-identification, show the person answering to be the one called, or

    (B) in the case of a business, the call was made to a place of business and the conversation related to business reasonably transacted over the telephone.

(7) **Public records or reports**. Evidence that a writing authorized by law to be recorded or filed and in fact recorded or filed in a public office, or a purported public record, report, statement, or data compilation, in any form, is from the public office where items of this nature are kept.

(8) **Ancient documents or data compilation**. Evidence that a document or data compilation, in any form,

    (A) is in such condition as to create no suspicion concerning its authenticity,

    (B) was in a place where it, if authentic, would likely be, and

    (C) has been in existence 20 years or more at the time it is offered.

(9) **Process or system**. Evidence describing a process or system used to produce a result and showing that the process or system produces an accurate result.

(10) **Methods provided by statute or rule**. Any method of authentication or identification provided by Act of Congress or by other rules prescribed by the Supreme Court pursuant to statutory authority.

Self-Authenticating Documents

Self-authenticating documents are those that the law automatically assumes were made for their apparent purpose. Usually a seal or some other indication of authenticity is on, or attached to, the document. Even with self-authenticating documents, the opposing side can show that they are fraudulent.

Rule 902 of the Federal Rules of Evidence lists 12 types of self-authenticating documents:

1. Domestic public documents under seal
2. Domestic public documents not under seal
3. Foreign public documents
4. Certified copies of public records
5. Official publications
6. Newspapers and periodicals
7. Trade inscriptions and the like
8. Acknowledged documents
9. Commercial paper and related documents
10. Presumptions under Acts of Congress
11. Certified domestic records of regularly conducted activity
12. Certified foreign records of regularly conducted activity

The most commonly used of these items are discussed here.

Sealed Government Documents

As used here, government documents include all public documents that are made by the federal, state, or local government. These government documents are self-authenticating if they bear an official seal and are signed by someone who states the document is genuine. Government documents are also self-authenticating if they have a signed and sealed statement attached that states that the original signature is genuine. Government documents from foreign countries are self-authenticating if they are either sealed or accompanied by a certificate of genuineness that is signed by an appropriate person and sealed.

Certified copies of public records are also self-authenticating. A certified copy is usually signed by someone working in the clerk's office. A paragraph is usually added to the document that states that it is a true copy of an official document. It is then signed and, in many states, sealed. Births, deaths, marriages, and divorces are usually established by certified copies. Prior convictions are also introduced into evidence by producing a certified copy of the original court record of the conviction.

Examples of Sealed Government Documents

- Judge's order convicting the defendant of a crime

  The court order must bear a seal of the court and a signed statement that the document is a true copy of the original.

- Death certificate

  Death certificates are usually signed by an attending physician or coroner and filed with a designated agency. When an "official" copy is requested, a clerk pulls the original, photocopies it, and attaches a certification to the photocopy stating that the copy is a true copy of the original death certificate.

- Birth certificate

  Doctor that delivers the baby is normally required to file a birth certificate with a designated agency. When an "official" copy is requested, a clerk pulls the original, photocopies it, and attaches a certification to the photocopy stating that the copy is a true copy of the original birth certificate.

Notarized Documents

Notarized documents may be self-authenticating. The statement added by the notary public usually states what the notary is declaring to be authentic. In many cases, the notary asks to see identification, such as a driver's license, and then notarizes the signature as being genuine. Sometimes a notary will state that the document is intended to be a deed or some other document. If so, the document is self-authenticating for that purpose.

Examples of Notarized Documents

• A deed signed by a person who is selling a parcel of land

The person who is selling the property signs the deed in the presence of the notary public. The notary verifies the identification of the person who signed the deed, and either inserts a statement at the bottom of the deed stating that the identity of the person was verified or signs a statement on a separate piece of paper and staples that form to the deed.

• A promissory note

A promissory note is a legal document in which one person acknowledges receiving money from another and promises to pay the money back. The note is signed in the presence of the notary. The notary verifies the identification of the person who signed the note, and either inserts a statement at the bottom of the promissory note stating that the identity of the person was verified or signs a statement on a separate piece of paper and staples that form to the promissory note.

Acknowledged Documents

The exact form of an acknowledgment is governed by state law (or federal law if made in a federal enclave). Wills are usually acknowledged. The person making the will must show the will to the witness and state that this document is intended to be his or her will. The witness then signs or acknowledges the will. The witness does not have to read the will or know what is in it. He or she needs to know only that the document was intended to be the maker's will.

Example of an Acknowledged Document

A will that is prepared by an attorney normally has a place on the last page where the witnesses sign the will. It also has a place for an acknowledgment.

To acknowledge a will, the person whose will it is must show the document to witnesses and say, "This is my will," or an equivalent statement. If a lawyer prepared the will, there usually will be a short paragraph explaining that the person making the will declared that this document was his or her will. The main reasons for having an acknowledgment in a will is to have witnesses who can testify that the person knew that the document was his or her will (was mentally competent) and that there was no undue influence used in order to get the person to sign the will.

Official Publications

Official government publications are self-authenticating. These documents include the officially published codes and case reporter. In many states, there is more than one publisher selling copies of the state's codes.

Law firms may purchase the one that has the best price. If it becomes necessary to take a volume of the code to court to prove the content of a code section, it is important to either take the official publication to court or to double check the unofficial one to make sure it matches the official one.

When it is necessary to establish a penal code section in court, the bound volume may be handed to the judge. Due to the fact that the judge can take judicial notice of all codes of the state where the court is located, it is rare for this to be done except when a law from another state is questioned. Although the judge may be shown the bound volume when a case is cited for precedent, it is more common for the attorneys to quote from the case and give the citation for the case in their briefs.

Examples of Official Publications

- A book, published by the official state publisher, titled *California Penal Code*.

  This book contains the wording of the penal code sections taken directly from the legislation that was signed by the governor.

- A book, published by the official state publisher, titled *Illinois Appellate Reports*.

  This book contains the official reports on the appellate court's decisions on appeals that it heard. In some states, all appellate court decisions are bound in one set of volumes. In others, there is one set of books for the Court of Appeals and another for the state's Supreme Court.

Other Self-Authenticating Documents

A variety of other documents are usually considered to have such a minimal likelihood of forgery that they are considered self-authenticating. Newspapers and periodicals are in this group. Note that the newspaper is self-authenticating but that does not guarantee that the stories are accurately reported. So are brand-name labels fastened to merchandise to show the name of the manufacturer. Commercial documents, such as letters of credit, are self-authenticating if they comply with the requirements stated in the Uniform Commercial Code.

Examples of Other Self-Authenticating Documents

- The page of the *New York Times* for the date in question giving the closing figures for stocks traded on the New York Stock Exchange.
- The page of the *Chicago Tribune* giving the weather for the local area for the day in question.
- A city sign, posted 500 feet before the crash site, reading "Speed Limit 55 Miles per Hour."

Documents Requiring Authentication

There are a variety of ways to authenticate documents. All of them are subject to challenge by the opposing side. The jury makes the final decision on authenticity.

Testimony of a Witness

The most obvious way to authenticate a document is to call one or more witnesses who can testify about the making of the document in question. If the document has been in the possession of the police, witnesses will also need to establish the chain of custody.

Examples of Using Testimony of a Witness to Authenticate a Document
- Friend of victim testified that she was at the victim's house and saw the extortion victim write a check to the person who was threatening him.
- Bank teller states that he observed the victim endorse the check before asking the teller to cash it.
- Caregiver for elderly woman testified that she was familiar with the woman's handwriting. She said that the signature of the feeble woman was now very difficult to read because her hand shook when she wrote, but she was positive that the signature on the check was the signature of the woman she cared for.

Lay Opinion on Handwriting

If any part of the document is handwritten (including the signature), anyone who is familiar with the handwriting of the person in question or who saw it being written or signed may authenticate it.

Examples of Using Lay Opinion to Authenticate a Document
- The witness states that the person who allegedly wrote the letter has been a friend for 10 years, and he recognizes the handwriting on the envelope to be that of his friend.
- A secretary testifies that she worked for the same boss for several years and she frequently signed her boss's name on letters and other unofficial documents. She testifies that the signature on the memo was her handwriting and not her boss's.
- The daughter of the deceased testifies that she was familiar with her father's handwriting. When shown a deed purporting to give a large tract of land to a person who had befriended her father for a very short period of time, she states that the signature was not her father's signature.

"Handwriting Expert"

A written document can also be authenticated by the testimony of a **forensics documents examiner** (formerly called a handwriting expert). To do this, it is usually necessary to provide the expert with a handwriting exemplar (sample) made by the person who allegedly wrote the document. More details on this type of authentication are given later in this chapter.

Examples of Using a "Forensics Document Examiner" to Authenticate a Document

- A forensics documents examiner testifies that she compared the allegedly forged check with a handwriting exemplar provided by the defendant, and it is her professional opinion that the defendant forged the signature on the check.
- A forensics documents examiner testifies that he examined the document and, in his expert opinion, the written portions of the document were made by more than one person.

Distinctive Characteristics

A document can be authenticated by showing that it contained distinctive characteristics, such as words, phrases, or "doodles," used by the person who allegedly made the document. The fact that it contains information known only to the maker, or a very small group of people, can also be used.

Examples of Using Distinctive Characteristics to Authenticate a Document

- Wife testifies that the signature on the check was not made by her husband because her husband's signature, although difficult to read, was very distinctive and not similar to the one on the forged check.
- Secretary testifies that she does not believe the will in question was prepared by the lawyer she works for because when he dictated a will, he always started with the phrase "being of sound mind and having the intent to distribute my earthly possessions to my loved ones" rather than the phrase found on the will in question.

Public Records

The fact that a report was made and filed in accordance with local law can be used to show that the event occurred. Police reports fall in this category. Since it is a crime to make a false police report, it is assumed that the event reported actually happened. Obviously, not all reports made to the police are true.

Examples of Using Public Records to Establish That an Event Occurred
- Birth certificate, signed by doctor who delivered the baby and filed with the county's Recorder of Vital Statistics.
- Death certificate, signed by personal physician of the deceased and filed with the state's Department of Vital Statistics.
- Report of suspected child abuse filed by a school teacher who is a mandated reporter of child abuse.

Ancient Documents

Ancient documents are accepted without authentication if they appear to be genuine and the document has been treated as if it were what it claims to be. A document appears to be genuine if there is no sign of alteration or forgery. The fact that the people who made the document have kept the document in an appropriate place, such as a safe deposit box, also shows they believed it was genuine.

At common law, a document had to be at least 30 years old to qualify as an ancient document. Many states still use this rule. Others have established a shorter time period. The Federal Rules of Evidence require the document to be 20 years old.

Examples of the Use of the Ancient Documents Rule
- Entry in family Bible stating that John and Martha were married on July 15, 1956. John and Martha lived together as husband and wife until John died in 2002.
- Deed dated August 1, 1957, stating that John and Martha purchased a house at 123 N. Main Street. John and Martha lived in this house for 40 years and paid off the mortgage.

Process or System Used

Some documents can only be authenticated by reliance on the process or system used to make them. The most common example of this is the X-ray. The court must rely on the technology involved in the X-ray machine. No independent proof of what the bones look like is usually available. Computer printouts are also subject to reliance on the operating system and software that produced them.

Forensics Documents Examiners[1]

A questioned documents examiner may testify if the authenticity of a document is challenged. When we mention questioned documents, we usually think of forged checks. The term can be used to apply to a broader range of things, including anything on paper, fabric, cardboard, or even written on walls. Although the most common cases involve written or typed materials, pictures, graffiti, and other forms of graphic presentations can also be examined. Fake passports, diplomas, and trademarks may be involved in a criminal case.

The forensics documents examiner evaluates the following in order to determine the document's validity: (1) handwriting (cursive and printing) and signatures; (2) typewriters, photocopiers, laser printers, and fax machines; (3) check writers, rubber stamps, price markers, and label makers; (4) printing processes; (5) ink, pencil, and paper; (6) alterations, additions, erasures, and obliterations; (7) indentations; and (8) sequence of strokes.

The questioned document should be delivered to the examiner in the same condition it was found. It should not be folded, cut, torn, marked, paper-clipped, or stapled. Documents should be kept in stiff, transparent folders or envelopes. They should be stored at room temperature in a dark place and delivered to the forensics lab as soon as possible. The chain of custody must also be maintained.

Handwriting Comparisons

As a child learns to write, his or her handwriting takes on habitual shapes and patterns. These form a unique subconscious pattern. Variations exist in angularity, slope, speed, pressure, letter and word spacing, relative dimensions of letters, connections, pen movements, writing skill, and finger dexterity. Additionally, a person may develop distinctive habits of arranging his or her writing on the page—margins, spacing, crowding, insertions, and alignments. Spelling, punctuation, phrasing, and grammar may also help identify the writer.

In order to determine who wrote a questioned document, the examiner must have an adequate sample of the suspect's handwriting. If possible, a handwriting exemplar should be obtained from the suspect. The normal procedure is to tell the suspect to copy, in his or her own handwriting, a paragraph provided by the examiner that contains all the letters in the alphabet. One sample may have from 500 to 1,000 different individual characteristics. A suspect cannot invoke the Fifth Amendment privilege against self-incrimination as grounds for refusing to provide an exemplar. A law enforcement agency cannot pick up the suspect and take him or her to the station in order to obtain the exemplar unless there is either probable cause to arrest the suspect or he or she consents to go to the station.

All handwriting characteristics found in the sample must be compared with those in the document in question. Although any one characteristic of the perpetrator's handwriting could be found in someone else's writing, the combination of many similar characteristics indicates that the suspect wrote both documents. The examiner will be able to make a more valid comparison if there is a large sample of the suspect's handwriting. If possible, the exemplar should be made with the same type of writing instrument (ballpoint pen, pencil, crayon, etc.) used in the questioned document. Exemplars made for the purpose of comparisons may not be useful if the suspect is intentionally trying to alter his or her normal writing style. Even then, if the exemplar is long enough, the suspect usually reverts to some of his or her normal handwriting characteristics.

As with fingerprint and ballistic comparisons, the number of matching characteristics is important in handwriting comparisons. Unfortunately, there is no specific number of matching characteristics that is used to show a positive comparison. The skill of the examiner and the facts of the individual case are used as the basis for the expert opinion. Obviously, if there are only a few matching characteristics, the opposing side will attempt to convince the jury that the expert's conclusion is wrong.

Typewriting Comparisons

The most common questions involving typewriter comparisons are the following: What make and model of typewriter was used to make the document? and Was the document typed on a specific typewriter? For many years there were only two common type sizes used on typewriters (pica and elite), but there were many minor variations between the typefaces used on different makes and models of typewriters.

Fifty years ago, typewriter companies made their own typebars. Most of these could be distinguished by comparing the document in question with a complete reference collection of typefaces used in typewriters. In a kidnapping, for example, this process could be used to determine if the model of typewriter the defendant owns could have been used to type the ransom note.

Today, many typewriter companies outsource the production of typebars. The result of this change is that different makes of typewriters may have the same typefaces. The use of interchangeable typing elements and daisy wheels has further complicated this process because one typewriter can use more than one typeface. This also makes it possible to destroy the element used to type a document without harming the typewriter. The advent of computer printers resulted in fewer documents being prepared on typewriters and necessitated the development of different comparison techniques.

Matching the document with one specific typewriter is based on the fact that the use of a typewriter, like all mechanical devices, results in wear and damage to moving parts. This results in unique type patterns. There may be variations in vertical and horizontal alignment of the letters (i.e., too high, too low, or too far to one side), perpendicular misalignment (i.e., letter leans to one side), or one or more of the characters may have a defect. An exemplar is made on the typewriter in question and then compared to the questioned document. Ideally, the exemplar should be made with the same typewriter ribbon as the questioned document. If the typewriter has variable touch control, the exemplar should include portions made at each setting. If it is not possible to make an exemplar on the typewriter in question, an examiner may be able to work from other documents known to have been typed on the same machine.

Alterations, Erasures, and Obliterations

Documents may be altered to change their meaning, alter the original intent of the maker, alter important dates, or perpetrate forgery. Erasers, sandpaper, razor blades, and knives are used for this purpose. All of these methods cause disturbances in the upper fibers of the paper that are apparent when the document is examined under a microscope. Although the microscope can show that an erasure has been made, it cannot show what the original document said if the erasure removed the original contents. If chemicals were used to obliterate portions of the original documents, tests can usually be performed to show what was removed. Infrared photography can also be used to reveal the contents of documents that have been charred in a fire.

Comparisons of Paper and Ink

Exact determination of the age of the ink used in a document is very difficult, but it is frequently possible to determine that two different inks were used in a document. If the two inks contain chemicals used in the manufacture of ink at different time periods, it is possible to state that part of the document was written at a later date. Many sophisticated tests have been developed for this purpose. A common problem in ink identification is that there is very little ink available for testing unless the handwritten portion of the document was lengthy.

The Bureau of Alcohol, Tobacco and Firearms (ATF) maintains an ink library. For many years, ink manufacturers have given samples of their ink to the library on a periodic basis. Every time a new ink is used, a sample is also sent to ATF. By comparing an ink sample to information in the library, it is possible to determine the approximate date when the ink was made. This is useful when trying to establish that a document was backdated or a forgery was made long after the year it is claimed to have been made. Since 1968, ATF has also encouraged ink manufacturers to add unique, nontoxic, chemically recognizable substances to their ink each year. When this is done, it is possible to determine the exact year the ink was manufactured.

The ink in typewriter ribbons can be tested in much the same manner as ink from pens. When the ink was manufactured and who manufactured it can be determined. It may also be possible to show that two different ribbons were used to type one document.

Although it may be possible to determine when the ink was manufactured, there is no reliable system to determine when a document was written. To determine how long ink has been on a document, it would be necessary to show temperature, humidity, and exposure to light and handling since the document was made. Testing is almost always impossible because all of these variables are seldom known.

Paper may be matched based on general composition, dates on forms, cutting marks, and thickness. The presence of synthetic brighteners, adhesive components, and synthetic fibers may also give some indication of when the paper was made. The exact formula used for paper varies enough that it is frequently possible to tell that two pieces of paper were not manufactured by the same company. Watermarks are imprinted on paper to identify the manufacturer. Since some manufacturers change watermarks yearly, these marks can be used to date a document. It is important to note that being able to determine the date the paper and ink were manufactured merely sets a starting point; it does not establish the date the document was written.

Introducing the Contents of Documents

The Best Evidence Rule was first established in approximately 1700. Its purpose was to prevent fraud. The origins of the rule date back to a time when the only way to make a duplicate was to copy the document by hand. In the process of copying, mistakes could be made either intentionally or accidentally. It was also believed that the document was a more accurate source of what was written down than the memories of the people who made the document. The Federal Rules of Evidence and many states no longer use the title "Best Evidence Rule," but most utilize the same concepts for establishing the admissibility of the contents of a document.

The law of evidence prefers that the original document be introduced in court when the content of the document is at issue. The same rule applies to all types of documentary evidence. Whether a letter, book, photograph, videotape, audiotape, or X-ray is involved, the original must be produced in court or accounted for. If for some reason it is necessary to show that the document was made, but proof of the contents of the document is not required, the rules in this section do not apply.

The Federal Rules of Evidence summarize the key terms used when introducing all types of documents. Pay careful attention to the definitions of writings, recordings, and photographs because these definitions do not reflect the way the same words are used in daily conversations.

Definitions Used in Court for Contents of Writings, Recordings, and Photographs

Federal Rules of Evidence, Rule 1001

For purposes of this article, the following definitions are applicable:
1. **Writings and recordings**. "Writings" and "recordings" consist of letters, words, or numbers, or their equivalent, set down by handwriting, typewriting, printing, photostating, photographing, magnetic impulse, mechanical or electronic recording, or other form of data compilation.
2. **Photographs**. "Photographs" include still photographs, X-ray films, videotapes, and motion pictures.
3. **Original**. An "original" of a writing or recording is the writing or recording itself or any counterpart intended to have the same effect by a person executing or issuing it. An "original" of a photograph includes the negative or any print therefrom. If data are stored in a computer or similar device, any printout or other output readable by sight, shown to reflect the data accurately, is an "original."
4. **Duplicate**. A "duplicate" is a counterpart produced by the same impression as the original, or from the same matrix, or by means of photography, including enlargements and miniatures, or by mechanical or electronic re-recording, or by chemical reproduction, or by other equivalent techniques that accurately reproduce the original.

Primary Evidence

The original document or a duplicate is considered **primary evidence** when the contents of the document are at issue in the case. The "original" is the document itself and any copies that the person making the document intended to have the same effect as the original. "Duplicate" (sometimes called duplicate original) refers to copies made with the same stroke of the pen (carbon copies), produced from the same negative or offset master, printed from the same set of fixed type, etc. The idea is that the contents are exactly the same. Photocopies made in the normal course of business are now generally accepted as duplicates. Microfilms and microfiches usually receive similar treatment. Note that the photocopies, microfilms, and microfiches need to be made in the normal course of business. Copies made for personal use, outside the business environment, are not admissible.

Definitions of Original and Duplicates

Based on the Federal Rules of Evidence

Rule 1002. Requirement of Original

To prove the content of a writing, recording, or photograph, the original writing, recording, or photograph is required, except as otherwise provided in these rules or by Act of Congress.

Rule 1003. Admissibility of Duplicates

A duplicate is admissible to the same extent as an original unless

1. A genuine question is raised as to the authenticity of the original or
2. In the circumstances it would be unfair to admit the duplicate in lieu of the original.

It would be very impractical to remove the original of a public record from the file and take it to court. For this reason, certified copies of public records, such as birth certificates, are usually admitted as originals.

Definition of Public Records When Establishing the Contents of the Document

Based on Federal Rules of Evidence

Rule 1005. Public Records

The contents of an official record, or of a document authorized to be recorded or filed and actually recorded or filed, including data compilations in any form, if otherwise admissible, may be proved by copy, certified as correct in accordance with Rule 902, or testified to be correct by a witness who has compared it with the original. If a copy which complies with the foregoing cannot be obtained by the exercise of reasonable diligence, then other evidence of the contents may be given.

Business records are often treated in a similar manner. If the custodian of the records prepares an affidavit stating that the photocopy is a true copy of the original, the original does not have to be sent to court. Some states require the custodian of the record to testify in court, whereas others allow the introduction of the documents based on the affidavit alone. This procedure does not apply to cases in which it is alleged that the business records have been altered.

Examples of Primary Evidence Used to Establish the Content of a Document
- The ransom note received by the parents of the kidnapped child.
- A photocopy of the original contract signed by the parties if the copy was made in the normal course of business.
- A carbonless copy of a sales receipt.
- A printout of a text message.
- The small printed receipt that the ATM dispenses after a customer is finished using the machine.

Most courts now admit duplicates in place of originals unless there is some indication that the original has been altered or for some other reason it would be unfair to admit the duplicate. Duplicates must be authenticated before they are accepted into evidence.

Computerized information storage obviously does not fit the original rule. Providing the jury with a floppy disk, flash drive, computer chip, or magnetic tape would be useless. Either by statute or by court decisions, a computer printout is now admissible to show the content of information and software stored in the computer. If the computer-generated document involved is lengthy, a summary of the contents may be used in court rather than introducing all of the material and asking the jury to analyze it. This procedure is used only if the opposing attorney is given ample time to review the original document and verify that the summary is accurate.

If there is any allegation that a printout is unreliable or does not accurately show the information in question, the opposing side is allowed to introduce its own evidence on the issue. Both sides may call expert witnesses to explain how the computer processes data. When authenticity is in doubt, some states require the side introducing the computerized information to carry the burden of proof on the validity of the printout.

Sometimes the defense refuses to produce a document. The prosecution would file a Motion for Discovery asking the judge to order production of the document. If the defense still has not produced the document by the time the case goes to court, the prosecution would be allowed to introduce testimony about the contents of the document. The same process would be used if the defense had unsuccessfully sought to obtain a document that is in the hands of the prosecution.

Secondary Evidence

Secondary evidence includes all other evidence that can be produced to establish the content of the original. This may be documents, such as the rough draft of a contract, or testimony about what was stated in the document. The Federal Rules of Evidence provide a summary of the rules on introducing secondary evidence.

Use of Secondary Evidence to Establish the Contents of Documents

Based on Federal Rules of Evidence

Rule 1004. Admissibility of Secondary Evidence at Trial

> The original is not required, and other evidence of the contents of a writing, recording, or photograph is admissible if

1. **Originals lost or destroyed**. All originals are lost or have been destroyed, unless the proponent lost or destroyed them in bad faith; or
2. **Original not obtainable**. No original can be obtained by any available judicial process or procedure; or
3. **Original in possession of opponent**. At a time when an original was under the control of the party against whom offered, that party was put on notice, by the pleadings or otherwise, that the contents would be a subject of proof at the hearing, and that party does not produce the original at the hearing; or
4. **Collateral matters**. The writing, recording, or photograph is not closely related to a controlling issue.

Testimony introduced to show the contents of a document is called **parol** (pronounced the same as *parole*) **evidence.** Parol evidence is not allowed to show the information in public records unless it is impossible to obtain certified copies. The majority of states follow the "American Rule," which prefers certain types of secondary evidence to others. Written copies, even rough drafts, are preferred rather than oral testimony. Immediate copies are usually preferred to more remote ones. The exact order of preference varies from state to state. The remaining states follow the "English Rule," which does not recognize degrees of secondary evidence. This allows any type of secondary evidence to be used when primary evidence is not available due to one of the reasons listed in the following discussion. The Federal Rules of Evidence follow the English Rule.

Examples of Secondary Evidence Used to Establish the Content of a Document

- The rough draft of a contract with penciled notes made by both parties.
- The disc from the dictating machine that the secretary used to type the contract.
- Testimony from the head accountant for the company that was the victim of embezzlement about the content of checks that the company did not authorize to be drawn on its account.
- Copies made from the bank's microfiche of checks that the bookkeeper destroyed.

One of the keys to convincing the judge to allow you to introduce secondary evidence is establishing that it is not your fault that the original is not available. If someone destroyed the original with the intent of preventing its use at trial, the opposing side will not have much trouble introducing secondary evidence. In the same vein, if it is impossible to obtain the document by using a subpoena *duces tecum* because the document has been taken out of state by the opposing party, it will be much easier to convince the judge that you should be able to introduce secondary evidence. The same policy would apply if the opposing side has the document and refuses to submit to the judge's discovery orders. On the other hand, if one side wants to introduce secondary evidence on a point that is not closely related to an important issue in the case, the judge is not likely to allow the use of this kind of evidence during trial.

When the contents of a large volume of records are relevant to the case, it is usually possible to present summaries, charts based on all of the records involved, or otherwise make it possible for the judge and jury to review them more quickly. If this is done, the opposing side must have the opportunity to review the original and verify that what is presented in court is accurate and not misleading.

Photographic Evidence[2]

Photographs must meet several requirements before they can be introduced into evidence. As is the case with every exhibit an attorney asks the judge to allow at trial, the content of the photo must be relevant to the case. The photos must accurately portray the scene; shots taken at angles that distort the scene will not be admissible. The requirements of the "Best Evidence Rule" must be met because photographs are documents. Although we normally think of still pictures when we use the term *photograph,* the same term applies to motion pictures and videotapes. X-rays are also photographs, but their admissibility is governed by the rules applied to scientific evidence.

Criteria for Admitting Photographic Evidence at Trial
1. Photo must be relevant to some point that is "at issue" in the trial.
2. Photo must accurately portray the scene.
3. Best Evidence Rule (or modern equivalent) must be satisfied.
4. Photo must not be unduly prejudicial.

The prosecutor or defense attorney cannot introduce pictures into evidence without laying the foundation for them. Pictures can either illustrate the testimony of a witness or be independent evidence in the case.

In both situations, it will be necessary to call witnesses to testify about what the jury will see in the pictures.

The proper foundation must be established before a photograph can be admitted into evidence. To do this, a witness must state that the photograph accurately depicts the scene as it existed when the photograph was taken; it must also accurately depict a scene that is relevant to the trial. Any witness who was at the scene can testify that the photo meets these criteria if he or she has a good memory of the details shown in the picture. It is not necessary to call the photographer to the witness stand. The judge retains the right to refuse to admit pictures that might confuse the jury or be unduly prejudicial. The number of photographs of the same scene that can be admitted is also within the discretion of the judge. Photographs that are merely cumulative are not admissible.

In some of the older cases, judges were cautious about introducing color photographs and enlargements for fear of swaying the jury. As color TV became a common feature in nearly every home, judges became less concerned about inflaming the jury. Now all forms of photography are judged by the same standards. They must accurately portray the scene without causing undue prejudice. Gruesome pictures taken at murder scenes cause the most problems. Pictures that emphasize the gory nature of the crime may be excluded because of their prejudicial impact on the jury. In these cases, the judge may limit the number of photographs that can be introduced.

Another problem with pictures is visual distortion. The angle of the camera, lighting, and other factors may result in deceptive representations of the scene. For example, an ordinary flight of stairs may appear very steep if the camera angle is altered; or the lighting at the time the picture was taken may indicate that visibility at the crime scene was much better (or worse) than it actually was at the time the crime occurred. The opposing side has the right to object to the admission of pictures that do not accurately show the facts. If there is no objection, the photographs will be admitted.

Enlargements and close-ups pose similar problems. Field evidence technicians usually include a ruler or some other standard-sized item in a picture as a point of reference. Aerial photographs are covered by the same considerations. The jury must be able to relate the picture to the total crime scene. These types of photographs are generally admissible as long as the picture will not mislead the jury.

Sometimes one side claims the pictures have been altered and do not represent the facts. This can be done by retouching the negative or superimposing one picture on another. It is usually necessary to call an expert witness to show that these techniques have been used.

Computer software has made it possible to alter photographs. These programs, some of which cost less than $100, make it possible to retouch photographs so that tampering cannot be detected. Photographs can be altered pixel by pixel. Possible alterations may be as slight as changing the shading or as overtly misleading as adding or removing a person or cleaning up a scene or a bloody victim. This potential for alteration makes it exceedingly important to maintain the chain of possession for both the photograph and the negative (if there is one) in order to show that the photograph introduced in court is tamper-free. One permissible use of altered photographs is to ask a witness during cross-examination to identify the photograph and then point out that the witness is so unobservant that he or she identified a picture in which important details had been changed.

More recently, motion picture or video reenactments of the crime have been produced. Videotapes of a drunk driving suspect taking the field sobriety test are now quite common. Whereas older court decisions required expert testimony about the process used to produce these films, they are now accepted without question. The accuracy of the facts depicted in the films must still be established by testimony at trial prior to admitting the films. If there is a question regarding the accuracy of the pictures or their prejudicial impact, the judge will usually preview the film out of the presence of the jury. In rare cases, it will be necessary to call expert witnesses who have examined the film to testify on whether or not the film has been spliced or altered.

Sound recordings are treated in the same manner as photographs. They must be relevant and meet the requirements for introducing the contents of documents. The tape used at trial must be accurate, and editing must not substantially alter the content of the conversation. Audiotapes of nonverbal sounds can also be used at trial. For example, a tape recording may contain the sound of screeching tires, screaming, or moaning and groaning.

Posed pictures are sometimes made to illustrate the facts of the case. For example, investigators may want pictures of the swollen, black-and-blue face of a battered wife. To give the bruises maximum impact, an investigator would need to photograph the victim 1 or 2 days after the assault because bruises do not turn "black and blue" immediately. Part of the foundation for these types of pictures will be testimony about when and where the photographs were taken. The pictures are usually admitted into evidence if they accurately reflect the testimony in the case. If they unfairly show controversial facts to the advantage of one side, they are frequently excluded.

Some cases even use animation to show the same events from different perspectives. Animation produced by computers is subject to the same foundation as any other computer-generated document. As advancing technology makes it possible to produce new audiovisual aids, the rules of evidence gradually develop methods to introduce them for the benefit of the jury.

Models, Maps, and Diagrams[3]

Most courts allow the witness to use models, maps, and diagrams to illustrate his or her testimony. Some states permit these objects to be formally introduced into evidence, whereas others do not. Each judge usually retains a great deal of discretion on this matter. Whenever models, maps, or diagrams are used, it is important for the attorney to state for the record what the witness was pointing to (e.g., "Let the record show that the witness pointed to the northeast corner of the intersection"). If this is not done, the record on appeal will be very confusing (i.e., the witness said "I was here, he was there"). This also applies when the witness places marks on the drawings to indicate where someone was standing or the location of an important object.

Witnesses are frequently allowed to use a chalkboard or chart paper to draw the crime scene. After this is done, the attorneys will ask questions related to the drawing. The drawing, if the witness has basic drawing skills, usually helps the jury visualize the location. When this type of drawing is done, it is rarely to scale. For this reason, it frequently is not introduced into evidence. The better practice is to have the drawing on paper or some other medium that can be saved for later reference if there are any additional questions. This also preserves it for appeal.

If scale drawings are desired, they are usually made before trial. They are made large enough so the jury can see them while the witness is testifying. If the police reports included the exact dimensions of the scene and where all relevant objects were located, the drawing could be based on these measurements. Otherwise, someone will have to go to the crime scene and take appropriate measurements. Since everything is to scale, judges are usually willing to admit the drawing into evidence after it has been authenticated.

Sometimes scale models are used. Examples could be the models that architects use to show proposed buildings and their surroundings or a three-dimensional model showing the inside of a room with all the furnishings done to scale. Anatomical models are also used to show the trajectory of bullets or the effects of other murder weapons. A key reason for admitting these types of models is to help the jury. The fact that they are to scale is important, but the judge can still decide that they are inadmissible if he or she believes the models would confuse the jurors more than help them.

Maps may be used to show the location of various places that are relevant to the case. Official survey maps, road maps, or maps drawn specifically for the trial can be used. Computer software is available that can generate street maps for most cities in the United States. Sometimes aerial photographs that show the relevant streets and buildings are introduced into evidence. Maps that are to scale are usually admissible.

Computer-generated diagrams and three-dimensional animated videos are now commonly used at trial. These types of demonstrative evidence, like their noncomputerized counterparts, must meet two requirements: They must be made to scale from evidence that is admitted in the case, and they must be relevant. For example, a defense attorney might produce a three-dimensional drawing depicting the positions of the attacker and the victim at the time the victim used a gun in self-defense. A program called Mannequin Designer, which creates three-dimensional human forms that can be positioned in virtually any manner and viewed from any angle, could be used for this purpose. For such a diagram to be admissible, the defense must show that the actual dimensions of the people depicted were entered accurately into the computer, the positions accurately reflect the facts of the case, and the software and hardware are reliable and accurate.

Summary

All documents must be authenticated (i.e., shown that they are what they claim to be). Many documents that bear seals, have acknowledgments, or are notarized are self-authenticating. Official government publications are also self-authenticating. When it is necessary to authenticate a document, several methods may be used: (1) testimony of a witness who has knowledge of the circumstances surrounding the making of the document; (2) testimony (expert or lay witnesses) that the handwriting in the document matches that of a specific person; (3) distinctive characteristics of the document; (4) document is public record; (5) the Ancient Document Rule applies; or (6) the process or system used to make the document is established in court.

A forensic document examiner may testify about the authenticity of a document. This expert can determine if the handwriting in the document matches that in an exemplar. Typewriter comparisons can also be made. Both ink and paper can be compared to establish their source and possible date. Computer-generated printouts made with ink jet, dot matrix, or laser printers can be compared. Tests can also be done to determine if a document has been altered or erased.

The Best Evidence Rule requires the original document to be introduced into evidence. Duplicates, such as carbon copies, are only admissible if the original is unavailable. Modern statutes have relaxed the rules on duplicates, especially for photocopies. When the original and duplicates are not available, secondary evidence may be admissible. Witnesses may testify (parol evidence) about the content of the document, but courts usually give preference to written documents that indicate the content of the missing original.

Photographs are admissible if they are relevant, satisfy the Best Evidence Rule, and are not unduly prejudicial. A witness must establish that the photograph accurately shows the scene, but the photographer is not required to testify. Color pictures, close-ups, enlargements, posed pictures, motion pictures, and videotapes are all admissible as long as they accurately represent relevant facts in the case. The judge has the discretion to refuse to admit photographs if they distort the facts.

Maps, models, and diagrams may be admitted into evidence if they are relevant and to scale. Witnesses may be allowed to draw on a chalkboard or butcher chart paper to help illustrate their testimony even if it is not done to scale, but these drawings are not usually admitted into evidence.

Review Questions

1. Define *authentication*. List three types of documents that are self-authenticating, and describe how a prosecutor authenticates the prior convictions of the defendant.
2. List five ways to authenticate a document.
3. Can a lay witness authenticate a handwritten document? Explain.
4. Explain how a forensics document examiner determines if a document and a handwriting exemplar were made by the same person.
5. Explain how a forensics document examiner can determine what make and model typewriter was used to make a document and how he or she can determine if a document was typed on the suspected typewriter.
6. How does a forensics document examiner determine if a document has been altered after it was originally made?
7. What evidence can a forensics document examiner find by examining the paper and ink used to make a document?
8. What is the Best Evidence Rule? When using this rule, what is primary evidence? What is secondary evidence?
9. Under the Best Evidence Rule, when may parol evidence be used to establish the contents of a document?
10. What foundation is necessary for the admission of a photograph?
11. Who determines how many and what type of photographs of the crime scene are admissible? What is the basis for this decision?
12. Are posed photographs admissible? Explain.

Writing Assignment

Go to www.cnn.com/crime. Look for a case that has some documentary evidence. If you have trouble finding a current case, go to www.crimelibrary.com and type the word *document* in the search box. Write a one-page (250-word) report pointing out the documentary evidence and discussing whether it is admissible in court.

Notes

1. K. Koppenhaver, *Forensic Document Examination, Principles and Practice* (Totowa, NJ: Humana Press, 2007); R. Saferstein, *Criminalistics: An Introduction to Forensic Sciences*, 9th ed. (Englewood Cliffs, NJ: Prentice Hall, 2006); D. Ellen, *Scientific Examination of Documents: Methods and Techniques*, 3rd ed. (Boca Raton, FL: CRC Press, 2005); R. Saferstein (Ed.), *Forensic Science Handbook*, vol. I, 2nd ed. (Englewood Cliffs, NJ: Prentice Hall, 2001), Chapter 13; J. Levinson, *Questioned Documents: A Lawyer's Handbook* (San Diego: Academic Press, 2001); R. Morris, *Forensic Handwriting Identification: Fundamental Concepts and Principles* (San Diego: Academic Press, 2000); "Questioned Document Examination." Downloaded June 10, 2007, from http://en.wikipedia.org/wiki/Questioned_document_examination.

2. H. L. Blitzer and J. Jacobia, *Forensic Digital Imaging and Photography* (San Diego: Academic Press, 2001); S. S. Phillips, C. Squiers, and M. Haworth-Booth, *Police Pictures: The Photograph as Evidence* (San Francisco: Chronicle Books, 1997); R. P. Siljander and D. D. Fredrickson, *Applied Police and Fire Photography*, 2nd ed. (Springfield, IL: Charles C. Thomas, 1997); S. Staggs, *Crime Scene & Evidence Photographer's Guide* (Springfield, IL: Charles C. Thomas, 1997).

3. M. Pollitt and S. Shenoi (Eds.), *Advances in Digital Forensics: IFIP International Conference on Digital Forensics, National Center for Forensic Science, Orlando, Florida, February 13–16, 2005* (New York: Springer-Verlag, 2005); S. P. Breaux, "Is Forensic Animation Right for Your Case? As the Capabilities of Computer Animation Grow, So Does Their Use at Trial. Here's How to Determine Whether This Tool Can Enhance Your Case Presentation," *Trial* 39(12): 66(2003); M. Reith, C. Carr, and G. Gunsch, "An Examination of Digital Forensic Models," *International Journal of Digital Evidence* 1(3)(2002); J. C. Russ, *Forensic Uses of Digital Imaging* (Boca Raton, FL: CRC Press, 2001; West Group, *Forensic Animation Evidence* (Eagan, MN: West Group, 1999); B. Galvin, "Photogrammetry Mapping for Crime Scenes." Downloaded June 12, 2007, from http://www.policeone.com/police-products/investigation/accident-investigation/articles/128028/; R. S. C. Leong, "Digital Forensics Investigation Framework That Incorporate Legal Issues." Downloaded June 12, 2007, from http://www.sciencedirect.com/science?_ob=ArticleURL&_udi=B7CW4-4KCPVBY-3&_user=10&_coverDate=09%2F30%2F2006&_rdoc=1&_fmt=&_orig=search&_sort=d&view=c&_acct=C000050221&_version=1&_urlVersion=0&_userid=10&md5=d9a4a118af1c2bc71f2f680c23c09d5c; S. Peisert, M. Bishop, S. Karin, and K. Marzullo, "Toward Models for Forensic Analysis." Downloaded June 13, 2007, from www.cs.ucsd.edu/groups/sysnet/miscpapers/PBKM-SADFE2007-ForensicModels.pdf.

CHAPTER 8

Hearsay and Its Exceptions

Feature Case: Robert Blake

Robert Blake was a child star who appeared in "Our Gang" short features. He was a 1967 Oscar nominee for "In Cold Blood," and he was the star of the long-running "Baretta" TV show. He was charged with the May 2001 murder of his wife, Bonny Lee Bakley.

Blake met Bonny in 1999. She became pregnant as the result of a one-night stand. They married after DNA tests confirmed parentage, but they lived in adjacent houses. Blake obtained a permit to carry a concealed weapon after Bonny claimed that a man was stalking her.

On May 4, 2001, they went out to dinner. After a pleasant meal, they walked back to their car. Blake opened the door for Bonny and then hurried back to the restaurant to get his gun. While Blake was gone to retrieve the gun, someone shot Bonny in the head.

Sixteen LAPD detectives were assigned to the case. Blake was interviewed three times in the first 2 days. Small discrepancies were found between his statements. Several days later, a Walther .38 PPK with its serial numbers partially filed off was found in a dumpster near the location of Bonny's murder. Ballistics tests revealed that the newly found gun was the murder weapon, not the one that Blake carried the night of the murder.

In April 2002, Robert Blake and Earle Caldwell, his bodyguard, were arrested. Blake was charged with murder, conspiracy to commit murder, and two counts of solicitation; Caldwell was charged with conspiracy to commit murder. The District Attorney alleged that Blake was the trigger man but did not seek the death penalty.

Witnesses at the preliminary hearing testified that between October 1999 and April 2001, Blake approached five people requesting their help with either killing Bonny or having her arrested and sent to prison. Twelve different plans had been floated by Blake, one almost identical to the way Bonny died.

During the 4-month trial, no eyewitnesses or blood or DNA evidence linked Blake to the crime. Tests on Blake's clothing showed no trace of Bonny's blood; insignificant amounts of gunpowder were found on his hands and boots.

The prosecution relied heavily on the testimony of two ex-stuntmen who claimed that Blake offered to pay them to kill Bonny. The defense impeached these witnesses based on their heavy drug use, hallucinations, and delusions. Other witnesses testified that Blake made statements indicating that he wanted Bonny dead. The defense successfully cross-examined these witnesses, pointing out their motives for testifying against Blake. Witnesses who saw Blake on the evening of the shooting testified about Blake's bizarre behavior. Blake did not testify at trial. Instead, the defense showed the jury a video of Barbara Walters interviewing Blake, during which he denied killing his wife.

After 36 hours of deliberation, the jury acquitted Blake on the charge of murdering his wife and one count of solicitation. Caldwell was also acquitted.

Bonny's family filed a wrongful death suit against Blake in civil court. The jury awarded them $30 million. Blake filed for bankruptcy.

Learning Objectives

After studying this chapter, you will be able to

- Define *hearsay*.
- List the requirements for the use of admissions and confessions.
- Identify three types of declarations against interest.
- Explain how to identify spontaneous statements and contemporaneous declarations.
- List the requirements for making a dying declaration admissible.
- Identify what falls under the Business Records Exception to the Hearsay Rule.
- Explain what is admissible hearsay to show character.
- Identify what is admissible as former testimony.
- Describe what prior statements are admissible to impeach and rehabilitate.
- Explain what is admissible as ancient documents.

Key Terms

- Admissions Exception
- Adoptive admission
- Ancient Documents Exception
- Authorized admission
- Business Records Exception
- Contemporaneous declaration
- Declarant
- Declaration against interest
- Double hearsay
- Dying declaration
- Excited utterance
- Former testimony
- Hearsay Rule
- Negative hearsay
- Past Recollection Recorded Exception
- Present sense impression
- Prior consistent statement
- Prior inconsistent statement
- Public Records Exception
- Reputation Exception
- Spontaneous statement
- Statement
- Tacit admission

Myths about Hearsay	Facts about Hearsay
A person cannot be convicted based on hearsay.	A conviction can be based on any type of admissible evidence, even hearsay.
Hearsay only applies to what people say.	Hearsay applies to both things that are said and things that are written down.
Hearsay only applies to what other people say.	Hearsay applies to what everybody says when they are not under oath.
Things that defendants in a criminal case say are not hearsay.	What the defendants say outside of court is hearsay, but there is an exception to the Hearsay Rule that makes these statements admissible.
Most states have done away with the Hearsay Rule.	Most states have expanded the exceptions to the Hearsay Rule so that more hearsay can be used in court.

Basic Hearsay Definitions

Our legal system usually requires that a case be decided solely on the basis of sworn testimony given in the presence of the trial judge or jury. The general rule is that out-of-court statements may not be used as evidence unless they fall under one of the exceptions to the **Hearsay Rule.** This chapter defines hearsay and discusses 14 of the most common exceptions to the rule.

People frequently misuse the term *hearsay*. This makes it very important for you to understand the term in its legal context. The definition in the Federal Rules of Evidence, which follows, has been adopted by approximately half of the 50 states.

To understand the Hearsay Rule, start by considering three things:

1. What is a statement?
2. Who is a declarant?
3. What is meant by "offered in evidence to prove the truth of the matter asserted"?

A **"statement"** may include several types of communication: oral, written, recorded on audio- or videotape, and nonverbal. In fact, anything a person says is a statement. So are his or her letters, business records, will, the deed to his or her house, etc. However, technically the legal word "statement" is even broader. It includes body movements done with the intent to communicate. Specifically, it includes actions such as shaking your head "no" or pointing in answer to the question, "Which way did he go?"

Statements are hearsay if they were not made in court at the hearing or trial that is currently being conducted. The common idea that "What you say is hearsay, but what I say is not" is not correct; statements originally made by a person while that person is not testifying in court are hearsay. This means that even the sworn testimony of the witness that was given at the preliminary hearing is hearsay when offered at the subsequent trial; the witness's account of what he or she said while the crime was being committed is also hearsay.

The **declarant** is the person who made the statement. If the witness is telling what he or she heard someone else say, the person who originally made the statement is the declarant and the statement is hearsay. If the person on the witness stand is telling what he or she previously said, the witness is the declarant and the statement is also hearsay. It is important to determine who the declarant is. The facts surrounding the declarant's statement are considered when determining if an exception to the Hearsay Rule applies.

Something is "offered to prove the truth of the matter asserted" when the attorney wants the jury to believe the answer. Most testimony is admitted for this purpose. Sometimes, however, an attorney will ask a question for some other reason.

Definitions of Basic Terms Used for Hearsay*

Statement

A "statement" is
1. An oral or written assertion or
2. Nonverbal conduct of a person, if it is intended by the person as an assertion.

Declarant

A "declarant" is a person who makes a hearsay statement.

Hearsay

"Hearsay" is
1. A statement,
2. Other than one made by the declarant while testifying at the trial or hearing,
3. Offered in evidence to prove the truth of the matter asserted.

*Based on Federal Rules of Evidence, Rule 801.

Examples of Statements That Are Hearsay
- Prosecutor asks a police officer to tell the jury what the defendant said during the interrogation.

  This is offered to show the truth of the matter asserted—that the defendant committed the crime as described in the confession: It is hearsay.

- Prosecutor wants to admit the note that was given to the teller during a bank robbery. This note says, "Hit the alarm button and you're dead."

  This is a written document that contains hearsay.

Examples of Statements That Are Not Hearsay
- If the defense wants to show that the defendant was insane, it might try to admit the defendant's statement, "I am Napoleon," to show that the defendant obviously did not know who he was.

  Since it is not used to show that it is true—in fact, it is was introduced for the purpose of showing that it is not true—the statement "I am Napoleon" is not hearsay.

- Prosecutor asks the witness to repeat the defendant's original alibi even though the defendant later changed her alibi.

  The purpose of this is to show that the defendant is a liar, not to show that the original alibi was true. When used for this purpose, the original alibi is not hearsay.

The Hearsay Rule

The Hearsay Rule is very simple—hearsay is not admissible in court. There are, however, many exceptions to this rule that are discussed later in this chapter. Most statements are admissible in court if they fall under one or more exceptions to the Hearsay Rule.

There are several reasons for the Hearsay Rule. The most important is a basic distrust of testimony that was not made under oath. Giving false testimony while under oath can be prosecuted as perjury. Since the hearsay statement was made without any fear of prosecution for perjury, it is not considered as trustworthy as statements that were made under oath.

Another reason courts are suspicious of hearsay is that the jury did not see the person while he or she was making the hearsay statement. Demeanor provides many clues that help jurors decide if the witness is telling the truth. All of those clues are missing if the person who originally made the statement does not testify. The fact that the person who originally made the statement is not testifying at trial also means that the defense attorney will not be able to cross-examine. Cross-examination is a key to determining whether a witness is telling the truth. The defense can question the person who testified to make sure he or she is accurately repeating what was said, but that is a weak substitute. For all of these reasons, hearsay is distrusted.

The Sixth Amendment to the U.S. Constitution gives the defense in a criminal trial the right to confront and cross-examine the people who accuse the defendant of a crime. This is called the Confrontation Clause. It includes the right to confront the people who told the police they saw the defendant commit the crime. When hearsay is improperly used at trial, the Sixth Amendment Confrontation Clause is violated. Judges are very cautious because erroneous rulings that allow the prosecution to admit hearsay have the potential for causing the conviction to be reversed due to a violation of the defendant's constitutional rights.

Despite the fact that there are very good arguments for not admitting hearsay into evidence, there are some situations in which out-of-court statements obviously should be used. These situations have been grouped together and form the exceptions to the Hearsay Rule. The exceptions to the Hearsay Rule that are used during criminal trials must be based on facts surrounding the making of the statement that show that the statement is trustworthy. Some are based on necessity, such as the dying declaration of the murder victim. Even so, these statements must be trustworthy.

Other exceptions to the Hearsay Rule are based on the concept of fair play. For example, it would be unfair to exclude the defendant's confession solely because it was not made under oath. It would also be unfair to allow one side to introduce an edited version of an out-of-court statement but deny the opposing side the right to introduce the portions of that statement that were intentionally left out.

Some states allow police officers to testify at the preliminary hearing and/or before the grand jury about conversations with victims and witnesses even though the officers could not give the same testimony at trial due to the Hearsay Rule. The purpose of this procedure is twofold: It makes the process more efficient; and it minimizes the inconvenience for victims and witnesses of taking time off work to testify in court. It does not interfere with the defendant's Sixth Amendment rights because the rule does not apply at trial.

Testimonial Hearsay

In two cases, *Crawford v. Washington* (541 U.S. 36 (2004)) and *Davis v. Washington* (547 U.S. 813 (2006)), the Supreme Court restricted the prosecutor's right to introduce testimonial hearsay. The Court relied heavily on the intent of the drafters of the Bill of Rights (called the "original intent doctrine") when it ruled that testimonial hearsay can be admitted at trial only if the person who made the hearsay statement testifies.

In *Davis* (2006) (which contained the Supreme Court's decisions on *Davis v. Washington* and *Hammon v. Indiana*), the Court explained its holdings:

> A critical portion of this holding, and the portion central to resolution of the two cases now before us, is the phrase "testimonial statements." Only statements of this sort cause the declarant to be a "witness" within the meaning of the Confrontation Clause. See id., at 51. It is the testimonial character of the statement that separates it from other hearsay that, while subject to traditional limitations upon hearsay evidence, is not subject to the Confrontation Clause. . . .
>
> Without attempting to produce an exhaustive classification of all conceivable statements—or even all conceivable statements in response to police interrogation—as either testimonial or nontestimonial, it suffices to decide the present cases to hold as follows: Statements are nontestimonial when made in the course of police interrogation under circumstances objectively indicating that the primary purpose of the interrogation is to enable police assistance to meet an ongoing emergency. They are testimonial when the circumstances objectively indicate that there is no such ongoing emergency, and that the primary purpose of the interrogation is to establish or prove past events potentially relevant to later criminal prosecution. (547 U.S. 819–820 (2006))

Both cases considered by the Supreme Court in *Davis* were domestic violence cases. In the first one, portions of the 911 tape were played for the jurors. The distraught woman could be heard telling the operator that she had been hit and the assailant was leaving. The court ruled that this was nontestimonial because the intent was to obtain police assistance during an emergency.

In the second case, police officers responding to a domestic disturbance call found the victim alone on the front porch. She appeared "somewhat frightened" but told the police that "nothing was the matter." The officers separated the parties and talked to them. After hearing the wife's account, the officers asked her to fill out and sign a battery affidavit. Her handwritten affidavit said

Broke our Furnace & shoved me down on the floor into the broken glass.
Hit me in the chest and threw me down. Broke our lamps & phone. Tore up
my van where I couldn't leave the house. Attacked my daughter.

Emphasizing that the emergency no longer existed, the Court ruled that
the affidavit was testimonial evidence and should not have been used at
trial because the person who made it did not appear in court.

In the aftermath of the Court's ruling in *Crawford*, advocates for
domestic violence victims argued that there should be a different rule
when the person who made the hearsay statement did not testify at trial
because of fear of the defendant. The Supreme Court refused to make such
a rule, but it pointed to a portion of the *Crawford* decision where it said,
"One who obtains the absence of a witness by wrongdoing forfeits the
constitutional right to confrontation" (541 U.S. at 62). Although the Court
refused to establish rules on what types of wrongdoing qualify for forfei-
ture, it pointed to Federal Rules of Evidence that state that hearsay can be
used in court if "a statement is offered against a party that has engaged
or acquiesced in wrongdoing that was intended to, and did, procure the
unavailability of the declarant as a witness" (Rule 804(b)(6)). The government must prove the defendant's wrongdoing by a preponderance of the
evidence prior to introducing the hearsay.

Unavailability of the Hearsay Declarant

Several exceptions to the hearsay rule are based on the declarant not
being available to testify in person. If the declarant is alive, the attorney
who wants to introduce the statement is expected to conduct a thorough
search for the witness and subpoena him or her to appear in court. This is
referred to as exercising due diligence. The judge will not declare a witness
unavailable if it appears that the side that wants to introduce the hearsay
failed to use due diligence to find the declarant.

Unavailability is a requirement under three hearsay exceptions discussed in this chapter: Declaration against Interest, Dying Declaration,
and Former Testimony. The Federal Rules of Evidence provide a list of five
situations that are considered sufficient reasons to allow nontestimonial
hearsay to be used in court even though the declarant could not be found.
Most states will accept similar reasons as long as no testimonial hearsay
is involved. When a prosecutor or defense attorney wants to introduce a
hearsay statement made by an unavailable witness, the judge will require
proof that one of these circumstances applies.

Person Whose Hearsay Is Sought at Trial May Be Declared Unavailable for One of These Reasons*

"Unavailability as a witness" includes situations in which the declarant
1. Is exempted by ruling of the court on the ground of privilege from testifying concerning the subject matter of the declarant's statement; or
2. Persists in refusing to testify concerning the subject matter of the declarant's statement despite an order of the court to do so; or
3. Testifies to a lack of memory of the subject matter of the declarant's statement; or
4. Is unable to be present or to testify at the hearing because of death or then existing physical or mental illness or infirmity; or
5. Is absent from the hearing and the proponent of a hearsay statement has been unable to procure the declarant's attendance by process or other reasonable means.

A declarant is not unavailable as a witness if exemption, refusal, claim of lack of memory, inability, or absence is due to the procurement or wrongdoing of the proponent of a statement for the purpose of preventing the witness from attending or testifying.

*Based on Federal Rules of Evidence, Rule 804(a).

Exceptions to the Hearsay Rule

Only statements that fall under one of the exceptions to the Hearsay Rule are admissible in court. When prosecutors review a case involving hearsay to decide if there is enough evidence to convict, one of the things they are really looking for are statements that fit within the exceptions to the Hearsay Rule.

Several other points should be kept in mind. Hearsay varies greatly. Some is so convincing it constitutes key evidence in the case. Other statements will be nearly frivolous. Finding the appropriate hearsay exception, so as to get certain evidence admitted, merely ensures that the jury will hear it. The jury, of course, will decide how much weight to give the evidence.

In some situations, more than one exception will apply. Examination of the requirements for the various exceptions may reveal technical reasons why one will be more appropriate to use than another.

Sometimes we come upon **"double hearsay."** Double hearsay is hearsay included in another hearsay statement. For example, if Jane told you what Mary said, whatever Jane told you is hearsay. But if Jane is repeating what Mary said that Alice told her, the portion about what Alice said is double hearsay. The only time when these types of statements are admissible is when there is a hearsay exception that applies to what Mary told Jane and an exception that covers what Jane told you.

All 50 states do not follow exactly the same exceptions to the Hearsay Rule. Approximately half of the states follow the Hearsay Rules listed in the Federal Rules of Evidence. The others follow their own rules, which may not be the same as the federal rules. Each student must do research and discover what rules apply in his or her local state courts. The Federal Rules list at least 30 exceptions to the Hearsay Rule. The most commonly used exceptions are discussed in this chapter.

Admissions and Confessions

Out-of-court statements made by the defendant appear to be within the definition of hearsay and are treated that way by some states. The Federal Rules of Evidence declare that statements made by parties to the lawsuit are not hearsay (Rule 801(d)(2)), thus avoiding the need to create an exception to the hearsay rule in order to use them at trial. States following this approach include Louisiana, Montana, Nebraska, Nevada, New Mexico, Oregon, Texas, and Wisconsin. Another approach is to use the standard definition of hearsay but state that statements by the parties are not excluded by the Hearsay Rule—that is, create an exception to the Hearsay Rule that allows statements made by the parties to be introduced in court. California, Florida, Kentucky, Pennsylvania, and Tennessee are among the states that follow this approach.

Definition

Admissions Exceptions to the Hearsay Rule*

A statement may be admissible under the Admissions Exception to the Hearsay Rule if it is used *against* a party to a law suit and the original statement falls under at least one of the following situations:

1. Admission of a Party

Statement was made by person who is a party to the lawsuit.

OR

2. Adoptive (Tacit) Admission

Party to the law suit adopted the statement or otherwise indicated a belief that the statement was true.

OR

3. Authorized Admission

Statement was made by a person authorized by a party to the law suit to make statements concerning the subject matter.

OR

4. Admission by Agent

Statement was made by a person who was the agent or servant of a party to the law suit, concerning a matter within the scope of the agency or employment, during the existence of the relationship.

OR

5. Admission by Co-conspirator

Statement was made by a co-conspirator of a party to the law suit during the course of the conspiracy in furtherance of the conspiracy.

*Based on Federal Rules of Evidence, Rule 801(d)(2).

Statements of a party (the defendant in a criminal case) will be admissible if the attorney establishes the appropriate foundation. This foundation for admissions is remarkably similar regardless of whether the statement must qualify under the **Admissions Exception** to the Hearsay Rule or the attorney introducing it must show that the statement is not considered hearsay. For that reason, it is important to understand the requirements for the Admissions Exception even when working in a state that does not recognize statements of parties as hearsay. Once the foundation is established, the statements are admissible even though there may not be any sign of their trustworthiness. The traditional rationale for allowing these statements to be considered by the jury is that a person would not make untrue statements that could be used against him or her.

Whereas admissions of a party may be used against the person making them, the reverse is not true. A party cannot introduce his or her own self-serving statements to bolster the case. The only questions that must be considered in court are whether the person made the statement and whether the person was mentally competent when the statement was made.

Admission of a Party

In a criminal case, the defendant is obviously a party to the lawsuit. The defendant's confessions and other statements may be admitted under the Admission of a Party Exception to the Hearsay Rule. By pleading "not guilty," the defendant denies committing the crime; therefore, any admission or confession the defendant made can be used against him or her. It is easy to remember that confessions can be admitted, but you must also remember that other statements that the defendant makes can also be used at trial. For example, during the first contact with the police, a suspect may give an alibi. Using hearsay terminology, this is an admission and it can be introduced at trial against the defendant.

Examples of Statements That Are Admissible under Admissions of a Party Exception to the Hearsay Rule

- On the morning after the crime occurred, the defendant told a friend, "I need you to cover for me. If anyone asks, tell them I was with you last night."
- After the police officer gave him the *Miranda* warnings, the defendant said, "Hey, I was there but I didn't do anything."
- When questioned at his home the day after the crime, the defendant told the police, "I don't know what you are talking about. Last night I went to visit my mother." The police left the house without making an arrest.

Examples of Statements That Are *Not* Admissible under Admissions of a Party Exception to the Hearsay Rule

- The defendant in a child abuse case wants to introduce the following statement she made to her best friend: "I would never do anything to hurt my kids."

  Self-serving statement—not admissible. Admissions can only be used *against* the person who made the statement.

- The defendant's neighbor told the police, "If you ask me, he's guilty."

  Statement is not an admission—it was made by a neighbor, not by someone who is a party to the case. It may be admissible under some other exception to the Hearsay Rule.

- After the police gave him the *Miranda* warnings, the suspect said, "I refuse to talk about it."

  Statement is an admission but the Supreme Court has specifically said that the fact that a person invoked the right to remain silent after being given the *Miranda* warnings cannot be used against that person.

In addition to complying with the requirements of the Admissions Exception to the Hearsay Rule, confessions are only admissible at trial if the police comply with the suspect's constitutional rights, such as giving *Miranda* warnings prior to custodial interrogation (see Chapter 14). When two or more defendants are being tried at the same time, it may be necessary to exclude confessions and/or admissions if the defendant who made these statements does not take the witness stand. Admitting a confession made by a defendant who decides not to testify would deny the co-defendant(s)'s Sixth Amendment right to cross-examine the person who made the statement. One solution to this problem is to "sanitize" the confession by removing all references to what the other defendant(s) did. Another solution is to have separate trials for the defendants.

Adoptive (Tacit) Admission

The **Adoptive (Tacit) Admission** applies when one person accepts a statement made by someone else. The definition of **adoptive admission** uses the phrase "manifested an adoption or belief in its truth." A simpler way to say that is "the person acted as though he or she believed the statement was true." This form of admission is based on the assumption that the statement was true because an innocent person would immediately deny a statement if it were untrue.

In the context of a criminal case, the adoptive admission applies when someone alleges that a person committed a crime and the alleged criminal does not reply that he or she did not do it (or an equivalent response). The person who is alleged to have committed the crime must be present when the statement is made. If the alleged criminal says something like "Yes, it was me" or "I agree with you," he or she is adopting the statement as true (i.e., making an adoptive admission). However, a person is not required to do anything that obvious. Actions that can be interpreted as showing a belief that the allegation is true are just as important. Failing to respond to the statement is considered an admission. Walking away without saying anything is considered a tacit admission.

Most textbooks only apply the Adoptive Admission Exception to the period during which the individuals remain face-to-face. The modern interpretation of the Adoptive (Tacit) Admission rule does not consider it an admission if a person fails to reply to an allegation made during a phone call, e-mail, fax, or letter.

Another situation in which failure to reply when confronted is not considered a tacit admission is when the person making the statement that alleges wrongdoing is an authority figure. The law recognizes that a person is more likely to remain silent in the presence of an authority figure. Police are considered authority figures; failure to respond to their allegations is not a tacit admission. Failure to admit a crime after being given *Miranda* warnings is not a tacit admission because the person has the constitutional right to remain silent.

Examples of Statements That Are Admissible under Adoptive (Tacit) Admissions Exception to the Hearsay Rule

- The salesclerk confronted the 10-year-old who had just stolen a candy bar and said, "I saw you do that! Don't you know it is wrong to steal?" The juvenile hung his head and didn't say anything.
- The juvenile's mother said, "Go to your room, you know better than to steal!" The juvenile went to his room without saying anything.
- The suspect stole a lawnmower from a neighbor who left his garage door open all night. The next day, the neighbor confronted him and said, "Why did you take it? Why?" The suspect quickly walked away without saying anything.

Examples of Statements That Are *Not* Admissible under Adoptive (Tacit) Admissions Exception to the Hearsay Rule

- The police officer told the shoplifter, "You're under arrest for theft." The shoplifter didn't say anything.

    The tacit admission exception to the Hearsay Rule does not apply when a person is confronted by an authority figure.

- The neighbor told a convicted drug dealer's mother, "Why does your kid do all those drugs?" The mother did not reply.

    The mother is not an agent of her child. Failure of the mother to reply is not a tacit admission.

- The day after discovering the embezzlement, the employer called the bookkeeper and said, "I've always treated you right; why did you steal from me?"

    To be an adoptive (tacit) admission, that allegation must be made face-to-face.

Authorized Admission

An **authorized admission** is a statement made by a person who is authorized to speak for a party to the law suit. In criminal cases, that means a person who is authorized to speak for the defendant. The exception means that if you authorized this agent to speak on your behalf, you are responsible for what the agent says—even if the agent says something incorrectly or something he or she was not authorized to say. For example, the president of a company is authorized to speak for the company, but the student intern is not. If the defendant in a criminal trial owned an apartment building, hired someone to be the manager, and gave the manager the duties of making repairs, advertising vacancies, showing units to prospective tenants, signing leases, collecting rent money, and evicting tenants who did not pay rent, the manager would be authorized to speak on behalf of the defendant as long as the discussion was about the apartment building. A person hired to make repairs, but not given all of these duties, would not be an agent of the owner.

Examples of Statements That Are Admissible under Authorized Admissions Exception to the Hearsay Rule

- The head of the public relations office of the company sent a letter to customers who had been victims of fraudulent advertising. The letter said, "We wish to apologize to our customers. The person responsible for the problem has been fired. In the future, you can rely on our ads." Criminal charges were filed against the corporation for fraud. The press release can be used at trial against the corporation as an authorized admission that the corporation engaged in misleading advertising.

- The store manager told the lady who slipped and fell while shopping, "I'm very sorry you got hurt. I'll tell my janitors to use a different kind of wax next time so the floors won't be so slippery." The lady later sued the store. The store manager's statement can be introduced against the company at a civil trial.

Examples of Statements That Are *Not* Admissible under Authorized Admissions Exception to the Hearsay Rule

- The cashier in the parts department told a customer who was returning a defective part, "I'm not surprised it didn't fit. We get a lot of that 'cause the company's so cheap. It buys knock-off parts just to save a few bucks."

  The cashier is not authorized to make statements on behalf of the company.

- The union leader said, "We are going on strike because XYZ Company always overloads its trucks. Those heavy trucks create a risk for our drivers and the public and we don't want any part in that."

  The union leader is authorized to speak for the union. The statement cannot be used by someone who is suing XYZ Company to show that the trucking company intentionally created the risk that harmed the plaintiff.

Admission by Agent

Admission by agent is the opposite of authorized admissions. Whereas authorized admission applied when the company authorizes an agent to speak on its behalf, admission by agent applies when someone is trying to hold a company liable based on what the agent or employee said. The authority flows the opposite way. As long as the companies and their agents do what they are supposed to do, there is no problem. When someone exceeds their authority, there is a problem.

The first question in these situations is what was the agent authorized to do? Once that is determined, the next question is, was the agent acting within the scope of what he or she was authorized to do? For example, in a company that sells used cars, the sales staff must have the details of a sale approved by "my manager." The review of the details by someone with more authority is designed to prevent the sale from being too generous. In this situation, the final sale is based on the deal the manager signs, not promises made by the person who meets the prospective client and talks to him or her. On the other hand, everything included in the sale that was authorized by the manager is enforceable against the owner of the car lot.

Example of Statements That Are Admissible under Admissions by an Agent Exception to the Hearsay Rule

- A couple who wanted to sell their house signed an agreement with a real estate company. The real estate agent told potential buyers that the house did not have termites. After they purchased the house, the new owners discovered extensive termite damage that made the house unsafe. The statements of the real estate agent could be used in a law suit by the new owners against the sellers. Real estate agents are normally authorized to make statements about the building that is being sold. On the other hand, if real estate law in the state requires all terms of the sale be approved by the owner, the purchaser cannot sue based on the agent's statements that were not in the written agreement.

- State law requires an insurance company to mail notices to clients 10 days before their policy will expire. An agent employed by the insurance company forgot to put a stack of expiration notices in the outgoing mail basket. Twelve days later, a lady whose notice had never been sent caused a serious traffic accident. The fact that the insurance agent did not follow required procedures can be used against the insurance company because it is considered likely that the lady would have renewed her policy if she had received the notice.

Example of Statements That Are *Not* Admissible under Admissions by an Agent Exception to the Hearsay Rule

- A sales representative works "in the field" and drives approximately 100 miles per day. One day, the rep runs some personal errands when he should have been working. During that time, he is involved in an accident. He hands the other driver his business card and says, "Call them; they will take care of everything."

This statement was not made within the scope of the sales rep's duties; therefore, it is not binding on the company. The situation might be different if the company routinely ignored the fact that sales reps ran personal errands as long as they completed the assigned calls on time.

- A delivery truck driver worked for a company that had a strict "no drinking on the job" policy. In the past, drivers had been fired for having one beer with lunch. A delivery driver had a pitcher of beer and a small pizza for lunch. An hour later, this driver was involved in an accident. She got out of the truck, handed the driver of the other car the truck's insurance ID card, and said, "Just call the insurance agent. He'll take care of everything."

The driver violated a strict "no drinking on the job" policy; therefore, the company is not responsible for the accident caused by the drunk driver. The driver's statement that the insurance agent would "take care of everything" did not create any liability for the company. If the company tolerated drinking on the job, then the outcome would be different.

Admission by Co-conspirator

Many states have a hearsay exception for statements made by co-conspirators. This rule closely mirrors the criminal law rule that makes each conspirator responsible for acts of other conspirators. Statements made by one conspirator during the conspiracy can be used against another conspirator.

The statement must be made within the scope of the conspiracy and in furtherance of the purpose of conspiracy.

Example of Statements That Are Admissible under Admission by Co-conspirator Exception to the Hearsay Rule

- Tom and Steve formed a conspiracy to rob a bank on Monday. Sunday afternoon, Steve was placing duct tape in a duffle bag to be used during the robbery when his girlfriend walked in. He winked at her and said, "Tomorrow Tom and I are applying for a big loan from the bank." This statement can be used against both Tom and Steve when the prosecution tries to show that Tom and Steve were involved in a conspiracy to rob the bank.
- Renee and Michelle formed a conspiracy to print counterfeit money. Renee sent e-mails to two vendors asking questions about the resolution that the printer could achieve and the colors of ink that were available. These e-mails can be used by the prosecution to show "acts" had been performed in furtherance of the conspiracy.

Example of Statements That Are *Not* Admissible under Admission by Co-conspirator Exception to the Hearsay Rule

- Mary and Jo agreed to kidnap Bruce, the boy Mary babysat, and hold him for $100,000 ransom. A week before the planned kidnapping, Jo called Mary and told her that she was leaving on vacation and wasn't going to help with the kidnapping. Mary went ahead with the kidnapping and signed Jo's name to the ransom note.

  The ransom note cannot be used to prove that there was a conspiracy because it was produced after Jo withdrew from the conspiracy.

- Bob talked to Mike about forming a production company to make "kiddie porn" DVDs. Mike acted like he was interested. Bob withdrew $50,000 from his savings account and bought an expensive camera and a machine to make 50 duplicate copies of a DVD at once. Meanwhile, Mike went to the FBI and told them about Bob's suggestion. The FBI agent told Mike to meet with Bob and get more information. Mike arranged to meet with Bob and recorded the entire conversation.

  Bob's statements cannot be used against him under the Admission by Co-conspirator Exception because there never was a conspiracy—Mike only pretended he was interested.

Declarations against Interest (Declarant Must Be Unavailable)

Unlike the Admissions Exception, which only applies to statements made by parties to the case, **declarations against interest** are admissible no matter who made them—but the declarant must be unavailable. If you look at the list of situations that qualify as "unavailable," the statement would be admissible if the defendant does not testify at trial.

Note that if a statement against personal interest is made by the defendant, the statement is admissible under either the Admissions Exception to the Hearsay Rule or as a declaration against interest. Most likely, the prosecutor will attempt to admit the statement under the Admissions Exception because it would not be necessary to show that the defendant is unavailable to testify. This makes it easier to introduce the statement at trial.

Definition

Declaration against Interest Exception (Also Called Statement against Interest Exception) to the Hearsay Rule*

A statement will be admissible under the Declaration against Interest Exception to the Hearsay Rule if, at the time the statement was made, it
1. Was contrary to the declarant's pecuniary or proprietary interest, OR
2. Tended to subject the declarant to civil or criminal liability, OR
3. Rendered invalid a claim by the declarant against another.

These factors are used to show that a reasonable person in the declarant's position would not have made the statement unless he or she believed the statement was true.

Note: A statement tending to expose the declarant to criminal liability and offered to exculpate the accused is not admissible unless corroborating circumstances clearly indicate the trustworthiness of the statement.

*Based on Federal Rules of Evidence, Rule 804(b)(3).

Examples of Statements That Are Admissible under Declaration against Interest Exception to the Hearsay Rule
- The fraud victim, who has since moved out of town and cannot be located, told a friend, "I can't tell my husband about this. I took money from an account at work to pay for those phony stocks. I feel like a fool falling for such an obvious swindle."
- A person who bought several stolen rings from the defendant told a friend, "Sure, I knew the rings were hot, but he was selling them so cheap, I just couldn't resist!" The suspect is now on trial for theft. The person who bought the rings has been charged with receiving stolen property and refuses to testify.

Examples of Statements That Are *Not* Admissible under Declaration against Interest Exception to the Hearsay Rule
- The victim of the fraud testified that he did not report the scam because it would be very embarrassing if his children learned that he did not read the small print on the contract.

Not admissible as declaration against interest because fraud victim is testifying; declaration against interest requires that the hearsay declarant is unavailable to testify.

- The foreign tourist who was arrested for soliciting a prostitute told the police, "Yes I paid her, but I had no idea hiring a prostitute was a crime; it isn't where I come from." The tourist had returned home and was not present to testify against the woman charged with prostitution.

    Although the tourist is unavailable, the declaration does not appear to be against his interest.

Originally, a statement was not considered to be against the interest of the person making it unless the statement could result in a financial loss for the declarant. In more recent years, the definition of "against interest" has expanded. Confessions to crimes are now generally included, as are statements that could be used against a person in civil court. A few states, such as Montana, Nevada, and Wisconsin, include statements that would make the person the subject of hatred, ridicule, or disgrace.

Declarations against interest are considered trustworthy because it is unlikely a person would make a statement that could be damaging unless the statement were true. Even then, testimony by the person who originally made the statement is preferred. It is only when the in-court testimony is not possible that the out-of-court statement is allowed.

Spontaneous Statements (Also Called Excited Utterances)

Some states consider **present sense impressions, spontaneous statements,** and **contemporaneous declarations** to be three separate exceptions to the Hearsay Rule. Other states include them in the *res gestae* (literally, "things done") exception to the Hearsay Rule that covers a variety of statements to explain the actions that were being done at the time the statement was made. We consider the two separately and note that they are quite similar.

Both of these exceptions to the Hearsay Rule are considered to be trustworthy because there was no time for the declarant to think about what he or she is saying. Unlike a statement that is contemplated and composed in order to present the case in a manner favorable to the declarant, the speed with which the spontaneous statement or contemporaneous declaration is made is believed to lower the probability that the declarant lied.

Sometimes the defendant in a criminal case makes a statement that would fall into the category of simultaneous statement or contemporaneous declaration. These exceptions to the Hearsay Rule are rarely used in these circumstances because it is easier to have the defendant's statements admitted under the Admissions Exception.

Definition

Spontaneous Statements Exception (Also Called Excited Utterance Exception) to the Hearsay Rule*

A statement will be admissible under the Spontaneous Statements Exception to the Hearsay Rule if, at the time the statement was made,

1. The statement related to a startling event or condition, AND
2. The statement was made while the declarant was under the stress of excitement caused by the event or condition.

*Based on Federal Rules of Evidence, Rule 803(2).

Examples of Statements That Are Admissible under the Spontaneous Statements (Also Called Excited Utterance) Exception to the Hearsay Rule

- Immediately after a traffic accident a bystander said, "Did you see that? He just ran the red light. He never tried to stop before he hit that car!"
- During a robbery the victim said, "No! No! Please don't take my money."
- The victim grabbed his stomach and said, "Oh, that hurts. Why did you hit me?"

Examples of Statements That Are *Not* Admissible under the Spontaneous Statements (Also Called Excited Utterance) Exception to the Hearsay Rule

- After she came home from work, a woman told her husband, "Some guy tried to rob the bank this morning. I'd just walked in there to cash a check. I was so scared when I saw he had a gun!"

This conversation took place several hours after the event—the woman was no longer under the stress or excitement of the event.

- A man told the police taking statements immediately after the bank robbery, "I was next in line for Teller No. 4. I saw the guy, but there wasn't anything to be afraid of. He didn't have a gun or anything."

This conversation occurred soon after the robbery was finished, but the man was never excited or frightened by the "robber."

- A man who observed a train wreck told a friend, "There was a train wreck last year. Right there, at the same spot. My wife was killed."

This man was speaking from the emotion of the moment, but he was talking about something that happened a year ago. This was not about the event that caused the excitement.

To qualify as a spontaneous statement, the declarant must have personally observed the event he or she is commenting about. This includes utilization of any of the five senses, although eyesight and hearing are the most common. Given the current level of "live" broadcasts by the media, it no longer is necessary for the declarant to be at the location where the event occurred.

The statement must be made very near (timewise) to the occurrence of the event in question. The person should still be responding to the event, or as some codes state, "in the excitement of the moment." The length of this interval will vary with the type of stimulus involved. There is no set time limit. The stronger the stimulus, the longer the "excitement of the moment" is likely to last. In some cases, this rule is applied to the time immediately following being told of an event, such as the death of a loved one.

Normally, the statement must be made without any questioning. The idea here is that there was no interrogation taking place. Polite questions such as "Are you OK?" would be less likely to defeat a request to introduce a statement as a spontaneous statement. Self-serving statements, such as statements the defendant made to make him- or herself look good, are not admissible under this exception even if all other criteria are met.

The defendant may make spontaneous statements, but this exception is normally used to admit statements by other people. Everything the defendant said is admissible against the defendant under the Admissions Exception to the Hearsay Rule.

Contemporaneous Declarations (Also Called Present Sense Impressions)

To be admissible under the Contemporaneous Declarations Exception (also called the Present Sense Impressions Exception) to the Hearsay Rule, the statement and the acts must occur at the same time (i.e., contemporaneously) and relate to the same event. There is no requirement, however, that the statements be made spontaneously. The statements will be admissible even if they are in response to a police officer's questions, such as "What are you doing?" and additional questions about what the person is doing, thinking, or feeling as the situation evolves. Communications with crisis intervention team members would qualify as long as they deal with current sensations. The same is true for a kidnapper's response to a hostage's questions or a written statement that the hostage taker prepared with the intent of reading it to the press. All of these statements may be edited (redacted) to remove portions that do not pertain to a present state of mind before they are presented in open court.

The Contemporaneous Declaration Exception covers answers to a list of questions that a patient prepared before going to the doctor. It applies to a person's recitation of current medical problems or attempts to explain the location of the pain and/or describe the type of pain the person is feeling. However, this exception to the Hearsay Rule would not cover statements about the past, such as the answer to the question, "When did the pain start?" The same would be true of psychological symptoms. The patient's response to a therapist's prompts would qualify, as would narrative as long as it focused on the current situation.

Definition

Contemporaneous Declaration Exception (Also Called Present Sense Impression Exception) to the Hearsay Rule*

A statement is admissible under the Contemporaneous Declaration Exception to the Hearsay Rule if

1. The statement describes or explains an event or condition made while the declarant was perceiving the event or condition, OR
2. The statement was made immediately after the declarant perceived the event or condition.

*Based on Federal Rules of Evidence, Rule 803(1).

Examples of Statements That Are Admissible under Contemporaneous Declaration (Also Called Present Sense Impression) Exception to the Hearsay Rule

- The doctor said, "I am going to have to operate to save your life."
- A man entered the bank and said, "This is a stick-up. Give me all the money."
- The victim said, "I'll give you the money; just don't shoot me!"

Examples of Statements That Are *Not* Admissible under the Contemporaneous Declaration (Also Called Present Sense Impression) Exception to the Hearsay Rule

- A woman told her friend, "I'm OK now, but I sure was scared this morning when that guy pointed the gun at me."

  This is not a contemporaneous declaration because the woman is telling her friend what happened earlier in the day.

- A man told his wife, "I look back on it, and it's awfully frightening thinking about how close I came to getting hit, but at the time I was pretty calm; all I thought about was grabbing that kid, pulling him to safety."

This is not contemporaneous. The man is trying to describe how he felt at the time he grabbed the kid, but that was in the past.

- A mother woke her child and gave him a hug, "Honey, you're OK. Mommy's here, you're safe. Don't cry. It was just a bad dream, no one's going to hurt you."

  This is not a contemporaneous declaration; the child was having a dream—the event never happened.

A statement may qualify under the Contemporaneous Declaration Exception to the Hearsay Rule and still not be admissible in court. If the statement is written in the doctor's notes or some other document, the document will need to be produced in court and be authenticated. If it is in a business record, someone from the records office will need to be called to testify about the process used to make the record. Another issue will arise if the declaration was made to an attorney, doctor, etc. because the statement may be privileged and at least one witness will need to waive the privilege before it can be introduced at trial (see Chapter 9).

Dying Declaration Exception (Also Called Statement under Belief of Impending Death; Declarant Must Be Unavailable)

The **dying declaration** is one of the oldest exceptions to the Hearsay Rule. It was based on the assumption that a person would not go to meet his Maker with a lie upon his lips. Hence, it was considered trustworthy. Obviously, not everyone is reluctant to use falsehoods at the moment of death, but the old assumption is still used to justify admitting the dying declaration into court.

The traditional rule allowed the use of dying declarations in criminal prosecutions of the declarant's killer but not in other criminal or civil trials. Over time, the admissibility of dying declarations was expanded to prosecution of crimes other than homicide and presentation in civil trials. The reasoning behind the expansion was that the trustworthiness of the dying declaration was based on the fear of imminent death. Therefore, the statement was equally trustworthy if, after making the statement, the person lived or died. Many states now allow dying declarations to be admitted into evidence in both criminal and civil trials. The Federal Rules (Rule 804(b)(2)) and a few states allow the statement to be used even if the declarant does not die.

Definition

Dying Declaration Exception (Also Called Statement under Belief of Impending Death) to the Hearsay Rule*

A statement is admissible in a homicide prosecution under the Dying Declaration Exception to the Hearsay Rule if

1. It was made when the declarant believed that death was imminent, AND
2. The statement concerned the cause or circumstances of what the declarant believed to be impending death.

Note: Many states add a third requirement: Declarant must die before trial.

*Based on Federal Rules of Evidence, Rule 804(b)(2).

Examples of Statements That Are Admissible under the Dying Declaration Exception to the Hearsay Rule
- The victim said, "I'm gonna die. That jerk, Peter, shot me."
- The victim said, "Get a priest. I need the Last Rites. John shot me after we had an argument over the money from the bank robbery."

Examples of Statements That Are *Not* Admissible under the Dying Declaration Exception to the Hearsay Rule
- A battered wife said, "He tried to kill me. I'm going to divorce that brute."

  This statement cannot be used as a dying declaration. The statement "I'm going to divorce that brute" indicates that she believes she will recover; therefore, this statement cannot be used as a dying declaration.

- The victim said, "I know I am dying. I want to confess to the bank robbery I committed last week and get it off my chest."

  This statement cannot be used as a dying declaration. The statement "I want to confess to the bank robbery I committed last week" indicates that the statement is not about the cause of death.

One of the keys to admissibility of dying declarations is the declarant's belief that he or she will die almost immediately. If the declarant has any hope of recovery, the statement will not fall under this exception. Neither will a statement that indicates the declarant believes death will not occur in the immediate future.

Dying declarations can only be about the events surrounding the death—usually it is a statement by the victim about who inflicted the fatal injury. Statements about past crimes or other things are not admissible unless the state expanded the rule. The declarant must speak from personal knowledge about things heard, seen, smelled, etc.

Another important aspect of the dying declaration is that the declarant must be mentally competent. Unlike the normal case in which only the competence of the person on the witness stand is at issue, in cases involving a dying declaration, both the hearsay declarant and the witness who is testifying must be mentally competent. Statements that qualify for this exception to the Hearsay Rule are treated the same as statements made in open court by a witness. If the dying person was in severe pain, under heavy medication, delusional, or exhibiting other signs of severe deterioration of his or her mental capacity, the question must be addressed.

Dying declarations do not have to be spontaneous. In fact, it is frequently necessary to ask the homicide victim questions in order to find out if he or she believes death is imminent. Questions regarding the crime are also allowed.

Mental or Physical State

The Mental or Physical State Exception to the Hearsay Rule is used to introduce statements made about mental, emotional, or physical states. The statement must relate to the declarant's mental, emotional, or physical state at the time the statement was made.

Definition

Mental or Physical State Exception to the Hearsay Rule*

A statement may be admissible under the Mental or Physical State Exception to the Hearsay Rule within the following guidelines:
1. A statement of the declarant's then existing state of mind, emotion, sensation, or physical condition (e.g., intent, plan, motive, design, mental feeling, pain, and bodily health) is admissible, but
2. A statement of memory or belief is not admissible to prove the fact remembered or believed.

   But a statement that relates to the execution, revocation, identification, or terms of declarant's will is admissible.

*Based on Federal Rules of Evidence, Rule 803(3).

Examples of Statements That Are Admissible under the Mental or Physical State Exception to the Hearsay Rule
- The robber said, "Give me your money or I will kill you."
- The battered woman screamed, "I hate you!"
- The torture victim repeatedly screamed, as if in extreme pain.

Examples of Statements That Are *Not* Admissible under the Mental or Physical State Exception to the Hearsay Rule
- A wife told her husband as she aimed a gun at him, "Do you remember how it used to be, back when we first got married, you were so gentle, always trying to make me smile?"

This does not qualify for the Mental or Physical State Exception because the wife is talking about mental state "back when we first got married."

- The paramedic asked the victim of a shooting who appeared to be gritting his teeth, "Do you want some pain medicine?" The man replied, "No, I'm no sissy."

This does not qualify for the Mental or Physical State Exception because the man is refusing to admit his current physical state.

- A paranoid boyfriend reads his girlfriend's homework for her fiction writing class, "I love him so much, I'd never hurt him!" and says, "You liar! You'd never hurt me! All you ever do is hurt me!"

This does not qualify for the Mental or Physical State Exception for two reasons: The girl supposedly wrote fiction, so the statement does not represent anyone's current mental state, and even if it did, it did not represent a current emotion—the essay had been written at some time in the past.

This exception to the Hearsay Rule is useful to show intent, plan, motive, design, emotions, pain, or health. The statement is admissible even if the declarant is available at the time of the trial. It must be noted that the statement is admitted to show that the declarant said it, but it is not admissible to show that what the declarant originally said was the truth.

Most states allow the admission of statements relating to physical or mental state that were made for the purpose of medical diagnosis or treatment. They must, of course, be relevant to the case. In some states, these statements are included in the Mental and Physical State Exception to the Hearsay Rule; in others, there is a separate exception for them. A few states have a separate exception to the Hearsay Rule for medical records. Where this does not exist, the issue of business records or public records must be addressed before they are admitted at trial. Another issue involved is whether or not the medical records can be excluded from evidence because they are privileged. Chapter 9 addresses this issue.

Statements showing irrational behavior are not usually admitted under the Mental or Physical State Exception to the Hearsay Rule. Although they are definitely relevant if the insanity defense is used, in most states they are not considered hearsay because they are not offered to show that what was said was true. In fact, they are offered to show just the opposite—that the declarant was irrational and did not know what was happening.

Business Records and Official Documents

Most businesses keep records on employees, inventory, customers, etc. A well-run business will have established procedures to collect this information, making it more trustworthy than information obtained by a less systematic method. Due to this apparent reliability, the **Business Records Exception** to the Hearsay Rule has been established. The same could be said for records maintained by many government agencies. Vital statistics (births, marriages, deaths, etc.) are a form of government record. However, they are normally treated separately because the record was filed with the appropriate government agency but in most cases a government employee did not participate in the event.

Business Records

The term *business* includes every kind of business, governmental activity, profession, or occupation and calling, whether conducted for profit or not. This is a very broad definition. Almost any organized activity can fit in it. It includes medical facilities (doctor's office, hospital, clinic, etc.), school (from preschool to university), the military and charities, as well as profit and nonprofit organizations.

Definition

Business Records Exception to the Hearsay Rule*

A document may be admissible under the Business Records Exception to the Hearsay Rule if

1. It is a memorandum, report, record, or data compilation, in any form, of acts, events, conditions, opinions, or diagnoses,
2. It was made at or near the time by, or from information transmitted by, a person with knowledge,
3. It is kept in the course of a regularly conducted business activity, and
4. It was the regular practice of that business activity to make the memorandum, report, record. or data compilation,
5. It is shown by the testimony of the custodian or other qualified witness, or by certification that complies with Rule 902(11), Rule 902(12), or a statute permitting certification,
6. The source of information or the method or circumstances of preparation does not indicate lack of trustworthiness.

Note: The term *business* as used in this paragraph includes business, institution, association, profession, occupation, and calling of every kind, whether or not conducted for profit.

*Based on Federal Rules of Evidence, Rule 803(6).

Examples of Statements That Are Admissible under the Business Records Exception to the Hearsay Rule

- Gun store records can be used to show that the defendant purchased the murder weapon several days prior to the death of the victim, thus showing premeditation.
- Time cards can be used to show that a person was at work on a specific day if the company mandates that its employees keep accurate time cards.

- Telephone records can be used to show that calls were made to the extortion victim from the defendant's telephone.

Examples of Statements That Are *Not* Admissible under the Business Records Exception to the Hearsay Rule

- Child pornography found on computer used by office manager is not admissible under Business Records Exception.

    These pictures are not admissible as business records because downloading them was not within the normal business use of the computer.

- A pile of sales records was found in a drawer in the accounting office.

    These sales records cannot be used as business records because normal business procedure calls for them to be entered into the "books"; leaving piles of them around the room is not part of normal business procedures.

- Records from the pharmacy showing that a client filled a prescription for a medicine that causes drowsiness.

    These records can be used to show that the client had a prescription filled but cannot be used to show that the person was under the influence of the medication at the time of the accident. Further evidence would need to be introduced showing that the person took the medicine on the day in question.

There are three keys to admissibility of a business record under the Federal Rules of Evidence. First, someone with firsthand knowledge must have made the record, or someone with firsthand information may communicate the information to another person who then includes it in a report. It is not necessary that the person who has firsthand information make the report. The Federal Rules of Evidence explicitly state that the report can be based on information transmitted by the person who has firsthand knowledge. Reports containing double hearsay, on the other hand, are not admissible. For example, the crime victim can tell the police officer what happened and then the police officer can include the information in the incident report. On the other hand, if someone approaches the police officer and reports what someone told him or her, it would be double hearsay if the officer included this in the incident report. Department policy will dictate what level of information should be in police reports. If the officer includes double hearsay in a report along with firsthand observations, the Business Records Exception requires excision of the portion of the report that is double hearsay, but the remainder of the report can be used in court.

The second key to admissibility is that the business record was made promptly after the event in question. The process for making "business records" includes filling out forms, writing reports, punching the keys of the cash register, making entries in a log book, adding an entry into a computer database, or dictating information to someone else, as well as a wide variety of other acts. Failure to make the record promptly makes the record less trustworthy, and therefore it is not admissible in court. One of the problems here is that there is no definition of "promptly"; therefore, there is no set length of time that makes the report untrustworthy. When the length of time it took to record the event is in question, lawyers for both sides will argue the case before the trial judge, and the judge will decide the issue. If the admission of the item is critical to the case, and the judge ruled against its introduction at trial, the post-trial appeal may raise the issue again. Allowing the trial judge the opportunity to rule on admissibility of the business record is important because issues cannot be raised for the first time on appeal.

Third, the records must be kept as a routine part of doing business. The procedures the business established must be followed. Even then, the court can rule information is not admissible if the opposing side is able to show that the business did "sloppy record keeping"—that is, it kept inadequate records, did not post entries promptly, allowed employees to abuse the record keeping function, or knew that fraudulent entries were entered into its records.

Another issue that may be raised when someone tries to introduce business records is that the record may have been made by someone who works for the company, but the record was not made in the "regular practice of that business activity." The advent of e-mail and text messaging has resulted in employees sending and receiving messages all day long. Telephone calls and voice mail messages raise the same issue. Some of these messages may qualify as business records, but many will not. The ones that are personal do not become business records because they are transmitted to a business or its employees, or they are saved on a business computer system.

One advantage of business records is that it is not necessary to have the person who made the record testify in court. Depending on how the business is organized and the type of record sought, the witness may be someone from personnel, accounting, or the records office. This person, called the "record custodian" in many codes, will testify about the methods used to make and record reports, as well as the security measures utilized to prevent tampering. Once it is established that the business has a reliable process for storing its records, the focus will shift to the particular record in question. The side offering the record into evidence will ask the record custodian the appropriate questions to establish that the report being introduced is a true copy of the original business record.

Business records can be used to establish many things. Some criminal cases, such as embezzlement, cannot be prosecuted without them. If a company keeps strict payroll records, the time card can be used to show that the employee was (or was not) at work at a given date and time. Hotel and airline records can be used to show that a person was at a given location on a given date. Although none of these is conclusive because someone could have used a false identity, the evidence can be admitted, and the other side will have to convince the jury that the defendant was (or was not) there.

Absence of a Business Record

If a company keeps good business records, the fact that it has no record of an event can be used as evidence that the event did not occur. For example, the fact that the defendant did not punch his time card can be used to show that he was not at work at that time. This is sometimes called **"negative hearsay."**

Definition

Absence of a Record Exception to the Hearsay Rule*

The fact that no record of an event was recorded in regularly made business records may be admitted into evidence to show that an event did not occur if
1. Evidence of a matter is not included in the memoranda, reports, records, or data compilations, in any form,
2. Records were kept in accordance with the provisions of paragraph (6)[Records of regularly conducted activity],
3. Absence of a record is used to prove the nonoccurrence or nonexistence of the matter,
4. The matter was of a kind of which a memorandum, report, record, or data compilation was regularly made and preserved,
5. The sources of information or other circumstances do not indicate lack of trustworthiness.

*Based on Federal Rules of Evidence, Rule 803(7).

Examples of Statements That Are Admissible under the Absence of Record Exception to the Hearsay Rule
- Cash register tape shows every item that was processed by the register. At the beginning of each transaction, the register prints the date and time. In a shoplifting case in which the defendant claims to have paid for the item, the tapes or computerized records from all registers in the store can be checked. If none of these sources show the item was purchased, this is proof that the defendant did not pay for the item in question.
- If the defendant works at a job that requires employees to "punch the clock" every time they report for work or leave, the fact that there is no record that the

defendant "punched the clock" can be used to show that the defendant was not at work on the date in question. The Court usually requires testimony about how the company handles time cards so the jurors will know how secure they are.

Examples of Statements That Are *Not* Admissible under the Absence of Record Exception to the Hearsay Rule

- Some companies are very lax about having employees "punch the clock" when reporting for work or leaving. For example, they may allow one employee to punch in for another employee when returning from lunch.

  In these circumstances, the fact that the defendant's time card had not been punched cannot be used in court to show that he or she was not at work because there was no systematic process that recorded attendance.

- Some teachers sporadically keep attendance.

  In these circumstances, the fact that the teacher did not put a mark beside a student's name cannot be used as evidence that the student was not in class on a particular day.

Public Records and Reports (Also Called Official Documents)

The Federal Rules of Evidence divide public records and reports into three categories. The first, "activities of the office or agency," covers a wide range of internal records and reports. Public agencies, ranging from the courts to the police department, the tax collector, and the dog catcher, are covered. Any report that these agencies make documenting their own activities falls in this category, much as the Business Records Exception covers reports a private agency makes in the normal course of business. On the other hand, any statement included in reports made by public agencies that is hearsay requires separate analysis. To be admissible, these embedded hearsay statements must be covered by some other exception to the Hearsay Rule. For example, if an officer records a dying declaration in a police report, the statements of the dying person are admissible under the Dying Declaration Exception, not the Public Records and Reports Exception.

Definition

Public Records and Reports Exception (Also Called Official Documents Exception) to the Hearsay Rule*

Records, reports, statements, or data compilations, in any form, of public offices or agencies, may be admissible under the Public Records and Reports Exception to the Hearsay Rule if they set forth

1. The activities of the office or agency, OR
2. Matters observed pursuant to duty imposed by law as to which matters there was a duty to report, excluding, however, in criminal cases matters observed by police officers and other law enforcement personnel, OR
3. In civil actions and proceedings and against the government in criminal cases, factual findings resulting from an investigation made pursuant to authority granted by law, unless the sources of information or other circumstances indicate lack of trustworthiness.

*Based on Federal Rules of Evidence, Rule 803(8)

Examples of Information Admissible under the Public Records and Reports Exception (Also Called Official Documents Exception) to the Hearsay Rule

- Police logs showing that Mary Jones reported domestic violence incidents on September 1, 2007; October 2, 2007; and November 3, 2007.
- Report by coroner's pathologist describing the autopsy that was done and stating that the unidentified person died at the hands of another.

Examples of Information *Not* Admissible under the Public Records and Reports Exception (Also Called Official Documents Exception) to the Hearsay Rule

- Statement in police report that says "Mary Smith told the undersigned officer that her sister Joy said that John Jones was having an affair with Lucy."

  This is double hearsay and is not made admissible by the fact that it is included in a public report.

- A neighbor submitted a report to Children's Protective Services alleging that Nancy Green neglected her children because Nancy's children went to school every day in January without jackets or lunch boxes.

  Mandatory Child Abuse Reporting Laws do not cover reports made by neighbors. Therefore, this is report is not a public report.

The second section of Federal Rule 803(8) does not apply to law enforcement agencies. This subsection covers mandatory reports filed with government agencies, not reports prepared by government employees about investigations they conducted. Child abuse reports, prepared by "mandatory reporters" and submitted to Children's Protective Services, fall into this category. The same is true of mandatory reports on elder abuse and also communicable disease reports that doctors, hospitals, and others are required to prepare. Individuals—doctors, nurses, teachers, day care workers, etc.—are mandated by state or federal law to prepare reports and forward them to specific government agencies. A "mandatory reporter" can be charged with a misdemeanor if he or she fails to report as required by law; this penalty is considered sufficient to make the reports trustworthy. Mandatory reports, prepared by hundreds or thousands of individuals who do not work for the government, thus become part of the files of numerous government agencies. These reports are covered by the Public Records and Reports Exception to the Hearsay Rule.

The third subsection of Rule 803(8) applies to the "factual findings resulting from an investigation made pursuant to authority granted by law." The result of this exception to the Hearsay Rule is that the reports of investigations conducted by government agencies may be admissible at trial. The agency could be the police department, coroner, grand jury, or any other department of a public agency that conducts investigations as a normal part of its operation. One caveat is attached to the admissibility of these investigative reports—that is, "unless the sources of information or other circumstances indicate lack of trustworthiness." The authors of the Federal Rules of Evidence put in a reminder that hearsay cannot be admitted into evidence if there is reason to doubt its trustworthiness. Their wording makes it clear that the report could lack trustworthiness because of the sources of the information or the way the investigation was conducted. This was a restatement of the standard rules that apply to hearsay, not a broad indictment of the way government conducts investigations.

Vital Statistics

"Vital statistics" are another form of government record. The most common documents in this category are certificates that record births, marriages, and deaths. Once again, the certificate is made by a person who conducts an activity as part of his or her profession—the practice of medicine or being a member of the clergy, for example—and files reports with the government about specific activities (delivering a baby, performing a marriage, etc.).

Definition

Records of Vital Statistics Exception to the Hearsay Rule*

Information from records of vital statistics is admissible under the Public Records Exception to the Hearsay Rule if it consists of
1. Records or data compilations, in any form,
2. Of births, fetal deaths, deaths, or marriages,
3. If the report thereof was made to a public office pursuant to requirements of law.

*Based on the Federal Rules of Evidence, Rule 803(9).

Examples of Vital Statistics That Are Admissible under the Vital Statistics Exception to the Hearsay Rule

- Marriage certificate filed with the county by a priest stating that he officiated at the marriage of John and Mary Jones on June 3, 2001.
- Death certificate filed with the county by Dr. Smith stating that he was present when Mary Jones died of a gunshot wound on December 4, 2007.
- Death certificate filed by Dr. Brown, deputy coroner for the county, stating his conclusion, after conducting the autopsy on Mary Jones, that she died at the hands of another (homicide).

Examples of Records That Are *Not* Admissible under the Vital Statistics Exception to the Hearsay Rule

- Certificate of marriage filed by Howard King.

  This marriage was determined to be void because Howard King was not a licensed member of the clergy.

- Birth certificate for Lonny Jordon was found in Dr. White's office after his death. Dr. White's executor filed it with the County Department of Vital Statistics.

  Birth certificate was not valid because Dr. White failed to sign it.

- Birth certificate of Nancy Black was proven to be no longer valid.

  Nancy Black was adopted on June 1, 2007, and as part of the adoption procedure, her original birth certificate was removed from vital statistics and replaced with one showing that she was the child of her adoptive parents.

Prior to 1900, very few states collected vital statistics. In the absence of legislatively established procedures, a variety of informal documents (written hearsay) were used when it was necessary to prove a person's age, marital status, and/or date of death. In the absence of such documentation, oral statements were admissible for these purposes. The most commonly used nongovernment sources were family Bibles or journals in which this information was recorded close to the time that the events occurred. Church records of baptisms, marriages, and funerals could be used to establish critical dates. Another source of vital statistics was U.S. Census records, which were compiled every 10 years, listing the names of the people living in the household and stating their ages.

Today, each state legislature has created a process that is used for maintaining vital statistics. Most mandate the forms that will be used and the procedures that must be followed. For example, the official birth certificate is completed by the doctor who delivered the baby, it is kept at the County Department of Vital Statistics, and a computer-readable copy is sent to the State Department of Vital Statistics. Other certificates may be prepared. For example, many hospitals give the parents an elaborate birth certificate.

The same is true for events held in churches, such as weddings and funerals. The family frequently assumes that the most elaborate certificate is the official one. This is not true. Only the one on a form mandated by the state qualifies for the Vital Statistics Exception to the Hearsay Rule. If the official form has been lost, other documents can be used to establish the event. Today, it is rare to resort to testimony of eye witnesses for information relating to births, marriages, and deaths.

Alternative procedures have been established for unusual occurrences. For example, in the aftermath of the September 11, 2001, terrorist attacks, many people were unaccounted for. Some investigators believed that the intensity of the initial explosion resulted in people being incinerated to unrecognizable ashes. It became obvious that an alternative procedure was needed so that the families that were left behind could go on with life, estates could be settled, and provisions could be made for business affairs. Bills were passed by the U.S. Congress and signed by the President that made provision for families to have a missing loved one officially declared dead.

In addition to establishing the procedures for recording vital statistics, it is important to establish a process for making duplicates that are acceptable in court. If each person who needed to establish a vital statistic were required to produce the original record, the integrity of the vital statistics files would be impinged. The possibility for lost records would be high. It would be easy to convince a jury that the absence of a document meant that the event never took place, when in reality the absence of the document meant that someone had removed the file and failed to return it. For this reason, the process for making certified copies was established. The process has been modified as more modern procedures have been introduced into the Vital Statistics Office.

Reputation

Reputation is what others say about someone. It is by its very nature hearsay. In fact, it is frequently nothing but gossip. Nonetheless, historically, there has been a hearsay exception for **reputation**. The terminology used is inconsistent. A "character witness" is called to testify about a person's reputation.

As a general rule, the character witness is not allowed to give his or her personal opinion about the person whose reputation is in question but should report on what the person's associates or the community thinks. "Associates" are the people who work with the person in question. "The community" refers to the residential and social community. These may be two completely different groups of people. (Refer to Chapter 4 for a discussion of when reputation is admissible.) A number of states now allow the witness to give his or her own opinion about the person's reputation or to cite specific incidents, but the Federal Rules of Evidence still follow the traditional rule.

Definition

Reputation Exception to the Hearsay Rule*

Statements are admissible under the Reputation Exception to the Hearsay Rule if they involve
1. Reputation of a person's character
2. Among associates or in the community.

*Based on Federal Rules of Evidence, Rule 803(21).

Examples of Statements That Are Admissible under the Reputation Exception to the Hearsay Rule

- Defense character witness said that defendant had a reputation in the community for being a peaceful, law-abiding person.
- Prosecution character witness said that defendant had a reputation among co-workers for being hot-tempered and violent.

Examples of Statements That Are *Not* Admissible under the Reputation Exception to the Hearsay Rule

- Character witness told jury her personal opinions about the defendant and cited incidents to support those opinions.

  Federal Rule allows testimony about reputation among associates or in the community, but it does not allow personal views of the character witness or testimony about specific incidents.

- Character witness told jury what the defendant's reputation was among other members of their fraternity while they were in college 10 years ago, but the witness admitted he had no current information about the defendant's character.

  Testimony about reputation in the fraternity would ordinarily be admissible, but when it is 10 years old and the witness has no recent information, the witness should not be allowed to testify.

The general rule is that the prosecution is not allowed to introduce testimony about the defendant's reputation. The purpose of this rule was to prevent the prosecution from asking the jury to infer that the defendant committed the crime because the criminal behavior charged would have been expected from a person with that reputation. The scene changes if the defendant introduces his or her own reputation into evidence. Since the defense opened the door to examine the defendant's reputation, the prosecution may call character witnesses to refute the ones the defendant called.

So far, we have talked about general character (e.g., the defendant is a nice guy who would not commit a crime). There are times when a specific character trait is in question because of the crime that has been alleged. If the defendant is on trial for a crime of violence, she might want to introduce character witnesses who testify that she has the reputation for being a very calm, nonviolent person. If the charge is theft, the defense may call a character witness who testifies that the defendant has the reputation for being a very honest person. The old rule applies: If the defense opens the door, then the prosecution can call witnesses who will testify that the defendant does not have the reputation the character witnesses claimed. Anyone who testifies as a character witness can be impeached. Ironically, a person who testifies that the defendant has a good reputation can be impeached based on his or her own bad reputation.

Occasionally, the reputation of the victim is at issue. This is most likely to happen when the defendant has been charged with an aggressive crime, such as aggravated battery, and is claiming that he was acting in self-defense. The defense would call character witnesses to testify that the victim had a reputation for being a bully and initiating fights. In cases in which a battered woman kills or seriously injures her batterer, the defense is frequently based on the prior violence that the victim has inflicted on the defendant. The defense may call character witnesses to help support the defendant's allegations.

Former Testimony (Witness Must Be Unavailable)

The **Former Testimony Exception** to the Hearsay Rule covers testimony taken under oath at a prior court appearance or other legislative authorized proceeding such as a deposition or arbitration proceeding. This is one of the easiest exceptions to the Hearsay Rule to justify. The statement was made under oath; therefore, it is considered trustworthy. The fact that the witness is no longer available makes the exception necessary. The use of this statement is restricted because the witness cannot be cross-examined. The jury will be deprived of the opportunity to watch the witness testify and observe possible signs of deception.

When this exception is used, the former testimony is introduced as evidence in the present case. If the former testimony is used to impeach, it comes in under the Prior Inconsistent Statement Exception to the Hearsay Rule.

In criminal cases, the Former Testimony Exception is most commonly used at trial to introduce testimony taken at the preliminary hearing. Testimony of any witness the defendant called at the preliminary hearing can be admitted by the prosecution. If it is the testimony of a prosecution witness, the defendant must have had the opportunity and motive to cross-examine. If the defense decided not to cross-examine, the testimony will still be admissible.

Definition

Former Testimony Exception to the Hearsay Rule*

A statement is admissible under the Former Testimony Exception to the Hearsay Rule if

1. Testimony was given as a witness

    a. at another hearing of the same proceeding OR

    b. in a different proceeding, OR

    c. in a deposition taken in compliance with law in the course of the same or another proceeding,

2. If the party against whom the testimony is now offered, or, in a civil action or proceeding, a predecessor in interest,

3. Had an opportunity and similar motive to develop the testimony by direct, cross, or redirect examination.

*Based on the Federal Rules of Evidence, Rule 804(b)(1).

Examples of Statements That Are Admissible under the Former Testimony Exception to the Hearsay Rule

- Transcript of testimony at preliminary hearing given by an elderly victim who died prior to trial.
- Transcript of testimony of defense witness at a prior trial. At the prior trial, this witness made statements indicating the defendant was not the person who committed the crime. The defendant was convicted in the prior trial. The conviction was reversed on appeal, and the case is currently being retried. The witness now refuses to testify.
- Transcript of testimony of prosecution witness at prior trial that ended in hung jury. The case is currently being retried. The prosecutor can introduced this transcript if the prosecution used due diligence but the witness could not be found.

Examples of Statements That Are *Not* Admissible under the Former Testimony Exception to the Hearsay Rule

- Eyewitness told the police that she saw the defendant hit the victim. The prosecutor wants to introduce the statement in the police report because the person who made the statement cannot be found.

To qualify for Former Testimony Exception to the Hearsay Rule, the statement must have been made under oath at a hearing designated in the code section. The statement in the police report was not made under oath; it was also not made at a hearing. Therefore, the statement in the police report is not admissible under the Former Testimony Exception to the Hearsay Rule.

- Transcript of prosecution witness at the preliminary hearing. The prosecution has made no effort to locate the witness.

This statement was made under oath at the prior hearing and the opposing side had the opportunity to cross-examine. The requirement that has not been met is that the witness is unavailable.

Testimony might also have come from a previous trial of the same case if there was a hung jury or the case was reversed on appeal. When there is more than one defendant, it is possible that the testimony came from the preliminary hearing of another defendant. In all of these situations, there must have been at least one defendant present with a motive to cross-examine that is similar to the motive of the current defendant.

Prior Inconsistent Statements

Prior inconsistent statements can be used to impeach a witness. When used for this purpose, opposing counsel asks questions about them during cross-examination (see Chapter 5). Many authorities on evidence claim that they are not hearsay because they are not offered to show that they are true. Instead, they are offered to show that the witness may not be telling the truth. The Federal Rules of Evidence (Rule 801(d)(1)(A)) and a number of states follow this approach. Some states list prior inconsistent statements as a separate exception to the Hearsay Rule, and for this reason they are discussed here. Under either approach, the prior statements are admissible.

The definition used in California Evidence Code Section 1235 is used to demonstrate how these statements are treated when they are considered evidence because there is no similar section in the Federal Rules of Evidence.

Definition

Prior Inconsistent Statements Exception to the Hearsay Rule*

Evidence of a statement made by a witness is admissible under the Prior Inconsistent Statements Exception to the Hearsay Rule if
1. Statement is inconsistent with his or her testimony at the hearing AND
2. Witness is given opportunity to explain inconsistency.

*Based on California Evidence Code Section 1235.

Examples of Statements That Are Admissible under Prior Inconsistent Statements Exception to Hearsay Rule

- Defendant gave Officer Green an alibi when questioned prior to arrest. On the witness stand, he gave a totally different account of where he was and denied having given the first alibi. Officer Green can be called to testify regarding what the defendant said.
- Defendant testified that she had never met the co-defendant prior to her arrest on February 10, 2007. On cross-examination she was asked if she remembered telling someone at her office on January 6, 2007, that the defendant was her new boyfriend. She admitted making the statement at her office. No other witness will be called regarding the statement.

Examples of Statements That Are *Not* Admissible under Prior Inconsistent Statements Exception to Hearsay Rule

- At trial the defendant gave an alibi that she had been at work when the robbery occurred. The prosecutor then asked the defendant why she refused to tell the officer about the alibi after being given *Miranda* warnings.

  The fact that the defendant refused to answer when given the *Miranda* warnings cannot be used as a prior inconsistent statement because the defendant had the right to refuse to talk to the officer.

- At trial the defendant refused to take the witness stand. The prosecutor wants to call witnesses to testify that the defendant told them that he had an alibi.

  The prosecutor had the right to introduce this information during the prosecution's case in chief. When the defendant does not take the stand, the prosecutor has no right to impeach the defendant.

If the witness admits the inconsistent statement, no other witnesses are called to impeach. However, if he or she denies making the statement, a witness may be called to restate what was said. The purpose of asking about the inconsistent statement first is to save court time. It also gives the witness a chance to explain if the statement has been taken out of context or is not accurate.

Identification made at pretrial lineup or showup procedures can be introduced as prior inconsistent statements if the person who made the identification at the pretrial procedure takes the stand and identifies a different person as the criminal. The same would be true if the person on the stand made an in-court identification of the defendant as the person who committed the crime but failed to identify the same person during a pretrial lineup.

Prior Consistent Statements

Prior consistent statements are used to rehabilitate a witness who has been impeached. The most common reason for using them is that the opposing side introduced prior inconsistent statements during cross-examination.

They can also be used if there is a charge that the witness recently fabricated his or her testimony, is biased, or has some other improper motive for testifying.

Prior consistent statements are offered to show that the person who is testifying made the statement, not that the statement is true. Rule 801(d)(1)(B) of the Federal Rules of Evidence and a number of states do not classify "prior consistent statements" as hearsay; other states consider them as hearsay but have an exception to the Hearsay Rule that allows these statements to be introduced at trial during redirect examination to rehabilitate a witness. Either way, the statements are admissible if the lawyer proposing that they be admitted correctly states the law when challenged by the opposition.

Prior consistent statements are discussed here because some states specifically list them as exceptions to the Hearsay Rule. The definition used in California Evidence Code Section 1236 is used to demonstrate how these statements are treated when they are considered evidence.

Definition

Prior Consistent Statements Exception to the Hearsay Rule*

1. Prior consistent statements are admissible if the statement is consistent with testimony by the present witness in this case AND

2. The consistent statement was made by the witness at this hearing

    a. Prior to the statement that was introduced to show inconsistent statements OR

    b. Prior to the express or implied charge that the testimony of this witness at this hearing has recently been fabricated

    OR

    c. Prior to the allegation that the witness at this hearing is influenced by bias or other improper motive AND

3. The statement was made before the inconsistent statement, bias, or motive for fabrication or other improper motive is alleged to have arisen.

*Based on California Evidence Code Section 1236.

Examples of Statements That Are Admissible under the Prior Consistent Statements Exception to the Hearsay Rule

• During cross-examination the prosecutor asked the witness questions designed to show that the defense witness altered his testimony due to a bribe he received on July 1, 2007.

On redirect the defense introduced a written statement made by the witness on May 3, 2007. Details of the document are the same as the testimony given during direct examination.

- During cross-examination the defense impeached the witness by showing that she was not able to identify the defendant at a police lineup.

  On redirect the prosecution was allowed to show that the witness had identified the defendant when the police took her to a showup the day before the lineup.

Examples of Statements That Are *Not* Admissible under the Prior Consistent Statements Exception to the Hearsay Rule

- On cross-examination, the defense introduced testimony that showed that the witness was a shareholder in the victim's company and would profit if the defendant was convicted because the stock would rise.

  In chambers, the prosecutor told the judge that he planned to introduce testimony that showed that stock in the victim's company had substantial gains during the period between the date of the alleged crime and the day the witness testified. At the defense's request, the judge ruled that testimony about the stock gains was not admissible because it did not address the issue of potential gains in the stock if the defendant was convicted.

- On October 22 during cross-examination, the prosecution successfully impeached the defense witness by asking questions about statements she made to the police on May 3. These statements were inconsistent with testimony the witness gave on October 20.

  At a conference in the judge's chambers, the defense informed the judge that he would ask questions during redirect about an entry in the witness's journal dated October 19 that was consistent with the testimony given on October 20. The prosecution objected to the testimony on the grounds that only journal entries dated before May 3, the date of the alleged crime, could be used to rehabilitate the witness. The judge ruled that the defense could not ask the proposed question during redirect.

Just as a prior inconsistent identification of a suspect at a lineup or showup can be used to impeach a trial witness, a prior consistent identification can be used to rehabilitate a witness. Care must be taken to use statements that fit the timeline (i.e., statements made prior to the "erroneous" identification). The same procedure may be used if there is an allegation that the witness was coached to identify the "correct" person or that the way the lineup was conducted led the witness to pick the wrong person; earlier consistent statements may be used to show that the person was able to identify the "correct" person prior to being coached or influenced by police misconduct.

Rehabilitating witnesses based on prior consistent statements is difficult unless there is a written, dated document that can be used for this purpose. Showing that a statement was made before the person who made it became biased or developed a bad motive is equally problematic. It is important to remember that rehabilitation occurs during redirect. Jurors are likely to become confused. Prior to attempting to rehabilitate a witness, it is important to consider how important the witness is to the total case and whether the jurors will be able to understand what the attorney is trying to prove.

Ancient Documents

The **Ancient Documents Exception** to the Hearsay Rule is necessary because after many years there is frequently no one available who can testify about the events that surrounded the making of the documents. This exception most commonly involves deeds and wills. The length of time to qualify for the Ancient Documents Exception varies and is usually set by the state's legislature. For example, both the Federal Rules and the Arizona Rules of Evidence require 20 years; Pennsylvania and Tennessee require 30 years.

Definitions

Ancient Documents Exception to the Hearsay Rule*

A record may be admissible under the Ancient Documents Exception to the Hearsay Rule if
1. Statement is in a document
2. The document was in existence for 20 years or more
3. Before the authenticity of the document is challenged.

*Based on Federal Rules of Evidence, Rule 803(16).

Examples of Documents That Are Admissible under the Ancient Documents Exception to the Hearsay Rule
- Deed dated 1975 showing that Sam Smith purchased a residential lot located at 123 Elm Street, Hometown, from John Doe. Deed does not appear to have been altered. Sam Smith and his family built a house and lived in it from 1975 until 2006.
- In a will dated 1945, Jane Doe gave land at 123 Elm Street, Hometown, to her son John. Will was probated without challenge and a deed was given to John.

Examples of Documents That Are *Not* Admissible under the Ancient Documents Exception to the Hearsay Rule
- In a will dated 1977, George Green disowned Gwendolyn, whom he treated as his favorite daughter, and gave his entire estate to Merry Widow, a woman none of George's family or friends had ever met or heard him talk about. George died in 2005. Merry Widow came to town with the will in 2007.

This will is more than 30 years old, but it will not be treated as an ancient document because the fact that all of his property was given to a complete stranger is not the normal way people handle their estates. It is also suspect because it was not kept in a location where George Green would have been likely to keep his will and was not probated in a timely manner.

- Merry Widow had a deed to George Green's house. George's heirs sent the deed to a forensics document examiner who discovered, among other things, that the name of the original grantee had been erased and Merry Widow's name had been typed over the erasure.

This deed did not appear genuine because of the erasure discovered by the forensic document examiner.

To qualify as an "ancient document," the document must appear to be genuine based on the observable characteristics of the document. Obviously, a document that has words crossed out will raise questions. Forensic tests may be performed to establish that the document could have been made at the time it is alleged to have been made. For example, suppose inkjet printers use unique ink. If one side of a law suit claims that the document was made in 1970, approximately 20 years before the inkjet printer was marketed, but the forensics lab could prove that the document was printed in a type of ink that is unique to inkjet printers, then the document will not be presumed to be valid under the Ancient Documents Exception to the Hearsay Rule. In this example, the differences in ink may not be observable to the naked eye, but tests from the forensics lab are permissible to establish this element of the Ancient Documents Exception.

One additional factor must be present in order for a document to qualify as an ancient document. The parties to the transaction must have acted as though the document was authentic. For example, a person normally lists friends and family members in a will. When a stranger's name appears in a rich man's will, the heirs will allege that the document is a forgery.

Past Recollection Recorded

The **Past Recollection Recorded Exception** to the Hearsay Rule can be used to introduce information even though the person who wrote it down can no longer remember the facts. Although it is unlikely that someone would forget the facts in a homicide investigation, it occurs at times with lesser crimes and traffic tickets.

The reason information in old reports is considered trustworthy is that the original report was accurately made near to the time the event occurred when memory was at its best. It does not have to be in the handwriting of the person who observed the event; it is also admissible if the report was dictated and someone else typed it.

Definition

Past Recollection Recorded Exception to the Hearsay Rule*

A written statement may be admissible into evidence under the Past Recollection Recorded Exception to the Hearsay Rule if

1. There is available a memorandum or record concerning a matter about which the witness once had knowledge AND
2. The witness now has insufficient recollection to enable the witness to testify fully and accurately AND
3. The document has been made or adopted by the witness AND
4. It was made when the matter was fresh in the witness's memory AND
5. It was made to reflect that knowledge correctly.

If admitted, the memorandum or record may be read into evidence but may not itself be received as an exhibit unless offered by an adverse party.

*Based on Federal Rules of Evidence, Rule 803(5).

Examples of Documents That Are Admissible under the Past Recollection Recorded Exception to the Hearsay Rule

- Police report for petty theft observed in progress by an officer. The officer has no current memory of the event. She testified that she always reviews her reports and corrects them before signing them. This report has been signed. Therefore, she can testify that the report is accurate.
- Notes that the witness made on a scrap of paper while talking to an extortionist on the telephone. He testified that he has blacked out the incident from his memory, but he remembers going over the demands twice and writing them down very carefully because the extortionist was threatening to kidnap his daughter.

Examples of Documents That Are *Not* Admissible under the Past Recollection Recorded Exception to the Hearsay Rule

- A robber handed the teller a demand note. The teller treated it as real and handed the person all the money that was in her drawer. The defendant, who allegedly committed the robbery, refused to take the witness stand.

  This document does not qualify for the Past Recollection Recorded Exception to the Hearsay Rule because the demand note was not written by the bank teller. The bank robber wrote the note.

- A police officer took a statement from the victim of the crime. She included the victim's statement in the incident report. At trial, the victim claimed he did not remember all the details. The prosecutor wants to introduce the police report under the Past Recollection Recorded Exception to the Hearsay Rule to establish the facts that the victim cannot remember.

  The reason the victim's statement in the police report cannot be introduced under the Past Recollection Recorded Exception is that the victim never adopted the police report, when the memory was fresh in his mind, as an accurate

representation of what he said. This police report might be admissible if offered
when the police officer who made it was on the stand if the officer could not testify
fully and accurately about the events in the police report.

As used here, a "report" is any writing. It includes both formal business
records and scraps of paper with notes written on them. Only things that
would otherwise be admissible can be admitted under this exception. In
other words, any parts of the report that are inadmissible hearsay, privileged, or not relevant would not be admissible.

A statement that a victim or witness made to the police may qualify
as past recollection recorded. The police report would need to pass two
tests. The officer who made the report would have to testify and meet
all the requirements for the Past Recollection Recorded Exception. The
person who made the hearsay statements that are included in the police
report would need to adopt them while these statements were fresh in his
or her memory. To do this, the officer would need to show the report, or
read it, to the person who made the statement and receive an affirmative
response to the question, "Is this an accurate report of what you told me?"
If the officer makes the report but does not run it by the person who made
the hearsay declaration, the Past Recollection Recorded Exception could
be used to admit personal observations of the officer if the officer had a
memory failure. The embedded hearsay could not to be used as "past recollection" of other people who had not adopted the report as accurate.

To use the Past Recollection Recorded Exception to the Hearsay Rule,
the trial witness must have little or no memory of the incident and at the
same time testify that the report is accurate. This sounds like a contradiction. The way it is accomplished in court is to show that the person testifying has a habit of making accurate reports. The prosecutor would ask a
police officer a series of questions, such as the following:

Prosecutor: Do you remember the facts in this case?
Officer: No, I went over my notes last night, but I have no indepen-
             dent memory of the events.
Prosecutor: Officer, when you write a report, do you automatically sign it?
Officer: No, I always re-read what I wrote to make sure it is correct.
             If I find any errors, I correct them before I sign it.
Prosecutor: I am handing you a report dated January 2, 2007. Did you
             write this report?
Officer: Yes, I did. That is my signature.
Prosecutor: Is this report accurate?
Officer: As I said, I have no independent memory of the events, but I
             signed the report. Therefore I know I reviewed it, and corrected
             any errors. I made sure it was accurate before I signed it.

At one time, most courts required that the witness have no memory at all about the incident. Now the more common view is that the witness has insufficient memory to be able to testify fully and accurately. The judge, of course, will determine when this occurs.

Once something has been ruled admissible as past recollection recorded, the report is read into the record. The document is not given to the jury unless the opposing side requests that the jury be allowed to see it. Allowing the jury to use it as an exhibit is believed to give the contents of the report more weight than it deserves.

Summary

The Hearsay Rule reflects the tremendous faith we put in our juries. By watching the witness testify under oath, the jury is expected to determine who is telling the truth. Out-of-court statements are therefore disfavored. Strict enforcement of this rule would be impractical, so many exceptions have been allowed.

One of the most important exceptions in criminal cases is the Admissions Exception, which allows the defendant's statements to be introduced. This includes statements of co-conspirators.

Statements people make against their own financial interest or that could cause them to be criminally prosecuted are admissible as a declaration against interest. These can only be used if the declarant is unavailable at trial.

Dying declarations cover statements made by a homicide victim after the fatal wound was inflicted. The declarant must believe that death is imminent. The statement must relate to the circumstances of the homicide; it typically identifies the person who inflicted the mortal injury.

Statements a person makes that accompany what he or she is doing or has just observed can be admitted under one of three exceptions: Spontaneous Statements, Contemporaneous Declarations, and Mental and Physical State. The lack of time to think up self-serving statements is considered to make these statements trustworthy.

The Business Records and Public Documents exceptions cover all types of records kept in the course of business and government as long as established procedures for recording events promptly have been complied with. Vital statistics, such as birth, marriage, and death records that the law requires doctors, the clergy, and others to report to the government, are also covered. The Past Recollection Recorded Exception also recognizes the value of good record keeping. This is helpful when the witness cannot remember an event. If accurate notes were made at the time of the event, the notes may be read to the jury.

The Former Testimony Exception permits the introduction of testimony previously taken under oath when the declarant is no longer available.

The Prior Inconsistent Statements Exception and Prior Consistent Statements Exception permit the introduction of statements for impeachment and rehabilitation.

The Ancient Documents Exception makes it possible to introduce old documents without trying to find witnesses from 20 or 30 years ago.

Review Questions

1. Define *hearsay*, and explain the rationale behind the Hearsay Rule.
2. Who is the declarant? List three exceptions to the Hearsay Rule that require the declarant to be unavailable.
3. What is an adoptive admission, and how does it differ from an authorized admission?
4. What types of interests are covered by declaration against interest?
5. What is a spontaneous declaration? Do contemporaneous statements have to be spontaneous?
6. When are statements of a person's mental state admissible?
7. What types of businesses are covered by the Business Records Exception? What types of public records are admissible hearsay?
8. What is admissible to show reputation?
9. What facts must be established at trial before an attorney can introduce the transcript of a witness's testimony at the preliminary hearing?
10. What must be shown before a prior inconsistent statement can be introduced?
11. List two situations in which prior consistent statements can be introduced at trial.
12. How old must a document be to qualify for the Ancient Documents Exception?
13. When is the Past Recollection Recorded Exception to the Hearsay Rule used?
14. What must the prosecutor show before a police report can be read to the jury under the Past Recollection Recorded Exception?

Writing Assignment

Go to www.cnn.com/crime and
1. Find a case that is currently on trial. Write a one-page (250-word) report on what has occurred in that trial during the past week and list the hearsay statements that were admitted at trial and identify which exception to the hearsay rule was used to admit them at trial.
OR
2. Find a case that has not gone to court and write a one-page (250-word) report analyzing the statements in the report and identify the hearsay exception that will let the statement into evidence at trial. Also list any hearsay statements that you do not think will be admitted due to the Hearsay Rule and explain why you drew that conclusion.

CHAPTER 9

Privileged Communications

Feature Case: President Bush Claims Executive Privilege

Between 2001 and 2007, the Bush administration has been widely seen as one of the most secretive and resistant to outside scrutiny in modern times. It has invoked executive privilege to prevent disclosure of its internal deliberations. The Bush administration claimed executive privilege as the reason it refused to relinquish documents during an investigation of a FBI regional office, documents related to the granting of pardons, and documents and testimony regarding the firing of nine United States attorneys. Vice President Cheney refused to release information regarding the development of his energy plan and other activities, and declared that neither Congress nor the executive branch had the power to inquire into his activities.

—Peter Nicholas, *Los Angeles Times*, July 29, 2007, Section A, p. 17

Learning Objectives

After studying this chapter, you will be able to

- Explain why the law regarding privileges allows relevant information to be excluded from trial.
- Identify conversations between an attorney and client that are privileged.
- List the privileges that apply to confidential communications between husband and wife.
- Recognize the privilege not to testify against one's spouse.
- Explain the physician–patient and clergy–penitent privilege.
- Describe the purpose and function of the police–informer privilege.
- Identify the reasons for considering police personnel files privileged.
- Describe what information obtained by the media is privileged.

Key Terms

- Attorney–client privilege
- Clergy–penitent privilege
- Confidential communication
- Executive privilege
- Husband–wife privileges
- News media privilege
- Physician–patient privilege
- Police informant privilege
- Police personnel files privilege

Myths about Privileges	Facts about Privileges
The privileges that we use in court today have been in use in the English court system since the Middle Ages.	A few of the privileges we use today have been in use in the English courts since the Middle Ages, but most of them were constructed fairly recently.
The priest–penitent privilege violates the First Amendment ban on government-sanctioned religion.	The priest–penitent privilege treats all religions in the same manner; therefore, it does not violate the Establishment Clause of the First Amendment.
The attorney–client privilege protects all conversations that a criminal suspect has with an attorney from disclosure in court.	The attorney–client privilege only applies to confidential communications. If the attorney meets a client in a public place and takes no precautions to keep the conversation from being overheard, the conversation will not be privileged because it was not confidential.
The doctor–patient privilege is superior to any law that mandates reporting of information to the government.	As long as there is a rational public health reason for requiring doctors to report their observations, conversations with patients, or lab test results, mandatory reporting laws will be upheld.

Basis for Privileges

Our legal system operates on the basic concept that what a person says can be used against him or her. One well-known exception is the privilege against self-incrimination (see Chapter 14). Another major exception is that privileged communications are excluded from evidence.

Over several centuries society has determined that there are certain relationships where it is important to maintain and encourage confidentiality. For example, in order to promote honest communications within a marriage, a husband–wife privilege was developed under common law. No matter how relevant the defendant's statement to his or her spouse may be, it is not admissible without the defendant's permission. Total confidentiality, however, would be contrary to public policy in some situations—for example, if the husband attempted to kill the wife. Therefore, exceptions were developed to make such statements admissible.

When a privilege is established, there is a corresponding rule that the holder of the privilege cannot be punished for invoking the privilege. The U.S. Supreme Court made this point in *Griffin v. California* 380 U.S. 609 (1965) by refusing to allow prosecutors to comment on the fact that a defendant had invoked the right to remain silent. It would be unjust to lead a jury to conclude that the only reason for invoking the privilege is that the defendant had something to hide.

The Federal Rules of Evidence say very little on the topic of privileges. Rule 501 is the only applicable rule. This rule acknowledges the power of the U.S. Constitution, statutes enacted by Congress, and rules needed to implement decisions of the U.S. Supreme Court to create privileges. When none of these apply, Rule 501 relies on the "principles of the common law as they may be interpreted by the courts of the United States in the light of reason and experience" to determine what relationships are privileged. Unlike hearsay, for example, there is no itemized list of privileges.

Two things must be shown in order to utilize privileges: (1) There must be a **confidential communication** and (2) the appropriate relationship must have existed between the parties.

Basic Rules for Privileged Communications
1. Statements must be made in circumstances that indicate confidentiality is expected.
2. Relationship between the individuals must be recognized as entitled to privilege.
3. Parties must not reveal confidential statements to others.
4. Privileged communications are admissible only if there is an exception to the privilege that covers the type of communication in question.

Other Evidentiary Rules That Must Be Considered
1. Statement must be relevant.
2. All privileged communications are hearsay.
3. Statements are admitted into evidence only if covered by an exception to the Hearsay Rule.
4. If the privileged communication is in writing:
   - Must authenticate the document.
   - Must satisfy rules on admitting contents of documents.

Although we usually think of privileged conversations, the rules extend to both oral and written communications including telephone calls and e-mail. The term *conversation* will frequently be used in this chapter to mean both oral statements and written communications. Confidentiality can be shown by the fact that two people excluded everyone else from the room while they talked or otherwise made an effort to keep anyone from overhearing what was said. On the other hand, if they were shouting at each other and someone heard the conversation, no privilege would apply. Written communications are confidential if delivered in sealed envelopes and stored in a manner so that others cannot see them; confidential material sent by fax or e-mail usually has a cover sheet stating that the information is privileged.

A person can voluntarily give up (waive) a privilege. Most commonly, this is done by revealing the privileged information to a third party. For example, if someone tells a friend all the details of a conversation he had with his attorney, the attorney–client privilege is waived. When a witness is called and voluntarily testifies to privileged communications, the privilege is considered waived both for the current and the future proceedings. There is one exception. If a trial witness claims a privilege and the judge incorrectly rules that the privilege does not apply, the witness must testify but the privilege is not waived.

Throughout the years, other privileges have developed that are not based on the idea that a close relationship requires confidential communication. Two of these involve law enforcement agencies: (1) The identity of police informants is frequently considered confidential, and (2) police personnel records are considered privileged. Only in special circumstances can these two types of information be used in court.

One of the newest privileges involves the news media. The U.S. Supreme Court has denied that there is a constitutional privilege for the press, but many states have statutory privileges that enable the media to protect their sources of information.

Communications covered by the various privileges are also hearsay. If an exception to the privilege applies, the communication is not automatically admissible. There must be both an exception to the privilege and an exception

TABLE **9-1** Comparison of Admissibility of Hearsay and Privileges

	Opposing Side Made a Contemporaneous Objection	Opposing Side Did Not Make a Contemporaneous Objection
Privilege— no exception applies	Statement is NOT admitted into evidence	Statement is admitted into evidence
Privilege— exception applies	Statement is admitted into evidence	Statement is admitted into evidence
Hearsay—no exception applies	Statement is NOT admitted into evidence	Statement is admitted into evidence
Hearsay— exception applies	Statement is admitted into evidence	Statement is admitted into evidence

to the hearsay rule before the information can be used in court. On the other hand, failure to make a contemporaneous objection when there is no applicable reason for admitting the statement will result in the statement being admitted into evidence when it should have been excluded. See Table 9-1.

At common law there were very few privileges. Gradually, however, state legislatures added new ones. Congress followed suit. This chapter discusses the most commonly used privileges. Students are encouraged to review their local laws and find out what privileges apply in their jurisdiction.

Attorney–Client Privilege

The **attorney–client privilege** dates back to the time of Elizabeth I in England and is firmly established in common law. It is based on the concept that an attorney cannot properly handle a case without full disclosure of the facts by a client.

The initial consultation is covered even if the client decides not to hire the attorney. Privilege does not depend on the payment of a fee for the lawyer's services. The privilege applies to conversations with a court-appointed attorney. If payment is received, it also does not matter who paid the lawyer. For example, if a father hires an attorney to represent his son, the son has the privilege—not the father. This is true even if the son is a minor.

Because the client is the holder of the privilege, the client can prevent the attorney from disclosing privileged information. Most states require the attorney to invoke the privilege unless the client has specifically ordered it waived. Many require the waiver to be in writing or made while the client is testifying at trial.

Attorney–Client Privilege Described

Attorney: A person the client reasonably believes is licensed to practice law. The fact that the attorney is not actually licensed does not invalidate the privilege.

Client: A person who consults with an attorney for the purpose of obtaining legal advice.

What is covered: Confidential communications between attorney and client regarding the legal services sought. Consultation in furtherance of future crimes is not privileged.

Who holds privilege: Client.

Exceptions to the privilege frequently found in criminal cases: Attorney's opinion sought to help a person commit a crime or escape punishment.

Examples of Use of Attorney–Client Privilege

- Defendant confessed to his defense attorney that he committed the crime.
- Defendant visited an attorney, outlined his case, and then decided to hire a different attorney.
- Business owner visited her attorney, outlined future business plans, and asked if the plans were legal.
- Man went to attorney, told about many personal problems, and asked for advice about filing for a divorce.
- Owner of a failing business went to attorney in order to file bankruptcy. During conversation a number of questionable business practices were revealed that did not amount to fraud.

The client must be seeking legal advice. Discussions with a lawyer as a business advisor, or as a friend, are not privileged. The more common view is that both what the client said and what the lawyer said are privileged. The lawyer can be compelled to give the names of clients and the dates the consultations occurred but not the reasons legal advice was sought. In most states, the privilege continues to exist even after the death of the client.

The privilege applies to communications between the attorney and client. What the attorney observed is not privileged. In a California case, the prosecutor wanted to call the defendant's former attorney as a lay witness to testify that when she was at the scene shortly after the crime, she saw the defense forensic expert pick up a small piece of evidence. The item was not listed in any of the expert's reports. No one else observed the incident. The appellate court ordered the attorney to testify about what she saw.[1] The decision was based on the fact that the testimony would not reveal any communication with the client; the fact that she was no longer the attorney in the case had no bearing on the outcome of the appeal.

To qualify as confidential communications, normally only the attorney and the client are present. The privilege will not apply if the client has a friend present while talking to the attorney unless some other privilege applies. For example, if a husband brought his wife with him when he visited an attorney, the husband–wife privilege would also apply.

There is another exception to the rule that prohibits extra people from participating in an attorney–client conference. Members of the attorney's office staff may be present during the interview and may have access to the case files. The work of secretaries, administrative personnel, law clerks, and paralegals is necessary to prepare court documents, conduct legal research, and summarize documents needed for trial. This exception also applies to expert witness(es) whom the attorney has retained for the case. It will be necessary for the attorney and the expert to discuss test results and other relevant issues while preparing for trial.

The privilege only applies to communications regarding legal services. The client cannot stretch the privilege by asking the attorney to hide incriminating physical evidence. For example, if a defendant hires an attorney to defend him on a robbery charge, their conversation regarding the robbery is privileged. However, if the client gives the attorney the gun used in the robbery, the gun will not be privileged. If the attorney becomes actively involved in concealing evidence, the attorney may face criminal charges as an accessory to the crime.

Although our legal system respects the right of every criminal defendant to have legal counsel at trial, it does not extend the attorney–client privilege to planning crimes or helping the client commit crimes. Arranging to have perjured testimony given at trial falls in this category. Not only is there no privilege for arranging for perjured testimony but also the attorney can be charged with a felony for doing so.

A controversial new exception to the attorney–client privilege has emerged. It applies if the attorney has reason to believe that the client will inflict serious bodily harm or death on a specific person in the near future. A few states impose a duty on attorneys to warn the person who is in danger and/or notify authorities. Once these warnings have been made, the confidentiality between attorney and client is broken and the same information can be introduced against the client in court.

Husband–Wife Privilege

In very early common law, neither the parties to the case nor their spouses were allowed to testify. The current version of the privilege emerged in approximately 1850. There are now two **husband–wife privileges.** One protects confidential communications between husband and wife that are made during the marriage. The other applies when one spouse is called to testify in court against the other.

The privilege for confidential communications between husband and wife restricts courtroom use of statements made in confidence during the marriage. It applies only if there is a valid marriage; most states apply the privilege to couples who are legally married even though they are not living together. The same states may refuse to apply this privilege to people who are living together but are not legally married. Some states officially recognize common-law marriages; in these states, the privilege also applies to parties to a valid common-law marriage. To date, the courts have refused to extend the privilege to couples who are merely living together unless they have a valid common-law marriage.

Husband–Wife Privilege for Confidential Communications Described

Husband and wife: Valid marriage is required. In states recognizing common-law marriages, parties to valid common-law marriage are covered.
What is covered: Confidential communications made during the marriage.
Who holds privilege: Both husband and wife. Either one can invoke it.
Exceptions to the privilege frequently found in criminal cases:

- Crimes one spouse committed against the other spouse.
- Crimes one spouse committed against the children of either spouse.
- Failure to support a spouse or a child.
- Bigamy.

Examples of Use of Husband–Wife Privilege for Confidential Communications

- While in the living room with no one there except his wife, the husband said, "I don't trust John. We just finished that job and I think he is planning on stealing the money from me."
- Wife whispered to husband, "I'm tired of you flirting with Mary. I'll get even with you someday."

Examples of When the Husband–Wife Privilege for Confidential Communications Would *Not* Apply

- After having a confidential conversation with his wife, the husband went to work the next day and told everybody what his wife had said.
- The night before their wedding, the bride told the groom about her inheritance while they were alone.

Approximately half of the states hold that confidential conversations that occurred during the marriage remain privileged even after the marriage has ended. In these states, a widow can refuse to disclose privileged conversations she had with her husband prior to his death. The same is true for divorced couples: They do not have to disclose confidential conversations they had during their marriage and they can prevent the former spouse from doing so in court.

The privilege covers all forms of communications (letters, phone calls, conversations, etc.) between husband and wife. They must, however, be made in a confidential situation. The presence of other family members, except for very young children, will usually defeat the privilege. The privilege is waived if the conversation is overheard because the husband and wife were in a public place, they are shouting at each other and could be heard by anyone in the area, or if personal letters, e-mails, or other documents were left where someone else could read them.

Many states hold that the privilege applies to actions as well as words. For example, if the wife saw her husband hide items stolen during a burglary, this would be considered privileged in states holding that actions are privileged.

Both husband and wife hold the privilege to refuse to disclose communications with a spouse and to prevent the spouse from disclosing those communications in court. Although the normal rule is that a privileged communication that has been disclosed to a third party is no longer privileged, the husband–wife privilege is not waived because one spouse betrayed the confidence by disclosing information. Only the spouse who disclosed the information has waived (given up) the privilege.

The policy reason for the privilege is that requiring one spouse to testify against the other would damage the marital relationship. The exceptions generally cover those situations in which the marriage is probably beyond repair.

There are several obvious situations in which the privilege cannot be applied. If one spouse commits a crime against the other, such as domestic violence, there is no public policy reason for preventing the victim from testifying. This is also true if either spouse victimizes any of the children in the family. If one spouse is charged with neglect or desertion of the family, the privilege is also waived. The same is true in bigamy cases. Many states also have exceptions to the privilege for planning crimes. This applies if one spouse told the other about his or her plans to commit a crime as well as situations in which both husband and wife were planning to commit a crime together. If a husband and wife are charged with conspiracy, either spouse may testify against the other.

The second husband–wife privilege is the privilege not to testify. This issue is raised when one spouse is on trial and the other is being called as a witness. To invoke the privilege, the parties must show that they are currently married. The privilege ends when the marriage ends.

Husband–Wife Privilege Not to Testify against Each Other Described

Husband and wife: Valid marriage is required. In states recognizing common-law marriages, parties to valid common-law marriage are covered.

What is covered: Testifying in court.

Who holds privilege: Legislature or case law designates which spouse holds this privilege; the most common rule is that the spouse who is being called to testify holds the privilege.

Exceptions frequently found in criminal cases:

- Crimes committed by one spouse against the other spouse.
- Crimes committed by one spouse against the children of either spouse.
- Failure to support a spouse or child.
- Bigamy.

Examples of Use of Husband–Wife Privilege Not to Testify against Each Other

- In states where spouse holds the privilege not to take the witness stand:

  Husband is on trial for robbery and wife is subpoenaed to testify. Wife may assert the privilege and refuse to take the witness stand.

- In states where defendant holds privilege to prevent spouse from taking witness stand:

  Husband is on trial for burglary. Prosecution subpoenaed wife to testify. Husband can assert the privilege and block wife from taking the witness stand.

Examples of When Husband–Wife Privilege Not to Testify against Each Other Would *Not* Apply

- In states where spouse holds the privilege not to take the witness stand:

  Husband is on trial for beating his wife. She does not want to take the witness stand and testify about the beating. Wife may not assert the privilege and refuse to take the witness stand because domestic violence is a crime for which the privilege does not apply.

- In states where defendant holds privilege to prevent spouse from taking witness stand:

  Husband is on trial for child abuse. Prosecution subpoenaed wife to testify. Husband cannot assert the privilege and block wife from taking the witness stand because child abuse is on the list of crimes for which the privilege does not apply.

There is considerable variation between the states with regard to who holds the privilege not to testify. Some jurisdictions allow the spouse who has been subpoenaed to refuse to testify; others allow the defendant to prevent his or her spouse from taking the witness stand. Several states do not recognize the testimonial privilege as separate from the confidential marital communication privilege.

The exceptions to the testimonial privilege are basically the same as those applicable to the confidential marital communication privilege. The same policy reasons apply. Some states do not allow this privilege to be invoked if the defendant got married for the purpose of preventing the new spouse from testifying.

A key distinction between the confidential communication privilege and the privilege not to testify is that the latter privilege is used to keep someone from taking the witness stand. The side that intends to invoke the privilege should notify the judge of this decision before the spouse is called as a witness. A hearing is held without the jury present. After each side argues its case, the judge rules on whether or not the spouse should take the stand. If the judge rules that the privilege not to testify applies, the witness is not sworn in. The jury is not told that the issue arose.

There must be a valid marriage on the date the privilege not to testify against a spouse is invoked. It does not matter whether the testimony would have been about events that occurred during the marriage or not. On the other hand, the confidential communication privilege prevents testimony about conversations that occurred during the marriage. In most states, the status of the marriage at the time of the court appearance is not important. Both privileges frequently apply; the result is that the spouse does not take the witness stand. See Table 9-2.

Physician–Patient Privilege

The **physician–patient privilege** did not exist at common law. It first appeared in a New York statute in 1828. Despite this fact, some of the federal courts allow evidence to be excluded under this privilege. Some recent cases also exclude physician–patient communications under the constitutional right of privacy.

In many ways, this privilege is similar to the attorney–client privilege. The patient is protected as long as there was a reasonable belief that the physician was licensed to practice medicine. The reason for the privilege is the belief that the doctor cannot adequately care for the patient unless he or she has complete information about the patient's condition. The privilege makes it more likely that the patient will be completely honest

TABLE **9-2** **Comparison of Privilege for Confidential Communications between Husband and Wife Versus Privilege Not to Testify against a Spouse**

	Confidential Communications between Husband and Wife*	Privilege Not to Testify against a Spouse
Statement boyfriend made to girlfriend in confidential setting—before they were married	N/A—not married	Applies if they are married* at the time the spouse is called to testify
Statement boyfriend made to girlfriend—not in confidential setting—before were married	N/A—not married and not confidential	Applies if they are married* at the time the spouse is called to testify
One spouse made a statement to the other spouse in confidential setting	Applies if they were married when the statement was made	Applies if they are married* at the time the spouse is called to testify
Statement one spouse made to the other spouse—not in confidential setting	N/A—not confidential	Applies if they are married* at the time the spouse is called to testify
Statement one spouse made to the other spouse in a confidential setting—they are now divorced	Applies if they were married when the statement was made	N/A—they were divorced at the time the spouse was called to testify
Statement one spouse made to the other spouse—not in confidential setting—they are now divorced	N/A—not confidential	N/A—they were divorced at the time the spouse was called to testify

* A legally valid marriage is required; in states that recognize common-law marriage, the relationship must qualify as a common-law marriage.

with the doctor. Although the definition varies slightly from state to state, it usually includes M.D.s as well as osteopaths, chiropractors, and possibly others. The doctor can be ordered to give names of patients and the dates that they consulted the doctor (but no information about their conversations) even if the communications are privileged.

Physician–Patient Privilege Described

Physician: Person reasonably believed by the patient to be licensed to practice medicine.

Patient: Person who consulted physician for purpose of diagnosis or treatment.

What is covered: Information obtained by the physician for the purpose of diagnosis or treatment of the patient.

Who holds the privilege: Patient.

Exceptions frequently found in criminal cases:

- Advice sought on how to conceal a crime.
- Advice sought to help plan crime.
- Information physician is required by law to report to authorities.

Notes
1. Some states do not allow the physician–patient privilege to be used in criminal cases.
2. If state law mandates that the doctor report a particular incident, the privilege does not apply in those cases. Incidents that must be reported vary from state to state; common examples are child abuse, gunshot wounds, etc.

Examples of Use of Physician–Patient Privilege
- Woman who had numerous lacerations and bruises went to doctor for treatment. When doctor asked how she sustained the injuries, she stated that she had been hiking and had a bad fall.
- Woman went to doctor for a HIV test. When asked why she wanted to be tested, she stated that she had been raped.
- Man told his doctor that he had not been sleeping well and that he was hearing voices telling him to attack people who went into an abortion clinic.

Examples of Situations *Not* Covered by Physician–Patient Privilege
- Blood and urine tests requested by the police in cases involving driving under the influence of alcohol.
- Blood tests done to obtain marriage licenses.
- Physical examinations done in order to obtain insurance.
- Court-ordered medical exams.
- Examinations done at the request of an attorney so that an expert witness can testify at trial.

Like the attorney–client privilege, the physician–patient privilege only exists if the physician and patient make reasonable attempts to keep the information confidential. Some states consider conversations privileged even though the patient is accompanied by a close family member. However, the presence of other people during the consultation will result in the information not being privileged unless some other privilege is involved. If the patient is accompanied by a spouse, the privilege for confidential communications between husband and wife would apply, but this privilege would not apply if an unmarried couple went to the doctor together.

The presence of a medical assistant during the examination does not violate the physician–patient privilege, and neither would the fact that the patient was sent to a laboratory for tests. It is also considered necessary for a member of the clerical staff to type the medical reports and someone to bill the insurance company. Much of this has been taken for granted, but recent federal laws mandate that patients be given information about their privacy rights.

Many states make information obtained by the physician privileged, rather than restricting the privilege to communications between the physician and patient. "Information" refers to what the doctor observed during the examination, such as bruises, as well as what the patient told the doctor.

The law recognizes that there are a variety of situations in which a person goes to a doctor. The only ones that are normally privileged are those in which the patient is seeking diagnosis or treatment. This includes referrals for a "second opinion." Consultation for purposes of giving the information to someone else, such as a physical exam required by the patient's employer, are not covered because the original intent was to disclose the information to someone else. Autopsy results are not usually covered by the privilege. This is based on the idea that a patient must be a living person; an alternative explanation is that autopsies are frequently mandated by state law when a person dies under suspicious circumstances. These reports were prepared to determine the cause of death and are made for the benefit of the state.

The physician–patient privilege belongs to the patient. If a doctor is on the witness stand and is asked about a privileged conversation, the doctor should assert the privilege on behalf of the patient. If the patient testifies in court that he or she waives the privilege, the doctor will answer the questions. The patient can claim the privilege even if the physician has died or the medical practice has been sold. The privilege also continues after the death of the patient.

Some states do not allow the physician–patient privilege to be used in criminal proceedings. In states that do not go so far as to abolish the privilege in criminal trials, the states may have an exception to the physician–patient privilege that applies when doctors help plan or conceal a crime. When a patient meets with a doctor for these purposes, the doctor can be compelled to testify about it in court. For example, plastic surgery used to help a suspect avoid arrest would not be privileged. Consultations regarding altering fingerprints would not be privileged. In some instances, the doctor has been charged as an accessory to the crime. The problem with this approach is that the doctor could claim the Fifth Amendment and refuse to testify.

Many states require doctors to report gunshot wounds, fetal deaths, sexually transmitted diseases, child abuse, and a variety of other things. The privilege cannot be used as a reason for not reporting, when the law mandates the event be reported. In these circumstances, the doctor can also be required to testify in court about the incident. Many states make it possible to charge a doctor or other mandated reporter with a misdemeanor if no report is filed.

Two variations of the physician–patient privilege are common: psychotherapist–patient privilege and psychologist–patient privilege. Some states include psychiatrists in the physician–patient privilege because psychiatry is a specialty within the practice of medicine; others have created separate statutory privileges. Practitioners of homeopathic medicine may also be included in the physician–patient privilege in a few states. The student should consult local law to determine how to proceed with cases involving therapists.

Clergy–Penitent Privilege

There was no **clergy–penitent privilege** at common law, but most states now accept it either by legislation or by case law.

Clergy–Penitent Privilege Described
Clergy: Priest, minister, or religious practitioner.
Penitent: Person who consults clergy for spiritual advice.
What is covered: Confidential communications.
Who holds the privilege: Both clergy and penitent.
Exceptions frequently found in criminal cases:

Traditionally: None.
Some states now require the clergy to report incidents of child abuse.

Examples of When Clergy–Penitent Privilege Would Apply
• Man went to confession and told the priest that he had robbed a bank.
• Woman met with her pastor in his study. She told him she had taken money from the Sunday School offering plate and asked if God would forgive her if she gave it back.

Examples of When Clergy–Penitent Privilege Would *Not* Apply
• Priest who taught in a school operated by the church noticed bruises on the face of a student. When he asked what had happened, the student replied that his father hit him.
• A woman met her rabbi at a party and told him that she had a bad habit. She loved to shop and frequently shoplifted.

The concept of a clergy–penitent privilege originated from the confidentiality of the Catholic confessional and gradually expanded. It now includes confidential communications with members of the clergy of all denominations. The courts usually look to the doctrines of the individual denominations to determine who is authorized to hear such communications. Many states only recognize the privilege if the denomination imposes a duty on the clergy to keep these communications confidential.

The communication must have been made in a confidential setting for the purpose of obtaining spiritual guidance. It does not cover situations in which a member of the clergy plays a different role, such as a marriage and family counselor (although a member of the clergy who is a licensed counselor may be covered by the privilege afforded therapists). It also does not apply to observations made in a nonconfidential setting—for example, seeing bruises on a child while shaking hands after the religious service or at the church picnic.

The clergy–penitent privilege is unique in that both the clergy and the penitent have the right to refuse to reveal what was said. The reason for giving a separate privilege to the clergy is that they are bound by the rules of their denominations not to disclose penitential communications. Corresponding to this respect for religious duties of the clergy is that traditionally there have not been any exceptions to this privilege. The result is that neither the prosecutor nor the defense can compel a member of the clergy to testify regarding the defendant's penitential communication. Recently, a number of states have expanded their child abuse reporting laws to mandate that members of the clergy report suspected child abuse. Therefore, members of the clergy, like doctors and teachers, are now required to file reports if they have at least a reasonable suspicion that someone has abused a child.

Media Reporter Privilege

The news media play a very important role in our society. We rely on them to keep us informed about what is going on around us and to investigate the misdeeds of government. The importance of their role is reflected in the First Amendment's protection of freedom of the press. The news media have unsuccessfully argued that the First Amendment gives them a privilege not to disclose their sources. This argument is based on the assumption that the news media would not be able to obtain sensitive information if the reporter could not guarantee that the identity of the informant would remain confidential.

There was no privilege for the press at common law. In *Zurcher v. Stanford Daily* (436 U.S. 547 (1978)) the U.S. Supreme Court held that the First Amendment does not mandate an absolute privilege. Since 1980, many states and the federal government have enacted statutes creating a **news media privilege.** Typically, there was no effort by the drafters of these statutes to differentiate based on the quality or circulation of the medium. A reporter for the *New York Times* is on the same footing as one hired by the *National Enquirer* or someone writing for the school newspaper. Although these laws are not identical, it is common to give reporters immunity from being cited for contempt of court if they refuse to tell the court or a grand jury the sources of information used in a story. The judge may hold an *in camera* (in chambers) hearing to determine if there is a right to invoke the privilege. A *subpoena duces tecum* (subpoena to produce documents in court) may also be used to attempt to obtain documents from a news agency.

If there were no privilege, a reporter could be subpoenaed to court and sworn in as a witness. If the reporter refused to answer questions about the source(s) for a particular story, the judge could hold the reporter in contempt. The reporter could be sent to county jail until he or she decides to answer the questions. The privilege, as enacted in most states, protects the reporter from going to jail for refusing to answer questions about informants and other sources used to prepare a news article.

Privilege for News Reporter Described

News reporter: Person employed by the media to investigate stories and report on them. Media includes print media as well as radio and television.

What is covered: Reporter's notes and identity of informants.

Who holds privilege: Reporter.

Exceptions frequently found in criminal cases:

Some states make an exception for prosecution of serious crimes if it can be shown that there is no other source for the information requested.

Examples of Ways Privilege for News Reporter Would Apply

- Notes the reporter made while investigating the case. What was published is no longer privileged because it was made available to the public, but notes on portions of the story that were not published are privileged.
- Film clips taken by a TV news crew that were not shown on the air.
- Audiotapes a reporter made of an interview done while researching a story. The newspaper later decided not to run the story.

Examples of Ways Privilege for News Reporter Would *Not* Apply

• Tape recordings a freelance journalist made of interview of suspect in murder case.

Most state laws only apply to people who are employed by the news media.

• Videotape a tourist made of police beating a motorist with their batons. Tourist tried to sell tape to the local TV station.

The person who made the tape does not qualify as a member of the news media.

When there is a statute in this area, it usually gives a very broad definition of "reporter." Publishers, editors, and reporters for newspapers, magazines, and periodicals are usually covered, as are those working for wire services. Similar protections are given to those working for radio, television, and cable networks. It is not clear whether the privilege extends to freelancers who are not employed by the media at the time they investigate or write stories.

The privilege generally covers all information discovered by the reporter that has not been published. This includes the sources directly related to the published story. It also covers items used only for background by the reporter and information collected, but not included, in the published version of the story. Notes, photographs, tapes, and outtakes (material edited out) are usually covered.

Some states require a reporter to give the names of sources if there is no other way to obtain vital information for the prosecution of a serious crime. The prosecution would have the burden of convincing the judge that there is no other way to obtain the evidence and that the reporter has enough relevant information to warrant violation of the confidence placed in him or her. This would be done at an *in camera* hearing.

There is an apparent conflict between this statutory privilege and the fact that the Supreme Court has allowed the police to obtain search warrants for newsrooms and reporters' desks. See Chapter 10 for a detailed discussion of the warrant process.

Executive Privilege

Numerous investigations of the President of the United States have been conducted in the twentieth century, but none stand out as much as the investigation of the Nixon administration.

A federal grand jury indicted a number of individuals involved in the Watergate scandal and other misdeeds, and it named President Nixon as an unindicted co-conspirator. Congress appointed a special prosecutor. At his request, the District Court issued a third-party subpoena *duces tecum* directing the President to produce tape recordings and documents relating to his conversations with aides and advisors for use at pending criminal trials. President Nixon moved to quash the subpoena on the grounds that the materials requested were covered by an **executive privilege** against disclosure of confidential communications.

In a unanimous opinion written by Chief Justice Warren Burger, the Supreme Court rejected Nixon's claim of absolute privilege. The Court stated,

> The expectation of a President to the confidentiality of his conversations and correspondence, like the claim of confidentiality of judicial deliberations, for example, has all the values to which we accord deference for the privacy of all citizens and, added to those values, is the necessity for protection of the public interest in candid, objective, and even blunt or harsh opinions in Presidential decision-making. A President and those who assist him must be free to explore alternatives in the process of shaping policies and making decisions and to do so in a way many would be unwilling to express except privately. These are the considerations justifying a presumptive privilege for Presidential communications. The privilege is fundamental to the operation of Government and inextricably rooted in the separation of powers under the Constitution. (*United States v. Nixon* 418 U.S. 683, 708–709)

> Nowhere in the Constitution, as we have noted earlier, is there any explicit reference to a privilege of confidentiality, yet to the extent this interest relates to the effective discharge of a President's powers, it is constitutionally based. (418 U.S. 683, 712)

> We conclude that when the ground for asserting privilege as to subpoenaed materials sought for use in a criminal trial is based only on the generalized interest in confidentiality, it cannot prevail over the fundamental demands of due process of law in the fair administration of criminal justice. The generalized assertion of privilege must yield to the demonstrated, specific need for evidence in a pending criminal trial. (418 U.S. 683, 714)

Within hours of the Court's denial of the claim of executive privilege, Nixon resigned the presidency of the United States.

This landmark case provides the framework for analyzing claims of executive privilege when documents are sought for use in criminal cases. First, it is presumed that the President has the right to refuse access to the confidential decision-making process. Second, statements requested in the subpoena that meet the test of admissibility and relevance must be isolated. Third, the District Court judge will hold an *in camera* hearing where the material that the executive branch claims is privileged will be examined.

Only the federal judge and an attorney representing the President will be present at this hearing. The outcome of this hearing will be an order detailing what, if anything, will be admissible at the criminal trial in question. During this process, the District Court has a very heavy responsibility to make sure that information reviewed *in camera* and determined to be privileged is accorded the "high degree of respect due the President of the United States" (418 U.S. 683, 716). The District Court has the responsibility for making sure that there are no leaks of the material that was reviewed but not ruled admissible at trial.

Privilege for Official Information

There was a common-law privilege for official government documents if disclosure would be against the "public interest." It was generally recognized to cover military and diplomatic secrets. It was not well developed in civil cases due to the fact that a person could not sue the government without the government's permission.

The federal Freedom of Information Act has made it easier to obtain many government documents. This statute, and many of its state counterparts, requires disclosure of information in government files but restricts access to facts about ongoing investigations. In some states, the identity of informants and locations where surveillance is being conducted are privileged. Legislation frequently makes personnel records of government employees privileged. Table 9-3 summarizes how privilege is applied to certain types of information.

T A B L E **9-3 Types of Information and How Privilege Is Applied**

Type of Information	Application of Privilege
Freedom of Information Act (federal)	Allows access to information retained by federal government. Exceptions apply.
Identity of informant	Police have privilege not to disclose identity of informants, but judge can order disclosure if it is crucial to defense.
Ongoing investigation	Police have right to refuse to disclose information about an ongoing investigation. Privilege ceases once investigation is finished.
Personnel records	Personnel records of government employees are privileged. Judge can order disclosure of relevant information.

These privileges apply to all levels and branches of law enforcement. It includes both traditional police forces and the investigative branches of other agencies, such as consumer affairs and environmental protection.

Privilege Not to Disclose Identity of Informant

The **police informant privilege** allows police officers to withhold the names of confidential informants—that is, people who supply the police with information with the understanding that they will not be called as witnesses. The information supplied is frequently used to develop other evidence that constitutes probable cause for an arrest.

Privilege Not to Disclose Identity of Informant Described
Police: Applies to all law enforcement agencies.
Informant: Person who supplies information to police with the understanding that his or her identity will not be made public.
What is covered: Name and address of the informer.
Who holds the privilege: Law enforcement agency that used the informant to help with a specific case.
Exceptions frequently found in criminal cases: Identity of informant must be disclosed if it is important in the defendant's case.

Examples of When Privilege Not to Disclose Identity of Informant Would Apply
- Mr. Jones called police and reported that the man who lived next door appeared to be dealing drugs. Police set up surveillance on the neighbor's house and an officer witnessed several drug deals.

  The police would not have to reveal the name of the informant because all crucial observations were made by the police.

Examples of When Privilege Not to Disclose Identity of Informant Would *Not* Apply
- As the result of a plea bargain agreement, Mr. Smith agreed to assist police in a stolen property investigation. Smith went "undercover" and made several purchases from burglars. Only Smith and the burglars were present when the purchases were made.

  The police would have to reveal Smith's name because his identity and the ability to attack his credibility at trial are crucial to the defense's case.

The U.S. Supreme Court in *McCrary v. Illinois* (386 U.S. 300 (1967)) held that there is a constitutional right to obtain the identity of an informant only if it is crucial to the defense. Circumstances that would trigger this exception would be that the informant was the only eyewitness to toxic waste dumping, or that the informant participated in a drug case by dressing in street clothes and doing the "buy." On the other hand, if the police used facts supplied by an informant to start an investigation, and as a result of this investigation they were able to establish probable cause, there is no need to disclose the identity of the informant.

When the defense demands the name of an informant, the judge will review the police files *in camera* (in chambers) with only the prosecutor and a representative for the police department present. The identity of the informant is given to the defense attorney only if the judge decides that there is a constitutional right to know this information. Even at this point, the police may refuse to disclose the identity of the informant, but refusal may result in dismissal of the case. The police and the prosecutor make the final decision on disclosing the identity of the informant; the informant cannot force them to withhold the information. If the life of the informant is in danger, or if concealing the identity of the informant is vital to other cases, it may be necessary to let the case be dismissed.

The police cannot prevent an informant from disclosing his or her own identity. If an informant does this, the relationship is no longer confidential and the police cannot continue to conceal the information.

Many states consider **police personnel files** privileged except when there is litigation between the employee and the employer. Certain facts, such as the dates of employment, are not privileged. The contents of these files are usually irrelevant in a criminal case.

There are a few recurring situations in criminal cases in which the contents of police personnel files are relevant. If the defense claims the officer is committing perjury, the fact that other people have filed complaints with the police department that the officer is untruthful is relevant. In a case in which the charges are assault and/or battery on a police officer, the defendant may claim that he or she only acted in self-defense. Prior allegations of police brutality against the officer will be relevant.

Privilege to Withhold Personnel Files Described

Personnel files: Permanent personnel records on an employee. Police personnel files include investigations of an officer conducted by internal affairs.

What is covered: Records concerning the performance of the officer and investigations of his or her conduct.

Who holds the privilege: Law enforcement agency.

Exceptions frequently found in criminal cases: Must disclose information relevant to the defense.

Examples of Ways Privilege for Police Personnel Files Would Apply

- The defendant claims the officer has falsified the evidence so the defense attorney subpoenaed the officer's personnel file. The judge reviewed the personnel file at the *in camera* hearing and determined that the only complaint against the officer was by his ex-wife, who stated he was not paying child support.

The defense would not be allowed to see the personnel file.

Examples of Ways Privilege for Police Personnel Files Would *Not* Apply

- The defendant was charged with assault on a police officer but the defendant claims she was acting in self-defense. The officer's personnel file was subpoenaed. The judge reviewed the personnel file at the *in camera* hearing and found two complaints of police brutality filed against the officer in the past 3 years.

The defense would be entitled to a copy of the two complaints of police brutality but would not have access to any other documents in the personnel file.

Police personnel files only become an issue in a case if the defense files a discovery motion asking for the police files. Many states mandate that this be done before trial. The motion would name the officer(s) involved in the case. If the police department refuses to give the files to the defense, a hearing will be conducted before the judge. The judge will review the files *in camera* and determine if there is anything in the officer's personnel file that is relevant. If there is, the judge will order that the relevant portions of the file be given to the defense. The order may include (1) dates and locations of alleged incidents, (2) names and addresses of victims, and (3) witnesses to these incidents. The opinions of internal affairs investigators are not given to the defense.

Many states have set limits on this type of disclosure. It is common to limit the period during which allegations of misconduct must be disclosed; a 5-year limit is common. If so, any material in the personnel file that relates to activities more than 5 years before the event in question is not shown to the judge. The defense may be required to give a plausible explanation for each file that is requested. Discovery may also be denied if there is a non-confidential source for the same information. For example, if the case was featured in the local newspaper, there is no justification for delving into the confidential personnel files of the officer(s) involved.

Summary

Privileges have been established to protect the need for confidential communications. Each legislature has decided which relationships should receive protection.

Even when a privileged relationship exists, the communication will be admissible unless the parties have attempted to keep the communications confidential. Voluntary disclosure defeats a privilege. The information will also be admissible if it falls under one of the exceptions to the privilege.

The attorney–client privilege protects confidential communications between an attorney and client. It covers discussions about crimes that have already occurred. This privilege, however, does not apply to conversations in which the client seeks advice on how to commit crimes or escape punishment.

Confidential communications between a husband and wife while they are married are privileged. Common exceptions cover situations in which one spouse is charged with committing a crime against the other spouse or their children.

Many states also allow one spouse to refuse to testify against the other spouse. Some reverse this and allow one spouse to refuse to let the other spouse testify against him or her. The same exceptions usually apply to this privilege and the privilege for confidential communications between husbands and wives. Unmarried cohabitants are not covered.

The physician–patient relationship usually has a privilege similar to the attorney–client relationship. Confidential communications are privileged except when planning or concealing a crime. Some states do not allow this privilege to be used in criminal cases at all.

There is a privilege for people who seek spiritual guidance from their clergy. Both the penitent and the clergy hold the privilege and can refuse to disclose their conversations.

Although there is no constitutional or common-law privilege for the news media, many states have enacted statutory privileges for the media. These laws usually take the form of giving the media immunity from citation for contempt when they refuse to identify the sources of information for a story. Some states make an exception if there is no other way to obtain information about a serious crime.

Confidential communications between the President of the United States and his immediate, high-level staff are presumed to be privileged. If a prosecutor can show that portions of those communications are relevant and otherwise admissible, an *in camera* hearing will be held in which the federal District Court judge reviews the communications in question. Based on this review, the judge will determine which confidential communications are covered by executive privilege and which ones will be available to the prosecution at trial.

Some government records are privileged. Two were discussed in this chapter: identity of police informants and police personnel files. The defendant has a constitutional right to know the identity of a police informant if the information this person provided is crucial to the defense. Police personnel files are privileged except where they contain information relevant to the case. The defense cannot obtain facts to be used in general character assassination of the police officer, but previous accusations that the officer committed perjury can be discovered; earlier allegations of police brutality are discoverable if relevant to the current case (e.g., the defendant is charged with assault on a police officer and claims he or she was acting in self-defense).

Review Questions

1. Define the attorney–client privilege, and list its exceptions.
2. Define the privilege for confidential communications between husband and wife, and list three exceptions.
3. Define the privilege of one spouse not to testify against the other, and give three exceptions.
4. Define the physician–patient privilege, and explain the common exceptions.
5. Define the clergy–penitent privilege, and explain the exceptions, if any.
6. When may the police keep the name of an informant secret?
7. Explain the procedure the defense would use to obtain the name of a police informant.
8. Identify two situations in which police personnel files would be relevant to a criminal case. Explain how a defendant can obtain the files.
9. Do the media have a First Amendment privilege to protect their sources? Explain.
10. Define the statutory privilege for the media to withhold the identity of their sources. Explain the procedure used to invoke the privilege.

Writing Assignment

Go to www.cnn.com/crime. Find a case involving the use of privilege. Write a one-page (250-word) report on the use of privilege in the case you found. If you have trouble finding a current case, go to www.crimelibrary.com and type the word *privilege* in the search box.

Notes

1. See, "To Avoid Jail, Former Lawyer for Phil Spector Testifies at Murder Trial." Downloaded on July 13, 2007 From http://www.courttv.com/trials/spector/071207_ctv.html.

CHAPTER 10

Developing Law of Search and Seizure

Feature Case: Murder of Christa Worthington

Christa Worthington, an ambitious, creative, honors graduate from Vassar, established a career as a fashion writer and editor for *Cosmopolitan* and *Woman's Wear Daily* before being sent to Paris as a reporter for *W* magazine. She moved on to London, where she worked as a freelance journalist. When she learned her mother was dying of cancer, she went to be near her, and a short while later she moved into her family's cottage in Truro, Massachusetts, a community of 1,600 near Cape Cod. Christa had an affair with a local man, but they broke up when he learned she was pregnant. Four days after her mother died of cancer, Christa gave birth to a girl whom she named after her mother. She gave up her career to be a full-time mom.

Two years later, a former boyfriend went to Christa's cottage and found her seminude body in a puddle of blood on the floor. Her daughter, who was by her side, reached up to him and said, "Mommy fell down." It appeared that the little girl had tried to revive her mother by giving her a drink from her sippy cup. The coroner estimated that Christa had been dead for 24–36 hours.

Several men who had dated Christa were the initial suspects, but all were cleared by DNA tests. DNA samples from other people who had contact with Christa were sent to the lab. The investigators were frustrated when DNA found under Christa's fingernails was shown to be from three unidentified men. Additionally, the killer left no fingerprints. Three years after the murder, the police appealed to male residents of the area to voluntarily submit DNA samples. Before DNA from these volunteers could be tested, the lab reported that a sample from the initial round of suspects matched the major DNA profile developed from saliva on the victim's breast and was consistent with the minor DNA profile developed from a vaginal swab. Christopher McCowen, a 33-year-old African American garbage collector who worked in Christa's neighborhood, was arrested for first-degree murder, aggravated rape, and armed assault. He had previously served time in Florida for crimes including car theft and burglary. Five women in the Cape Code area had obtained domestic violence restraining orders against him.

Two detectives handled McCowen's 7-hour interrogation. McCowen signed a waiver form after being given his *Miranda* rights, but he requested that the interview not be tape recorded. The detectives reminded him of his right to call his attorney on several occasions, and a telephone was on the table in the interview room for his use. He did not avail himself of these opportunities to exercise his privileges. Twice the detectives offered him something to drink, and on one occasion they offered to get food for him. McCowen initially denied knowing Christa. During the interrogation, he gradually changed his story but always claimed that the sexual encounter was consensual. He blamed the murder on a friend. The interview was stopped while the detectives verified his friend's alibi. Twice the detectives indicated that the interview was over, but on both occasions McCowen told them that he wanted to talk some more in order to clear things up.

A pretrial hearing on McCowen's Motion to Suppress the Confession due to a violation of his rights lasted nearly 4 days. The judge's 13-page ruling carefully detailed what the police did, how McCowen's rights were protected, and McCowen's behavior. After this detailed recap of the hearing, the judge ruled that McCowen was neither intoxicated nor under the influence of drugs or medications during the interrogation. Furthermore, the judge found that the detectives had been calm and in no way intimidated or coerced McCowen during the interrogation. The judge concluded that the *Miranda* warnings had been given correctly and that McCowen made a knowing, intelligent, and voluntary waiver of his rights. McCowen's statements in the interview room were admissible at trial.

During the trial, the prosecution presented evidence from the crime scene, McCowen's statements, and testimony from other witnesses. The pathologist testified that there were minor defensive wounds on Christa's hands, cuts and bruises on her face and torso, and blunt force trauma to her head; he concluded that the cause of death was a knife wound that cut her left lung and pierced her heart. The force of the knife was so strong that the knife nicked the floor under the victim's body. There was no evidence of trauma to her genitals; hence, the pathologist could not rule out consensual sex.

The defense based its case on the contamination of the crime scene, racial prejudice that made it impossible for the detectives to believe that the affluent white woman would have consensual sex with the black garbage collector, and the "unjust" arrest of McCowen who was but one in a long line of men who had sex with Worthington. The defense also introduced evidence that it claimed showed the police coerced McCowen while he was under the combined influences of alcohol, marijuana, and Percocet. It was also alleged that he had an IQ of 78 and did not have the capacity to make a valid waiver of his *Miranda* rights. According to the defense attorney, McCowen's low IQ, combined with being under the influence of prescription painkillers and marijuana during the interview, made it impossible for him to understand his rights. The jury convicted McCowen.

Learning Objectives

After studying this chapter, you will be able to
- Describe the history of the Fourth Amendment.
- List what acts of law enforcement are considered to be "searches" and "seizures."
- Define *probable cause* and how it is used in arrest and search situations.
- Define the legal meaning of the term *standing*.
- Identify what information is needed to obtain a search warrant and explain how a search warrant is executed.
- Define the Exclusionary Rule and its effect on evidence.
- Identify the Fruit of the Poison Tree Doctrine, its exceptions, and application.
- Define the independent source rule.
- Identify those court proceedings in which the Exclusionary Rule is not used.
- Explain the constitutional limits placed on the use of physical force to obtain evidence.

Key Terms

- Affidavit
- Anonymous informant
- Confidential informant
- Exclusionary Rule
- Execution of a warrant
- Fruit of the Poison Tree Doctrine
- Good Faith Exception
- Independent Source Exception
- Inevitable Discovery Exception
- Knock-and-announce procedure
- Probable cause
- Protective sweep
- Public Safety Exception
- Return (of search warrant)
- Substantial compliance
- Valid on its face

Myths about Warrants, Exclusionary Rule, and the Fruit of the Poison Tree	Facts about Warrants, Exclusionary Rule, and the Fruit of the Poison Tree
If the police wish to conduct a search, they must obtain a search warrant.	There are numerous exceptions to the search warrant requirement.
For a judge to issue a valid search warrant, there must be sworn testimony from at least one eyewitness to the crime.	The U.S. Supreme Court allows judges to issue search warrants based on the totality of the circumstances. If all of the facts in the affidavit for the warrant, taken as a whole, provide probable cause that evidence of the crime is currently at a specific location, a judge can issue a warrant to search the premises. One type of evidence is not preferred above another kind, as long as the evidence is credible.
When serving a search warrant, the police may only seize things that are specifically listed in the warrant.	In addition to the items specified in the search warrant, the police have the right to seize anything that falls under the Plain View Doctrine.
The Exclusionary Rule is no longer used in the United States.	The Exclusionary Rule is still in use in the United States, but decisions of the U.S. Supreme Court during the past 45 years have narrowed the application of the rule.
The authority of local police officers to use force when making an arrest is solely governed by state laws.	In addition to state laws, the Fourth Amendment and the Due Process Clause of the Fifth and Fourteenth Amendments place restrictions on a police officer's right to use force when making an arrest and/or recovering evidence.

History and Development of Fourth Amendment

The principle that "a man's home is his castle" existed in England long before the colonies were settled in America. The English Bill of Rights was enacted by Parliament in 1689 and gave even the poorest peasant the right to exclude the King from his home. Yet, in Colonial America the British freely used the "general warrant," which gave unlimited rights for soldiers to search homes for whatever evidence they might find.

Many of the original states expressed their disapproval of the general warrant by including a prohibition against unreasonable searches and seizures in their constitutions. When the U.S. Constitution was ratified, it did not contain any mention of searches and seizures or any of the other protections now in our Bill of Rights. Many of the states that ratified the Constitution insisted that additional protections against the power of the federal government be included. The first 10 amendments to the Constitution, known collectively as the Bill of Rights, were added in 1791, only 4 years after the Constitution was ratified. Their wording has not been changed since.

Fourth Amendment

The right of the people to be secure in their persons, houses, papers and effects, against unreasonable searches and seizures, shall not be violated, and no Warrants shall issue, but upon probable cause, supported by Oath or affirmation, and particularly describing the place to be searched, and the persons or things to be seized.

There are three broad concepts in this amendment:

1. Protection is provided for the person, home, and belongings.
2. Unreasonable searches and seizures are prohibited.
3. Warrants must be based on probable cause and specifically describe the place to be searched and what is to be seized.

These concepts are explained in this chapter and in Chapters 11–13.

Definitions

Prior to considering what police conduct violates the Fourth Amendment, four basic definitions must be discussed: search, seizure, probable cause, and standing.

Definitions

Search:

An examination of a person, his or her house, personal property, or other locations when conducted by a law enforcement officer for the purpose of finding evidence of a crime.

Seizure:

The act of taking possession of a person or property.

Probable cause:

A reasonable belief that a person has committed or is committing a crime or that a place contains specific items connected with a crime. Under the Fourth Amendment, probable cause must be shown before an arrest warrant or search warrant may be issued.

Standing:

Standing is a party's right to make a legal claim or seek judicial enforcement of a duty or right.

Search

A search involves the act of looking for something that otherwise would not be seen. Finding something that was left out where the police could see it is the opposite of a search. If the officer has the right to move things, then anything seen while moving those items is in plain view and is not the product of a search.

Even if there is a search, it may not violate the Fourth Amendment. Only unreasonable searches are prohibited. The Supreme Court has spent a great deal of time deciding what is "reasonable" and what is not. If a search is illegal, it is also unreasonable. The result is that items found during an illegal search are not admissible in court. This is discussed later in this chapter.

Examples of Searches

- Police officer orders the suspect to empty his pockets and carefully examines each item that is produced.

  If the officer did this before arresting the suspect, it is unreasonable.
  If the officer arrested the suspect before ordering the pockets emptied, the officer's actions would be a reasonable search. See Chapter 11.

- A police officer sees a suspicious car parked behind a store late at night. The officer opens the unlocked door and looks for stolen merchandise.

  If the officer does this based on probable cause that stolen merchandise is in the car, it would be a reasonable search. See Chapter 12.
  If the officer does not have probable cause that there was anything in the car that he had the right to seize, the search would be unreasonable.
  The fact that the car was parked in violation of a local ordinance would empower the officer to write a citation. In these circumstances, the officer would not be authorized to open the door or search the interior of the car.

- A police officer goes to a farm and finds a field of marijuana plants.

  If the officer searches close to the farmhouse, his actions are unreasonable.
  If the officer searches open fields that are not near a dwelling, the actions are reasonable. See Chapter 12.

Examples of Actions That Are *Not* Searches

- A police officer was walking down the sidewalk and saw a wallet that appeared to be lost. She picked up the wallet.

  Finding the wallet and picking it up would not be a search.
  Opening the wallet and looking for ID would have been a search.
    The search would be considered reasonable because the purpose of opening the wallet was to help locate the owner and return the wallet. See Chapter 12.

- A police officer was walking through the park and observed a young man smoking a cigarette. The air was full of the smell of marijuana smoke.

The park was a public place; therefore, what the officer observed while walking through the park was not a search.

Picking up the man's backpack and looking inside for marijuana would be a search. Searching the backpack would be considered unreasonable because it was an invasion of the man's privacy.

> If the smell of marijuana was so strong that it provided probable cause justifying an arrest, the officer could legally search the backpack immediately after the arrest. See Chapter 11.

- An officer was called to a house to investigate a recent burglary. The resident invited the officer into the house and took him to the kitchen to show him a broken window where he believed the burglar entered the house. While talking to this person, the officer noticed several sheets of uncut $20 bills on the kitchen table.

The officer had been invited into the house to take a burglary report. Therefore, he was legally there.

Making an observation from a location where the officer had the legal right to be was not a search.

Picking up the sheets of $20 bills to look at them more closely would have been a search.

Examining a sheet of $20 bills would be considered unreasonable because the officer had no right to pick it up.

> If the officer's observation of the sheet of $20 bills (without picking them up) was sufficient to establish probable cause that they were counterfeit, and there was probable cause to believe that the person he was talking to was involved in counterfeiting, the officer could make an arrest.
>
> Immediately after the arrest, he could seize the sheets of $20 bills if they were within arm's reach of the person who was arrested. See Chapter 11.
>
> Information about the sheets of $20 bills could be included in an affidavit used to obtain a warrant to search the house for evidence of counterfeiting.

Seizure

Police "seize" evidence when they take it into their possession. When a person is seized, it is called an arrest. Even when there is no search (for example, something was left out in plain view where the police could see it), officers still must have probable cause to seize it.

For example, if a police officer observes something inside a house by looking through a window, there is no right to enter the house to seize it without a search warrant. Another example would be information that is recorded while circling the area in an aircraft. Observing back yards and fields in this manner is not a search because there is no physical entry onto the property of another person. There must be sufficient evidence to obtain a search warrant in order to enter private property and seize the items that were observed. Abandoned property goes by a different rule because no one currently owns it (or has a possessory interest in it). Evidence left in a public place can be seized without a search warrant because there is no invasion of anyone's property interests. It does not matter whether the items were in transparent or opaque trash sacks or other forms of packaging.

Examples of Seizures

- Police stop a man carrying an object that appears to be a gun. They immediately seize the object. An arrest can be made as soon as it is determined that the man does not have a permit to carry the gun.
- When the suspect is booked into the city jail, officers remove all personal belongings in the suspect's possession.
- Officers go to a bank and obtain a copy of the suspect's checking account records. A court order is needed in order to make this a legal seizure.

Examples of Actions That Are *Not* Seizures

- Police stop a man walking down the street at 11:30 p.m. in an industrial area. They ask for identification and the reason that the man is at the location. The man explains that he works the midnight to 8:00 a.m. shift at a factory approximately a quarter mile from the location. After copying the information from the man's driver's license, they return it to the man and allow him to continue his legal activity.

  The man was briefly detained, which may be considered a seizure. The police copied information from the driver's license, but returned the license. There was no seizure of the ID.

- A police officer observed a box in a shopping bag in a trash barrel on the curb for the garbage truck to pick up the next morning. The officer picked up the sack, examined the contents, and put it in an evidence bag.

  Everything in the trash barrels has been discarded by the owner. It no longer belongs to anyone; therefore, picking it up is not a seizure.

Probable Cause

In criminal cases, **probable cause** is required in three key situations:

1. Probable cause that a crime was committed.
2. Probable cause that the suspect is the person who committed the crime.
3. Probable cause that evidence is at a specific location.

The Fourth Amendment specifically refers to issuing warrants based on probable cause. It is also an important prerequisite for many police activities conducted without warrants.

Examples of Probable Cause to Make an Arrest

- Police arrive at scene and observe the suspect hitting another person with a baseball bat.
- Woman calls 911. When the police arrive at her house, they observe that the woman has red marks on her face indicating she has recently been hit. The woman tells the officers that her husband hit her six times with his open hand.

Examples of Facts That Did *Not* Make Probable Cause

- Police arrive at the scene and discover the front door is open. They cautiously walk though the house but see nothing amiss.

   The police officers have no idea why the front door is open. The owner may have left it open or someone else may have opened it.
   There is no indication that a crime has been committed.
   The officers do not have probable cause to make an arrest.

- Police officers receive a message from the dispatcher to go to 123 Maple Street and investigate a possible dead body in the back yard.

   Upon arrival at 123 Maple Street, officers go into the back yard and see a white female in a prone position on the lawn.
   The odor of alcohol is detected when they approach the body. As one officer gently probes the body with a gloved hand, the woman begins to move.
   It is determined that the woman drank a large quantity of beer and "passed out" in her back yard.
   Having determined that no crime was committed, the officers leave.

Standing

"Standing" refers to the right to ask the court to take legal action. Only a person with standing can activate the Exclusionary Rule by asking the judge to rule that evidence cannot be used at trial because it was illegally seized. After many years of struggling with the concept, the U.S. Supreme Court adopted "reasonable expectation of privacy" as a guide and no longer uses the term "standing." A person can only ask to have evidence excluded due to a violation of the Fourth Amendment if it can be shown that his or her privacy was violated by the police. The results of having standing and having one's reasonable expectation of privacy violated are frequently the same.

Some examples illustrate this approach. If a person's house is searched unconstitutionally, the resident's reasonable expectation of privacy has been violated; the person who lives in the house can have the evidence suppressed if charges were filed against him or her. An overnight guest who was present when the house was searched also has an expectation of privacy that was violated when his or her personal belongings were searched. The overnight guest can have the illegally seized evidence suppressed. On the other hand, if a friend left something in the house prior to the search but was not present when the illegal search was conducted, the friend had no reasonable expectation of privacy. This conclusion is based on the rationale that by giving up possession of property, the owner gives up control of the items that were left behind. The friend hoped that his or her personal items would be treated with respect, but the people in the house were free to do whatever they wanted with their friend's property once he or she left. Therefore, the friend had no expectation of privacy. Without an expectation of privacy, the friend cannot ask the court to suppress items from evidence that were left at another person's house. This is true even though the police seized the items during a search that was conducted illegally. The Supreme Court also ruled that people who stop briefly at a home or apartment for business purposes have no expectation of privacy in the residence they are visiting. Due to the fact that they do not have an expectation of privacy, business visitors cannot have property that the police seized illegally suppressed.

Rights under the Fifth Amendment are also personal. Only the person who made the confession can successfully make a motion to suppress it. If the confession implicated someone else in the crime, the person who was implicated would not have the right to have the confession suppressed even though *Miranda* had been violated.

Examples of the Right to Have Evidence Suppressed

- Sam was illegally stopped by the police and his car was searched. Sam has standing to ask the court to suppress evidence that was found illegally.
- Mary, who is a suspect in a theft investigation, is spending the weekend with her brother Ned. Police enter Ned's apartment without a search warrant and find the items that Mary stole.

Examples of Individuals Who Do *Not* Have the Right to Have Evidence Suppressed

- At a party, Pete gave Rosie a small bag containing illegal drugs and asked her to put it in her purse. The police raided the party and found the drugs.

  Rosie would have standing to ask the judge to suppress the drugs at her trial because they were in her possession. The judge would rule on whether or not Rosie's Fourth Amendment rights had been violated by the police when they raided the party.
  Pete does not have standing to ask the judge to suppress the drugs at his trial because they were not in his possession. When he gave Rosie possession of the drugs, he gave up the right to challenge any search of Rosie that produced the drugs.

- Tom, a salesman, was visiting the home of Victor, his client. Tom had just placed a thick notebook containing a sales prospectus and samples of his products on the kitchen table when the police entered Victor's home and searched the living room and kitchen. The police carefully examined the contents of the notebook and arrested Tom for receiving stolen merchandise, a felony.

Victor could successfully have the evidence suppressed if it was found during an illegal search that was conducted in violation of the Fourth Amendment.

Tom could not have the evidence in the notebook suppressed, even if the search violated the Fourth Amendment, because the Supreme Court has ruled that a casual business visitor does not have an expectation of privacy in a building that is searched.

For the same reason, Tom could not have the evidence in the notebook suppressed because the officer's examination of the notebook violated the Plain View Rule.

Warrant Requirements

The Fourth Amendment specifically states that (1) no warrant shall be issued unless there is probable cause, (2) probable cause must be established under oath or affirmation, and (3) the warrant must particularly describe the place to be searched and the person or things to be seized. It does not say that all searches must be authorized by warrants.

The Supreme Court has decided many cases addressing the issue of whether or not warrants are required. It has stated a preference for warrants, but it has also recognized that there are situations in which officers do not have to obtain them. Search warrants may be issued to search nearly any location, including residences, newsrooms, and doctors' and lawyers' offices.

In noncriminal situations, such as inspections to determine if buildings conform to electrical codes, search warrants are also required if no one will consent to the inspection. For these "administrative warrants," probable cause is satisfied if there is a reasonable legislative purpose for the inspection.

The basic principle is that warrants are mandatory except when the facts fit within one of the exceptions to the warrant requirement. This chapter deals with the procedures used to obtain warrants. The numerous exceptions authorized by the Supreme Court are dealt with in Chapters 11 and 12.

Information Needed to Obtain a Warrant

The warrant process was created to allow a neutral magistrate to review the facts and decide if the police should be authorized to conduct a search or make an arrest. To do this, the magistrate must have the facts of the case. The Fourth Amendment requires that these facts be taken under oath or affirmation. The written document used for this purpose is called an **affidavit.**

Prior to the 1960s, some judges relied on the officer's decision that there was probable cause. For example, the affidavit might read, "This officer has received information from a reliable informant which causes me to conclude that there is probable cause to search the house located at 123 N. Main St., Hometown, for stolen property." In 1964, the Supreme Court ruled that this was not acceptable.[1] It held that a warrant is only valid if the judge determined that probable cause existed. To do this, the judge must personally review the facts.

Search Warrants

Facts given in an affidavit are usually very detailed and must convince the judge that there is evidence that the officers have a legal right to seize. The warrant may authorize a search for illegal drugs or other contraband, fruits of the crime, items used to commit the crime, or other items that can be used in the case. The facts need to provide detailed information about the crime involved, as well as an explanation of why the officers want to seize the items in question.

In addition to showing what is to be seized, the affidavit must give facts that show where the items to be seized are located. The description of the location to be searched must be as exact as possible. Since the reason for requiring search warrants is to protect people's privacy, the warrant should be worded so that the police are restricted to as small an area as possible. Figure 10-1 shows what can and cannot be searched with a search warrant that authorizes the search of a garage for an assault rifle and a 55-gallon drum of methamphetamine pills. The officers may open the refrigerator, for example, because it would be possible to conceal the assault rifle in there if the shelves had been removed; they may not open the washer and dryer because their interiors are too small to hide the rifle, but officers could look behind them to see if the assault rifle was stashed there. Since the search warrant authorized officers to look for a 55-gallon drum, and not small quantities of pills, cupboards and boxes too small to conceal this large drum or the assault rifle cannot be searched.

Street addresses are usually given, but the location should be described even more precisely, if possible. For example, "the living room of the house at 456 S. Grand Ave." or "the garage of the house at 789 W. First St." Case law generally upholds warrants that include a correct description of the location even when the street address is wrong. Examples would include "the blue house on the corner of Market and Third, with the address of 301 N. Market" even though it turned out that 301 N. Market was the wrong

Figure 10-1
Execution of a Search Warrant
The search warrant stated that officers may search this garage for an assault rifle and a 55-gallon drum of methamphetamine pills.

address, or "the apartment at the head of the stairs on the third floor of the building at 321 S. Broadway," when it turned out that the apartment number given in the warrant was wrong.

A problem unique to search warrants is the requirement that the information be fresh. If the facts are stale, they may not be a reliable indicator of where the items to be seized are currently located. In a drug case in which the dealer is known to do a high volume of business and change locations frequently, information 2 or 3 days old may be stale. If the case involves the use of stolen building materials at a construction site, the information is not likely to become stale if the stolen property is being incorporated into a building. It is important for the police to have current information to avoid rejection of the affidavit due to staleness.

Example of Facts the U.S. Supreme Court Ruled Were Sufficient to Establish Probable Cause to Obtain a Search Warrant

Massachusetts v. Sheppard 468 U.S. 981 (1984)

The badly burned body of Sandra Boulware was discovered in a vacant lot in the Roxbury section of Boston at approximately 5 a.m. Saturday, May 5. An autopsy revealed that Boulware had died of multiple compound skull fractures caused by blows to the head. After a brief investigation, the police decided to question one of the victim's boyfriends, Osborne Sheppard. Sheppard told the police that he had last seen the victim on Tuesday night and that he had been at a local gaming house (where card games were played) from 9 p.m. Friday until 5 a.m. Saturday. He identified several people who would be willing to substantiate the latter claim.

By interviewing the people Sheppard had said were at the gaming house on Friday night, the police learned that although Sheppard was at the gaming house that night, he had borrowed an automobile at approximately 3 a.m. Saturday morning in order to give two men a ride home. Even though the trip normally took only 15 minutes, Sheppard did not return with the car until nearly 5 a.m.

On Sunday morning, police officers visited the owner of the car Sheppard had borrowed. He consented to an inspection of the vehicle. Blood stains and pieces of hair were found on the rear bumper and within the trunk compartment. In addition, the officers noticed strands of wire in the trunk similar to wire strands found on and near the body of the victim. The owner of the car told the officers that when he last used the car on Friday night, shortly before Sheppard borrowed it, he had placed articles in the trunk and had not noticed any stains on the bumper or in the trunk.

Note: The previous facts were held sufficient to issue a search warrant for Sheppard's residence for the victim's clothing, rope and/or wire matching samples found on the body, a blunt instrument used to kill the victim, and blood-stained clothing.

Example of Facts the U.S. Supreme Court Ruled Were *Not* Sufficient to Establish Probable Cause to Obtain a Search Warrant

United States v. Leon 468 U.S. 897 (1984)

In August 1981, a confidential informant of unproven reliability informed an officer of the Burbank Police Department that two persons known to him as "Armando" and "Patsy" were selling large quantities of cocaine and methaqualone from their residence at 920 Price Drive in Burbank, California. The informant also indicated that he had witnessed a sale of methaqualone by "Patsy" at the residence approximately 5 months earlier and had observed at the time a shoebox containing a large amount of cash that belonged to "Patsy." He further declared that "Armando" and "Patsy" generally kept only small quantities of drugs at their residence and stored the remainder at another location in Burbank.

On the basis of this information, the Burbank police initiated an extensive investigation focusing first on the Price Drive residence and later on two other residences as well. Cars parked at the Price Drive residence were determined to belong to Armando Sanchez, who had previously been arrested for possession of marijuana, and Patsy Stewart, who had no criminal record. During the course of the investigation, officers observed an automobile belonging to Ricardo Del Castillo, who had previously been arrested for possession of 50 pounds of marijuana, arrive at the Price Drive residence. The driver of the car entered the house, exited shortly thereafter carrying a small paper sack, and drove away. A check of Del Castillo's probation records led the officers to Alberto Leon, whose telephone number Del Castillo had listed as his employer's. Leon had been arrested in 1980 on drug charges, and a companion had informed the police at that time that Leon was heavily involved in the importation of drugs into this country. Before the current investigation began, the Burbank officers had learned that an informant had told a Glendale police officer that Leon stored a large quantity of methaqualone at his residence in Glendale. During the course of the investigation, Burbank officers learned that Leon was living at 716 South Sunset Canyon in Burbank.

Subsequently, the officers observed several persons, at least one of whom had prior drug involvement, arrive at the Price Drive residence and leave with small packages; observed a variety of other material activity at the two residences as well as at a condominium at 7901 Via Magdelena; and witnessed a variety of relevant activity involving respondents' automobiles. The officers also observed Sanchez and Stewart board separate flights for Miami. The pair later returned to Los Angeles together, consented to a search of their luggage that revealed only a small amount of marijuana, and left the airport.

Note: This warrant application was found insufficient because the facts used to corroborate the reliability of the informant were either stale or only related to innocent activity.

Arrest Warrants

For an arrest warrant, facts must be given to establish every element of each crime listed in the warrant. Additional information must be included to show that the person named is the one who committed the crime(s). The physical description of the person to be arrested, along with his or her date of birth (if available) or approximate age, is usually required so the officers making the arrest can verify that they have the correct person. It is possible to obtain an arrest warrant even if the name of the suspect is not known if a detailed description, usually including an alias or street name, is given.

In several sexual assault cases, it was possible to successfully run a DNA test but the authorities did not know the name of the suspect. An arrest warrant was obtained based on the DNA report rather than a name. In at least one case, the person was later identified and charged with the crime.

Process to Obtain an Arrest Warrant
- Draft affidavit(s) that contains facts to establish

    Probable cause that crime occurred.
        Must have probable cause that each element in the definition of the crime occurred.

Probable cause that the person named in the arrest warrant committed the crime. Reasons why the judge should believe the information is true.

Affidavit must be signed under penalty of perjury.
Arrest warrant is prepared so it will be ready for the judge to sign.

- Present affidavits and draft arrest warrant to the judge.

The judge may have officer sworn in and ask for additional facts.
If the judge is satisfied that requirements for warrant have been met, the judge signs the warrant.

The judge can change the crimes listed on the warrant that the officers prepared for the judge's signature.

- Officers may execute the arrest warrant.

Example of Way to Establish Probable Cause for an Arrest Warrant

While on routine patrol on the evening of December 10, 2007, the undersigned officer observed a person in the alley behind 123 North Park Ave., Hometown. Said individual had an object in his hand that appeared to be a tire iron. The individual was using the object to pry open a garage door. The undersigned officer aimed the patrol car's flood light on the individual and ordered the individual to halt. The individual paused, looked at the undersigned officer for approximately ten (10) seconds, and then ran. The undersigned officer was unable to apprehend him. A tire iron was recovered at the scene.

Latent fingerprints were recovered from the tire iron by Officer Fred Smith. Based on a comparison made by Officer Fred Smith, fingerprints recovered from the tire iron match fingerprints in the files of this department taken when John Q. Doe was booked on May 2, 2001.

Officer Smith prepared a photo array of six (6) pictures of men who resembled John Q. Doe's booking picture. When undersigned officer viewed the photo array, he selected the picture of John Q. Doe immediately and unequivocally.

For the reasons stated above, an arrest warrant is requested for John Q. Doe for the offense of attempted burglary, Penal Code Section 459, at 123 North Park Ave, Hometown, on December 10, 2007.

Example of Facts That Did *Not* Establish Probable Cause for an Arrest Warrant

On October 10, 2007, the undersigned officer responded to a "robbery now" call at a 7-11 convenience store located at 654 North Juniper Ave, Hometown. Alice Woods, the clerk working at the store at the time I arrived, told me that a male juvenile robbed her. According to Woods, a male juvenile wearing a white T-shirt and blue jeans entered the store about 6:15 p.m., picked up a bottle of beer, and loitered near the refrigerator case until another customer went to the check-stand.

When Woods was busy with that customer, the juvenile tried to sneak out the front door. Woods said that she yelled, "Hey, come back here!" but never left the cash register. Three juveniles were standing outside the store when I took the report, but Woods did not recognize any of them as the juvenile who took the beer. Woods could not give a more detailed description of the juvenile who walked out of the store with the bottle of beer.

For the reasons stated above, an arrest warrant is requested for John Q. Doe for the offense of robbery, Penal Code Section 211, at 654 North Juniper Ave., Hometown, on October 11, 2007.

Reliability of Facts in Affidavit

Due to the fact that the affidavit is usually reviewed by a judge without a chance to question the person providing the information, the affidavit must also convince the judge that the facts are reliable. If the officer making the affidavit observed the facts firsthand, the fact that the affidavit is made under oath is sufficient to establish reliability. Information provided by crime victims and eyewitnesses is usually assumed to be reliable unless there is a motive to falsify. One problem that frequently occurs with victims is that they do not provide enough details to identify the suspect.

Informants who are themselves criminals create the biggest problem. Due to their past convictions, or a bad motive for incriminating someone else, they lack credibility. In *Spinelli v. United States* the Supreme Court established a rule that required applications for warrants to establish probable cause for the action sought (search or arrest) and separate probable cause that the informant is credible.[2] Some states still follow this rule, whereas others have adopted the more lenient standard established in *Illinois v. Gates.*

When a warrant is sought in a state that follows the *Spinelli* standard, facts stated in the affidavit must establish the reliability of the informant. The most common method used to do this is to give specific examples of useful information that the informant has given the officers in the past. If, in previous cases, officers checked out the facts supplied by the informant and found they were correct, the informant's reliability in the current case is enhanced. Another method is to verify the information provided in the present case. When reliability is established by verifying facts, the Supreme Court insisted in *Spinelli* that the facts that were checked showed criminal activity. Merely verifying innocent facts, such as addresses and telephone numbers, is not enough.

In 1983, in *Illinois v. Gates*, the Supreme Court ruled that anonymous tips could be used to obtain search warrants.[3] The Court relaxed the older rule that required that facts supporting the informant's reliability be given in the affidavit. In states that follow this rule, it is possible to support the reliability of the information by showing that the facts given are so detailed that they must be true. When an anonymous informant is used, it is especially important that as many facts as possible be given in the affidavit. Even so, the police must verify as much of the information as possible prior to seeking a warrant.

A distinction must be made between confidential informants and anonymous ones. **Confidential informants** give police information on the condition that their names will not be revealed. This information can be used in a warrant without giving the name of the person who provided it. At a later time, the defendant may request the name of the informant, but the judge will only require the police to disclose it if the identity of the informant is crucial to the case (*McCray v. Illinois*).[4]

People whose identities are unknown, referred to as **anonymous informants,** frequently provide information to the police. They may call a hotline, such as "We Tip," and leave a message on an answering machine, or they may talk directly to an officer on the phone without identifying themselves. It would be impossible for the police to give the names of these people to the defense. It is also impossible, of course, to establish their prior reliability.

Procedure to Obtain a Warrant

The Fourth Amendment merely requires that a warrant be issued by a neutral magistrate. In most policing agencies, however, the case is reviewed by the officer's supervisor prior to seeking a warrant. Additionally, the prosecutor frequently reviews the file to determine if a warrant should be sought. Sometimes the prosecutor prepares the proper forms and helps police draft the required affidavits.

The completed warrant application is presented to a judge or magistrate who must be neutral and not part of any law enforcement agency. Many years ago, some states authorized high-ranking police officials and members of their attorney's general staff to issue warrants. This procedure was specifically disapproved in *Coolidge v. New Hampshire* because all personnel in law enforcement agencies are considered to have a vested interest in apprehending criminals.[5] The Supreme Court considered this to create a potential conflict of interests that could interfere with an objective review of the facts in the affidavit.

Most states restrict a judge's authority to issue warrants. The rules for arrest warrants and search warrants differ and may result in two or more judges being involved in the same case. Judges are usually restricted to granting search warrants for locations within the court's geographical jurisdiction. Arrest warrants may only be issued for crimes that occurred within the court district.

If there is more than one judge in the jurisdiction, each judge has equal power to issue a warrant. Although there is no constitutional requirement that a warrant be issued by a judge who is assigned to criminal trials, judges who are not assigned to the criminal calendar usually defer to those who are.

Once a request for a warrant has been rejected by a judge, it may not be taken to another judge in hopes of obtaining a more favorable decision. However, new affidavits containing more facts can be drafted and the process started again. This may require more work for the police in order to develop additional information, or it might merely mean that a careful review of the file shows that the original affidavit left out some key facts.

Many states require that search warrants be executed in the daytime (typically defined as 6 a.m. to 10 p.m.) unless the judge specifically indicates they may be served at night. Arrest warrants for misdemeanors commonly cannot be served at night unless the suspect is in a public place. There are usually no similar restrictions on felony warrants.

Search warrants must be served within a few days after they are issued. State laws vary, but search warrants usually expire within 10 days. The reason for this short time period is the same as the policy that rejects affidavits containing stale information. The only reason to invade a person's privacy is to obtain evidence that can lawfully be seized by the police. If there is too much delay, there is no longer any reason to believe that the evidence is at the location.

Arrest warrants must be obtained before the statute of limitations expires on the crime in question. State laws establish how long an arrest warrant is valid. Misdemeanor warrants frequently do not expire for at least 1 year; most felony warrants are valid for 3 years or more depending on the charge. Warrants for murder and a few other crimes may be valid indefinitely. The reason for enforcing old arrest warrants, but not search warrants, is that stale information may not be used to obtain a search warrant, but the passage of time usually does not change the probable cause that the suspect committed the crime. If new facts indicate that the person named in the warrant did not commit the crime, the warrant should be withdrawn.

Process to Obtain a Search Warrant

- Draft affidavit(s) that contains facts to establish

  Probable cause that crime occurred;
  > Must have probable cause that each element in the definition of the crime occurred.

  Probable cause that evidence that is relevant to this crime is currently at the location to be searched. Evidence includes

Items used to commit the crime

Clothing and other items witnesses observed during the crime

Items taken from the scene of the crime, including property that was stolen.

Reasons why the judge should believe the information is true;

Reasons why the judge should believe the information is not "stale."

Affidavit must be signed under penalty of perjury.

Search warrant is prepared so it will be ready for the judge to sign.

• Present affidavits and draft search warrant to judge.

The judge may have officer sworn in and ask for additional facts.

If the judge is satisfied that requirements for warrant have been met, the judge signs the warrant.

The judge can change the items to be seized or the location to be searched on the draft warrant before the judge signs the search warrant.

• Officers may execute the arrest warrant.

Must execute warrant before it expires.

Knock-and-announce applies to houses.

Protective sweep applies in any type of building.

Plain View Doctrine applies as long as officers execute search warrant properly.

• Return must be filed after warrant was executed.

States when search warrant was executed.

Who executed it.

Inventory of items seized when search warrant was executed.

Example of Proper Procedures to Obtain a Search Warrant

On February 1, 2008, patrol officers observed Apartment #4 at 987 South Seventh Street for 90 minutes. While they watched, they saw 5 people enter the apartment. From their viewpoint a block away, it appeared that people came out of the apartment carrying small bags. They wrote a memo notifying the Narcotics Bureau detailing their observations.

Narcotics officers set up a stakeout that lasted 15 hours spread over 3 days. Between February 4 and 7, 2008, officers on the stakeout observed 29 people enter Apartment #4 at 987 South Seventh Street; 27 of these people exited after staying less than 10 minutes; each of these 27 people carried a small paper bag.

An undercover narcotics officer went to Apartment #4, 987 South Seventh Street, on February 8, 2008. After entering through the front door, he was directed to the kitchen where he purchased a substance the seller said was "meth." The purchase was made with marked money. While in the kitchen, the narcotics officer observed an apparatus of the type commonly used to make tablets, a large plastic bag containing a white powdery substance was to the left of the apparatus, a clear plastic canister approximately 12 inches high and 16 inches in diameter containing tablets similar to the ones purchased, approximately 100 zip lock bags approximately 2 × 3 inches in size, and a package of brown paper bags of the type frequently used for lunches. No weapons were observed. When the person who was believed to have sold the controlled substance to the officer exited the apartment at 11:51 p.m., she was arrested. The search incident to arrest produced $579 in cash, including the two marked $10 bills used by the undercover officer to purchase the drugs. No weapons were found on the person who was arrested. Laboratory tests conducted on February 9 indicated that the tablets purchased contained a total of 19.2 grams of methamphetamine plus various fillers.

The undercover officer signed an affidavit and prepared a search warrant for the search of the kitchen of Apartment #4 at 987 South Seventh Street. The warrant authorized the search for methamphetamine powder and pills, equipment and paraphernalia used to make pills, cash, weapons, and other items that were contraband.

The judge reviewed the affidavit and concluded that there was probable cause that methamphetamine tablets were being made and sold in Apartment #4 at 987 South Seventh Street. The judge found no reason to believe that weapons were being used, so the portion of the warrant that authorized the search for weapons was crossed out before the judge signed the search warrant.

Example of Procedures Used to Obtain a Search Warrant That Were *Not* Appropriate

On February 1, 2008, patrol officers observed Apartment #4 at 987 South Seventh Street for 90 minutes. While they kept the location under surveillance, they saw five people enter the apartment. From their viewpoint a block away, it appeared that people came out of the apartment carrying small bags.

They quickly drafted an affidavit stating the above facts and requesting a warrant so they could search the apartment for narcotics and narcotics paraphernalia. When they presented the affidavit to a local judge, she looked at it and told them that the affidavit did not contain probable cause to issue a search warrant.

Execution of Search Warrants

A warrant directs a peace officer to take specific action (i.e., search or make an arrest). The act of doing this is called the **execution of a warrant.** If necessary, a police officer may take civilians along when executing the search warrant; for example, if the warrant authorizes a search for jewelry stolen during a residential burglary, the owner of the jewelry may go along to help identify the items in question. On the other hand, taking the news media along when officers enter a private home violates the privacy of the residents.

The officer executing the warrant is responsible for verifying that the warrant is **valid on its face.** This means that the warrant looks like it was legally issued, and it has not expired. The officer is not liable in a subsequent civil case if a judge issued a warrant without probable cause *unless* the officer knew there was a problem with the warrant. For example, in *Groh v. Ramirez* (2004), an officer prepared an affidavit that supplied probable cause for a search warrant but the warrant did not indicate the location to be searched or the items to be seized; the court found that this warrant was not valid on its face and the officer was not entitled to immunity when sued for violating the suspect's Fourth Amendment rights.[6]

Even with a warrant, officers are expected to respect people's privacy. This results in five requirements:

1. Absent an emergency or consent of the occupants, a warrent is required to enter a home;
2. Prior to entering a home, officers must comply with knock-and-announce procedures;
3. A protective sweep may be conducted for the safety of the officers immediately after entering a building;
4. Searches must be restricted to the area described in the warrant;
5. A return must be completed after the search and sent to the courthouse.

Preference for Warrant When Entering a Dwelling

The Fourth Amendment specifically requires that search warrants "particularly describe" the location to be searched and the items to be seized. When executing the warrant, officers must restrict their movement to locations where they are reasonably likely to find the things specified in the search warrant. If a large item, such as a 25-inch color television, is to be seized, officers may not look in drawers or other places that are obviously too small to conceal such an item.

If the warrant mentions the location of the evidence, such as the kitchen, officers may not search other rooms. Although the courts have been quite strict in interpreting these requirements, they have given officers the right to seize evidence they find while legally conducting a search. For example, if drugs are found in plain view while officers are looking for the stolen television, the drugs can be seized and appropriate charges filed. This is called the Plain View Doctrine. It is discussed in more detail in Chapter 12.

Right to Enter

The ancient "home is one's castle" doctrine has been interpreted in *Payton v. New York* to mean that a person can prevent police from entering his or her home unless the officer(s) has a warrant or there is an emergency.[7] An arrest warrant is needed to enter the suspect's home in order to arrest him or her; if the suspect is hiding in someone else's home, a search warrant is needed to enter that dwelling. Emergencies that would permit entry without a warrant include hot pursuit of someone who just entered the house or someone inside the house calling for help.

Mincey v. Arizona held that there is no automatic right to enter a dwelling even if it is the scene of a murder or other serious crime.[8] The officers are justified in entering if there is a possibility that there are injured people inside who need assistance. Once it is determined that no further emergency aid is needed, the officers must either obtain consent from someone who lives in the dwelling or secure a search warrant.

Knock-and-Announce

Prior to entering a house, officers must comply with the knock-and-announce procedure unless special situations exist.[9] This rule applies to the service of warrants as well as actions done while investigating crimes and making warrantless arrests. The procedure is only required for residential buildings.

The proper **knock-and-announce procedure** requires four basic actions: (1) Police must knock or otherwise announce that they are there; (2) they must identify their official capacity (e.g., "Police."); (3) announce why they are there (e.g., "We have a warrant for your arrest."); and (4) wait long enough for a cooperative person to open the door. The length of the wait will vary, of course, with the circumstances. If no one responds, officers may resort to forced entry if necessary.

Two types of situations permit officers to enter without complying with the full knock-and-announce procedures. First, if there are explicit facts that indicate that the officer's life, or the life of someone else in the house, may be in danger, immediate entry may be allowed. Following an armed suspect to the house would be an example of this type of emergency. Similar exceptions are allowed if taking the time to comply is very likely to result in the destruction of evidence or escape of a suspect. To qualify for total avoidance of knock-and-announce, the facts must clearly indicate that there is an immediate danger. Mere suspicion or the fact that criminals usually destroy the evidence is not enough. In *Richards v. Wisconsin* (1997), the Supreme Court refused to allow judges to automatically waive knock-and-announce procedures when issuing search warrants in drug cases.[10]

Second, **substantial compliance** is permitted if the facts that develop while officers are giving the appropriate announcements indicate that there is danger. This follows the same basic situations mentioned in the previous paragraph: (1) danger to the police, (2) destruction of evidence, (3) escape of a suspect, or (4) danger to people in the house. Substantial compliance is only authorized if the officers, in good faith, have attempted to comply with the law, and while they are doing this the suspect does something to indicate that further delay would jeopardize the case. Common examples are hearing someone running away from the door while the officers are announcing their presence, the sound of toilets flushing when the officers are attempting to serve a search warrant in a drugs case, or hearing someone in the house screaming for help. In these situations, the Supreme Court indicated that the crucial question is how long it would take the suspect to destroy the evidence, not how long it would take a cooperative person to come to the door.[11]

Protective Sweep

Officers may conduct a **protective sweep** in order to prevent attacks on them when they execute a search warrant (*Maryland v. Buie*).[12] When executing a search warrant in a house, they may quickly look in adjoining areas to make sure no one is hiding there. To go to more distant parts of the building, the officers must have reasonable suspicion that someone might ambush them. A protective sweep does not allow officers to look in drawers or other areas too small to conceal a person. The Plain View Doctrine does, however, apply to things found when checking appropriate places.

Return

Lastly, officers must file a **"return"** on the search warrant. The return is a document, sometimes printed on the back of the search warrant, that tells the court what actions were taken. The time and date the warrant was served are listed. If anything was seized, an inventory of all items taken is included in the return. Copies of the warrant and the return are given to the person whose premises were searched. If no one was there at the time of the search, the copies are left at the scene in a conspicuous place.

If no one executed the search warrant, this fact is indicated on the return. After the officers complete the return, it is filed with the court and becomes part of the official record of the case.

Exclusionary Rule

Although the U.S. Supreme Court has had the power to interpret the Constitution and the Bill of Rights since its inception, few cases were decided prior to 1914 that dealt with the Fourth Amendment. *Weeks v. United States*,[13] decided that year, declared that evidence obtained by federal agents in violation of the Fourth Amendment could not be used in federal court. The rule, however, did not apply to state and local police. In fact, the rule was so narrow that the so-called "Silver Platter Doctrine" emerged. This doctrine, which lasted until 1960, allowed evidence obtained unconstitutionally by local law enforcement officers to be used in federal court.

In 1949, the U.S. Supreme Court declared that the Fourth Amendment was binding on state and local law enforcement officers. At the same time, however, it refused to rule that evidence illegally obtained under the Fourth Amendment had to be excluded from trials in state courts.

Exclusionary Rule and the Fruit of Poison Tree Doctrine

Mapp v. Ohio,[14] decided in 1961, finally made the **Exclusionary Rule** binding on state courts. Although *Mapp* made unconstitutionally obtained evidence inadmissible, it did not provide guidelines to help the police determine when the Fourth Amendment had been violated. The Court issued many decisions in the years following *Mapp* in an effort to clarify the application of the Fourth Amendment.

Throughout the years, the Supreme Court has followed two key rationales in applying the Exclusionary Rule: (1) deterrence of unconstitutional police conduct and (2) judicial integrity. The deterrence rationale excludes evidence based on the belief that police officers will be more careful if they know their errors may mean they cannot convict the criminal. The reverse of this has also been seen: If the Court believes that application of the rule would have little deterrent value in a specific situation, the Court allows the evidence to be used even though it was obtained in violation of the Fourth Amendment.

The judicial integrity approach excludes evidence because the courts should not be tainted by unconstitutional acts of the police. If this were the only basis for excluding evidence, the effect of the court action on future police conduct would not be considered. Very few cases have made judicial integrity the sole basis for their decision. In the 1970s, some Supreme Court cases did not even mention it. Recent cases usually mention judicial integrity, but the dominant rationale is deterrence.

The Supreme Court's language in *Mapp* indicated that illegally seized evidence is totally inadmissible in court. Two years later in *Wong Sun v. United States*,[15] the Court went even further and declared that evidence derived from illegally obtained evidence was also inadmissible. This is called the **Fruit of the Poison Tree Doctrine.**

Example 1

Aaron's briefcase was seized during an unconstitutional search. The briefcase and its contents would be inadmissible under the Exclusionary Rule. While searching the contents of the briefcase, the police found a key for a storage locker. They located the storage locker and discovered that it contained stolen televisions. The stolen televisions would be inadmissible

TABLE **10-1** Seizure of Briefcase during Unconstitutional Search

Exclusionary Rule	Fruit of the Poison Tree Doctrine
Illegally seized Aaron's briefcase and its contents.	The key to the storage locker was found in the illegally seized briefcase. Stolen TV sets were found when they unlocked the door to the storage locker.
Briefcase and its contents will not be admissible at trial due to the Exclusionary Rule.	The key was part of an illegal seizure. Therefore, items discovered when the key was used are inadmissible under the Fruit of the Poison Tree Doctrine.

under the Fruit of the Poison Tree Doctrine. Table 10-1 illustrates how the Exclusionary Rule and Fruit of the Poison Tree Doctrine apply to these facts.

Example 2

All items found during the search of Bob immediately following an illegal arrest would be inadmissible under the Exclusionary Rule. If Bob was given *Miranda* warnings immediately after his arrest and he confessed, the confession is usually inadmissible as "fruit of the poison tree" (Table 10-2).

At some point, the taint of the original unconstitutional act evaporates. Various factors have caused this result: passage of time; exercise of free will by a person giving the police information; the fact that a person has been released from police custody; a lengthy chain of events; etc. No one event automatically stops the Fruit of the Poison Tree Doctrine. The courts analyze all of the facts.

Example 3

The *Wong Sun* Case.[16] Narcotics agents had a tip from Hom Way that Blackie Toy was selling heroin. They illegally entered Blackie Toy's living

TABLE **10-2** Giving *Miranda* Warnings Immediately after an Illegal Arrest

Exclusionary Rule	Fruit of the Poison Tree Doctrine
Search incident to Bob's illegal arrest.	Statements Bob made during interrogation conducted immediately after the illegal arrest are inadmissible even if *Miranda* warnings were given correctly.
	Statements are the fruit of the illegal arrest.

quarters and interrogated him. Mr. Toy indicated that Johnny Yee sold drugs and kept heroin in his bedroom. Mr. Yee was arrested and surrendered nearly an ounce of heroin to the agents. He told officers that his supplier was Wong Sun. When Wong Sun was arrested, the officers who searched his apartment did not find any narcotics. Toy, Yee, and Wong Sun were arraigned on narcotics charges and released. A few days later when he voluntarily returned to the agent's office, Wong Sun was advised of his rights, including the right to have an attorney present. He made damaging admissions that were used at his trial. Table 10-3 shows how the Exclusionary Rule and Fruit of the Poison Tree Doctrine apply to the Wong Sun case.

Despite the broad language in *Mapp* and *Wong Sun*, there are many situations in which unconstitutionally seized evidence is admitted in court.

Good Faith Exception

In 1984, the Supreme Court recognized a **Good Faith Exception** to the Exclusionary Rule *(United States v. Leon; Massachusetts v. Sheppard)*.[17] Officers must be acting under an objective belief that what they are doing is constitutional. They must stay up to date on the law of searches, seizures, and confessions. The facts must be such that a reasonable officer could have made an honest mistake. If the officer has an ulterior motive, this exception does not apply.

T A B L E   **10-3** Application of Exclusionary Rule and Fruit of the Poison Tree Doctrine to the Facts in *Wong Sun v. United States*

Exclusionary Rule	Fruit of the Poison Tree Doctrine
Illegal entry into Toy's living quarters.	**Inadmissible**
Entry was held to be illegal because Hom Way was not a reliable informant.	• Statements made by Toy • Arrest of Yee • Heroin that Yee gave to agents at time of his arrest • Arrest of Wong Sun
	Admissible because taint of original illegal actions had dissipated
	• Statements made by Toy, Yee, and Wong Sun after arraignment while they were released from custody on their own recognizance. Agents asked them to come to headquarters for questioning. They were interrogated and made incriminating statements.

T A B L E   **10-4** **Good Faith Exceptions to the Exclusionary Rule**

Exclusionary Rule	Good Faith Exception to the Exclusionary Rule
Warrant was obtained to search Charlie's house based on an affidavit that did not contain enough facts to establish probable cause.	Evidence seized in plain view while executing the warrant at Charlie's house will be admissible if the warrant appeared to be valid on its face and the officers executing the warrant did not know there was a problem with the warrant.
Dan was arrested based on a statute that the arresting officer believed to be valid.	Evidence found during the search incident to Dan's arrest will be admissible if the officer in good faith relied on the statute even though the statute was declared unconstitutional after the arrest was made.
Eve was arrested based on information the officers received from the dispatcher indicating that there was an outstanding warrant for her arrest. This information was erroneous; the warrant had previously been recalled but someone forgot to remove it from the database.	Evidence found in Eve's purse during the search incident to her arrest will be admissible in court if the officers in good faith made the arrest based on information in a normally reliable database.

However, acting in good faith is not enough. The rule only applies in a few distinct situations. It has been applied to actions done under search warrants that appeared to be valid on their face. An arrest made under a statute that appeared valid but was later ruled unconstitutional by the courts was also upheld. An arrest based on a check of computerized files that indicated there was an outstanding warrant for the suspect was held to fall under the Good Faith Exception even though it was later determined that the warrant had been recalled before the arrest was made. Table 10-4 gives several examples of the application of the Good Faith Exception to the Exclusionary Rule.

Inevitable Discovery

The **Inevitable Discovery Exception** to the Exclusionary Rule is based on the idea that the police would have found the evidence even if they had not used unconstitutional procedures. In *Nix v. Williams*,[18] the case that the Supreme Court used to establish the rule, the fact that hundreds of volunteers were searching for a missing child was used to show that the discovery of the body was inevitable. The fact that improper interrogation procedures were used to induce the suspect to tell police where the body was located did not make the body inadmissible because the police would have discovered it anyway. Each case will, of course, turn on its unique facts. The prosecution

TABLE **10-5** Inevitable Discovery Exception to the Exclusionary Rule

Exclusionary Rule	Inevitable Discovery Exception to the Exclusionary Rule
Illegally obtained statements made by Williams told the officers where to find the body of the victim.	The body of the victim, and any evidence discovered on it, was admissible because there were hundreds of people searching for the victim and it was inevitable that the body would have been found legally.

bears the burden of convincing the judge that the evidence would inevitably have been found by legal methods. Table 10-5 shows the relationship between the Exclusionary Rule and Inevitable Discovery Exception.

Independent Source

To admit evidence under the **Independent Source Exception,** the prosecution must convince the judge that the police discovered the evidence without relying on unconstitutional procedures. In *Segura v. United States*,[19] evidence had been illegally seized when the police entered the suspect's apartment immediately after arresting him. Later, the police obtained a search warrant based on legally obtained information, authorizing the search of the same apartment. Evidence not observed during the first search was seized. The Supreme Court found that the search warrant provided an independent source for the evidence seized during the second search. This would not have been so if the illegally seized evidence had been used to obtain the warrant. Table 10-6 shows the relationship between the Exclusionary Rule and the Independent Source Exception.

TABLE **10-6** Independent Source Exception to the Exclusionary Rule

Exclusionary Rule	Independent Source Exception to the Exclusionary Rule
Evidence observed in Frank's apartment immediately after his illegal arrest is not admissible.	Officers legally obtained a search warrant based on facts that were obtained independent of the search of Frank's apartment immediately after his illegal arrest. When executing this search warrant in Frank's apartment, they found the same evidence the other officers had observed but not seized.

The Independent Source Exception was also applied in *Murray v. United States*.[20] Federal agents illegally entered Murray's warehouse and observed numerous bales of marijuana. They did not seize anything at that time. Instead, they obtained a search warrant based on legally obtained information. When executing the search warrant, the marijuana they had previously seen was seized. The Court affirmed the admission of the marijuana at trial.

As the Court pointed out in *Murray*, the ultimate question is whether the facts in the affidavit and the execution of the search warrant are genuinely independent of the prior unconstitutional activity. The credibility of the police officer(s) involved is the crucial factor in this analysis.

Public Safety

The **Public Safety Exception** is based on the idea that the police are justified in acting to protect the public from immediate danger, even if it is necessary to violate someone's constitutional rights to do so (*New York v. Quarles*).[21] In this situation, there must be an immediate danger, such as a gun left where children can play with it. The fact that the area is closed to the public at the time the questioning is conducted does not change the rule because the danger will continue until the weapon is found.

In *Quarles*, the police arrested a man suspected of rape who was believed to be armed. They found an empty holster but no gun. An officer immediately asked the suspect where the gun was; the suspect indicated the location. Introducing the gun in court was upheld based on the Public Safety Exception to the Exclusionary Rule even though the *Miranda* warnings had not been given prior to questioning. Another example of the Public Safety Exception would be asking the suspect, immediately after an arrest for kidnapping, where the victim was being held. Only brief, urgently needed questions are permitted under this exception; attempts to get a full confession would not qualify. Table 10-7 illustrates the interaction of the Exclusionary Rule and the Public Safety Exception.

Knock-and-Announce Exception

The Knock-and-Announce Exception, which applies when a search warrant is being served, is based on the Court's conclusion that the Exclusionary Rule is designed to deter seizure of evidence using methods that violate the Fourth Amendment. When the police obtain a valid search warrant, the main purpose of the Exclusionary Rule has been fulfilled. The Supreme Court went on to say, "What the knock-and-announce rule has

T A B L E **10-7 Public Safety Exception to the Exclusionary Rule**

Exclusionary Rule	Public Safety Exception to the Exclusionary Rule
Police arrested George for attempted murder shortly after the crime. They noticed he was wearing a holster that was empty. They asked him where the gun was without giving him the *Miranda* warnings.	George's statement about the location of the gun was admissible because there was an important public safety interest in recovering the gun before anyone could be harmed.

never protected, however, is one's interest in preventing the government from seeing or taking evidence described in a warrant."[22] The Court balanced the interest of knock-and-announce against the burden of excluding otherwise legally seized evidence, and it concluded that violations of knock-and-announce when serving a warrant would not make otherwise legally obtained evidence inadmissible at trial.

Procedural Exceptions

A variety of situations have been found to be outside the scope of the Exclusionary Rule.

Harmless Error

Cases are not automatically reversed because the judge admitted unconstitutionally obtained evidence that should have been excluded. The Harmless Error Rule applies to most constitutional violations (*Chapman v. California*).[23] The case will be reversed *only if* the appellate judges are convinced, beyond a reasonable doubt, that the erroneously admitted evidence influenced the jury's decision in the case.

Harmless error is usually the last issue considered on appeal. Before an appellate court considers the issue of harmless error, it must determine whether constitutional errors occurred. If they did, the next step is to determine how much weight the jury gave this evidence. The justices look at the weight of the evidence, not at the personalities of the individual jurors. They consider all of the evidence that was introduced against the defendant. The question that must be answered is whether the jury would have convicted the defendant if the evidence that was erroneously admitted had *not* been introduced. The burden of proof is high: In order to reverse a case, a majority of the appellate judges must conclude beyond a reasonable

T A B L E   **10-8** Harmless Error Exception to the Exclusionary Rule

Exclusionary Rule	Harmless Error Exception to the Exclusionary Rule
Illegally seized gun was admitted at Hal's trial.	If the trial judge erroneously allowed the illegally seized gun to be introduced into evidence at Hal's trial, the appellate court will reverse Hal's conviction only if a majority of the justices are convinced beyond a reasonable doubt that the admission of the gun influenced the jury's decision to convict Hal.

doubt that the erroneously admitted evidence influenced the jury's verdict. If the evidence against the defendant is overwhelming, the justices easily conclude that the erroneously introduced evidence was harmless. If the evidence barely established guilt, the case is likely to be reversed. The weight of each piece of evidence that was erroneously admitted is evaluated before the justices can decide the outcome of the appeal when neither of these extremes apply. Table 10-8 illustrates the relationship between an error at trial and an appellate court's decision to reverse.

Grand Jury

The right of the grand jury to investigate criminal cases is deeply embedded in our legal history. In *United States v. Calandra*,[24] the Supreme Court held that this tradition is stronger than the Exclusionary Rule. Unconstitutionally obtained evidence may be introduced for the grand jury to consider when returning an indictment, even though the same evidence will be inadmissible at trial. This ruling allows cases to proceed into the phase of the case in which most plea bargaining is done. Table 10-9 gives an example of the use of illegally seized evidence at a grand jury hearing.

Impeachment

Although the Exclusionary Rule prevents the prosecution from using illegally obtained evidence to establish its case, the rule is not a license for the defendant to commit perjury. In *Harris v. New York*,[25] the Court held that if a defendant testifies during trial, statements he or she made to the police can be used for impeachment. The statements must relate to the topics raised during direct examination. Confessions obtained by coercion may not be used for impeachment, however, because they are inherently untrustworthy and violate due process. The right to use unconstitutionally obtained statements

T A B L E **10-9 Grand Jury Exception to the Exclusionary Rule**

Exclusionary Rule	Grand Jury Exception to the Exclusionary Rule
Police illegally arrested Ingrid. During the search incident to Ingrid's arrest, cocaine was found in her pocket. The illegally seized cocaine would *not* be admissible at trial.	The illegally seized cocaine *could* be introduced when the grand jury decides whether to indict Ingrid.

for impeachment only applies to the defendant; the credibility of other witnesses may not be challenged in this manner (*James v. Illinois*).[26] Table 10-10 gives an example of how statements obtained in violation of the *Miranda* warnings can be used to impeach the suspect at trial.

In a few cases, this rule also applies to the results of illegal searches (*United States v. Havens*).[27] Evidence previously excluded must be relevant to a specific issue in the current case. For example, a suspect had been arrested on drug possession charges, but the case was dismissed because illegal methods were used to find the drugs. In a later case, the same suspect took the stand and categorically denied ever being involved with drugs. The arresting officer, who made an earlier seizure of a large quantity of drugs that the suspect was carrying, was allowed to testify in order to impeach this testimony.

Civil Cases

The Exclusionary Rule does not apply in civil cases. This is true even if the evidence was seized by the police. In *United States v. Janis*,[28] police illegally seized evidence while investigating gambling. After the prosecutor refused to file charges, the evidence was turned over to the Internal Revenue Service

T A B L E **10-10 Impeachment Exception to the Exclusionary Rule**

Exclusionary Rule	Impeachment Exception to the Exclusionary Rule
Police interrogated Jeff after his arrest and did not give him the *Miranda* warnings. Jeff admitted his role in committing the burglary. This statement would *not* be admissible during the prosecution's case-in-chief to establish that Jeff committed the crime.	During the defense's case-in-chief, Jeff took the witness stand and denied any involvement in the crime. During cross-examination, the prosecution *could* use Jeff's statement to the police in order to impeach him. **Note:** Jeff's statement would not have been admissible if Jeff had not taken the witness stand.

T A B L E **10-11 Civil Case Exception to the Exclusionary Rule**

Exclusionary Rule	Civil Case Exception to the Exclusionary Rule
Police illegally entered Karl's residence and seized evidence of illegal gambling. The prosecutor refused to file criminal charges against Karl because the evidence would be inadmissible in criminal court.	After the prosecutor refused to file criminal charges against Karl, the IRS sued him in civil court for tax evasion based on the same evidence the criminal court ruled was inadmissible. The evidence would be admissible because the IRS case is in civil court.

(IRS). The IRS filed civil charges of tax evasion, relying on the illegally obtained evidence. The Supreme Court held that this did not violate the Fourth Amendment. It justified its decision on the deterrence rationale: Police do not seize evidence for the purpose of civil suits; therefore, exclusion of the evidence would have no deterrent value. Table 10-11 gives an example of the use of illegally seized evidence at a civil trial for tax evasion.

Deportation

The Supreme Court also ruled that unconstitutionally obtained evidence could be used in hearings held by U.S. Immigration and Customs Enforcement (ICE) to deport aliens. The ruling in *Immigration and Naturalization Service v. Lopez-Mendoza*[29] applies to both civil and criminal ICE proceedings. Table 10-12 gives an example of a situation in which illegally seized evidence could be used at a deportation hearing.

Sentencing

Although the Supreme Court has not specifically ruled on the question, many lower courts permit illegally obtained evidence to be used at sentencing hearings.[30] The reason given for these rulings is that only marginal

T A B L E **10-12 Deportation Case Exception to the Exclusionary Rule**

Exclusionary Rule	Deportation Exception to the Exclusionary Rule
Police illegally detained Larry and searched him. A large quantity of illegal drugs was found in Larry's backpack. A criminal court judge ruled that the drugs are *not* admissible because they were seized illegally.	If it was discovered that Larry was a resident alien in the United States, the illegal drugs *could* be used in court in an attempt to deport Larry due to his involvement in the illegal drug trade.

T A B L E **10-13** Sentencing Exception to the Exclusionary Rule

Exclusionary Rule	Sentencing Exception to the Exclusionary Rule
Police legally arrested Mike. When conducting the search incident to the arrest, the officers found a stolen watch worth $50 in Mike's pocket. They extended their search into the next room and found $10,000 worth of stolen jewelry. The $10,000 worth of jewelry would *not* be admissible at Mike's trial because the search incident to the arrest went beyond what is legally authorized.	The $10,000 worth of jewelry found in Mike's home *could* be used at the sentencing hearing in an attempt to convince the judge to give Mike a longer sentence than he would have received for the theft of the $50 watch.

deterrence would result from excluding the evidence. The courts believe that police conduct their investigations for the purpose of obtaining convictions. Excluding evidence from sentencing hearings would have a deterrent effect only if the police obtained it solely for use at the sentencing hearing. The Court did not believe this was the case. Therefore, it ruled that evidence obtained in violation of the Fourth Amendment could be used at a sentencing hearing. Table 10-13 illustrates how illegally seized evidence can be used at a sentencing hearing.

Parole Revocation Hearings

The Exclusionary Rule does not apply at parole revocation hearings.[31] The Supreme Court weighed the need to deter unlawful conduct by parolees against the likelihood that law enforcement officers would be motivated to conduct illegal searches so that parole would be revoked, and it decided in favor of maintaining controls on parolees. Similar standards would logically apply to probation revocation hearings. Table 10-14 gives an example of the use of evidence seized in violation of the Fourth Amendment at a parole violation hearing.

Search by Private Person

The Bill of Rights was designed to protect people from an overbearing central government. Since *Mapp*, the Fourth Amendment has also been used to protect people in the United States against actions by state and local governments. Even with this expansion, the Fourth Amendment does not protect against actions by people who are not working for a government agency. Evidence seized by a "private person" does not become inadmissible

T A B L E   **10-14** Parole Revocation Exception
to the Exclusionary Rule

Exclusionary Rule	Parole Revocation Exception to the Exclusionary Rule
Nancy, who was on parole, was illegally detained while walking down the street. She was searched and marijuana was found in her pocket. The marijuana would *not* be admissible at trial if Nancy was charged with possession of marijuana.	Nancy's parole officer filed a petition to revoke her parole because Nancy violated a condition of parole that required that she violate no laws. The marijuana *could* be used at the parole revocation hearing.

under the Exclusionary Rule.[32] To qualify for this exception, the private person must be acting on his or her own. If the police encourage a person to do what the police cannot do due to *Mapp*, the evidence is treated the same way it would have been treated if the police had conducted the search themselves. Table 10-15 gives two examples of the use of evidence obtained by private persons.

Impermissible Methods of Obtaining Evidence

There are certain boundaries imposed by our society that cannot be crossed by the police in their search for criminals. The Supreme Court ruled that the police may not use methods that "shock the conscience" or "offend the sense of justice." These concepts come from the due process clause rather than any one amendment. *Rochin v. California*[33] is the landmark case in this area. Rochin attempted to swallow the evidence. The police responded by having his stomach pumped. The Court found that this procedure was very painful and could not be tolerated in a civilized society. The use of the "third degree" to obtain confessions is on similar footing. Due process is violated when coercion is used during interrogation (*Hayes v. Washington*).[34]

More recently, the Court considered the question of performing surgery on the suspect to obtain evidence (*Winston v. Lee*).[35] The case involved the recovery of a bullet that lodged in the suspect's arm when he was shot by the crime victim. A search warrant or other court order was a necessary prerequisite to performing the operation without the subject's permission.

Although the Court has not totally ruled out the use of surgery, it established a balancing test that heavily favors the privacy of the individual. Surgical procedures that pose any threat to the suspect's health cannot be done. The prosecution must show a compelling need for the evidence. If there are other witnesses who can supply the needed information, surgery

T A B L E   **10-15 Search by Private Person Exception to the Exclusionary Rule**

Exclusionary Rule	Search by Private Person Exception to the Exclusionary Rule
Ollie was suspected of buying stolen merchandise. When he left his garage door open, the police entered the garage, looked through several boxes, and discovered 100 stolen watches. The recovered watches are *not* admissible in court because the police illegally searched the garage.	Paul, Ollie's next-door neighbor, heard rumors that Ollie was buying stolen property. When Paul saw that Ollie left his garage door open, he went into the garage and looked through several boxes. Paul found a bag containing 100 watches with the price tags still on them. Paul took the bag and its contents to the police station. The watches were identified as stolen from a Federal Express shipment. These watches *could* be used at trial if it is established that the police did not direct Paul to search Ollie's garage.
Quint was dealing drugs out of the back door of his restaurant. The police were unable to obtain a search warrant because they did not have probable cause to search Quint's restaurant. Roxanne, the owner of the shop next to Quint's restaurant, called the police to tell them her suspicion that Quint was dealing drugs. The police told Roxanne, "We are sorry, but we cannot do anything about it. But if you brought us a sample of the drugs that Quint is selling, we could have it tested and obtain a warrant to arrest Quint." The next night, Roxanne surreptitiously entered the kitchen area of Quint's restaurant, put a sample of the drugs into a zip lock bag, and gave it to the local police.	The local police encouraged Roxanne to obtain drugs from Quint's restaurant. When Roxanne responded by trespassing on Quint's property to obtain evidence, the court treats Roxanne as if she was acting at the direct command of the police. Evidence that Roxanne obtained for the police is suppressed using the same standards that would apply if a police officer quietly entered Quint's restaurant and obtained the evidence. In these circumstances, evidence that Roxanne obtained is *not* admissible at trial.

is not a reasonable alternative. Surgery also would not be allowed if the facts indicate that there is a high probability that it will not be possible to conduct conclusive tests on the evidence once it is recovered.

Table 10-16 analyzes two situations in which the police sought to obtain physical evidence from the body of the suspect. Note that both the officers' actions and the reasons for their actions are important.

High-speed police pursuits are dangerous and occasionally result in fatal accidents. The Supreme Court ruled that reckless driving by the police does not raise constitutional issues. Due process is implicated *only if* the officer intentionally tried to cause harm unrelated to the legitimate objective of arresting the suspect (*County of Sacramento v. Lewis*).[36]

T A B L E **10-16** Impermissible Methods of Obtaining Evidence

Action	Analysis
Sam was shot by a police officer when he tried to escape from the scene of a robbery he had committed. The bullet lodged in his stomach. The area where the bullet was embedded became infected and made Sam very ill. He was taken to a hospital and the bullet was removed and the infected area cleansed.	The court would authorize surgery to remove the bullet in these circumstances. Even though abdominal surgery posed risks to Sam's health, it was done for medical reasons that aimed at speeding Sam's recovery.
Tom was arrested for driving under the influence of alcohol. He was taken to the emergency room so that a blood sample could be drawn for a blood alcohol test. Tom became very combative. Three officers subdued Tom and pinned him to the floor long enough for a medical technician to draw the blood sample.	The purpose of drawing blood was to obtain evidence to be used against Tom. The only possible benefit to Tom would be a showing that his blood alcohol was below the legal limit. If the officers used excessive force to pin him down so that the blood sample could be drawn, the court would rule that the methods used were excessive, shocked the conscience, and offended the sense of justice. Testimony about the results of the blood alcohol test would *not* be admissible at Tom's trial.

Summary

The Fourth Amendment was enacted to protect citizens from an oppressive central government. It mandates that warrants be issued by neutral magistrates based on facts given under oath or affirmation. To satisfy the Fourth Amendment, the judge must review the affidavits and determine whether the facts establish probable cause to issue the warrant. The judge also needs to know why the information in the affidavit is reliable. Search warrants cannot be based on stale facts. The area to be searched must be described in as much detail as possible so that officers will not unnecessarily invade someone's privacy.

When serving a warrant at a residence, officers must comply with "knock-and-announce" unless there is an immediate threat of harm to the officers, destruction of the evidence, or escape of the suspect. If no one responds to the knock, the officers may use force to enter.

While executing a search warrant, the officers must confine their search to places where the evidence listed in the warrant could be located. This includes staying out of areas where the warrant does not authorize entry, as well as restricting the search to places where items of the size indicated could be hidden.

The Exclusionary Rule prevents unconstitutionally seized evidence from being admitted at trial. The Fruit of the Poison Tree Doctrine excludes evidence derived from illegally obtained evidence. Even though the police violated constitutional rights, evidence may be admitted at trial if the violation was done in "good faith" reliance on an apparently valid warrant, a statute that was believed to be constitutional, or computerized information indicating that there was an outstanding arrest warrant for the suspect.

Evidence will be admitted under the Inevitable Discovery Exception if the court is convinced that it would have been found even if there was no unconstitutional activity. The Independent Source Exception also allows evidence to be admitted despite unconstitutional actions. To qualify under this rule, there must have been a genuinely independent and constitutional search that led to the evidence.

If immediate action is required to save someone's life, police may act under the Public Safety Exception. This exception authorizes only brief questioning aimed at preventing serious injury.

Cases are not dismissed for violations of the Exclusionary Rule if the Harmless Error Rule applies. This rule allows cases to be affirmed if the appellate judges are convinced that the introduction of inadmissible evidence at trial did not affect the verdict.

The Exclusionary Rule is not applied in a variety of situations. Grand juries may use unconstitutionally obtained evidence. The prosecutor can use it to impeach a witness or at the defendant's sentencing hearing. Unconstitutionally obtained evidence can be used in civil suits and in U.S. Immigration and Customs Enforcement (ICE) cases (formerly Immigration and Naturalization Service). None of the protections of the Fourth Amendment apply to actions of private persons acting on their own.

Evidence may not be obtained by means that offend our sense of justice. Surgery and other medical procedures that are particularly painful or dangerous are carefully scrutinized by the courts. Confessions may not be coerced. These situations violate due process.

Review Questions

1. Define:
    (a) Search
    (b) Seizure
    (c) Probable cause
    (d) Standing
2. Explain what must be in an affidavit for a search warrant. How does a judge determine if an affidavit is reliable?
3. Explain what procedures must be followed prior to entering a house to serve a search warrant.
4. What areas may be searched when executing a search warrant?
5. Describe two situations in which police may enter a residence without a warrant.
6. Explain when officers are allowed to conduct a protective sweep when executing a search warrant.

7. Explain the Exclusionary Rule and the Fruit of the Poison Tree Doctrine.
8. Explain the Inevitable Discovery Exception to the Exclusionary Rule. How does it differ from the Independent Source Exception to the Exclusionary Rule?
9. Explain three exceptions to the Exclusionary Rule that are not listed in Question 8.
10. Explain two types of police tactics prohibited by due process.

Writing Assignment

Go to www.cnn.com/crime and find a case in which the defense made a motion to suppress evidence. If you have trouble finding a current case, go to www.crimelibrary.com and type the words *Fourth Amendment* in the search box. Prepare a one-page (250-word) report explaining the legal rationale the defense used when it asked to have the evidence suppressed and the judge's ruling on this issue.

Notes

1. *Aguilar v. Texas* 378 U.S. 108, 12 L.Ed. 2d 723, 84 S.Ct. 1509 (1964).
2. *Spinelli v. United States* 393 U.S. 110, 21 L.Ed. 2d 637, 89 S.Ct. 584 (1969).
3. *Illinois v. Gates* 462 U.S. 213, 76 L.Ed. 2d 527, 103 S.Ct. 2317 (1983).
4. *McCray v. Illinois* 386 U.S. 300, 18 L.Ed. 2d 62, 87 S.Ct. 1056 (1967).
5. *Coolidge v. New Hampshire* 403 U.S. 443, 29 L.Ed. 2d 564, 91 S.Ct. 2022 (1971).
6. *Groh v. Ramirez* 540 U.S. 551, 157 L.Ed. 2d 1068, 124 S.Ct. 1284 (2004).
7. *Payton v. New York* 445 U.S. 573, 63 L.Ed. 2d 639, 100 S.Ct. 1371 (1980).
8. *Mincey v. Arizona* 437 U.S. 385, 57 L.Ed. 2d 290, 98 S.Ct. 2408 (1978).
9. *Wilson v. Arkansas* 514 U.S. 927, 131 L.Ed. 2d 976, 115 S.Ct. 1914 (1995).
10. *Richards v. Wisconsin* 520 U.S. 385, 137 L.Ed. 2d 615, 117 S.Ct. 1416 (1997).
11. *United States v. Banks* 540 U.S. 31, 157 L.Ed. 2d 343, 124 S.Ct. 521 (2003).
12. *Maryland v. Buie* 494 U.S. 325, 108 L.Ed. 2d 276, 110 S.Ct. 1093 (1990).
13. *Weeks v. United States* 232 U.S. 383, 58 L.Ed. 652, 34 S.Ct. 341 (1914).
14. *Mapp v. Ohio* 367 U.S. 643, 6 L.Ed. 2d 1081, 81 S.Ct. 1684 (1961).
15. *Wong Sun v. United States* 371 U.S. 471, 9 L.Ed. 2d 441, 83 S.Ct. 407 (1963).
16. *Wong Sun v. United States* 371 U.S. 471, 9 L.Ed. 2d 441, 83 S.Ct. 407 (1963).
17. *United States v. Leon* 468 U.S. 897, 82 L.Ed. 2d 677, 104 S.Ct. 3405 (1984); *Massachusetts v. Sheppard* 468 U.S. 981, 82 L.Ed. 2d 737, 104 S.Ct. 3424 (1984). See also *Illinois v. Krull* 480 U.S. 340, 94 L.Ed. 2d 364, 107 S.Ct. 1160 (1987); *Arizona v. Evans* 514 U.S. 1, 131 L.Ed. 2d 34, 115 S.Ct. 1185 (1995).
18. *Nix v. Williams* 467 U.S. 431, 81 L.Ed. 2d 377, 104 S.Ct. 2501 (1984).
19. *Segura v. United States* 468 U.S. 796, 82 L.Ed. 2d 599, 104 S.Ct. 3380 (1984).
20. *Murray v. United States* 487 U.S. 533, 101 L.Ed. 2d 472, 108 S.Ct. 2529 (1988).
21. *New York v. Quarles* 467 U.S. 649, 81 L.Ed. 2d 550, 104 S.Ct. 2626 (1984).
22. *Hudson v. Michigan,* 126 S.Ct. 2159; 165 L. Ed. 2d 56 (2006).

23. *Chapman v. California* 386 U.S. 18, 17 L.Ed. 2d 705, 87 S.Ct. 824 (1967).
24. *United States v. Calandra* 414 U.S. 338, 38 L.Ed. 2d 561, 94 S.Ct. 613 (1974).
25. *Harris v. New York* 401 U.S. 222, 28 L.Ed. 2d 1, 91 S.Ct. 643 (1971).
26. *James v. Illinois* 493 U.S. 307, 107 L.Ed. 2d 676, 110 S.Ct. 648 (1990).
27. *United States v. Havens* 446 U.S. 620, 64 L.Ed. 2d 559, 100 S.Ct. 1912 (1980).
28. *United States v. Janis* 428 U.S. 433, 49 L.Ed. 2d 1046, 96 S.Ct. 3021 (1976).
29. *Immigration and Naturalization Service v. Lopez-Mendoza* 468 U.S. 1032, 82 L.Ed. 2d 778, 104 S.Ct. 3479 (1984).
30. *United States v. Butler* 680 F. 2d 1055 (5th Cir. 1982); *United States v. Larios* 640 F. 2d 938 (9th Cir. 1981).
31. *Pennsylvania Board of Probation & Parole v. Scott* 524 U.S. 357, 141 L.Ed. 2d 344, 118 S.Ct. 2014 (1998).
32. *Burdeau v. McDowell* 256 U.S. 465, 65 L.Ed. 1048, 41 S.Ct. 574 (1921); *United States v. Jacobsen* 466 U.S. 109, 80 L.Ed. 2d 85, 104 S.Ct. 1652 (1984).
33. *Rochin v. California* 342 U.S. 165, 96 L.Ed. 183, 72 S.Ct. 205 (1952).
34. *Hayes v. Washington* 373 U.S. 503, 10 L.Ed. 2d 513, 83 S.Ct. 1336 (1963).
35. *Winston v. Lee* 470 U.S. 753, 84 L.Ed. 2d 662, 105 S.Ct. 1611 (1985).
36. *County of Sacramento v. Lewis* 523 U.S. 833, 140 L.Ed. 2d 1043, 118 S. Ct. 1708 (1998).

CHAPTER **11**

Field Interviews, Arrests, and Jail Searches

Feature Case: The Trial of Ivory John Webb Jr.

On January 29, 2006, Senior Airman Elio Carrion, who was home on leave after a 6-month tour of duty in Iraq, attended a family barbeque. It was the night before he was due to return to his base. Carrion and a high school friend, both 21 years old, were intoxicated when they left the barbeque. Although he had a suspended license, the friend borrowed a blue Corvette and sped through neighboring towns, passing a deputy at more than 100 mph. The deputy gave chase but was unable to catch them. Deputy Webb heard the chase on his police radio and took over the pursuit until the Corvette hit a dip, jumped a curb, swiped a fence, and rolled into a wall. The driver remained in the car, but Carrion jumped out the passenger door and lay beside the car.

Webb stood over Carrion with his gun drawn and the beam of his flashlight shining on Carrion's face. Webb repeatedly shouted, "Shut up!" but the men repeatedly talked back. Carrion gestured with one hand and told Webb "We mean you no harm" and "We are on your side." Carrion said that he was in the military and had more training than Webb. What happened next is recorded on 1 minute and 15 seconds of grainy videotape that was shown to the jury repeatedly in slow motion and freeze frame. The outcome is not in dispute: Webb shot Carrion in the leg, chest, and shoulder. In a statement prepared by Webb and read to the jury, he described how he felt during the encounter:

> My heart is going crazy—where were my guys [my backup]? I say to myself, "He's getting up." I'm getting lightheaded.... I can't get the

words out, I'm saying "Get up," I'm thinking "Don't get . . . " In my mind I'm shouting out, shouting it out, shouting it out, but . . . I've spent so much energy I can't—I can't get it out. . . . He turns toward me and I'm thinking to myself, "What is he doing?" And I see the hand, I'm dead, I'm, I'm dead.

According to the prosecution, Carrion had both hands on the ground just before Webb told him, twice, clearly to get up. As he got to his knees, Webb fired three shots. A prosecution expert inferred that the half-second pause between the shots was evidence of deliberate intent.

The defense emphasized that throughout the encounter, one of Carrion's hands was often in motion, either gesturing or, at two points, reaching toward Webb within inches of his weapon. At another point, Carrion reached into his oversized Raiders jacket and Webb thought he was pulling a gun. The defense attorney emphasized that Webb was in fear of his life, and regardless of what he said, he believed he was telling Carrion to get his hands back on the ground where Webb could see them. The defense asserted, "In that position—in that level of fear—no human being is held to a standard of having to articulate perfectly."

Both sides called experts on police training and tactics to analyze the tape and report on the appropriateness of Webb's actions.

At the end of the 4-week trial, Webb was acquitted of charges of attempted voluntary manslaughter and assault with a firearm that could have resulted in more than 18 years in prison if he had been convicted.

Learning Objectives

After studying this chapter, you will be able to
- Recognize the standard that allows police to detain a person without making an arrest.
- Describe the extent of the search permitted when police stop a person who is not under arrest.
- Define the standard for making legal arrests.
- Describe the extent of the search police may conduct when an arrest is made.
- Explain when a warrant is needed to make an arrest.
- Identify the type of search permitted when someone is booked into jail.
- List the types of searches permitted in a jail without a search warrant.

Key Terms

- Booking search
- Canine searches
- Citizen's arrest
- Field interview
- Frisk

- Jail search
- Plain feel
- Probable cause
- Protective sweep
- Reasonable force

- Reasonable suspicion
- School searches
- Search incident to arrest
- Temporary detention

Myths about Arrests and Detentions	Fact about Arrests and Detentions
If a fleeing felon fails to stop when told to do so, the police may shoot.	Police are only allowed to shoot if someone is in danger of imminent death or serious bodily injuries that are likely to cause death.
The police may not detain a person unless there is probable cause to make an arrest.	The police may temporarily detain someone for questioning if there is reasonable suspicion that the person is involved in criminal activity. "Reasonable suspicion" is a lower standard than probable cause.
The police have the right to automatically frisk anyone whom they detain.	The police only have the right to frisk (pat down outer clothing for weapons) if the officer has reasonable suspicion that the person is armed.
The police need an arrest warrant to make an arrest for a crime that was not committed in their presence.	Police can make felony arrests based on probable cause even if the crime did not occur in their presence. In most states, they need an arrest warrant to arrest for a misdemeanor that was not committed in the officer's presence.
When there is no emergency, police are required to obtain arrest warrants.	The only time the Supreme Court has required police to obtain an arrest warrant is when they will enter a dwelling to make the arrest.

This chapter focuses on the authority the police have to detain people against their will. Inherent in the right to detain is the right to use reasonable force to do so. The Supreme Court has ruled that the Fourth Amendment sets limits on the amount of force that officers may use.

The Fourth Amendment places boundaries on the rights of police officers to stop individuals. This chapter focuses on stops based on "reasonable suspicion" and "probable cause." Every time the police are allowed to detain someone, officers are also given the right to conduct at least a limited search if the circumstances indicate it is needed for their protection. The rights of the police vary according to the reasons for detaining the person. Three types of situations cover most police encounters: field interviews, arrests, and booking. Searches of jail and prison inmates are also discussed.

Right to Use Force to Detain or Arrest Suspects

Anytime an officer has the right to detain someone, the officer has the right to use reasonable force to prevent that person from leaving. This applies to both temporary detentions for questioning and arrests. The **force** used must always be **reasonable** under the circumstances. Deadly force is only justified if a life (including the officer's life) is in danger. The Supreme Court set this standard in *Tennessee v. Garner*,[1] a case that dealt with the right to use deadly force to make an arrest. The justification for the use of force is even less when officers are only investigating to determine if a crime has occurred. Only a situation perceived as life threatening will ever justify using deadly force.

The Fourth Amendment also controls the right to use less than lethal force. As the Court pointed out in *Graham v.* Connor,[2] when force is used, it must be reasonable under the circumstances. Although the rules on the use of force can be reduced to a short list, the rapidly changing situations that law enforcement officers face dictate that officers be well trained on the issues involved before they have to make split-second judgment calls on whether to shoot.

What Should Be Considered before Using Physical Force

Factors that *must* be considered when using physical force:
1. Reasonable person
2. Reasonable appearances
3. Reasonable force

Factors that should *never* be considered:
1. Get even
2. Revenge
3. Retaliation
4. "Teach 'em a lesson"

Reasonable Person

When the topic is the right to use force, the reasonable person is the reference point. A hypothetical reasonable person has all of the physical attributes of the person who must decide whether or not to use force. In addition, the reasonable person is in the same situation as the person in question, has the same weapons available, and the same people are present. The reasonable person will have reasonable emotional reactions to the situation. The reasonable person is neither overly timid nor overly brave.

If a strong, young policeman with a 9 mm gun in his holster is being attacked by a person who is high on PCP and the backup officer has an estimated time of arrival of 15 minutes, then the reasonable person is a strong, young policeman with a 9 mm gun confronted by a person who is high on PCP with no one to assist him for 15 minutes. If the officer is facing a hostile group of people, so is the reasonable person. If the question is whether a frail, 86-year-old woman who is cornered in her home has the right to shoot a group of muscular, young gang members, then the reasonable person has the same physical attributes as that frail, 86-year-old woman; is cornered in her home; and is confronted by the same number of muscular, young gang members.

Reasonable Appearances

When analyzing the right to use force, the facts are not as important as what the facts reasonably appear to be. In other words, if it reasonably appears that the menacing, tattooed juvenile has a gun in his pocket, the reasonable person will formulate a response based on the belief that the assailant has a gun. The analysis does not change if the postmortem reveals that the tattoos were temporary rub-ons and the juvenile had a water pistol.

Reasonable Force

Supreme Court decisions, resting on the Fourth Amendment, set two limits on a police officer's right to use force. First, officers may never use deadly force unless the officer's life, or the life of someone nearby, is in imminent danger. By inference, deadly force is never authorized to apprehend individuals for misdemeanors and nonviolent felonies. The offender's actions are more important than the offenses committed. Second, whatever force that an officer uses must be reasonable force.

Reasonable force is the level of force that a reasonable person would use to safely extricate him- or herself from a situation. If it appears the officer can talk his or her way out of the problem, then a resort to even minimal force would be unreasonable. Reasonable force is usually a higher level of force than the assailant is using because if both parties used exactly the same amount of force, there would be a standoff.

These situations are usually fluid and require new analysis every time the facts change. Consider the situation in which an officer is trying to talk an armed person into surrendering. When the gun is aimed at the officer and it appears that an emotionally distraught person is about to pull the trigger, it may be reasonable for the officer to shoot in order to save his life. A few moments later, when the person is apparently calm and has put the gun down, the officer would not be justified in shooting. If the person retrieves the gun and starts talking about suicide, the facts must be reviewed anew. During the course of the afternoon, there may be a dozen different situations that arise from the same location. Table 11-1 provides an analysis of appropriate use of force.

T A B L E **11-1 Analysis of Appropriate Use of Force**

A police officer told Zev he was under arrest and started to handcuff him. Zev became combative and swung his arm, hitting the officer in the head twice with the loose handcuff. When a second officer arrived, Zev tried to run away.	The issue of what level of force is reasonable must be considered based on what appeared to be happening when the force was applied. The first officer had the right to use reasonable force in self-defense when Zev was hitting him. If the other officer had been present during this assault, that officer would have been allowed to use reasonable force to stop Zev's attack. When the second officer arrived and Zev ran, the analysis changes because Zev is no longer attacking anyone. The officers should not continue to use the same level-of-force analysis that applied when Zev was attacking the first officer.
Yvette pulled a gun when a store employee stopped her for shoplifting. A standoff occurred until the police arrived. When an officer turned on the car's exterior speaker and said, "Put down the gun!" Yvette turned toward the police car and fired a shot. From the look on her face, it appeared that she was surprised that the gun went off. Her hand dropped to her side, and she stood there motionless, with the lights of the police car in her eyes, crying.	In a life-threatening situation, the police are allowed to use reasonable deadly force. This vignette illustrates the fluid nature of these situations. At the time the police arrived, Yvette was aiming a gun at the store employee. This could have been interpreted as a threat to the employee's life that justified deadly force, but before the police acted, Yvette changed her position. The analysis must also change. The next scenario involves Yvette aiming the gun at the police car and shooting. If the police had acted at that moment, they would have been entitled to shoot Yvette because she posed a very real threat to the lives of the officers. The final situation has Yvette with the gun at her side, crying. The officers must decide if it reasonably appears that she is an imminent threat to the lives of the officers, the store employee, or bystanders.
Will tried to kill a member of a rival gang. When the police arrived, Will sprinted down the street and over three fences. Based on the way he used both hands to vault over fences, the officers concluded that Will no longer had a weapon. None of the officers at the scene were able to keep up with Will. Fearing that Will would escape, an officer fired three shots at Will, killing him.	The issue of what level of force is reasonable must consider what reasonably appeared to be happening. If the officer shot Will when he believed that Will was not armed and did not pose a threat to the lives of the officers if he escaped, the shooting would be in violation of the Fourth Amendment.

Criminal Charges for Using Excessive Force

If someone uses more force than is reasonably necessary, the force that is beyond what would be considered reasonable is called excessive force. This is an important distinction because an officer can be charged with criminal conduct if he or she uses excessive force. If the excessive force results in death, the officer can be charged with manslaughter or even murder.

The prosecutor determines what charges to file, but the case will be decided by the jury (unless there is a plea bargain). Expert witnesses frequently have conflicting analyses of the facts. Review the Ivory Webb case. Even though the prosecution thought it had a strong case, the jury decided the officer should not be jailed as punishment for a mistake. In some situations, the U.S. Attorney will file federal charges for violating a suspect's constitutional rights if there was a flagrant violation and the local authorities did not treat the matter seriously. The officer cannot claim double jeopardy as a defense when this is done. Both state and federal charges were filed in the Rodney King case.

Field Interviews

Police frequently observe something that indicates that further investigation is called for. Many times the initial observation does not give the police officer enough information to arrest someone but indicates there is definitely something going on that needs to be checked out. Based on what they find during the **field interview,** the police may either make an arrest or release the person involved.

Right to Detain

The U.S. Supreme Court agreed with the police that officers should have the power to act even though the facts do not indicate that an arrest should be made. The leading case is *Terry v. Ohio.*

Standard for Temporary Detention

The police may temporarily detain someone for questioning if there are specific articulable facts that would lead a reasonable police officer to believe that criminal activity is occurring.[3]

The standard for this type of stop is frequently called **reasonable suspicion.** It differs from the standard for making an arrest in several ways. Reasonable suspicion does not require as many facts as are needed to make an arrest. The officer must be able to cite specific facts that caused him or her to believe criminal activity was present, but it is not necessary to identify a specific crime believed to be in progress. To make an arrest, the officer must believe that it is more probable than not that the suspect committed a crime. Reasonable suspicion only requires that a reasonable officer would believe that some criminal activity is occurring. An arrest is based on what a "reasonable person" would conclude; temporary detention can be based on what a "reasonable officer" would believe.

Even though the Court allowed the police to detain someone against his or her will without making an arrest, the police still cannot stop people any time they feel like it. An officer may stop someone based on reasonable suspicion but not randomly, on "mere suspicion," or based on a hunch. The officer must have specific facts that can be stated to justify detention—sometimes called "articulable suspicion."

The Court has never set a specific time limit on **temporary detentions.** The length of time must allow the officer to conduct a brief investigation. How long that investigation may take varies with the circumstances. One case involving a 90-minute detention was ruled unreasonably long. Cases involving 20-minute stops have been upheld. The detention should last no longer than necessary to determine if the person stopped was actually involved in a crime. The important thing is that the police diligently pursued reasonable investigative techniques in order to decide if the suspect should be arrested.

The courts have interpreted the temporary detention standard quite freely, permitting many police actions. For example, the Supreme Court held that the fact that a person ran from the scene when a police officer approached is sufficient grounds to detain the individual for questioning (*Illinois v. Wardlow*).[4] Merely associating with other known criminals or loitering in a high-crime area, however, is not sufficient to justify a stop.

Although most temporary detentions are based on the police officer's firsthand observations, often someone else provides the information. The Supreme Court, in *Adams v. Williams*, indicated that the police may use facts supplied by others if there is sufficient reason to believe the person supplying the facts is reliable.[5] The totality-of-the-circumstances test is used to make this determination, even if the information came from an anonymous informant. An anonymous tip, unconfirmed by the police, is not enough to detain someone even though the informant stated that the suspect was armed (*Florida v. J. L.*).[6]

The right to detain temporarily is not restricted to crimes in progress. Police may also stop someone on the basis of a wanted flyer (*United States v. Hensley*).[7] In these situations, the wanted flyer usually creates reasonable suspicion; additional details supplied by the law enforcement agency circulating the flyer establish probable cause for the arrest. If the flyer turns out to be based on insufficient evidence, the arrest is illegal (*Whiteley v. Warden*).[8]

Examples of Temporary Detentions

Legal Detentions
- Police observed two suspects, who appeared to be armed, outside a liquor store intently watching the clerk count money.
- Police saw a car with lights out driving rapidly away from the scene of a "burglary now" call.
- Police saw a person matching the description of a robbery suspect running away from the scene shortly after the robbery occurred.

Illegal Detentions
- Police stopped a person who was standing on a corner near the location where drug dealers frequently made sales.
- Police saw a car driving slowly in a residential area, stopping frequently to look at numbers painted on the curb in front of houses.
- Police stopped a person who was jogging at night in an industrial area.

Searches during Temporary Detention

The Supreme Court, recognizing that it is frequently necessary to search suspects in order to protect the officer, established standards governing these searches.

This limited search, frequently called a **frisk** or a "pat down," is designed solely for the protection of the officer. There is no automatic right to search every person stopped. Officers must have a reasonable suspicion that the search is needed for their protection. If a person is stopped, for example, because there is reasonable suspicion that a violent crime has been committed or is in progress, the right to search logically follows. If the situation involves a property crime, there may be little or no right to search.

Standard for Search during Temporary Detention
During a temporary detention, a search for weapons may be done *if, and only if,* the officer has a reasonable suspicion that the suspect is armed or dangerous. The officer may conduct a pat down of outer clothing for weapons. If the officer feels an object believed to be a weapon, he or she may reach into the clothing and remove it.

The scope of the search is limited to what is necessary to protect the officers. As previously indicated, in most cases, this involves "patting down" the suspect for weapons. If officers feel something they believe is a

Figure 11-1
Search during Temporary Detention
There was recently a shooting in the area, and the police officer is reasonably suspicious that this person may be armed.

weapon, then they may retrieve it. Sometimes this search may be slightly broader. For example, in *Terry v. Ohio* the suspects were wearing heavy coats because it was a cold winter day. The Court approved a search that included checking inner pockets for items that could not be detected during a pat down because of the bulky nature of the coats. Figure 11-1 depicts the extent of a legal search when a person driving a car was detained based on *Terry v. Ohio* and there was reasonable suspicion that he was armed or that there were weapons in the car.

When police, acting on reasonable suspicion, retrieve what they believe is a weapon, it is a legal search. This falls under the Plain View Doctrine. If, in fact, the object they seize is not a weapon, whatever they seize will still be admissible. The right to retrieve items in "plain view" was expanded slightly in *Minnesota v. Dickerson*.[9] The officers were allowed to remove items that did not feel like weapons if, by their distinctive feel, it could be determined that the items were contraband. This has been called **plain feel.**

Examples of Searches during Temporary Detentions

Legal Searches

- Officers observe bulge in suspect's pocket. During pat down, officer feels hard object the shape of a knife. When the object is retrieved, it turns out to be a package of rock cocaine.
- Robbery victim describes the robber and states that he had a gun. Officers stop a man who fits the description given by a robbery victim approximately 10 minutes after the robbery and approximately half a mile from where it occurred. An officer immediately frisked the suspect and retrieved a gun from the pocket in his pants.

Illegal Searches

- Officer who has no reason to believe suspect is armed conducts a pat down.
- During a legal pat down, an officer feels a lump of something that he or she cannot identify in the suspect's pocket. He orders the suspect to empty the pocket and discovers that the lump was a package containing methamphetamine.

Special Situations

A variety of situations have been before the Supreme Court. You should be familiar with the rights of the police to act in each of them.

Car Stops

There is no special right to stop a car or other vehicle. Nor do police have the right to randomly stop a car merely to check vehicle registration or to see if the driver has a valid license (*Delaware v. Prouse*).[10] In *Pennsylvania v. Mimms*,[11] the Court recognized the right of the police officer to order the driver to get out of a vehicle during a traffic stop. Other occupants may be ordered out of the car without particularized suspicion that they are involved in criminal activity (*Maryland v. Wilson*).[12] Someone may be searched if there is reasonable suspicion that that person is armed; for example, a bulge in the driver's pocket resembles a gun. Complete searches of the suspect and the passenger compartment of the vehicle are authorized if an arrest is made.

Cars are frequently stopped because of vehicle code violations. Depending on the state code, an officer may be authorized to stop a car and issue a citation based on something as minor as the license plate light being out. The officer needs at least reasonable suspicion of a code violation in order to make one of these stops; once the car has stopped, the officer will verify that the equipment is not functioning properly. If the driver will be released, the only rationale for a search is reasonable suspicion that the person is armed or has weapons in the vehicle. The passenger compartment can be searched for weapons in the same manner that it could if the stop had been based on *Terry v. Ohio*.

At other times, the facts may indicate that there is reasonable suspicion that the occupants of a car are involved in criminal activity. These cars can be stopped under the authority of *Terry* to detain suspects temporarily. When this occurs, officers have the authority to conduct a search of the passenger compartment for weapons only if there is an articulable and objectively reasonable belief that the suspect is potentially dangerous (*Michigan v. Long*).[13] This right to look for weapons exists even if the officers have decided to release the suspects. The rationale for this is that a suspect who has been released may return to the car, retrieve a weapon, and use it to harm the officers.

Examples of Car Stops

Legal
- Officer observed a car go through an intersection without stopping for a red traffic light.
- Officer observed a car driving at night without the headlights on.
- Officer observed a car go slowly down a residential street, stopping at every garage that had the door open.

Notes
In all three of these situations, the officer could conduct a pat down of the driver for weapons *only if* the officer had a reasonable suspicion that the driver has a weapon.

In all three of these situations, the officer could conduct a search of the passenger compartment for weapons *only if* the officer had reasonable suspicion that there is a weapon in the vehicle.

Illegal
- Officer observed a car being driven 5 miles below the speed limit on a street in an industrial area on a weekend. The car was stopped and immediately the entire vehicle was searched.

The facts stated do not indicate that there was a valid reason for the car stop. If there had been a legal stop and reasonable suspicion that there were weapons in the vehicle, the search should have been limited to the passenger compartment.

- Officer stopped a truck because the driver made an illegal U-turn at an intersection. The driver was pulled from the cab and searched thoroughly.

The officer had the right to make the stop of an illegal U-turn. In order to search the driver, the officer needed reasonable suspicion that the driver was armed. Even if there was reasonable suspicion that the driver was armed, the search should have been limited to a pat down for weapons.

- Officer saw the passenger of a car throw a paper sack from a fast-food restaurant out the window. The passenger was cited for littering and the passenger compartment and trunk were searched.

The officer had the right to make a stop for littering. In order to legally search the car, the officer needed reasonable suspicion that weapons were in the car. Search of vehicle should have been confined to a search of the passenger compartment for weapons.

Fingerprinting

The Supreme Court, in *Davis v. Mississippi* and *Hayes v. Florida*, heard cases involving taking suspects to the police station for fingerprinting.[14] Both times the Court ruled that this may not be done without probable cause to arrest. The most recent case indicated that it would, however, be legal to fingerprint a person at the scene.

Examples of Fingerprinting

Legal
- Suspect who is under arrest is taken to the police station and fingerprinted.
- Suspect who is stopped because he matched the description of a person who was seen leaving a nearby house that was burglarized 10 minutes earlier is fingerprinted at the location where he was detained.

Illegal
- Suspect detained on reasonable suspicion is taken to the police station and fingerprinted.
- All the people who work at a store where expensive electronic equipment is missing are taken to the police station without their consent and fingerprinted.

Interrogation

Miranda warnings are not required when an officer questions a suspect during a temporary detention based on reasonable suspicion. The warnings will be required for questioning after an arrest is made. *Dunaway v. New York*[15] held that transportation to the station for questioning can only be done if the suspect consents or has been arrested.

Examples of Interrogation during Detention

Legal
- A man is stopped based on reasonable suspicion that he is selling drugs and questioned for 10 minutes. The police officer did not give the man the *Miranda* warnings.

Illegal
- A woman is stopped based on reasonable suspicion that she used a stolen credit card, taken to the police station, and questioned for 10 minutes.

School Searches

Searches by school officials are governed by standards similar to those that apply to temporary detentions. There must be reasonable suspicion that the student has broken the law or violated a school regulation. These searches are not restricted to weapons. In *New Jersey v. T.L.O.*,[16] the Supreme Court affirmed the search of a 14-year-old girl's purse for cigarettes.

Examples of Searches at School

Legal

- A girl is detained in the vice principal's office and questioned about smoking in the restroom. She denies it. The vice principal dumps the contents of her purse onto the desk and searches the items from the purse for cigarettes.
- A boy is detained in the vice principal's office because a teacher reported seeing the boy sell marijuana. He is told to empty his pockets and backpack onto the counter. The teacher searches the things he put on the counter for marijuana.

Illegal

- When a fifth-grade student reported that her lunch money is missing, all the students in the classroom were searched because the teacher had no idea who took the money.
- Teachers randomly selected students in their high school and searched their belongings.

Canine Searches

The Supreme Court has allowed customs agents to briefly detain luggage in order to have narcotics detection dogs check it for drugs.[17] *United States v. Place* held that there must be reasonable suspicion that the suitcases contain drugs. The luggage may not be opened prior to the canine inspection. Additionally, the detention must not be unreasonably long. The fact that a reliable, properly trained dog indicates drugs are present will establish probable cause.

Examples of Canine Searches

Legal

- Dogs trained to sniff for drugs are stationed near the luggage carousel at the airport and allowed to sniff luggage as it is delivered from incoming airplanes.

  The luggage is being processed in the normal manner; therefore, the dog may sniff it without any particularized suspicion. Reasonable suspicion is needed to detain the luggage for the dog to sniff it.

Illegal

- A car suspected of being used to smuggle narcotics into the United States is stopped in the desert for an hour while the officers wait for a dog trained to sniff out narcotics to arrive.

  The car could be briefly detained based on reasonable suspicion.
  An hour detention was too long.

Arrests

In Fourth Amendment terms, an arrest is the seizure of a person. More commonly, it is thought of as taking a person into custody for committing

TABLE **11-2** **Comparison of Field Interview and Arrest**

	Field Interview Based on Reasonable Suspicion	**Custodial Arrest Based on Probable Cause**
Grounds to initiate contact	Reasonable suspicion—sufficient facts that would make a reasonable officer believe criminal activity is afoot.	Probable cause—sufficient facts to convince a reasonable person that a crime has been committed and this is the person who did it.
Warrant requirement	None.	Arrest warrant is mandated when officers will enter a home to make an arrest. Many states require a warrant to arrest for a misdemeanor not committed in the officer's presence.
Miranda warnings	*Miranda* warnings are not required.	*Miranda* warnings are mandated for all questioning after the person is taken into custody.
Right to use force	Officer may use reasonable non-deadly force to detain the person. Officers are restricted to the lowest level of force that will contain the situation. Deadly force may be used *only if* there is imminent danger to the life of the officer or a bystander.	Officer may use reasonable non-deadly force to arrest a person. Deadly force is never authorized to make a misdemeanor arrest. For felony arrests, deadly force is justified *only if* there is imminent danger to the life of the officer or a bystander.
Length of stop	Brief detention in order to ask the suspect questions. At the end of questioning the officers must decide whether to arrest the suspect or release him or her.	Once the arrest is made, the officers may take the time that is necessary to secure the scene and complete necessary paperwork. The suspect is then transported to the station and booked.

a crime. All arrests must be based on **probable cause.** Officers do not need to personally evaluate probable cause for the arrest if they are executing an arrest warrant or acting at the direction of another officer. Table 11-2 compares the field interview discussed in the previous section with an arrest.

Probable Cause to Arrest

Probable cause consists of a group of facts that makes a reasonable person more certain than not that an event occurred. In an arrest situation, that reasonable person must be more certain than not that the person arrested committed a specific crime. This requires a higher level of certainty than the reasonable suspicion needed for a field interview. It is a considerably lower level of proof, however, than the "beyond a reasonable doubt" required for a conviction.

To decide if there is probable cause, the officer must determine that there is probable cause for each element of the crime. In many cases, an arrest is made for one crime, but different charges are filed by the prosecutor. This may be due to new evidence, such as drugs found when the suspect was searched incident to the arrest. It can also be due to information discovered by the police between the time of arrest and when the charges are filed. The arrest is still valid if, at the time of the arrest, the officer had probable cause to believe that the suspect committed the crime for which he or she was arrested. This same rule applies even if the prosecutor refuses to file charges. The fact that the defendant was acquitted does not prove that the arrest was illegal; proof beyond a reasonable doubt that is required to convict is a much higher standard than probable cause for a legal arrest.

Powers of Arrest

At common law and in many states today, an officer may arrest without an arrest warrant if there is probable cause to believe a felony has been committed. For misdemeanors, officers are also required to have probable cause but can only arrest without a warrant if the crime is committed in their presence. When the crime has occurred before the officer arrived at the scene, the arrest must be made by someone who witnessed it or the facts must be presented to a judge who can issue an arrest warrant.

Having someone who witnessed the crime make the arrest (often the victim) is commonly called a **citizen's arrest.** For felonies, a citizen's arrest can be made by a person who knows of the existence of the crime even though he or she did not observe it occurring. Many states give the person making a citizen's arrest immunity from being sued for making the arrest only if the person making the arrest was correct in assessing the facts. In other words, a police officer can make an arrest based on probable cause, but a person who is not a police officer must be 100% certain. Most states require the police to take custody of a person who has been arrested in this manner, although citations are now issued for many nonviolent misdemeanors.

Another approach to the problem of misdemeanors not committed in the officer's presence is to have the victim and/or witnesses state the facts in an affidavit. The victim or the police can then go to the prosecutor. This is commonly referred to as "swearing out a complaint." A judge will review the affidavit and, if probable cause has been established, issue an arrest warrant. This procedure can be used if it is not possible to make a citizen's arrest because the suspect left the scene. It is also used if the victim does not want to press charges at the time the crime occurs but later decides to pursue the case.

Although the Supreme Court repeatedly has stated that obtaining a warrant is the preferred procedure, it has never required the police to obtain arrest warrants in cases in which they have probable cause, even if there is no emergency requiring swift action. Neither is there a requirement that they arrest as soon as they believe they have enough evidence to establish probable cause.

Officers are required to obtain a warrant if the arrest is to be made in a home. This rule, which the Supreme Court stated in *Payton v. New York*,[18] applies whether officers are looking for the suspect in his or her own home or in someone else's house (*Stegald v. United States*).[19] Either an arrest or a search warrant can be used to enter the suspect's home to arrest him or her; a search warrant is needed if the officers must enter any other home to make the arrest. The foundation for this rule is the right of people to privacy in their homes. There is an emergency exception to the rule that applies if someone inside the house is calling for help, screaming, or apparently being attacked. If officers are in hot pursuit and the suspect runs into a house, the emergency exception also applies.

Examples of Situations in Which Police Have Authority to Make Arrest without an Arrest Warrant (Based on Traditional Rules)
- Man flags down police officer and states that a man just pulled a knife on him and stole his wallet. Officer reviews the facts and concludes that robbery, a felony, has been committed.
- Officer responds to a domestic disturbance call. As the officer walks past the front window, she observes a man hit a woman in the face. The officer concludes that a domestic battery has occurred in her presence.

Examples of Situations in Which Police Do *Not* Have Authority to Make Arrest without an Arrest Warrant (Based on Traditional Rules)
- Woman flags down a police car and tells the officer that her boyfriend just beat her up. The officer reviews facts and concludes that a misdemeanor battery occurred, but the crime did not occur in the officer's presence.
- Drunken man flags down a police car and tells the officer that someone stole his wallet. When the officer questions the man, he notes that the man is giving inconsistent statements and concludes that it is more likely that the wallet was lost.

Search Incident to Arrest

Between 1914 and 1969, the Supreme Court repeatedly changed the rules on how far the police may search when they make an arrest. The current rule, which was established in *Chimel v. California* (1969),[20] was originally based on three main criteria: (1) protection of the officer, (2) preventing

Figure 11-2
Search Incident to Arrest
This person was arrested in a living room, and the police officer will conduct a search of the area.

destruction of evidence of the crime, and (3) seizure of contraband. It allows officers to thoroughly search the person and area under the immediate control of the person being arrested (Figure 11-2).

Standard for Search Incident to a Custodial Arrest
Immediately following an arrest, officers may conduct a thorough search of the person arrested and the area under the arrestee's immediate control.

The crime the suspect was arrested for has no bearing on the extent of the **search incident to arrest** (*United States v. Robinson; Gustafson v. Florida*).[21] The Supreme Court no longer follows the original rationale that one of the justifications for the search incident to an arrest is to seize evidence of the crime. Even for offenses that have no physical evidence, such as driving without a license, if the person is arrested and taken into custody, the search may include the person and area under his or her immediate control. This rule applies to all crimes for which an officer has the authority to take someone into custody, even minor ones such as driving without a seat belt (*Atwater v. City of Lago Vista*).[22]

The justification for the search is the arrest. Therefore, items found during the search cannot be used as a basis for the arrest. The search must be done contemporaneously with the arrest. Only searches done at the scene immediately after the arrest qualify. Those done later must be justified on some other grounds.

Unlike the protective search done during field interviews, there are no restrictions on the thoroughness of the search conducted when the suspect is arrested and taken into custody. Only the area searched is restricted. Anywhere the person arrested could reach to obtain weapons or destroy evidence can be searched. This "arm's reach" rule (also called the "wing-span" rule) is applied without considering the fact that the suspect was handcuffed prior to the search. Anywhere he or she could reach if not restrained is included. Some courts have permitted searches up to 10 feet from the suspect. Officers are not restricted to places where evidence is believed to be. They may open drawers, look under sofa cushions, check in the clothes dryer, or check anything else provided it is within arm's reach. Table 11-3 compares the officer's right to search during a field interview with the search that is allowed when making a custodial arrest.

T A B L E   **11-3 Comparison of Right to Search during Field Interview and Incident to Arrest**

	Right to Search during Field Interview Based on Reasonable Suspicion	**Search Incident to Custodial Arrest Based on Probable Cause**
Right to search	Officer must have reasonable suspicion that the suspect is armed.	Search is allowed anytime a person is arrested and taken into custody. No suspicion that person is concealing evidence is required.
Reason for search	Sole justification of search is to retrieve weapons that could be used to harm the officer.	Originally the Supreme Court stated the purpose of the search was to retrieve evidence of the crime, weapons, and contraband. Later cases have allowed the search whenever there is a valid custodial arrest even if there were no grounds to believe the person was concealing anything.
Timing	Search must be done during the brief detention allowed by *Terry*.	Search must be contemporaneous with the arrest.
Search of the person	Pat down of person for weapons.	Thorough search of the person.
Search of surrounding area	None.	Officers may search all items within the suspect's immediate control.
Search of vehicle	If person was in vehicle when detained, officers may search passenger compartment for weapons *if* there is reasonable suspicion that weapons are in the vehicle.	If person was in vehicle at time of arrest, officers may conduct thorough search of passenger compartment.

Search Incident to Arrest

Legal

- Suspect was arrested in a bank for forgery. Everything was removed from the purse she was carrying and closely inspected. Three forged checks were found in a bank deposit envelope in the lining of the purse.
- Suspect was arrested for selling drugs. In addition to a search of the suspect, officers thoroughly searched the passenger compartment of the car the suspect was driving at the time of the arrest. Five stolen credit cards were found wedged between the back seat and the arm rest.

Illegal

- Suspect was arrested for robbery. An officer drove the suspect to the station and booked her. The officer then returned to the location where the arrest was made and searched the area within 3 feet around where the suspect stood at the time of the arrest.

To qualify for a search incident to arrest, the search must be done at the time and place of the arrest.

- A car was stopped for speeding. After the driver signed the citation, one officer detained the driver at the curb while her partner thoroughly searched the passenger compartment of the car.

A search incident to arrest can only be done if there is a custodial arrest. In this case, the driver was going to be released on a citation; therefore, the only search that would apply is the one discussed under *Terry v. Ohio*. If the officers had reasonable suspicion that the driver was armed, the driver could be patted down for weapons. If there was reasonable suspicion that weapons were in the car, the passenger compartment could be searched for weapons.

Whatever is found on the person or under his or her immediate control during the search incident to an arrest is admissible evidence. It does not have to be evidence of the crime for which he or she was arrested. In many cases, the search incident to the arrest produces drugs or other contraband. Illegal weapons and evidence of totally unrelated crimes may be discovered. Additional charges may be sought based on what is found; it does not matter that the new charges are more serious than the ones that caused the arrest.

The search incident to arrest may overlap a protective sweep, but the timing of the search and what the officer is looking for are different. A protective sweep is normally done as soon as the officers arrive at the location. Its purpose is to locate people who are present who may ambush the officers. On the other hand, the search incident to an arrest must be done after the arrest and contemporaneous with it. The officer does a thorough search of the person and the area under that person's immediate control and may seize anything of evidentiary value. The right to search a person at the time of his or her arrest does not rely on any type of threat to the arresting officer.

Whether or not a physical arrest is made is important. When the state law authorizes a custodial arrest, it shows the offense is considered sufficiently serious to justify a major invasion of the individual's privacy. If the state deems the action less offensive, officers may be authorized to cite and release the suspect on the spot. Obviously, a citation is a much smaller invasion of the suspect's privacy. Accordingly, intrusive searches are not permitted. Traffic stops present a typical example. If the suspect is released at the scene, the officers may not invade the suspect's privacy by doing a thorough search. The officers can, however, order the occupants to get out of the car. The right to search in these situations is similar to what can be done during a field interview (i.e., protective pat down for weapons), but even this is allowed *only if* there is reasonable suspicion that the person is armed. Due to the fact that the officers are only with the offender briefly, their need to protect themselves is not the same as when the offender is taken into custody.

Arrests frequently involve either the driver or the passenger of a car. In the 1981 case of *New York v. Belton*,[23] the Supreme Court held that the entire passenger compartment, including the glove box and console, may be searched incident to the custodial arrest of an occupant of the car. *Thornton v. United States*[24] expanded the rule to include situations in which the person being arrested is a "recent occupant" of the vehicle. The search must be done at the time of the arrest, but the suspect may be removed from the car before the search begins. The Court also authorized an extensive search of anything in the passenger compartment, including luggage and other parcels. The Closed Container Rule (see Chapter 12) does not apply. Other parts of the car, such as the trunk, require some other justification.

When an arrest is made in a home or other building, officers may make a **protective sweep.** A protective sweep is a quick, visual check for people who may be hiding nearby. At the time of an arrest and without additional facts indicating danger, officers may look in the area immediately adjoining the place where the arrest was made, such as a closet where someone could hide. To go beyond that, the Supreme Court requires that the officer conducting the search has a reasonable belief based on specific articulable facts that, taken together with the rational inferences from those facts, lead a reasonable officer to believe someone is present who might attack the officer (*Maryland v. Buie*) (see Table 11-4).[25]

T A B L E **11-4** Comparison of Protective Sweep with Search Incident to Arrest

	Protective Sweep	Search Incident to Arrest
When search is conducted	When the officers arrive at the location	After an arrest
Rationale for search	Protect officers from being ambushed when searching or making an arrest	Protect officer; prevent destruction of evidence of the crime; and seize contraband
Area that may be searched	Area adjacent to where officers will be performing their duties	Person and area under that person's immediate control
What officers are looking for	People who are hiding and may harm the officers	Anything of evidentiary value

Examples of Searches Incident to Arrest

Legal Searches
- Immediately after the arrest, officers searched the suspect and found a small envelope containing heroin hidden in a cigarette pack in the suspect's shirt pocket.
- Suspect was driving a car when arrested on an outstanding warrant. Officers placed the suspect in the police car and searched the entire passenger compartment of the suspect's car. Counterfeit money was found in the console.
- Suspect was standing near a desk when arrested. Officers searched the desk drawers and found records of a bookmaking operation.

Illegal Searches
- Suspect was stopped for speeding (noncustodial arrest). Officers searched the suspect and found a stolen ring hidden in a handkerchief.
- Suspect was arrested on the front lawn. Officers entered the house and found a bank money bag taken in a robbery in the kitchen.
- Suspect was arrested at her home. After booking, officers returned to the house and conducted a detailed search of the area where the suspect had been standing when arrested.

Booking

Booking occurs when the person who has been arrested enters the jail or a holding facility. It also happens if a person reports directly to the jail to serve all or part of a sentence. Inmates who serve weekends or leave the facility daily on work furlough are included. Whether the person has been searched recently or not, the right to search at the time of booking is the same.

The reason for allowing **booking searches** is to prevent weapons and contraband from entering the jail. Searches done at the time of booking are usually divided into two types: (1) search of the person, and (2) search of property.

Scope of Search at Booking
A booking search may include a thorough search of the person and any items in his or her possession at that time.

Search of the Person

The booking search is usually the most extensive search of the person that occurs. Although both searches incident to arrest and booking searches allow thorough searches of the person, the booking situation provides the privacy necessary to do strip searches.

Due to the fact that weapons and drugs can easily be hidden, strip searches and searches of body cavities are permitted. Reasonable attempts to preserve privacy, such as shielding the strip search area from public view and having searches conducted by officers of the same gender as the suspect, are still required. Combative inmates who defy control by booking personnel or those who attempt to flee the booking area waive protections of their privacy.

Several states have enacted legislation limiting the right to conduct strip searches and body cavity searches when inmates are booked into the jail. Many of these laws were triggered by public outcry over how an "average citizen," arrested for a very minor offense, was humiliated during a strip search. Most of the states that have enacted restrictions allow full searches for felonies but limit them for misdemeanors. In misdemeanor cases, the police usually must have cause to believe that weapons or contraband will be discovered in order to do a strip search. Sometimes the statutes allow complete searches anytime the suspect is booked for drug or weapons charges but require a factual showing to justify a strip search in all other cases. These restrictive statutes frequently require a court order prior to conducting a body cavity search. Several federal appellate courts have applied similar restrictions to booking searches of felony suspects, but the U.S. Supreme Court has not considered this precise issue.

Examples of Searches of a Person at Booking

Legal Search
- During search of a woman booked for theft, rock cocaine was found sewn into the hem of her shirt.

- During the search of a man booked for driving under the influence of alcohol, a small packet of methamphetamine tablets was found hidden behind his ear.
- During a search of a woman arrested for prostitution, cash was found in her bra.
- During a strip search of a man arrested for dealing drugs, a balloon of heroin was found taped to his thigh.

Illegal Searches

Note: The U.S. Supreme Court has given police the authority to conduct invasive searches at the time a person is booked. Some state legislatures, however, have restricted this authority. These laws limiting booking searches most frequently apply to people who are booked for misdemeanors. Check your local law to determine if special rules apply in your state.

Property Searches

At booking, it is common to inventory and store all of the suspect's property, including clothing. Jail uniforms are frequently issued. These measures help keep weapons and contraband out of the jail facility and also reduce problems in the jail caused by thefts.

The Supreme Court has considered two cases dealing with inmate property at the time of booking. One dealt with sending clothing the inmate was wearing when booked to a forensics laboratory for examination. In *United States v. Edwards*,[26] the Court held that anything in the inmate's possession that could have been searched at the time of arrest could be searched in the jail without a warrant. No distinction was made between searches done at the time of booking and those done at a later time.

The second case, *Illinois v. Lafayette*,[27] involved searching a shoulder bag that the inmate carried at the time of booking. The Court held that any container or other article the inmate has in his or her possession at the time of booking can be searched. The Closed Container Rule does not apply at booking. Everything taken from the inmate may be listed in an itemized inventory. Inventorying property at the time of booking is viewed as necessary to prevent theft by jail employees; it also reduces the number of inmates making unfounded reports of theft. Information found during the inventory is also useful in positively identifying the person being booked.

Examples of Searches of Property at Time of Booking

Legal Searches

- Inmate's clothing and everything she was carrying were thoroughly searched at the time of booking.
- Inmate booked for felony drug charges was strip searched by an officer of the same gender in a room in the booking area where no one else could observe.
- Purse inmate was carrying at time of arrest was searched during booking.

- Items removed from inmate's pockets at time of booking were searched at a later time.

Illegal Searches

Note: No examples of illegal booking searches are listed here because the authorities who operate the jail have the right to search any property that will be introduced into the jail.

Jail and Prison Searches

Once a person has been booked, his or her expectation of privacy is greatly reduced. In fact, it nearly disappears. The Supreme Court generally allows **jail searches** if a valid administrative reason can be given.

Inmates may be searched at any time. The randomness of these searches is seen as an important factor in maintaining security and reducing the flow of contraband in jails and prisons. *Bell v. Wolfish* held that even slight grounds to believe that an inmate may be concealing contraband can justify body cavity searches.[28]

Cell searches may also be done without cause. Inmates have no reason to expect privacy in their cells (*Hudson v. Palmer*).[29] The need to maintain order and security within the facility justifies the intrusion into the inmate's cell. Some courts have allowed limited privacy interests in legal papers and diaries inmates keep in their cells.

This same need to maintain security in correctional facilities has justified limitations on what an inmate can possess. Many items that are legal outside the prison can be seized as contraband; for example, large paper clips may be prohibited because of the possibility they can be sharpened and bent to form weapons. Prison officials can also restrict what inmates receive from visitors and through the mail. Due process, however, requires that inmates be given reasonable notice of the rules.

Examples of Searches in Jail or Prison

Legal Searches
- Correctional officer stopped an inmate who was walking down a hall in jail and did a pat down. A makeshift knife was found in his pocket.
- Two correctional officers ordered all of the inmates to leave their cell block. They then searched every cell. Illegal drugs were found hidden in two cells.
- Correctional officers in the visiting room routinely do thorough strip searches of inmates before and after contact visits.
- Individuals who enter the prison for contact visits with inmates may be strip searched before and after the visit.
- Attorneys who visit inmates may be searched.

Illegal Searches

Note: No examples of illegal jail or prison searches are listed because the officers who run jails and prisons have the authority to conduct any search that promotes the safe operation of the facility. This includes unannounced strip searches and body cavity searches.

Summary

Police may briefly stop a person for questioning if there are specific, articulable facts that would lead a reasonable officer to believe that criminal activity is afoot. When this type of detention is made, a pat down of the outer clothing may be conducted for weapons *if* there is a reasonable suspicion that the detainee is armed. If a car is stopped, the officers have the right to search the passenger compartment for weapons *if* there is a reasonable suspicion that the car contains weapons. The right to detain a person for a field interview does not include the right to transport the suspect to the station for fingerprinting or interrogation.

All arrests must be based on probable cause. The officer must have facts that would cause a reasonable person to conclude that a specific crime has been committed and that this is the person who committed it. A totality-of-the-circumstances test will be used to determine if the officer had enough facts to justify the arrest.

Police usually have the right to arrest if there is probable cause to believe a felony has been committed, but in most states arrests for misdemeanors are restricted to situations in which the officers observed the crime in progress. If the officers were not present when the crime occurred, the victim or someone else who observed the misdemeanor needs to make the arrest or swear out a complaint.

A warrant is normally needed to make an arrest inside a house. An emergency (sometimes called "exigent circumstances"), such as officers following a suspect into the house in hot pursuit or someone screaming for help, permits entry without a warrant.

When a custodial arrest is made, a search of the person and area under his or her immediate control is allowed. The search must be done at the time and place of arrest. Anything found is admissible. If the person was arrested while riding in a car, the entire passenger compartment may be searched.

A thorough search of the person (and anything in his or her possession) may be done at the time of booking. The Closed Container Rule does not apply. Strip searches and searches of body cavities must be done in a manner that protects the inmate's privacy.

Once the inmate enters the prison population, there are very few restrictions on searches. Probable cause is not required. The need to maintain security and control contraband justifies random searches of inmates and cells.

Review Questions

1. What is the standard for stopping a suspect for brief questioning when there are no grounds for an arrest? Explain.

2. How much force may be used to detain someone for a field interview? For an arrest? Explain.
3. Explain when a search is permitted during a temporary detention. How extensive may the search be? Explain.
4. When may a person be transported to the police station for fingerprinting or interrogation? Explain.
5. What is the standard for an arrest and when is a warrant required? Explain.
6. What area may be searched at the time of arrest? Explain.
7. What search is permitted if a person is arrested in a car? Explain.
8. Explain the extent of the search permitted at booking.
9. Can property seized at booking be searched at a later time without a search warrant? Explain.
10. Explain the right to search inmates in prisons and jails.

Writing Assignment

Go to www.cnn.com/crime and find a case of a celebrity who was recently arrested. What was found during the search incident to the arrest? Write a one-page (250-word) report on the case that you found.

Notes

1. *Tennessee v. Garner* 471 U.S. 1, 85 L.Ed. 2d 1, 105 S.Ct. 1694 (1985).
2. *Graham v. Connor* 490 U.S. 386, 104 L.Ed. 2d 443, 109 S.Ct. 1865 (1989).
3. *Terry v. Ohio* 392 U.S. 1, 20 L.Ed. 2d 889, 88 S.Ct. 1868 (1968).
4. *Illinois v. Wardlow* 528 U.S. 119, 145 L.Ed. 2d 570, 120 S.Ct. 673 (2000).
5. *Adams v. Williams* 407 U.S. 143, 32 L.Ed. 2d 612, 92 S.Ct. 1921 (1972); *Alabama v. White* 496 U.S. 325, 110 L.Ed. 2d 301, 110 S.Ct. 2412 (1990).
6. *Florida v. J. L.* 529 U.S. 266, 146 L.Ed. 2d 254, 120 S.Ct. 1375 (2000).
7. *United States v. Hensley* 469 U.S. 221, 83 L.Ed. 2d 604, 105 S.Ct. 675 (1985).
8. *Whiteley v. Warden* 401 U.S. 560, 28 L.Ed. 2d 306, 91 S.Ct. 1031 (1971).
9. *Minnesota v. Dickerson* 508 U.S. 366, 124 L.Ed. 2d 334, 113 S.Ct. 2130 (1993).
10. *Delaware v. Prouse* 440 U.S. 648, 59 L.Ed. 2d 660, 99 S.Ct. 1391 (1979).
11. *Pennsylvania v. Mimms* 434 U.S. 106, 54 L.Ed. 2d 331, 98 S.Ct. 330 (1977).
12. *Maryland v. Wilson* 519 U.S. 408, 137 L.Ed. 2d 41, 117 S.Ct. 882 (1997).
13. *Michigan v. Long* 463 U.S. 1032, 77 L.Ed. 2d 1201, 103 S.Ct. 3469 (1983).
14. *Davis v. Mississippi* 394 U.S. 721, 22 L.Ed. 2d 676, 89 S.Ct. 1394 (1969); *Hayes v. Florida* 470 U.S. 811, 84 L.Ed. 2d 705, 105 S.Ct. 1643 (1985).
15. *Dunaway v. New York* 442 U.S. 200, 60 L.Ed. 2d 824, 99 S.Ct. 2248 (1979).
16. *New Jersey v. T.L.O.* 469 U.S. 325, 83 L.Ed. 2d 720, 105 S.Ct. 733 (1985).
17. *United States v. Place* 462 U.S. 696, 77 L.Ed. 2d 110, 103 S.Ct. 2637 (1983).
18. *Payton v. New York* 445 U.S. 573, 63 L.Ed. 2d 639, 100 S.Ct. 1371 (1980).
19. *Stegald v. United States* 451 U.S. 204, 68 L.Ed. 2d 38, 101 S.Ct. 1642 (1981).
20. *Chimel v. California* 395 U.S. 752, 23 L.Ed. 2d 685, 89 S.Ct. 2034 (1969).
21. *United States v. Robinson* 414 U.S. 218, 38 L.Ed. 2d 427, 94 S.Ct. 467 (1973); *Gustafson v. Florida* 414 U.S. 260, 38 L.Ed. 2d 456, 94 S.Ct. 488 (1973).
22. *Atwater v. City of Lago Vista* 532 U.S. 318, 149 L.Ed. 2d 549, 121 S.Ct. 1536 (2001).

23. *New York v. Belton* 453 U.S. 454, 69 L.Ed. 2d 768, 101 S.Ct. 2869 (1981).
24. *Thornton v. United States* 541 U.S. 615, 158 L.Ed. 2d 905, 124 S.Ct. 2127 (2004).
25. *Maryland v. Buie* 494 U.S. 325, 108 L.Ed. 2d 276, 110 S.Ct. 1093 (1990).
26. *United States v. Edwards* 415 U.S. 800, 39 L.Ed. 2d 711, 94 S.Ct. 1234 (1974).
27. *Illinois v. Lafayette* 462 U.S. 640, 77 L.Ed. 2d 65, 103 S.Ct. 2605 (1983).
28. *Bell v. Wolfish* 441 U.S. 520, 60 L.Ed. 2d 447, 99 S.Ct. 1861 (1979).
29. *Hudson v. Palmer* 468 U.S. 517, 82 L.Ed. 2d 393, 104 S.Ct. 3194 (1984).

CHAPTER 12

Plain View, Consent, Vehicle, and Administrative Searches

Feature Case: Snoop Dogg Arrested at Airport

On September 27, 2006, rapper Snoop Dogg was arrested as he was about to board a plane for New York because a collapsible baton was found in his computer bag during security screening. He told authorities that the baton, which could fold down to 8 inches in length, was a prop for a video he planned to film.

The 35-year-old rapper pled guilty to felony possession of a dangerous weapon. His sentence included 160 hours of community service, 3 years' probation, $1,000 in fines and court costs, and a $10,000 donation to a county charity for troubled children. His community services would be done at a local park where he would pick up trash, rake leaves, paint benches, etc. under the supervision of a park ranger.

The felony conviction would be reduced to a misdemeanor if he did not break the law for 1 year.

Learning Objectives

After studying this chapter, you will be able to

- Explain the Plain View Doctrine.
- Define the Open Fields Doctrine.
- Describe the right to search abandoned property and consent searches.
- List situations in which police have a right to search cars.
- Identify the exceptions to the administrative warrant requirement.

Key Terms

- Abandoned property
- Administrative warrant
- Aerial search
- Apparent authority
- Consent search
- Open Fields Doctrine
- Plain View Doctrine
- Right to inventory
- Roadblock

Myths about the Procedures Discussed in This Chapter	Facts about the Procedures Discussed in This Chapter
Under the Plain View Doctrine, an officer can seize anything that is in plain view when a search is conducted.	In order to seize an item under the Plain View Doctrine, the officer must be legally at the location and have probable cause that the item is either contraband or evidence of a crime.
Evidence officers find while trespassing is not admissible in court.	Under the Open Fields Doctrine, evidence is admissible even if the officers were trespassing. Searches done near a residential structure do not qualify for the Open Fields Doctrine.
Police must warn individuals of their Fourth Amendment rights before asking for consent to search personal possessions.	Police are not required to advise anyone of Fourth Amendment rights.
Only the owner of a building can give valid consent for the police to conduct a search without a warrant.	Anyone with apparent authority over an area can give valid consent for police to conduct a search without a warrant.
Police must obtain a warrant to search a car unless there is an emergency situation.	If police have probable cause to search a car, they can legally conduct the search without obtaining a search warrant.
Police are only allowed to search a car if they believe the car is being used for illegal purposes.	There are several exceptions to the warrant requirement that allow police to search cars that are not suspected of being involved in criminal activity.
Warrants that are obtained for administrative purposes must satisfy the same probable cause standards as search warrants.	Administrative warrants can legally be issued if there is a reasonable legislative purpose for the search as long as the officers are *not* investigating criminal activity.

Plain View and Open Fields Doctrines

The **Plain View Doctrine,** established in *Washington v. Chrisman, Coolidge v. New Hampshire,* and other cases, is one of the most well-known and useful exceptions to the warrant requirement.

Plain View Doctrine Defined

It is not an unreasonable search for officers who are legally on the premises to observe items left where they can be seen. Probable cause is needed to seize the objects observed in plain view.[1]

The Plain View Doctrine has three key elements:

1. Objects must be where officers can observe them.
2. The officers must be legally at the location where the observation was made.
3. There must be probable cause to seize what was observed.

The Observation

Finding objects in plain view is not considered a search because they are not hidden. However, under the Plain View Doctrine, officers are not allowed to move things or otherwise examine them for identifying marks (such as serial numbers). The item must be at a location where the officer can see it without disturbing anything. This does not prevent the officer from moving to a better vantage point to observe an item—for example, walking around the room, stretching or bending—as long as the officer stays in an area where he or she is legally entitled to be. Most courts also allow the use of flashlights and binoculars.

In *Horton v. California* the Supreme Court made it clear that items do not have to be discovered inadvertently to qualify for the Plain View Doctrine.[2] In that case, officers had requested a search warrant to search for stolen property and weapons, but the judge had issued a warrant only authorizing a search for stolen property. While executing the search warrant, officers did not find any stolen property, but they did find weapons. The court held that these weapons were in plain view and legally seized, even though the officers suspected that they were there before going to the location.

Examples of Observations Covered by Plain View Doctrine

- During a stop authorized by *Terry v. Ohio*, an officer believed the suspect was armed and did a "pat down." A hard object in his jacket pocket was believed to be a gun, but when the officer retrieved it, it turned out to be a roll of counterfeit $20 bills.
- While executing a search warrant for a large quantity of fake ATM cards, an officer opened a drawer and found 50 packets of heroin.
- A car was stopped for speeding. The officer looked through the window as he approached the driver and saw an illegal assault rifle on the back seat.

Examples of Observations *Not* Covered by Plain View Doctrine

- A police officer stopped a car illegally. Marijuana clippings were observed on the floor behind the driver's seat.

  Plain View does not apply because the officer was not legally at the location.

- A police officer was executing a search warrant. He went into a portion of the house not covered by the search warrant and noticed a stack of credit cards.

  Plain View does not apply because the officer was not legally there—he went into a portion of the house that was not covered by the search warrant.

- An officer made an illegal arrest. During a search incident to an arrest, the officer found narcotics in the suspect's pocket.

  Plain View does not apply because the arrest was not legal; therefore, the officer could not legally conduct the search.

Legally on Premises

For the Plain View Doctrine to operate, the officers must be legally at the location where the observation was made. Probably the most common situations involve making arrests, field interviews, car stops, and executing search warrants. If the officer illegally entered the house, for example, nothing observed inside qualifies for the Plain View Doctrine.

Aerial searches are an extension of this concept. In *California v. Ciraolo*, the Supreme Court held that observations made from a police aircraft qualify for the Plain View Doctrine.[3] The fact that the defendant built a fence around his backyard indicated a subjective expectation of privacy, but the Court found that this did not matter when the police observed some marijuana plants with the naked eye from public airspace. Since this case arose from observations made from a chartered aircraft, it is clear that the observation does not have to be made during routine patrol or from a frequently used flight path.

Examples of Being Legally on the Premises for Plain View Doctrine

- Officers arrived at a house to serve an arrest warrant. They complied with "knock-and-announce" before entering. Three feet inside the front door they observed a stack of uncut sheets of counterfeit $20 bills.
- Officers arrested the driver of a car for driving under the influence of alcohol. While they were inventorying the car prior to having it towed away, they opened the trunk and discovered 10 bricks of marijuana.
- Officers discovered the suspect's car in a public parking lot. They walked around it and checked for damage consistent with it being involved in a recent hit-and-run accident.
- Officers chartered a helicopter and flew over the suspect's house. Parked in the backyard partially covered by a tarp, they observed a vehicle matching the description of the getaway car from a recent robbery.

Examples of *Not* Being Legally on the Premises for Plain View Doctrine

- Officers suspected that the house at 301 S. First Street was being used to grow marijuana. They climbed a fence so they could look in the windows at the rear of the house.

  Plain View does not apply because the officers were trespassing when they looked into the rear windows.

- An eyewitness to a hit-and-run accident gave the police the license number of the car that left the scene. An officer used this information to obtain the address where the car was registered. When the officer arrived at the location, he walked into the open garage and checked the car for paint transfers and damage to the front bumper.

  Plain View does not apply because the officer was trespassing when he went into the garage.

Probable Cause to Seize

The fact that the item was in plain view and the officers were legally present indicates that there has been no unreasonable search. The final issue deals with the right to seize the item. To do this, there must be probable cause (*Arizona v. Hicks*).[4] Reasonable suspicion is not enough.

This probable cause requirement means the facts must indicate it is more likely than not that the item is evidence of a crime or is contraband. This decision must be made without searching the item for clues such as serial numbers. If probable cause exists, the item can be seized on the spot without a warrant.

Even when the facts do not establish probable cause, the observation may still be useful. It may provide leads in the investigation. The observation can also be included, along with other facts, in an affidavit used to obtain a warrant to conduct a full search of the location.

Examples of Probable Cause to Seize Item under the Plain View Doctrine

- When conducting a booking search of the suspect, an officer emptied the backpack that the suspect had been carrying. The officer carefully inspected everything and discovered a watch that exactly matched the description of a unique watch taken in a recent robbery.
- While executing a search warrant for equipment used to make counterfeit money, an officer discovered seven TV sets. By walking around the TVs, the officer was able to copy down serial numbers. The officer had the dispatcher run the serial numbers and confirmed that they matched those on TVs taken during a recent burglary of an appliance store.
- An officer inventoried a car found abandoned in the street prior to having the car towed to an impound lot. The officer found three hand-rolled marijuana cigarettes in the ash tray.

Examples of *Not* Having Probable Cause to Seize Item under the Plain View Doctrine

- While executing a search warrant, an officer found a zip lock bag with an odd colored powder in it. Having no idea what it was, she put the zip lock in an evidence envelope.

  The fact that the officer had no idea what was in the bag indicates that there was no probable cause to seize the zip lock bag.

- While frisking a suspect during a *Terry* stop, an officer placed a paper bag that the suspect was carrying into an evidence envelope without opening it.

  Probable cause is needed to seize anything under Plain View. This officer did not have probable cause because he did not know what was in the paper bag.

Open Fields Doctrine

The **Open Fields Doctrine,** established in *Oliver v. United States* and *United States v. Dunn,*[5] relies heavily on history and the wording of the Fourth Amendment. Since farmland and other open spaces are not included in the "persons, houses, papers, and effects" specified in the Fourth Amendment, they are not protected. Historical protection of the "curtilage," or enclosed area immediately around the house, expands the amendment to those areas but not beyond to open fields. Figure 12-1 illustrates where police officers can seize evidence under the Open Fields Doctrine.

Open Fields Doctrine Defined

Evidence found by officers in open areas that are not close to homes can be seized. This evidence is admissible even though the officers were trespassing at the time they seized it.

Figure 12-1
Open Fields Doctrine

The Open Fields Doctrine has little use in the urban setting, but it can be used in rural areas. It is very useful in the search for clandestine marijuana cultivation. The Open Fields Doctrine applies even though fences have been built and "No Trespassing" signs posted. Areas where there are no established roads can also be searched under this doctrine.

Examples of Application of Open Fields Doctrine
- Officers suspected that a farmer was growing marijuana in the portion of his field farthest from the road. They walked down the rural road, climbed a fence that had a "No Trespassing" sign, and went to the back of the field. They found approximately 100 healthy marijuana plants growing there.
- Police chartered a helicopter and flew over the suspect's farm. Approximately 500 yards from the house they observed 10 cars in various stages of being dismantled.

Examples of Situations That Would *Not* Qualify for the Open Fields Doctrine
- Officers were on private property when they found a large growth of marijuana plants. As they continued to investigate, they discovered a small cabin. Through the open curtains they saw equipment used to manicure marijuana and package it.

  Looking into the cabin's windows is not allowed under the Open Fields Doctrine.
- While responding to a call to take a burglary report, officers noticed that small marijuana plants were growing in the planter beside the front door.

  The planter beside the front door is not in an open field.

Abandoned Property

One of the key points in the Supreme Court's analysis of search and seizure issues is the expectation of privacy. Both an objective and a subjective expectation of privacy must exist. The subjective part of the analysis focuses on the efforts a person took to protect his or her privacy. The objective aspect of privacy means that a privacy interest exists that society is willing to protect.

Seizing **abandoned property** is not an unreasonable search because there is neither an objective nor a subjective expectation of privacy. In most cases, the fact that the property has been abandoned clearly indicates that the previous owner no longer has any interest in it. This is clear when the property has been left in a public place.

A more difficult question arises when trash has been sealed in opaque plastic bags and left at the curb for pickup by a garbage truck. Although the opaque plastic may indicate a subjective expectation of privacy, the Supreme Court, in *California v. Greenwood*, ruled that there is no objective basis for this expectation.[6] This rests on the fact that strangers, animals, and snoops are free to look through trash. The person throwing out the trash also has no authority to prevent the garbage collectors from rummaging through it or giving it to the police. Leaving items for recycling results in the same conclusion because it should be anticipated that someone will sort through it.

The final part of this analysis is determining when something has been abandoned. Dumping it in a trash can in a public place or littering the highway are obvious examples of abandonment. A person who merely puts an item in a waste basket inside a private home still has the right to reclaim it. Hiding something in an open area that is accessible to the public, such as under a rock in the forest, could be considered either way. Items that a person discards while being pursued by police, but prior to arrest, are considered abandoned.[7]

Examples of Situations in Which Abandoned Property Rule Applies

- As a police officer chased the suspect, the suspect threw something away. After detaining the suspect, the officer went back to the location and found a small plastic bag containing illegal drugs.
- Police suspected that a man was involved in bookmaking. They put his house under surveillance and watched him put his trash bags at the curb and go back inside. They seized the trash bags and searched them for anything indicating bookmaking.

Examples of Situations in Which Abandoned Property Would *Not* Apply

- Officers searching for evidence from a bank robbery found a cloth bag full of marked money carefully hidden under a dumpster.

  The fact that the bag was carefully hidden indicates that it was not abandoned.

- Officers looking for evidence of drug trafficking went into the suspect's backyard and searched his garbage cans.

  The garbage cans were still in a private party's backyard, so the contents cannot be considered abandoned.

Consent Searches

Officers do not need a warrant if they have obtained consent to search. On the other hand, probable cause to search cannot be based solely on the fact that a person refused to give consent.

Consent Search Defined

A search conducted based on the voluntary consent of a person with apparent authority over the area to be searched does not require a search warrant or other justification.

Three key points must be considered to determine if a search can be based on consent:

1. The standard for obtaining consent.
2. Who can give consent.
3. What can be searched based on the consent given.

Standard for Consent

Schneckloth v. Bustamonte established that consent must be given voluntarily.[8] The Supreme Court has, however, specifically refused to require officers to warn suspects that there is a constitutional right to refuse to give consent for a search. Each case must be analyzed on the totality of the circumstances that were present when the officers asked for permission to search. Officers do not need reasonable suspicion to approach a person and ask for consent to search.

Consent may be implied from a person's conduct. It is well-known that everyone goes through a security check before boarding a commercial airplane or being admitted to a rock concert. The Snoop Dogg case is an example. An illegal weapon was found when his carry-on luggage was searched at the airport. He could have avoided the search by selecting a different mode of transportation; he also could have reduced his chance of being arrested by placing contraband in luggage that was not subject to routine search.

Some factors clearly indicate that the consent is coerced. Consent is not voluntary if the police inform someone that they have a search warrant. Allowing the police to enter in these circumstances is considered to be merely acquiescing to authority (*Bumper v. North Carolina*).[9] By stating that they have a warrant, the police, in effect, inform people that they do not have the right to refuse entry.

More commonly, the courts will consider all of the facts present when the request for consent was made. The fact that officers had their guns drawn weighs very heavily against the consent being voluntary. Other applicable factors include the education and intelligence of the suspect, attempts by the police to intimidate the suspect, and the fact that the suspect already knew his or her rights. For example, in *Florida v. Bostick*, uniformed officers approached a person on a bus and asked for permission to search his luggage.[10] The officers testified that they informed Bostick that he had the right to refuse to consent, and they never drew their guns or threatened Bostick in any manner with a gun. Bostick testified that he did not feel free to leave the bus. The Court held that consent was valid and saw no distinction between a stop in the close confines of a bus and one on the street.

Examples of Consent Search

- During a routine traffic stop, the officer politely asked the driver, "Do you mind if I look in the trunk?" The driver replied, "OK."
- An officer handling a domestic violence call arrived after the batterer left. The officer asked the battered woman, "Do you mind if I look to see if there are any guns in the house? I can take the guns into custody so he won't be able to shoot you." The woman said, "Yes, please do!"

Examples of Situations That Would *Not* Be Considered Valid Consent Searches

- When officers arrived at the suspect's apartment, both the suspect and her roommate were there. The roommate told the officers that they were welcome to search the living room. The suspect refused to give consent for the search.

  When the suspect is at the location, the suspect's refusal to give consent cannot be countermanded by another person who lives there.

- An officer went to a suspect's home when he knew the suspect was at work. Holding up a folded piece of paper, the officer told the elderly gentleman who answered the door, "Search warrant. May I come in?"

  There is no valid consent when someone allows a search because an officer feigns having a search warrant.

Who Can Consent

Consent must be given by someone with **apparent authority** over the area to be searched (*United States v. Matlock* and *Illinois v. Rodriguez*).[11] Officers may rely on reasonable appearances that a person lives in a house or owns a business.

Ownership, however, is not essential. In fact, the owner may not be able to consent. The key again is reasonable expectation of privacy. Landlords cannot consent to searches of a tenant's apartment, nor can hotel personnel grant permission to search a guest's room. Police cannot rely on consent from people whose personal privacy is not at stake.

If two people have equal rights to a location, either may consent to a search. This commonly applies to husband–wife and roommate situations. For example, either roommate can consent to a search of the kitchen, but if they have separate bedrooms one cannot consent to a search of the other's room.

The parent–child relationship is more complicated. If a young child is living at home, the parent can consent to a search of the child's room and possessions. Older children, however, may have their own privacy interests. Paying rent or the fact that the parents recognize the child's right to exclude them from the room may indicate that a parent cannot give consent. Even if the parent can consent to police entering the room, teenagers may still have an expectation of privacy regarding locked containers kept in their rooms.

Very young children do not have the authority to consent to police entering the house. Children generally do not have the right to consent to searches of their parents' room or other private areas of the house.

Probationers and parolees pose a different question. Some states permit searches of probationers and parolees on less than probable cause. Others make consent to searches a condition of probation or parole. In *Griffin v. Wisconsin*, the Supreme Court approved of this practice because it is necessary to facilitate rehabilitation and deter criminal activity.[12] In the case before the Court, searches based on "reasonable grounds," but less than probable cause, were authorized under the supervision of the probation officer.

Examples of Who Can Consent to a Search

- A father called the police because he was afraid his 15-year-old son was using drugs. The police talked to the father while the son was not home. The father told the officer that his son stayed in the garage a lot. The officer asked if he could search the garage. The father gave the officer permission.
- Two roommates got into a fight, but one left before the police arrived. The neighbors called the police. Roommate A told the police that Roommate B was selling drugs. The officer asked where the drugs were kept. When told that they were in the freezer in the kitchen, an officer asked Roommate A for permission to look in the freezer. Roommate A said yes.
- A car carrying three adult males was stopped because a man who lived nearby complained that the car was cruising the area all evening. The officer had all of them get out of the car. He then asked the driver if he could search the car. The driver said yes.

Examples of Who *Cannot* Consent to a Search

- A woman was washing windows when the police arrived. An officer asked her, "Can we go in?" She nodded her head.

  There is no indication that the woman lived at the location or that she understood what the officers said. If either one of these factors is missing, the consent is not valid.

- The police stopped at the manager's office and asked for a key before going to the suspect's apartment. The manager gladly gave it to them.

  The manager is not the person whose privacy will be invaded; therefore, consent given by an apartment manager is not valid consent.

Scope of the Search

The area to be searched and how long officers can search may be very broad or very limited. These factors are governed by the conditions that accompanied the consent. Once consent has been given, officers can search anything in that area (including closed containers) unless the person giving the consent has placed restrictions on what may be searched.[13] Consent can be withdrawn at any time and no justification needs to be given for terminating the consent to search.

What is found during the search may create probable cause for an additional search. If so, this probable cause can be considered by the officers when seeking a search warrant. It may also indicate that some other exception to the warrant requirement applies. Plain view accompanies a consent search. Anything seen during the search can be seized if there is probable cause to tie it to a crime.

Examples of the Scope of the Search When There Is a Consent Search

- During a routine traffic stop the officer asked to look in the trunk. The driver consented. When the officer was searching the trunk, the driver suddenly yelled, "Stop. Get out of my trunk. Now!" Consent was taken away and the officer had to stop the search.
- Officers entered a pawn shop and asked the sales clerk, "Do you mind if we look around?" The clerk nodded agreement. The officers slowly inspected everything behind the counter, writing down serial numbers so they could check them later.

Examples of Searches That Are *Not* Valid Because Officers Went Beyond the Scope of the Consent

- After obtaining consent to search the dorm room from a college student who lived there, the officer pretended not to hear what was said when the student told the officer to leave.

  The officer cannot extend the consent beyond a reasonable attempt to revoke it.

- When the driver of the car that was stopped for speeding could not find the vehicle registration, the officer asked if she could look for it in the glove compartment. The driver agreed. While pretending to look in the glove compartment, the officer searched for narcotics under the passenger seat and in the door pocket.

  When the officer asked for consent to search a specific area, the consent was limited to that area.

Vehicle Searches

Cars and other vehicles have become very important parts of our daily lives and are highly visible and heavily regulated. Their extensive exposure to public view, coupled with detailed licensing requirements and safety inspections, has resulted in a lesser expectation of privacy in vehicles than in homes. The mobility of vehicles is viewed as creating an urgency not present when evidence is found in buildings. For all of these reasons, the rules for searching vehicles are somewhat different than those for other locations.

Motor homes are usually treated like vehicles. *California v. Carney*[14] concluded that even though motor homes possess many of the characteristics of houses, they still have the ability to leave the scene. This creates an urgency not present with more traditional dwellings. If, on the other hand, the motor home is hooked up to utilities or otherwise immobilized, it is treated like a dwelling.

Vehicle Search Incident to Arrest

The search incident to a custodial arrest normally covers the person and area under his or her immediate control. If the occupant of a car is arrested, *New York v. Belton* [15] permits the search to cover the person and the passenger compartment of the car. *Thornton v. United States* [16] expanded this rule to situations in which the person arrested is a "recent occupant" of the vehicle. The entire passenger compartment is viewed as the area where the person may reach to obtain a weapon and/or destroy evidence or contraband. Unlike the nonvehicle arrest, the person arrested can be removed from the vehicle prior to the search. This does not change the requirement that the search be contemporaneous with the arrest.

Right to Search a Vehicle as Incident to Arrest Defined
When an occupant of a car is arrested, officers may conduct a thorough search of the person arrested and the entire passenger compartment.

The passenger compartment is easily identified in a traditional sedan. It includes the area around the front and back seats, the glove compartment, and the console. It does not extend to the trunk, the area under the hood, or to other parts of the vehicle. Vans, sports utility vehicles, and other models that do not have a physical barrier separating the driver and occupants from storage space require a factual determination of what is the equivalent of the passenger compartment.

Everything within the passenger compartment may be thoroughly searched. This includes items, such as briefcases, that would normally fall under the Closed Container Rule. The glove compartment and console may be opened. Since both weapons and other evidence may be seized, areas too small to hide a gun or knife may also be searched.

Examples of Vehicle Searches Done Incident to Arrest
- An officer arrested the passenger in a car based on an outstanding warrant. Prior to taking the person to jail, the officer conducted a very careful search of the entire passenger compartment.
- An officer arrested the driver of a car for driving under the influence of alcohol, handcuffed him, and placed him in the back seat of the police car. An officer legally parked the car at the curb. While one officer watched the driver, the other very thoroughly searched the passenger compartment of the vehicle.

Examples of Vehicle Searches That Would *Not* Qualify as Search Incident to Arrest

- A patrol officer in New Jersey stopped a car for driving erratically. When the driver's license was run through the National Crime Information Center database, it indicated the driver had an outstanding arrest warrant for felony assault in New York. The driver was arrested and the entire car searched.

  Incident to a custodial arrest, the passenger compartment may be searched. In this case, the officers extended their search to the entire car.

- A traffic officer stopped a car for speeding. After writing a citation, the officer searched the passenger compartment of the car.

  The right to search the passenger compartment incident to an arrest only applies if there is a custodial arrest. The only search that applies when the driver is given a citation is the search for weapons authorized in *Terry v. Ohio.*

Vehicle Searches Based on Probable Cause

Primarily due to the mobility of cars and other vehicles, the Supreme Court in *Chambers v. Maroney* authorized searches without a warrant if the police have probable cause to believe that evidence is in the vehicle.[17] Subsequent cases make it clear that these searches do not require any type of emergency to justify the failure to obtain a search warrant (*Michigan v. Thomas* and *Maryland v. Dyson*).[18] In fact, a probable cause search may be conducted after a car has been impounded for a reason totally unrelated to the case.

Right to Search Vehicle Based on Probable Cause Defined

Officers may conduct a search of a vehicle without a warrant if there is probable cause to believe that the vehicle contains something of evidentiary value that can legally be seized. The search is restricted to areas where there is probable cause to believe the items are located. It may be done at the scene or later at a more convenient location.[19]

The scope of a probable cause search of a vehicle is directly tied to the facts. For example, if an officer saw someone run from the scene of a robbery, throw something in the trunk of a car, and then flee the scene on foot, there would be probable cause to believe evidence of the robbery may be in the trunk of the car. The trunk may be searched immediately based on this probable cause. These facts, however, do not provide any justification to search other parts of the car. It is important to note that once a search is justified, the officer can search anything in the car that is large enough to conceal the item(s) sought. This would justify searching a purse that belongs to a passenger in the car who is not yet suspected of criminal activity (*Wyoming v. Houghton*).[20]

Sometimes probable cause searches and searches incident to arrests overlap. For example, if police pursue a getaway car leaving the scene of a burglary with occupants matching the description of the suspects, they will have probable cause to arrest the occupants and probable cause to search the car. On the other hand, if a person in a car is arrested on an old warrant, there will be no probable cause to search the car.

There is no time limit on when a probable cause vehicle search must be done. It can be done at the scene or later. Officers can tow the car to a storage yard, the police station, or some other convenient location before searching it. One evidentiary issue must be considered, however. If the search is not done immediately, the prosecution will have the burden of showing that no one tampered with the vehicle or "planted" the evidence between the time the car was impounded and the search was conducted.

United States v. Ross held that the search of a vehicle based on probable cause can be as extensive as the one a judge could authorize if presented with an affidavit stating the facts known to the officers.[21] Closed containers can be searched on the spot. Officers are not required to seize them and obtain a warrant before opening them.

Examples of Vehicle Searches Done on Probable Cause

- Police saw a man run from a store with a clerk chasing him shouting "Thief! Thief!" The man threw something through the open window of a car and ran away. An officer reached through the open window and retrieved a brand new watch with the sales tags still on it.
- Police stopped a car for speeding. As the officer walked up to the driver, he smelled a strong odor of marijuana coming from the trunk. The officer demanded the keys to the trunk, opened it, and found 500 pounds of marijuana.
- Police observed what they thought was a drug deal. When they stopped the suspect's car, they observed approximately 25 baggies of marijuana on the passenger seat. The car was impounded. Two days later, they searched the entire passenger compartment and found a number of other drugs packaged for sale.

Examples of Vehicle Searches That Would *Not* Qualify as Probable Cause Searches

- The driver of a car was arrested based on an outstanding arrest warrant for robbery. Based on the fact that they had probable cause to arrest the driver, the police searched the passenger compartment and the trunk.

Probable cause to make an arrest does not give officers the right to conduct a probable cause search of the car. The search of the passenger compartment was appropriate because it was done incident to a custodial arrest. Searching the trunk went beyond what is allowed because there was no probable cause to believe that there was anything in the trunk that the officers could seize.

- After a foot pursuit, a police officer arrested a burglary suspect as she was unlocking the door to her car. The officers impounded the car and searched the trunk thoroughly.

  To do a probable cause search of the trunk of the car, there must be probable cause that something of evidentiary value is in the trunk. Here, the suspect had just arrived at the car, and the officers had no evidence indicating that she placed anything in the trunk of the car.

- A car was found abandoned in the middle of the street. Police impounded it and conducted a thorough search of the entire vehicle.

  When a car is impounded, the officers are allowed to conduct an inventory of what is in the car. This is different from the search that is done based on probable cause that something of evidentiary value is in the car.

Vehicle Search—Inventory of Impounded Vehicles

Whenever a car is legally impounded it may be inventoried. The reason for impounding the vehicle has no bearing on the **right to inventory.** The Supreme Court, in *South Dakota v. Opperman*,[22] based the right to conduct the inventory on the protection of both the owner of the vehicle and the police. The police protect the owner by accounting for everything that is present and removing valuable items. The police are protected against unfounded claims of theft because a detailed report is available stating exactly what was in the vehicle at the time it was taken into custody.

Right to Inventory Vehicles Defined

Anytime a vehicle is impounded, officers may inventory its contents. The inventory consists of making an itemized list of what is in the car.

Any evidence found during the inventory is admissible. The primary question is whether the police were searching for evidence or conducting a legitimate inventory. Department policies that require all cars to be inventoried are usually admissible on this point. In general, the courts are satisfied that an inventory was being conducted if the police systematically go over the entire car. The inventory is more likely to be considered a pretext to search if the officers stopped as soon as evidence was found. Closed containers may be opened during an inventory if the department's policy indicates that this action is authorized.[23]

Another distinction between a search and an inventory is the extent of the search. An inventory usually involves merely itemizing observable items that could be removed from the car. This commonly includes opening the glove compartment and trunk. It does not involve inspecting the inside of the spare tire, removing rocker panels, or cutting the upholstery open to see if they contain drugs. Such acts would be considered searches.

Examples of Vehicle Searches during the Inventory of an Impounded Vehicle

- Police had a car towed away because it was blocking a fire lane. When it arrived at the impound lot, they inventoried it. They found a jack, a tire iron, a spare tire, and a sack containing 100 counterfeit CDs in the trunk.
- Police had a car towed away because it was inoperable after an accident. They inventoried it prior to the arrival of the tow truck and found 10 forged checks and false IDs in the glove compartment.
- Police arrested a suspected bank robber after a high-speed chase. The car was impounded as evidence. Prior to towing it, the car was inventoried. In the trunk they found a bank bag from the bank that was robbed and money wrappers from the same bank.

Examples of Vehicle Searches That Would *Not* Qualify as the Inventory of an Impounded Vehicle

- The driver of a car was arrested for driving under the influence of alcohol and the car was impounded. An officer started by searching the trunk. As soon as he found narcotics in the trunk, the officer stopped the inventory.

  A search only qualifies as an inventory if the officer systematically inventories everything in the vehicle. When the officer stopped the process after finding the narcotics, the inventory was nullified.

- At the scene of a traffic accident the officer indicated that the vehicles would be impounded. After the inventory was complete, the car that was in operable condition was released to its owner.

  The right to inventory a vehicle only applies if the vehicle is impounded.

Vehicle Search during Stop Based on Reasonable Suspicion

Michigan v. Long[24] stated two prerequisites for the search of a car for weapons during a field interview:

1. There must have been specific articulable facts that caused the officers to believe that at least one of the occupants of the vehicle was involved in criminal activity AND
2. There must have been at least a reasonable suspicion that the vehicle contained weapons the suspect might use against the officers.

Right to Search Vehicles during Stops Based on Reasonable Suspicion Defined

During a field interview, the passenger compartment of a vehicle may be searched for weapons if there is reasonable suspicion that the vehicle contains weapons.

Although this type of vehicle search permits police to search the entire passenger compartment, it is more limited than the search incident to a custodial arrest. Weapons are the only things officers are justified in looking for. This means that only areas large enough to conceal a weapon can be searched. Anything found while the officers are properly conducting this type of search is admissible under the Plain View Doctrine.

The search for weapons can be done while the suspects are out of the car if they will be permitted to return to it. This is allowed because as soon as the suspect is released, he or she may retrieve weapons from the car and attack the officer.

Noncustodial arrests, such as traffic tickets, also fall under this rule. It is important to note that the second prerequisite, reasonable suspicion that the vehicle contains weapons, is not an automatic conclusion when a noncustodial arrest is made. Officers must be able to state specific facts that caused them to suspect that weapons were present.

Examples of Vehicle Search during Stop Based on Reasonable Suspicion

- A car is stopped based on reasonable suspicion that the occupants are about to paint graffiti on a nearby wall. Based on the behavior of the suspects, the officers believe they have weapons in the car. The passenger compartment is searched; two knives and 6 ounces of cocaine are recovered.
- A car is stopped because officers believe the occupants are about to commit a drive-by shooting. The passenger compartment of the car is immediately searched for weapons. The officers find a sawed-off shotgun under the driver's seat.

Examples of Vehicle Search That Would *Not* Qualify as Search Based on Reasonable Suspicion

- A traffic officer pulled a car over because it was driving at night without any tail lights. The officer ordered the driver and passenger out of the car and immediately did a thorough search of the passenger compartment.

  In order to search a car based on reasonable suspicion, the officer must have reasonable suspicion that there are weapons in the car. Driving without any tail lights, without more facts, does not create suspicion that the driver and/or a passenger is armed.

- A patrol officer stopped a car in an industrial area where it was parked behind a factory. When the driver was asked to exit the car, he became belligerent. The officer immediately pulled the man out of the car and did a thorough search of the passenger compartment and the trunk.

  The search that is allowed based on reasonable suspicion that there are weapons in the vehicle is limited to a search of the passenger compartment for weapons. The search of the trunk exceeds this allocation.

Vehicle Search—Outside of Vehicle

The outside of a car parked in a public place falls under the Plain View Doctrine (*Cardwell v. Lewis; New York v. Class* [25]). What is seen may be used to establish probable cause for further action. For example, paint on the car may indicate that it has been in a collision. Samples may be taken, either at the original location or later at the impound lot, and sent to a forensics laboratory for testing. This rule also allows officers to look for vehicle identification numbers. It is important to note that this rule does not apply to cars parked on a private property.

Right to Search the Outside of a Vehicle Defined
Officers may inspect the outside of a vehicle that is parked in a public place.

Examples of Vehicle Search—Outside of the Vehicle
- While a police officer questioned the suspect, another officer went outside and looked at the suspect's car, which was parked on the street. A dent and paint the color of the vehicle that had been pushed over a cliff were found on the front bumper.
- The police had the suspect under surveillance and noted that she always parked at the curb in front of her apartment. After the suspect went inside, an officer looked at the tags on the license plate and determined that they were not the ones issued for the car.

Examples of Vehicle Search That Would *Not* Qualify as Legal Search of Outside of the Vehicle
- The police suspected that John's car had been used to transport a kidnap victim. An officer went into the underground parking garage of the building where John lived and looked through the car windows for any items the victim indicated were in the car when she escaped.

  The right to look at the outside of a vehicle only applies when the vehicle is in a public place. The officer did not have the right to go into a private parking garage to look at the car.

- An officer saw a car parked on a red curb outside a bank and became suspicious that it was a "getaway" car for a robbery. She forced open the trunk and found six bricks of marijuana.

  The only search that is allowed under this exception is observation of the exterior of the car. Opening the trunk is not allowed.

Vehicle Search during Non-Criminal Investigation

The Supreme Court authorized searches not related to the investigation of a crime as part of the "community caretaking function" of the police (*Cady v. Dombrowski* [26]). The case involved searching an impounded car in an unguarded lot for a gun that the driver had the legal right to possess. The search was considered justified because it was done to prevent vandals from stealing the gun. During the search, much to the surprise of the officers, evidence of an unreported murder was discovered.

Right to Search Vehicle during Non-Criminal Investigation Defined

In some circumstances, cars may be searched if there is a legitimate reason for the search not related to the investigation of a crime.

This is an exception to the search warrant requirement that has not been fully developed by the Supreme Court. Officers should be very cautious in relying on it.

Examples of Vehicle Searches during Non-Criminal Investigations

- Police officers find a car parked beside a rarely used road. It appears the vehicle has been there a long time. They open the door in order to find the registration. Once inside, they detect the smell of marijuana.
- A Department of Motor Vehicles officer is checking paperwork at a local car dealer against the cars on the lot to verify that the dealer is paying appropriate fees. One car does not have any license plates. The agent opens the trunk to locate the plates and finds several stolen car stereos.

Examples of Vehicle Searches That Would *Not* Qualify as Legal Search during Non-Criminal Investigations

- An officer finds a dirty car without license plates parked on a city street. Suspecting that the car is stolen, he opens the door to look for the vehicle registration and finds an illegal gun.

  The fact that the officer suspects that the car is stolen indicates that the search is part of a criminal investigation.

- An officer is notified that a car has been parked in the same location for at least a week. Noting that the car matches one belonging to a person who has been reported missing, the officer conducts a thorough search of the car to determine if there is any evidence that indicates that the person met with "foul play."

  The fact that the officer was trying to determine if the person met with foul play indicates that this search was part of a criminal investigation.

Vehicle Stops at Roadblocks

The seemingly contradictory rule that allows the police to stop all cars without cause but not to randomly stop a few cars was *dicta* in *Delaware v. Prouse*,[27] a case that expressly prohibited random car stops for the purpose of checking drivers' licenses and vehicle registrations. It suggested that stopping all cars traveling on the street to check licenses and registrations would be legal.

Right to Stop Vehicles at Roadblocks Defined

Vehicles may not be stopped randomly when there is no suspicion of illegal activity, but in some situations roadblocks may be established and all cars stopped briefly. Officers may also set up roadblocks in order to distribute information about a recent crime that occurred in the area.[28]

Roadblocks have been used to conduct inspections of safety equipment, such as brakes and tail lights. Roadblocks are not authorized, however, merely to check for outstanding arrest warrants. The Supreme Court approved the use of roadblocks for sobriety checkpoints after balancing the need to prevent drunk driving against the minimal intrusion such roadblocks make on the rights of individual motorists.[29] In another case, however, the Court refused to allow stopping cars at roadblocks that were set up to detect illegal drugs.[30] On the other hand, officers may set up a roadblock for the purpose of soliciting information from the public about a recent crime.[31]

Examples of Legal Vehicle Stops at Roadblocks

- Officers set up a roadblock and stopped every fourth car in order to give the driver a breath alcohol test. Arrests were made for drivers whose blood alcohol was over the legal limit. Officers also arrested people when the officers observed drugs through the windows of the car.
- Officers set up a roadblock so they could check safety equipment on the cars— brake lights, head lights, and turn signals. If the car did not have operative safety equipment, the driver was given a "fixer" ticket. People were also cited if they were not wearing seat belts when they drove into the roadblock.

Examples of Vehicle Stops That Would *Not* Qualify as Legal Roadblocks

- Officers set up a roadblock in an area where there had been numerous drug arrests within the past 2 weeks. They stopped each car and searched it for narcotics.

  Checking cars for narcotics is considered part of ordinary police work. The Supreme Court ruled that roadblocks could not be used for this purpose.

- Officers set up a roadblock for "drunk drivers." Every car was stopped. All drivers were given sobriety tests and the cars were searched for open containers of alcohol.

  Roadblocks can be used for "drunk drivers," but searching the cars for open containers of alcohol goes beyond what can legally be done.

Administrative Searches

There are many reasons to search a building that are not related to normal police activity. For example, inspectors may need to check for compliance with the fire and building codes. The Supreme Court, in *Camara v. Municipal Court* and *See v. City of Seattle*,[32] designed a modified warrant procedure for these situations.

The probable cause needed for an **administrative warrant** is very different from that mandated for search warrants. The purpose of the warrant is to protect people's privacy from invasion by public officials. It is also designed to prevent harassment by frequent, needless inspections.

Requirements for Administrative Warrant

Probable cause for an administrative warrant requires a reasonable legislative purpose for the search. This legislative purpose does not have to show that there is reason to suspect that there are violations in any specific building.

The statement of legislative purpose merely restates the reason the law was created that authorized the search. For example, if the sanitation district is authorized to inspect each building once every 4 years, the fact that the quadrant of the city where the house in question is located is scheduled for inspection this year is sufficient probable cause. There is no need to state that there are facts indicating that the sanitation code is being violated at the address named in the warrant application.

Although the administrative warrant procedure applies to both residential and commercial buildings, use of these warrants is rare. Most people are willing to permit inspectors to enter the building and perform their duty. When admission is denied, a warrant can be used to complete the inspection. The process can be used for building and wiring codes, inspection of restaurants for health code violations, sanitation inspections for rodents and other pests, and inspections to determine if the fire regulations are being complied with.

Supreme Court cases establish exemptions from the administrative warrant requirement for firearms dealers (*United States v. Biswell*),[33] establishments selling alcoholic beverages (*Colonnade Catering Corp. v. United States*),[34] junkyards that dismantle cars (*New York v. Burger*),[35] and safety inspections under the Federal Mine Safety and Health Act of 1977 (*Donovan v. Dewey*).[36]

These are all businesses that are typically heavily regulated. The common theme for permitting warrantless inspections is the following:

1. The regulatory scheme is supported by a substantial government interest.
2. The warrantless inspections are necessary to further the regulatory scheme.
3. The statute must limit official discretion and advise the owners of businesses of the limits on their privacy.

Immigration and Naturalization Service agents were also exempted from the use of warrants when they enter businesses to check for undocumented workers employed there (*Immigration and Naturalization Service v. Delgado*).[37] The Court found that, unlike the other exemptions, entering the business, including blocking the exits, did not constitute a seizure. If specific individuals were detained for questioning, normal Fourth Amendment standards would apply.

Several Supreme Court cases have refused to grant exemptions from the administrative warrant requirement. One is for Occupational Safety and Health Administration inspections. Inspectors may not enter a business to check for violations of health and safety rules without consent or an administrative warrant (*Marshall v. Barlow's, Inc.*).[38]

Fire inspectors pose several interesting problems. Firefighters trying to put out a blaze, and those involved in the mop-up operation, obviously do not need any type of warrant. Inspections that are primarily regulatory in nature require administrative warrants. An administrative warrant is also required if there is suspicion of arson. Once arson investigators have probable cause to believe arson in fact occurred, they need a regular search warrant to enter the structure (*Michigan v. Tyler*; *Michigan v. Clifford*).[39] Burned-out structures may still have a protected privacy interest if the owners have tried to board them up or otherwise keep people out.

Examples of Legal Administrative Searches

- The fire department is checking all businesses for compliance with fire regulations. When Business X refused to allow the inspection, the fire department obtained an administrative warrant and did the inspection anyway.
- The health department checks restaurants for compliance with sanitary requirements. When Big Burgers refused to allow the inspectors into the kitchen, the health department obtained an administrative warrant in order to inspect the kitchen.
- The Federal Bureau of Alcohol, Tobacco and Firearms (ATF) went to Gun Shop to check its records against the stock on hand. The owner of Gun Shop refused to allow the search. ATF agents forced their way into Gun Shop and searched it because firearms dealers are exempt from the administrative warrant requirement.

Examples of Searches That Would *Not* Qualify as Legal Administrative Searches

- The fire marshal suspects that the fire at the local dry cleaners was set by an arsonist. An administrative warrant is obtained authorizing the fire marshal to search the burned-out dry cleaners.

The fire marshal can use administrative warrants to enter businesses or residences in order to check for violations of the fire code. Once there is probable cause that arson was involved, a regular search warrant must be used.

- The police suspect that Hank is hiding undocumented workers in several garages at his apartment building. They obtain an administrative warrant to check the garages for failure to obtain a building permit before the garages were converted to apartments.

An administrative warrant would be appropriate if they intend to check for building code violations such as installing plumbing in garages without a building permit. If the intent is to search for undocumented workers, a regular search warrant should be obtained.

Summary

It is not a search to observe something that is in plain view. The Plain View Doctrine applies to whatever officers see without searching while they are legally on the premises. There must be probable cause in order to seize an item. A related rule, called the Open Fields Doctrine, admits evidence observed by officers even while trespassing. To qualify, the area must not be near a dwelling.

No matter where abandoned property is found, it is admissible. The Fourth Amendment does not apply to abandoned property due to the fact that no one's expectation of privacy is involved.

A search is legal if it is done with the consent of a person with apparent authority over the area. Officers must reasonably believe this person has a privacy interest in the area to be searched. The consent must be voluntary, but officers do not need to inform anyone of his or her constitutional right to refuse to consent. The person giving the consent may limit the area to be searched and/or restrict the length of time the police may spend searching.

The Supreme Court does not recognize as great a privacy interest in vehicles as in houses. If an occupant of a car is arrested, the entire passenger compartment may be searched. Specific parts of a car may be searched, immediately or after impounding the vehicle, if there is probable cause to believe evidence is concealed there. Any impounded vehicle may be inventoried. Evidence found during the inventory is admissible. If a car is stopped on reasonable suspicion that it is involved in criminal activity and there is also reasonable suspicion that weapons are in the vehicle, the passenger compartment may be searched for weapons. The exterior of a car parked in a public place may be inspected under the Plain View Doctrine.

A special search warrant must be obtained to enter a building to do an administrative inspection if no one will give consent. Probable cause for this warrant is established if there is a reasonable legislative purpose for the inspection. Gun dealers, junkyards, and establishments selling alcohol may be entered for inspection without the warrant.

Review Questions

1. What are the requirements for the Plain View and Open Field Doctrines?
2. When may police search abandoned property? Explain.
3. What is the standard for determining if consent to search is valid? Who may consent? How detailed a search is permitted? Explain.
4. What areas may police search if they arrest the driver of a car? Explain.
5. When may officers search a car without a warrant? When may officers inventory a car? Explain.
6. What areas may be searched if a car is stopped because there is reasonable suspicion that a passenger is involved in criminal activity? Explain.
7. May officers randomly stop cars to check registration? Explain.
8. Can roadblocks be set up to check for drunk driving? Explain.
9. When is an administrative warrant required? How do officers obtain one? Explain.
10. Name three types of businesses that are generally exempt from the administrative warrant requirement. What is the common rationale for such exemptions?

Writing Assignment

Go to www.cnn.com/crime and find a case that has either a vehicle search or a consent search. Write a one-page (250-word) report on the case that you found.

Notes

1. *Washington v. Chrisman* 455 U.S. 1, 70 L.Ed. 2d 778, 102 S.Ct. 812 (1982). See also *Coolidge v. New Hampshire* 403 U.S. 443, 29 L.Ed. 2d 564, 91 S.Ct. 2022 (1971).
2. *Horton v. California* 496 U.S. 128, 110 L.Ed. 2d 112, 110 S.Ct. 2301 (1990).
3. *California v. Ciraolo* 476 U.S. 207, 90 L.Ed. 2d 210, 106 S.Ct. 1809 (1987).
4. *Arizona v. Hicks* 480 U.S. 321, 94 L.Ed. 2d 347, 107 S.Ct. 1149 (1987).
5. *Oliver v. United States* 466 U.S. 170, 80 L.Ed. 2d 214, 104 S.Ct. 173 (1984); *United States v. Dunn* 480 U.S. 480 294, 94 L.Ed. 2d 326, 107 S.Ct. 1134 (1987).
6. *California v. Greenwood* 486 U.S. 35, 100 L.Ed. 2d 30, 108 S.Ct. 1625 (1988).
7. *California v. Hodari D.* 499 U.S. 621, 113 L.Ed. 2d 690, 111 S.Ct. 1547 (1991).
8. *Schneckloth v. Bustamonte* 412 U.S. 218, 36 L.Ed. 2d 854, 93 S.Ct. 2041 (1973).
9. *Bumper v. North Carolina* 391 U.S. 543, 20 L.Ed. 2d 797, 88 S.Ct. 1788 (1968).
10. *Florida v. Bostick* 501 U.S. 429, 115 L.Ed. 2d 389, 111 S.Ct. 2382 (1991).
11. *United States v. Matlock* 415 U.S. 164, 39 L.Ed. 2d 242, 94 S.Ct. 988 (1974); *Illinois v. Rodriguez* 497 U.S. 177, 111 L.Ed. 2d 148, 110 S.Ct. 2793 (1990).
12. *Griffin v. Wisconsin* 483 U.S. 868, 97 L.Ed. 2d 709, 107 S.Ct. 3164 (1987).
13. *Florida v. Jimeno* 500 U.S. 248, 114 L.Ed. 2d 297, 111 S.Ct. 1801 (1991).
14. *California v. Carney* 471 U.S. 386, 85 L.Ed. 2d 406, 105 S.Ct. 2066 (1985).
15. *New York v. Belton* 453 U.S. 454, 69 L.Ed. 2d 768, 101 S.Ct. 2869 (1981).

16. *Thornton v. United States* 541 U.S. 615, 158 L.Ed. 2d 905, 124 S. Ct. 2127 (2004).
17. *Chambers v. Maroney* 399 U.S. 42, 26 L.Ed. 2d 419, 90 S.Ct. 1975 (1970).
18. *Michigan v. Thomas* 458 U.S. 259, 73 L.Ed. 2d 750, 102 S.Ct. 3079 (1982); *Maryland v. Dyson* 527 U.S. 465, 144 L.Ed. 2d 442, 119 S. Ct. 2013 (1999).
19. *Chambers v. Maroney* 399 U.S. 42, 26 L.Ed. 2d 419, 90 S.Ct. 1975 (1970).
20. *Wyoming v. Houghton* 526 U.S. 295, 143 L.Ed. 2d 408, 119 S. Ct. 1297 (1999).
21. *United States v. Ross* 456 U.S. 798, 72 L.Ed. 2d 572, 102 S.Ct. 2157 (1982).
22. *South Dakota v. Opperman* 428 U.S. 364, 49 L.Ed. 2d 1000, 96 S.Ct. 3092 (1976).
23. *Michigan v. Long* 463 U.S. 1032, 77 L.Ed. 2d 1201, 103 S.Ct. 3469 (1983).
24. *Michigan v. Long* 463 U.S. 1032, 77 L.Ed. 2d 1201, 103 S.Ct. 3469 (1983).
25. *Cardwell v. Lewis* 417 U.S. 583, 41 L.Ed. 2d 325, 94 S.Ct. 2464 (1974); *New York v. Class* 475 U.S. 106, 89 L.Ed. 2d 81, 106 S.Ct. 960 (1986).
26. *Cady v. Dombrowski* 413 U.S. 433, 37 L.Ed. 2d 706, 93 S.Ct. 2523 (1973).
27. *Delaware v. Prouse* 440 U.S. 648, 59 L.Ed. 2d 660, 99 S.Ct. 1391 (1979).
28. *Illinois v. Lidster* 540 U.S. 419, 157 L.Ed. 2d 843, 124 S. Ct. 885 (2004).
29. *Michigan Dept. of State Police v. Sitz* 496 U.S. 444, 110 L.Ed. 2d 412, 110 S.Ct. 2481 (1990).
30. *City of Indianapolis v. Edmond* 531 U.S. 32, 148 L.Ed. 2d 333, 121 S.Ct. 447 (2000).
31. *Illinois v. Lidster* 540 U.S. 419, 157 L.Ed. 2d 843, 124 S. Ct. 885 (2004).
32. *Camara v. Municipal Court* 387 U.S. 523, 18 L.Ed. 2d 930, 87 S.Ct. 1727 (1967); *See v. City of Seattle* 387 U.S. 541, 18 L.Ed. 2d 943, 87 S.Ct.1737 (1967).
33. *United States v. Biswell* 406 U.S. 311, 32 L.Ed. 2d 87, 92 S.Ct. 1593 (1972).
34. *Colonnade Catering Corp. v. United States* 397 U.S. 72, 25 L.Ed. 2d 60, 90 S.Ct. 774 (1970).
35. *New York v. Burger* 482 U.S. 691, 96 L.Ed. 2d 601, 107 S.Ct. 2636 (1987).
36. *Donovan v. Dewey* 452 U.S. 594, 69 L.Ed. 2d 262, 101 S.Ct. 2534 (1981).
37. *Immigration and Naturalization Service v. Delgado* 466 U.S. 210, 80 L.Ed. 2d 247, 104 S.Ct. 1758 (1984).
38. *Marshall v. Barlow's, Inc.* 436 U.S. 307, 56 L.Ed. 2d 305, 98 S.Ct. 1816 (1978).
39. *Michigan v. Tyler* 436 U.S. 499, 56 L.Ed. 2d 486, 98 S.Ct. 1942 (1978); *Michigan v. Clifford* 464 U.S. 287, 78 L.Ed. 2d 477, 104 S.Ct. 641 (1984).

CHAPTER 13

USA PATRIOT Act, Foreign Intelligence, and Other Types of Electronic Surveillance Covered by Federal Law

Feature Case: Jose Padilla[*]

In a 3-month trial, Jose Padilla, Adham Amin Hassoun, and Kifah Wael Jayyousi were accused of being part of a North American support cell that provided supplies, money, and recruits to groups of Islamic extremists. The defense contended that the three men were trying to help persecuted Muslims in war zones by sending them humanitarian aid.

When Padilla was first detained in 2002, the Bush administration portrayed him as a U.S. citizen and Muslim convert who was a committed terrorist. Claiming that he was part of an al-Qaida plot to detonate a radioactive "dirty bomb" in the United States, the administration claimed that his detention was an important victory in the war against terrorism.

The charges brought in civilian court in Miami, however, were much less serious than those initial claims, in part because Padilla was interrogated

[*]Based on story downloaded November 3, 2007, from http://www.courttv.com/news/2007/0816/jose_padilla.html.

with no attorney present while he was held in military custody as an enemy combatant for 3½ years. An additional problem was that he was not read his *Miranda* rights.

Padilla's attorneys fought for years to get his case into federal court. In late 2005, shortly before the U.S. Supreme Court considered President Bush's authority to continue detaining him, Padilla was added as a defendant in the case against a Miami terrorism support group. He had lived in south Florida in the 1990s and was supposedly recruited by Hassoun to become a mujahedeen fighter while he was there.

The key piece of physical evidence was a five-page form Padilla supposedly filled out in July 2000 when he was petitioning to attend an al-Qaida training camp in Afghanistan. This camp linked Padilla to the other two defendants as well as Osama bin Laden's terrorist organization. The form, recovered in Afghanistan by the CIA in 2001, contained seven of Padilla's fingerprints and several other personal identifiers, such as his birthdate and his claim that he was able to speak Spanish, English, and Arabic.

Padilla's lawyers insisted that the form was far from conclusive, and they denied that he was a 'star recruit' of the North American support cell that allegedly intended that he become a terrorist. They said Padilla traveled to Egypt in September 1998 to learn Islam more deeply and become fluent in Arabic. "His intent was to study, not to murder," said Padilla's attorney Michael Caruso.

Central to the investigation were approximately 300,000 FBI wiretap intercepts collected from 1993 to 2001, mainly involving Padilla's co-defendants Hassoun and Jayyousi and others. Most of the conversations were in Arabic and purportedly used code such as "tourism" and "football" for violent jihad or "zucchini" and "eggplant" instead of military weapons or ammunition. The bulk of these conversations and other evidence concerned efforts in the 1990s by Hassoun and Jayyousi, both 45 years old, to assist Muslims in conflict zones such as Chechnya, Bosnia, Somalia, Afghanistan, and Lebanon. Jayyousi also ran an organization called American Worldwide Relief and published a newsletter called the *Islam Report* that provided details of battles and political issues in the Muslim world.

Padilla was convicted.

Learning Objectives

After studying this chapter, you should be able to

- Define the Misplaced Reliance Doctrine.
- List the requirements for obtaining an electronic surveillance warrant.

- Explain how the USA PATRIOT Act applies to wiretapping and foreign intelligence operations.
- State the requirements for obtaining an electronic surveillance warrant based on the current version of the Wiretap Act.
- Explain the differences between the Wiretap Act of 1968 (as currently amended) and the current version of the Foreign Intelligence Surveillance Act.

Key Terms

- Bumper Beeper
- Covert entry
- Foreign Intelligence Surveillance Act
- Electronic surveillance
- Misplaced Reliance Doctrine
- Pen Register
- Title III
- Trap and Trace Device
- USA PATRIOT Act
- Wiretap Act

Myths	Facts
The USA PATRIOT Act created a new vehicle for investigating terrorism.	Many of the items in the USA PATRIOT Act amended existing federal laws. A few new statutes were added.
The USA PATRIOT Act replaced all existing federal laws regulating the issuance of electronic surveillance warrants.	The USA PATRIOT Act amended some portions of the Wiretap Act of 1968, but most of the provisions of the original Act are still in place.
Search warrants must be obtained when using undercover officers.	Based on the Misplaced Reliance Doctrine, search warrants are not required if someone voluntarily allows an undercover officer to observe or participate in criminal activity.
The Foreign Intelligence Surveillance Act (FISA) was enacted to exempt the CIA and other U.S. agencies involved in foreign intelligence gathering from the Fourth Amendment.	FISA was enacted to create a vehicle that would enable federal judges to issue electronic surveillance warrants for use by U.S. agencies that investigate activities of foreign governments and their agents.
The President of the United States can authorize wiretaps for foreign intelligence purposes without asking a judge for approval.	The President can order the installation of wiretaps for foreign intelligence purposes, but it is still necessary to obtain approval from the Foreign Intelligence Court.
An electronic surveillance warrant is required to obtain e-mail records and stored e-mail messages.	Obtaining e-mail records and stored e-mail is covered by the Electronic Communication Privacy Act, which was modified by the USA PATRIOT Act. When seeking e-mail that the provider has placed in long-term storage, law enforcement can use a subpoena. This is easier than obtaining a search warrant.

Law enforcement's interest in conducting wiretaps and other forms of electronic surveillance has increased with the rapid growth of new forms of electronic communications. Since September 11, 2001, fear of terrorist attacks has made ongoing seizures of international communications necessary.

This chapter first discusses the Misplaced Reliance Doctrine, which applies to eavesdropping; this investigative technique can be used without a warrant. Next, it briefly recounts the history of electronic surveillance warrants and their recent expansion. A number of major federal laws are reviewed, including the Wiretap Act of 1968 (also referred to as Title III), the Foreign Intelligence Surveillance Act of 1978, the USA PATRIOT Act (2001), and legislation enacted in 2006 that extended the life of the PATRIOT Act. Many of these pieces of legislation are long (the original PATRIOT Act was 323 pages) and provide amendments for many older laws, so delving into all of the intricate subparts is difficult. Discussion will focus on what the laws currently authorize. Portions of these laws that are of most significance to law enforcement agencies fighting terrorism are covered, as is the Wiretap Act, which is the primary vehicle for obtaining electronic surveillance warrants. No attempt is made to cover electronic surveillance legislation at the state level.

Eavesdropping and Electronic Surveillance

Eavesdropping has probably been done since people began keeping secrets from each other. Electronic surveillance, however, only emerged after the technology developed. Both involve the seizure of private conversations. The key distinction noted in Supreme Court cases is that the person making the comments knows whether a listener is present but is unlikely to know whether electronic equipment is being used. Violation of trust by one party to a conversation is all that it takes to make what was said admissible in court.

Misplaced Reliance Doctrine

In situations in which the suspect knew someone was listening, the Supreme Court has placed the burden on the suspect to make sure that he or she can trust everyone who can hear what is said. This is called the **Misplaced Reliance Doctrine.** It applies whether or not tape recorders or radio transmitters are used. The person who overhears the conversation may carry tape recorders, radio transmitters, or other high-tech equipment without prior authorization from a judge.

Misplaced Reliance Doctrine Defined

No warrant is required to obtain conversations that can be overheard by the police or their agents based on the misplaced reliance of the suspect. Each person bears the burden of restricting his or her conversations to people who will not reveal them to the authorities.

The facts from two cases help explain this doctrine. *Hoffa v. United States* is one of the leading cases.[1] When Jimmy Hoffa was on trial in what is called the "Test Fleet" case, the U.S. Justice Department had another union official named Partin released from prison. Partin was instructed to join Hoffa's entourage and report on Hoffa's out-of-court activities. No electronic monitoring equipment was used. Partin frequented Hoffa's hotel suite and overheard conversations about plans to tamper with the jury. The "Test Fleet" case ended with a hung jury. Evidence supplied by Partin was used in a subsequent case in which Hoffa was charged with attempting to bribe jurors. The Supreme Court found this was a case of misplaced reliance. Hoffa knew Partin was present and took the risk that Partin might report the jury tampering to the authorities. The fact that the Justice Department had planted Partin had no legal significance.

Federal narcotics agents used concealed radio transmitters in *United States v. White*, another leading case.[2] They recorded conversations between agents and the defendant in public places, restaurants, the defendant's home, and the informant's car. The informant also allowed an agent to hide in a kitchen closet and transmit conversations between the informant and the defendant. All of these recorded conversations were found admissible under the Misplaced Reliance Doctrine. Defendant White should have been more careful in deciding whom he could trust. This even applied to the agent in the closet. White should not have relied on his friend who allowed the agents to hide there.

Examples of Situations Covered by Misplaced Reliance Doctrine

- Mary told her friend Liz that she had stolen an expensive ring. Liz reported what Mary said to the police.
- Nancy got in an argument while talking to Phil on her cell phone. She became so upset that she started shouting. A passerby who heard Nancy threaten to kill Phil reported it to the police.
- Rick was arrested for selling drugs. He tried to plea bargain. Officers told him that they would drop the charges if he wore a "body mike" while buying drugs from his supplier. Rick wore the body mike and the police obtained enough evidence to convict the supplier.

Examples of Situations *Not* Covered by Misplaced Reliance Doctrine

- Police had been watching Sam as he collected "protection money." At the end of the day he always stopped at the pay phone on 3rd and Main and made a call. Without obtaining a warrant, the police put a wiretap on that phone and recorded his calls.

  This was a public phone and no one gave permission. Therefore, the police must obtain a wiretap warrant in order to legally record the calls.

- Tom, the basketball coach at a nationally ranked university, was a suspect in a sports betting operation. A police officer contacted a cooperative janitor, who unlocked the door so that a listening device could be installed in Tom's office. The recorded calls indicated that Tom was involved in rigging the point spread at crucial games.

  The janitor did not have the authority to authorize the installation of the listening device. Therefore, the information obtained from the listening device would not be admissible against Tom in court.

Electronic Surveillance and Wiretap Act of 1968

Electronic surveillance has particularly troubled the Supreme Court because it has a great potential for abuse. In both wiretap and bugging cases, the victim may be totally unaware that the government is listening. The key decisions on this topic were made in the late 1960s and early 1970s. Since that time, new laws have been needed because technology has rapidly advanced, creating opportunities for electronic eavesdropping that are much greater than those that existed previously.

Reasonable expectation of privacy, the current standard for Fourth Amendment protections, originally came from a wiretap case. Prior to that time, electronic surveillance cases had focused on trespassing. Anything the police could accomplish without physically trespassing on the suspect's property was permitted. Sometimes this went to the extreme of measuring how far a "spike mike" had gone into the common wall between two apartments in order to determine if there had been a trespass.

In *Katz v. United States*,[3] agents had probable cause to believe that the suspect was using a telephone booth as part of an interstate gambling operation. A listening device was placed on the outside of a public telephone booth. There was no trespass. Even so, the Supreme Court held that the government violated the Fourth Amendment. Katz had a reasonable expectation of privacy because he entered the telephone booth, closed the door, and kept his voice down.

The issuing of warrants permitting electronic surveillance was reviewed by the Supreme Court in *Berger v. New York*.[4] Statutes authorizing this specialized search warrant must provide very precise requirements, including a description of the offense and the types of conversations the officers expect to seize. The warrant must be limited to a short period of time. Although the Court did not specifically state what the maximum length of time was, it found that 2 months was too long. Extensions of the original warrant must be based on a showing that probable cause exists for the continuance of the surveillance. The warrant must have a return that reports on the interceptions made while the listening equipment was in place.

Warrant Requirement for Electronic Surveillance Defined

An electronic surveillance warrant is required to install wiretaps and electronic listening devices that invade a person's reasonable expectation of privacy. The warrant must contain a detailed statement of probable cause, including a showing of why other investigative techniques will not work. The warrant must not permit electronic monitoring for extended periods of time.

Examples of Electronic Surveillance That Is Conducted Legally

- Based on a wiretap warrant, the police department had the telephone company connect a device that would record all conversations on the lines listed in the warrant.
- Based on an electronic surveillance warrant, the federal agents had a device secretly installed in the suspect's living room. The device contained a radio transmitter so that the agents were able to monitor the conversations from a surveillance van parked a block away.
- Based on an electronic surveillance warrant, the police had a device installed that recorded all messages left on the suspect's home phone.

Examples of Electronic Surveillance That Is *Not* Conducted Legally

- Based on a search warrant, police entered a house and installed a recording device in the telephone receiver.

  Installation of a recording device requires an electronic surveillance warrant. A search warrant is not sufficient.

- The police asked the local phone company to install a wiretap on a suspect's phone.

  Consent by the phone company is not sufficient because it is not the phone company's privacy that is being invaded. An electronic surveillance warrant is required.

Not all electronic devices that transmit information are covered by the same legal rationale. **Pen registers** record the numbers dialed for outgoing calls; **"trap and trace"** devices record the phone numbers on incoming calls. Neither is covered by the Fourth Amendment or the Wiretap Act (*Smith v. Maryland*; *United States v. New York Telephone Co.*)[5] because these devices do not seize (record) conversations. The Supreme Court found no expectation of privacy in the telephone numbers because the telephone company has access to them. Congress, however, passed laws regulating their use during criminal investigations. This legislation mandates that a warrant be obtained before installing pen registers and "trap and trace" devices. In order to obtain this specialized warrant, an application must be submitted that contains

1. the identity of the attorney for the government or the name of the state law enforcement or investigative officer making the application, and the identity of the law enforcement agency conducting the investigation; and

2. a certification by the applicant that the information likely to be obtained is relevant to an ongoing criminal investigation being conducted by that agency.[6]

The process is similar to the one federal investigators follow when seeking search warrants. Note that it is not necessary to establish probable cause; investigators need only show that the information obtained will be relevant to an ongoing criminal investigation. The extra requirements imposed on applicants for electronic surveillance warrants do not apply.

The Fourth Amendment also does not apply to transponders (also called "**bumper beepers**") as long as they do not enter residences (*United States v. Karo*; *United States v. Knotts*).[7] A transponder emits a signal that makes it possible to track a vehicle or package without keeping it under visual surveillance. The Supreme Court held that the electronic device merely facilitates the surveillance process. It drew the line, however, when the container with the transmitter in it entered the suspect's home.

Examples of Use of Federal Legislation on Electronic Surveillance

- FBI agents are investigating organized crime's involvement in gambling. They have been able to trace banking records to a specific person, but attempts to place this person under surveillance have failed. They obtain a Title III warrant for a wiretap on the person's home phone for 30 days.
- City police officers are investigating a kidnap for ransom case. They were assisted by the FBI because interstate transportation of the victim was suspected. The kidnapper is calling the parents and trying to arrange the delivery of the ransom money. FBI agents obtain a warrant to install a "trap and trace" device on the phone in order to determine where the kidnapper is calling from.
- Federal agents believe that a person who is involved with a terrorist cell sponsored by a foreign government is plotting to blow up a federal building in the near future. The U.S. Attorney General authorizes a wiretap for 90 days.

Federal Legislation on Electronic Surveillance[8]

Immediately after *Katz* and *Berger* indicated the need for carefully drafted legislation authorizing electronic surveillance, Congress enacted the Omnibus Crime Control and Safe Streets Act of 1968. Title III of this act, officially called the Wiretap Act of 1968,[9] was devoted to electronic surveillance. The Wiretap Act has been amended several times, including changes authorized by the **USA PATRIOT Act** (2001) and its reauthorization statute in 2006.

Wiretap Act of 1968

The code sections. The **Wiretap Act** of 1968,[10] sometimes referred to as **Title III**, made it a federal felony to willfully intercept any wire or oral communication by electronic or mechanical devices unless an electronic surveillance warrant has been obtained.[11] Oral communications are currently defined as any utterance by a person exhibiting an expectation that such communication is not subject to interception in circumstances justifying such expectation; electronic communications are not covered by this definition.[12] The PATRIOT Act extended the Wiretap Act to cover voice mail messages, and records of telephone or Internet/e-mail service providers that record customers' names, addresses, and other information about their accounts including the length of service and source of payments (credit card and bank account numbers). Wire communications include any communication made in whole or in part by wire, cable, or other connection operated by a common carrier.[13] Employees of the telephone company or other common carriers, such as telephone operators who legally intercept conversations, are prohibited from disclosing them.[14]

The Wiretap Act set detailed requirements that must be followed in order to obtain an electronic surveillance warrant. Although this statute only applies to federal agents, it has much broader implications because many states have either authorized their officers to proceed under identical laws or have used it as a basis for state statutes. Federal rules may also apply if local police officers are part of a task force that includes federal agents. In such situations, it is likely that if electronic surveillance warrants are needed, they will be obtained using the Wiretap Act.

Electronic surveillance warrants may only be issued by federal judges for the investigation of crimes specified in the Wiretap Act. The following list contains approximately half of the crimes that are enumerated:

> Any offense punishable by death or by imprisonment for more than 1 year relating to the enforcement of the Atomic Energy Act of 1954; sabotage of nuclear facilities; espionage; kidnapping; protection of trade secrets;

sabotage; treason; riots; destruction of vessels; piracy; murder, robbery, or extortion; bribery of public officials, witnesses, bank officials, and sporting contests; unlawful use of explosives; transmission of wagering information; influencing or injuring an officer, juror, or witness; assassination of the President, Presidential staff, members of Congress, or Supreme Court justices; transactions involving nuclear materials or biological weapons; interference with commerce by threats or violence; use of interstate commerce facilities in the commission of murder for hire; laundering of monetary instruments; embezzlement from pension and welfare funds; sex trafficking of children by force, fraud, or coercion; sexual exploitation of children; selling or buying of children; child pornography; interstate transportation of stolen property; hostage taking; computer fraud and abuse; production of false identification documentation; procurement of citizenship or nationalization unlawfully; reproduction of naturalization or citizenship papers; any offense involving counterfeiting; manufacture, importation, receiving, concealment, buying, selling, or otherwise dealing in narcotic drugs, marijuana, or other dangerous drugs; destruction of a natural gas pipeline; aircraft piracy; smuggling of aliens; chemical weapons; or terrorism.[15]

The USA PATRIOT Act added several categories of crimes to this list, but the majority of them were in the bill when it was passed in 1968.

Realizing that several states passed laws that in effect made the Wiretap Act their state's law on electronic surveillance, Congress added a list of the state-level felonies for which electronic surveillance warrants can be issued. Those crimes are murder, kidnapping, gambling, robbery, bribery, extortion, or dealing in narcotic drugs, marijuana, or other dangerous drugs, or other crimes dangerous to life, limb, or property.[16] States that enact their own electronic surveillance laws may alter this list.

More facts must be included in an application for a Wiretap Act warrant than for a normal search warrant. The code is very specific about what should be included:

1. The identity of the law enforcement officer making the application.
2. The name of the senior officer who reviewed the application and authorized its presentation to the court.
3. A full and complete statement of the facts and circumstances relied on by the applicant to justify his or her belief that an order should be issued, including
   a. details as to the particular offense that has been, is being, or is about to be committed,
   b. particular description of the nature and location of the facilities from which or the place where the communication is to be intercepted,

c. particular description of the type of communications sought to be intercepted,

d. the identity of the person, if known, committing the offense and whose communications are to be intercepted.

4. A full and complete statement as to whether or not other investigative procedures have been tried and failed or why they reasonably appear to be unlikely to succeed if tried, or it would be too dangerous to try them.

5. A statement of the period of time for which the interception is required to be maintained.

6. A full and complete statement of the facts concerning all previous applications known to the individuals authorizing and making the application, involving any of the same persons, facilities, or places specified in the application, and the action taken by the judge on each such application.[17]

An applicant can request a warrant without listing the location where the wiretap will operate. To obtain a warrant in these circumstances requires a strong showing justifying deviation from normal procedure.[18]

If an extension is needed for an existing warrant, the application must comply with the previous list and give a detailed description of what has been obtained during previous wiretaps. If the surveillance produced few results, the application for the extension must give a reasonable explanation why efforts to date were not more productive.[19]

Another step that must be completed when seeking a wiretap warrant is that the application must be reviewed before it is submitted to the judge.[20] Federal law enforcement agents must have their warrant applications screened by a senior member of the Attorney General's staff. The U.S. Attorney General now has the flexibility to designate someone with the rank of Deputy Assistant Attorney General, or higher, in the criminal division to review these applications.[21] If a state empowers its officers to act under the federal Wiretap Act, the state Attorney General reviews applications by officers with statewide agencies, and the principal prosecuting attorney of the county does corresponding reviews for local police departments.[22] The entire warrant application must be reviewed by the screener before it can be submitted to a judge.

The Court may direct a common carrier, such as the telephone company, to cooperate with the agents executing the warrant.[23] The maximum length of interception under the warrant is 30 days.[24] Shorter periods are preferred.

If there is reason to suspect that there is immediate danger of death or serious physical injury to any person, conspiratorial activities threaten the nation's security interest, or there are conspiratorial activities characteristic of organized crime, an emergency procedure is available.[25] There must be sufficient grounds to obtain a warrant before an emergency interception begins. An application must be made for a warrant within 48 hours of the start of an interception. If a wiretap warrant is obtained, it will retroactively apply and any communications seized will be admissible in court. If the application is denied, or if no application is made, the interception must stop immediately; anything obtained during the interception will be inadmissible in court.

The communications obtained under the electronic surveillance warrant must be tape recorded or otherwise retained.[26] The recordings must be done in a manner that prevents later editing or alteration. These recordings must be made available to the judge when the surveillance has been completed. They must be kept for 10 years and may not be destroyed without an order from a judge.

The person(s) whose conversations were intercepted must be served with a limited inventory within 90 days of the end of surveillance. The person must be told

1. That an order was entered or the application was made.
2. The date of the entry, and the period of authorized, approved or disapproved interception, or the denial of the application.
3. The fact that during the period, wire, oral, or electronic communications were, or were not, intercepted.[27]

The judge has the discretion to permit the persons whose communications were seized to see the application for the warrant and to hear the taped interceptions.[28] If evidence obtained during the surveillance is to be used in court, all parties must have access to the application and warrant at least 10 days before the testimony is introduced.[29]

Title III contains its own exclusionary rule. It is stricter than the one created by the Supreme Court. Illegally obtained conversations may not be used in any hearing, trial, or other proceeding before any court, grand jury, government agency, regulatory body, or legislative committee of the United States or any of the states, counties, or cities. Anyone whose telephone or premises was monitored, as well as anyone whose conversations were seized, has standing.[30]

The case law on the Wiretap Act. The Supreme Court has decided several cases regarding the Wiretap Act. Probably the most important to local law enforcement is *Dalia v. United States*.[31] The issue was whether agents using an electronic surveillance warrant could covertly enter a home to install listening devices. Congress had not addressed the issue. The Court found that the right to enter was a fundamental part of the right to use electronic devices. Re-entry to service the equipment and/or retrieve it at the end of the surveillance was also included. No separate search warrant was required. Neither was it necessary to ask for authorization for **covert entries** when the original surveillance warrant was obtained.

Minimization is done to protect privacy by limiting the monitoring of conversations. One aspect of this is the requirement that the suspects be named in the application for a surveillance warrant. Listing prime targets is not enough. *United States v. Donovan* applied this to all persons the government has probable cause to believe are involved in the crime and whose conversations are likely to be seized.[32] This does not make conversations inadmissible if police knew a person, such as the wife of the suspect in *United States v. Kahn*, was likely to be using the telephone but had no reason to suspect that she was involved in criminal activity.[33] Each case is to be decided based on an objective review of the facts. The officer's subjective intent is not binding (*Scott v. United States*).[34]

Although the Wiretap Act has an emergency provision that can be used in cases involving national security, the Supreme Court has narrowly interpreted it. Neither the President, Attorney General, nor anyone else can authorize wiretaps on U.S. citizens, even "domestic dissidents," without judicial review (*United States v. United States District Court (Keith)*).[35]

Foreign Intelligence Surveillance Act of 1978 (FISA)[36]

In response to *Keith*, Congress passed the **Foreign Intelligence Surveillance Act** (FISA) in 1978. It started as a platform for issuing electronic surveillance warrants, but it has been amended several times. It is now a key piece of legislation in the post-9/11 war against terrorism.

FISA was enacted in order to provide a "secure framework by which the Executive Branch may conduct legitimate electronic surveillance for **foreign intelligence** purposes within the context of this nation's commitment to privacy and individual rights."[37] FISA created the Foreign Intelligence Surveillance Court (FISC), which currently consists of 11 judges appointed by the Chief Justice of the Supreme Court. The Foreign Intelligence Surveillance Court of Review (FISCR), which has jurisdiction to review FISA applications that the FISC denied, was also part of the original design. The Supreme Court theoretically has the final word, although to date no petitions for certiorari have been made. FISCR published its first opinion in 2006; the number of unpublished opinions is unknown.

The applicant for a FISA warrant must complete an extensive application:

(1) The identity of the Federal officer making the application;

(2) The approval of the Attorney General to make the application to the court;

(3) The identity, if known, or a description of the target of the electronic surveillance;

(4) A statement of the facts and circumstances relied on by the applicant to justify his belief that—

   (A) the target of the electronic surveillance is a foreign power or an agent of a foreign power; and

   (B) each of the facilities or places at which the electronic surveillance is directed is being used, or is about to be used, by a foreign power or an agent of a foreign power;

(5) A statement of the proposed minimization procedures;

(6) A detailed description of the nature of the information sought and the type of communications or activities to be subjected to the surveillance;

(7) Certification(s) by the Assistant to the President for National Security Affairs or an executive branch official or officials designated by the President:

   (A) that the certifying official deems the information sought to be foreign intelligence information;

   (B) that a significant purpose of the surveillance is to obtain foreign intelligence information;

   (C) that such information cannot reasonably be obtained by normal investigative techniques;

   (D) that designates the type of foreign intelligence information being sought according to the categories described in section 1801 (e) of this title; and

   (E) including a statement of the basis for the certification.

(8) A statement of the means by which the surveillance will be effected and a statement whether physical entry is required to effect the surveillance;

(9) a statement of the facts concerning all previous applications that have been made to any judge under this subchapter involving any of the persons, facilities, or places specified in the application, and the action taken on each previous application;

(10) a statement of the period of time for which the electronic surveillance is required to be maintained, and if the nature of the intelligence gathering is such that the approval of the use of electronic surveillance under this subchapter should not automatically terminate when the described type of information has first been obtained, a description of facts supporting the belief that additional information of the same type will be obtained thereafter; and

(11) whenever more than one electronic, mechanical, or other surveillance device is to be used with respect to a particular proposed electronic surveillance, the coverage of the devices involved, and what minimization procedures apply to information acquired by each device.[38]

Prior to presenting it to the court, it must be approved by the Attorney General. The application is then submitted to the FISC by a federal officer.

The definition of probable cause that applies when FISA warrants are sought is different than the one used for other Fourth Amendment purposes. The applicant must establish that the target of the electronic surveillance is a foreign power and no "United States person" is being considered a foreign power or foreign agent because of activities protected by the First Amendment. When the judge evaluates probable cause, the target's past activities, as well as facts and circumstances relating to current and future activities, may be considered.[39]

Another difference between FISA wiretaps and those authorized by the Wiretap Act is that a judge can issue the warrant without restricting it to a specific telephone number(s) and locations listed in the application. These roving warrants increase the investigator's ability to obtain valid intelligence data. Low-cost cell phones, dubbed disposable phones, have made the change necessary.

A confusing feature of FISA is that surveillance can be authorized for different periods of time. Unless an exception applies, warrants are valid for a maximum of 90 days.[40] Warrants targeting foreign powers may be valid for a maximum of 1 year;[41] for foreign agents, the corresponding period is 120 days.[42] In all cases, the warrant terminates if the stated objective is reached before the expiration date.

Similar to Wiretap Act warrants, FISA provides for emergency warrants. If the Attorney General determines that "an emergency situation exists with respect to the employment of electronic surveillance to obtain foreign intelligence information before an order authorizing such surveillance can with due diligence be obtained," the surveillance can be started immediately.[43] If a FISA warrant is obtained within 72 hours, it will apply retroactively.

In matters of national security, FISA permits the President to authorize the Attorney General to conduct electronic surveillance for up to 1 year without a warrant. This includes the right to conduct "wiretaps" and intercept e-mail as well as utilizes pen registers and "trap and trace" devices. Monitoring must be limited to channels used exclusively between foreign powers. The Attorney General must certify in writing under oath that there is "no substantial likelihood that the surveillance will acquire the contents of any communication to which a United States person is a party."[44] Nonverbal technical intelligence can also be seized.

For electronic surveillance of foreign agents not utilizing the exclusive channels mentioned previously, the President must provide a written authorization for the Attorney General to petition a special federal court for permission to use such techniques. The surveillance order is normally good for no more than 120 days; extensions can be for up to 1 year.[45]

In the only case published by the United States Foreign Intelligence Surveillance Court of Review since it was created in 1978, the court ruled that when FISA is used to issue wiretap orders, the information gathered can be shared with other government agencies for use in prosecuting crimes. Unlike some lower courts, the appellate court found no basis in the statute, or debates when it was enacted by Congress, to warrant creating a wall between the intelligence community and law enforcement.[46]

Physical Searches

FISA was amended in 1994 to make it possible to obtain warrants for physical searches done in connection with foreign intelligence investigations. The process is similar to the one outlined previously for FISA electronic surveillance warrants. The application to the FISC must include a statement of the nature of the foreign intelligence sought and the manner in which the physical search is to be conducted. Review by the Attorney General is mandated. The assistant to the President for National Security Affairs, or designee, must certify

(A) that the certifying official deems the information sought to be foreign intelligence information;

(B) that a significant purpose of the search is to obtain foreign intelligence information;

(C) that such information cannot reasonably be obtained by normal investigative techniques;

(D) that designates the type of foreign intelligence information being sought according to the categories described in section 1801 (e) of this title; and

(E) includes a statement explaining the basis for the certifications required by subparagraphs (C) and (D).[47]

The application is reviewed by a FISC judge and issued if there is probable cause. As used here, probable cause means

(A) the target of the physical search is a foreign power or an agent of a foreign power, except that no United States person may be considered an agent of a foreign power solely upon the basis of activities protected by the First Amendment to the Constitution of the United States; and

(B) the premises or property to be searched is owned, used, possessed by, or is in transit to or from an agent of a foreign power or a foreign power.[48]

When evaluating probable cause, the judge is allowed to consider past activities of the target, as well as facts and circumstances relating to current or future activities of the target.[49]

FISA also has a provision originally designed to obtain business records. It now has a broader definition:

> Application for an order requiring the production of any tangible things (including books, records, papers, documents, and other items) for an investigation to obtain foreign intelligence information not concerning a United States person or to protect against international terrorism or clandestine intelligence activities, provided that such investigation of a United States person is not conducted solely upon the basis of activities protected by the First Amendment to the Constitution.[50]

The application can be filed with the FISC or any U.S. Magistrate. The orders are routinely granted if they meet the procedural specifications of the code section. Unlike search warrants, probable cause is not required—only the certification that there is an ongoing investigation that complies with existing Executive Orders. Once issued, the order is served on the record holder, much like a subpoena to produce documents for a grand jury. The person who receives the order is bound by federal law to maintain secrecy about the order.

National Security Letters[51]

During a span of 30 years, Congress passed legislation that allowed the Executive Branch to obtain records from banks and many other institutions; all of them were revised as part of the USA PATRIOT Act. Referred to as National Security Letter (NSL) statutes, what they have in common is that they enable a federal investigative agency, usually the FBI, to obtain records stored with a third party. No prior judicial authorization is required. The entity that is served with an NSL is required to maintain secrecy about the request and/or compliance with it.

Although the materials requested must be relevant to an ongoing investigation, all that the investigator need put in most NSL requests is the following quote: "such information is sought for the conduct of an authorized investigation to protect against international terrorism or clandestine intelligence activities."[52] Table 13-1 summarizes five NSL statutes that are part of the USA PATRIOT Act.

T A B L E **13-1** National Security Letters

Authorizing Legislation[a]	Who Can Use This Law	Standard for Issuing NSL	Type of Agency	Type of Information
Right to Financial Privacy Act of 1978 (RFPA)	FBI	Relevance	Banks, credit unions, pawnbrokers, travel agencies, automobile dealers, U.S. Postal Service, and casinos	Financial records
Fair Credit Reporting Act (FCRA)	FBI	Relevance	Consumer reporting agencies	Names and addresses of all financial institutions at which consumer maintains or has maintained an account
Fair Credit Reporting Act (FCRA)	Any government agency authorized to conduct investigations of international terrorism	Information is necessary for the agency's conduct of investigation Restricted to international terrorism and clandestine intelligence activities	Consumer reporting agencies	Consumer report on a consumer and all other information in the consumer's file
Electronic Communications Privacy Act (ECPA)	FBI	Relevance	Telecommunications providers	Information regarding wire and electronic communications, such as routing and addressing information Does not cover content of communications
Intelligence Authorization Act for Fiscal Year 1995	FBI	Must have reasonable grounds to believe, based on credible information, that the person might be sending classified information to foreign powers or agents	Financial agencies, financial institutions, consumer reporting agencies	Information about finances including records of travel Limited to government employees who hold security clearances

[a]Acts have been amended by the USA PATRIOT Act (2002).
Based on N. A. Sales, "Secrecy and National Security Investigations," *Alabama Law Review* 58 (2007).

Summary

Eavesdropping is covered by the Misplaced Reliance Doctrine. Anything overheard is admissible. The person speaking bears the burden of restricting his or her conversations to trustworthy people. This rationale applies even if someone is surreptitiously carrying electronic recording equipment.

Wiretapping and other electronic monitoring of conversations require a special warrant. Only specific serious crimes justify this type of invasion of privacy. Police must show that other types of investigative techniques are inadequate. The warrant is good for a maximum period of 30 days. Once the electronic surveillance warrant has been obtained, officers may covertly enter to install, maintain, and retrieve the equipment. The Wiretap Act of 1968 was designed to enable federal courts to issue electronic surveillance warrants. The Foreign Intelligence Surveillance Act of 1978 covers wiretaps and other devices used on agents working for foreign governments and terrorists. Both of these statutes were amended by the USA PATRIOT Act so that they can be used in the fight against terrorism.

Review Questions

1. Is a warrant required if an informer is going to carry a tape recorder when talking to a suspect who has not been arrested? Explain.
2. When is an electronic surveillance warrant required? Explain.
3. Explain the requirements for obtaining a warrant under the Wiretap Act of 1968 (Title III).
4. Explain the requirements for conducting electronic surveillance under the Foreign Intelligence Surveillance Act.
5. Explain how the FBI, while investigating terrorism by foreign agents, can gain access to bank account information and other personal records of the suspected terrorist.

Writing Assignment

Go to the websites that we have used previously and find a case in which a wiretap was used. Write a one-page report on it. Include why the wiretap was used and whether useful information was obtained from the wiretap.

Notes

1. *Hoffa v. United States* 385 U.S. 293, 17 L.Ed. 2d 374, 87 S.Ct. 408 (1966).
2. *United States v. White* 401 U.S. 745, 28 L.Ed. 2d 453, 91 S.Ct. 1122 (1971).
3. *Katz v. United States* 389 U.S. 347, 19 L.Ed. 2d 576, 88 S.Ct. 507 (1967).
4. *Berger v. New York* 388 U.S. 41, 18 L.Ed. 2d 1040, 87 S.Ct. 1873 (1967).
5. *Smith v. Maryland* 442 U.S. 735, 61 L.Ed. 2d 220, 99 S.Ct. 2577 (1979). See also *United States v. New York Telephone Co.* 434 U.S. 159, 54 L.Ed. 2d 376, 98 S.Ct. 364 (1977).
6. 18 U.S.C. 3121(b).
7. *United States v. Karo* 468 U.S. 705, 82 L.Ed. 2d 530, 104 S.Ct. 3296 (1984); *United States v. Knotts* 460 U.S. 276, 75 L.Ed. 2d 55, 103 S.Ct. 1081 (1983).
8. N. Abrams, "The US Crosses the Rubicon: The Military Commissions Act 2006," *Journal of International Criminal Justice* 5: 1(2007, March); S. Blasberg, "Legal Update: Law and Technology of Security Measures in the Wake of Terrorism," *Boston University Journal of Science and Technology Law* 8: 721 (2002, Summer); E. Broxmeyer, "Note and Comment: The Problems of Security and Freedom: Procedural Due Process and the Designation of Foreign Terrorist Organizations under the Anti-Terrorism and Effective Death Penalty Act," *Berkeley Journal of International Law* 22: 439 (2004); G. Christensen, "Government Information Collection: Federal Data Collection, Secure Flight, the Intelligence Reform and Terrorism Prevention Act, and the Reauthorization of the USA PATRIOT Act," *I/S: A Journal of Law and Policy for the Information Society* 2: 485 (2006, Fall); J. X. Dempsey, "Communications Privacy in the Digital Age: Revitalizing the Federal Wiretap Laws to Enhance Privacy," *Albany Law Journal of Science & Technology* 8: 65 (1997); S. N. Herman, "The USA PATRIOT Act and the Submajoritarian Fourth Amendment," *Harvard Civil Rights–Civil Liberties Law Review* 41: 67 (2006, Winter); J. Jaffer, "Symposium: Secret Evidence and the Courts in the Age of National Security: Panel Report: Secret Evidence in the Investigative Stage: FISA, Administrative Subpoenas, and Privacy," *Cardozo Public Law, Policy & Ethics Journal* 5: 7 (2006, Fall); C. Metzler, "Providing Material Support to Violate the Constitution: The USA PATRIOT Act and Its Assault on the 4th Amendment," *North Carolina Central Law Journal* 2006, 29 N.C. Cent. L.J. 35; S. A. Osher, "Privacy, Computers and the Patriot Act: The Fourth Amendment Isn't Dead, But No One Will Insure It," *Florida Law Review* 54: 521 (2002, July); K. Oyama, "Cyberlaw: Note: E-Mail Privacy after *United States v. Councilman*: Legislative Options for Amending ECPA," *Berkeley Technology Law Journal* 21: 499 (2006); S. H. Rackow, "Comment: How the USA PATRIOT Act Will Permit Governmental Infringement upon the Privacy of Americans in the Name of 'Intelligence' Investigations," *University of Pennsylvania Law Review* 150: 1651 (2002, May); R. Shulman, "Note: USA Patriot Act: Granting the U.S. Government the Unprecedented Power to Circumvent American Civil Liberties in the Name of National Security," *University of Detroit Mercy Law Review* 80: 427 (2003, Spring); C. Truehart, "Case Comment: *United States v. Bin Laden* and the Foreign Intelligence Exception to the Warrant Requirement for Searches of 'United States Persons' Abroad," *Boston University Law Review* 82: 555 (2002, April); J. W. Whitehead and S. H. Aden, "Forfeiting 'Enduring Freedom' for 'Homeland Security': A Constitutional Analysis of the USA PATRIOT Act and the Justice Department's Anti-Terrorism Initiatives," *American University Law Review* 51: 1081 (2002, August).
9. 18 U.S.C. 2510 et. seq.
10. Id.
11. 18 U.S.C. 2511(1).
12. 18 U.S.C. 2510(2).
13. 18 U.S.C. 2510(1).
14. 18 USC 2511(2).
15. 18 U.S.C. 2516(1).
16. 18 U.S.C. 2516(2).

17. 18 U.S.C. 2516

18. 18 U.S.C. 2518(11).

19. 18 U.S.C. 2518(6).

20. 18 U.S.C. 2516(1).

21. Id.

22. 18 U.S.C. 2516(2).

23. 18 U.S.C. 2518(12).

24. 18 U.S.C. 2518(5).

25. 18 U.S.C. 2518(7).

26. 18 U.S.C. 2518(8).

27. 18 U.S.C. 2518(8)(d).

28. 18 U.S.C. 2518(8)(d)(3).

29. 18 U.S.C. 2518(9).

30. 18 U.S.C. 2515.

31. Dalia *v. United States* 441 U.S. 238, 60 L.Ed. 2d 177, 99 S.Ct. 1682 (1979).

32. *United States v. Donovan* 429 U.S. 413, 50 L.Ed. 2d 652, 97 S.Ct. 658 (1977).

33. *United States v. Kahn* 415 U.S. 143, 39 L.Ed. 2d 225, 94 S.Ct. 977 (1974).

34. *Scott v. United States* 436 U.S. 128, 56 L.Ed. 2d 168, 98 S.Ct. 1717 (1978).

35. *United States v. United States District Court, Eastern Michigan (Keith)* 407 U.S. 297, 32 L.Ed. 2d 752, 92 S.Ct. 2125 (1972).

36. The Foreign Intelligence Surveillance Act of 1978 can be found at 50 U.S.C. 1801 et. seq.

37. B. Hund, "Note: Disappearing Safeguards: FISA Nonresident Alien 'Loophole' Is Unconstitutional," *Cardozo Journal of International and Comparative Law* 15: 169, 182 (2007, Winter).

38. 50 U.S.C. 1804.

39. 50 U.S.C. 1805(a)(3).

40. 50 U.S.C. 1805(e)(1).

41. 50 U.S.C. 1805(e)(1)(A).

42. 50 U.S.C. 1805(e)(1)(B).

43. 50 U.S.C. 1805.

44. 50 U.S.C. 1802.

45. 50 U.S.C. 1805(e)(2)(B).

46. *In re: Sealed Case No. 02-001.* United States Foreign Intelligence Surveillance Court of Review (November 18, 2002).

47. 50 U.S.C. 1823(a)(7).

48. 50 U.S.C. 1824(a)(3).

49. 50 U.S.C. 1824(b).

50. 50 U.S.C. 1861(a)(1).

51. N. Sales, "Secrecy and National Security Investigations," *Alabama Law Review* 58: 811 (2007).

52. 12 U.S.C. 3414(a)(5)(A).

CHAPTER **14**

Self-Incrimination

Feature Case: Central Park Jogger Attack

In 1989, five African American and Hispanic teenagers from Harlem who had been implicated in a series of muggings were arrested, interrogated by police, and later convicted of raping and beating nearly to death a Caucasian female jogger in New York's Central Park. Despite the youths' assertion of innocence during and after trial, the case received extraordinary attention primarily because of the brutal nature of the crime, the fact that four of the teens' confessions were videotaped, and colorful media descriptions of the teens acting like "animals" "wilding" as in a "wolf pack" looking for "prey" during a period when violent crime was perceived to be an out-of-control epidemic plaguing New York City.

However, on December 19, 2002, the convictions of the five youths were vacated when convicted rapist and murderer Matias Reyes admitted responsibility for the Central Park attack and exonerated the teens, providing a confession that was corroborated by physical evidence indicating he had acted alone. Consequently, the case directly questioned police interrogation techniques that employ extensive questioning, isolation, deceptive tactics, and use of false promises made to young, immature, uneducated, or other so-called "vulnerable" suspects.

Learning Objectives

After studying this chapter, you will be able to

- Define the scope of the Fifth Amendment protection against self-incrimination.
- Explain how the Fifth Amendment applies to nontestimonial evidence.
- State the *Miranda* warnings and explain when they should be given.

- Describe the standard for a waiver of *Miranda* rights.
- Explain how *Miranda* rights apply to sequential interrogations.
- List the procedures that are required prior to interrogating a person who has been indicted or arraigned.

Key Terms

- Custodial interrogation
- Double jeopardy
- Immunity
- Indigent suspect
- *Miranda* booking exceptions

- *Miranda* public safety exception
- *Miranda* waiver
- *Miranda* warnings
- Right to counsel

- Right to have attorney present
- Right to remain silent
- Self-incrimination
- Testimonial evidence
- Tolling statute of limitations

Myths about *Miranda* Rights	Facts about *Miranda* Rights
Police are always required to provide *Miranda* warnings when arresting a suspect.	*Miranda* warnings are only required at the time of arrest if the suspect will be interrogated immediately after arrest.
Miranda warnings must be read verbatim because any mistake in advising a suspect will result in the waiver being invalid.	Although officers are encouraged to use standardized warnings, a suspect's waiver will be valid as long as he or she understood the nature of the *Miranda* warnings and made a knowing, intelligent, and voluntary waiver of those rights.
Once a suspect invokes his or her right to remain silent, police cannot initiate questioning again.	Police may re-advise a suspect of his or her rights and reinitiate questioning as long as the suspect agrees to talk and does not ask for legal counsel.
The police must give *Miranda* warnings at traffic stops, detentions, and similar field interviews.	*Miranda* warnings are only required for custodial interrogations or their "functional equivalent" and are *not* needed during limited detentions, such as traffic stops, where there is no coercive atmosphere.

Scope of the Privilege against Self-Incrimination

The Fifth Amendment protects a suspected criminal from being compelled to give testimony that might incriminate him- or herself. It does not apply in civil cases.

Privilege against Self-Incrimination Defined

No person can be required to make statements that can be used against him or her in a criminal proceeding.

Situations Not Covered by the Fifth Amendment

Self-incrimination applies only if criminal charges could be based on the confession or admission. It does not apply in three situations that arise in criminal cases in which it is impossible to file charges:

1. The statute of limitations has run.
2. The witness has been granted immunity.
3. The witness cannot be prosecuted due to double jeopardy.

It must be noted that even in these cases due process prevents police from using coercion to obtain confessions.

Statute of Limitations

If the statute of limitations has run, no charges can be filed. Due to the fact that the **statute can be tolled** (stopped) if a suspect flees the jurisdiction to avoid prosecution, it is possible for the statute to have run against one suspect but not another. A similar situation occurs when one suspect committed a felony and another person involved in the same crime spree only committed a misdemeanor that has a shorter statute of limitations. When either of these situations occurs, the police may be interested in obtaining a statement from the suspect for whom the statute has expired in order to use the information against someone who can still be prosecuted. In these circumstances, a suspect cannot refuse to talk on the grounds that it might incriminate him or her.

Immunity

A witness with immunity cannot be prosecuted for what he or she said, provided the confession is within the scope of the **immunity.** In most states, the prosecutor can grant immunity, but defense counsel does not have similar powers. Grand juries can also grant immunity. The formal documents filed with the court when immunity is granted specify the scope of the immunity. The most common types of immunity are use immunity (what is stated by the witness cannot be used against him or her) and transaction immunity (the witness cannot be prosecuted for the crimes specified; neither his or her statements nor evidence the police obtain independently can be used). A grant of immunity from federal prosecution carries with it immunity from state prosecution for the same offense, and vice versa.

If the witness is careless enough to tell about crimes not covered by immunity, charges can be filed. On the other hand, the immune witness cannot refuse to testify merely to protect a friend or save face. Refusal to testify is grounds for holding the witness in contempt of court. This type of contempt usually results in sending the witness to jail until he or she is willing to testify. Since the witness can be released as soon as the testimony is given, the witness is said to "hold the key" to the jail.

Double Jeopardy

Double jeopardy protects a person who has been either convicted or acquitted of a crime. The same crime, or lesser included charges, cannot be re-filed. The fact that the jury convicted the defendant of a lesser included offense when the more serious charge was filed implies an acquittal on the more serious offense.

When there are multiple parties to the crime who are tried separately, the testimony of an accomplice who has already been tried and either convicted or acquitted can be very useful. Once again, there is no right to refuse to testify based on self-incrimination. As a practical matter, the prosecutor may delay using this approach until after the conviction has been affirmed on appeal. It is important to note that only convictions or acquittals activate this rule. Failing to file charges, winning suppression motions, or dismissing the case without prejudice do not qualify; neither does a trial ending in a "hung jury."

Examples of Situations *Not* Covered by Fifth Amendment

- Mary was charged with murder because she hired Harry, a "hit man," who killed her wealthy husband. She convinced the trial jury of her innocence and was acquitted. If called to testify at Harry's trial, Mary cannot invoke the Fifth Amendment because double jeopardy will protect her from being prosecuted for the murder twice.

  Mary could claim Fifth Amendment protection against double jeopardy if charges were filed against her again for the murder of her husband.

  Mary *cannot* claim Fifth Amendment self-incrimination and avoid testifying at Harry's trial because no charges can be filed against her after her acquittal.

- Carrie stole sweaters from a department store. Shelby, a sales clerk, was charged with fraud for doctoring the sales records. The detective handling the cases lost both files. When he found them 18 months later, charges could not be filed against Carrie, but Carrie was called to testify about the theft at Shelby's trial for felony fraud.

  Carrie has protection against charges being filed against her based on the 1-year statute of limitations for the misdemeanor theft.

  Assume that all felonies, except murder, have a statute of limitations of 3 years.

  Shelby can be prosecuted for fraud (a felony) because the statute of limitations has *not* run on the fraud.

  Assume that Carrie *cannot* be prosecuted for anything related to the fraud that Shelby committed except the theft.

  Carrie *cannot* claim the Fifth Amendment self-incrimination privilege to avoid testifying at Shelby's trial.

• Ian was given "transaction immunity" when he agreed to testify against fellow gang members about a rape they both participated in. The week before the trial, he received a letter threatening to kill him if he testified. At trial he was sworn in as a witness. When the prosecutor asked him a question about the rape, Ian claimed the Fifth Amendment. The judge instructed Ian that he could not claim the Fifth Amendment and told Ian that he would be held in jail if he refused to testify.

Ian *cannot* claim the Fifth Amendment self-incrimination privilege and avoid testifying because he has immunity.

> Ian cannot refuse to testify about incidents covered by the immunity. When a person with immunity refuses to testify, that person can be placed in jail until he or she decides to testify.

How the Privilege against Self-Incrimination Is Invoked

The appropriate way to invoke the privilege against **self-incrimination** varies with the stage of the criminal justice system where it is used. Prior to arrest and during field interviews, a person may refuse to answer questions, but the police have no duty to inform the suspect that he or she may do so. The suspect's use of the privilege at this stage depends on his or her prior knowledge of these rights. If the suspect wants to seek advice from an attorney at this phase of the investigation, it must be done at his or her own expense.

During custodial interrogations, the police must inform the suspect of his or her constitutional rights. In order to continue the questioning, a knowing, intelligent, and voluntary waiver must be obtained from the suspect. Coercion may not be used to persuade a suspect to talk. An indigent suspect has the right to have counsel appointed at government expense during custodial interrogation if he or she so desires.

At trial, the proper procedure depends on who is invoking the Fifth Amendment privilege. If it is the defendant, the defense attorney indicates this indirectly by not calling him or her to the witness stand. Although it is obvious to the jury that the defendant did not testify, the Supreme Court in *Griffin v. California* made it clear that no inference of guilt may be drawn from the invocation of this constitutional right.[1] The prosecutor may not ask the jury to infer that the only reason the defendant did not testify is that he or she is guilty. If the defendant makes a timely request, the judge must instruct the jurors that they may not draw this conclusion (*Carter v. Kentucky*).[2]

There is one exception to this procedure. If the defense counsel claims during the closing statement that the defendant never had an opportunity to explain his or her side of the case, the prosecution may inform the jury that the defendant had the right to testify but chose not to (*United States v. Robinson*).[3]

Other witnesses must take the stand, even if they have already said they refuse to testify. The privilege against self-incrimination is asserted in response to each question. In most cases, the reason for invoking the privilege is obvious and no explanation is given in open court. If it appears there is no basis for invoking this privilege, the judge may ask the witness, outside the hearing of the jury and attorneys, to explain why the privilege applies.

Witnesses have the right to have their own attorneys present to give advice on how to answer questions. When a witness who does not have an attorney present starts to make an incriminating statement, the judge usually will stop the proceedings briefly to determine if the witness understands the gravity of what is happening. The judge, or the prosecutor at the judge's direction, frequently advises the witness of his or her right to remain silent by giving the *Miranda* warnings.

If the defendant takes the witness stand and lies under oath, he or she can be punished. The obvious approach is to file charges for perjury. Another approach is to use the fact that the defendant committed perjury as an enhancement when calculating the sentence for the crime for which he or she was on trial. The Supreme Court approved this practice but noted that an enhancement could not be imposed if it appeared that the testimony was inaccurate due to confusion, mistake, or faulty memory. If the defendant objects to the enhancement, there must be an independent finding by the judge that the testimony was a willful obstruction of justice, or an attempt to do so, that falls within the definition of perjury (*United States v. Dunnigan*).[4] This would occur at the sentencing hearing and does not necessitate a new trial.

Examples of How the Fifth Amendment Is Invoked

• Kevin was stopped approximately 100 yards from a building where the burglar alarm had just gone off. The police legally stopped him based on reasonable suspicion but did not have probable cause to arrest him. They questioned him without giving the *Miranda* warnings. Kevin said, "Sorry, I refuse to answer any more questions. Fifth Amendment." The police stopped the questioning.

When a person is stopped on reasonable suspicion, the police are *not* required to give the person the *Miranda* warnings.

A person stopped on reasonable suspicion has the right to refuse to answer questions and the right to have an attorney present during questioning, but the police are not required to provide this information.

At this stage of the proceedings, the person must pay for the attorney.

• Libby was on trial for embezzlement. Her attorney told her that the Fifth Amendment gave her the right to refuse to testify. She decided that was a good idea. During the defense case-in-chief, the defense attorney did not call Libby to testify.

Everyone has the right *not* to testify during his or her own criminal trial.

The decision not to testify is made during a conference with the attorney. No specific mention is made in open court about the defendant's decision not to testify. It becomes clear that he or she will not testify when the defense attorney announces, "The Defense rests," without calling the defendant.
The prosecutor does not have the right to call the defendant to the stand.
The prosecutor cannot comment about the fact that the defendant did not testify or tell the jurors that a defendant would refuse to testify only if he or she was guilty.

- Martin helped Lizzy alter the company books. He had not been arrested or charged with his part in the crime. The prosecutor called Martin as a witness. He answered the questions that he thought were safe. When the prosecutor asked an incriminating question, Martin asked to talk to his lawyer. After doing so, Martin told the judge that he refused to answer the question because of the Fifth Amendment. The prosecutor went on to another question.

  Martin cannot refuse to take the witness stand. Only the defendant is allowed to invoke the privilege in that manner.
  Martin can invoke the Fifth Amendment and refuse to answer specific questions if he and his attorney believe that the answers to those questions could be used against him.

Note: Some states have statutes that require the witness to declare his or her intent to invoke the Fifth Amendment before taking the witness stand. In these states, a hearing is held before the witness takes the stand so the judge and attorneys can decide whether the person should be allowed to testify.

Nontestimonial Compulsion

The Supreme Court has repeatedly held that the Fifth Amendment privilege against self-incrimination applies only to **testimonial evidence.** Most commonly, this means statements that a person makes that are admissions or confessions. These may be either oral or written. The privilege does not apply to other incriminating evidence that may be obtained from a person.

Body Fluids

The results of blood, urine, or breath tests can be used in cases involving driving under the influence of alcohol. A variety of tests are done on blood and semen samples in sexual assault cases. DNA samples may be tested. Many other tests are used less frequently. All of these tests rest on the same basis as far as the Fifth Amendment is concerned. Although the results may be very incriminating, no privilege can be asserted as grounds for refusing to take the tests because they are nontestimonial.[5]

Three other types of challenges can be used. If the arrest was illegal, usually due to lack of probable cause, body fluids can be excluded on the grounds of an illegal search and seizure. The Fruit of the Poison Tree Doctrine could then be used to exclude the laboratory tests. Due process could be asserted as a reason for excluding the test results if excessive force was used to obtain the samples. A variety of other rules of evidence can be invoked if the fluids were not handled in a manner that established the chain of custody, if the laboratory personnel were not adequately trained, or if the equipment used was not properly maintained.

Identifying Features

A person's appearance is also not testimonial evidence. The most commonly used identification procedure involves fingerprints. Due to the high scientific reliability of fingerprint identification, a match is very incriminating. Once again, the Fifth Amendment provides no protection because no testimony is required. The Fourth Amendment protects the suspect to the extent that the police may not take a suspect to the station for the purpose of obtaining fingerprints for comparison purposes unless there is consent or probable cause to make an arrest (*Hayes v. Florida*).[6] This does not prevent the police from rolling a set of prints at the scene where a legal field interview is conducted. The fingerprint cards made any time a person was legally arrested are very useful for the purpose of identifying fingerprints found at a crime scene. Print cards in government files for other purposes, such as applications for state licenses, can also be used.

Visual identification by victims and witnesses to the crime are treated in a similar manner. They are not testimonial (*United States v. Wade*).[7] The suspect cannot invoke the Fifth Amendment as a grounds for refusing to participate in a lineup or showup. The police do not violate the suspect's rights by showing mug shots or other photographs. Due process protects the suspect from unduly suggestive techniques used by the police. This is discussed in more detail later in this chapter.

Handwriting and Voice Exemplars

Handwriting exemplars and voice exemplars, also referred to as samples, are frequently used for identification purposes. Neither is testimonial (*United States v. Mara*).[8] The suspect is told what to write or say. For this reason, the content of the exemplar is not an indication of guilt and cannot be incriminating. The visual or audio characteristics of the exemplar are incriminating, but these factors are not testimonial.

Sobriety Tests

Sobriety tests, whether conducted at the scene where a car is stopped on suspicion of drunk driving or later during booking, are not covered by the Fifth Amendment privilege. Actions in the sobriety test that indicate lack of muscle coordination, such as poor balance and slurred speech, are not testimonial. Questions that call for incriminating answers, such as "How many drinks did you have?" require *Miranda* warnings. Videotapes of the sobriety test are admissible in court, but segments that would be considered interrogation must be excluded (*Pennsylvania v. Muniz*).[9]

Examples of Nontestimonial Compulsion

- Erin was arrested on suspicion of driving under the influence of alcohol. The officer took her to the nearest emergency room and had a nurse draw a blood sample.

  Erin *cannot* invoke the Fifth Amendment self-incrimination privilege as grounds for refusing to give the blood sample because blood is not testimonial evidence.

  Drawing blood for a sobriety test is considered an emergency because the alcohol will dissipate over time as part of a normal body function that cannot be stopped in a living person.

  No search warrant is required because of this emergency.

  The police need probable cause in order to arrest a person and take the person to an appropriate facility to have blood drawn.

  Absent consent, blood cannot be drawn during a detention based on reasonable suspicion.

- Frank is a suspect in a rape case. The arresting officer used a swab to obtain a tissue sample from the inside of Frank's cheek. If the DNA test is positive, this tissue sample will be very incriminating.

  Frank *cannot* invoke the Fifth Amendment self-incrimination privilege because tissue samples are not testimonial evidence.

  Unreasonable force *cannot* be used to obtain the tissue sample.

  Probable cause is needed to detain Frank in order to take the tissue sample.

  Many states require that medical personnel take the tissue sample, not the arresting officer.

  Investigating officers must comply with both the U.S. Supreme Court decision and state law.

- Phyllis was arrested for forgery. She was asked to copy a paragraph the officer handed her, using her own handwriting. If a forensic documents examiner determines that the handwriting exemplar indicates that Phyllis wrote the forged documents, it will be very incriminating.

  Phyllis cannot invoke the Fifth Amendment self-incrimination privilege as grounds for refusing to make the exemplar because exemplars are not testimonial evidence.

  Officers must have probable cause to take Phyllis to the station to obtain the exemplar.

Miranda Warnings

Miranda v. Arizona[10] is one of the best known Supreme Court cases, yet there are many details surrounding the *Miranda* decision that still cause confusion. To help clear up some of these problems, four key areas are addressed:

1. What are the *Miranda* warnings?
2. When must they be given?
3. How does a suspect waive his or her *Miranda* rights?
4. What rules apply to sequential interrogations?

Content of *Miranda* Warnings

Each officer must fully understand the **Miranda warnings** so that he or she can explain them correctly to each suspect. The Supreme Court has permitted paraphrasing but has been quite intolerant of misleading warnings. This includes answers to a suspect's questions about these rights. Although the police would obviously feel it is best to make a full confession, it is the job of the defense attorney to decide the best tactic for the suspect to take. Police officers should not attempt to give legal advice.

Miranda Warnings Defined

Prior to custodial interrogation the suspect must be warned that
1. You have the right to remain silent.
2. Anything you say can and will be used against you in a court of law.
3. You have the right to have an attorney present during questioning.
4. If you cannot afford an attorney, one will be appointed at no charge to assist you during questioning.

The **right to remain silent** includes the right to refrain from making both oral and written statements. Nodding the head "yes" or "no" would also be covered. The suspect retains the right to refuse to answer questions at any time. Even though he or she agreed to talk at the beginning of the interview, the right to remain silent enables the suspect to stop the interrogation at any time.

Second, anything that the suspect says can be used against him or her in court. For emphasis, many departments warn the suspect that statements "can and will" be used against you in court. Statements that are not confessions can be used if they have any evidentiary value. Attempts to incriminate another person frequently are used to show guilty knowledge. Anything that is inconsistent with other statements made by this suspect can be used to impeach him or her at trial. Attempts to talk to the police "off the record" indicate that the suspect does not understand the warnings.

Third, the suspect has the **right to have an attorney present** during questioning. Law enforcement officers may not continue questioning a suspect after he or she has requested an attorney. The fact that an attorney will be appointed at arraignment is not enough. It should be noted, however, that this right is not a guarantee that an attorney will meet with the suspect immediately. The police have two alternatives—stop questioning or give the suspect an attorney. Since most attorneys routinely tell their clients not to make any statements to the police, it is not uncommon for the interrogation to be stopped when an attorney is requested. The suspect is returned to his or her cell but no attorney is called. This does not violate the suspect's rights.

Lastly, if the suspect cannot afford an attorney, one will be provided at no cost to the suspect. The purpose of this warning is to inform the **indigent suspect** that his or her lack of money will not prevent him or her from having an attorney present during questioning. It is not the duty of the police, however, to review the financial status of the suspect and give advice on whether he or she is eligible for a free attorney. The court usually makes this determination of eligibility at the arraignment. Neither is it appropriate for the police to tell the suspect that the court has the authority to order a person to repay the cost of the attorney. If the suspect requests an attorney, the police should proceed in the same manner regardless of the suspect's apparent wealth (or lack thereof): Questioning must stop.

Many law enforcement agencies have the *Miranda* warnings printed on pocket size cards so officers can read them to each suspect. The purpose of the card is to ensure that the warnings are given uniformly. However, merely reciting the Court's language is not enough. The warnings must be given so that the suspect can understand them. The prosecution bears the burden of convincing the judge that the warnings were correctly explained to the suspect. This must be established by a preponderance of the evidence.

For juveniles, this means explaining the warnings in very simple terms. Similar problems may occur with illiterate and mentally impaired suspects. Intoxicated and mentally ill suspects also pose a challenge. If the suspect does not speak English fluently, an interpreter may be necessary. Care must be taken to make sure the interpreter and the suspect speak the same dialect. Subtle differences, if not clearly understood by the suspect, may make the warnings void.

Sample Dialogue Used to Give *Miranda* Warnings

Det. Dawson:	I have some questions for you, but before we begin I need to give you the *Miranda* warnings.
Johnny Johnson:	Oh, neat. I saw that on TV.
Det. Dawson:	I want you to pay close attention. This is not TV. You were arrested for a serious crime.
Johnny Johnson:	OK.
Det. Dawson:	Here is a *Miranda* card I want you to read while I read it out loud. Item No. 1 says, "You have the right to remain silent." Do you know what that means?
Johnny Johnson:	Sure. It means I do not have to answer your questions.
Det. Dawson:	Good. Look at No. 2. It says "Anything you say can and will be used against you in a court of law." Do you know what that means?
Johnny Johnson:	I think it means that if I confess, you will tell about it when I go to trial.
Det. Dawson:	Well, that is part of it. But you need to understand that anything you say, not just a confession, can be used against you in court. Got that?
Johnny Johnson:	Yeah, I understand that.
Det. Dawson:	Now let's look at No. 3. It says, "You have the right to have an attorney present during questioning." Do you understand?
Johnny Johnson:	Well, yes and no. It says I have the right to have an attorney here while you question me. But I don't have an attorney so it doesn't apply to me.
Det. Dawson:	Yes, I know you don't have an attorney. But that is covered in No. 4. Look at it very closely. It says, "If you cannot afford an attorney, one will be appointed at no charge to assist you during questioning."
Johnny Johnson:	Oh, I see. I sure can't afford an attorney but if I want one I get one free. Right?
Det. Dawson:	Yes, that's right. All you have to do is ask.

When *Miranda* Warnings Are Required

The key to giving *Miranda* warnings at the correct time is to watch for **custodial interrogation.** The suspect must be in custody at the time, and the police must be interrogating him or her.

Custody, for the purposes of *Miranda,* is the equivalent of a custodial arrest (*Berkemer v. McCarty*).[11] It does not include traffic stops in which citations are issued and the violator is released at the scene (*Pennsylvania v. Bruder*).[12] Brief field interviews based on reasonable suspicion are not covered. Neither does it apply to situations in which the suspect is being questioned at the police station but is not under arrest (*Oregon v. Mathiason*).[13] Whether there is a custodial arrest is judged by an objective test; the subjective intent of the officer is not important.[14]

On the other hand, *Orozco v. Texas* held that it does not matter why the suspect is in custody.[15] Warnings are required if a suspect was arrested for a minor crime and questioned regarding a very serious one. Questioning by a different law enforcement agency also requires the warnings. *Miranda* warnings are even required if the suspect is questioned while in jail serving time on a totally unrelated offense.

In *Rhode Island v. Innis* and *Brewer v. Williams*, the Supreme Court defined interrogation as the process of questioning, or its functional equivalent.[16] *Miranda* warnings are required prior to any interrogation that is done while the suspect is in custody. Asking questions about a crime is clearly interrogation. So is requesting a narrative statement. The Court has also included indirect attempts to obtain information. For example, if two officers engage in a conversation with the intent of being overheard and eliciting a response, this is the functional equivalent of interrogation. So is telling a suspect, "I want you to think about this . . . " but never asking a specific question. Trial judges are left with the task of deciding which conversations were indirect questioning and which ones accidentally resulted in a response from the suspect.

As with the Fourth Amendment, the Fifth Amendment protections only apply to acts by government employees and their agents. If an accomplice, who has decided to cooperate with the police, questions the suspect, the same rules apply as if the police had done it themselves. Questioning done by a private person that the police did not authorize or condone does not require *Miranda* warnings. Informants from the jail population can provide very useful information. They may report on anything they hear.

A 1990 Supreme Court case held that *Miranda* warnings are not required when an inmate is questioned by an undercover police officer. Voluntary statements made in this type of situation are admissible because none of the coercive elements of police interrogation are present when the inmate does not know he or she is being questioned by law enforcement personnel (*Illinois v. Perkins*).[17]

Miranda warnings may even be required prior to questioning by non-police personnel. The need for the warnings prior to a polygraph examination conducted by the police is fairly obvious. Warnings are not required if the defense requests the examination or the defendant consents to it, but it is still a good idea to give them. *Estelle v. Smith* held that psychiatric examinations conducted on behalf of the prosecution, or ordered by the court, also must be preceded by *Miranda* warnings.[18]

Volunteered statements are admissible even though *Miranda* warnings were not given. They are also admissible if a suspect who refused to talk, or requested an attorney, later comes forward and volunteers information. As used in this context, *volunteered* means the suspect came forward on his or her own initiative and made a statement. The Supreme Court used the example of a person who came to the police station and immediately blurted out a confession to the desk officer. A suspect in a holding cell who bangs on the bars and wants to talk to an officer is another example. It is important to be aware, however, that any detailed questioning that follows the volunteered information is considered interrogation.

The courts recognize a minor exception to *Miranda* for the **booking** process. Questions related to name, address, person to notify in case of an emergency, date of birth, and a few other biographical facts are permitted without giving any warnings. Warnings would be required if questioning at booking is extended in order to obtain information needed for a criminal investigation.

Another exception recognized by the Supreme Court in *New York v. Quarles* is for **public safety**.[19] Brief questioning is permitted without giving *Miranda* warnings if it is done in order to obtain information that is needed immediately in order to protect others from harm. Asking where the suspect hid a gun would fit under this exception if the question was asked in order to prevent innocent people from being hurt by the gun.

Examples of When *Miranda* Warnings Are and Are *Not* Required

Miranda Warnings Required

- Don was arrested for an assault that occurred the previous day. After arriving at the station, the police decided to question him. Prior to starting questioning they gave him the *Miranda* warnings.

  Miranda warnings are required prior to custodial interrogation. The arrest in this case did not occur on the day of the crime. That does not change the rule. Don is in custody and the officers plan to interrogate him: *Miranda* warnings must be given before the questioning starts.

- Mike was arrested by an officer from City E Police Department. The day after the arrest, officers from City M Police Department came to the jail and wanted to question Mike. The first thing they did after seating Mike in the interrogation room was give him the *Miranda* warnings. Mike asked, "Why did you do that?" An officer replied, "We have to give warnings any time we question someone who is in custody." Mike replied, "But you didn't arrest me." The officer replied, "It doesn't matter. If you are in custody and we question you, we have to give you the warnings."

  Miranda warnings must be given prior to custodial interrogation. In this case, an officer from City E arrested Mike. The next day, officers from City M came to question Mike. Clearly Mike was in custody. Unless they are positive that correctly worded *Miranda* warnings were given the day before and Mike still remembers them, the officers from City M need to give Mike the *Miranda* warnings before questioning him.

Miranda Warnings Not Required

- Police were questioning Adam at his home about a recent arson. Adam answered a few questions, but when he realized he was the suspect in the case he said, "No more questions. I know my Fifth Amendment rights. If you want to talk to me again, call my attorney. Now leave my house."

  The police did not need to advise Adam of his rights because he was not under arrest.

  The police did not need to provide Adam an attorney because he was not under arrest.

  Adam had the right to call his own attorney and/or to demand that his own attorney be present during the interview. The government does not have to pay for Adam's attorney at this stage of the proceedings.

- Bruce was stopped for speeding. The traffic officer asked, "Do you know how fast you were driving?" Bruce laughed and said, "Wait. Wait. You can't ask me questions unless you give me my *Miranda* warnings!" The officer replied, "Sorry, Mister. The D.A. says that we only have to give *Miranda*s after we arrest someone." Bruce groaned; the officer was right.

  Bruce did not have the right to have the officers read the *Miranda* warnings because he was not in custody.

  The Supreme Court explicitly stated that *Miranda* warnings are not required at a traffic stop.

- Carl was caught trying to break into a house. He was arrested for attempted burglary. An officer handcuffed Carl and placed him in the back seat of the patrol car. During the drive to the station Carl said, "Hey, I'm going to win this case. You didn't give me the *Miranda* warnings." The officer replied, "Wrong! You only have the right to *Miranda*s if we question you after your arrest."

  Miranda warnings have to be given prior to custodial interrogation. Once a person is under arrest, he or she is in custody. *Miranda* warnings would have to be given prior to interrogation. Since Carl was not under interrogation, the officer was not required to give the *Miranda* warnings.

Waiver of *Miranda* Rights

Once *Miranda* warnings have been correctly given to a suspect who is in custody, the police may try to obtain a waiver of the suspect's rights. This must be a **knowing, intelligent,** and **voluntary** waiver.

To have a knowing waiver, the suspect must have been correctly advised of his or her rights. The courts have uniformly required that the police show that they have done this. It is not presumed that anyone knows the *Miranda* warnings. Even though it may seem ridiculous for a police officer who arrests a prominent defense attorney or judge to advise him or her of the *Miranda* rights, it is still the best way to ensure that any statements obtained can be used in court.

"Intelligent," as used in this context, means that the person had the basic intelligence necessary to understand his or her rights. This may be an issue if a young juvenile is involved. It is also an issue if the suspect is mentally impaired. Similar problems occur when the suspect is extremely intoxicated (either from alcoholic beverages or drugs). Only the most extreme cases qualify for suppression on the basis of lack of an intelligent waiver. This is especially so in intoxication cases—the courts generally admit confessions except when the suspects totally lack the ability to understand what is going on.

"Voluntary" is somewhat difficult to define in this context. No coercion may be used to obtain a confession. The courts have taken a fairly rigid stance against coercion used to obtain a waiver of *Miranda* rights. During the interrogation that follows the waiver, police have been permitted more leeway in using deceptive tactics as long as the will of the suspect is not overborne.

Colorado v. Connelly limited the prohibition against coercion to acts of the police or their agents.[20] Factors outside the control of the police that are coercive will not cause a confession to be suppressed. For example, the fact that the suspect confessed after hearing "voices from heaven" ordering him or her to do so does not make the confession involuntary. On the other hand, a confession was held to be coerced when an informant, whom the police had asked to help them obtain a confession, told the suspect that he could protect the suspect from gang violence only if a full confession of past crimes was made.[21]

"Third-degree" tactics offend due process. Physical force cannot be used to obtain a confession. Deprivation of food and/or sleep for long periods is not allowed. Neither are false promises of leniency, such as offers to drop charges or assurances that the suspect will get a light sentence if he or she confesses.

Absent one of these obviously coercive acts, the courts consider the totality of the circumstances. The key concept is that the police are not allowed to overbear the will of the suspect. This balances the acts of the police against the vulnerability of the defendant. What may be coercive when done to a naive teenager may be considered acceptable when applied to a streetwise ex-convict.

Lies and half-truths may be permitted. The police do not have to tell the suspect all of the crimes being investigated (*Colorado v. Spring*).[22] Neither do they have to inform him or her that someone has arranged for an attorney to come to the jail to provide counsel (*Moran v. Burbine*).[23]

The last issue involving the waiver of *Miranda* rights is the procedure used to obtain the waiver. The Supreme Court has not set a protocol. In fact, in *North Carolina v. Butler* the Court found a valid waiver based on the suspect's conduct.[24] The suspect had responded in the affirmative when asked if he understood his rights but did not reply when asked if he wished to waive them. The indication that he understood the warnings, coupled with the fact that he answered the questions asked by the police, was enough to convince the Court that a valid waiver had been obtained. In another case, the Court decided that the confession was admissible when the suspect gave an oral confession, even though his reply to the request for a waiver was that he refused to make a written confession (*Connecticut v. Barrett*).[25]

Despite these cases that condone less than explicit waivers, each officer should attempt to obtain as much evidence of a valid waiver as possible. Many agencies have the suspect sign a card that has the warnings printed on it. Although the signature on the form is not conclusive (the suspect can still allege that he or she was forced to sign the card), it does provide an impressive exhibit that can be used at trial. Having the suspect initial each of the warnings on the *Miranda* card provides even stronger evidence of a waiver. Copious notes taken during the interrogation help. Tape recording the interrogation, including the process of giving *Miranda* warnings and requesting a waiver, is also useful.

Sample Dialogue Used to Obtain a Waiver of *Miranda* Rights

Det. Dawson:	OK, we've gone over all the warnings and you understand them. Is that correct?
Johnny Johnson:	Yeah, I understand them.
Det. Dawson:	Are you currently intoxicated or under the influence of any type of drugs?
Johnny Johnson:	No. I'm cold sober. I gave up doing drugs after I spent that time in detox.
Det. Dawson:	Do you read English well?
Johnny Johnson:	I do OK. I never finished high school but I was always good at reading.
Det. Dawson:	So you read the *Miranda* card and understand it.
Johnny Johnson:	Yeah, I read it. I didn't understand it all but I do now, after you explained it.
Det. Dawson:	I want to ask you some questions about why you were arrested. But I need to know if you think that I am forcing you to talk to me. Am I?
Johnny Johnson:	No. You aren't forcing me to talk. I'd shut up real fast if I thought you were trying to force me to talk.

Det. Dawson:	One last detail before I can ask you those questions. Look at the *Miranda* card, at the very bottom. There is a short paragraph there that says that you understand your rights and you are willing to talk to me. And that you are doing this voluntarily. All you need to do is sign it and then we can get on with the questions.
Johnny Johnson:	OK. I see it. Give me a pen and I'll sign it.

Sequential Interrogations

It is not uncommon for the police to interrogate a suspect more than once. The procedures that the police should follow at second (or later) interrogation sessions depend largely on what occurred previously.

Prior Interrogation without Valid *Miranda* Waiver

At one time, many courts held that none of the confessions following a statement obtained in violation of *Miranda* could be used to establish the prosecution's case. This was based on the "cat out of the bag" theory. Once the suspect had confessed, the courts believed the suspect was likely to confess again because he or she knew the police already knew he or she was guilty.

In 1985, the Supreme Court decided *Oregon v. Elstad*, which held such a theory did not apply.[26] If the first confession was involuntary, all subsequent confessions are inadmissible. On the other hand, if the first confession was voluntary but in violation of *Miranda*, a subsequent confession may be admissible if a new set of properly administered *Miranda* warnings were given and the suspect waived his or her rights. Each case is considered on its merits. *Miranda* warnings given only seconds after obtaining the inadmissible confession will not be viewed as effective. Using the first confession as the primary focus of the second interrogation session would likely trigger the Fruit of the Poison Tree Doctrine. A voluntary confession obtained several days after the suspect was released from custody will more than likely be admissible. The more scrupulous the police are in obtaining the second confession, the better chance they have of using it in court. No matter what the police do, the original confession obtained in violation of *Miranda* will remain inadmissible except for impeachment purposes.

Sample Dialogue Used to Start Interrogations When Prior Interrogation Was Conducted without Valid *Miranda* Waiver

Det. Dawson:	Johnny, have you been questioned since you were arrested yesterday?
Johnny Johnson:	Yes. Det. Smith asked me a bunch of questions right after they brought me here.
Det. Dawson:	OK. That was what I had heard. I want you to forget about talking to Det. Smith. Whatever you told him will not be used to convict you. I want you to just focus on the questions that I am going to ask. Can you do that?
Johnny Johnson:	I'll try.
Det. Dawson:	Now we just went over your *Miranda* rights. You understand them, right?
Johnny Johnson:	Yeah, I already told you that I do. I don't forget stuff that fast!
Det. Dawson:	And you are willing to answer my questions?
Johnny Johnson:	Yes. Just get on with it.

Prior Interrogation with Valid *Miranda* Waiver

If the first interrogation was conducted legally and the suspect agreed to talk, a subsequent interrogation can be conducted rather routinely. The Supreme Court has not required a new set of *Miranda* warnings every time questioning is resumed. The warnings are needed if the suspect is not likely to remember his or her rights. If there has been a lengthy delay between two interrogations, warnings should be administered again so the suspect cannot claim in court that he or she forgot his or her rights. It is also a good idea to give the warnings again if someone else gave them the first time. This serves as a guarantee that the warnings were given correctly.

Sample Dialogue Used to Start Interrogation When There Was a Prior Interrogation with a Valid *Miranda* Waiver

Det. Dawson:	Hi, Johnny. Did you have a good lunch?
Johnny Johnson:	It was OK, I guess. The food in here isn't great.
Det. Dawson:	Do you remember what we were talking about before lunch?
Johnny Johnson:	You talked a lot about my *Miranda* rights. Then you started asking questions about what I did yesterday.
Det. Dawson:	Why did we stop talking?
Johnny Johnson:	Because it was lunch time.
Det. Dawson:	I want to ask you some more questions. Is that OK?
Johnny Johnson:	Yeah, it's OK. This is taking too long.

Suspect Invoked Right to Remain Silent

Police must stop interrogation immediately if the suspect invokes the right to remain silent. This rule applies whether the suspect invoked the right to remain silent at the time the *Miranda* warnings were initially given or asserted the right after custodial interrogation was in progress. This does not mean, however, that the police may never try to resume questioning.

In *Michigan v. Mosley,* the Supreme Court insisted that the suspect's rights be scrupulously honored.[27] Police may not badger the suspect with frequent attempts to get the suspect to talk, but after a reasonable time they may ask the suspect if he or she would like to continue the interrogation. A new waiver of the *Miranda* rights is mandatory at this point.

No specific guidelines have been established for renewing questioning after the suspect refused to talk. In the leading case, there was a 2-hour gap between the interrogations; the second interview was conducted by different officers on a different floor of the police building and focused on a different crime. Each case will turn on its own facts. A reasonable time period must follow the request to remain silent. Tactics that appear to harass the suspect are not tolerated.

Sample Dialogue to Start Interrogation after the Suspect Invoked Right to Remain Silent

Det. Dawson:	Welcome back, Johnny. Have you thought about what you told me yesterday?
Johnny Johnson:	Yeah, I thought about it a lot last night.
Det. Dawson:	Yesterday you said you didn't want to talk to me anymore. Is that right?
Johnny Johnson:	Yeah, that's what I said.
Det. Dawson:	Would you like to talk to me now?
Johnny Johnson:	Yeah, I thought about it a lot and I have some things to say to you now.
Det Dawson:	I'm glad to hear that, but before we start I need to read the *Miranda* warnings to you again. When I finish you can sign the waiver form and we can talk. OK?
Johnny Johnson:	OK.

Suspect Invoked Right to Attorney

Edwards v. Arizona establishes a rule that applies when a suspect who is in custody and being questioned requests an attorney: Questioning must stop and can resume only if an attorney is present.[28] This is a distinctly different rule than the one that applies if the suspect refuses to speak to officers: If the attorney was requested, the request cannot be revoked unless there is an attorney present; a lapse of time cannot be used to justify renewing questioning without an attorney present.

One of the major problems with the rule about requesting an attorney is determining when it applies. An unambiguous request for counsel automatically invokes it (*Smith v. Illinois*).[29] Unfortunately, suspects frequently make equivocal statements. In *Oregon v. Bradshaw*, the Supreme Court found that the suspect's question, "Well, what is going to happen now?" permitted the officers to continue the interrogation.[30] Each case will have to be decided on its own facts. It is important, however, that officers avoid the temptation to ignore a request for counsel and attempt to convince the suspect that he or she does not need or want an attorney.

Sample Dialogue Used to Determine If Suspect Has Invoked Right to an Attorney

Det. Dawson:	What did you just say?
Johnny Johnson:	I said, "Maybe I need an attorney."
Det. Dawson:	So, do you want an attorney?
Johnny Johnson:	Oh, gee, I'm not sure. You said I could have one. When you ask me all those questions I get scared. But I don't trust attorneys. It's so confusing. Maybe I should have one. What do you think?
Det. Dawson:	I just want to know if you want an attorney right now, at this minute. Give me a straight answer—yes or no.

If the officer determines that the suspect wants an attorney, the suspect must have an opportunity to speak with an attorney before questioning can continue; the attorney will also have to be present when a new waiver is sought. This rule applies in two situations: (1) the suspect asked for an attorney, and (2) the suspect refused to talk to the officer and requested an attorney. The time that elapses between interviews is no substitute for contact with an attorney. Questioning may resume only if the defendant has an attorney present (*Minnick v. Mississippi*).[31]

Sample Dialogue Used to Start Interrogation after Suspect Invoked Right to Attorney

Det. Dawson:	OK, Johnny. It's 4:00 p.m. When I was talking to you earlier you asked for an attorney. What happened after that?
Johnny Johnson:	You stopped talking to me and had some guy take me back to the holding cell.
Det. Dawson:	Have you had a chance to talk to an attorney?
Johnny Johnson:	Yes. I called the Public Defender's Office and talked to Mr. Brown.
Det. Dawson:	Is Mr. Brown an attorney?

Johnny Johnson:	Yes.
Det. Dawson:	Is Mr. Brown in this room right now?
Johnny Johnson:	Yes. He is sitting beside me. Sorry, I forgot to introduce you.
Det. Dawson:	Are you ready to talk to me now?
Johnny Johnson:	Mr. Brown doesn't want me to talk, but I need to tell you some stuff.
Det. Dawson:	OK. I'm giving you another *Miranda* card. Read it and sign it if you want to talk to me. Mr. Brown can stay here with you if you want.
Johnny Johnson:	Yeah, I know. You give me lots of those cards to sign.

In 1988, the Supreme Court made it clear in *Arizona v. Roberson* that the fact that the subsequent interrogation was about a different crime did not alter this rule.[32] The suspect had been arrested at the scene of a burglary. Immediately after the arresting officer gave the *Miranda* warnings, the suspect demanded to see his lawyer. Three days later, a different officer, who did not know the suspect had invoked his *Miranda* rights, questioned him about a different burglary. The confession was ruled inadmissible even though the second officer obtained a *Miranda* waiver before the suspect made an incriminating statement. The Supreme Court clearly stated that it intended to follow the bright line rule in *Edwards* without exceptions. This makes it imperative that officers communicate the request for an attorney to all potential interrogators. Noting it on the booking slip may be helpful.

Sample Dialogue Used to Interrogate Suspect Who Has Already Asked for an Attorney

Conversation between Det. Jones and Officer White who is in charge of the holding cells

Det. Jones:	I'm here to question Johnny Johnson. Please have him sent to Interrogation Room No. 3.
Officer White:	Let me check his file. Wait. There is a note that says he asked for an attorney when Det. Dawson interrogated him this morning.
Det. Jones:	Wow. I'm glad you told me that. If I'd gone ahead and questioned him the judge would have thrown it all out. Forget about sending him to the interrogation room.

Special Situations

Several situations require special attention: whether proper *Miranda* warnings are sufficient to make a confession admissible when the suspect was illegally arrested; procedures that should be modified when juveniles are questioned; and the use of confessions for impeachment purposes. Complying with normal *Miranda* procedures may not be enough in these situations.

Suspect Illegally Arrested

The Supreme Court refused to rule that all confessions made after a valid *Miranda* waiver are admissible. If the arrest was illegal, *Miranda* will not automatically make the confession admissible (*Lanier v. South Carolina*; *Brown v. Illinois*; *New York v. Harris*).[33] Instead of making all of these confessions admissible, the Court utilized the Fruit of the Poison Tree Doctrine. Confessions obtained after an illegal arrest are only admissible if the facts show that the taint of the unconstitutional act has dissipated. Each case must be reviewed on its own merits. Confessions obtained after the suspect has been released from custody are quite likely to be admissible. On the other hand, if any form of police brutality was present during the arrest, the confession will probably be suppressed. Relevant considerations include observance of *Miranda*, the temporal proximity of the arrest and the confession, the presence of intervening circumstances, and particularly, the purpose and flagrancy of the official misconduct.[34]

Sample Dialogue Used to Start Interrogation after Suspect Was Illegally Arrested

Det. Dawson:	Good morning, Mr. Green.
Mr. Green:	Good morning.
Det. Dawson:	I've been reading your file. It looks like Officer Swenson arrested you last week but the D.A. refused to file charges. Some technicality about the arrest.
Mr. Green:	I don't know anything about technicalities. I just know they let me go home.
Det. Dawson:	What day did they let you go home?
Mr. Green:	Last Thursday. Four days ago.
Det. Dawson:	And why are you at the police station today?
Mr. Green:	You called me and said you wanted to talk to me and hear my side of it. It sounded like a good idea, so I came down.
Det. Dawson:	You are free to leave when you want to. Did you know that?
Mr. Green:	Yeah, sort of. Unless you arrest me first.
Det. Dawson:	That's right. So now, let's start talking.

Note: *Miranda* warnings are not required in this scenario because the suspect is not under arrest. Warnings are not required when the suspect is at the police station but not under arrest.

Interrogating Juvenile Suspects

All but very young juveniles are capable of waiving their *Miranda* rights. Whereas the question of whether the suspect is in custody is the same for adults and juveniles,[35] the question of whether there was a valid waiver of *Miranda* rights will be considered on the totality of the circumstances. The clarity of the warnings given is very important. Other factors include the age and intelligence of the juvenile. Prior contacts with the police and other evidence of sophistication related to the criminal justice system are relevant. Police tactics that intimidate or coerce are carefully scrutinized.

If juveniles ask to speak to their parents, the questioning must stop. The courts have treated this type of request as the equivalent of an adult demanding an attorney. *Fare v. Michael C.* held that requests to speak to a probation officer, on the other hand, have no conclusive effect.[36] It is important to take notice of any request the juvenile makes, however, because it may be considered as an indication that the suspect wants to terminate the questioning.

Sample Dialogue Used to Start Interrogation of a Juvenile

Det. Dawson:	Hello, Michelle.
Michelle:	Hi.
Det. Dawson:	I'm here to talk to you about why you were arrested. Before I do that, I need to explain your rights to you. OK?
Michelle:	OK.
Det. Dawson:	How old are you, Michelle?
Michelle:	I'm 15. My birthday was last week.
Det. Dawson:	Do you go to school?
Michelle:	Yes. Wilson High.
Det. Dawson:	What grade are you in?
Michelle:	I'm a sophomore.
Det. Dawson:	What kind of grades do you get?
Michelle:	Mostly Cs and Ds. But they keep telling me I'm really smart and I could do better if I studied. School is so boring.
Det. Dawson:	Have you ever been in trouble with the law before?
Michelle:	Yeah. I was in Juvie last year.
Det. Dawson:	So you know about your rights.
Michelle:	Yeah. The Public Defender told me all about them when I was in Juvie waiting for my trial.
Det. Dawson:	OK. I'm going to go over your *Miranda* rights with you. I want you to listen real close because this is very important. OK?
Michelle:	OK. But don't use any big words. I get lost when people use too many big words.

Impeachment

Statements a suspect makes during an interrogation can be used to impeach his or her trial testimony as long as the statement was voluntary (*Harris v. New York*).[37] Coerced statements cannot be used in court, but any voluntary statement made during an interrogation that violated other aspects of *Miranda* can be used to impeach.

This rule is only activated if the person who was interrogated takes the witness stand and testifies in a manner that conflicts with the prior statements. It is important that the prosecutor be aware of any statements the police obtained even though they now realize that inappropriate procedures were followed.

Sample Court Dialogue Used to Introduce a Confession for Impeachment

Prosecutor:	The People call Det. Dawson.

Court clerk swears in Det. Dawson and he takes the witness stand.

Prosecutor:	Det. Dawson, did you interrogate Sean O'Neil on February 2, 2008?
Det. Dawson:	Yes, I did.
Prosecutor:	Did Sean O'Neil make any statements to you?
Defense attorney:	Objection. Judge Wilson ruled that the statements Mr. O'Neil made to Det. Dawson are inadmissible because the *Miranda* warnings were not given correctly.
Prosecutor:	Your Honor, I am attempting to introduce Mr. O'Neil's statements for impeachment. The U.S. Supreme Court ruled in *Harris v. New York* that voluntary statements are admissible for impeachment purposes even if *Miranda* warnings were not given properly.
Judge:	Objection overruled. You may proceed, Mr. Prosecutor.
Prosecutor:	Det. Dawson, please answer the question.
Det. Dawson:	Yes, Sean O'Neil made several statements to me.
Prosecutor:	On direct examination, Sean stated that he was at his girlfriend's house between 8:00 p.m. and midnight on February 1, the night of the drive-by shooting. Is that what he told you on February 2?
Det. Dawson:	No. He told me that he was hanging out with some friends at a strip club. He claimed he arrived at 9:00 p.m. and stayed until it closed at 2:00 a.m. He never mentioned his girlfriend.

Post-Arraignment Confessions

The **right to counsel** attaches at the beginning of adversary court proceedings (*United States v. Gouveia*).[38] This is the arraignment unless
some other proceeding, such as indictment by the grand jury, occurs first.
From the time the right to counsel attaches, police may not interview a
suspect without an attorney present unless there is a waiver of the right
to counsel. It does not matter whether the interrogation takes place in a
custodial setting.

Interrogation after Right to Counsel Attaches
Once formal court proceedings have begun, a suspect must waive the right to
counsel prior to custodial or noncustodial interrogation. *Miranda* warnings may
be used for this purpose.

The leading case is *Massiah v. United States.*[39] Massiah had been indicted
by a federal grand jury for smuggling narcotics. He retained a lawyer, entered
a "not guilty" plea, and was released on bail. Colson, his co-defendant,
decided to cooperate with federal agents and allowed them to conceal a
radio transmitter under the front seat of his car. While seated in Colson's
car, Massiah and Colson discussed their upcoming trial and Massiah made
several incriminating statements. The Supreme Court held that these statements were not admissible because they were obtained in violation of
Massiah's right to counsel.

For interrogations that occur after arraignment or indictment, the
key questions are, Was the accused made sufficiently aware of the right
to have counsel present during questioning? and Was he or she aware
of the possible consequences of the decision to forgo the assistance of
counsel? In *Illinois v. Patterson*, the Supreme Court said that a knowing,
intelligent, and voluntary waiver of *Miranda* satisfies these criteria.[40] A
similar problem arises if the defendant has been indicted prior to being
arrested: Statements that officers deliberately elicit anytime after the
indictment without the suspect's attorney present are not admissible at
trial.[41]

The Court refused to hold that the defendant must actually meet
with an attorney prior to making this decision. If, on the other hand, the
suspect demands to see an attorney or to have one present during questioning, interrogation must stop and cannot be resumed unless there is an
attorney present.

For defendants who remain in custody, the rules that govern *Miranda*
warnings apply whether or not an arraignment has occurred. Officers
must be particularly alert, however, if the suspect has been arraigned but

is currently not in custody. In these situations, even though there is no custodial interrogation, *Miranda* warnings or some other form of advice regarding the right to counsel must be given and a waiver obtained before discussing the case that has been filed. Table 14-1 compares the rights to counsel under *Miranda* and *Massiah*.

Since the right to counsel does not attach until the court proceedings begin, the normal *Miranda* rules apply to questioning conducted after the

TABLE **14-1 Comparison of Right to Counsel under *Miranda* and *Massiah***

	Miranda	*Massiah*
When must suspect be advised of his or her rights?	Prior to custodial interrogation.	Prior to interrogation that occurs after the first court appearance. Rule applies to suspects who are in custody and those who have been released but still have charges pending in court.
When does the suspect have the right to have an attorney present?	During any questioning by authorities that occurs after the suspect asks for an attorney.	At all interrogation sessions after the first court appearance.
What charges are covered?	Once the attorney is requested, there must be an attorney present during custodial interrogation about any crime.	Right to counsel applies to charges that have been filed in court. Right to have an attorney present during questioning on other crimes is governed by normal *Miranda* procedures.
Procedure for waiving right to counsel	Before suspect requests attorney: Suspect can waive right without attorney present. After suspect requests attorney: Attorney must be present when suspect waives right to have counsel present.	Defendant can waive right to have attorney present on his or her own without an attorney present.
Warnings that must be given	Police must give *Miranda* warnings.	Police must advise defendant of the right to have an attorney present and obtain a waiver. *Miranda* warnings may be used for this purpose but the Court has not specified that they are the only warnings that can be used.

arraignment about charges that have not been filed. It may be difficult to determine which charges have been filed, particularly if the suspect has cases pending in several jurisdictions. Therefore, the safest practice is to give *Miranda* admonitions whenever talking to a suspect who has been arraigned.

Sample Dialogue Used to Start Interrogation to Obtain a Post-Arraignment Confession

Det. Dawson: Good morning, Johnny. I haven't seen you for a long time.

Johnny Johnson: Yeah. That's because I've been in county jail for several months. But they finally let me out.

Det. Dawson: Did you go to court while you were in jail?

Johnny Johnson: Yes. I had an arraignment in June and a preliminary hearing in July.

Det. Dawson: Was this all about those burglaries I arrested you for last April?

Johnny Johnson: Yes. They filed two counts of burglary. No other charges were filed, though. I guess I got lucky.

Det. Dawson: Did they give you an attorney at the arraignment?

Johnny Johnson: Yes. His name is Mr. Nelson. I have his card here in my wallet somewhere.

Det. Dawson: OK. You are out of jail and you have an attorney. When you called I got the impression that you wanted to talk to me about your case. Is that true?

Johnny Johnson: Yes. You always treated me fair.

Det. Dawson: Before I can discuss anything, I need you to waive your right to have Mr. Nelson, your attorney, present. Or we can call him and ask him to come down here, if you prefer.

Johnny Johnson: No, that's OK. The reason I called you was that I wanted to talk to you without him telling me what to do.

Det. Dawson: The easiest way to handle this is to go over the *Miranda* warnings and then you can waive them, if you want to talk to me, that is.

Johnny Johnson: Sure. I know my *Miranda*s by heart, you have given them to me so many times.

Det. Dawson: Just the same, here is the *Miranda* card. Let's go over it to make sure we get everything right.

Summary

The Fifth Amendment privilege against self-incrimination only applies to statements that can be used against a person in a criminal trial. It does not apply if the statute of limitations has expired, the witness has immunity, or double jeopardy prevents refiling the charges.

Testimonial acts are covered: oral and written statements as well as assertive gestures. The following are not covered because they are not considered testimonial: body fluids (blood, urine, breath, etc.), identifying features (physical appearance and fingerprints), exemplars (handwriting and voice), DNA samples, and sobriety tests.

Miranda v. Arizona established that a suspect must be advised of his or her constitutional rights. These rights include the right to remain silent, the clear warning that anything said can be used against the suspect in court, the right to have an attorney present during questioning, and the right to have an attorney at public expense if the suspect is indigent.

Miranda rights need only be given prior to custodial interrogation, but it does not matter why the suspect is in custody. Interrogation includes both direct and indirect questions. To be valid, a waiver of *Miranda* rights must be knowing, intelligent, and voluntary. There is no required procedure that must be used to obtain the waiver. It may be oral, written, or inferred from the suspect's conduct.

Volunteered statements do not fall under *Miranda*. There is also an exception that permits biographical questions to be asked during booking. Another exception permits officers to ask urgent questions immediately following arrest in order to protect members of the public from danger.

If a suspect waives his or her *Miranda* rights, interrogation may be resumed at any time. An indication that the suspect wishes to remain silent must be scrupulously honored, but the police may ask for a new *Miranda* waiver at a later time. When the suspect requests a lawyer, the police may not attempt to question the suspect again unless there is a lawyer present.

Miranda warnings will not automatically make a confession admissible if the suspect was illegally arrested. Each case is considered on its facts.

Care should be taken when advising juveniles of their *Miranda* rights. A valid waiver can be obtained only if the juvenile fully understood the warnings. A juvenile's request to speak with a parent(s) is considered the same as an adult's request for an attorney.

Statements made after incorrect *Miranda* warnings, or even when the warnings were not given, can be used to impeach. To be admissible for this purpose, the statements must have been made without coercion.

The right to counsel attaches at the first formal court appearance. This usually means arraignment or indictment. From that time on, the police may not question the suspect unless he or she waives the right to have an attorney present. This rule applies to both custodial interrogation and questioning that occurs in noncustodial settings. *Miranda* warnings can be used to obtain a waiver of the right to counsel for this purpose.

Review Questions

1. Define the *privilege against self-incrimination*, and list three situations in which a suspect cannot invoke it.
2. List three types of evidence obtained from a suspect that are not considered testimonial.
3. State the *Miranda* warnings, and explain when they are required.
4. What is the standard for a valid *Miranda* waiver? Explain the acceptable procedures for obtaining a valid *Miranda* waiver.
5. Is it necessary to give a new set of *Miranda* warnings if the suspect has already waived his or her rights? Explain.
6. If the suspect invoked the right to remain silent, may officers attempt to interrogate him or her at a later time? Explain.
7. If the suspect asked for an attorney, may officers attempt to question him or her at a later time? Explain.
8. Can confessions be used in court if the suspect was illegally arrested prior to the interrogation? Explain.
9. Can a statement that was obtained in violation of *Miranda* be used in court? Explain.
10. What special procedures are required prior to interrogating a suspect who has already been arraigned in court? Explain.

Writing Assignment

With the prevalence of reality police shows on television, it seems that everyone knows the protections outlined in the *Miranda* decision. Use the Internet (www.findlaw.com) to find the U.S. Supreme Court's decision in *Dickerson v. United States* 530 U.S. 528 (2000). Then conduct an informal survey by interviewing at least 10 people you know to determine if the public understands their actual self-incrimination rights. Ask each person (1) to recite the protections established in *Miranda*, (2) whether the police must always provide the warnings when arresting a suspect, and (3) whether the police must provide a person with an attorney if one is requested. Write a one-page (250-word) essay about your research.

Notes

1. *Griffin v. California* 380 U.S. 609, 14 L.Ed. 2d 106, 85 S.Ct. 1229 (1965).
2. *Carter v. Kentucky* 450 U.S. 288, 67 L.Ed. 2d 241, 101 S.Ct. 1112 (1981).
3. *United States v. Robinson* 485 U.S. 25, 99 L.Ed. 2d 23, 108 S.Ct. 864 (1988).
4. *United States v. Dunnigan* 507 U.S. 87, 122 L.Ed. 2d 445, 113 S.Ct. 111 (1993).
5. *Schmerber v. California* 384 U.S. 757, 16 L.Ed. 2d 908, 86 S.Ct. 1826 (1966).
6. *Hayes v. Florida* 470 U.S. 811, 84 L.Ed. 2d 705, 105 S.Ct. 1643 (1985).
7. *United States v. Wade* 388 U.S. 218, 18 L.Ed. 2d 1149, 87 S.Ct. 1926 (1967).
8. *United States v. Mara* 410 U.S. 19, 35 L.Ed. 2d 99, 93 S.Ct. 774 (1973).
9. *Pennsylvania v. Muniz* 496 U.S. 582, 110 L.Ed. 2d 528, 110 S.Ct. 2638 (1990).
10. *Miranda v. Arizona* 384 U.S. 436, 16 L.Ed. 2d 694, 86 S.Ct. 1602 (1966).
11. *Berkemer v. McCarty* 468 U.S. 420, 82 L.Ed. 2d 317, 104 S.Ct. 3138 (1984).
12. *Pennsylvania v. Bruder* 488 U.S. 102, 102 L.Ed. 2d 172, 109 S.Ct. 205 (1988).
13. *Oregon v. Mathiason* 429 U.S. 492, 50 L.Ed. 2d 714, 97 S.Ct. 711 (1977). See also *California v. Beheler* 463 U.S. 1121, 77 L.Ed. 2d 1275, 103 S.Ct. 3517 (1983).
14. *Stansbury v. California* 511 U.S. 318, 128 L.Ed. 2d 293, 114 S.Ct. 1526 (1994).
15. *Orozco v. Texas* 394 U.S. 324, 22 L.Ed. 2d 311, 89 S.Ct. 1095 (1969).
16. *Rhode Island v. Innis* 446 U.S. 291, 64 L.Ed. 2d 297, 100 S.Ct. 1682 (1980). See also *Brewer v. Williams* 430 U.S. 387, 51 L.Ed. 2d 424, 97 S.Ct. 1232 (1977).
17. *Illinois v. Perkins* 496 U.S. 292, 110 L.Ed. 2d 243, 110 S.Ct. 2394 (1990).
18. *Estelle v. Smith* 451 U.S. 454, 68 L.Ed. 2d 359, 101 S.Ct. 1866 (1981).
19. *New York v. Quarles* 467 U.S. 649, 81 L.Ed. 2d 550, 104 S.Ct. 2626 (1984).
20. *Colorado v. Connelly* 479 U.S. 157, 93 L.Ed. 2d 473, 107 S.Ct. 515 (1986).
21. *Arizona v. Fulminante* 499 U.S. 279, 113 L.Ed. 2d 302, 111 S.Ct. 1246 (1991).
22. *Colorado v. Spring* 479 U.S. 364, 93 L.Ed. 2d 954, 107 S.Ct. 851 (1987).
23. *Moran v. Burbine* 475 U.S. 412, 89 L.Ed. 2d 410, 106 S.Ct. 1135 (1986).
24. *North Carolina v. Butler* 441 U.S. 369, 60 L.Ed. 2d 286, 99 S.Ct. 1755 (1979).
25. *Connecticut v. Barrett* 479 U.S. 523, 93 L.Ed. 2d 920, 107 S.Ct. 828 (1987).
26. *Oregon v. Elstad* 470 U.S. 298, 84 L.Ed. 2d 222, 105 S.Ct. 1285 (1985).
27. *Michigan v. Mosley* 423 U.S. 96, 46 L.Ed. 2d 313, 96 S.Ct. 321 (1975).
28. *Edwards v. Arizona* 451 U.S. 477, 68 L.Ed. 2d 378, 101 S.Ct. 1880 (1981).
29. *Smith v. Illinois* 469 U.S. 91, 83 L.Ed. 2d 488, 105 S.Ct. 1285 (1984).
30. *Oregon v. Bradshaw* 462 U.S. 1039, 77 L.Ed. 2d 405, 103 S.Ct. 2830 (1983).
31. *Minnick v. Mississippi* 498 U.S. 146, 112 L.Ed. 2d 489, 111 S.Ct. 486 (1990).
32. *Arizona v. Roberson* 486 U.S. 675, 100 L.Ed. 2d 704, 108 S.Ct. 2093 (1988).
33. *Lanier v. South Carolina* 474 U.S. 25, 88 L.Ed. 2d 23, 106 S.Ct. 297 (1985); *Brown v. Illinois* 422 U.S. 590, 45 L.Ed. 2d 416, 95 S.Ct. 2254 (1975); *New York v. Harris* 495 U.S. 14, 109 L.Ed. 2d 13, 110 S.Ct. 1640 (1990).
34. *Kaupp v. Texas* 538 U.S. 626, 155 L.Ed. 2d 814, 123 S.Ct. 1843 (2003).
35. *Yarborough v. Alvarado* 541 U.S. 652, 158 L.Ed. 2d 938, 124 S.Ct. 2140 (2004).
36. *Fare v. Michael C.* 422 U.S. 707, 61 L.Ed. 2d 197, 99 S.Ct. 2560 (1979).
37. *Harris v. New York* 401 U.S. 222, 28 L.Ed. 2d 1, 91 S.Ct. 643 (1971).
38. *United States v. Gouveia* 467 U.S. 180, 81 L.Ed. 2d 146, 104 S.Ct. 2292 (1984).
39. *Massiah v. United States* 377 U.S. 201, 12 L.Ed. 2d 246, 84 S.Ct. 1199 (1964).
40. *Illinois v. Patterson* 487 U.S. 285, 101 L.Ed. 2d 261, 108 S.Ct. 2389 (1988).
41. *Fellers v. United States* 540 U.S. 519, 157 L.Ed. 2d 1016, 124 S.Ct. 1019 (2004).

CHAPTER 15

Identification Procedures

Feature Case: Centennial Olympics Suspect Richard Jewell

In the summer of 1996, with the Olympic Games underway in Atlanta, Georgia, a pipe bomb exploded in the city's Centennial Park, killing one person and injuring more than 110 bystanders. In the following days, law enforcement officials began to focus their suspicions on a security guard named Richard Jewell, who had initially been praised for helping evacuate the area shortly after the explosion. Within 72 hours of the incident, newspapers and television networks began reporting that Jewell had become the focus of the investigation. In the face of extensive media coverage, Jewell maintained his innocence, passed a polygraph test administered by a retired FBI expert, and insisted he was wrongly identified as the perpetrator.

As media attention on him intensified, Jewell broke down in tears at one television news conference as he explained that the false accusation and extensive media coverage had ruined his life and made him a prisoner in his own home. Even Jewell's mother publicly urged President Bill Clinton to intervene and exonerate her son, but Jewell remained a "suspect."

In October 1996, the U.S. Attorney's Office officially informed Jewell he was no longer a "target" of the investigation.

Several years later, the FBI identified Eric Robert Rudolph, an anti-government extremist, as the person responsible for the Centennial Park Olympic bombing. Rudolph was also a suspect in the bombings of a gay nightclub, an abortion clinic in the Atlanta area (both done in 1996), and a clinic in Birmingham, Alabama, in 1997. The press release referred to

Rudolph as the "most notorious American fugitive on the FBI's 'Most Wanted' List."

In May 2003, after a massive manhunt in the hills of North Carolina and offers of a $1 million reward for his apprehension, Rudolph was arrested, and in 2005 he pled guilty to the bombings and provided information about the location of more than 250 pounds of buried dynamite and other explosives in exchange for a sentence of life in prison without parole.

Richard Jewell subsequently became a Deputy Sheriff for Meriwether County, which is just outside Atlanta. He received an undisclosed amount from civil lawsuits filed against NBC, CNN, and the *New York Post* about their coverage of the Olympic bombing investigation.

On the 10th anniversary of the bombings, the governor of Georgia, Sonny Perdue, said, "The bottom line is this: His actions saved lives that day. Mr. Jewell, on behalf of Georgia, we want to thank you for keeping Georgians safe and doing your job during the course of those Games."

Learning Objectives

After studying this chapter, you will be able to

- Define and differentiate between lineup, showup, and photographic lineup.
- Explain Fourth Amendment rights applicable to identification procedures.
- Explain Fifth Amendment rights applicable to identification procedures.
- Explain Sixth Amendment rights applicable to identification procedures.
- Explain the due process guarantees that apply to identification procedures.

Key Terms

- Due process
- Lineup
- Photographic lineup
- Showup
- Unduly suggestive

Myths about Identification Procedures	Facts about Identification Procedures
Eyewitness identification of crime suspects is one of the most reliable methods in correctly determining the perpetrator of a crime.	Studies suggest mistaken identification of the wrong person by victims and witnesses is one of the most common errors leading to the arrest and conviction of innocent people.
Most perpetrators are quickly identified by analysis of forensic evidence left behind and collected by police at crime scenes.	Even where forensic evidence is found at a crime scene, identifying the perpetrator often takes a great deal of time and investigative resources if the suspect is not already known.

Myths about Identification Procedures	Facts about Identification Procedures
Lineups and photographic lineups (also called "six packs") involve a victim or witness identifying a suspect from a random array of other persons or photographs.	To encourage accurate identifications, the array of persons or photos presented must be similar in appearance without being unduly suggestive of the person the police believe committed the crime.
During a "showup," police simply present a suspect to the victim or witness and ask if this is the person who committed the crime.	Victims or witnesses are usually transported to the location where the suspect is and admonished that it is just as important to exonerate someone who is innocent as it is to identify the person they believe committed the crime.

Definitions Used for Identification Procedures

Law enforcement officers use a variety of techniques to identify the perpetrators of crimes. In addition to conducting identification procedures in a manner that ensures accurate identification of the suspect, Fourth, Fifth, Sixth, and Fourteenth Amendment rights must be protected.

There are three basic procedures used to allow victims or witnesses to identify the person who committed the crime:

- Lineups
- Showups
- Photographic lineups

These terms are defined for the purpose of this chapter to avoid confusion with other usages of the terms. Appropriate procedures for conducting these activities are discussed later in this chapter.

Lineups

A **lineup** is a procedure in which the victim or eyewitness is asked to view a group of people and select the one who committed the crime. Figure 15-1 shows an example of a lineup. Many police departments and jails have viewing rooms set aside for this purpose. These rooms may include marks on the wall to indicate height, special-effects lighting that can simulate whatever illumination existed at the crime scene, and one-way mirrors so the suspects cannot see the people making the identification. On the other hand, a lineup may also be done by merely having the group of people stand in front of the person who saw the crime being committed. Due to the need to assemble several people, lineups are rarely done in the field.

Figure 15-1
An Example of a Lineup

Showups

A **showup** is a much simpler procedure. One suspect is shown to the person who is to make the identification. This can be done in the field or at a police facility. Figure 15-2 shows an example of a showup.

Photographic Lineups

Photographic lineups involve showing pictures. Figure 15-3 presents an example of a photographic lineup. The suspect does not need to be in custody when this is done. It may be done by handing the witness a few carefully selected photographs or by allowing him or her to look through mug books. High school yearbooks are also used if the suspect is a juvenile or young adult. Although the photographs may be from any source, booking pictures are used most frequently because the police have easy access to them. If a tentative identification is made, the police may decide to hold a lineup.

Is this the person who hit you?

Figure 15-2
An Example of a Showup

Figure 15-3
An Example of a Photographic Lineup

Fourth Amendment Rights during Identification Procedures

The police do not have the authority to detain a suspect in order to conduct a lineup or showup unless the detention complies with the Fourth Amendment. Random and "hunch" stops are not allowed. Neither may people be detained just because they fit a general description so that there will be enough people to make a valid lineup.

Fourth Amendment Rights during Identification Procedures Defined
Absent consent, there must be reasonable suspicion to stop a suspect in the field for a showup. If there is probable cause to arrest, the suspect may be transported to the police station for either a lineup or a showup.

A suspect may be detained briefly based on reasonable suspicion. Identification procedures may be conducted at the scene of this detention, but the suspect may not be transported to the station during this type of detention.[1] Victims and witnesses can be transported to the location in order to conduct a showup.

Probable cause to arrest is necessary in order to transport the suspect to the police station. Once there, either a lineup or a showup may be conducted. The identification procedures do not have to be related to the crime for which the suspect was arrested. For example, a suspect who was arrested for burglary can be put in a lineup by officers investigating a murder. It is also permissible to use inmates that are already in custody to provide an adequate number of people for a valid lineup.

The Fourth Amendment applies to detentions and arrests by the police. Photographic lineups are normally conducted using pictures that the police already have in their files. No one is detained in order to conduct this type of procedure. For this reason, Fourth Amendment rights do not apply to photographic lineups.

Examples of Protecting Fourth Amendment Rights during Identification Procedures

- A police officer arrived at a "robbery now" call. The suspect fled the scene as the police car approached. Melody, the victim, gave the officers a good description of the robber. Another officer patrolling approximately two blocks away saw a man running down the street who matched the description broadcast by the officer at the scene. The man was detained while the victim was transported to the scene. As soon as Melody saw the suspect she screamed, "That's him!"

- A traffic officer arrested James for drunk driving. After the blood test, James was taken to the station for booking. An officer who walked through the booking area commented, "That guy over there looks just like the artist's drawing they are circulating in the serial rape cases." James was placed in a lineup and the rape victims were asked to tell the officers if the rapist was in the lineup. Three women selected James; the others were not sure.

Examples of Violating Fourth Amendment Rights during Identification Procedures

- The clerk at a 7-11 store gave the police a vague description of the man who stuck a gun in her back and took all the money in the cash register. The police detained all the gang members loitering a block away and took them to the 7-11 and asked the cashier which one did the robbery.

  The clerk's description was too vague to give the police the right to detain a suspect. Even if the detention were legal, the police do not have the right to transport the suspects to the 7-11.

  In addition to the Fourth Amendment errors, there is a due process problem with this scenario. The wording of the officer's request for the cashier to identify the robber is suggestive.

- A woman arrived home and found a man ransacking her house. When she walked into the house, the man ran out the door. When the police arrived, she gave them a good description of the burglar. A patrol officer stopped a man carrying a bulging pillow case a half mile from the burglary. The man, who was sweating and appeared to be out of breath, was taken to the police station and placed in a lineup with five other men.

  The officer had reasonable suspicion to stop the man, but probable cause is required to take the man to the station (unless he consents). Therefore, being in a lineup at the station violated the man's Fourth Amendment rights.

Fifth Amendment Rights during Identification Procedures

Being identified by an eyewitness is very incriminating. Unfortunately for the criminal, this is not enough to activate the Fifth Amendment. The privilege not to incriminate oneself only applies to testimonial communications.

Fifth Amendment Rights during Identification Procedures Defined

A suspect has no Fifth Amendment right to refuse to participate in a lineup or showup. He or she may not refuse to pose, wear appropriate clothing, or give voice exemplars.

In *United States v. Wade* and *Gilbert v. California*, the Supreme Court held that a legally arrested suspect has no Fifth Amendment right to refuse to participate in a lineup.[2] Neither may he or she refuse to put on clothing worn by the suspect when the crime was committed. The suspect can also be required to walk, take a particular stance, or make gestures observed during the commission of the crime.

Voice exemplars are not covered by the Fifth Amendment. Although they require the suspect to speak, he or she is told what to say. Therefore, the content of the speech is not incriminating. For this reason, the participants in a lineup or showup can be required to repeat what the victim claims the criminal said during the commission of the crime. For example, "Put the money in the bag" or "Scream and I'll kill you."

Distinctive features of the suspect may be re-created. Obviously, this cannot be done if it harms the people participating in the lineup or showup. If the crime was committed by a person with tape on his or her face, tape may be put on each participant's face. A make-up artist can create realistic scars, tattoos, etc. Realistic-looking wigs, toupees, and fake beards may be used.

Although none of these procedures violates the Fifth Amendment, due process demands fundamental fairness. If special effects are used on one person in a lineup, similar techniques must be applied to other participants if necessary to make them all have similar features.

Examples of Protecting Fifth Amendment Rights during Identification Procedures

• Jason was put in a lineup after his arrest for theft. He was very uncooperative and told the officers, "I know my Fifth Amendment rights. I demand to be taken back to my cell."

The officers were correct when they refused to comply with his demands because Jason does not have a Fifth Amendment right to refuse to participate in a lineup.

- Zoe was arrested for passing counterfeit bills. She was placed in a lineup and told to put on a jacket that was found at the crime scene. She refused and said, "My lawyer told me that I do not have to do this because I have a privilege not to incriminate myself."

The officers were correct when they told her she had to put the jacket on because wearing clothing found at the crime scene is not covered by the Fifth Amendment. She could refuse to make incriminating statements but she could not refuse to participate in the lineup.

- Duane was arrested for bank robbery. He was placed in a lineup and each person was told to say, "This is a stickup. Give me your money. If you yell I'll shoot you." Duane refused to say anything.

The officers were correct when they told each person to say what the robber told the teller. The Fifth Amendment protects individuals when they are asked to incriminate themselves.

Repeating what the officers told them to say so the victim can identify their voice is not the same as making a statement that is incriminating.

Sixth Amendment Rights during Identification Procedures

The suspect has a right to counsel during a lineup only if adversary court proceedings have begun (*Kirby v. Illinois*).[3] This usually occurs at an arraignment or indictment. Although the Supreme Court has not explicitly addressed the right to counsel at a showup, it can be inferred that the suspect has the right to have an attorney present only if he or she has already been arraigned or indicted.

Sixth Amendment Rights during Identification Procedures Defined

A suspect who has been arraigned or indicted has the right to have an attorney present at a lineup or showup. There is no right to counsel at a photographic lineup if the suspect is not present.

Moore v. Illinois held that the defendant also has the right to have counsel present during in-court identifications procedures.[4] This applies when a witness is asked if the person who committed the crime is present in the courtroom. The same rule is used at arraignments, preliminary hearings, and trials. It also covers asking someone who is not on the witness stand to identify the suspect in the courtroom. It does not matter whether the identification is made before, during, or after the court hearing.

On the other hand, there is no right to counsel during an identification procedure if the suspect is not present. *United States v. Ash* held that photographic lineups do not activate the right to counsel.[5] The rule is the same whether the pictures are shown before or after arraignment. There is no right to counsel even if the prosecutor decides to show the witness pictures immediately before testifying at trial.

Although there is a right to have an attorney present at some lineups and showups, the attorney does not have the right to run the show. Neither can he or she advise the suspect not to cooperate. The lawyer plays the role of an observer. In addition to not being allowed to tell the police how to conduct the lineup, the attorney does not have any duty to tell them to stop doing things that violate the suspect's rights. Whatever the attorney observes can be used in court to challenge the admissibility of identifications made at the lineup.

Examples of Protecting Sixth Amendment Rights during Identification Procedures

- Wendy was stopped when she attempted to flee the scene of a hit-and-run accident. A police officer transported a person who witnessed the accident to where Wendy was. Upon seeing the officer approach, she said, "Wait a minute. I want my attorney here before that guy tries to put the blame on me." The officer who was detaining her said, "Sorry, but you do not have the right to have an attorney during showups that we do before your first court appearance."

  The officer is correct. There is no right to an attorney at a showup held before the first court appearance or indictment.

- Steve was arrested for several burglaries and booked at the police station. The next day, the police held a lineup and asked eyewitnesses from several recent burglaries to tell them if the person they saw commit the crime was present in the lineup. When being taken to the lineup room, Steve said, "I demand an attorney." The officer replied, "You can have your attorney when you are arraigned tomorrow, but we do not have to provide one for a lineup held before the arraignment."

  The officer is correct. There is no right to an attorney at a lineup held before the first court appearance or indictment.

- Approximately 1 week before trial was scheduled to start, the prosecutor decided that a lineup should be held to determine if the eyewitness and victim still remembered what the attacker looked like. When Danny's attorney heard that the lineup was planned, he called the prosecutor and said, "What do you think you are doing? You know you can't hold a lineup now without me being there! He's already been arraigned!" The prosecutor said, "You're right. I'd forgotten about that. The lineup is set for 2:00 p.m. tomorrow. Be there."

  The defense attorney was right. The suspect has the right to have an attorney present during a lineup held after arraignment or indictment.

Due Process Rights during Identification Procedures

The purpose of the Fourteenth Amendment's due process clause is to ensure that the justice systems in the 50 states are based on fundamental fairness. Similar Fifth Amendment protections apply to cases in federal courts. In the area of identification procedures, **due process** means that the police must not use unnecessarily suggestive techniques (*Foster v. California*).[6] Testimony about eyewitness identification will not be admissible in court if there is a substantial likelihood of mistaken identification.

Due Process Rights at Lineups and Photographic Lineups

Lineups and photographic lineups have many of the same problems. Nothing in the way these procedures are conducted may point to one individual. This usually involves two areas: how the participants are selected and how the witnesses are handled.

Due Process Rights during Identification Procedures Defined
Identification procedures must not be unduly suggestive. There must not be a substantial likelihood of mistaken identification.

One of the first rules is that there must be an adequate selection of individuals with similar characteristics. From five to seven individuals is adequate. The participants are usually drawn from the jail population and/ or employees working near the viewing room. Each of them must match the general description of the perpetrator of the crime. For example, if the eyewitness said the crime was committed by an African American male, no white males should be in the lineup. Obviously, it will not be possible to find five identical matches; in fact, using identical twins would defeat the purpose of a lineup. The goal is to have participants who are sufficiently similar so there is no clue as to which one is the suspect. Anything that makes the suspect stand out is prohibited because it is **unduly suggestive**. Figure 15-4 illustrates how due process is applied to lineups.

If any participant in the lineup has a particularly noticeable scar or tattoo, the lineup could be invalid unless something is done to either hide it or simulate the characteristic on all participants. Make-up artists can be used for this purpose. Similarity in hairstyles and facial hair is also necessary. Wigs and fake beards may be used for this provided they appear real.

Additional problems arise if the same witness views more than one lineup, photographic lineup, or showup. The fact that the witness sees one suspect twice may cause him or her to draw the inference that the person who was in both lineups is the one the police believe committed the crime.

Lineup that satisfies due process

Lineup that is unduly suggestive

The first lineup satisfies due process because there is nothing about it that suggests which suspect to select. Each person in the lineup has the same basic characteristics. The viewer must rely on memories of the event in question when making a choice. No one is singled out as the only possible match.

The second lineup does not satisfy due process because it is unduly suggestive. Only one suspect has all of the characteristics described by the person who gave a description of the person seen at the crime scene. A lineup would also be invalid if the eyewitnesses gave such vague descriptions that too many individuals could match the description given.

Figure 15-4
How Due Process Applies to Lineups

This is unduly suggestive because many people will conclude that if the police believe a person committed the crime, he or she must be the one who did it; they may distrust their memory and pick the person who was in multiple lineups. A better way to test the witness's memory is to place the suspect in one lineup and then conduct a "blank" lineup. The blank lineup contains people meeting the general description, but none of them is a suspect in the case. The witness, it is hoped, will not identify anyone in the blank lineup.

Care must be taken to prevent witnesses from drawing their conclusions based on the way the identification procedures were conducted rather than on their memory of the crime scene. Making an identification is not a committee assignment. Each witness must make an independent decision. It is best to separate witnesses, usually by allowing only one to be present in the viewing area at a time. Witnesses should not be allowed to tell each other which participant in the lineup is believed to be the criminal or even that the person seen committing the crime was (or was not) in the lineup.

The officers conducting the lineup or photographic lineup must be careful not to indicate which participant is believed to be the criminal. Each person in a lineup must be asked to do and say the same things. Equal time should be devoted to each participant. Avoid statements such as, "Look at No. 3 again" or "Don't you think No. 5 looks like the person who robbed you?" Police officers should also avoid making comments to each other that might be overheard by the observer.

A detailed report should be made on each identification procedure that was conducted. If possible, this should include a photograph taken while the lineup was in progress. All pictures used in a photographic lineup should be saved and attached to the report. The name and description of the person each witness identified must be included in the report. This is true whether or not the witness picked the "right" suspect.

Altering some of the pictures using a felt-tip pen is not permissible because it is obvious what has been done, but new computer scanners and software now make it possible to add realistic-looking beards, change hairstyles, etc. Pictures showing booking numbers are not recommended because the fact the person has been booked may unduly prejudice the viewer. Placing booking pictures in window envelopes that hide indications of their source is permissible. The lack of suitable pictures may make it impossible to have a photographic lineup in some cases.

Due Process Rights at Showups

Many of the protections against unduly suggestive lineups do not apply to showups because the witness usually views only one person. Some rules govern both types of identification procedures: Police should not coach the witnesses, and witnesses must arrive at their conclusions independently. Figure 15-5 is an example of a showup that would satisfy due process.

Stovall v. Denno, the Supreme Court's first case about showups, involved a murder case.[7] Two people had been attacked: One was dead and the other in grave condition and being prepared for surgery. Doctors told the investigator that the patient had a very low chance of surviving the

Figure 15-5
Showup That Satisfies Due Process

surgery. At that point, the police brought the suspect to the hospital room and asked the patient if this was the person who attacked her and killed her husband. The Court's decision in the case appeared to restrict showups to emergencies, but *Neil v. Biggers* made it clear that the police can conduct showups when there is no emergency forcing them to do so. Instead, the due process analysis focuses on the reliability of the identification.[8] Factors the courts have considered include the following:

1. Opportunity of the witness to view the crime (including lighting and the length of time the witness was with the suspect)
2. Degree of attention the witness paid to the suspect while the crime was in progress
3. Level of certainty of the witness
4. Accuracy of the witness's prior description of the suspect
5. Prior inaccurate identifications made by the witness
6. Length of time between showup and crime

The same approach was used in a case in which only one photograph was shown for identification purposes (*Manson v. Brathwaite*).[9] Although the Court criticized the police for using only one picture because it was suggestive, the conviction was upheld because the totality of the circumstances indicated that the witness was not swayed by it. The witness was a police officer who purchased heroin from the suspect while working undercover. Based on a general description, another officer left the suspect's picture on the undercover officer's desk. The justices concluded that the officer was not susceptible to the subtle inference that the person in the picture was the one the police believed committed the crime.

Example of Protecting Due Process Rights during a Showup

Veronica was the victim of a home invasion robbery. She called the police 5 minutes after the robbers left. When questioned by the police, she told them that she was held captive in the brightly lit bathroom for 30 minutes by the shorter suspect while the taller one ransacked the house. Neither robber wore a mask. She gave the following descriptions: One robber was a white male between 18 and 20 years old, between 5 feet 8 inches and 5 feet 10 inches tall, slender build, blond hair, and wearing a black sweatshirt and black denim pants; the other robber was an Hispanic male, approximately 25 years old, between 5 feet 10 inches and 6 feet tall, black hair, muscular build, and wearing a navy blue hooded sweatshirt and navy blue sweat pants. The robbers left carrying several items of expensive jewelry in a black sock.

Several hours later, the police stopped a car for speeding and became suspicious that the two males in the car were the men who robbed Veronica. Another patrol car picked Veronica up and brought her to the scene. An officer warned her that the men might, or might not, be the ones that robbed her, and she should not presume that the men were guilty of the crime. She looked at the two men as they stood under a street light. After nearly a minute, Veronica said, "I'm sure the short guy is the one that forced me into the bathroom and stayed there to make sure I didn't get out. I got a good look at him for a long time. The other guy is the right size, but I didn't get much chance to see his face, so I can't say for sure that he is the one."

> The police had reasonable suspicion to stop the two men because Veronica gave the officers good descriptions of the robbers.
>
> The officers helped protect the suspect's due process rights by advising Veronica that the fact the men were detained did not mean they were guilty.
>
> Veronica took her time and truthfully told the officers that she was not sure about the second man.

Use of Identification Testimony at Trial

A witness may testify about any properly conducted identification procedure. Whereas the prosecutor will ask about situations in which the witness correctly identified the suspect, the defense attorney will try to show as many misidentifications as possible. The ability of the witness to identify the suspect may be challenged. This includes bad eyesight, poor memory, and a variety of other factors.

Some courts even allow psychologists to give expert testimony on the inherent problems with eyewitness identification. These problems include perception, memory, emotional state of the witness, and both conscious and unconscious motivation to identify someone as the perpetrator of the crime. The impact of stereotypes and prejudice may also be covered.

Experts may be allowed to testify about the brain functions involved in memory and recall and explain why memory is not always accurate. Occasionally, the results of psychological research on recall are also introduced into evidence.[10]

A hearing must be held if there is a question regarding the constitutional validity of the identification procedure (*Watkins v. Sowders*).[11] Testimony in the presence of the jury regarding lineups or showups that violate the right to counsel is grounds for automatic reversal of a conviction (*Gilbert v. California*).[12] The Harmless Error Rule applies to other violations. Fourth Amendment and due process errors result in reversals if there is a substantial chance that they influenced the outcome of the case.

The Fruit of the Poison Tree Doctrine has been applied to in-court identifications that followed improper pretrial procedures. If the in-court testimony is not influenced by the unconstitutional procedure, the witness may testify about the crime scene and make an in-court identification of the defendant. State courts frequently permit this type of testimony. The prosecutor may not ask questions about the improperly conducted lineup or other procedure, but the defense may ask about it on cross-examination.

United States v. Owens allowed testimony regarding a pretrial photographic lineup, even though the witness did not remember why he picked the defendant's picture.[13] He also did not remember seeing the defendant commit the crime. The victim's memory had been severely impaired due to the crime that involved a beating with a metal pipe. The defense attorney introduced evidence that, while in the hospital, the victim had named another person as the assailant. The court held that the photographic lineup was admissible because there was no evidence that it was suggestive. The fact that the witness was available for cross-examination, even though he could not answer questions due to loss of memory, satisfied the Sixth Amendment's Confrontation Clause. The defense could not prevent the witness from taking the stand. Obviously, it could argue to the jury that the witness lacked credibility.

Sample Dialogues for Introducing Identification Testimony at Trial

Introducing Testimony about a Showup That Was Conducted Properly

Prosecutor: Mrs. Worth, did the police ever ask you to identify the man who hit you?

Mrs. Worth: Yes, they did. They called me at home one day and said they had someone they wanted me to look at. They wanted me to do that before they decided whether to file charges.

Prosecutor: When was that?

Mrs. Worth: Right after I got out of the hospital.

Prosecutor: How long was that after he hit you?

Mrs. Worth: A week.

Prosecutor: Where did this identification procedure take place?

Mrs. Worth: At the police station. I was sitting in what they said was an interview room when an officer brought in a man in jail clothing.

Prosecutor: Who else was present?

Mrs. Worth: Nobody. Just me, the officer, and the guy they brought in.

Prosecutor: What did the officer say to you at the time?

Mrs. Worth: She said, "I want you to look at this man. Tell me if he is the person who hit you. Take your time and think about it. If you are sure that this is the man, tell me so. If you are not sure, tell me that, too. I don't want you guessing on this. This may be the right man, but it might also not be the right one." Or something like that.

Prosecutor: How long did it take you to make a decision?

Mrs. Worth: My first impression was that it was him, but I spent a couple of minutes thinking back to the night of the attack and trying to remember exactly what he looked like.

Prosecutor: And what did you finally tell Officer Bartlett?

Mrs. Worth: I told her that the man standing there was the one who hit me. I was very sure it was him.

Prosecutor: And is that man in the courtroom today?

Mrs. Worth: Yes. [Points at defendant.] That is him sitting next to the defense attorney.

In-Court Identification of the Suspect by Witness Who Viewed a Lineup That Was Not Conducted Properly

Prosecutor: Dr. Morgan, you have testified that your office was robbed. Did the police ever ask you to view a lineup and pick out the person who robbed you?

Dr. Morgan: Yes, they had me attend a lineup.

Prosecutor: Now, I know this will sound strange, but I want you to do your best to forget about what happened at that lineup. I want you to focus solely on what is occurring here in the courtroom today. OK?

Dr. Morgan: OK. I will try.

Prosecutor: Thinking about the day that you were robbed, did you get a good chance to see the person's face?

Dr. Morgan: Yes. I looked up from my desk and he was standing there, staring at me. I must have looked at him for a full minute before he blindfolded me.

Prosecutor: And could you identify that person today if you saw him?

Dr. Morgan: Yes, I could. I'll never forget that face.

Prosecutor: Now, using only the face you saw during the robbery as a guide, is the person who robbed you in the courtroom today?

Dr. Morgan: Yes, he is. He is right over there. [Pointing]

Prosecutor: I need you to state for the record who you are pointing at.

Dr. Morgan: I am pointing at the man in the blue shirt seated at the table with the sign that says "Defense."

Prosecutor: Thank you, Dr. Morgan. That will be all.

Judge: Defense. You can cross-examine the witness now.

Summary

The police frequently use three procedures to help eyewitnesses identify criminals: lineups, showups, and photographic lineups. Lineups involve showing the witness a group of possible suspects. Photographic lineups provide a selection of pictures of possible suspects for the witness to choose from. Showups are done by showing one suspect to the witness.

The Fourth Amendment prohibits stopping people without cause unless they consent. To detain someone for a showup in the field, there must be at least a reasonable suspicion that this person committed a crime. Suspects may only be transported to a police station for identification procedures if there is probable cause to arrest them.

The Fifth Amendment protection against self-incrimination does not apply to identification procedures. The suspect may not refuse to participate in a lineup or showup. He or she can be required to speak, stand in a particular pose, or wear appropriate clothing.

Suspects can invoke the Sixth Amendment right to counsel during lineups and showups held after they have been arraigned or indicted. They have the right to have an attorney present, but the attorney only participates as an observer.

Due process requires identification procedures to be fundamentally fair. Anything the police do that suggests which person in a lineup or photographic lineup is the suspect violates due process. There should be enough people who are similar in appearance in the lineup to force the witness to demonstrate his or her memory and ability to observe. The police must not attempt to focus the viewer's attention on any one individual or coach the witness; no one else should be allowed to do so, not even other victims and witnesses from the same crime.

Showups are judged on the totality of the circumstances. Identifications are usually admissible if the witness had a good opportunity to observe the crime and could give a good description of the suspect. There does not have to be an emergency to justify the failure to conduct a full lineup.

Introduction of testimony at trial regarding identification procedures that violate the right to counsel is grounds for automatic reversal of a conviction. Other mistakes are judged by the Harmless Error Rule. The Confrontation Clause of the Sixth Amendment gives the defense the right to cross-examine witnesses who testify about lineups, showups, and photographic lineups.

Review Questions

1. Define *lineup*, and explain what constitutional rights apply.
2. Define *showup*, and explain each applicable constitutional right.
3. Define *photographic lineup*, and explain what constitutional rights apply.
4. What types of errors in identification procedures will cause reversal of a conviction? Explain.
5. Assume that a person viewed an improperly conducted lineup. Will that person be allowed to testify in court? To make an in-court identification of the suspect? Explain.

Writing Assignment

Prepare your own lineup or photographic lineup by selecting one of your classmates, family members, or friends to be a "suspect" for demonstration purposes, having them stand up in front of class or provide their individual photograph. Then select five other people to serve as subjects in your lineup or photo array by either standing next to the "suspect" or providing individual photos for you to arrange next to the "suspect" photograph. After comparing either the lineup or photographic lineup you have created, write a 250-word (one-page) essay telling what characteristics you looked for in selecting your subjects, what attributes are similar or different between your subjects and suspect that would be considered by a victim or witness, and what other things you could have done to prevent this identification technique from being "unduly suggestive."

Notes

1. *Hayes v. Florida* 470 U.S. 811, 84 L.Ed. 2d 705, 105 S.Ct. 1643 (1985); *Dunaway v. New York* 422 U.S. 200, 60 L.Ed. 2d 824, 99 S.Ct. 2248 (1979).
2. *United States v. Wade* 388 U.S. 218, 18 L.Ed. 2d 1149, 87 S.Ct. 1926 (1967); *Gilbert v. California* 388 U.S. 263, 18 L.Ed. 2d 1178, 87 S.Ct. 1951 (1967).
3. *Kirby v. Illinois* 406 U.S. 682, 32 L.Ed. 2d 411, 92 S.Ct. 1877 (1972). See also *United States v. Wade,* supra.
4. *Moore v. Illinois* 434 U.S. 220, 54 L.Ed. 2d 424, 98 S.Ct. 458 (1977).
5. *United States v. Ash* 413 U.S. 300, 37 L.Ed. 2d 619, 93 S.Ct. 1568 (1973).
6. *Foster v. California* 394 U.S. 440, 22 L.Ed. 2d 402, 89 S.Ct. 1127 (1969).
7. *Stovall v. Denno* 388 U.S. 293, 18 L.Ed. 2d 1199, 87 S.Ct. 1967 (1967).
8. *Neil v. Biggers* 409 U.S. 188, 34 L.Ed. 2d 401, 93 S.Ct. 375 (1972).
9. *Manson v. Brathwaite* 432 U.S. 98, 53 L.Ed. 2d 140, 97 S.Ct. 2243 (1977).
10. National Institute of Justice, *Eyewitness Evidence: A Guide for Law Enforcement* (Washington, DC: U.S. Department of Justice, 1999); S. L. Sporer, R. S. Malpass, and G. Koehnken (Eds.),

Psychological Issues in Eyewitness Identification (Mahwah, NJ: Erlbaum, 1996); B. L. Cutler and S. D. Penrod, *Mistaken Identification: The Eyewitness, Psychology, and the Law* (New York: Cambridge University Press, 1995); M. Zalman and L. Siegel, "The Psychology of Perception, Eyewitness Identification, and the Lineup," *Criminal Law Bulletin* 27(2): 159–176 (1991).

11. *Watkins v. Sowders* 449 U.S. 341, 66 L.Ed. 2d 549, 101 S.Ct. 654 (1981).

12. *Gilbert v. California,* supra.

13. *United States v. Owens* 484 U.S.554, 98 L.Ed. 2d 951, 108 S.Ct. 838 (1988).

CHAPTER 16

Preparing the Case for Court

Feature Case: The Perjury of Los Angeles Police Department Detective Mark Fuhrman

Former Los Angeles Police Department homicide detective Mark Fuhrman, a 20-year law enforcement veteran, was one of the initial investigators assigned to the 1994 murders of Nicole Brown Simpson and Ronald Goldman, allegedly committed by retired football star and personality O.J. Simpson.

In June 1994, Detective Fuhrman and his partner responded to the Brentwood, California, crime scene and, along with other evidence, found one of the alleged killer's bloody gloves. Later, Detective Fuhrman and other investigators executed a search warrant at Simpson's home and reported finding additional evidence, including drops of blood and a matching glove. Simpson was indicted and charged with two counts of murder.

During the criminal trial, Detective Fuhrman became one of the most controversial witnesses when, during cross-examination, he specifically and repeatedly denied using the "N" word when describing someone of the African American race in the preceding 10 years.

The defense called four witnesses to testify about instances in which Fuhrman used the racial epithet during the preceding 10 years, and it played a recorded interview in which the detective not only used the "N" word but also demonstrated a so-called "negative attitude" toward African Americans. Simpson's defense attorneys re-called Fuhrman to testify. When

Fuhrman refused to answer any questions and asserted his constitutional right not to incriminate himself, the defense imputed the credibility of the entire Los Angeles Police Department investigation. Later, the prosecution denounced Fuhrman as a "bad cop" during closing arguments.

On October 3, 1995, the jury acquitted Simpson of the murders.

Following the trial, Mark Fuhrman pled "no contest" to felony charges of committing perjury. He apologized "from the bottom of [his] heart" that he had used racist terms and denied ever having been a racist. Fuhrman left the Los Angeles Police Department and has denied planting any evidence, maintaining, "There was never a shred, never a hint, never a possibility—not a remote, not a million, not a billion-to-one possibility—I could have planted anything. Nor would I have reason to."

Learning Objectives

After studying this chapter, you will be able to

- Describe how the prosecutor evaluates a case when deciding if it should be filed.
- List what precautions must be taken to ensure that physical evidence will be admissible in court.
- Explain the process for subpoenaing witnesses.
- Identify the proper dress and demeanor of a peace officer in court.
- Describe what contacts an officer should have with lawyers, witnesses, and jurors.
- Explain how an officer should deal with the media.

Myths about Criminal Court Proceedings	Facts about Criminal Court Proceedings
If a person is arrested or given a citation, the case will automatically be prosecuted and he or she must stand trial for all the offenses alleged by the police.	The decision whether or not to prosecute, including what charges should be filed, rests with the discretion of the prosecutor (or grand jury).
If there is probable cause to arrest a person, there is sufficient evidence to support a conviction in a criminal trial.	Although probable cause is necessary for an arrest, the standard for a conviction is higher. There must be sufficient evidence to satisfy each element of a crime beyond a reasonable doubt to obtain a conviction.
Criminal cases sometimes take a long time to get to trial because the prosecution has to finish its investigation and has requested repeated continuances of the trial.	The accused enjoys a right to a speedy trial. Absent extraordinary circumstances, long delays in proceeding to trial usually require a waiver by the accused. Many delays are due to a defense request.

Introduction

It is very important that a peace officer know the law of arrest, search and seizure, and confessions while working in the field. Proper techniques for preserving physical evidence at the crime scene are crucial. Understanding what is relevant and who is competent to testify are important in deciding to seek a criminal complaint.

Learning all of these things, however, may be wasted if the officer does not know how to prepare the case for trial. This is true even though many cases are plea bargained and never go to trial. If defense attorneys sense that the police cannot convince the jury that the defendant is guilty beyond a reasonable doubt, they usually will not persuade their clients to plea bargain. This chapter is designed to help police officers understand their duties in preparing the case for court.

Reviewing Facts of the Case

Police must have probable cause in order to make an arrest. The report prepared soon after the arrest is made normally sets out the facts used to establish it. Supplemental reports usually detail what is discovered after the arrest. All of these reports must be reviewed in order to determine what charges should be sought.

Reviewing the case in preparation for presenting it to the prosecutor requires objectivity. Police sometimes make errors. Frequently, these errors are caused by the stress of fast-breaking events. Constitutional rights may have been violated. Becoming defensive and denying the mistakes that were made will not delude an experienced prosecutor. Officers given the responsibility for presenting cases to the prosecutor must be able to review the case file and determine what evidence is admissible. Based on this, they should decide what charges to seek. This, of course, requires a good working knowledge of the penal code or other relevant statutes.

Most prosecutors carry a heavy case load. Due to this and other factors, they usually do not want to file cases that they cannot win. Judges may also pressure prosecutors not to waste court time on weak or trivial cases. Prosecutors are more concerned with determining whether or not a jury will convict the defendant.

Probable cause to make an arrest is not a sufficient reason to file criminal charges. A conviction requires much stronger evidence than what is needed for a valid arrest. To arrest someone, there must be probable cause, which means it is more likely than not that the person committed the crime. At a minimum, this equates to 51% certainty. To convict, there must

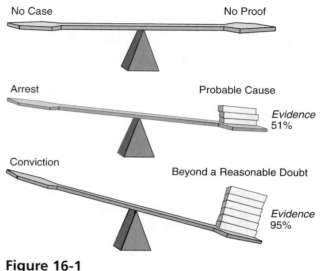

Figure 16-1
Likelihood of Conviction

be proof beyond a reasonable doubt. Although the jurors do not need to feel 100% sure, the facts need to make them feel approximately 95% sure that the defendant is guilty. Figure 16-1 illustrates how the strength of evidence is related to the likelihood of getting a conviction.

The facts should be carefully assessed to determine if each element of each charge sought can be established beyond a reasonable doubt. If there is a doubt, lesser included offenses should be considered. For suspects who are on probation or parole, the potential sentence for the current offense should be weighed against the consequences of revoking probation/parole. The person asking the prosecutor to file charges should be able to discuss the request in detail and provide the criminal history of the suspect. Habitually requesting charges that cannot be supported by the evidence only decreases the credibility of the police department in the eyes of the prosecutor.

Outlining the charges is very helpful. A computer database is useful for this purpose. A convenient layout for reviewing the charges is a screen with three columns. Figure 16-2 shows a sample screen. In the first column, enter every element of each charge sought. In the second column, opposite each element, note all evidence that can be used to establish it. The third column is used for comments related to strengths and/or weaknesses of the evidence. Any other important facts should also be noted. If a computerized system is not available, these comments can be made on 5 × 8-inch cards. The database or cards should be updated as new evidence develops

| Case No. 08-1234 | Court File No. | SE 66-44-22 |
| Suspect: George Green | Charge: | Burglary |

Other cases pending against suspect: 08-1111 (murder)

Elements of Offense	Evidence	Comments
Entry	Pry marks on door.	Unable to match pry marks to items in evidence.
	Suspect's fingerprints found on drawer where cash was kept in house.	Suspect had access to house before forced entry occurred.
Structure	Home of John Smith 123 Broadway	
Intent	Theft of following items from the dwelling: Stereo, TV, and $500	No ID numbers on TV

Other facts: Burglary reported on 1/2/08. Victim had been out of town from 12/24/07 to 1/2/08. No eyewitnesses. John Smith has prior perjury conviction. Suspect was a friend of Smith until 12/20/07 when they had a violent argument. Suspect frequently visited Smith at his home while they were friends and may have left fingerprints prior to the date the crime occurred.

Figure 16-2
Sample Computer Screen for Outline of Charge

in the case. If this is done, the case can easily be reviewed when it is time to prepare for trial.

Credibility of the witnesses is critical. The fact that the investigating officer believes the witness is not enough. The jury must also believe him or her. Objectively advising the prosecutor of factors that enhance or detract from the credibility of witnesses is important. Hiding weaknesses of the witnesses from the prosecutor will not help win the case. Defense attorneys specialize in demolishing the credibility of weak witnesses.

Working with the Prosecutor

In addition to investigating the case and asking the prosecutor to file the charges, the police are usually responsible for preserving the physical evidence and serving subpoenas on witnesses. Both of these tasks have one thing in common—keeping track of the location of potential evidence.

Preparing Physical Evidence

In order to introduce physical evidence at trial, the prosecutor must know where the item has been, who has had access to it, and anything that has been done with it since it came into police custody. This will be needed to establish the "chain of custody" prior to admitting the item into evidence.

The prosecutor also needs to know the evidentiary significance of each piece of physical evidence. Probably the two most important facts will be where each item of evidence was found and what tests have been done on each item. For example, the bullet was taken from the brain of the deceased during an autopsy, and ballistic tests show it was fired from the gun found in the defendant's possession at the time of her arrest. Once again, it is very important to keep the prosecutor advised of all facts related to the physical evidence.

If the police tell the prosecutor about the positive tests conducted at the forensics laboratory but do not mention the negative tests, the prosecutor may falsely believe the case is very strong. Facts not known to the prosecutor may also give the defense an added edge during cross-examination. In fact, the prosecutor's lack of knowledge may even result in dismissal of the case if the defense can convince the judge that it was denied its constitutional right to discovery.

Physical evidence is prone to motions to suppress based on illegal search and seizure. For this reason, the prosecutor needs to know all the facts on how each item was obtained.

Keeping track of all of the previously mentioned details for each item of potential evidence is not easy, particularly when an item may be relevant to two or more crimes or there are multiple suspects. A computerized database is ideally suited for this task. Each time an event, such as a new court date or results of a laboratory test, is entered, every screen that uses that information will be updated. Figure 16-3 presents a sample screen. If a card system is used, the information will have to be posted to each card involved.

The database, whether electronic or paper, should contain sections for the following:

1. Description of item
2. Where it was obtained
3. Facts justifying its seizure
4. Chain of custody
5. Tests that have been performed

Adequate space for other information that may be useful should also be provided. If the computer database is kept current on each item of evidence, the officer should be able to answer any questions the prosecutor may have.

Case No. 08-1234   Court File No.   SE 66-44-22
Suspect: George Green   Charge: Burglary

Other cases pending against suspect: 08-1111 (murder)

Evidence Tag No. 08-04   **Location:**   Bin 387

Description of item: RCA portable stereo model 345678X23.

Where obtained: In possession of George Green at time of his arrest.

Justification for seizure: Suspect stopped for running a red light. Record check showed that suspect had outstanding warrant. Search of car incident to arrest on warrant revealed RCA portable stereo listed above. Serial number run by dispatcher and found to match item stolen during burglary reported by John Smith on 1/2/08.

Chain of custody: Officer David A. Doe seized item on 1/2/08 at time of arrest and ran serial number. He sealed item in plastic and stored in station evidence locker bin 387. Officer Jane E. Jones removed item from evidence locker 1/4/08 and checked it for fingerprints. She sealed it in plastic and returned it to evidence locker bin 387 on 1/4/08. Item taken to forensics laboratory on 1/8/08 by Officer Sam Smith. Blood and tissue scrapings taken from item at forensics lab. Officer Sam Smith sealed it in plastic and returned it to evidence locker bin 387 on 1/10/08.

Tests performed: Fingerprints on item do not match suspect's prints; unable to identify fingerprints. Blood tests show the presence of human blood type O positive. Tissue samples: inconclusive.

Comments: Suspect had several recent bruises at time of arrest and matched description of person who was involved in a fight in the parking lot of Joe's Pool Hall on 1/1/08. One person was shot during that altercation who had type O positive blood. See Case No. 08-1111.

Figure 16-3
Sample Computer Screen for Physical Evidence

Witnesses

Many prosecutors will ask the police for a list of witnesses. If time permits, a meeting may be set up to discuss which witnesses should be called. The prosecutor's office usually handles the paperwork for issuing subpoenas. The police frequently are asked to serve the subpoenas.

The prosecutor must be prepared for the impeachment of his or her witnesses. This requires a thorough knowledge of witnesses' backgrounds, including prior statements to police about the case, previous arrests, and convictions. Other problems, such as poor eyesight or hearing, must also be brought to the prosecutor's attention. A thoroughly prepared case

Case No.	08-1111	Court File No.	SE 66-44-22

Case No.   08-1111   **Court File No.**   SE 66-44-22
Defendant: George Green   **Charge:**   Murder
Witness: Suzie Q. Adams
Other cases involving witness: none
Other cases pending against this suspect: 08-1234 (burglary)

Home address: **Work address:**
789 E. Main St.   543 S. First St.
Anytown, CA   Anytown, CA
(123) 456-7890   (123) 987-6543
                                                  Works 9-5 weekdays

Other places to locate witness:
Mother lives at 399 S. Tenth St., Anytown (123) 246-8102.
Witness frequents Joe's Pool Hall.

Testimony: Ms. Adams was a customer at Joe's Pool Hall on 1/1/08. She was
interviewed by the police 15 minutes after the shooting and described the assailant
as a 5'10" tall white male weighing 200 lbs., wearing a green turtleneck sweater and
blue jeans. She picked George Green out of a line-up held on 1/3/08.

Strengths and Weaknesses: Ms. Adams admitted having 4 drinks between 9:00
p.m. and midnight on 1/1/08. She is an LVN who works in a doctor's office and
routinely takes heights and weights of patients.

Figure 16-4
Sample Computer Screen for Witness

includes notations about evidence that can be introduced to rehabilitate
the witnesses. This obviously means that officers must be familiar with the
rules for impeachment and rehabilitation.

Once again, the police should keep accurate records on what a witness
can testify about and where the witness can be located. The computer database that already contains the outline of the charges and the description
of the physical evidence can also be used for this information. Figure 16-4
shows a sample screen. It should contain at least three things:

1. Current address of witness and other places witness might be found
2. Facts witness can testify about
3. Strengths and weaknesses of witness

It is quite possible that witnesses will move while the case is awaiting
trial. If a key witness cannot be located, the case may have to be dismissed
or result in an acquittal. This places one more burden on the police—
keeping track of the witnesses. Addresses and telephone numbers must be
kept current. Many courts now have victim–witness specialists who help
with this, but the police cannot neglect these details if they hope to win
the case.

Unfortunately, some witnesses become frustrated with the court proceedings and decide not to cooperate with the investigation. Frequent trips to the courthouse, particularly if they appear unnecessary because the defendant obtained a continuance, discourage witnesses. Once again, the burden falls on the police. Sometimes victim–witness assistance programs can help. Inconvenience to the victim should be reduced as much as possible. Positive attitudes are important. A witness who feels that he or she is on trial or being unfairly treated by "the system" may testify unfavorably at trial.

Witnesses who cannot remember crucial events complicate the court proceedings. In major cases, it is good police procedure to talk with all witnesses a few days before trial or other court appearances in order to determine what they can recall. Attempts may be made to refresh their memories, but officers must never give the appearance of coaching the witness on what to say. Officers should have a working knowledge of both "present memory refreshed" and "past recollection recorded" when talking with these witnesses. The prosecutor must be made aware of these potential problems so tactical decisions can be made on how to handle the case. Another type of problem is presented if the witness alters his or her testimony or refuses to testify. Although a subpoena will give the court the power to force the witness to take the stand, the prosecutor needs to be aware of these problems in advance so a decision can be made on whether or not to risk calling the witness to the stand. Some states still follow the common law rule that you cannot impeach your own witness. Under this rule, the prosecutor could not try to show a prosecution witness is lying or has a poor memory. Even if the state will allow the prosecutor to impeach the witness, the extra time and testimony may not be worth the effort. There is always a hazard that the jury may believe the untruthful answer. It may also confuse the jury or convince them that the case is weak.

If police officers suspect a witness plans to lie, they can warn him or her of the penalty for perjury. The prosecutor should be alerted immediately. Police protection and restraining orders can be sought if a witness is being harassed or intimidated. However, the fact that the witness may be prosecuted for perjury or the defendant charged with intimidating the witness is not much help at this stage. The jury cannot be told of these possibilities.

Dress and Demeanor

During the investigation of the crime, officers focus on obtaining the facts. The prosecutor screens the case to determine if there is sufficient evidence to prove the crime beyond a reasonable doubt. Officers must not forget another important role of the jury—to assess the credibility of the witnesses. "Truth" does not always win if the jurors have a negative impression of the witness. This includes the officers who testify. For this reason, it is important that each officer consider his or her own appearance and demeanor when preparing for court.

Appearance

"Dress for success," the "power suit," and many other expressions reflect the importance of a person's physical appearance in business situations. The same is true in the courtroom. The jury's first impression of the witness will be based on physical appearance. For many jurors, this may be the single most important factor used to weigh the testimony. Good grooming is therefore crucial.

Officers who do not wear a uniform in their normal assignment, such as detectives, usually appear in court in civilian clothing. Opinions differ on whether patrol officers should testify in uniform. Some believe that the public respects law enforcement officers, and the uniform adds credibility to the witness. Others believe that a uniformed officer, especially one visibly wearing a gun, smacks of authoritarianism and has a negative impact on jurors. Community attitudes toward the police will have a lot to do with determining what an officer should wear. Formal or informal policies of the police department or prosecutor's office may provide guidance.

Whether the officer wears a uniform or civilian clothes, the clothing should be clean, neat, and fit appropriately. Jurors may infer that an officer who dresses in a sloppy manner is also sloppy in investigating the crime and handling the evidence.

If civilian clothing is worn, it is best to dress in conservative business attire. Flamboyant and gaudy clothing detracts from what the witness says. Officers must look professional. What is considered appropriate in a large, metropolitan area may be out of place in a rural farming community and vice versa.

The same rule applies to all aspects of the officer's appearance. Jewelry, cosmetics, and fragrances should be appropriate for a daytime business meeting. Hair, beards, and mustaches should be neatly styled in an appropriate manner. Even fingernails should be inspected to make sure they are clean and properly manicured.

Demeanor

The courtroom places high demands on the officer's professionalism. Each officer needs to remain polite and civil to everyone involved. The officer should be an unbiased pursuer of truth, not a persecutor of the defendant. This is not easy under cross-examination when the defense is trying to make painstaking detectives appear to be incompetent liars or "Keystone Cops."

Each officer must realize that the attorneys in the case are playing the roles assigned them by the criminal justice system. It is the duty of the defense attorney to impeach each witness if possible. During cross-examination, the officer should try to remember that the defense is not attacking him or her personally, although it may appear to be so at the time.

Good grammar is essential. Jurors may judge the intelligence of the witness by the grammar used. Vocabulary is also important. Each officer needs to select words that accurately answer the attorney's questions. A varied vocabulary also helps keep the jurors from being bored. Excessively technical language and police jargon ("cop talk") may confuse the jurors. Therefore, officers should avoid language that would not be understood by the average person.

While testifying, officers must make certain that they understand the question before answering it. If necessary, they should ask to have it repeated. Misinterpreting the question, or answering before the question has been completely stated, can result in testimony that confuses the jury. It can also make the officer look foolish and/or dishonest. Either of these impressions is damaging to credibility. A good witness pauses briefly after a question has been asked for three reasons: to allow time to think about the question, to give the jury the impression that the witness is thoughtfully deciding what to say, and to allow the attorneys time to make appropriate objections to the question before the answer is heard by the jury.

Most people, including jurors, dislike arrogance. Even though the officer firmly believes that he or she has conducted a perfect investigation and the defendant is obviously guilty, the officer must not appear smug while testifying. Care should also be taken to avoid letting the defense attorney lead the officer into stating that he or she never makes errors. This is a favorite tactic used to make small mistakes in the investigation look bigger.

Another trap officers fall into is appearing to be "professional witnesses." Due to frequent court appearances, most veteran officers develop set patterns of speech while on the stand. Many appear to be almost testifying from rote memory. Some use short, clipped sentences spoken in a monotone. Defense attorneys like to infer that the testimony is less than honest because it appears to be memorized and used in case after case. This type of testimony may also cause jurors to become bored and unconsciously allow their attention to drift away from what is being said.

Any appearance of personal animosity toward the defendant or defense attorney should be avoided. It is the officer's duty to bring the guilty to justice, not to have a personal vendetta against criminal suspects. Although most jurors have a general knowledge of the role of police in our society, they may favor the "underdog." If the "poor little defendant" is being picked on by the "mean policeman," the jurors may side with the defendant. Additionally, an officer who displays ill will toward the defendant is a prime candidate for impeachment on bias. The defense will strongly imply to the jury that the officer is either lying or exaggerating.

No one is expected to have total recall. "Present memory refreshed" was designed to help people recall things that had slipped from their memory. A witness should be ready to honestly admit refreshing his or her memory. The prosecutor should be prepared to ask relevant questions to show that this was legitimately done. Redirect can be used to show that the officer has not merely memorized an old police report or made up the testimony to conveniently fit the facts that have already been admitted into evidence. During closing arguments, the prosecutor can emphasize the fact that any normal person forgets from time to time.

Example of Present Memory Refreshed

Prosecutor: Ms. Adams, do you clearly recall what happened on January 4, 2008?

Ms. Adams: Yes, I do.

Prosecutor: Have you done anything to help you remember the events that occurred that day?

Ms. Adams: Yes. I read the journal entries that I wrote that day, and the next day, too. Oh, I also read the newspaper clippings that I kept in the pocket of my journal.

Prosecutor: Have you talked to anyone about the events in question?

Ms. Adams: Yes, I talked to Det. Dawson.

Prosecutor: I don't want you to repeat what the detective said, but can you tell us what you discussed with Det. Dawson?

Ms. Adams: Well, he stopped by where I work. He asked if I remembered what happened. When I said I didn't remember it all, he let me read the police report.

Prosecutor: So you refreshed your memory by reading your journal, the newspaper clippings, and the police report?

Ms. Adams: Yes.

Prosecutor: Did you talk to anyone else about it?

Ms. Adams: No, just Det. Dawson.

Prosecutor: And at this time, right now in court, you clearly recall what happened that day?

Ms. Adams: Yes.

Demeanor off the witness stand is also important. Jurors frequently see the witnesses in the halls and elevators, and even the courthouse cafeteria and parking lot. If they observe horseplay, lewd remarks, and off-color jokes, they may decide the officer is immature or prejudiced and lose respect for the officer. Any negative impression may affect the weight given the officer's testimony. Care should be taken to make a favorable impression at all times.

Contacts with Lawyers, Witnesses, and Jurors

The police usually have more contact with the prosecutor than anyone else in the courtroom. Sometimes friction develops between them. Officers who have conducted a lengthy investigation may be upset to find that the prosecutor is not totally familiar with the case. Sometimes there is a difference of opinion on the tactics the prosecutor is using or anger about how the prosecutor's office has previously handled cases. No matter what type of problem arises, it is essential that it not come to the attention of the defense attorney or jurors.

It is a good idea, if possible, to talk about the case with the prosecutor before court begins. This should be done in a location where privacy is assured so that the case can be thoroughly discussed. During trial, it may be necessary to write messages on a legal pad or pass notes to the prosecutor. This should be done in as unobtrusive a manner as possible. The jury's attention needs to remain focused on the witness and not on what is happening at the prosecutor's table.

Attorneys who come to the police station to talk with their clients may attempt to discuss the case with the officers. Once the defendant has been arraigned, however, the defense attorney should deal directly with the prosecutor. Police officers must direct any communications from the defense attorney or defendant to the prosecutor. Attempts by the prosecutor or police to contact the defendant directly are viewed as interfering with the attorney–client relationship. During this time period, if the police need to contact the defense attorney or defendant, it is necessary to channel communications through the prosecutor's office. Figure 16-5 illustrates the flow of communication after arraignment between the people involved in a case.

Cordial relationships between officers and attorneys are necessary in court. Even though the defense attorney is obviously trying to defeat the case, officers must remain polite. There are two reasons for this. One is that those who work in the criminal justice system should respect each others'

Police officer

communication

Prosecutor

communication

Defense attorney

communication

Defendant

Figure 16-5
Communication with Defendant after Arraignment

professionalism. The other is the jury. If jurors observe open hostility against the defense, they may decide the officers lack objectivity and their testimony is biased.

Impressions the jurors might receive also mandate avoiding excessive familiarity with the defense counsel and other courtroom personnel. Watching a group of good friends merely going through the motions of a trial may convince the jurors that the case is a sham or that it does not deserve to be taken seriously. Either of these opinions is bound to hurt the prosecution's case during jury deliberations.

Witnesses for both sides must be treated with common courtesy. This is important to maintain the dignity of the court proceeding as well as to avoid biasing the jury. On the other hand, constantly talking to the witnesses may convince the jurors that the police are setting up the testimony. This must be avoided.

Victims and witnesses frequently complain that they are forgotten by the criminal justice system. Keeping them informed of the progress of the case is important. Familiarizing witnesses with the court procedures before they are called to testify may help them better understand what is happening. It cannot be assumed that witnesses can learn the process by arriving early and watching the court proceedings; witnesses are usually excluded from the courtroom until they testify. Comfortable waiting rooms should be provided at the courthouse. All possible efforts should be made to avoid unnecessarily subpoenaing them. On-call subpoenas reduce the amount of time spent idly waiting in the courthouse or taking time off work to go to court only to find that the case has been continued.

Whenever officers are in the courthouse, they must be alert to the presence of jurors. When not in the jury box, they may be almost anywhere. Jurors should only hear about the case from the witness stand. If they overhear conversations about the case, particularly relating to suppressed evidence, it may cause a mistrial. Jurors have been known to stop officers in the hall and ask about the evidence in the case. A polite explanation that the rules do not allow the officer to answer these types of questions must be given. The officer must remember two things: Never answer the out-of-court questions, and never be rude to the jurors.

Example of Officer Contact with Juror

A woman approaches a uniformed officer in the hallway outside the courtroom.

Juror: Officer! Officer!

Officer: Yes, Ma'am.

Juror: I have a question about what you said in court. Did you find anything when you searched that man?

Officer: I'm sorry, ma'am, but I can't answer any questions.

Juror: But this is important. What was in his pocket?

Officer: I can't answer anything outside of court. I know you would like to know that, but the jury is only allowed to consider the facts that are introduced in the trial. Jurors aren't allowed to ask witnesses questions outside of court. Please don't think I am being rude, but I must go now so there is no appearance of impropriety.

Press Coverage

The First Amendment governs freedom of the press. The Supreme Court has affirmed the media's right to cover almost all criminal court hearings, but the media may be excluded in juvenile cases. A judge must give strong justification whenever part of a hearing is closed.

On the other hand, prejudicial pretrial publicity may endanger a conviction. The Supreme Court has allowed narrowly defined "gag" orders that prevent parties to the case, including attorneys and the police, from commenting to the media. Again, a strong justification is needed to make these orders. The Supreme Court has also upheld the constitutionality of state bar disciplinary rules that prohibit attorneys from making statements to the press that pose a substantial likelihood of prejudicing the case.

Most cases do not arouse sufficient media curiosity to be a problem. For this reason, many officers are unprepared for those cases that do. Each department needs guidelines on how to handle the media. Every officer must be familiar with them. Courtesy is required because an angry reporter can distort the facts and make the police appear incompetent, vindictive, or corrupt.

Care must also be taken to avoid "trying the case in the press." Statements given to reporters must be accurate, but the facts should be carefully reviewed to avoid inflammatory statements. It is usually wise to avoid disclosing the contents of confessions due to the sensationalism they may cause. Publication of a confession that is later held inadmissible runs a high likelihood of endangering the objectivity of the jury and causing a reversal of the conviction. This also applies to items that may have been seized illegally. Few juries are sequestered during the entire trial. Although the judge instructs the jurors to avoid listening to radio or television accounts of the case or reading about it in newspapers, the possibility of a juror finding out about the coverage of the case in the media must be considered. The police should avoid giving statements to the media during trial. A mistrial could be declared or a conviction reversed if a juror learned about these out-of-court statements before reaching a verdict.

Summary

Officers must carefully review the facts of the case prior to presenting it to the prosecutor for filing. They must be sure that there is evidence to establish probable cause for each element of the crime. The same is true when preparing for the trial: The prosecutor must consider the best way to use the available evidence to establish every element of the offense(s) beyond a reasonable doubt. Witnesses must be available to establish the chain of custody for each item of physical evidence. The evidentiary value of each item must be analyzed after considering all available information, including the results of any laboratory tests that were performed.

All physical evidence must be reviewed and the chain of custody must be established for each item. Evidentiary value must also be determined after reviewing all relevant information. including the results of forensic laboratory tests that were conducted.

Information must be maintained on each potential witness. It is important to know both what the witness is competent to testify about and where the witness can be located. It may also be necessary to interview each witness again to test his or her memory if there has been a lengthy delay between the occurrence of the crime and the trial.

Officers must appear neat and well groomed in court. Good grammar and vocabulary are important. Testimony must be in language the jurors can understand and not laced with police jargon. Overt hostility toward the defendant is unprofessional and may cause the jurors to become protective of the defendant.

Once a case has been filed, there should be no direct communication between the police and the defense attorney or the defendant unless the prosecution has authorized it. Requests for discovery and other information must be channeled through the prosecutor.

Victims and witnesses should be afforded every professional courtesy. Subpoenaing them for court hearings should be restricted as much as possible in order to avoid causing them inconvenience. They should be kept informed on the progress of the case and their role in all court proceedings.

Officers must be cautious to avoid contact with jurors. Although jurors must be treated courteously, they should not be given any opportunity to hear out-of-court conversations related to the case. Any request they have for additional information must be given to the judge—direct communications with the police are prohibited during trial.

The First Amendment gives the media the right to cover criminal trials, but the Sixth Amendment gives the defendant the right to an impartial jury. Prejudicial pretrial publicity must be avoided. Accurate descriptions of the crimes may be released to the media, but sensationalism may cause a mistrial. Any evidence that has a high potential for suppression because of the methods used to obtain it (*Miranda* violations, search and seizure problems, etc.) should not be disclosed. Any information to be released to the media should be funneled through press relations officers who are trained to deal with these situations.

Review Questions

1. Describe how an officer should evaluate the facts in a case prior to taking it to the prosecutor for filing.
2. What facts are necessary to establish the chain of custody for physical evidence? Explain.

3. What information does an officer need to maintain on potential witnesses in a case? How are subpoenas obtained for witnesses? Explain.
4. How should an officer dress and act in court? Explain.
5. List three things that may cause jurors to discredit the testimony of an officer.
6. Describe the relationship that should exist during trial between the defense attorney, the defendant, and the police.
7. Explain what can be done to help the witnesses prepare for trial.
8. How should an officer handle contacts with the jurors outside the courtroom? Explain.
9. Should the media have access to everything in the police department's files about the investigation of a crime? Explain.
10. Do members of the media have a constitutional right to be present during trial? Explain.

Writing Assignment

Use the Internet (www.findlaw.com) to research the different stages associated with a criminal case, including arrest, booking and bail, arraignment, plea bargaining, preliminary hearing, pretrial motions, trial, sentencing, and appeals. In 250 words or less (one page), summarize what happens and describe the respective roles of police officers, prosecutors, and defense attorneys at each stage of the proceedings.

GLOSSARY

A

abandoned property   Items that have been discarded and currently do not belong to anyone are referred to as abandoned property. The Fourth Amendment does not prevent searches of abandoned property; neither probable cause nor reasonable suspicion is required to do this type of search.

administrative warrant (or administrative search warrant)   An administrative warrant is required to conduct a noncriminal inspection when consent has not been given. The probable cause requirement is met by showing a judge that there is a reasonable legislative purpose for authorizing the inspection. Administrative warrants are used for inspections related to health and safety regulations, building and fire codes, and other noncriminal governmental functions. If the investigation is being done because there is suspicion that criminal activity is occurring on the premises, a regular search warrant is required.

Admissions Exception to the Hearsay Rule   The Admissions Exception to the Hearsay Rule makes a statement admissible if (1) it was made by a person who is a party to the lawsuit (in a criminal case, the defendant), and (2) the statement is used against the person who made it.

adoptive admission   An adoptive admission (also called a tacit admission) refers to actions that indicate a person is adopting a statement made by someone else. If a person remains silent after being accused of wrongdoing in circumstances in which an innocent person would be expected to deny the allegation, it is assumed that the person is admitting that the statement is true. Adoptive admissions are admissible if they meet the criteria established in the Admissions Exception to the Hearsay Rule.

aerial searches   Aerial searches involve observations made from helicopters and airplanes. As long as the flight is in public air space and in compliance with FAA rules, there is no need to obtain a warrant or have probable cause to justify the intrusion. This rule applies even though the observed items were in the backyard of a residence surrounded by a high fence.

affidavit   An affidavit is a written statement signed under oath or penalty of perjury. When officers seek arrest warrants and search warrants, they must give the judge affidavits containing enough facts to establish probable cause.

ancient documents   Older documents may be admissible without calling witnesses to authenticate them if there are no indications that the documents have been altered or tampered with. State law varies, but documents more than 30 years old are usually referred to as "ancient documents." There is a separate exception to the Hearsay Rule that permits these documents to be admitted at trial.

Ancient Documents Exception to the Hearsay Rule   A document is admissible under the Ancient Documents Exception to the Hearsay Rule if it meets three criteria: (1) The document appears to be genuine, (2) people have acted as if it is genuine, and (3) it is at least as old as required by the legislature. State legislatures typically require that the document in question be at least 20–30 years old.

anonymous informant   A person who provides the police with information but does not give his or her name is called an anonymous informant.

apparent authority   When requesting permission to conduct a search, officers may rely on consent given by a person with apparent authority over the area. If it reasonably appears to the officers that the person has authority over the area, the search will be valid even though the person misled the officers about his or her power to give consent.

arraignment   The arraignment is the first court appearance in a criminal case. At the arraignment the defendant is informed of the charges, a plea is entered, bail is set (if it is a bailable offense), the defendant is given the opportunity to obtain an attorney, and the next court date is set. The right to counsel "attaches" at arraignment—the defendant has the right to have counsel present during any meeting with police or prosecutor after arraignment as well as during all court appearances.

arrest warrant   An arrest warrant authorizes any peace officer to arrest a specific person for committing a specific crime. Obtaining an arrest warrant tolls the statute of limitations and extends the period of time during which an arrest may be made. In order to obtain an arrest warrant, affidavits must be presented to a judge that establish probable cause that a crime has been committed and probable cause that a specific person committed the crime. Information must be included describing the suspect so that the arresting officer can determine that the correct person is being arrested.

at issue   Something is "at issue" in a case if it is disputed. If the defendant pleads "not guilty," all facts necessary to establish the crime are "at issue." If the defense stipulates to facts, those facts are no longer "at issue." Example: In a rape case involving an attack by a stranger, the identity of the attacker is "at issue" and DNA tests can be introduced at trial to establish that semen recovered at the scene came from the defendant. In a "date rape" case in which consent of the victim is at issue but the identity of the person who had sex with the victim is not, DNA tests would be inadmissible because their only purpose is to establish a fact that is not "at issue."

attorney–client privilege   A client can prevent his or her attorney from testifying regarding information the client revealed in confidence. Key terms: (1) attorney: a person the client reasonably believes is licensed to practice law; (2) client: a person who consults with an attorney for the purpose of obtaining legal advice; (3) what is covered: confidential communications between attorney and client regarding the legal services sought; (4) who holds the privilege: client. Exceptions: Attorney's opinion sought to help a person commit a crime or escape punishment is not privileged.

authentication   Authentication is showing that a writing (document) is what it is claimed to be.

authorized admission   An authorized admission is a statement made by a person who is authorized to speak on behalf of another person. Example: A statement by the CEO of Company X is admissible against Company X at trial. These statements are admissible if they meet the criteria established in the Admissions Exception to the Hearsay Rule.

B

ballistics expert   A ballistics expert is a person with specialized training and experience in testing weapons and ammunition.

beyond a reasonable doubt   Proof "beyond a reasonable doubt" is proof that leaves the jury firmly convinced. In criminal cases, the accused's guilt must be established "beyond a reasonable doubt."

blood alcohol   Blood alcohol tests determine the percentage of alcohol in the blood. This test is frequently used to establish that a person was driving under the influence of alcohol but may be used in any case in which intoxication is at issue. To be relevant, the blood sample must be taken in a medically approved manner as soon after the crime as possible.

body fluids   Body fluids include blood, urine, semen, etc. A suspect cannot use the Fifth Amendment as a reason to refuse to provide samples of body fluids to be used for laboratory tests.

booking process exception to *Miranda*   An officer or clerk who is filling out a booking slip may ask the suspect for name, address, and other necessary information without giving *Miranda* warnings. Extensive questioning would require *Miranda* warnings and a waiver.

booking search   The search done at the time a person is booked into the jail can include a thorough search of the person as well as anything the person has in his or her possession at that time. Any containers carried by the person being booked can be searched. Skin searches and body cavity searches are permitted based on U.S. Supreme Court decisions, but some states restrict searches of people booked solely on misdemeanor charges.

burden of persuasion   While the prosecution has the burden of proof in criminal cases on almost all issues, the defense has the burden of persuasion.

The prosecution must prove the defendant's guilt. The defense does not have to prove that the defendant is innocent, but it must persuade the jury that the prosecution has not established the defendant's guilt beyond a reasonable doubt. This can be done by discrediting prosecution witness and/or calling defense witnesses.

burden of proof   Proof that precludes every reasonable hypothesis except that which the law requires for the case. In a criminal case, the accused's guilt must be established "beyond a reasonable doubt," which means that facts proven must, by virtue of their probative [tending to prove] force, establish guilt.

Business Records Exception to the Hearsay Rule   A document is admissible under the Business Records Exception to the Hearsay Rule if it meets five criteria: (1) It was made at or near the time of the underlying event; (2) it was made by, or from information transmitted by, a person with first-hand knowledge acquired in the course of a regularly conducted business activity; (3) it was made and kept entirely in the course of a regularly conducted business activity; (4) it was made pursuant to a regular practice of that business activity; and (5) all the above are shown by the testimony of the custodian of the business records or other qualified witness.

C

canine searches   Searches by reliable, trained dogs can be used to establish probable cause. If there is a reasonable suspicion that luggage at an airport or other location contains drugs, it may be detained briefly to allow a narcotics-trained dog to sniff it.

case law   Case law is the collection of appellate court opinions. Lawyers and judges study case law in order to find opinions that are relevant to the current case. Based on *stare decisis*, these decisions are binding on lower courts until reversed, vacated, or overruled.

chain of custody   The chain of custody (also called chain of possession or continuity of possession) accounts for everyone who has had possession of an item of real evidence from the time it came into police custody until it is introduced into court. It is used to show the judge and jury that the evidence has not been tampered with.

challenge for cause   A challenge for cause is used to remove a prospective juror from the jury on the grounds that he or she is unable to decide the case solely on the facts admitted at trial and the law the judge will give as jury instructions. The attorney's decision to use a challenge for cause is based on juror's answers to questions during *voir dire*, and the attorney must be able to convince the judge that the juror has formed opinions that will prevent him or her from deciding the case on information presented at trial.

character   Character describes what a person's moral traits really are. Since there is virtually no way to determine this, reputation is introduced at trial if relevant. "Character witnesses" testify about the person's reputation.

charge bargaining   Charge bargaining is the process of working out an agreement between the prosecution and defense on what charges will be filed. Charge bargaining is similar to plea bargaining except that it occurs before the charges are filed.

circumstantial evidence   Circumstantial evidence indirectly proves a fact. It requires the trier of the facts to use an inference or presumption in order to conclude that the fact exists.

citizen's arrest   An arrest made by someone who is not a peace officer is referred to as a "citizen's arrest." Citizenship is not required. The person making the arrest must have observed the crime take place and have sufficient facts to establish that the person arrested committed the crime. Citizen's arrests are most common in misdemeanors because police officers usually lack the authority to make arrests for misdemeanors that were not committed in their presence.

Civil Case Exception to the Exclusionary Rule   Evidence seized by police officers in violation of the Fourth and Fifth Amendments can be introduced in civil cases.

clergy–penitent privilege   A penitent may prevent a member of the clergy from testifying about what the penitent revealed in confidence. Key terms: (1) clergy: priest, minister, or religious practitioner; (2) penitent: person who consults clergy for spiritual advice; (3) what is covered: confidential communications where the penitent sought spiritual guidance; (4) who holds the privilege: both the clergy and the penitent hold this privilege. Exceptions: traditionally, none. Some states now require the clergy to report incidents of child abuse.

clerk's transcript   The clerk's transcript is a copy of all documents filed with the court in the case, including the entries the clerk made during court days. It does not include a verbatim record of what occurred at each hearing.

closed container   Any box, suitcase, or other container that can be securely closed and thereby hide the contents from view is considered a closed container. Under the closed container rule, police officers may seize a closed container if they have probable cause to believe that it contains contraband. They may not open a closed container until a judge has granted a search warrant for that purpose. Exceptions to the closed container rule allow officers to open the container without a search warrant. The following situations are exceptions to the closed container rule: booking searches, search of a vehicle incident to arrest, search of a vehicle based on probable cause, search of a vehicle based on reasonable suspicion, and inventory of an impounded vehicle.

competent witness   A person is competent to be a witness in court if that person (1) understands the duty to tell the truth and (2) can narrate the events in question.

computing/digital forensics   The specialist in computing/digital forensics has extensive training in recovering data as well as many other ways to search the computer. A Certified Forensics Computer Examiner, or someone with similar credentials, has passed examinations given by a professional organization in this field. A person who specializes in computing/digital forensics can determine if files have been deleted from a computer or other digital device. Hidden files can also be found. This includes searching for pictures, documents, and e-mail messages.

conclusive presumption   A conclusive presumption mandates that the jury draw a specific inference if the basic fact has been established. The opposing side may try to disprove the basic fact, but it is not allowed to introduce evidence to disprove the presumed fact when this type of presumption is used.

confidential communication   As used in the law of privileges, any communication made in circumstances that protect the confidentiality of what is said or done is considered a confidential communication. The confidential nature of the communication is not violated if an attorney or doctor has necessary office staff present during the communication or staff does necessary work on the case. The communication is no longer confidential if the holder of the privilege voluntarily discloses the information to a person not covered by a privilege.

confidential informant   A person who provides information for the police on the condition that the police will not disclose his or her identity is called a confidential informant.

consent search   A consent search is a search based on permission from at least one person with apparent authority over the area. If the suspect is present and refuses to consent, the fact that another person is willing to consent will not constitute valid consent for a search. Consent must be given voluntarily, but officers are not required to inform a person about the right to refuse consent. Officers do not need probable cause or any other legal justification for the search if they have consent.

Contemporaneous Declaration Exception to the Hearsay Rule   A statement is admissible under the Contemporaneous Declaration Exception to the Hearsay Rule if it meets two criteria: (1) It was made by the declarant to explain what he or she was doing, and (2) it was made at the time the declarant was performing the act that he or she was trying to explain.

Contemporaneous Objection Rule   The Contemporaneous Objection Rule requires that attorneys state their objections to questions immediately after the witness is asked the questions. The purpose of the rule is to allow the judge to make a ruling on the objection before the witness answers. This prevents the jury from hearing what might be prejudicial information. The Contemporaneous Objection Rule applies to both sides in all court proceedings.

continuity of possession   See *chain of custody*.

controlled delivery   A controlled delivery is the delivery of a package (or other object) while it is under surveillance by the police. The package usually has been legally seized prior to the delivery and the delivery is conducted in order to gain additional evidence and establish the identity of the intended receiver. Setting up a controlled delivery does not require a search warrant unless activities inside a home will be monitored.

corroboration (also called corroborative evidence)   Corroborative evidence supports the prior testimony of another witness by providing additional evidence to confirm what the previous witness said without merely duplicating it. For example, if an eyewitness testified that he saw John at the scene of the crime, testimony by a police officer that John's fingerprints were found at the location would provide corroboration for the witness's testimony.

credibility of the witness   The trier of the facts evaluates the credibility of the witness. After listening to the testimony, observing the witness's "body language," listening to the opposing side's attempts to impeach the witness, and considering the testimony of other witnesses, the jurors (or judge, in a trial without a jury) decide if the witness is telling the truth.

crime scene warrant   There is no exception to the warrant requirement for crime scenes that are on private property. Officers have the right to enter a crime scene to provide aid for the injured and arrange for the coroner to remove the deceased, but once these tasks have been accomplished, either consent or a search warrant is necessary if the officers want to stay at the location to conduct an investigation.

cumulative evidence   Evidence is said to be cumulative if it merely restates what has already been admitted into evidence. The judge has discretion to limit the amount of cumulative evidence that can be admitted at a trial. Example: If there were 10 witnesses to a crime and all gave similar statements, the judge would probably rule that 2 or 3 witnesses could testify but not all 10 of them.

custodial interrogation   Officers must give the *Miranda* warnings prior to custodial interrogation. Custody means the person is under arrest or otherwise deprived of his or her freedom. Interrogation is the process of questioning. Both direct and indirect questions require *Miranda* warnings. Temporary detention (field interviews) authorized by *Terry v. Ohio* (1968) does not require *Miranda* warnings. *Miranda* warnings are not required for questioning of an inmate by an undercover officer as long as the inmate does not know that he or she is being questioned by a law enforcement officer and the inmate has not been arraigned for the crime under discussion.

D

declarant   As used in the Hearsay Rule, the declarant is the person who made the statement. When determining whether hearsay is admissible, the rules governing the exceptions to the Hearsay Rule are applied to the declarant—regardless of who is testifying about the statement at trial.

Declarations against Interest Exception to the Hearsay Rule   A statement is admissible under the Declarations against Interest Exception to the Hearsay

Rule if it meets two criteria: (1) The person making the statement is not available to testify in court, and (2) the statement is against the interest of the person making the statement. A statement is considered to be against the interest of the person making it if it could result in criminal prosecution, monetary loss, or impairment of an interest in real estate. See your state law for complete list.

Deportation Exception to the Exclusionary Rule   Evidence seized in violation of the Fourth and Fifth Amendments can be introduced at deportation hearings.

digital image processing   Many new techniques and software are available to help investigators improve the quality of pictures. Using digital image processing, what were once discarded as blurry pictures can now be enhanced so that an identification can be made.

direct appeal   A direct appeal is an appeal that is taken immediately after the conviction and is based solely on what happened at trial and other court hearings in the case. Transcripts of the original trial are used; no witnesses are called. No new evidence can be introduced during a direct appeal.

direct evidence   Direct evidence is based on personal knowledge or observation of the person testifying. No inference or presumption is needed. If the testimony is believed by the jury, the fact it relates to is conclusively established.

direct examination   Direct examination is the questioning of a witness by an attorney for the side that called the witness. During the prosecution's case in chief, the prosecutor conducts direct examination. This will be followed by cross-examination by the defense attorney.

discovery   Discovery is the pretrial process whereby one side is able to find out what evidence the other side has. Some states require each side to disclose nearly all evidence that it has in its possession (except material protected by the Fifth Amendment and other privileges) and give the opposing side copies of statements that have been made by witnesses. Lists of witnesses each side intends to call to testify at trial are also exchanged. The defense cannot be required to disclose the defendant's statement or tell the prosecution in advance that the defendant will or will not testify at trial.

documentary evidence   Written and printed items are called documentary evidence; this is a subset of real evidence. Photographs, video and audiotapes, motion pictures, and computer-generated reports and graphics are also included in documentary evidence.

double hearsay   Double hearsay refers to a hearsay statement that is embedded in another hearsay statement. Example: In the statement "D said that E told her what F said," what F originally said is hearsay; when D attempts to repeat what E said, it is double hearsay.

double jeopardy   Being tried for the same crime twice is double jeopardy. This defense applies if the defendant has either been convicted (and the conviction upheld on appeal) or acquitted on the same charge or a lesser included offense. The view in the United States is that double jeopardy does not prevent re-filing charges and seeking a new conviction if the defendant's conviction is reversed on appeal.

due process at lineup or showup   Due process, as applied to lineups and showups, prohibits procedures that are unduly suggestive. Violations of due process result from disparities in height, weight, race, age, or other factors. Comments by the police or other people that are overheard by the person viewing the lineup or showup may be unduly suggestive if they influence the selection of the person who allegedly committed the crime.

Dying Declaration Exception to the Hearsay Rule   A statement is admissible under the Dying Declaration Exception to the Hearsay Rule if it meets four criteria: (1) At the time the statement was made, the declarant had a sense that he or she would die very soon; (2) the declarant had firsthand knowledge of what he or she was saying; (3) the statement is about the cause and circumstances of the death; and (4) the declarant is now dead.

E

electronic surveillance   Electronic surveillance involves the seizure (recording) of conversations by electronic transmitting devices and/or recording equipment. It usually involves wiretaps or other types of listening devices. The Wiretap Act of 1968 (Title III of the Omnibus Crime Control and Safe Streets Act of 1968) allows federal judges to issue electronic surveillance warrants if there is a strong showing of need for this technique in the investigation of serious federal felonies and organized crime activities listed in Title III. The warrant application must be screened by the U.S. Attorney General or his or her designee. An electronic surveillance warrant is valid for a maximum of 30 days but can be renewed based on a showing that probable cause still exists for the monitoring activity. Some states have electronic surveillance laws nearly identical to Title III; others are more restrictive. Unless specifically prohibited by the legislature, no warrant is required for a person to wear a transmitting or recording device or to conceal these types of devices on his or her premises if the person has agreed to cooperate with authorities.

evidence   Something that proves or disproves allegations and assertions. Evidence, in the legal sense, includes only what is introduced at trial. The testimony of witnesses, documents, and physical objects can all be evidence.

Excited Utterance Exception to the Hearsay Rule   Excited utterances are also referred to as spontaneous declarations. A statement is admissible under the Spontaneous Statement Exception to the Hearsay Rule if it meets two criteria: (1) It tells about something the declarant observed with one of the five senses, and (2) it was made spontaneously while the declarant was still under the stress and excitement of the event.

Exclusionary Rule   The Exclusionary Rule prohibits the use of unconstitutionally obtained evidence at trial. For example, if it is established that drugs were found by officers who conducted an illegal search, the drugs are suppressed (not allowed into court). The U.S. Supreme Court applied the Exclusionary Rule to the federal courts in the 1914 case of *Weeks v. United States* and to state courts in the 1961 case of *Mapp v. Ohio*.

execution of a warrant   A warrant is executed when peace officers act as directed by the warrant. A search warrant is executed when the search is conducted; an arrest warrant is executed when the arrest is made.

executive privilege   *United States v. Nixon* 418 U.S. 683, 708-709 (1974) provides the framework for analyzing claims of executive privilege when documents are sought for use in criminal cases. First, it is presumed that the President has the right to refuse access to the confidential decision-making process. Second, statements requested in the subpoena that meet the test of admissibility and relevance must be isolated. Third, the District Court judge will hold an *in camera* hearing in which the material that the executive branch claims is privileged will be examined. Only the federal judge and an attorney representing the President will be present at this hearing. The outcome of this hearing will be an order detailing what, if anything, will be admissible at the criminal trial in question. During this process, the District Court has a very heavy responsibility to make sure that information reviewed *in camera* and determined to be privileged is accorded the "high degree of respect due the President of the United States" (418 U.S. 683, 716). The District Court has the responsibility for making sure that there are no leaks of the material that was reviewed but not ruled admissible at trial.

exemplars   The most common exemplars used in the investigation of crimes are handwriting exemplars and voice exemplars. These samples, which the suspect is told how to prepare, are used for identification purposes. Example: If there was a demand note during a bank robbery, the suspect may be required to give a handwriting exemplar so a forensic document examiner can compare it to the ransom note and attempt to determine if the two documents were made by the same person.

experiment   An experiment attempts to screen out all extraneous variables so that the experimenter can measure the impact of one factor. Only results of experiments that replicate all relevant conditions of the crime scene are admissible in court.

expert witness   An expert witness is a person who is called to testify about a relevant event based on his or her special knowledge or training. Expert witnesses are only allowed if some evidence in the case is beyond the understanding of the average juror.

F

Federal Rules of Evidence   The Federal Rules of Evidence were enacted by the U.S. Congress to govern the admission of evidence in federal court. The Federal Rules of Evidence are a part of the United States Code. Several states have adopted the Federal Rules.

field interview   A field interview (also referred to as a temporary detention) is a brief detention for the purpose of determining whether a crime has occurred and the person detained should be arrested. Officers must have specific, articulable facts that lead them to believe that criminal activity is afoot. If there is reasonable suspicion that the person is armed, officers may frisk the person for weapons. *Terry v. Ohio* (1968) is the leading case.

field sobriety test   See *sobriety test.*

fingerprints   If an officer has the right to detain a person in the field based on reasonable suspicion (*Terry v. Ohio*), the person may not be transported to the station for the purpose of taking fingerprints. If the officer has the necessary supplies available, the officer can make a fingerprint exemplar card at the location where the person was stopped. If a person has been arrested, he or she can be taken to the police station and fingerprinted there.

force   An officer may use reasonable force to detain a person. What force is reasonable will depend on the circumstances, but deadly force is only authorized to protect someone whose life is in danger.

Foreign Intelligence Surveillance Act of 1978 (FISA)   Electronic surveillance on activities of foreign governments and their agents is controlled by FISA. It authorizes a small group of federal judges to issue warrants for wiretaps and other surveillance activities. FISA was amended by the USA PATRIOT Act in order to give federal agents greater powers to conduct surveillance of suspected terrorists.

forensic accountant   A forensic accountant is used in fraud and embezzlement cases to determine if financial records have been falsified or altered. A Certified Fraud Examiner (CFE) or a Fraud Certified Public Accountant (FCPA) has extensive training and experience in this type of work.

forensic anthropologist   The forensic anthropologist works with pathologists and odontologists to estimate age, sex, ancestry, stature, and unique bony features of the deceased. Specialists in facial reconstruction may make three-dimensional sculptures of the face based on a portion of a skull.

forensic footwear analysis   Making plaster casts of footprints dates back nearly 100 years. Current advancement in forensic footwear focuses on details in the wear pattern of the shoe to estimate the height, weight, and physical impairments of the suspect.

Former Testimony Exception to the Hearsay Rule   A statement is admissible under the Former Testimony Exception to the Hearsay Rule if it meets three criteria: (1) The statement was recorded under oath at the prior court hearing, (2) the person whose testimony is introduced is not available to testify at the present court proceeding, and (3) the former testimony is offered either against a person who introduced the prior testimony or against a person who had the right and opportunity to cross-examine at the prior hearing.

Fourth Amendment   The right of the people to be secure in their persons, houses, papers and effects, against unreasonable searches and seizures, shall not be violated, and no Warrants shall issue, but upon probable cause, supported by Oath or affirmation, and particularly describing the place to be searched, and the persons or things to be seized.

frisk   Patting down the outer clothing for weapons is referred to as a frisk. A frisk is allowed during a temporary detention if the officers have reasonable suspicion that the suspect is armed.

Fruit of the Poison Tree Doctrine   Evidence derived from unconstitutionally obtained evidence is said to be the "fruit of the poison tree." It is inadmissible at trial unless the taint of the illegal acts has dissipated. Example: Officers failed to give *Miranda* warnings in a timely manner and the suspect told them where the murder weapon was hidden. Officers used this information to seize the murder weapon. The confession is inadmissible because of the *Miranda* error. The murder weapon will not be admissible in court because it is the fruit of an illegally obtained confession.

G

geographic profiling   Geographic profiling operates on the assumption that serial murderers (or rapists, etc.) balance the desire to kill (or rape) far from home and avoid recognition with the desire to remain in familiar territory. Mapping of the locations of serial crimes is facilitated by software developed for this purpose. It is estimated that use of the software helps police narrow their target zone by 95%.

Good Faith Exception to the Exclusionary Rule   Permits the use of unconstitutionally obtained evidence if officers were acting in good faith when seizing it. The Supreme Court has limited the Good Faith Exception to situations in which there was reliance on a warrant that appeared to be valid on its face; arrests made under statutes that were later held unconstitutional; and arrests made after a records check revealed an outstanding warrant even though the fact that the warrant had been recalled had accidentally been omitted from the database.

Grand Jury Exception to the Exclusionary Rule   Evidence that has been seized in violation of the Fourth or Fifth Amendments can be presented to the grand jury when the prosecutor is seeking an indictment. This is an exception to the Exclusionary Rule; the same evidence is not admissible at trial.

H

habeas corpus   *Habeas corpus* proceedings are held in civil court when a person challenges the legality of his or her confinement. These proceedings may be filed only if the petitioner is currently being held in custody. Examples: denial of reasonable bail, failure to release an inmate at the expiration of a sentence, a conviction obtained when the defendant was denied the right to counsel, and confinement in a mental hospital after the person has regained mental competence.

Harmless Error Rule   The Harmless Error Rule states that an error will not cause a case to be reversed on appeal unless the appellate court believes the error was likely to affect the outcome of the case. Appellate courts frequently rule that errors occurring during a trial are harmless.

Hearsay Rule   The Hearsay Rule makes hearsay declarations inadmissible at trial. There are many exceptions to the Hearsay Rule. An attorney who wishes to introduce hearsay at trial must be able to state which exception to the Hearsay Rule is applicable to the statement.

held to answer   If the judge at the preliminary hearing is convinced that there is enough evidence that the crime was committed and the defendant is the perpetrator, the defendant will be "held to answer" on the charge. This means that the judge authorizes the prosecution to proceed to trial with the case.

husband–wife privileges   There are two husband–wife privileges. **Privilege for confidential communications**: A husband or wife may prevent the other from testifying about communications made in confidence during their marriage. Key terms: (1) husband and wife: valid marriage is required (in states recognizing common-law marriages, common-law marriages are covered); (2) what is covered: confidential communications made during the marriage; (3) who holds the privilege: either spouse; and (4) exceptions to the privilege in criminal cases: crimes committed by one spouse against the other spouse; crimes committed by one spouse against the children of either spouse; failure to support a spouse or child; and bigamy. **Privilege not to testify**: Depending on state law, either the defendant's spouse has the right to refuse to take the witness stand and testify against his or her spouse or the defendant has the right to prevent his or her spouse from taking the witness stand. Key terms: (1) husband and wife: valid marriage is required (in states recognizing common-law marriages, valid common-law marriages are covered); (2) what is covered: testifying in court during the time the marriage exists; (3) who holds the privilege: usually the person being called to testify (consult law in your state); and (4) exceptions in criminal cases: crimes committed by one spouse against the other spouse; crimes committed by one spouse against the children of either spouse; failure to support a spouse or child; and bigamy.

hypothetical question   A hypothetical question states a group of facts and asks an expert witness to draw conclusions based on the facts given in the question. All of the facts in the hypothetical question must have been introduced into evidence in the case. It is not necessary for the expert witness to have personally examined the evidence mentioned in the hypothetical question.

I

identifying features   Identifying features include how a person looks (in person or a photograph) as well as other distinctive things used for identification such as fingerprints. The Fifth Amendment does not protect the suspect from use of identifying features.

immunity   When a person is granted immunity, he or she is guaranteed that no criminal charges will be filed. Immunity is formally granted by the prosecutor. Transaction immunity protects the person from prosecution for specific crimes no matter how the evidence is obtained. Use immunity prevents the prosecution from using the immune statements against the person who made them, but it does not prevent the prosecutor from filing charges and obtaining a conviction if evidence is available from other sources.

impeachment   Impeachment is the process of attacking the credibility of a witness. Six main methods of impeachment are allowed: (1) bias or prejudice, (2) prior felony convictions, (3) immoral acts and uncharged crimes, (4) prior inconsistent statements, (5) inability to observe, and (6) reputation.

Impeachment Exception to the Exclusionary Rule   Confessions obtained in violation of *Miranda* can be used to impeach the defendant if the defendant takes the stand during trial. This is a limited exception; the statements are covered by the Exclusionary Rule and cannot be offered by the prosecution to establish the defendant's guilt.

Independent Source Exception to the Exclusionary Rule   To admit evidence under the Independent Source Exception to the Exclusionary Rule, the prosecution must be able to convince the judge that the police discovered the evidence in question without relying on unconstitutional procedures.

indictment   An indictment is the formal document stating the charges the grand jury has decided the defendant should face at trial.

indigent suspect   An indigent suspect, as used when considering *Miranda* rights, is a suspect who cannot afford to hire an attorney.

Inevitable Discovery Exception to the Exclusionary Rule   The U.S. Supreme Court recognizes an exception to the Exclusionary Rule that allows unconstitutionally seized evidence to be admitted in court if the judge is convinced that it was inevitable that the evidence would have been found legally.

inference   An inference is a conclusion that is drawn from the facts. When circumstantial evidence is used, the jury must infer that a fact exists based on other evidence that logically causes the jury to draw that conclusion.

Information   The document filed by the prosecution after the preliminary hearing is called the Information. It is similar in format to the criminal complaint but only contains charges that the defendant was "held to answer" on at the end of the preliminary hearing.

interrogation after right to counsel attaches   Once formal court proceedings have begun, a suspect must waive the right to counsel prior to custodial or noncustodial interrogation. *Miranda* warnings may be used for this purpose.

interview   An officer has the authority to transport a suspect to the station for questioning only if there is probable cause to arrest that person or the person has consented. If the person is detained based on reasonable suspicion, the officer may conduct a brief interview in the field but may not take the suspect to the station for questioning. When an interview is conducted in the field prior to arrest, the officer is not required to give *Miranda* warnings.

inventory vehicle   See *vehicle search—inventory of impounded car.*

J

jail searches   Officer may search an inmate or any place in the jail or prison if there is an administrative reason for the search. Probable cause is not required. The need to maintain security and stop the flow of contraband justifies nearly all searches in custodial facilities. Only slight suspicion is needed to conduct body cavity searches of inmates; less intrusive searches can be done without suspicion.

judicial discretion   When applying the law to fact situations and making appropriate rulings there is a great deal of judicial discretion. This means that the judge has the authority to consider the facts and make a ruling for a specific case. Examples: The Sixth Amendment gives the defense the right to cross-examine witnesses, but if the judge determines that the right is being abused he or she may limit cross-examination; when a judge sentences a criminal defendant, the judge usually has discretion in setting the length of the sentence, granting probation, etc.

judicial notice   Judicial notice is usually limited to facts that are public knowledge, commonly known scientific facts, and federal, local, and international laws. When a judge utilizes his or her authority to take judicial notice of a fact, the jurors are instructed that they must conclude that that fact exists. No evidence is introduced at trial to prove the fact that has been judicially noticed.

K

knock-and-announce procedure (also called knock notice)   Prior to entering a house, officers are required to comply with the knock-and-announce procedure. They must knock or otherwise announce their presence, state who they are, and state why they are there. The notice requirements do not apply if the facts indicate an immediate threat to the officer's safety, strong likelihood of immediate destruction of evidence, imminent escape of the suspect, or danger to innocent people in the house. The Supreme Court has refused to authorize exceptions based solely on the nature of the crime under investigation. If officers are in the process of complying with knock and announce and any of the above situations develop, the "substantial compliance" rule allows them to proceed without completing the warnings. The test for how long the officers must wait before entering is how long it would take a suspect to destroy the evidence or escape, not how long it would take a cooperative person to come to the door.

L

latent prints   The term *latent prints* refers to fingerprints that are recovered at the crime scene or from other items of evidence. They are compared to fingerprints that are on file in order to determine the identity of the person who left the latent prints.

lay witness A lay witness is a person who observed an event that is relevant to the case on trial. Lay witnesses are allowed to testify about any relevant event that was observed with one or more of the five senses (sight, hearing, smell, touch, or taste). Lay witnesses are not allowed to give opinions.

laying the foundation Laying the foundation is the process of establishing the preliminary facts that are required before evidence can be admitted. Example: before a gun found at a homicide scene can be admitted, it must be established that this is the same weapon found at the crime scene, it is in the same condition that it was at the time it was found, and no one has had an opportunity to tamper with it.

leading question Leading questions are questions that suggest the desired answer. Leading questions are permitted during cross-examination. During the prosecution's case in chief, the defense attorney is allowed to ask leading questions when cross-examining the prosecution witnesses.

limited admissibility Limited admissibility describes the situation in which evidence is introduced at trial but the jury is instructed that it may use this evidence for one purpose but not any other. For example, evidence may be introduced to show that a witness lied. This can be used to attack the credibility of the witness but may not be used to prove that the defendant is guilty of the crime.

lineup A lineup involves showing a victim or eyewitness a group of people to determine if he or she can identify the person who allegedly committed the crime. There must be a sufficient number of people in the lineup to give a valid opportunity for witnesses to make an identification. The people placed in the lineup should be of similar physical appearance and dressed so that no one stands out as the suspect. The suspect has the right to have an attorney present at a lineup if the lineup is held after the suspect has been arraigned or indicted.

M

material evidence Evidence is considered material if it is relevant to some fact that is at issue in the case and it has more than just a remote connection to the fact.

matter of law Legal issues are decided by the judge; such decisions are sometimes referred to as a "matter of law." They include rulings on the law, such as the admissibility of evidence, application of the Hearsay Rule, privileges, etc. They also include facts that are admitted into evidence by the use of stipulations and judicial notice. When a fact becomes a "matter of law," the judge instructs the jury that they must conclude that the fact has been proven.

media reporter privilege See *news reporter privilege.*

***Miranda* booking exception** Police are not required to obtain a waiver of the *Miranda* rights when asking routine booking questions.

***Miranda* public safety exception** At the time of arrest, officers are allowed to ask a few pointed questions without obtaining a *Miranda* waiver if this is necessary to protect the public from imminent harm. This exception is most likely to arise when a weapon is believed to be at the scene or a kidnap victim has not been found.

Miranda **waiver** Any waiver of *Miranda* rights must be knowing, intelligent, and voluntary. The person making the waiver must know his or her constitutional rights, have sufficient intelligence to understand them, and waive them without coercion.

Miranda **warnings** The U.S. Supreme Court in the case of *Miranda v. Arizona* (1966) ruled that prior to custodial interrogation the suspect must be given the following warnings:

1. You have the right to remain silent;
2. Anything you say can and will be used against you in a court of law;
3. You have the right to have an attorney present during questioning; and
4. If you cannot afford an attorney, one will be provided free.

A knowing, intelligent, and voluntary waiver of these rights must be obtained before questioning for any statements the suspect makes to be admissible in court.

Misplaced Reliance Doctrine No warrant is required to obtain conversations that can be overheard by the police or their agents based on the misplaced reliance of the suspect. Each person bears the burden of restricting his or her conversations to people who will not reveal them to the authorities.

mitochondrial DNA (mtDNA) analysis mtDNA analysis can be used on samples that cannot be submitted for restriction fragment length polymorphism, polymerase chain reaction, or short tandem repeat analysis because mtDNA does not rely on nuclear DNA. mtDNA analysis uses DNA extracted from another cellular organelle called mitochondrion and can be used to test hair, bones, and teeth. All mothers have the same mitochondrial DNA as their daughters; therefore, mtDNA analysis can be done on cells of unidentified human remains and any female relative of a missing person.

models The most common models used at trial are maps and diagrams. To be admissible, models must be to scale and accurately depict the item in question.

modus operandi *Modus operandi* literally means the method of operation. Many criminals become creatures of habit and commit the same crimes in the same way. This distinctive method of committing a crime is referred to as a *modus operandi*. When the suspect has a known *modus operandi*, the prosecutor may be allowed to introduce testimony about other crimes the defendant is known to have committed. If distinctive features of the prior crimes match those of the crime for which the defendant is on trial, the jury may infer that the defendant committed the present crime.

N

national security letters (or NSL statutes) A number of federal statutes authorize the issuance of "national security letters," which are the equivalent of subpoenas. No prior judicial approval is required. NSL can be used to obtain records in the hands of another party, such as banking records, credit histories, account numbers, travel records, information about wire and electronic communications, etc.

negative hearsay   Negative hearsay is the use of the fact that no record of an event was found to show that the event did not occur. Example: the fact that John's time card was punched on Monday is hearsay that can be used to show that John was at work on Monday; the fact that John's time card was not punched on Tuesday can be used as negative hearsay to show that he did not go to work on Tuesday.

news reporter privilege   Many states give members of the news media protection from being cited for contempt of court if they refuse to reveal confidential sources of information gathered while working on a news story. Key terms: (1) reporter: person employed by the media to investigate stories and report on them (media includes print media as well as radio and television); (2) what is covered: reporter's notes and identity of informants; (3) who holds privilege: reporter; and (4) exceptions in criminal cases: some states make an exception in the prosecution of serious crimes if it can be shown that there is no other source for the information requested.

nontestimonial compulsion   The self-incrimination clause of the Fifth Amendment does not protect a person against nontestimonial compulsion. The following procedures are considered in this category: blood, breath, and urine tests; taking samples for DNA testing; photographs and fingerprints; participating in lineups, showups, and photographic lineups; handwriting and voice exemplars; and field sobriety tests.

O

Open Fields Doctrine   The Open Fields Doctrine adopted by the U.S. Supreme Court allows law enforcement officers to search open areas not adjacent to a residence. This applies even if the field is fenced and/or posted with "no trespassing" signs.

Opinion Rule   The Opinion Rule states that opinions of the witnesses are not admissible because it is the function of the trier of the facts to draw their own conclusions (inferences). Lay witnesses may not give opinions, but expert witnesses are allowed to give professional opinions.

P

parol evidence   The term *parol evidence* refers to testimony that is introduced to establish the contents of a document. The original or duplicate of a document are preferred over parol evidence. If a satisfactory explanation can be provided for the absence of the original and duplicate, the judge may allow parol evidence.

Parole Revocation Exception to the Exclusionary Rule   Evidence obtained in violation of the Fourth and Fifth Amendments can be introduced at parole revocation hearings.

Past Recollection Recorded Exception to the Hearsay Rule   A document is admissible under the Past Recollection Recorded Exception to the Hearsay Rule if it meets six criteria: (1) the statement would be admissible if the declarant testified at the current trial; (2) the witness currently has insufficient present recollection to testify fully and accurately; (3) the report was made at a time when the facts were fresh in the memory of the witness; (4) the report was made by the witness, someone under his or her direction, or by another person for the purpose of recording the witness's statement; (5) the witness can testify that the report was a true statement of the facts; and (6) the report is authenticated.

peremptory challenges   Peremptory challenges are used to remove prospective jurors from the jury on the basis of the prosecutor or defense attorney's subjective opinions. The attorneys are not required to state why they use peremptory challenges. Peremptory challenges may not be used to exclude jurors based on race or gender. The number of peremptory challenges that can be used in a case is set by state law.

photographic lineup   A photographic lineup involves showing a victim or eyewitness pictures of potential suspects and asking him or her to indicate whether a picture of the person who allegedly committed the crime is in the group viewed. A sufficient variety of pictures should be used to permit valid identification. The pictures should be sufficiently similar in appearance to avoid being unduly suggestive. There is no right to have an attorney present at a photographic lineup, no matter when it is conducted.

physical evidence   See *real evidence.*

physician–patient privilege   A patient has the right to prevent his or her physician from testifying regarding confidential communications made while the patient was seeking diagnosis or treatment. Key terms: (1) physician: person reasonably believed by the patient to be licensed to practice medicine; (2) patient: person who consulted physician for purposes of diagnosis or treatment; (3) what is covered: information obtained by the physician for the purpose of diagnosing or treating the patient; (4) who holds the privilege: patient; and (5) exceptions in criminal cases: advice sought on how to plan or conceal a crime, and information the physician is required by law to report to authorities. Many states do not allow the defendant to use this privilege in criminal cases.

plain feel   When an officer is conducting a pat down based on reasonable suspicion that a person is armed, the officer may seize an item if he or she can tell by the distinctive feel of the object that it is contraband. This rule applies even though the item in question does not feel like a weapon. Officers are not allowed to manipulate or squeeze the item to determine if it is contraband.

Plain View Doctrine   It is not a search for officers to observe items that were left where the officers can see them while the officers are legally on the premises. The Plain View Doctrine requires that: (1) the officer must be legally at the spot where the observation was made; (2) the officer did not pick up or examine an item to determine whether it is contraband, stolen, etc., and (3) the officer must have probable cause in order to seize items found in plain view.

plea bargaining Plea bargaining is the process whereby the prosecution and defense work out an agreement for the defendant to plead guilty to one or more charges without a trial if the prosecutor will drop some of the original charges or support a lighter sentence.

police informant privilege The police have a privilege not to disclose the identity of their confidential informants unless the identity of the informant is crucial to the defendant's case. Key terms: (1) police: applies to all law enforcement agencies; (2) informant: person who supplies information to police in confidence; (3) what is covered: name and address of the informant; (4) who holds the privilege: law enforcement agency; and (5) exceptions: identity of informant must be disclosed if it is important in the defendant's case.

police personnel files Police and other governmental agencies have a privilege not to disclose the contents of their personnel files unless the information is relevant to the defendant's case. Key terms: (1) personnel files: permanent personnel records of an employee (police personnel files include investigations of an officer conducted by internal affairs); (2) what is covered: records concerning performance of officer and investigations of his or her conduct; (3) who holds the privilege: law enforcement agency; and (4) exceptions: must disclose information relevant to the defense.

polling the jury Polling the jury is the process of asking each juror if he or she agrees with the verdict that has just been read. The jurors are polled in the courtroom after the verdict for each charge is read and then they are dismissed.

polymerase chain reaction (PCR) analysis PCR analysis reproduces the cells in the sample until there are enough to conduct a DNA test. It can be done on a sample as small as a few cells. This test is not harmed by environmental factors, but great care must be exercised to avoid contamination by other biological materials when collecting and preserving the sample.

posed picture (photograph) A posed picture is a photograph that was made to illustrate a fact in the case. It may come from a re-enactment of the crime. Posed pictures are usually admissible if they accurately depict the facts of the case. The jury will be told that they are posed and were not taken during the crime.

post-arraignment confession Attempts to obtain a confession from a suspect after arraignment or indictment are covered by *Massiah v. United States* (1964). Prior to interrogation, police must obtain a waiver of the suspect's right to counsel. This rule applies whether or not the suspect is in custody. The attorney does not need to be present when the waiver is given. If the suspect is in custody, *Miranda* also applies.

preliminary hearing (also called preliminary examination) Hearing held before a judge to determine if there is sufficient admissible evidence to justify making the defendant face a criminal trial on the charges. If it is determined that sufficient evidence has been presented, the defendant will be "held to answer" on the charges. In most states, a preliminary hearing is not held if the case has been presented to a grand jury or if all charges are misdemeanors.

present memory refreshed Present memory refreshed refers to the process of refreshing the memory of a witness, either before or during trial. After the memory has been refreshed, the witness can testify based on his or her memory of the events. The witness is subject to cross-examination about what was done to refresh his or her memory.

present sense impression A statement is admissible under the Contemporaneous Declaration (also called a present sense impression) Exception to the Hearsay Rule if (1) it was made by the declarant to explain what he or she was doing, and (2) it was made at the time the declarant was performing the act he or she was trying to explain.

presumption A presumption is a conclusion that the law requires the jury to draw from facts that have been established at trial. The judge instructs the jurors when they are to use a presumption.

prima facie The prosecution has established a *prima facie* case if it has introduced sufficient evidence to convince the judge that it is more probable than not that the defendant committed the crime charged. The prosecution must establish a *prima facie* case at the preliminary hearing. It is a lower burden of proof than what will be required at trial.

primary evidence *Primary evidence* is a term that refers to an original document or a duplicate.

Prior Consistent Statement Exception to the Hearsay Rule A statement is admissible under this exception to the hearsay rule if (1) the witness has been impeached on the basis of prior inconsistent statements (a consistent statement that was made before the alleged inconsistent statement may be admissible to rehabilitate the witness), (2) cross-examiner has alleged that the witness recently changed his or her testimony (prior consistent statement made before the alleged change may be used to rebut this allegation), or (3) cross-examiner has alleged that the witness altered his or her testimony due to bias or other bad motive (prior consistent statement made before the alleged bias/motive arose can be introduced).

Prior Identification Exception to the Hearsay Rule A statement is admissible under the Prior Identification Exception to the Hearsay Rule if it meets three criteria: (1) the witness has testified that he or she accurately identified the person who committed the crime, (2) the witness identified the defendant or another person as the person who committed the crime, and (3) the identification was made when the crime was fresh in the witness's memory.

Prior Inconsistent Statements Exception to the Hearsay Rule A statement is admissible under the Prior Inconsistent Statements Exception to the Hearsay Rule if it meets two criteria: (1) the statement is inconsistent with testimony given on the witness stand by the person who made the prior statement, and (2) the witness was asked about the inconsistent statement and given a chance to explain.

prison searches Prison searches do not violate the Fourth Amendment as long as there is a valid administrative reason for the search. Neither reasonable suspicion nor probable cause is required.

privilege against self-incrimination The privilege against self-incrimination is a key feature of the Fifth Amendment. It only applies if a statement can be used in criminal court against the person who made it. The *Miranda* warnings were designed to help suspects subject to custodial interrogation to be aware of the privilege against self-incrimination.

privilege not to disclose identity of informant The privilege not to disclose the identity of an informant applies to all law enforcement agencies. Key definitions: (1) informant: person who supplies information to police with the understanding that his or her identity will not be made public; (2) what is covered: name and address of the informer; (3) who holds the privilege: law enforcement agency that used information provided by the informant to help with a specific case; and (4) exceptions frequently found in criminal cases: identity of informant must be disclosed if it is important in the defendant's case.

privilege to withhold personnel files Personnel files are normally privileged. Key definitions: (1) permanent personnel records on an employee: personnel files include investigations of an officer conducted by internal affairs; (2) what is covered: records concerning the performance of the officer and investigations of his or her conduct; (3) who holds the privilege: law enforcement agency; and (4) exceptions frequently found in criminal cases: must disclose information relevant to the defense, such as prior allegations of excessive force or perjury.

probable cause A reasonable belief that a person has committed or is committing a crime or that a place contains specific items connected with a crime. Under the Fourth Amendment, probable cause must be shown before an arrest warrant or search warrant may be issued.

probative force Probative force means that an item of evidence tends to prove a fact that is at issue in the case. Various pieces of evidence will have different amounts of probative force. Examples: in a rape case, DNA tests matching semen stains left at the scene with the defendant's DNA have great probative force; the testimony of a witness who identified the rapist based on a fleeting glance under poor lighting conditions will have much less probative force than the DNA test results.

probative value A fact has probative value if it tends to prove (or disprove) the existence (or nonexistence) of something that is at issue in the case.

protective sweep A "protective sweep" is a search of the premises for the safety of the officer. It is limited to a visual inspection of places in which a person might be hiding. A protective sweep is limited to the immediate adjoining area unless there is reasonable suspicion that someone is hiding in a more remote spot.

Public Records Exception to the Hearsay Rule   A document is admissible under the Public Records Exception to the Hearsay Rule if it meets three criteria: (1) a public employee made the document within the scope of his or her duty, (2) the document was made at or near the time the event occurred, and (3) the sources of the information and method and time of preparation indicate the record is trustworthy. Records of vital statistics (births, deaths, marriages, etc.) are admissible if (1) the maker of the record is required by law to report the event to a governmental agency, and (2) the report was made and filed as required by law.

Public Safety Exception to the Exclusionary Rule   The U.S. Supreme Court recognizes an exception to the Exclusionary Rule that allows unconstitutionally obtained evidence to be admitted in court if there was brief questioning or searching at the time of arrest for the purpose of protecting the public or rescuing the victim. This exception has been used to locate weapons that the suspect hid and to help find kidnap victims. Detailed questions are not allowed without *Miranda* warnings.

R

real evidence   Anything that can be perceived with the five senses (except testimonial evidence) that tends to prove a fact at issue is called real evidence. Another name frequently used for real evidence is physical evidence.

reasonable deadly force   A police officer may only use deadly force when it reasonably appears that the life of the officer, or another person nearby, is in danger. Imminent life-threatening injuries are treated the same as imminent death. When officers use deadly force in circumstances that are not life threatening, they violate the Fourth Amendment.

reasonable force   An officer may only use reasonable force to detain a person. What force is reasonable will depend on the circumstances, but deadly force is only authorized if someone's life is in danger. Using more force than is reasonable under the circumstances is a violation of the Fourth Amendment.

reasonable person   Many areas of the law use a reasonable person as their reference point. When discussing the use of force, the standard is based on what a reasonable person would do in the same circumstances. The reasonable person has the same physical characteristics and resources that the person in question had at the time it was necessary to make a decision on how much force to use. The reasonable person is allowed to consider reasonable appearances when deciding what to do. Thus, the facts as the reasonable person could reasonably believed them to be are more important than the actual facts.

reasonable suspicion   An officer may detain someone briefly for questioning based on reasonable suspicion. Police must have specific, articulable facts that indicate that criminal activity is afoot.

rebuttable presumption   A rebuttable presumption is not conclusive. Once the side relying on a rebuttable presumption introduces evidence to establish the presumed fact, the opposing side may introduce evidence to either disprove the basic fact or disprove the presumed fact.

rebuttal   Rebuttal is the part of the trial when the prosecution calls witnesses in an attempt to disprove what the defense witnesses said during the defense's case in chief.

rehabilitation   Rehabilitation is the process of trying to prove to judge and jury that a witness should be believed even though the witness has already been impeached.

rejoinder   Rejoinder is the part of the trial when the defense is allowed to call witnesses and attempt to cast doubt on what prosecution witnesses testified about during rebuttal.

relevant evidence   Any evidence that tends to prove or disprove any disputed fact in the case is relevant evidence. To be relevant, an item merely needs to show that it is more probable that the fact exists than it appeared before the evidence was introduced. No single piece of evidence has to make a fact appear more probable than not.

reporter's transcript   The reporter's transcript is a verbatim record of what occurred in court. It is made from notes taken by the court reporter.

reputation   A person's reputation is what other people believe about that person's character. It may or may not be an accurate reflection of character. If reputation is relevant, "character witnesses" may be called to testify about the person's reputation for traits that are relevant to the case, such as honesty, brutality, etc.

Reputation Exception to the Hearsay Rule   A statement is admissible under the Reputation Exception to the Hearsay Rule if it is about the reputation of a person among his or her associates at work or in the community. Some states also allow the witness to testify regarding his or her personal opinion about the person whose reputation is at issue.

restriction fragment length polymorphism (RFLP)   RFLP was one of the first DNA tests used in forensic investigation. It is not used as much now because it requires a larger DNA sample (as large as a quarter) to conduct the test. Samples degraded by environmental factors, such as dirt or mold, do not work as well for RFLP.

return (of search warrant)   A return is a document, usually printed on the back of a search warrant, in which the police state when the warrant was executed. An itemized inventory of what was seized is also included.

right to counsel   The right to counsel attaches at the first court appearance. After that time, officers must obtain a waiver of the right to counsel prior to interrogation. This rule applies to custodial and noncustodial interrogation conducted after the arraignment or indictment.

right to have an attorney present   A suspect has the right to have an attorney present during custodial interrogation. If he or she requests an attorney, questioning must stop and may only resume if there is an attorney present. If questioning is stopped for this reason, the police do not have to call an attorney unless they intend to resume questioning. If the suspect has already been arraigned or indicted, he or she has the right to have an attorney present at lineups, showups, and during questioning regarding the charges that have already been filed (whether or not the suspect is in custody at the time of this interrogation).

right to inventory a vehicle   Whenever a vehicle is legally impounded, the authorities have the right to inventory its contents. This results in an itemized list of all items present in the vehicle at that time. Inventories are allowed regardless of the reason the vehicle was impounded.

right to remain silent   A suspect has the right to remain silent during custodial interrogation. Even if a suspect waives his or her *Miranda* rights, the suspect retains the right to refuse to answer specific questions or to stop the interrogation at any time. If a suspect invokes the right to remain silent, officers must stop questioning but may request a new *Miranda* waiver after waiting long enough to indicate to the suspect that his or her rights will be scrupulously honored.

roadblock   A roadblock involves the stopping of all vehicles traveling on a street or highway. Officers may stop all vehicles or stop a percentage of the cars (such as every fourth car). The U.S. Supreme Court has approved the use of roadblocks to check for drunk drivers but has refused to authorize stopping vehicles to check for drugs. Roadblocks for the purpose of handing out "wanted flyers" soon after a crime have been upheld.

S

school searches   School officials may search students if there is reasonable suspicion that a student has broken the law or violated a school rule. This search is not confined to a pat down for weapons. Purses and other personal items may be searched.

search   A search is an examination of a person, his or her house, personal property, or other locations when conducted by a law enforcement officer for the purpose of finding evidence of a crime.

Search by a Private Person Exception to the Exclusionary Rule   Evidence obtained during a search conducted by a private person who is not acting at the urging of a police officer is admissible at trial. This evidence is not covered by the Exclusionary Rule even though the private person may have violated someone's reasonable expectation of privacy.

search incident to arrest   Contemporaneous with an arrest, officers may search the person arrested and the area under his or her immediate control. This search may be as thorough as necessary. It is not restricted to looking for weapons or evidence of the crime for which the person was arrested. If a person is in a vehicle at the time of arrest, or has been a recent occupant of a vehicle, the officers may conduct a thorough search of the passenger compartment of the vehicle incident to the arrest.

search of person during temporary detention   When an officer makes a temporary detention based on reasonable suspicion (*Terry v. Ohio*), the officer may conduct a pat down of the suspect's outer clothing for weapons if the officer has reasonable suspicion that the person is armed.

search of vehicle during temporary detention   When an officer makes a temporary detention of a person in a vehicle based on reasonable suspicion (*Terry v. Ohio*), the officer may search the passenger compartment of the vehicle for weapons if the officer has reasonable suspicion that weapons are concealed in the vehicle.

secondary evidence   Secondary evidence refers to all types of evidence used to establish the contents of a document when neither the original document nor a duplicate is available. This would include rough drafts as well as testimony about what the document said.

seizure   The act of taking possession of a person or property.

self-authenticating   Self-authenticating documents can be introduced into evidence without calling witnesses to authenticate them. Examples: documents bearing the government seal, notarized documents, and official publications.

self-incrimination   Self-incrimination is the making of a statement (oral or written) that can result in criminal liability for the person who made it. The privilege against self-incrimination comes from the Fifth Amendment of the U.S. Constitution. It does not cover physical evidence such as fingerprints, blood samples, DNA, or handwriting exemplars; it also does not apply if it is not possible to prosecute the person making the statement due to double jeopardy, expiration of statute of limitations, or a grant of immunity.

sequestered   A jury is sequestered when it is kept away from people who are not on the jury. In high-publicity cases, the jury may be housed in a local hotel for the duration of the trial. It is more common to sequester the jurors while they are deliberating on the verdict. Many juries are not sequestered at all.

short tandem repeat (STR)   STR technology is used to evaluate specific regions (loci) within nuclear DNA. Variability in STR regions can be used to distinguish one DNA profile from another. The FBI uses a standard set of 13 specific STR regions for CODIS, the database that can be accessed at the local, state, and national level for convicted offenders, unsolved crime scene evidence, and missing persons. The odds of two individuals having the same 13-loci DNA profile are approximately 1 in 1 billion.

showup   A showup involves having a victim or eyewitness view one person in order to make an identification of the person who allegedly committed the crime. The suspect has the right to have an attorney present at a showup if the showup is held after the suspect has been arraigned or indicted.

sobriety tests   Sobriety tests are frequently given to determine if a person is intoxicated. The most commonly used ones involve breath, blood, and urine. The U.S. Supreme Court has ruled that a suspected drunk driver cannot claim the Fifth Amendment as grounds to refuse to participate in a sobriety test. Field sobriety tests are given to drivers stopped on suspicion of driving under the influence of alcohol or drugs. An officer asks the driver to perform a variety of movements that would likely be impaired if a person were intoxicated.

Spontaneous Statement Exception to the Hearsay Rule   A statement is admissible under the Spontaneous Statement Exception to the Hearsay Rule if it meets two criteria: (1) it tells about something the declarant observed with one of the five senses, and (2) it was made spontaneously while the declarant was still under the stress and excitement of the event. Spontaneous statements are also referred to as "excited utterances."

standing   Standing is a party's right to make a legal claim or seek judicial enforcement of a duty or right.

stare decisis   In our common-law system, prior decisions of appellate courts are considered binding on lower courts (until reversed, vacated, or overruled). This is called *stare decisis.*

statement   As used in the Hearsay Rule, a statement refers to all types of communications: oral, written, those recorded on audio- or videotape or on computer disks, and nonverbal gestures.

statute of limitations   The statute of limitations is established by the legislature. It sets time limits for filing criminal charges. For example, in most states misdemeanor charges must be filed with the court clerk within 1 year of the day the crime was committed; for felonies the period is longer (frequently 3–6 years), and for some crimes, such as murder, there is no statute of limitations and the charges can be filed at any time. If the period specified in the statue of limitations has expired, the person who committed the crime cannot claim the Fifth Amendment as a reason not to answer questions about the crime; therefore, *Miranda* warnings are not required. See also *tolling the statute of limitations.*

stipulation   A stipulation is an agreement between all sides to a lawsuit to allow the jury to conclude that a fact exists. Once a stipulation is made, no evidence will be introduced to prove the stipulated fact. The judge will instruct the jurors that they must conclude that the stipulated fact exists.

substantial compliance   Substantial compliance with knock-and-announce procedures prior to entering a house is sufficient if, while the required procedures are being conducted, officers hear or see something that indicates further delay would result in physical harm to the officers, destruction of evidence, escape by the suspect, or harm to an innocent person inside the residence.

suppression hearing   The suppression hearing is a court hearing, usually held prior to the trial, for the purpose of deciding whether evidence may be used at trial. Evidence that the judge rules may not be used is suppressed. Suppression hearings are common if there are questions about whether the police complied with search and seizure rules and/or properly obtained a confession.

T

tacit admission   As used in the hearsay rule, a tacit admission occurs when a statement is made by someone else and then a person adopts it as his or her own statement. This is usually done by remaining silent when accused of wrongdoing in circumstances in which an innocent person would be expected to deny the allegation. Tacit admissions are also referred to as "adoptive admissions."

temporary detention   A person may be detained temporarily if there is reasonable suspicion that he or she is involved in criminal activity. If there is reasonable suspicion that the person is armed, officers may frisk the person for weapons. Temporary detentions are also referred to as field interviews.

testimonial evidence   1. Statements made by a competent witness, testifying under oath or affirmation in a court proceeding, are called testimonial evidence. Affidavits and depositions are frequently included in testimonial evidence. 2. Testimonial evidence, as the term is used when discussing the *Miranda* warnings, means oral and written statements that a suspect makes in response to questions. Handwriting and voice exemplars are not testimonial evidence because someone dictates what the suspect should say or write.

Title III   The Wiretap Act of 1968 was Title III of the Omnibus Crime Control and Safe Streets Act of 1968. For this reason, the Wiretap Act of 1968 is sometimes called Title III.

tolling the statute of limitations   The statute of limitations establishes a deadline for filing charges. Some events "stop the clock" on the statute of limitations; this is referred to as tolling the statute of limitations. Many states toll the statute of limitations if a person leaves the state in order to avoid apprehension and/or prosecution.

trier of the facts   The role of the trier of the facts is to evaluate the evidence and decide which facts have been sufficiently proven. In a jury trial, the jurors are the triers of the facts. In a trial held without a jury, the judge is both the trier of the facts and the trier of the law.

trier of the law   The role of the trier of the law is to decide what law applies to a given case. This includes giving the jury instructions on the definitions of the crimes(s) charged, ruling on objections made at trial (such as hearsay), and deciding whether *Miranda* and search and seizure rules were correctly followed by the police. In a trial, the trier of the law is the judge.

U

unduly suggestive   A lineup or photographic lineup is unduly suggestive if it points out one person as the suspected criminal. This could be caused by disparities in height, weight, race, age, or other factors. Comments and coaching by the police or other people viewing the identification procedure that indicate which person is believed to have committed the crime would also be unduly suggestive. Unduly suggestive lineups and photographic lineups violate due process.

USA PATRIOT Act of 2001   The USA PATRIOT Act, passed by Congress soon after the events of September 11, 2001, made many changes in the Foreign Intelligence Surveillance Act, the Wiretap Act, and numerous other federal statutes to facilitate the detection of terrorists and stop terrorist attacks. USA PATRIOT is an acronym for Uniting and Strengthening America by Providing Appropriate Tools Required to Intercept and Obstruct Terrorism.

V

valid on its face　A statute or warrant is valid on its face if it appears to be constitutional. Officers may act in reliance on these statutes and warrants until they learn that they are unconstitutional. If it can be determined by the wording that a warrant or statute is defective, police are not authorized to act pursuant to them.

vehicle search—incident to an arrest　If a person is in a vehicle at the time he or she is arrested, the officers may conduct a thorough search of the passenger compartment of the vehicle contemporaneous to the arrest.

vehicle search—inventory of impounded car　When a vehicle is legally impounded for any reason, the car may be inventoried in order to provide a complete list of what was in the car at the time it was taken into custody.

vehicle search—noncriminal purpose　If officers inspect a vehicle for a noncriminal purpose, any evidence of a crime that they find can be used in court.

vehicle search—outside of car　Officers may examine the exterior of a car that is on public property. Anything found in plain view can be used in court.

vehicle search—probable cause there is evidence in the vehicle　When officers have probable cause that there is evidence or contraband in a vehicle, they may search the portion of the car where the evidence or contraband is believed to be. No warrant is required; the officer may conduct as thorough a search as a judge could authorize after reviewing the facts.

vehicle search—stop based on reasonable suspicion　When a person in a car is detained based on reasonable suspicion, the passenger compartment of the vehicle can be searched for weapons if there is reasonable suspicion that weapons are concealed in the vehicle. This rule applies whether or not the person driving the car will be released at the scene.

vehicle stop at roadblock　Police may stop vehicles at a roadblock established to arrest drivers who are intoxicated. The Supreme Court balanced the benefit to society against the intrusion on the individual's privacy and determined that DUI roadblocks were justified. Roadblocks conducted to find narcotic users were not approved because the Court classified them as part of normal police activity. On the other hand, roadblocks set up to distribute wanted flyers for a recent crime were considered justified.

Vital Statistics Exception to the Hearsay Rule　Records of vital statistics (births, deaths, marriages, etc.) are admissible if (1) the maker of the record is required by law to report the event to a governmental agency, and (2) the report was made and filed as required by law.

voir dire　*Voir dire* is the process of asking questions in order to determine if someone is qualified. During *voir dire* of the jury, the prospective jurors are asked questions in order to determine if they have formed opinions about the defendant's guilt and other relevant issues. Information obtained during *voir dire* is used by prosecution and defense attorneys when exercising challenges for cause and peremptory challenges. A *voir dire* hearing is also held to determine whether a person is qualified to testify as an expert witness.

voluntary consent   To be valid, consent for a search must be voluntary. All the factors applicable to giving consent will be considered when the Court determines if the consent was voluntary. Officers can obtain valid consent without advising a person of his or her Fourth Amendment right to refuse to give consent for a search. A person who gives voluntary consent for a search retains the right to revoke the consent.

W

weight of each piece of evidence   The trier of the facts determines the weight to be given to each piece of evidence. One of the key factors influencing this decision is the credibility of the witness(es) who testified about the item. The jurors (or judge, in a trial without a jury) can disregard evidence even if there is no other evidence presented on the issue, if they believe the witness is not telling the truth. Based on their own common sense, jurors also decide how much weight to give each piece of evidence: One item might be conclusive, another so trivial that they disregard it.

Wiretap Act of 1968   Following the Supreme Court's declaration that electronic surveillance warrants were required whenever a person's reasonable expectation of privacy was invaded by electronic "bugs," Congress passed the Wiretap Act of 1968, which authorized federal judges to issue electronic surveillance warrants for wiretaps and other forms of electronic monitoring. Because the Wiretap Act was Title III of the Omnibus Crime Control and Safe Streets Act of 1968, the Wiretap Act is sometimes referred to as Title III.

Y

Y chromosome analysis   The Y chromosome is passed directly from father to son, so the analysis of the genetic markers on the Y chromosome is useful for tracing relationships among males or for analyzing biological evidence involving multiple male contributors.

INDEX